murach's
JavaScript
and jQuery

4TH EDITION

Mary Delamater

Zak Ruvalcaba

BEGINNER TO PRO

murach's
JavaScript
and jQuery

4TH EDITION

Mary Delamater

Zak Ruvalcaba

MIKE MURACH & ASSOCIATES, INC.

3730 W Swift Ave. • Fresno, CA 93722

www.murach.com • murachbooks@murach.com

Editorial team

Authors: Mary Delamater
                   Zak Ruvalcaba

Editors: Anne Boehm
                   Joel Murach

Production: Juliette Baylon

Books for web developers

Murach's HTML and CSS

Murach's PHP and MySQL

Murach's ASP.NET Core MVC

Murach's Java Servlets and JSP

Books on programming languages

Murach's Python Programming

Murach's Java Programming

Murach's C#

Murach's C++ Programming

Books for database programmers

Murach's MySQL

Murach's SQL Server for Developers

Murach's Oracle SQL and PL/SQL for Developers

Books for data analysis

Murach's R for Data Analysis

Murach's Python for Data Analysis

For more on Murach books,
please visit us at www.murach.com

10 9 8 7 6 5 4 3 2
ISBN: 978-1-943872-62-6

Contents

Contents

Expanded contents

Section 2   jQuery essentials

Resources

Introduction

Today, JavaScript is used on most pages of most modern websites, from small individual sites to the largest commercial sites. And wherever you find JavaScript, there's a good chance you'll also find jQuery, the classic JavaScript library that makes it easier to develop JavaScript applications.

That's why this book presents the JavaScript and jQuery skills that every web developer should have today. It works if you're a web designer who's coming from an HTML and CSS background and has no programming experience. But it also works if you're a server-side programmer who has experience with a language like Java, C#, PHP, or Python. Either way, you'll end up with a solid set of the JavaScript and jQuery skills that you'll need on the job.

What this book does

This book is divided into four sections, and each takes you to a new level of expertise:

- Section 1 presents a seven-chapter course in JavaScript that gets you off to a great start. This section works for programming novices as well as experienced programmers because it lets you set your own pace. If you're a beginner, you'll move slowly and do all the exercises. If you have some experience, you'll move more quickly as you focus on the differences between JavaScript and the other languages that you've used. When you finish this section, you'll have a solid set of JavaScript skills, including the skills that help you get the most from jQuery.

- Section 2 presents the jQuery skills that every web developer should have. The first chapter presents the core jQuery skills, and the next three chapters focus on effects and animations, forms and data validation, and jQuery plugins and UI widgets.

- Section 3 presents more skills that every professional JavaScript programmer should have. Here, you'll learn more about working with numbers, strings, and dates...how to handle exceptions and use regular expressions...when and how to use browser objects, cookies, and web storage...more about using arrays...how to use sets and maps...and how to create and use your own objects. To do that, this section presents these skills in conjunction with the jQuery skills presented in section 2. Because that's the way applications are often coded in the real world, this is an excellent way to learn these skills.

- Section 4 presents more skills that take your JavaScript programming to the next level. To start, it presents expert-level skills like how to use closures and modules to safely share your code with other programmers. Then, it shows how to use Ajax with the Fetch API and Promise objects to asynchronously update a web page with data from a web server, without reloading the entire page. Finally, this section shows how to use Node.js to run JavaScript on a server so it can be used for server-side scripting.

Why you'll learn faster and better with this book

Like all our books, this one has features that you won't find in competing books. That's why we believe you'll learn faster and better with our book than with any other. Here are a few of those features.

- This book is designed to teach you the skills you're going to need on the job without wasting your time on skills that you aren't likely to need. That sounds simple, but most JavaScript books either overwhelm you with information that you'll never need or trivialize the subject by avoiding all of the complications. For instance, this book shows you the basics of DOM scripting with JavaScript, but then it shows you how to use jQuery to simplify DOM scripting.

- If you page through this book, you'll see that all of the information is presented in "paired pages," with the essential syntax, guidelines, and examples on the right page and the perspective and extra explanation on the left page. This helps you learn faster by reading less...and this is the ideal reference format when you need to refresh your memory about how to do something.

- To show you how JavaScript and jQuery work, this book presents dozens of complete applications that range from the simple to the complex. We believe that studying the code for complete applications is critical to the learning process...and yet you won't find programs like ours in other JavaScript and jQuery books.

- Of course, this book also presents dozens of short examples, so it's easy to find an example that shows you how to do what you want to do. In addition, our paired pages make it easier to find the examples that you're looking for when compared to traditional books that embed the examples in the text.

- The exercises at the end of each chapter give you hands-on experience by letting you practice what you've learned. These exercises also encourage you to experiment and to apply what you've learned in new ways...just as you'll have to do on the job.

What software you need

To develop JavaScript applications, you can use any text editor. However, a text editor that includes syntax coloring and auto-completion helps you develop applications more quickly and with fewer errors. That's why we recommend Visual Studio Code (VS Code). Although VS Code is free, it provides many powerful features.

Then, to test a web page, we recommend that you do your primary testing with Google's Chrome browser. That's because Chrome provides excellent developer tools for testing and debugging your JavaScript applications.

If you decide to use VS Code, chapter 1 presents a short tutorial that gets you started right. And to help you install Chrome and VS Code, appendixes A and B provide the set-up procedures that you need for the Windows and macOS operating systems.

How our downloadable files can help you learn

If you visit www.murach.com, you can download all of the files that you need for getting the most from this book. This includes the files for:

- the applications presented in this book
- the starting points for the exercises presented at the end of each chapter
- the solutions to those exercises

These files let you test, review, and copy the code. If you have any problems with the exercises, you can refer to the solutions to help you over the learning blocks, an essential part of the learning process. And in some cases, the solutions might show you a more elegant way to handle a problem, even when you've come up with a solution that works. Here again, appendixes A and B show you how to download and install these files on Windows and macOS.

Support materials for instructors and trainers

If you're a college instructor or corporate trainer who would like to use this book as a course text, we offer a full set of the support materials you need for an effective course. That includes:

- instructional objectives that help your students focus on the skills that they need to develop
- test banks that let you measure how well your students have mastered those skills
- extra exercises that let your students prove how well they have mastered those skills
- case studies that let your students develop substantial JavaScript and jQuery applications
- PowerPoint slides that you can use to review the content of the book

Instructors tell us that this is everything they need for a course without all the busywork that they get from other publishers.

To learn more about these instructor's materials, please visit www.murachforinstructors.com if you're an instructor. Or if you're a trainer, please visit www.murach.com and click the *Courseware for Trainers* link, or contact Kelly at 1-800-221-5528 or kelly@murach.com.

Please remember, though, that the primary component for a successful course is this book. Because your students will learn faster and more thoroughly when they use our book, they will have better questions and be more prepared when they come to class. Because our guided exercises start from partial applications, your students will get more practice with new skills in lab. And because our paired pages work so well for reference, your students will be able to review for tests and do their projects more efficiently.

Companion books

Besides JavaScript and jQuery, the best web developers also master HTML5 and CSS3. To that end, you'll find that *Murach's HTML5 and CSS3* is the perfect companion to this JavaScript and jQuery book. With both books at your side, you'll be able to develop web pages that use HTML5, CSS3, JavaScript, and jQuery the way the best professionals use them.

We also offer books on server-side programming in languages like Java, C#, PHP, and Python. To learn more about our new books and latest editions, please visit www.murach.com. There, you'll find the details for all of our books, including complete tables of contents.

Please let us know how this book works for you

From the start of this project, we had three primary goals. First, we wanted to present the JavaScript and jQuery skills that every web developer should have, all in a single book. Second, we wanted to do that in a way that works for web designers with no programming background as well as experienced programmers. Third, we wanted to make this the best on-the-job reference you've ever used.

Now, we think we've succeeded. We thank you for buying this book. We wish you all the best with your JavaScript and jQuery programming. And if you have any comments, we would appreciate hearing from you.

Mary Delamater, Author
maryd@techknowsolve.com

Mike Murach
Publisher

Section 1

JavaScript essentials

This section presents the essential JavaScript skills. This subset of skills will get you off to a fast start with JavaScript. And this subset of JavaScript skills is the least you need to know for using jQuery effectively.

Chapter 1 in this section presents the concepts and terms that you need for developing JavaScript applications. It also shows you how to use Visual Studio Code, which is one of the many source code editors that are available for developing JavaScript applications.

Then, chapter 2 presents a starting subset of the JavaScript language. Chapters 3 and 4 complete that subset. Chapter 5 shows you how to test and debug your JavaScript applications. Chapter 6 shows you how to use that subset for DOM scripting, the predominant use of JavaScript. And chapter 7 shows you how to work with images and timers.

At that point, you'll be well on your way to developing JavaScript applications at a professional level. Then, you can dive right into jQuery by moving on to section 2.

1

Introduction to web development

This chapter presents the background concepts, terms, and skills that you need for developing JavaScript applications. That includes a quick review of the HTML and CSS skills that you need, and a tutorial on how to use Visual Studio Code, which is the source code editor that we used to develop the JavaScript apps for this book.

If you have some web development experience, you should be able to go through this chapter quickly by skimming the topics that you already know. But if you're new to web development, you should take the time to master the concepts and terms of this chapter.

How a web application works

A web application consists of many components that work together as they bring the application to your computer or mobile device. Before you can start developing JavaScript applications, you should have a basic understanding of how these components work together.

The components of a web application

The diagram in figure 1-1 shows that web applications consist of *clients* and a *web server.* The clients are the computers, tablets, and mobile devices that use the web applications. They access the web pages through *web browsers.* The web server holds the files that make up a web application.

A *network* is a system that allows clients and servers to communicate. The *Internet* is a large network that consists of many smaller networks. In a diagram like the one in this figure, the "cloud" represents the network or Internet that connects the clients and servers.

In general, you don't need to know how the cloud works. But you should have a general idea of what's going on.

To start, networks can be categorized by size. A *local area network* (*LAN*) is a small network of computers that are near each other and can communicate with each other over short distances. Computers in a LAN are typically in the same building or adjacent buildings. This type of network is often called an *intranet*, and it can be used to run web applications for use by employees only.

By contrast, a *wide area network* (*WAN*) consists of multiple LANs that have been connected. To pass information from one client to another, a router determines which network is closest to the destination and sends the information over that network. A WAN can be owned privately by one company or it can be shared by multiple companies.

An *Internet service provider* (*ISP*) is a company that owns a WAN that is connected to the Internet. An ISP leases access to its network to companies that need to be connected to the Internet.

The components of a web application

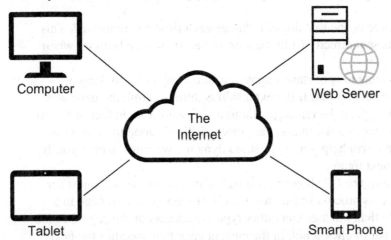

Description

- A web application consists of clients, a web server, and a network.
- The *clients* use programs known as *web browsers* to request web pages from the web server. Today, the clients can be computers, smart phones like the iPhone, or tablets like the iPad.
- The *web server* returns the pages that are requested to the browser.
- A *network* connects the clients to the web server.
- An *intranet* is a *local area network* (or *LAN*) that connects computers that are near each other, usually within the same building.
- The *Internet* is a network that consists of many *wide area networks* (*WANs*), and each of those consists of two or more LANs. Today, the Internet is often referred to as "the Cloud", which implies that you really don't have to understand how it works.
- An *Internet service provider* (*ISP*) owns a WAN that is connected to the Internet.

Figure 1-1   The components of a web application

How static web pages are processed

A *static web page* is one that doesn't change each time it is requested. This type of web page is sent directly from the web server to the web browser when the browser requests it.

You used to be able to spot static pages in a web browser by looking at the extension in the address bar. If the extension is .htm or .html, the page was probably a static web page. Increasingly, though, this isn't true. In fact, it's hard to find a static web page on the internet anymore. Still, it's good to know how they work, since that will help you understand dynamic websites, which you'll learn about in the next figure.

The diagram in figure 1-2 shows how a web server processes a request for a static web page. This process begins when a client requests a web page in a web browser. To do that, the user can either type the address of the page into the browser's address bar or click a link in the current page that specifies the next page to load.

In either case, the web browser builds a request for the web page and sends it to the web server. This request, known as an *HTTP request*, is formatted using the *HyperText Transfer Protocol* (HTTP), which lets the web server know which file is being requested.

When the web server receives the HTTP request, it retrieves the requested file from the disk drive. This file contains the *HTML (HyperText Markup Language)* for the requested page. Then, the web server sends the file back to the browser as part of an *HTTP response*.

When the browser receives the HTTP response, it *renders* (translates) the HTML into a web page that is displayed in the browser. Then, the user can view the content. If the user requests another page, either by clicking a link or typing another web address into the browser's address bar, the process begins again.

How a web server processes a static web page

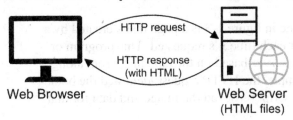

Web Browser   Web Server
                               (HTML files)

Description

- *Hypertext Markup Language* (*HTML*) is the language used to define the content for the web pages of an application.

- A *static web page* is an HTML document that's stored on the web server and doesn't change.

- When the user requests a static web page, the browser sends an *HTTP request* to the web server that includes the name of the file that's being requested.

- When the web server receives the request, it retrieves the HTML for the web page and sends it back to the browser as part of an *HTTP response*.

- When the browser receives the HTTP response, it *renders* the HTML into a web page that is displayed in the browser.

Figure 1-2   How static web pages are processed

How dynamic web pages are processed

A *dynamic web page* like the one in figure 1-3 is a page that's created by a program or script on the web server each time it's requested. This program or script is executed by an *application server* based on the data that's sent along with the HTTP request. In this example, the HTTP request identified the book that's shown. Then, the program or script retrieved the image and data for that book from a *database server*.

The diagram in this figure shows how a web server processes a dynamic web page. The process begins when the user requests a page in a web browser. To do that, the user can either type the URL of the page into the browser's address bar, click a link that specifies the dynamic page to load, or click a button that submits a form containing the data the dynamic page should process.

In each case, the web browser builds an HTTP request and sends it to the web server. This request includes whatever data the application needs for processing the request. If, for example, the user has entered data into a form, that data will be included in the HTTP request.

When the web server receives the HTTP request, the server examines the file extension of the requested web page to identify the application server that should process the request. The web server then forwards the request to the application server that processes that type of web page.

Next, the application server retrieves the appropriate program or script from the hard drive. It also loads any form data that the user submitted. Then, it executes the script. As the script executes, it generates the HTML for the web page. If necessary, the script will request data from a database server and use that data as part of the web page it is generating. The processing that's done on the application server can be referred to as *server-side processing*.

When the script is finished, the application server sends the dynamically generated HTML back to the web server. Then, the web server sends the HTML back to the browser in an HTTP response.

When the web browser receives the HTTP response, it renders the HTML and displays the web page. Note, however, that the web browser has no way to tell whether the HTML in the HTTP response is from a static page or a dynamic page. It just renders the HTML.

When the page is displayed, the user can view the content. Then, when the user requests another page, the process begins again. The process that begins with the user requesting a web page and ends with the server sending a response back to the client is called a *round trip*.

A dynamic web page at amazon.com

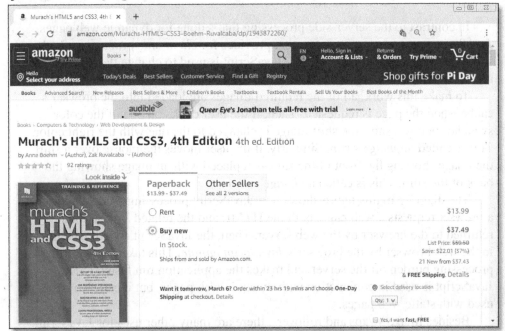

How a web server processes a dynamic web page

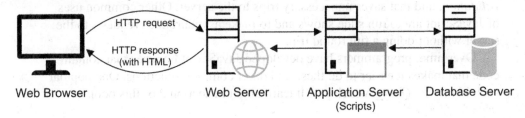

Web Browser   Web Server   Application Server   Database Server
                                         (Scripts)

Description

- A *dynamic web page* is a web page that's generated by a program or script that is running on a server.

- When a web server receives a request for a dynamic web page, it looks up the extension of the requested file to find out which *application server* should process the request.

- When the application server receives a request, it runs the specified script. Often, this script uses the data that it gets from the web browser to get the appropriate data from a *database server*. This script can also store the data that it receives in the database.

- When the application server finishes processing the data, it generates the HTML for a web page and returns it to the web server. Then, the web server returns the HTML to the web browser as part of an HTTP response.

Figure 1-3   How dynamic web pages are processed

How JavaScript is used for client-side processing

In contrast to the server-side processing that's done for dynamic web pages, *JavaScript* is a *scripting language* that provides for *client-side processing*. In the web page in figure 1-4, for example, JavaScript is used to change the images that are shown without using server-side processing.

To make this work, all of the required images are loaded into the browser's cache when the page is requested. Then, if the user clicks on one of the color swatches below a shirt, the shirt image is changed to the one with the right color. This is called an *image swap*. Similarly, if the user moves the mouse over a shirt, the image showing the front of the shirt is replaced with an image showing the back of the shirt. This is called an *image rollover*.

The diagram in this figure shows how JavaScript processing works. When a browser requests a web page, both the HTML and the related JavaScript are returned to the browser by the web server. Then, the JavaScript code is executed in the web browser by the browser's *JavaScript engine*. This takes some of the processing burden off the server and makes the application run faster. Often, JavaScript is used in conjunction with dynamic web pages, but it can also be used with static web pages.

Besides image swaps and rollovers, there are many other uses for JavaScript. For instance, another common use is to validate the data that the user enters into an HTML form before it is sent to the server for processing. This is called *data validation*, and that saves unnecessary trips to the server. Other common uses of JavaScript are to run slide shows and to make asynchronous requests to the server without doing a full round trip.

Over time, programmers have developed JavaScript libraries that contain code that makes it easier to do these and other common functions. One popular such library is *jQuery*, which you'll learn about in section 2 of this book.

A web page with image swaps and rollovers

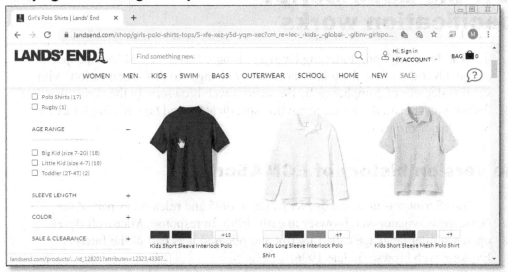

How JavaScript fits into this architecture

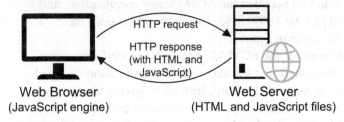

Three of the many uses of JavaScript and jQuery

- Data validation
- Image swaps and rollovers
- Slide shows

Description

- *JavaScript* is a *scripting language* that is run by the *JavaScript engine* of a web browser and controls the operation of the browser.

- When the browser requests an HTML page that contains JavaScript or a link to a JavaScript file, both the HTML and the JavaScript are loaded into the browser.

- Because JavaScript runs on the client, not the server, its functions don't require a trip back to the server. This helps an application run more efficiently.

- *jQuery* is a JavaScript library that makes it easier to do many of the common functions that JavaScript is used for.

Figure 1-4   How JavaScript is used for client-side processing

How the ECMAScript specification works

The JavaScript programming language is based on the ECMAScript specification. Over the years, there have been many changes to this specification, with varying degrees of compliance by the various web browsers. In the topics that follow, you'll learn the basics about this specification and how it's implemented by the major browsers.

The version history of ECMAScript

JavaScript was invented by NetScape in 1995 and released as part of the Netscape Navigator web browser in early 1996. In response, Microsoft developed a similar language called JScript and released it as part of the Internet Explorer web browser in late 1996.

Since there were differences between the two scripting languages, Netscape gave JavaScript to the *European Computer Manufacturers Association (ECMA)* to develop a standard. The standard is called the *ECMAScript specification,* and the first version was released in June 1997. Since then, several versions have been released, as shown in the table in figure 1-5.

In June 2015 the sixth version of the ECMAScript, or ES, specification was released. At the same time, the committee in charge of the specification changed how it would release new versions going forward. Instead of having a set specification that they would release when all the features were completed, they moved to yearly releases of features that had been approved to that point. Thus, the version released in 2015 was officially named ECMAScript 2015, although you'll often see it referred to as ES6. After that, the versions are usually referred to by the year, such as ECMAScript 2016, or ES2016.

ES5 and ES6 represented significant updates to the ECMAScript specification, while ES2016 added only a handful of smaller features. Since then, ES2017, ES2018, ES2019, and ES2020 added several important features. Many of these features are listed in this figure. In this book, you'll learn how to use the most useful features of all the releases, including ES2020.

The versions and release dates of the ECMAScript specification

Version	AKA	Release date
1		June 1997
2		June 1998
3	ES3	December 1999
4		Abandoned (never released)
5	ES5	December 2009
5.1		June 2011
2015	ES2015, ES6	June 2015
2016	ES2016, ES7	June 2016
2017	ES2017, ES8	June 2017
2018	ES2018, ES9	June 2018
2019	ES2019, ES10	June 2019
2020	ES2020, ES11	June 2020

Some of the important additions in the recent versions

ES5

- Allows you to run in strict mode.
- Adds several methods that make it easier to work with arrays and objects.
- Adds a built-in way to work with JavaScript Object Notation (JSON).

ES2015 (ES6)

- Adds several syntactic improvements that make code easier to read and understand.
- Adds block scope and easier ways to work with classes.
- Adds arrow functions, iterators, and Promises for working with asynchronous code.

ES2016

- Adds a simpler syntax for computation with powers.
- Adds a method to check if an array includes a specified element.

ES2017

- Adds async functions and the await keyword for working with Promises.

ES2018

- Adds asynchronous iteration.
- Adds more regular expression features.

ES2019

- Adds new string, array, and object methods.
- Adds improvements to the JSON object.

ES2020

- Adds a new BigInt data type.
- Adds new operators for dealing with nulls.

Figure 1-5   The version history of ECMAScript

Browser support for ECMAScript

The table in figure 1-6 presents the versions of the major browsers that support the ECMAScript specification through ES2019. These browsers also support the major new features of ES2020. This means that these browsers support all the ECMAScript features that you'll learn about in this book

However, for earlier versions of these browsers, or for other browsers, the support for the later versions of the ECMAScript specification may be spottier. In particular, the Internet Explorer (IE) browser struggles to support the more recent versions of ECMAScript. Earlier versions of IE, such as IE6, were notoriously noncompliant with the specification. Later versions had better compliance, but still lagged behind the other browsers, and that continues to this day.

So, if you want your web pages to support web browsers that aren't included in this table, you'll need to make some adjustments. To start, you can go to the website at the URL in this figure to see which browsers support which features. Then, you can use only those features that are supported by the browsers you want to support.

The other approach is to add workarounds to your code that will make many of the ECMAScript features work in browsers that don't support them. You can also learn more about that by going to the website at the URL in this figure.

The browsers that support the ECMAScript specification

Browser	Version
Chrome	79 and above
Edge	79 and above
Firefox	68 and above
Opera	66 and above
Safari	12.1 and above

The URL for a browser compatibility table

`http://kangax.github.io/compat-table/`

Description

- At the time of this writing, the features of ECMAScript through ES2020 are supported by all the modern browsers listed here. Because of that, you can safely use the JavaScript presented in this book with these browsers.

- If you want to support other browsers, such as IE, or older versions of these browsers, you can use the website presented here to see which features are supported by which browsers.

- The website presented here also provides information about polyfill files and transpilers that you can use to allow browsers that don't fully support the ECMAScript specification to use your website.

Figure 1-6   Browser support for ECMAScript

The components of a JavaScript application

When you develop a JavaScript application, you use HTML to define the content and structure of the page. You use CSS to format that content. And you use JavaScript to do the client-side processing. This is illustrated by the Email List application that is presented in the next three figures.

Figure 1-7 starts with the user interface for the application. It asks the user to make three entries and then click on the Join List button. The asterisks to the right of the text boxes for the entries indicate that these entries are required.

When the user clicks on the button, JavaScript checks the entries to make sure they're valid. If they are, the entries are sent to the web server for server-side processing. If they aren't, messages are displayed so the user can correct the entries. This is a common use of JavaScript called *data validation* that saves a trip to the server when the entries are invalid.

You might have noticed that the user interface in this figure isn't much to look at. This is what a plain HTML document with no formatting looks like. In the next figure, though, you'll see how applying some CSS can improve its appearance.

The HTML

HyperText Markup Language (*HTML*) is used to define the content and structure of a web page. In figure 1-7, you can see the HTML for the Email List application. In general, this book assumes that you are already familiar with HTML, but here are a few highlights.

First, note that this document starts with a DOCTYPE declaration. This declaration is the one you'll use with HTML5, and you must code it exactly as it's shown here. In this book, all of the applications use HTML5.

Second, in the head section of the HTML document, you can see a meta element that specifies that UTF-8 is the character encoding that's used for the page. After that, there's another meta element that sets the viewport to help the page display properly on mobile devices. Then, there's a title element that contains the text that will display in the browser's tab. Finally, there's an HTML comment indicating that any link and style elements go here in the head element. You'll see an example of a link element for a CSS file in the next figure.

Third, in the body section, you can see the use of a main element, which is one of the HTML5 elements that we'll be using throughout this book. Within this element, you can see the use of h1, form, div, label, input, and span elements. The body section ends with an HTML comment indicating that any script elements go at the end of this section. Although script elements can also go in the head element, it's considered a best practice to put them at the end of the body section. In figure 1-9, you'll see an example of a script element for a JavaScript file.

In this book, as you've just seen, we refer to *HTML elements* like the <link>, <script>, <main>, and <h1> elements as the link, script, main, and h1 elements.

The HTML file in a browser before CSS is applied to it

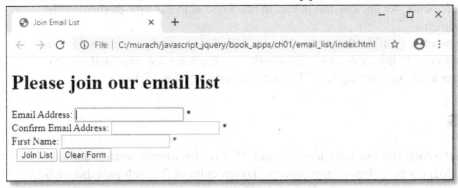

The code for the HTML file named index.html

```html
<!DOCTYPE html>
<html>
<head>
    <meta charset="UTF-8">
    <meta name="viewport" content="width=device-width, initial-scale=1">
    <title>Join Email List</title>
    <!-- link and style elements go here -->
</head>
<body>
    <main>
        <h1>Please join our email list</h1>
        <form id="email_form" action="join.html" method="get">
            <div>
                <label for="email_1">Email Address:</label>
                <input type="text" id="email_1" name="email_1">
                <span id="email_1_error">*</span>
            </div>
            <div>
                <label for="email_2">Re-enter Email Address:</label>
                <input type="text" id="email_2" name="email_2">
                <span id="email_2_error">*</span>
            </div>
            <div>
                <label for="first_name">First Name</label>
                <input type="text" id="first_name" name="first_name">
                <span id="first_name_error">*</span>
            </div>
            <div>
                <label> </label>
                <input type="submit" id="join_list" value="Join List">
                <input type="button" id="clear_form" value="Clear Form">
            </div>
        </form>
    </main>
    <!-- script elements go here -->
</body>
</html>
```

Description

- *HTML (HyperText Markup Language)* defines the structure and content of a web page.

Figure 1-7   The HTML for the web page

However, to prevent confusion when referring to one-letter elements like the p and a elements, we enclose the letters in brackets, as in the <p> element or the <a> element.

In practice, you'll often hear *elements* called *tags* so you can think of them as synonyms. In this book, we occasionally use the term *tag*, especially when referring to an opening tag like <h1> or a closing tag like </h1>.

The CSS

In the early days of web development, HTML documents were coded so the HTML not only defined the content and structure of the web page but also the formatting of that content. However, this mix of structural and formatting elements made it hard to edit, maintain, and reformat the web pages.

Today, *Cascading Style Sheets* (*CSS*) let you separate the formatting from the content and structure of a web page. As a result, the formatting that was once done with HTML should now be done with CSS.

In figure 1-8, then, you can see the link element that links the external CSS file to the HTML. As you saw in figure 1-7, this link element goes in the HTML head element. You can also see how this CSS has changed the appearance of the page in the browser.

After that, you can see the CSS that's used to format the HTML in the last figure. Here again, this book assumes that you are already familiar with CSS, but here is a quick description of what this CSS is doing.

In the style rule for the body element, the font-family property sets the font for the entire document, the background-color property sets the background color of the browser window, the margin property centers the body in the browser window, the width property sets the width of the body to 670 pixels, the border property puts a blue border around the body, and the padding property puts space between the contents and the right, left, and bottom borders. This is typical CSS for the applications in this book.

Similarly, the style rules for the h1, div, label, input, and span elements are intended to make these elements look better. For instance, the style rule for the h1 element sets the font color to blue, and the style rule for div elements sets the bottom margin so there's horizontal space after each div.

The style rule for the labels makes them display as block elements, so things like width can be applied to them, but also as inline elements, so they can be on the same line as other elements. Then, this style rule sets the width of the labels to 11ems, and it aligns the text for the labels on the right.

The style rule for the input elements sets the left margin so there's space between the labels and the text boxes. It also sets the right margin so there's space between the text boxes and span elements.

Last, the style rule for the span elements sets the text color to red. When the HTML page is first loaded, these span elements only contain asterisks (*) to indicate that these entries are required. But the JavaScript changes those asterisks to error messages if the related entries are invalid, and it removes the asterisks if the related entries are valid.

The web page in a browser after CSS has been applied to it

The link element in the HTML head element that applies the CSS file

```html
<link rel="stylesheet" href="email_list.css">
```

The code for the CSS file named email_list.css

```css
body {
    font-family: Arial, Helvetica, sans-serif;
    background-color: white;
    margin: 0 auto;
    width: 670px;
    border: 3px solid blue;
    padding: 0 2em 1em;
}
h1 {
    color: blue;
}
div {
    margin-bottom: 1em;
}
label {
    display: inline-block;
    width: 11em;
    text-align: right;
}
input {
    margin-left: 1em;
    margin-right: 0.5em;
}
span {
    color: red;
}
```

Description

- *Cascading Style Sheets* (*CSS*) are used to control how web pages are displayed by specifying the fonts, colors, borders, spacing, and layouts of the pages.

Figure 1-8   The CSS for the web page

The JavaScript

Figure 1-9 shows how this application looks in a browser if the JavaScript finds any invalid data after the user clicks the Join List button. Here, you can see that error messages are displayed to the right of the user entries for the second and third text boxes. In other words, the JavaScript has actually changed the contents of the span elements.

When JavaScript changes the HTML for a page, it is called *DOM scripting*. That's because the JavaScript is actually changing the *Document Object Model* (or *DOM*) that's generated by the browser when the page is loaded. This DOM represents all of the elements and attributes that are coded in the HTML. Then, when JavaScript changes any aspect of the DOM, the change is immediately made to the browser display too.

After the browser display, this figure shows the script element that links the external JavaScript file to the HTML. This element is typically coded at the end of the body section, as shown in figure 1-7.

Then, this figure shows the JavaScript for this application. Since you are going to learn how all of this code works in the next six chapters, you may want to skip over this code right now. But if you have any programming experience, it may be worth taking a quick look at it. In that case, here are a few highlights.

To start, this code consists of four *functions* that consist of blocks of code. You'll learn more about how to code functions as you progress through this book. For now, just know that the $() function gets an element from the page, the joinList() function executes when the user clicks on the Join List button, the clearForm() function executes when the user clicks on the Clear Form button, and the anonymous function runs when the DOM has been loaded into the browser.

In the joinList() function, you can see four if-else statements that provide most of the logic for this application. Here, you can see that the if-else structures are similar to those in any modern programming language like Java, C#, or PHP. You can also see that declaring a variable or constant and assigning a value to it is done in a way that's similar to the way that it's done in other programming languages.

What's different about JavaScript is that it provides methods and properties that let you modify the DOM. For instance, the $() function uses the querySelector() method to get the first element in the document that matches the CSS selector that's passed to the function. Then, the first statement in the joinList() function uses the $() function to get the object that represents the first text box in the HTML. This statement also uses the value property to get the value that the user entered into that text box.

Later, the first if statement checks whether that value is an empty string (""), which means the user didn't make an entry. If it is, the JavaScript replaces the * in the span element for that text box with an error message. To do that, it uses this code:

```
$("#email_1_error").textContent = "Email is required.";
```

The web page in a browser with JavaScript used for data validation

The script element in the HTML body element that adds the JavaScript file

```
<script src="email_list.js"></script>
```

The code for the JavaScript file named email_list.js

```javascript
const $ = selector => document.querySelector(selector);

const joinList = evt => {
    // get user entries from text boxes
    const email1 = $("#email_1").value;
    const email2 = $("#email_2").value;
    const firstName = $("#first_name").value;

    // check user entries
    let isValid = true;
    if (email1 == "") {
        $("#email_1_error").textContent = "Email is required.";
        isValid = false;
    } else {
        $("#email_1_error").textContent = "";
    }
    if (email1 != email2) {
        $("#email_2_error").textContent = "Emails must match.";
        isValid = false;
    } else {
        $("#email_2_error").textContent = "";
    }
    if (firstName == "") {
        $("#first_name_error").textContent = "First name is required.";
        isValid = false;
    } else {
        $("#first_name_error").textContent = "";
    }

    // cancel form submit if any user entries are invalid
    if ( !isValid ) {
        evt.preventDefault();
    }
};
```

Figure 1-9   The JavaScript for the web page (part 1)

The final if statement checks if any of the user's entries are invalid. If so, it uses the preventDefault() method to cancel the default method of the Join List submit button, which is to post the data in the form to the server. This prevents unnecessary round trips to the server.

In the clearForm() function, you can see three groups of code statements that modify the DOM. The first three statements clear any values in the text boxes, while the next three statements clear any error messages in the span elements. Finally, the last statement moves the browser's cursor to the first text box.

The last block of code is a call to the addEventListener() method, which attaches an anonymous function as the event handler for the DOMContentLoaded event. Then, within the anonymous function, the joinList() and clearForm() functions are attached as event handlers for the click events of the Join List and Clear Form buttons.

Although this code may look daunting right now, you'll see that it's all quite manageable. You'll also come to realize that DOM scripting is where JavaScript get its power.

The code for the JavaScript file named email_list.js (continued)

```javascript
const clearForm = () => {
    // clear text boxes
    $("#email_1").value = "";
    $("#email_2").value = "";
    $("#first_name").value = "";

    // clear span elements
    $("#email_1_error").textContent = "*";
    $("#email_2_error").textContent = "*";
    $("#first_name_error").textContent = "*";

    // set focus on first text box after resetting the form
    $("#email_1").focus();
};

document.addEventListener("DOMContentLoaded", () => {
    // hook up click events for both buttons
    $("#join_list").addEventListener("click", joinList);
    $("#clear_form").addEventListener("click", clearForm);

    // set focus on first text box after the form loads
    $("#email_1").focus();
});
```

Figure 1-9   The JavaScript for the web page (part 2)

The HTML skills that you need for this book

Although this book assumes that you are already familiar with HTML, the next three topics present a quick review of the HTML skills that you're going to need for this book. If you don't already have these skills and you can't pick them up from the topics that follow, we recommend that you use *Murach's HTML5 and CSS3* as a reference while you're learning JavaScript.

How to use the HTML5 semantic elements

All of the applications in this book use the HTML5 semantic elements whenever they're appropriate. If you aren't already using them or at least familiar with them, figure 1-10 summarizes what you need to know.

In particular, the applications in this book may use the main, section, aside, and nav elements. That makes it easier to apply CSS to these elements because you don't have to code id attributes that are used by the CSS. Instead, you can apply the CSS to the elements themselves.

The primary HTML5 semantic elements

Element	Contents
header	The header for a page.
main	The main content of a page. Can only appear once per page, and cannot be the child of an article, aside, footer, header, or nav element.
section	A generic section of a document that doesn't indicate the type of content.
article	A composition like an article in the paper.
aside	A portion of a page like a sidebar that is related to the content that's near it.
nav	A portion of a page that contains links to other pages or placeholders.
figure	An image, table, or other component that's treated as a figure.
footer	The footer for a page.

A page that's structured with header, main, and footer elements

```
<body>
    <header>
        <h1>San Joaquin Valley Town Hall</h1>
    </header>
    <main>
        <p>Welcome to San Joaquin Valley Town Hall. We have some
            fascinating speakers for you this season!</p>
    </main>
    <footer>
        <p>&copy; San Joaquin Valley Town Hall.</p>
    </footer>
</body>
```

The page displayed in a web browser

San Joaquin Valley Town Hall

Welcome to San Joaquin Valley Town Hall. We have some fascinating speakers for you this season!

© San Joaquin Valley Town Hall.

Description

- HTML5 provides *semantic elements* that you should use to structure the contents of a web page. Using these elements can be referred to as *HTML5 semantics*.
- All of the HTML5 elements are supported by the modern browsers.
- This book also uses standard HTML elements like h1 and h2 elements for headings, img elements for images, <a> elements for links, and <p> elements for paragraphs.

Figure 1-10   How to use the HTML5 semantic elements

How to use the div and span elements

If you've been using HTML for a while, you are certainly familiar with the div element. It has traditionally been used to divide an HTML document into divisions that are identified by id attributes. Then, CSS can use the ids to apply formatting to the divisions.

But now that HTML5 is available, div elements shouldn't be used to structure a document. Instead, they should only be used when the HTML5 semantic elements aren't appropriate.

Note, however, that div elements are often used in JavaScript applications. If, for example, a section element contains three h2 elements with each followed by a div element, JavaScript can be used to display or hide a div element whenever the heading that precedes it is clicked. This structure is illustrated by the first example in figure 1-11, and you'll see how this works in chapter 6.

Similarly, span elements have historically been used to identify portions of text that can be formatted by CSS. By today's standards, though, it's better to use elements that indicate the contents of the elements, like the cite, code, and <q> elements.

But here again, span elements are often used in JavaScript applications, as shown by the second example in this figure. In fact, you've just seen this in the Email List application. In that application, JavaScript puts the error messages in the appropriate span elements.

Notice that this code also uses div elements. Unlike in the first example, though, these elements are used so they can be formatted with CSS, and they're used because none of the HTML5 semantic elements are appropriate.

The div and span elements

Element	Description
div	A block element that provides a container for other elements.
span	An inline element that lets you identify text that can be formatted with CSS.

Div elements in the HTML for a JavaScript application

```
<section id="faqs">
    <h1>jQuery FAQs</h1>
    <h2>What is JavaScript?</h2>
    <div>
        // contents
    </div>
    <h2>What is jQuery?</h2>
    <div>
        // contents
    </div>
    <h2>Why is jQuery so popular?</h2>
    <div>
        // contents
    </div>
</section>
```

Span elements in the HTML for a JavaScript application

```
<div>
    <label for="email_1">Email Address:</label>
    <input type="text" id="email_1" name="email_1">
    <span id="email_1_error">*</span>
</div>
<div>
    <label for="email_2">Re-enter Email Address:</label>
    <input type="text" id="email_2" name="email_2">
    <span id="email_2_error">*</span>
</div>
<div>
    <label for="first_name">First Name</label>
    <input type="text" id="first_name" name="first_name">
    <span id="first_name_error">*</span>
</div>
```

Description

- Before HTML5, div elements were used to define the structure within the body of a document. The ids for these div elements were then used by the CSS to apply formatting to the elements.

- Today, the HTML5 semantic elements should be used to make the structure of a page more apparent. However, you will still use div elements to define blocks of code that are used in JavaScript applications.

- Before HTML5, span elements were often used to identify portions of text that you could apply formatting to.

- Today, a better practice is to use specific elements to identify content. However, you will still use span elements for some JavaScript applications.

Figure 1-11   How to use the div and span elements

How to use the basic HTML attributes

Figure 1-12 presents the HTML *attributes* that are commonly used in JavaScript applications. You should already be familiar with the *id attribute* that identifies one HTML element and with *class attributes* that can be applied to more than one HTML element. You should also be familiar with the *for attribute* that relates a label to an input element and with the *title attribute* that can be used to provide a tooltip for an element.

When you use JavaScript, you will commonly use the *name attribute* so the server-side code can access the data that is submitted to it. You will sometimes add or remove class attributes to change the formatting of elements. And you will sometimes use title attributes to provide text that's related to elements.

In practice, you usually use the same value for the id and name attributes of an element. For instance, the example in this figure uses "email" as the value of both the id and name attributes for the text box. That makes it easier to remember the attribute values.

The basic HTML attributes

Attribute	Description
`id`	Specifies a unique identifier for an element that can be referred to by CSS.
`class`	Specifies one or more class names that can be referred to by CSS, and the same name can be used for more than one element. To code more than one class name, separate the class names with spaces.
`name`	Specifies a unique name for an element that is commonly used by the server-side code and can also be used by the JavaScript code.
`for`	In a label element, this attribute specifies the id of the control that it applies to.
`title`	Specifies additional information about an element. For some elements, the title appears in a tooltip when the user hovers the mouse over the element.

HTML that uses these attributes

```
<body>
    <h1>San Joaquin Valley Town Hall</h1>
    <h2 class="first_h2">Welcome to San Joaquin Valley Town Hall.</h2>
    <p>Please enter your e-mail address to subscribe to our
        newsletter.</p>
    <form id="email_form" name="email_form"
            action="join.html" method="get">
        <label for="email">E-Mail: </label>
        <input type="text" id="email" name="email"
                title="Enter e-mail address here.">
        <input type="button" value="Subscribe">
    </form>
</body>
```

The HTML in a web browser with a tooltip displayed for the text box

San Joaquin Valley Town Hall

Welcome to San Joaquin Valley Town Hall.

Please enter your e-mail address to subscribe to our newsletter.

E-Mail: [   ] [Subscribe]

[Enter e-mail address here.]

Description

- An *attribute* consists of an attribute name, an equals sign, and the value of the attribute enclosed in either single or double quotation marks.

- The *id* and *class attributes* are commonly used to apply CSS formatting. The id attribute is also commonly used by JavaScript code to access an element.

- The *name attribute* is commonly used by server-side code to access data.

- The *for attribute* in a label element is used to identify the control that it applies to.

Figure 1-12   How to use the basic HTML attributes

The CSS skills that you need for this book

Although this book assumes that you are already familiar with CSS, the next three topics present a quick review of the CSS skills that you're going to need for this book. If you don't already have these skills and you can't pick them up from the topics that follow, we recommend that you use *Murach's HTML5 and CSS3* as a reference while you're learning JavaScript.

How to provide the CSS styles for an HTML page

Figure 1-13 shows two ways that you can include CSS styles for an HTML document. First, you can code a link element in the head section of an HTML document that specifies a file that contains the CSS for the page. This is referred to as an *external style sheet*, and this is the method that's used for the applications in this book.

Second, you can code a style element in the head section that contains the CSS for the page. This can be referred to as *embedded styles*. In general, it's better to use external style sheets because that makes it easier to use them for more than one page. However, embedded styles can be easier to use for simple applications like the ones in this book because you don't need to create an extra file.

In some cases, you may want to use two or more external style sheets for a single page. You may even want to use both external style sheets and embedded styles for a page. In these cases, the styles are applied from the first external style sheet to the last one and then the embedded styles are applied.

Two ways to provide styles

Use an external style sheet by coding a link element in the head section

```
<link rel="stylesheet" href="styles/main.css">
```

Embed the styles in the head section

```
<style>
    body {
        font-family: Arial, Helvetica, sans-serif;
        font-size: 87.5%; }
    h1 { font-size: 250%; }
</style>
```

The sequence in which styles are applied

- Styles from an external style sheet
- Embedded styles

A head element that includes two external style sheets

```
<head>
    <title>San Joaquin Valley Town Hall</title>
    <link rel="stylesheet" href="../styles/main.css">
    <link rel="stylesheet" href="../styles/speaker.css">
</head>
```

The sequence in which styles are applied

- From the first external style sheet to the last

Description

- When you use *external style sheets*, you separate content (HTML) from formatting (CSS). That makes it easy to use the same styles for two or more pages.

- If you use *embedded styles*, you have to copy the styles to other documents before you can use them in those documents.

- If more than one declaration for the same property is applied to the same element, the last declaration overrides the earlier declarations.

- When you specify a relative URL for an external CSS file, the URL is relative to the current file.

Figure 1-13   How to provide the CSS styles for an HTML page

How to code the basic CSS selectors

Figure 1-14 shows how to code the basic CSS selectors for applying styles to HTML elements. To start, this figure shows the body of an HTML document that contains a main and a footer element. Here, the two <p> elements in the main element have class attributes with the value "blue". Also, the <p> element in the footer has an id attribute with the value "copyright" and a class attribute with two values: "blue" and "right". This means that this element is assigned to two classes.

The four style rules in the first group of CSS examples are type selectors. To code a type selector, you just code the name of the element. As a result, the first style rule in this group selects the body element. The second style rule selects the main element. The third style rule selects the h1 element. And the fourth style rule selects all <p> elements.

In these examples, the first style rule changes the font for the body, and all of the elements within the body inherit this change. This style rule also sets the width of the body and centers it in the browser. Then, the second style rule puts a border around the main element and puts some padding inside the border. It also makes the main element a block element. This is necessary for IE because IE doesn't treat the main element as a block element.

The third style rule that uses a type selector sets the margins for the heading. In this case, all the margins are set to zero except for the bottom margin. Last, the style rule for the paragraphs sets the margins for the top, bottom, and left side of the paragraphs. That's why the paragraphs in the main element are indented.

The style rule in the second group of CSS examples uses an id selector to select an element by its id. To do that, the selector is a pound sign (#) followed by the id value that uniquely identifies an element. As a result, this style rule selects the <p> element that has an id of "copyright". Then, its one property declaration sets the font-size for the paragraph to 90% of the default font size.

The two style rules in the last group of CSS examples use class selectors to select HTML elements by class. To do that, the selector is a period (.) followed by the class name. As a result, the first style rule selects all elements that have been assigned to the "blue" class, which are all three <p> elements. The second style rule selects any elements that have been assigned to the "right" class. That is the paragraph in the footer. Then, the first style rule sets the color of the font to blue and the second style rule aligns the paragraph on the right.

One of the key points here is that a class attribute can have the same value for more than one element on a page. Then, if you code a selector for that class, it will be used to format all the elements in that class. By contrast, since the id for an element must be unique, an id selector can only be used to format a single element.

As you probably know, there are several other selectors that you can use with CSS. But the ones in this figure will get you started. Then, whenever an application in this book requires other selectors, the selectors will be explained in detail.

HTML that can be selected by element type, id, or class

```
<body>
    <main>
        <h1>The Speaker Lineup</h1>
        <p class="blue">October 19: Jeffrey Toobin</p>
        <p class="blue">November 16: Andrew Ross Sorkin</p>
    </main>
    <footer>
        <p id="copyright" class="blue right">Copyright SJV Town Hall</p>
    </footer>
</body>
```

CSS style rules that select by element type, id, and class

Elements by type

```
body {
    font-family: Arial, Helvetica, sans-serif;
    width: 400px;
    margin: 1em auto; }
main {
    display: block;
    padding: 1em;
    border: 2px solid black; }
h1 { margin: 0 0 .25em; }
p { margin: .25em 0 .25em 3em; }
```

One element by ID

```
#copyright { font-size: 90%; }
```

Elements by class

```
.blue { color: blue; }
.right { text-align: right; }
```

The elements displayed in a browser

The Speaker Lineup

October 19: Jeffrey Toobin
November 16: Andrew Ross Sorkin

Copyright SJV Town Hall

Description

- You code a selector for all elements of a specific type by naming the element. This is referred to as a *type selector*.

- You code a selector for an element with an id attribute by coding a pound sign (#) followed by the id value. This is known as an *id selector*.

- You code a selector for an element with a class attribute by coding a period followed by the class name. Then, the style rule applies to all elements with that class name. This is known as a *class selector*.

Figure 1-14   How to code the basic CSS selectors

How to code CSS style rules

Figure 1-15 presents the CSS for the Email List application that was presented earlier in this chapter. This is typical of the CSS for the applications in this book. Since the focus of this book is on JavaScript, not CSS, the CSS for the book applications is usually limited. For instance, the CSS in this example doesn't require id or class selectors.

Just to make sure we're using the same terminology, this CSS contains six *style rules*. Each style rule consists of a selector, a set of braces { }, and one or more *property declarations* within the braces. Also, each property declaration consists of a *property name*, a colon, the value or values for the rule, and an ending semicolon.

For instance, the first style rule is for the body element. It consists of six property declarations that set the font, background color, margins, width, border, and padding for the body. Here, the declaration for the margin property sets the top and bottom margins to zero and the right and left margins to "auto", which means the body will be centered in the browser window. And the declaration for the padding property sets the padding around the contents to 2 ems on the right and left and 1 em on the bottom. (An *em* is a typesetting term that is approximately equal to the width of a capital letter M.)

The second style rule is for the h1 element, and its one property declaration sets the color of the font to blue. Similarly, the one property declaration of the third style rule sets the bottom margin of div elements to 1 em.

The fourth style rule is for the label elements, and the fifth style rule is for the input elements. The style rule for label elements sets the display property to inline-block and the width property to 11 ems, and it aligns the text in the labels on the right. The style rule for input elements sets the left margin to 1 em, and it sets the right margin to .5 em.

The last style rule is for the span elements that follow the input elements. It just sets the color of the text in these elements to red because these elements will display the error messages for the application.

Beyond this brief introduction to CSS, this book will explain any of the CSS that is relevant to the JavaScript for an application. So for now, if you understand the style rules in this figure, you're ready to continue.

The CSS file for a typical application in this book

```
body {
    font-family: Arial, Helvetica, sans-serif;
    background-color: white;
    margin: 0 auto;
    width: 670px;
    border: 3px solid blue;
    padding: 0 2em 1em;
}
h1 {
    color: blue;
}
div {
    margin-bottom: 1em;
}
label {
    display: inline-block;
    width: 11em;
    text-align: right;
}
input {
    margin-left: 1em;
    margin-right: 0.5em;
}
span {
    color: red;
}
```

Description

- Because the focus of this book is JavaScript, not CSS, the CSS that's used in this book is usually simple. We just apply enough CSS to make each application look okay and work correctly.

- In fact, for most of the applications in this book, you won't have to understand the CSS so it won't even be shown. Whenever the CSS is critical to the understanding of the JavaScript application, though, it will be explained in detail.

- At the least, you should know that the CSS for an HTML document consists of one or more *style rules*. Each of these style rules starts with the selector for the style rule followed by a set of braces { }. Within the braces are one or more property declarations.

- You should also know that each CSS *property declaration* consists of a *property name*, a colon, the value or values for the property, and a semicolon.

- Many programmers use the popular Bootstrap CSS framework for their websites. Bootstrap's basic module allows you to lay out web pages using predefined classes. While beyond the scope of this book, Bootstrap is easy to use. You can search the Internet for more information.

Figure 1-15   How to code CSS style rules

How to test a JavaScript application

Next, you'll learn how to test a JavaScript application. To do that, you run the HTML for the web page that uses the JavaScript.

How to run a JavaScript application

When you develop a JavaScript application, you're usually working on your own computer or your company's server. Then, to run the application, you use one of the four methods shown in figure 1-16. Of the four, it's easiest to run the HTML page from the IDE or text editor that you're using to develop the HTML, CSS, and JavaScript files. You'll learn more about how to use VS Code to do that in a moment.

Otherwise, you can open the HTML file from your browser. To do that, you can press Ctrl+O to start the Open command. Or, you can find the file using File Explorer (Windows) or Finder (macOS) and then double-click on it. That will open the page in your system's default browser. Of course, you can also run a new page by clicking on the link to it in the current page.

After an application has been uploaded to an Internet web server, you can use the second set of methods in this figure to run the application. The first way is to enter a *Uniform Resource Locator (URL)* into the address bar of your browser. The second way is to click on a link in one web page that requests another page.

As the diagram in this figure shows, the URL for an Internet page consists of four components. In most cases, the *protocol* is HTTP or HTTPS. If you omit the protocol, the browser uses HTTP or HTTPS as the default.

The second component is the *domain name* that identifies the web server that the HTTP request will be sent to. The web browser uses this name to look up the address of the web server for the domain. Although you can't omit the domain name, you can often omit the "www." from the domain name.

The third component is the *path* where the file resides on the server. The path lists the folders that contain the file. Forward slashes are used to separate the names in the path and to represent the server's top-level folder at the start of the path. In this example, the path is "/ourwork/".

The last component is the name of the file. In this example, the file is named index.html. If you omit the filename, the web server will search for a default document in the path. Depending on the web server, this file will usually be named index.html, default.htm, or some variation of the two.

The web page at javascript_jquery/book_apps/ch01/email_list/index.html

Four ways to run an HTML page that's on your own server or computer

- From your browser, use the Ctrl+O shortcut key combination to start the Open command. Then, browse to the HTML file and double-click on it.
- Use File Explorer (Windows) or Finder (macOS) to find the HTML file, and double-click on it.
- Use the features of your text editor or IDE.
- Click on a link in the current web page to load the next web page.

Two ways to run an HTML page that's on the Internet

- Enter the URL of the web page into the browser's address bar.
- Click on a link in the current web page to load the next web page.

The components of an HTTP URL on the Internet

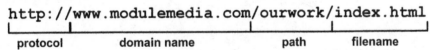

```
http://www.modulemedia.com/ourwork/index.html
```
   protocol   domain name   path   filename

What happens if you omit parts of a URL

- If you omit the protocol, the default of http:// or https:// will be used.
- If you omit the filename, the default document name for the web server will be used. This is typically index.html, default.htm, or some variation.

Description

- When you are developing JavaScript applications, you usually store them on your own computer instead of the Internet. So when you test the applications, you run them from your own computer.
- Later, after the applications are deployed to your Internet web server, you can run the applications from the Internet.

Figure 1-16   How to run a JavaScript application

How to find errors in your code

As you test even the simplest of applications, you're likely to have errors in your code. When that happens, the JavaScript may not run at all, or it may run for a short while and then stop. That's why figure 1-17 shows you how to find the errors in your code.

As this figure shows, if a JavaScript application doesn't run or stops running, you start by opening the *developer tools*. Although there are several ways to do that, you'll use the F12 key most of the time. That's why the developer tools for Chrome and other browsers are often referred to as the *F12 tools*.

Next, you open the Console panel of the developer tools to see if there's an error message. In this figure, the console shows a message for an error that occurred when the user started the Email List application, clicked on the Join our List button, and nothing happened.

Then, if you click on the link to the right of the error message, the Sources panel is displayed with the JavaScript statement that caused the error highlighted. In this case, the problem is that "email" should be "email_2" since that's the id of the second text box in the HTML.

Note that the Sources panel in this figure doesn't show the Debugging pane that's typically displayed at the right side of the panel. If you're not using this pane, you can close it by clicking on the Hide Debugger button at the right above the JavaScript code. To redisplay it, you can click the Show Debugger button.

In chapter 5, you'll learn more about testing and debugging, but the technique shown in this figure will be all that you need until your applications get more complicated.

Chrome with an open Console panel that shows an error

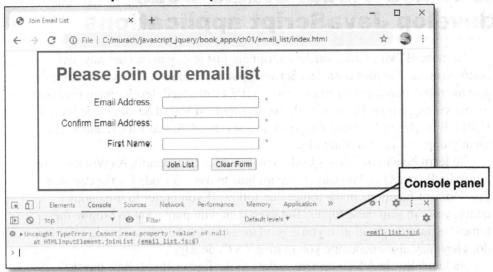

The Sources panel after the link in the Console panel has been clicked

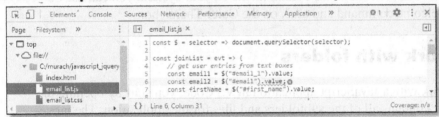

How to open or close Chrome's developer tools

- To open, press F12 or Ctrl+Shift+I. Or, click on the Menu button in the upper right corner of the browser, and select More Tools→Developer Tools.
- To close, click on the X in the upper right corner of the tools panel or press F12.

How to find the JavaScript statement that caused the error

- Open the Console panel by clicking on the Console tab. You should see an error message like the one above along with the line of code that caused the error.
- Click on the link to the right of the error message that indicates the line of code. That will open the Sources panel with the portion of JavaScript code that contains the statement displayed and the statement highlighted.

Description

- Chrome's *developer tools* provide some excellent debugging features, like identifying the JavaScript statement that caused an error.
- Because you usually start the developer tools by pressing the F12 key, these tools are often referred to as the *F12 tools*.

Figure 1-17   How to find errors in your code

How to use Visual Studio Code to develop JavaScript applications

Because HTML, CSS, and JavaScript are just text, you can use any text editor to create the files for a JavaScript application. However, a better editor or an *Integrated Development Environment* (*IDE*) can speed development time and reduce coding errors. For this book, we recommend Visual Studio Code (or VS Code). It is a free editor that runs on Windows, macOS, and Linux, and it can greatly improve your productivity.

To learn how to install VS Code, you can refer to appendix A (Windows) or appendix B (macOS). You can also learn how to use VS Code for the common development functions in the topics that follow. If you prefer to use another editor, you can skip these topics. But even then, you may want to browse these topics because they will give you a good idea of what an editor should be able to do. They may also encourage you to give VS Code a try.

Incidentally, the VS Code screenshots in the figures that follow use the light Visual Studio color theme. In contrast, the default theme for VS Code is dark. If you want to change the default theme on your system, you can use the Help→Welcome command and click on the Color Theme box.

How to work with folders

To work with a JavaScript application in VS Code, you start by opening the folder that contains all of the subfolders and files for the application. The procedure for doing that is described in figure 1-18.

After you open the folder for an application, it's subfolders and files are displayed in the Explorer window at the left side of VS Code's main window. In this example, the folder is for the Email List application presented in this chapter. If you open another folder, it replaces the folder that's currently open.

To make it easier to work with the applications for this book, we recommend that you use VS Code to open the folder that contains all of the applications. This is illustrated by the dialog box in this figure. After you do that, all of the chapter folders will be listed in the Explorer window, as you'll see in the next figure. Then, you'll be able to expand these folders to view and work with the subfolders and files that they contain. You'll get a chance to do this in exercise 1-3 at the end of this chapter.

This figure also shows how to add, rename, and delete folders. Note here that the technique for adding a folder to the main folder, in this case, the Email_List folder, is different from the technique for adding a folder to another folder. Finally, this figure shows how to close a folder.

The dialog box for choosing a folder in VS Code

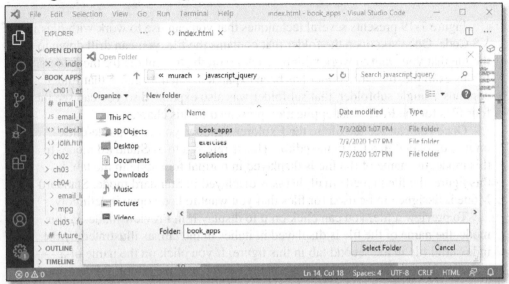

How to open a folder

1. Start VS Code and select File→Open Folder from the menu system.
2. Use the resulting dialog box to select the folder that contains the files you want to work with and then click Select Folder.

How to close a folder

- Select File→Close Folder from the menu system.

How to add, rename, or delete a folder

- To add a folder to the main folder, point to the name of the folder in the Explorer window and click the New Folder icon that's displayed to its right. Then, enter a name for the folder.
- To add other folders, right-click on a folder in the Explorer window and select New Folder. Then, enter a name for the folder.
- To rename a folder, right-click on it and select Rename. Then, edit the name.
- To delete a folder, right-click on it and select Delete.

Description

- *Visual Studio Code* (also known as *VS Code*) is a text editor that you can use to work with a variety of file types, including JavaScript, HTML, and CSS.
- All of the files for the applications presented in this book are stored in this folder:
  `\murach\javascript_jquery\book_apps`

Figure 1-18   How to work with folders in VS Code

How to work with files

Figure 1-19 presents several techniques that you can use to work with files in VS Code. Once you open the folder that contains the file, you can drill down to the file that you want to work with by clicking on the **>** symbols for the folders. In this example, the ch01 folder has been expanded. Then, because that folder contains a single subfolder, that subfolder was also expanded so you can see the four files for the Email List application presented in this chapter.

Once you can see the file in the Explorer window, you can double-click on it to display it in a tab in the editor. This is referred to as Standard mode. In this mode, the name of the file is displayed in normal font style in the tab. In this figure, the file named email_list.js is displayed in Standard mode. Standard Mode is designed to be used for files that you want to keep open indefinitely.

To preview a file, you can click on it to display it in Preview mode. In this mode, the name of the file is displayed in italics in the tab, as illustrated by the index.html file in the second tab in this figure. If you click on the name of a different file, VS Code loads that file in the same tab of the editor. Preview mode provides an excellent way to quickly view and edit various files, especially those files that you don't want to keep open for a long time.

When two or more files are displayed in an editor, you can switch between them by clicking on the tab for the file you want to display. Alternatively, you can select a file from the Open Editors list at the top of the Explorer window. This list includes all of the files that are currently displayed in an editor.

To close a file, you can use one of the techniques described in this figure. If you try to close a file and it has changes that haven't been saved, you'll be asked if you want to save the changes. You can also save changes to one or more files without closing them as described in this figure. You might want to do that if you're making more than just a few changes and you want to be sure the changes you've already made aren't lost.

This figure ends by showing how to add, rename, or delete a file. The skills for doing that are identical to the skills for adding, renaming, or deleting a folder, except that when you add a file, you click the New File icon or select New File. Note that when you add a file, you must include an extension (.html, .css, or .js) depending on whether it is going to be an HTML, CSS, or JavaScript file. Then, VS Code will know what type of file it is, and its editor will be adjusted to the syntax of that type of file when it is opened.

When you add a new file, you should realize that VS Code doesn't generate any code for it. Because of that, you have to enter all of the code yourself. Another option, though, is to copy code from another file and paste it into the new file. Or, you can open a similar file and then select File→Save As to save it with a new name. Then, you can delete the code you don't need and add code you do need.

VS Code with files in Standard and Preview mode

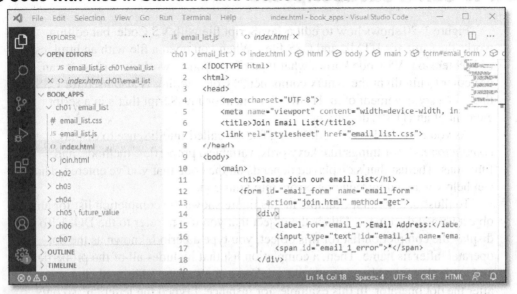

How to preview or open a file

- To open a file, double-click on it in the Explorer window. This displays the file in a tab in the editor with the name of the file in normal font style, indicating that you are in Standard Mode.

- To preview a file, click on it in the Explorer window. This displays the file in a tab in the editor with the name of the file in italics, indicating that you are in Preview Mode. If you open or preview another file, VS Code reuses the tab.

- To display a file that's already open, click on its tab or select it from the Open Editors list at the top of the Explorer window.

How to close or save a file

- To close a file, click the X in the upper right corner of the tab for the file, click the X to the left of the file name in the Open Editors list, or select File→Close Editor.

- If you close a file with changes, you'll be asked if you want to save the changes.

- If you want to saves changes without closing a file, select File→Save. To save changes to more than one file, select File→Save All.

How to add, rename, or delete a file

- To add a file, you use the same skills as you do for adding a folder except that you click the New File icon or select New File. When you name the file, be sure to include an extension.

- VS Code doesn't generate any starting code for new files. As a result, you must enter all code for the file yourself or use similar code from another file.

- To rename or delete a file, you use the same skills as you do for renaming or deleting a folder.

Figure 1-19   How to work with files in VS Code

How to edit a JavaScript file

Figure 1-20 shows how to edit a JavaScript file with VS Code, but editing works the same for HTML and CSS files. When you open a file with an html, css, or js extension, VS Code knows what type of file you're working with so it can use color to highlight the syntax components. Color coding is also used for CSS that's in a style element of an HTML document or JavaScript that's in a script element of an HTML document.

As you enter code, VS Code uses a feature called IntelliSense to display *completion lists* for things like keywords, variables, properties, methods, and functions. The list that's displayed depends on the code that you've entered. That can help you avoid introducing errors into your code.

To illustrate, the first example in this figure shows the completion list for an object named document. This is the object that you use to refer to the DOM. To display the completion list for this object, you type a period, known as the dot operator, after its name. Then, a completion list that includes all of the properties and methods of the object are displayed. You can also type additional characters after the dot operator. In this example, for instance, I typed the letter "q" so only the properties and methods that contain this letter are displayed.

When a completion list is displayed, you can insert an item by clicking on it. Alternatively, you can highlight the entry you want by using the arrow keys to scroll through the list. Then, you can complete the entry by pressing the Tab or Enter key.

This also works with HTML and CSS entries. If, for example, you type "<s" in an HTML document, VS Code presents a list of the elements that start with the letter *s*. Then, if you select one of the elements and enter a right angle bracket, VS Code adds the closing tag. This feature also works when you start an attribute.

Similarly, if you start to enter the name of an element for a CSS style rule, VS Code presents a list of the elements with the letters you enter. If you enter one or more letters to start a property declaration, VS Code presents a list of the properties that start with those letters. And if you start an entry for a property value, VS Code will present a list of values.

If VS Code detects an error as you type, it displays a red wavy line under the error as shown in the second example. Here, the else keyword is underlined because the preceding if block doesn't end with a right brace (}). To display the description of an error, you can hover the mouse over the red wavy underline. Alternatively, you can open the Problems window to display a list of all the errors. Then, you can click on an error to display it in the file.

The Explorer window also indicates if a file contains errors. To do that, it displays the name of the file, as well as the name of the folder that contains the file, in red. In addition, it displays the number of errors in the file to the right of the filename.

As you work with VS Code, you'll see that it has the same type of interface that you've used with other programs. So if you want to do something that isn't presented in this chapter, try right-clicking on an item to see what menu options are available and see what's available from the menu system. With a little experimentation, you'll find that this program is easy to use.

The completion list for selecting a property or method of an object

The Problems window with an error displayed

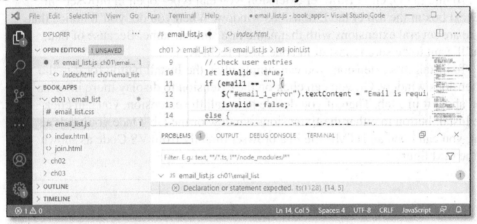

How to use the IntelliSense feature

- IntelliSense displays *completion lists* for things like keywords, variables, properties, methods, and functions as you type so you can enter them correctly.
- To insert an item from a completion list, click on it or highlight it and then press the Tab or Enter key.
- If you enter an opening parenthesis or brace, the closing parenthesis or brace is added automatically.

How to identify the errors that are marked by VS Code

- If VS Code detects a syntax error, it underlines it with a red wavy line.
- To get the description for an error, hover the mouse over the red wavy line.
- To see all the errors in a file, you can display the Problems window (View→Problems). Then, you can click on an error to take you to it in the file.

Description

- VS Code simplifies the task of editing JavaScript code by providing features like IntelliSense, error checking, and color coding.

Figure 1-20   How to edit a JavaScript file in VS Code

How to install the Open in Browser extension

As you develop JavaScript applications, you'll want to open the HTML files that contain the script elements in one or more browsers. Unfortunately, VS Code doesn't provide a way to do that out of the box. Because of that, we recommend that you install an extension to VS Code that lets you open HTML files in a browser. One popular extension is Open in Browser from TechER, and figure 1-21 shows how to install it.

To start, you click the Extensions icon in the left sidebar. Then, the Extensions window is displayed in place of the Explorer window. This window lists any extensions that are already installed as well as any recommended extensions.

To find the Open in Browser extension, you can type "open in browser" in the text box at the top of the Extensions window. When you do, you'll notice that there are several extensions with that name or a similar name. Because of that, you'll want to be sure to install the one from TechER.

To install this extension, you can simply click the Install button for it in the Extensions window. Or, you can click on the extension to display more information about it in a tab. Then, if you decide to install the extension, you can click the Install button in either the Extensions window or the tab. Once you've done that, you can open an HTML file in a browser directly from VS Code as shown in the next figure.

VS Code as the Open in Browser extension is installed

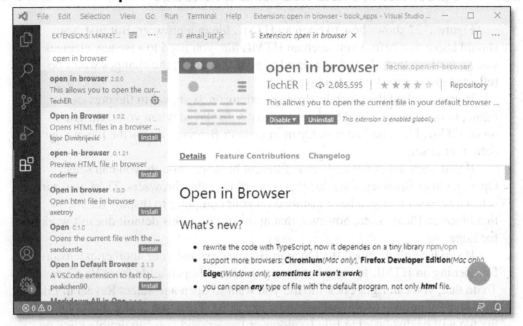

How to install the Open in Browser extension

1. Click the Extensions icon in the left sidebar.
2. Enter "open in browser" in the text box at the top of the Extensions window to filter the available extensions.
3. Click the Install button for the Open in Browser extension from TechER. Or, click on the extension to display information about it in a tab, and then click the Install button in the tab.

Description

*   By default, VS Code doesn't provide a way to open an HTML file in a browser so you can test the JavaScript code it uses.
*   To make it easier to open an HTML file in a browser, you can install an extension to VS Code. One popular extension is the Open in Browser extension developed by TechER.

Figure 1-21   How to install the Open in Browser extension

How to open an HTML file in a browser

Figure 1-22 shows how to open an HTML file in a browser. But first, you should know that before you open an HTML file, you need to save any changes you've made to that file and its related files. If you don't, the changes won't be reflected in the page that's displayed.

If you installed the Open in Browser extension as shown in the previous figure, two items are added to the menu that's displayed when you right-click on an HTML file. The first one, Open in Default Browser, opens the file in your default browser.

If you want to open the file in a different browser, though, you can select Open in Other Browser. This displays a list of the other browsers. Then, you can select a browser that you have installed on your computer to display the file in that browser. Please note, however, that at this writing, this default doesn't work for Edge.

If you haven't installed the Open in Browser extension or another extension for opening an HTML file in a browser, you can still open a file from VS Code. To do that, you can right-click the file you want to open and select Reveal in File Explorer (Windows) or Reveal in Finder (macOS). Then, the folder that contains the file will be displayed in File Explorer or Finder, and you can double-click on the file to open it.

When you open an HTML file from File Explorer or Finder or by using the Open in Browser extension, a new browser or browser tab is opened each time. But in most case, that's not what you want. To avoid that, you can open the file just once. Then, after you find and fix the errors in VS Code, you can save the changes, switch to the browser, and click on the Reload or Refresh button in the browser to reload the file with the changes. That way, you use the same tab or Browser instance each time you test the application.

How to open an HTML file using the Open in Browser extension

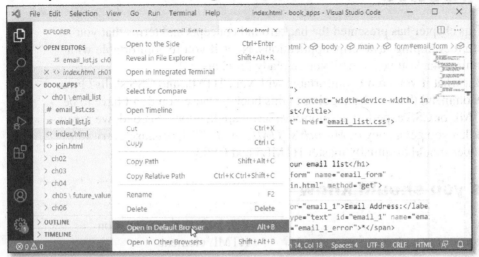

The web page in Chrome

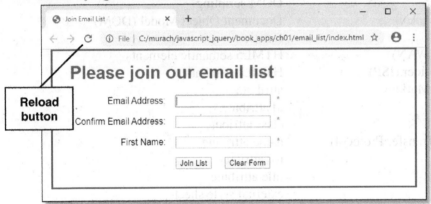

Description

- If you installed the Open in Browser extension as shown in the previous figure, you can open an HTML file by right-clicking on the file in the Explorer window and selecting Open in Default Browser to open the file in your default browser.

- If you select Open in Other Browsers when you're using the Open in Browser extension, you can select the browser in which you want the file to be opened. Note, however, that at this writing, this doesn't work for Edge.

- If you haven't installed the Open in Browser extension, you can right-click on the file in the Explorer window and select Reveal in File Explorer (Windows) to display it in File Explorer or Reveal in Finder (macOS) to display it in Finder. Then, you can double-click the file to open it.

- Every time you open an HTML file from VS Code, another browser instance or browser tab is opened. Another alternative is to save the corrected files in VS Code, switch to the browser, and click its Reload or Refresh button.

Figure 1-22   How to open an HTML file in a browser

Perspective

This chapter has presented the background concepts and terms that you need for developing JavaScript applications. Now, if you're comfortable with everything that you've learned, you're ready for chapter 2.

But what if you aren't comfortable with your HTML and CSS skills? First, we recommend that you keep going in this book because you don't have to be an HTML or CSS expert to develop JavaScript applications. Second, we recommend that you get a copy of *Murach's HTML5 and CSS3*, because every web developer should eventually master HTML5 and CSS3.

Terms you should know

client
web browser
web server
network
intranet
local area network (LAN)
Internet
wide area network (WAN)
Internet service provider (ISP)
HTML (HyperText Markup
    Language)
static web page
HTTP (HyperText Transfer Protocol)
HTTP request
HTTP response
render a web page
dynamic web page
application server
database server
server-side processing
round trip
JavaScript
JavaScript engine
scripting language
client-side processing
image swap
image rollover
data validation
jQuery
European Computer Manufacturers
    Association (ECMA)

ECMAScript specification
HTML element
tag
CSS (Cascading Style Sheets)
DOM scripting
Document Object Model (DOM)
function
HTML5 semantic elements
HTML5 semantics
attribute
id attribute
class attribute
name attribute
for attribute
title attribute
external style sheet
embedded styles
CSS selector
type selector
id selector
class selector
style rule
property declaration
property name
URL (Uniform Resource Locator)
protocol
domain name
path
developer tools
IDE (Integrated Development
    Environment)

Summary

- A web application consists of clients, a web server, and a network. *Clients* use *web browsers* to request web pages from the web server. The *web server* returns the requested pages.

- A *local area network* (*LAN*) connects computers that are near to each other. This is often called an *intranet*. By contrast, the *Internet* consists of many *wide area networks* (*WANs*).

- To request a web page, the web browser sends an *HTTP request* to the web server. Then, the web server gets the HTML for the requested page and sends it back to the browser in an *HTTP response*. Last, the browser *renders* the HTML into a web page.

- A *static web page* is a page that is the same each time it's retrieved. By contrast, the HTML for a *dynamic web page* is generated by a server-side program or script, so its HTML can change from one request to another.

- *JavaScript* is a *scripting language* that is run by the *JavaScript engine* of a web browser. It provides for *client-side processing*. *jQuery* is a JavaScript library that makes it easier to code many common functions.

- JavaScript is commonly used to modify the *Document Object Model* (*DOM*) that's built for each web page when it is loaded. This is referred to as *DOM scripting*. When the DOM is changed, the browser immediately changes its display so it reflects those changes.

- The ECMAScript specification provides the standards that JavaScript implements. At this writing, most modern browser support all of the important features through ES2020.

- HTML (HyperText Markup Language) is the language that defines the structure and contents of a web page. CSS (Cascading Style Sheets) is used to control how the web pages are formatted.

- You can view a web page that's on your own computer or server or on an Internet server. To view a web page on an Internet server, you can enter the URL (Uniform Resource Locator) that consists of the protocol, domain name, path, and filename into a browser's address bar.

- To help find errors when you test a JavaScript application, you can use the Console panel in Chrome's developer tools.

- To develop JavaScript applications, you can use an Integrated Development Environment (IDE) or a text editor like VS Code.

Before you do the exercises for this book...

Before you do the exercises for this book, you should download and install the Chrome browser as well as the applications for this book. If you're going to use VS Code, you should also download and install that product. The procedures for installing the software and applications for this book are in appendix A (Windows) and appendix B (macOS).

Exercise 1-1   Run the Email List application

In this exercise, you'll run the Email List application that's presented in figures 1-7 through 1-9.

Open the application in Chrome

1. Start Chrome if it isn't already open. Then, use the Ctrl+O key combination to open this HTML file:

    `murach\javascript_jquery\book_apps\ch01\email_list\index.html`

2. To test what happens when you don't enter any data, just click the Join List button without entering any data.

3. Enter an email address in the first text box and invalid data in the second text box and click the Join List button to see what error messages are displayed.

4. Enter valid data for all three text boxes and click on the button. Then, the data is submitted for processing and a new web page is displayed.

Preview the developer tools

5. To rerun the application, click the browser's Back button. This should reset the entries.

6. Enter an email address in the first text box, leave the other text boxes empty, and click the Join List button. Then, press F12 to open Chrome's developer tools. Display the Console tab by clicking on it, and note that it doesn't contain any error messages.

7. Click on the Sources tab. Then, if it's not already displayed, click on the email_list.js file in the left pane to see the JavaScript code for the page. Do the same for the index.html file to see the HTML for the page.

8. Click on the Elements tab, and drill down to see the HTML elements within the form element for the page. In the span elements, you can see the error messages that are displayed, not the starting values in the HTML. That's because the Elements tab represents the Document Object Model for the page, and JavaScript has changed that model.

9. Do more experimenting if you want. These are powerful debugging tools that you'll use a lot as you go through this book, so it's good to become familiar with them. When you're through, press the F12 button to close the tools.

Exercise 1-2   Run other section 1 applications

This exercise has you run two of the applications presented in chapters 6 and 7. That will give you some idea of what you'll be able to do when you complete this section.

Run the FAQs application of chapter 6

1. Open this file in the Chrome browser:
   `murach\javascript_jquery\book_apps\ch06\faqs\index.html`

2. Click on the first heading to display the text for it, and click the heading again to hide the text.

3. Tab to the next heading and press the Enter key to display the text for it, and press the Enter key again to hide the text.

Run the Image Swap application of chapter 7

4. Open this file in the Chrome browser:
   `murach\javascript_jquery\book_apps\ch07\image_swap\index.html`

   Notice the four small images near the top of the page, and notice that a larger version of the first image is displayed below the smaller images.

5. Click on the second image to see that a larger version of that image is now displayed.

6. Tab to the next image and press the Enter key to display a larger version of that image.

Exercise 1-3   Get started with VS Code

This exercise is for readers who are going to use VS Code with this book. It guides you through the process of using VS Code to work with the files for the JavaScript book applications and exercises that you've downloaded. Before you do this exercise, you need to install VS Code as shown in Appendix A or B.

Start VS Code and consider changing the color theme

1. Start VS Code. Then, if the Welcome page isn't displayed, use the Help→Welcome command to open it. Now, click on the Color Theme box and review the color themes. If you want to change the theme, do that now.

Open the folders for this book

2. Use the procedure in figure 1-18 to open the book applications that are stored in this folder:
   `murach\javascript_jquery\book_apps`

   After you open this folder, you should see the chapter folders within this folder listed in the Explorer window.

3. Use the same procedure to open the exercise starts that are stored in this folder:

```
javascript_jquery\exercises
```

When you do that, notice that the folder that contains the book applications is closed.

Test the Email List application

4. Use the procedure in figure 1-21 to install the Open in Browser extension.

5. In the Explorer window, click on the > symbol before ch01 to display the files for the Email List application.

6. Right-click the file named index.html, and select Open in Default Browser to open that file in your default browser.

7. Switch back to VS Code. If you have another browser installed on your computer, right-click on the index.html file again, but this time select Open in Other Browsers. Then, click on the other browser to open the file in that browser. But remember that at this writing, this doesn't work for Edge.

Edit the JavaScript code

8. In the Explorer window, double-click on the file named email_list.js to open that file, and note the colors that are used for syntax highlighting.

9. In the JavaScript file, delete the right parenthesis in the first line of code. This should display a red wavy line under the semicolon at the end of the line. Then, hover the mouse over this line to display the error description. This illustrates VS Code's error-checking feature. Now, undo the change that you made. (To undo a change with the keyboard, press Ctrl+Z.)

10. In the JavaScript file, after the third statement that starts with const in the joinList() function, start a statement on a new line with these characters:

```
if (e
```

This should insert the closing parenthesis and display a list of the possible entries that start with the letter e. Here, you can see that email1 and email2 are included in the list. These are the constants that are created by the first two const statements in this function, and this illustrates VS Code's IntelliSense feature. Now, undo this change.

11. Enter the statement that follows on a new line that comes right before the last line of the JavaScript code, which consists of just a right brace followed by a right parenthesis and a semicolon:

```
alert("The DOM has now been built");
```

12. To test the statement that you added, select File→Save from the menu system to save your changes. Then, switch to your browser and click on the Reload or Refresh button. When you do, a dialog box should be displayed indicating that the DOM has been built. To close this dialog box, click on its OK button.

13. If you're curious, do more experimenting. Then, exit from VS Code and close the browser or tab.

2

Get started fast with JavaScript

The goal of this chapter is to get you off to a good start with JavaScript, especially if you're new to programming. If you have programming experience with another language, you should be able to move rapidly through this chapter. Otherwise, take it easy and do the exercises at the end of this chapter.

How to include JavaScript in an HTML document

In chapter 1, you saw how to use the script element to include the JavaScript for an application that's in a separate file. But you can also code JavaScript directly within a script element. You'll learn more about both ways to use the script element now.

How to use the script element

The table in figure 2-1 presents two attributes of the script element. As you saw in the last chapter, you use this element to include the JavaScript that's in a separate *external file*.

In the script element, the src attribute is used to refer to the external file. You can also code a type attribute with the value "text/javascript" to tell the browser what kind of content the file contains. But with HTML5, that attribute isn't needed because the assumption is that all files that are referred to in script elements contain JavaScript. However, you might see the type attribute in legacy code or in online examples.

In the first example in this figure, the src attribute refers to a file named calculate_mpg.js. The assumption here is that this file is in the same folder as the HTML file. Otherwise, you need to code a relative URL that provides the right path for the file. If, for example, the JavaScript file is in a folder named javascript and that folder is in the same folder as the HTML file, the src attribute would be coded this way:

```
<script src="javascript/calculate_mpg.js"></script>
```

This works the same as it does for any other file reference in an HTML document.

The second example in this figure shows another way to include JavaScript in an HTML document. Here, the JavaScript is coded directly within the script element. This can be referred to as *embedded JavaScript*.

Your applications will work the same whether the JavaScript is embedded in the script element or included from an external file. However, it's a better practice to use external files. That's because an external file separates the JavaScript from the HTML. Another benefit is that it makes it easier to reuse the code in other pages or applications.

As you can see, the script elements in both of the examples in this figure are coded at the end of the body element. You can also code script elements in the head element of an HTML document. However, it's recommended that you code your script elements in the body element after any other HTML elements. That way, your scripts have access to those HTML elements if they need them. In addition, all of the HTML will load before the JavaScript code is executed, which can prevent a blank page from being displayed for long-running scripts.

Two attributes of the script element

Attribute	Description
src	Specifies the location (source) of an external JavaScript file.
type	With HTML5, this attribute can be omitted. If you code it, use "text/javascript" for JavaScript code.

A script element that includes JavaScript that's in an external file in an HTML page

```
<body>
    ...
    <script src="calculate_mpg.js"></script>
</body>
```

A script element that embeds JavaScript in an HTML page

```
<body>
    ...
    <script>
        alert("The Calculate MPG application");

        let miles = prompt("Enter miles driven");
        miles = parseInt(miles);

        let gallons = prompt("Enter gallons of gas used");
        gallons = parseInt(gallons);

        let mpg = miles/gallons;
        mpg = parseFloat(mpg);

        alert("Miles per gallon = " + mpg);
    </script>
</body>
```

Description

- You can use a script element to identify an *external JavaScript file* that should be included with an HTML page. This is the more common way of including JavaScript.

- You can also use a script element that contains the JavaScript statements to be included in an HTML page. This can be referred to as *embedded JavaScript.*

- When a script element identifies an external JavaScript file, the JavaScript code in that file runs as if it were embedded in the script element.

- If you code more than one script element, the JavaScript code is included in the sequence in which the elements appear.

- You can also code script elements in the head element of an HTML document. However, it's recommended that you include your script elements at the end of the body element.

Figure 2-1   How to use the script element

How to use the noscript element

In the last figure, you learned how to include JavaScript in an HTML document. However, if a user has JavaScript disabled in their browser, then your JavaScript code won't run and your website won't function properly.

You can use the HTML noscript element to include the content in a web page that you want to display when a user has JavaScript disabled in their browser. In that case, the content within the noscript element is displayed. However, when JavaScript is enabled, the browser ignores the noscript element.

Programmers used to use noscript elements to create an alternate experience for users without JavaScript. However, over time websites became more reliant on JavaScript code to function, and that JavaScript code became more complex, making this strategy harder to implement. Today, noscript elements are used more often to notify a user that they need to enable JavaScript to use the website.

Figure 2-2 shows an HTML page with two noscript elements. The first one is within a header element. It displays a message that the website won't function properly if JavaScript isn't enabled in the browser.

The second noscript element is within the footer element, after a script element with embedded JavaScript that gets and displays the current date. Here, the noscript element provides an alternate experience to displaying the current date.

Next, this figure shows how this HTML page looks in a browser with JavaScript enabled. As you can see, none of the content within the noscript elements is sent to the browser. By contrast, the date produced by the embedded JavaScript code in the script element is sent to the browser.

Next, this figure shows how this HTML page looks in a browser with JavaScript disabled. This time, the content within both noscript elements is sent to the browser, while the embedded JavaScript code in the script element doesn't execute.

If you include noscript elements in your HTML page, it can be useful to run your browser with JavaScript disabled so you can make sure these elements work the way you want them to. This figure shows how to disable and enable JavaScript in the Chrome browser.

An HTML page with two noscript elements

```
<body>
    <header>
        <h1>Welcome to my website!</h1>
        <noscript>
            <h2>To get the most from this website, please enable JavaScript
            in your browser.</h2>
        </noscript>
    </header>
    <!-- main HTML for page goes here -->
    <footer>
        <script>
            const today = new Date();
            document.write(`Today is ${today.toDateString()}.`);
        </script>
        <noscript>
            Today is the first day of the rest of your life.
        </noscript>
    </footer>
</body>
```

How the page looks in a browser with JavaScript enabled

Welcome to my website!

Today is Tue May 18 2021.

How the page looks in a browser with JavaScript disabled

Welcome to my website!

To get the most from this website, please enable JavaScript in your browser.

Today is the first day of the rest of your life.

How to disable JavaScript in Chrome

1. Click the menu button in the upper right corner of the browser window.
2. Select Settings, then scroll to the "Privacy and security" section.
3. Expand Site Settings, then scroll to and expand the JavaScript item.
4. Toggle the Allowed switch to Blocked.

How to enable JavaScript in Chrome

- Follow the procedure above, but toggle the Blocked switch to Allowed.

Description

- You can use the noscript element to display content when JavaScript is disabled. This creates an alternate experience for non-JavaScript users.
- More often, you'll use noscript elements to let users know they need to enable JavaScript.
- You can test your noscript elements by disabling JavaScript in your browser.

Figure 2-2   How to use the noscript element

The JavaScript syntax

The *syntax* of JavaScript refers to the rules that you must follow as you code statements. If you don't adhere to these rules, your web browser won't be able to interpret and execute your statements.

How to code JavaScript statements

Figure 2-3 summarizes the rules for coding *JavaScript statements*. The first rule is that JavaScript is case-sensitive. This means that uppercase and lowercase letters are treated as different letters. For example, *salestax* and *salesTax* are treated as different names.

The second rule is that JavaScript statements should end with a semicolon. That way, it will be easier to tell where one statement ends and the next one begins. To help remind you to include semicolons, many IDEs issue a warning if you omit them.

The third rule is that JavaScript ignores extra whitespace in statements. Since *whitespace* includes spaces, tabs, and new line characters, this lets you break long statements into multiple lines so they're easier to read.

Be careful, though, to follow the guidelines in this figure about where to split a statement. If you don't split a statement at a good spot, JavaScript will sometimes try to help you out by adding a semicolon for you, and that can lead to errors.

Finally, JavaScript has a *strict mode* that restricts the sorts of things you can do in your JavaScript code. For instance, later in this chapter you'll learn how to declare a variable using keywords. In non-strict mode, JavaScript also allows you to declare a variable without using a keyword. However, doing so leads to some unexpected behavior, which can lead to bugs that are hard to track down. In strict mode, though, if you try to declare a variable without a keyword, JavaScript throws an error. This alerts you to problems right away and helps you write safer code.

To enable strict mode, you code the "use strict" directive at the top of a code file or at the top of a function like the one shown in this figure. You should always use strict mode unless you've got a good reason not to. All of the applications for this book include the "use strict" directive at the top of every JavaScript code file.

A block of JavaScript code

```
const joinList = () => {
    "use strict";

    const emailAddress1 = $("#email_address1").value;
    const emailAddress2 = $("#email_address2").value;
    const firstName = $("#first_name").value;

    if (emailAddress1 == "") {
        alert("Email Address is required.");
    } else if (emailAddress2 == "") {
        alert("Second Email Address is required.");
    } else if (emailAddress1 != emailAddress2) {
        alert("Second Email entry must equal first entry.");
    } else if (firstName == "") {
        alert("First Name is required.");
    } else {
        $("email_form").submit();
    }
};
```

The basic syntax rules

- JavaScript is case-sensitive.
- Each JavaScript statement ends with a semicolon.
- JavaScript ignores extra whitespace within statements.
- When JavaScript is in *strict mode*, it disallows certain JavaScript features and coding practices that are considered unsafe.

How to split a statement over two or more lines

- Split a statement after:
  an arithmetic or relational operator such as +, −, *, /, =, ==, >, or <
  an opening brace ({), bracket ([ ), or parenthesis
  a closing brace (})
- Do not split a statement after:
  an identifier, a value, or the *return* keyword
  a closing bracket ( ]) or closing parenthesis

Description

- A JavaScript *statement* has a syntax that's similar to the syntax of Java.
- *Whitespace* refers to the spaces, tab characters, and return characters in the code, and it is ignored by the compiler. As a result, you can use spaces, tab characters, and return characters to format your code so it's easier to read.
- In some cases, JavaScript will try to correct what it thinks is a missing semicolon by adding a semicolon at the end of a split line. To prevent this, follow the guidelines above for splitting a statement.
- *Strict mode* helps you write safer, cleaner code. To enable strict mode, you can include the "use strict" directive at the top of a code file or the top of a function.

Figure 2-3   How to code JavaScript statements

How to create identifiers

Variables, constants, functions, objects, properties, methods, and events must all have names so you can refer to them in your JavaScript code. An *identifier* is the name given to one of these components.

Figure 2-4 shows the rules for creating identifiers in JavaScript. Besides the first four rules, you can't use any of the JavaScript *reserved words* (also known as *keywords*) as an identifier. These are words that are reserved for use within the JavaScript language. You should also avoid using any of the JavaScript global properties or methods as identifiers, which you'll learn more about as you progress through this book.

Besides the rules, you should give your identifiers meaningful names. That means that it should be easy to tell what an identifier refers to and easy to remember how to spell the name. To create names like that, you should avoid abbreviations. If, for example, you abbreviate the name for monthly investment as mon_inv, it will be hard to tell what it refers to and hard to remember how you spelled it. But if you spell it out as monthly_investment, both problems are solved.

Similarly, you should avoid abbreviations that are specific to one industry or field of study unless you are sure the abbreviation will be widely understood. For example, mpg is a common abbreviation for miles per gallon, but cpm could stand for a number of different things and should be spelled out.

To create an identifier that has more than one word in it, many JavaScript programmers use a convention called *camel casing*. With this convention, the first letter of each word is uppercase except for the first word. For example, monthlyInvestment and taxRate are identifiers that use camel casing.

An alternative is to use a convention called *snake casing*. With this convention, all the words in an identifier are lower case and separated by underscore characters. For example, monthly_investment and tax_rate are identifiers that use snake casing. If the standards in your shop specify one of these conventions, by all means use it. Otherwise, you can use whichever convention you prefer...but be consistent.

In this book, snake casing is used for the ids and class names in the HTML, and camel casing is used for all JavaScript identifiers. That way, it will be easier for you to tell where the names originated.

Rules for creating identifiers

- Identifiers can only contain letters, numbers, the underscore, and the dollar sign.
- Identifiers can't start with a number.
- Identifiers are case-sensitive.
- Identifiers can be any length.
- Identifiers can't be the same as *reserved words*.
- Avoid using global properties and methods as identifiers. If you use one of them, you won't be able to use the global property or method with the same name.

Valid identifiers in JavaScript

```
subtotal          index_1              $
taxRate           calculate_click      $log
```

Camel casing versus snake casing

```
taxRate           tax_rate
calculateClick    calculate_click
emailAddress      email_address
futureValue       future_value
```

Naming recommendations

- Use meaningful names for identifiers. That way, your identifiers aren't likely to be reserved words or global properties.
- Be consistent: Either use camel casing (taxRate) or snake casing (tax_rate) to identify the words within the variables in your scripts.
- If you use snake casing, use lowercase for all letters.

Reserved words in JavaScript

```
abstract      else         instanceof    switch
arguments     enum         int           synchronized
boolean       eval         interface     this
break         export       let           throw
byte          extends      long          throws
case          false        native        transient
catch         final        new           true
char          finally      null          try
class         float        package       typeof
const         for          private       var
continue      function     protected     void
debugger      goto         public        volatile
default       if           return        while
delete        implements   short         with
do            import       static        yield
double        in           super
```

Description

- *Identifiers* are the names given to variables, functions, objects, properties, and methods.
- In *camel casing*, all of the words within an identifier except the first word start with capital letters. In *snake casing*, all words are lower case and separated by underscores.

Figure 2-4   How to create identifiers

How to use comments

Comments let you add descriptive notes to your code that are ignored by the JavaScript engine. Later on, these comments can help you or someone else understand the code whenever it needs to be modified.

The example in figure 2-5 shows how comments can be used to describe or explain portions of code. At the start, a *block comment* describes what the application does. This kind of comment starts with /* and ends with */. Everything that's coded between the start and the end is ignored by the JavaScript engine when the application is run.

The other kind of comment is a *single-line comment* that starts with //. In the example, the first single-line comment describes what the JavaScript that comes before it on the same line does. By contrast, the second single-line comment takes up a line by itself. It describes what the function that comes after it does.

In addition to describing JavaScript code, comments can be useful when testing an application. If, for example, you want to disable a portion of the JavaScript code, you can enclose it in a block comment. Then, it will be ignored when the application is run. This can be referred to as *commenting out* a portion of code. Later, after you test the rest of the code, you can enable the commented out code by removing the markers for the start and end of the block comment. This can be referred *uncommenting*.

Comments are also useful when you want to experiment with changes in code. For instance, you can make a copy of a portion of code, comment out the original code, and then paste the copy just above the original code that is now commented out. Then, you can make changes in the copy. But if the changes don't work, you can restore your old code by deleting the new code and uncommenting the old code.

When should you use comments to describe or explain code? Certainly, when the code is so complicated that you may not remember how it works if you have to maintain it later on. This kind of comment is especially useful if someone else is going to have to maintain the code.

On the other hand, you shouldn't use comments to explain code that any professional programmer should understand. That means that you have to strike some sort of balance between too much and too little.

One of the worst problems with comments is changing the way the code works without changing the related comments. Then, the comments mislead the person who is trying to maintain the code, which makes the job even more difficult.

A portion of JavaScript code that includes comments

```
/* this application validates a user's entries for joining
   our email list
*/
"use strict";

const $ = selector => {                          // the $ function
    return document.querySelector(selector);
};
// this function gets and validates the user entries
const joinList = () => {
    const emailAddress1 = $("#email_address1").value;
    const emailAddress2 = $("#email_address2").value;
    const firstName = $("#first_name").value;
    let isValid = true;                          // set default value

    // validate the first entry
    if (emailAddress1 == "") {
        $("email_address1_error").textContent = "This field is required.";
        isValid = false;                         // set valid flag to off
    } else {
        $("email_address1_error").textContent = "";
    }

    // validate the second entry
    ...
    ...
};
```

The basic syntax rules for JavaScript comments

- Block comments begin with /* and end with */.
- Single-line comments begin with two forward slashes and continue to the end of the line.

Guidelines for using comments

- Use comments to describe portions of code that are hard to understand.
- Use comments to disable portions of code that you don't want to test.
- Don't use comments unnecessarily.

Description

- JavaScript provides two forms of *comments*: *block comments* and *single-line comments*.
- Comments are ignored when the JavaScript is executed.
- During testing, comments can be used to *comment out* (disable) portions of code that you don't want tested. Then, you can remove the comments when you're ready to test those portions.
- You can also use comments to save a portion of code in its original state while you make changes to a copy of that code.

Figure 2-5   How to use comments

How to work with data

When you develop JavaScript applications, you frequently work with data, especially the data that users enter into the controls of a form. In the topics that follow, you'll learn how to work with three of the seven types of JavaScript data.

The primitive data types

JavaScript provides for seven *primitive data types*, which are summarized in the table in figure 2-6. The *number data type* is used to represent numerical data, which can be either integer or decimal values. *Integers* are whole numbers, and *decimal values* are numbers that can have one or more decimal digits. The value of either data type can be coded with a preceding plus or minus sign. If the sign is omitted, the value is treated as a positive value. A decimal value can also include a decimal point and one or more digits to the right of the decimal point.

As the last example of the number types in this figure shows, you can also include an exponent when you code a decimal value. If you aren't familiar with this notation, you probably won't need to use it because you won't be working with very large or very small numbers. On the other hand, if you're familiar with scientific notation, you already know that this exponent indicates how many places the decimal point should be moved to the left or right. Numbers that use this notation are called *floating-point numbers*.

The *string data type* is used to store character data. To represent string data, you code the *string* within single or double quotation marks (quotes). Note, however, that you must close the string with the same type of quotation mark that you used to start it. If you code two quotation marks in a row without even a space between them, the result is called an *empty string*, which can be used to represent a string with no characters in it.

The *Boolean data type* is used to store true and false values. To represent Boolean data, you code either the word *true* or *false* with no quotation marks. This data type can be used to represent one of two states.

These first three data types are the ones you'll use the most, which is why this figure and the ones that follow focus on them. However, you should be familiar with the rest of the primitive data types as well.

The *symbol data type* was introduced in ES6, and it can be used to create unique identifiers as properties for objects. This helps ensure that an object doesn't have an identifier with the same name as one in another object. You'll learn how to work with symbols in chapter 12.

The *null data type* and the *undefined data type* are similar in that they both represent the absence of a value. However, they're used differently. The undefined value is used by JavaScript to indicate that an object hasn't been assigned a value by the programmer. The null value, by contrast, is used by programmers to indicate that an object has been intentionally set to no value. You'll see examples of this later in this chapter and book.

The *bigint data type* was introduced in ES2020 (released in June 2020). It represents very large and very small numbers.

JavaScript's primitive data types

Data type	Represents...
Number	an integer or a decimal value that can start with a positive or negative sign.
String	character (string) data.
Boolean	a value that has two possible states: true or false.
Symbol	a unique value that can't be changed.
Null	no value.
Undefined	a value that hasn't been assigned.
BigInt	an extremely large or extremely small number.

Examples of number values

```
15             // an integer
-21            // a negative integer
21.5           // a decimal value
-124.82        // a negative decimal value
-3.7e-9        // floating-point notation for -0.0000000037
```

Examples of string values

```
"JavaScript"   // a string with double quotes
'String Data'  // a string with single quotes
""             // an empty string
```

The two Boolean values

```
true           // equivalent to true, yes, or on
false          // equivalent to false, no, or off
```

The number data type

- A number value can be an *integer*, which is a whole number, or a *decimal value*, which can have one or more decimal positions to the right of the decimal point.

- In JavaScript, decimal values are stored as *floating-point numbers*. In that format, a number consists of a positive or negative sign, one or more significant digits, an optional decimal point, optional decimal digits, and an optional exponent.

- If a result is stored in a number data type that is larger or smaller than the data type can store, it will be stored as the value Infinity or -Infinity.

The string data type

- A string value is surrounded by double quotes or single quotes. The string must start and end with the same type of quotation mark.

- An *empty string* is a string that contains no characters. It is entered by typing two quotation marks with nothing between them.

The Boolean data type

- A *Boolean value* can be true or false. Boolean values are often used in conditional statements, as you'll see in chapter 3.

Figure 2-6   The primitive data types

How to declare and initialize variables and constants

A *variable* stores a value that can change as the program executes. To *declare* a variable in JavaScript, you code the *let* keyword followed by the identifier (or name) that you want to use for the variable. JavaScript also provides an older keyword, *var*, that you can use to declare and initialize variables. As you'll see in a moment, though, it's recommended that you use *let* instead.

When you declare a variable, you should also assign an initial value to it. To *initialize* a variable, you code an equals sign (the *assignment operator*) and a value after the variable name. The value that you assign to a variable determines its data type.

The first two statements in the first group of examples in figure 2-7 show how to declare a variable and initialize it with a numeric value. To do that, you assign a *numeric literal* to the variable, which consists of an integer or decimal value. Here, the first statement declares a variable named count and assigns an integer value of 1 to it. The second statement declares a variable named subtotal and assigns a decimal value of 74.95 to it.

The third and fourth statements show how to declare a variable and initialize it with a string value. To do that, you assign a *string literal* to the variable. A string literal consists of a value that's enclosed in single or double quotes. The third statement, for example, declares a variable named name and assigns a value of "Joseph" to it. The fourth statement is similar, except no value is included between the quotes. As you learned in the last topic, this represents an empty string that doesn't contain any characters.

The fifth statement shows how to declare a variable and initialize it with a Boolean value. To do that, you assign the keyword true or false to the variable. Here, the value false is assigned to a variable named isValid.

The sixth statement shows that, in addition to assigning a *literal value* to a variable, you can assign another variable to it. In this case, the value of the subtotal variable in the second statement is assigned to a variable named total. You can also assign an expression to a variable, which you'll see a bit later.

The last statement shows that you can declare and initialize two or more variables in a single statement. To do that, you code *let* followed by the variable name, an equals sign, and a value for each variable, separated by commas.

It's also possible to declare a variable without initializing it. In this case, JavaScript initializes the variable with undefined. However, this is considered a poor practice because uninitialized variables are a frequent source of bugs. As a result, you should always initialize your variables, even if you just assign a null value.

A *constant* (sometimes called, somewhat inaccurately, a *constant variable*) stores a value that cannot change once it's been initialized. The syntax for declaring a constant is the same as for a variable, except you use the *const* keyword. In addition, a constant must be initialized when it's declared.

Once a variable is initialized, you can use the assignment operator to reassign its value as shown here. If the new value is a different data type, the

How to declare and initialize a variable

Syntax

```
let variableName = value;
```

Examples

```
let count = 1;                 // integer value of 1
let subtotal = 74.95;          // decimal value of 74.95
let name = "Joseph";           // string value of "Joseph"
let email = "";                // empty string
let isValid = false;           // Boolean value of false
let total = subtotal;          // assigns value of subtotal variable
let x = 0, y = 0;              // declares and initializes 2 variables
```

How to declare and initialize a constant

Syntax

```
const constantName = value;
```

Examples

```
// same as above but with const keyword
```

How to reassign the value of a variable

```
let count = 1;
count = count + 1;             // value of count is now 2
```

What happens when you try to reassign the value of a constant

```
const count = 1;
count = count + 1;             // TypeError: Assignment to constant variable.
```

Description

- A *variable* stores a value that can change as the program executes. A *constant* (or *constant variable*) stores a value that may not be reassigned once it's been created.

- To *declare* a variable, code the keyword *let* and a variable name. To *initialize* a variable, use the *assignment operator* (=) to assign a value to it.

- To declare and initialize a constant, do the same but use the *const* keyword.

- You can also declare a variable with the *var* keyword, but that's not recommended.

- The data type of a variable or constant is determined by the value that's assigned to it.

- Although you can declare a variable without initializing it, that's not recommended. A constant must be initialized when it's declared.

- You can use commas to declare more than one variable or constant in a single statement.

- The value that's assigned to a variable or constant can be a *literal value*, or *literal*, another variable or constant, or an expression like the ones you'll learn in a moment.

- To code a *string literal*, you enclose it in single or double quotes. To code a *numeric literal*, you code an integer or decimal value that isn't enclosed in quotes.

- To assign a Boolean value to a variable, you use the true and false keywords.

Figure 2-7   How to declare and initialize variables and constants

data type of the variable changes. By contrast, you can't reassign the value of a constant. If you try, JavaScript throws an error.

Many programmers consider it a best practice to use constants instead of variables unless they're certain they need to change a value. That's because changing a variable's value during program execution can be a source of bugs.

If you use constants and you try to change a constant's value, JavaScipt will alert you by throwing an error. Then, you can evaluate your code and decide if you really need to change that value. If so, you can change the constant to a variable by changing the *const* keyword to *let*.

How JavaScript handles variables and constants

Figure 2-8 presents some basic information about how JavaScript treats the variables and constants that you declare in your code. Understanding this can save you trouble later on.

When JavaScript code loads, the JavaScript engine scans it and stores any variables or constants declared with the *let*, *const*, or *var* keyword in memory first. Then, it rescans and executes the code in the order that the code appears. This process is called *hoisting*, because it seems as if the variables and constants have been "hoisted" to the top of the file.

For variables declared with *var*, JavaScript also initializes them to undefined when they're hoisted. As a result, if your code refers to one of these variables before it's declared, JavaScript won't tell you that it doesn't exist. This is shown in the first group of examples in this figure.

In the first example in this group, the first statement displays the value of a variable named val1 in the browser. Then, the second statement declares and initializes that variable. Because val1 is declared with *var*, JavaScript hoists it and initializes it to undefined. As a result, this code displays "undefined" in the browser. In the second example, the variable is declared and initialized before it's used. As a result, this code displays "value".

By contrast, variables declared with *let* and constants declared with *const* aren't initialized when they're hoisted. Because of that, they can't be used until you initialize them, even though they exist in memory. This period of time, from when JavaScript scans and stores a variable or constant to when you initialize it, is called the *temporal dead zone*, or *TDZ*. If you try to access a variable or constant in the TDZ, JavaScript throws an error.

This is shown in the second group of examples in this figure. In the first example in this group, the first statement displays the value of a variable named val1 in the browser. Then, the second statement declares and initializes the variable. As a result, the val1 variable is in the TDZ until the second statement runs. Because of that, trying to access it in the first statement causes an error.

To avoid these kinds of problems, you should always declare and initialize a variable or constant before you use it. In addition, you should use the *let* keyword to declare variables. That way, if you accidentally try to use a variable before you declare it, JavaScript will let you know by throwing an error.

How JavaScript processes variable and constant declarations

- JavaScript places all variable and constant declarations in memory first. This is called *hoisting*.

- When a variable that's declared with the *var* keyword is hoisted, JavaScript initializes it with a value of undefined. Because of this, you can access the variable before you declare it, but its value will be undefined.

- When a variable that's declared with the *let* keyword is hoisted, JavaScript doesn't initialize it. That's also true of a constant. Because of this, you can't access the variable or constant before you declare it.

A variable declared with the var keyword

Accessed before it's declared

```
alert(val1);                    // displays "undefined"
var val1 = "value";
```

Accessed after it's declared

```
var val1 = "value";
alert(val1);                    // displays "value"
```

A variable declared with the let keyword

Accessed before it's declared

```
alert(val2);                    // ReferenceError - nothing displays
let val2 = "value";
```

Accessed after it's declared

```
let val2 = "value";
alert(val2);                    // displays "value"
```

Description

- When the JavaScript engine interprets a script, it scans the code and puts all variable and constant declarations in memory first. This is called *hoisting*, because it's as if the variables and constants are 'hoisted' to the top of the script.

- Variables declared with *var* are initialized when they're hoisted, while variables declared with *let* and *const* are not.

- A variable declared with *var* is always accessible. That is, JavaScript won't throw an error if you try to access it before you declare it. However, this usually isn't what you want, and it can lead to hard-to-find bugs.

- A variable declared with *let* or *const* is inaccessible between the time it's hoisted and when you declare it. This period is called the *temporal dead zone,* or *TDZ*.

- If you try to access a variable in the TDZ, JavaScript will throw an error. This is more helpful behavior, as it lets you know that you're doing something you shouldn't.

- To avoid problems, you should declare and initialize your variables before you use them.

- In general, you should avoid using the *var* keyword in new code. However, you'll see it often in legacy code and in online examples.

Figure 2-8   How JavaScript handles variable and constant declarations

How to work with expressions

In the preceding figures, you learned how to declare variables and constants and assign literal values and the values in other variables or constants to them. Now, you'll learn how to assign expressions to a variable or constant. An *expression* uses *operators* to perform operations on values.

How to code arithmetic expressions

An *arithmetic expression* can be as simple as a single value or it can be a series of operations that result in a single value. In figure 2-9, you can see the operators for coding arithmetic expressions. If you've programmed in another language, these are probably similar to what you've been using. In particular, the first four *arithmetic operators* are common to most programming languages.

Most modern languages also have a *modulus operator* that calculates the remainder when the left value is divided by the right value. In the example for this operator, 13 % 4 means the remainder of 13 / 4. Then, since 13 / 4 is 3 with a remainder of 1, 1 is the result of the expression.

In contrast to the first five operators in this figure, the increment and decrement operators add or subtract one from a variable. To complicate matters, though, these operators can be coded before or after a variable name, and that can affect the result. To avoid confusion, then, it's best to only code these operators after the variable names and only in simple expressions like the one that you'll see in the next figure.

When an expression includes two or more operators, the *order of precedence* determines which operators are applied first. This order is summarized in the second table in this figure. For instance, all multiplication and division operations are done from left to right before any addition and subtraction operations are done.

To override this order, though, you can use parentheses. Then, the expressions in the innermost sets of parentheses are done first, followed by the expressions in the next sets of parentheses, and so on. This is typical of all programming languages, as well as basic algebra, and the examples in this figure show how this works.

JavaScript's arithmetic operators

Operator	Name	Description
+	Addition	Adds two operands.
–	Subtraction	Subtracts the right operand from the left operand.
*	Multiplication	Multiplies two operands.
/	Division	Divides the right operand into the left operand. The result is always a floating-point number.
%	Modulus	Divides the right operand into the left operand and returns the remainder.
++	Increment	Adds 1 to the operand.
––	Decrement	Subtracts 1 from the operand.

The order of precedence for arithmetic operations

Order	Operators	Direction	Description
1	++	Left to right	Increment operator
2	––	Left to right	Decrement operator
3	* / %	Left to right	Multiplication, division, modulus
4	+ –	Left to right	Addition, subtraction

Examples of simple arithmetic expressions

Example	Result
5 + 7	12
5 – 12	-7
6 * 7	42
13 / 4	3.25
13 % 4	1
counter++	counter = counter + 1
counter--	counter = counter – 1
3 + 4 * 5	23 (the multiplication is done first)
(3 + 4) * 5	35 (the addition is done first)
13 % 4 + 9	10 (the modulus is done first)
13 % (4 + 9)	0 (the addition is done first)

Description

- An *arithmetic expression* consists of one or more operands that are operated upon by arithmetic *operators*.

- An arithmetic expression is evaluated based on the *order of precedence* of the operators. To override the order of precedence, you can use parentheses.

- Because the use of increment and decrement operators can be confusing, it's best to only use these operators in expressions that consist of a variable name followed by the operator as shown above.

Figure 2-9   How to code arithmetic expressions

How to use arithmetic expressions in assignment statements

Now that you know how to code arithmetic expressions, figure 2-10 shows how to use these expressions with variables and constants as you code *assignment statements*. Here, the first two examples show how you can use the multiplication and addition operators in JavaScript statements.

This is followed by a table that presents three of the *compound assignment operators*. These operators provide a shorthand way to code common assignment statements. For instance, the += operator modifies the value of the variable on the left of the operator by adding the value of the expression on the right to the value of the variable on the left. When you use this operator, the variable on the left must already exist and have a value assigned to it.

The other two operators in this table work similarly, but the -= operator subtracts the result of the expression on the right from the variable on the left. And the *= operator multiplies the variable on the left by the result of the expression on the right. The first group of examples after this table illustrates how these operators work.

The second example after the table shows three ways to increment a variable by adding 1 to it. As you will see throughout this book, this is a common JavaScript requirement. Here, the first statement assigns a value of 1 to a variable named counter.

Then, the second statement uses an arithmetic expression to add 1 to the value of the counter. This shows that a variable name can be used on both sides of the = operator. The third statement adds one to the counter by using the += operator. When you use this operator, you don't need to code the variable name on the right side of the = operator, which makes the code more concise.

The last statement in this example uses the ++ operator shown in the previous figure to add one to the counter. This illustrates the best way to use increment and decrement operators. Here, the numeric expression consists only of a variable name followed by the increment operator.

The last example illustrates a potential problem that you should be aware of. Because decimal values are stored internally as floating-point numbers, the results of arithmetic operations aren't always precise. In this example, the salesTax result, which should be 7.495, is 7.495000000000001. Although this result is extremely close to 7.495, it isn't equal to 7.495, which could lead to a programming problem if you expect a comparison of the two values to be equal. The solution is to round the result. You'll learn one way to do that later in this chapter.

Code that calculates sales tax

```
const subtotal = 200;
const taxPercent = .05;
const taxAmount = subtotal * taxPercent;     // 10
const total = subtotal + taxAmount;          // 210
```

Code that calculates the perimeter of a rectangle

```
const width = 4.25;
const length = 8.5;
const perimeter = (2 * width) + (2 * length)     // (8.5 + 17) = 25.5
```

The most useful compound assignment operators

Operator	Description
+=	Adds the result of the expression to the variable.
-=	Subtracts the result of the expression from the variable.
*=	Multiplies the variable value by the result of the expression.

Statements that use the compound assignment operators

```
let subtotal = 74.95;
subtotal += 20.00;                // subtotal = 94.95

let counter = 10;
counter -= 1;                     // counter = 9

let price = 100;
price *= .8;                      // price = 80
```

Three ways to increment a variable named counter by 1

```
let counter = 1;                  // counter = 1
counter = counter + 1;            // counter now = 2
counter += 1;                     // counter now = 3
counter++;                        // counter now = 4
```

A floating-point result that isn't precise

```
const subtotal = 74.95;           // subtotal = 74.95
const salesTax = subtotal * .1;   // salesTax = 7.495000000000001
```

Description

- Besides the assignment operator (=), JavaScript provides for *compound assignment operators*. These operators are a shorthand way to code common assignment operations.

- JavaScript also offers /= and %= compound operators, but you won't use them often.

- When you do some types of arithmetic operations with decimal values, the results aren't always precise, although they are extremely close. That's because decimal values are stored internally as floating-point numbers. The primary problem with this is that an equality comparison may not return true.

Figure 2-10   How to use arithmetic expressions in assignment statements

How to concatenate strings

Figure 2-11 shows how to *concatenate*, or *join*, two or more strings. This means that one string is added to the end of another string.

To concatenate strings, you can use the + sign as a *concatenation operator*. This is illustrated by the first example in this figure. Here, the first code statement assigns string literals to the constants named firstName and lastName. Then, the next statement creates a *string expression* by concatenating lastName, a string literal that consists of a comma and a space, and firstName. The result of this concatenation is

`Hopper, Grace`

which is stored in a new constant named name.

In the second example, you can see how the += operator can be used to get the same results. When the expressions that you're working with are strings, this operator does a simple concatenation.

Another way to concatenate strings is to use a *template literal*. A template literal is like a string literal, except it's enclosed in tick marks (` `` `) rather than single or double quotes. Then, you embed string literals, variables, or constants within the template literal. To do that, you enclose the embedded string within braces ({}) that are preceded by a dollar sign ($).

In the third example, you can see how this works. Here, the lastName and firstName constants are embedded within a template literal that contains a comma and a space.

Sometimes, the strings you're concatenating are so long that your code needs to be on more than one line. The last example in this figure shows how to do that with the + operator and with a template literal. The important thing to note here is that when you use the + operator, you need to code a + operator at the end of each line that will continue to a new line. When you use a template literal, though, you don't need to do anything special at the end of lines.

Note that the constants to be concatenated in this example aren't all strings. Instead, the greeting constant is a string, the price constant is a number, and the isValid constant is a Boolean. When you concatenate a string and any other data type, the other type is converted to a string and then the strings are concatenated.

The concatenation technique you use is mostly a matter of personal preference. In general, though, template literals are more readable, while the + and += operators perform slightly faster.

When working with multiple lines, however, you should know that the spaces and line breaks in your code are preserved in a template literal. This won't matter if you're outputting the string as HTML, but it can cause formatting issues in the dialog boxes produced by the alert() and prompt() methods of the window object. You'll learn about these methods in figure 2-13.

The concatenation operators for strings

Operator	Description
+	Concatenates two values.
+=	Concatenates the result of the expression to the end of the variable.

Constants used for the first three examples

```
const firstName = "Grace", lastName = "Hopper";
```

How to concatenate string variables with the + operator

```
const name = lastName + ", " + firstName;          // name is "Hopper, Grace"
```

How to concatenate string variables with the += operator

```
let name = lastName;            // name is "Hopper"
name += ", ";                   // name is "Hopper, "
name += firstName;              // name is "Hopper, Grace"
```

How to concatenate string variables with a template literal

```
const name = `${lastName}, ${firstName}`;          // name is "Hopper, Grace"
```

How to concatenate on multiple lines

```
const greeting = "Hello";
const price = 15.99;            // number data type
const isValid = true;          // boolean data type
```

With the + operator

```
const message = greeting + "! Is the price really " +
    "just " + price + "? Answer: " + isValid + ".";
// message is "Hello! Is the price really just 15.99? Answer: true."
```

With a template literal

```
const message = `${greeting}! Is the price really
    just ${price}? Answer: ${isValid}.`;
// message is "Hello! Is the price really just 15.99? Answer: true."
```

Description

- To *concatenate*, or *join*, two or more strings, you can use the + or += operator.

- You can also use a *template literal*, which allows you to embed strings directly within a string that functions as a template.

- A template literal is enclosed in tick marks (` `` `) rather than quote marks. Then, within the template literal, the embedded strings are enclosed in braces ({}) that are preceded by a dollar sign ($).

- You can concatenate strings with values of other data types, like numbers or Booleans. When you do, JavaScript converts the non-string value to a string and then concatenates it.

- You can concatenate long strings on multiple lines with the + operator or with a template literal.

- A template literal is easier to read, but the + and += operators perform faster.

Figure 2-11   How to concatenate strings

How to include special characters in strings

The first table in figure 2-12 summarizes four of the many *escape sequences* that you can use when you work with strings. These sequences let you put characters in a string that you can't put in just by pressing the appropriate key on the keyboard. For instance, the \n escape sequence is equivalent to pressing the Enter key in the middle of a string. And the \' sequence is equivalent to pressing the key for a single quotation mark.

Escape sequences are needed so the JavaScript engine can interpret code correctly. For instance, since single and double quotations marks are used to identify strings in JavaScript statements, coding them within the strings would cause syntax errors. But when the quotation marks are preceded by escape characters, the JavaScript engine can interpret them correctly.

The code examples below the table show some strings with escape sequences that are passed to the alert() method. You'll learn more about this method in the next figure. For now, just know that it causes the browser to display a dialog box like the two shown below the code examples. Note how the escape sequences in the strings are displayed in these dialog boxes.

The second table in this figure summarizes four of the many codes that you can use to include *Unicode characters* in strings. These codes let you include letters from other languages in a string, like letters that include accents, umlauts, and tildes. They also let you include middle Eastern script and Korean, Chinese, and Japanese ideographs, as well as symbols like the copyright symbol and the registered trademark symbol.

The code example below the table shows a string with Unicode characters. If you study the dialog box that displays this string, you can see that it contains a heart symbol, a trademark symbol, a smiley face symbol, and a copyright symbol. You can use the URL at the bottom of this figure to look up the codes for more Unicode characters.

Some of the escape sequences that can be used in strings

Operator	Description
\n	Starts a new line in a string. Doesn't affect HTML but does work with the text in alerts and prompts.
\'	Puts a single quotation mark in a string.
\"	Puts a double quotation mark in a string.
\\	Puts a backslash in a string.

How escape sequences can be used in a string

```
alert("This isn\'t the time to talk about this.");
alert("The file is in the javascript\\strings directory.");
```

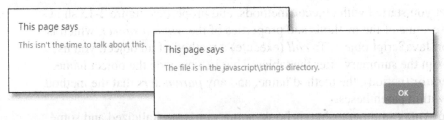

Some of the codes for Unicode characters

Code	Character	Description
\u00A9	©	Copyright
\u00AE	®	Registered trademark
\u263A	☺	Smiley face
\u2665	♥	Heart

How Unicode characters can be used in a string

```
alert("I \u2665 Murach\u00AE Publishing! \u263A \n(\u00A9 2020)");
```

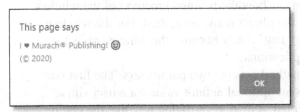

A website that lists all the Unicode characters

https://en.wikipedia.org/wiki/List_of_Unicode_characters

Description

- You can use *escape sequences* to insert special characters within a string, like a return character that starts a new line or a quotation mark.

- You can use *Unicode characters* to include letters, punctuation, scripts, and ideographs from most languages, as well as some symbols.

Figure 2-12   How to include special characters in strings

How to use objects, methods, and properties

In simple terms, an *object* is a collection of methods and properties. A *method* performs a function or does an action. A *property* is a data item that relates to the object. When you develop JavaScript applications, you will often work with objects, methods, and properties. You'll learn how to use the methods and properties of many objects as you progress through this book.

Introduction to objects, methods, and properties

To get you started with objects, methods, and properties, figure 2-13 shows how to use some of the methods and properties of the *window object*, which is a common JavaScript object. To *call* (execute) a method of an object, you use the syntax in the summary after the tables. That is, you code the object name, a *dot operator* (period), the method name, and any *parameters* that the method requires within parentheses.

In the syntax summaries in this book, some words are italicized and some aren't. The words that aren't italicized are keywords that always stay the same, like *alert*. You can see this in the first table, where the syntax for the alert() method shows that you code the word alert just as it is in the summary. By contrast, the italicized words are the ones that you need to supply, like the string parameter you supply to the alert() method.

In the first example after the syntax summary, you can see how the alert() method of the window object is called:

```
window.alert("This is a test of the alert method");
```

In this case, the one parameter that's passed to it is "This is a test of the alert method". So that message is displayed in the alert dialog box.

In the second example, you can see how the prompt() method of the window object is called. This time, though, the object name is omitted. For the window object (but only the window object), that's okay because the window object is the *global object* for JavaScript applications.

As you can see, the prompt() method accepts two parameters. The first one is a message, and the second one is an optional default value for a user entry. When the prompt() method is executed, it displays a dialog box like the one in this figure. Here, you can see the message and the default value that were passed to the method as parameters. At this point, the user can change the default value or leave it as is, and then click on the OK button to store the entry in the constant named userEntry. Or, the user can click on the Cancel button to cancel the entry, which returns a null value.

To access a property of an object, you use a similar syntax. However, you code the property name after the dot operator as illustrated by the second syntax summary. Unlike methods, properties don't require parameters in parentheses. This is illustrated by the statement that follows the syntax. This statement uses the alert() method of the window object to display the location property of the window object.

Common methods of the window object

Method	Description
alert(*string*)	Displays a dialog box that contains the string that's passed to it by the parameter along with an OK button.
prompt(*string*,*default*)	Displays a dialog box that contains the string in the first parameter, the default value in the second parameter, an OK button, and a Cancel button. If the user enters a value and clicks OK, that value is returned as a string. If the user clicks Cancel, null is returned.

One property of the window object

Property	Description
location	The URL of the current web page.

The syntax for calling a method of an object

```
objectName.methodName(parameters)
```

A statement that calls the alert() method of the window object

```
window.alert("This is a test of the alert method");
```

A statement that calls the prompt() method with the object name omitted

```
const userEntry = prompt("This is a test of the prompt method", 100);
```

The prompt dialog box that's displayed

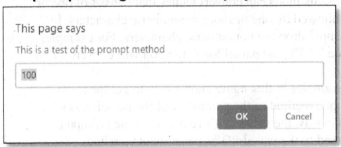

The syntax for accessing a property of an object

```
objectName.propertyName
```

A statement that displays the location property of the window object

```
alert(window.location);        // Displays the URL of the current page
```

Description

- An *object* has *methods* that perform functions that are related to the object as well as *properties* that represent the data or attributes that are associated with the object.

- When you *call* a method, you may need to pass one or more *parameters* to it by coding them within the parentheses after the method name, separated by commas.

- The *window object* is the *global object* for JavaScript, and JavaScript lets you omit the object name and *dot operator* (period) when referring to the window object.

Figure 2-13   Introduction to objects, methods, and properties

How to use the parseInt() and parseFloat() methods of the window object

The parseInt() and parseFloat() methods are used to convert strings to numbers. The parseInt() method converts a string to an integer, and the parseFloat() method converts a string to a decimal value. If the string can't be converted to a number, the value *NaN* is returned. NaN means "Not a Number". You'll learn one way to check whether a value is a number in the next chapter.

These methods are needed because the values that are returned by the prompt() method and the values that the user enters into text boxes are treated as strings. This is illustrated by the first group of examples in figure 2-14. For this group, assume that the default value in the prompt() method isn't changed by the user. As a result, the first statement in this group stores 12345.6789 as a string in a variable named entryA. Then, the third statement in this group converts the string to an integer value of 12345.

Note that the object name isn't coded before the method name in these examples. Again, that's okay because window is the global object for JavaScript. Note too that the parseInt() method doesn't round the value. It just removes, or truncates, any decimal portion of the string value.

The last four statements in the first group of examples show what happens when the parseInt() or parseFloat() method is used to convert a value that isn't a number. In that case, the value NaN is returned.

Note, however, that these methods can convert values that consist of one or more numeric characters followed by one or more nonnumeric characters. In that case, these methods simply drop the nonnumeric characters. For example, if a string contains the value 72.5%, the parseFloat() method will convert it to a decimal value of 72.5.

The second group of examples in this figure shows how to get the same results by coding the prompt() method as the parameter of the parseInt() and parseFloat() methods. In this way, the value that's returned by the prompt() method is immediately passed to the parseInt() or parseFloat() method.

Note in the first group of examples that entryA, entryB, and entryC are variables because their values change. By contrast, in the second group of examples, entryA, entryB, and entryC are constants because their values don't change. Because working with constants is safer, the second group of examples is preferable. However, if you find that coding a method as a parameter for another method makes your code hard to read, it's OK to use variables and be less concise.

Two methods of the window object

Method	Description
parseInt(*string*)	Converts the string it receives to an integer data type and returns that value. If it can't convert the string to an integer, it returns NaN.
parseFloat(*string*)	Converts the string it receives to a decimal data type and returns that value. If it can't convert the string to a decimal value, it returns NaN.

Examples that use the parseInt() and parseFloat() methods

```
let entryA = prompt("Enter any value", 12345.6789);
alert(entryA);                               // displays 12345.6789
entryA = parseInt(entryA);
alert(entryA);                               // displays 12345

let entryB = prompt("Enter any value", 12345.6789);
alert(entryB);                               // displays 12345.6789
entryB = parseFloat(entryB);
alert(entryB);                               // displays 12345.6789

let entryC = prompt("Enter any value", "Hello");
alert(entryC);                               // displays Hello
entryC = parseInt(entryC);
alert(entryC);                               // displays NaN
```

A more concise way to code these examples

```
const entryA = parseInt(prompt("Enter any value", 12345.6789));
alert(entryA);                               // displays 12345

const entryB = parseFloat(prompt("Enter any value", 12345.6789));
alert(entryB);                               // displays 12345.6789

const entryC = parseInt(prompt("Enter any value", "Hello"));
alert(entryC);                               // displays NaN
```

Description

- You can use the parseInt() or parseFloat() method to convert string data to numeric data.
- *NaN* is a value that means "Not a Number". It's returned by the parseInt() and parseFloat() methods when the value that's being parsed isn't a number.
- To make your code concise, you can embed one method as the parameter of another. For instance, you can code the prompt() method as the parameter for the parseInt() or parseFloat() method.

Figure 2-14   How to use the parseInt() and parseFloat() methods

How to use the write() method of the document object

Figure 2-15 shows how to use the write() method of the *document object*. This method writes its data into the body of the document so it's displayed in the browser window.

The example in this figure shows how to use the write() method. Here, an HTML page contains two script elements, each with embedded JavaScript code that uses the write() method to send some data to the document. Then, this figure shows what the HTML and embedded JavaScript look like in the browser.

Each script element in this example is placed at the spot in the HTML that the data it sends to the document should go. So, the first script element writes the current date within a <p> element in the main section, and the second script element writes a copyright notice in the footer. Also note that the JavaScript code in the second script element can access the today object that's in the first script element.

Although not shown here, you can also include HTML elements within the parentheses of the write() method. For instance, you could code the first write() method like this:

```
document.write(`<b>${today.toDateString()}</b>`);
```

Then, the date would be displayed in bold in the browser.

How to use the toFixed() method of the Number object

Figure 2-15 also shows how to use the toFixed() method of the Number object. You'll learn more about the Number object in chapter 4. For now, just know that you can use the toFixed() method with variables and constants of the number data type to round a decimal value and convert it to a string.

The code example below the table shows how this works. Here, a constant named pi is initialized with a decimal value that has five decimal places. As a result, the data type of pi is numeric.

Then, the alert() method is called, and the value returned by calling the toFixed() method of pi is passed as the parameter. The toFixed() method is passed the numeric literal 3, which means that it will round the value of pi to 3 decimal places. The result is that the value of 3.14159 is rounded to 3.142, and the rounded result is displayed in the browser.

A method of the document object

Method	Description
write(*string*)	Writes the string that's passed to it into the document.

An example that uses the write() method

```
<body>
    </main>
        <h1>Hello!</h1>
        <p>Today's Date is
            <script>
                const today = new Date();
                document.write(today.toDateString());
            </script>
        </p>
        <p>We hope you enjoy our website!</p>
    </main>
    <footer>
        <script>
            document.write(`Copyright \u00A9 ${today.getFullYear()}`);
        </script>
    </footer>
</body>
```

The output in a browser

Hello!

Today's Date is Tue May 18 2021

We hope you enjoy our website!

Copyright © 2021

A method of the Number object

Method	Description
toFixed(*n*)	Rounds a number to *n* decimal places and converts it to a string.

An example that uses the toFixed() method

```
const pi = 3.14159;
alert(pi.toFixed(3));              // displays 3.142
```

Description

- The *document object* is the object that lets you work with the Document Object Model (DOM) that represents all of the HTML elements of the page.

- To output text or HTML directly to your page, place script elements where you want the text or HTML to appear and call the write() method.

- The Number object provides methods for working with numeric data. You can use its toFixed() method to produce a string that's rounded to a specified number of digits.

Figure 2-15   How to use the write() method and the toFixed() method

Two illustrative applications

This chapter ends by presenting two applications that illustrate the skills that you've just learned. These aren't realistic applications because they get the user entries from prompt statements instead of from controls on a form. However, these applications will get you started with JavaScript.

The Miles Per Gallon application

Figure 2-16 presents a simple application that issues two prompt statements that let the user enter the number of miles driven and the number of gallons of gasoline used. Then, the application calculates the miles per gallon (MPG) and displays the user's entries and the MPG calculation in the HTML document.

In the JavaScript, you can see how the user's entries are parsed into decimal values and then stored in constants named miles and gallons. After that, miles is divided by gallons, parsed into a decimal, and stored in a constant named mpg. Last, a template literal is used to create a string that contains the user's entries and the calculation within three <p> elements. Then, this string is sent to the document using the write() method of the document object. Notice that the script element is below the h1 element so the data is written below that element.

Can you guess what will happen if the user enters invalid data in one of the prompt dialog boxes? Then, the parseFloat() method will return NaN instead of a number, and the calculation won't work. Instead, the MPG value will display as NaN. Unlike other languages, though, the JavaScript will run to completion instead of crashing when the calculation can't be done, so the web page will be displayed.

Incidentally, the dialog boxes in this figure are the ones for a Chrome browser. When you use other browsers, the dialog boxes will work the same but look slightly different.

The two prompts of the Miles Per Gallon application

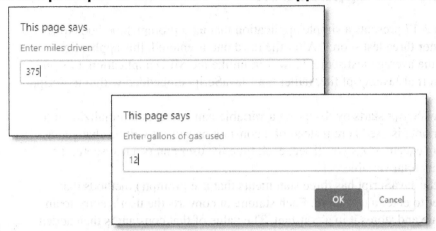

The results displayed in the browser

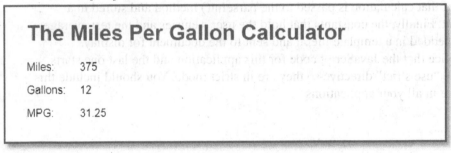

The body element of the HTML file with embedded JavaScript

```
<body>
    <h1>The Miles Per Gallon Calculator</h1>
    <script>
        "use strict";

        // get miles driven from user
        const miles = parseInt(prompt("Enter miles driven"));

        // get gallons used from user
        const gallons = parseInt(prompt("Enter gallons of gas used"));

        // calculate mpg
        const mpg = parseFloat(miles/gallons);

        const html = `<p><label>Miles: </label>${miles}</p>
                    <p><label>Gallons: </label>${gallons}</p>
                    <p><label>MPG: </label>${mpg.toFixed(2)}</p>`;
        document.write(html);
    </script>
</body>
```

Figure 2-16   The Miles Per Gallon application

The Test Scores application

Figure 2-17 presents a simple application that uses prompt() methods to let the user enter three test scores. After the third one is entered, this application calculates the average test score. However, unlike the MPG application, this one uses an external JavaScript file, rather than JavaScript embedded within its script element.

The JavaScript starts by declaring a variable name total and initializing it to zero. A variable is used here instead of a constant because it will be changed as the program executes. As you'll see, each time the user enters a test score, it's added to this total variable.

Next, the JavaScript has three statements that use prompt() methods that ask the user to enter a test score. Each statement converts the user's entry to an integer value and stores it in a constant. The value of that constant is then added to the total variable.

Then, the total variable is divided by 3 to calculate the average score. The result of that calculation is passed to the parseInt() method and stored in a constant. Finally, the constants that hold the user's entries and the test average are embedded in a template literal and sent to the document for display.

Notice that the JavaScript code for this application and the last one starts with the "use strict" directive so they are in strict mode. You should include this directive in all your applications.

The first prompt of the Test Scores application

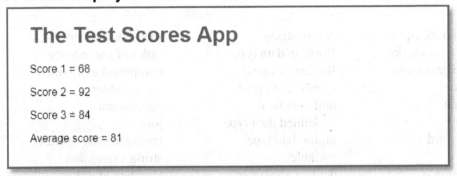

The results displayed in the browser

The Test Scores App

Score 1 = 68

Score 2 = 92

Score 3 = 84

Average score = 81

The body element of the HTML with an external JavaScript file

```html
<body>
    <h1>The Test Scores App</h1>
    <script src="test_scores.js"></script>
</body>
```

The test_scores.js file

```javascript
"use strict";

let total = 0;              // initialize total variable

const score1 = parseInt(prompt("Enter test score"));
total += score1;

const score2 = parseInt(prompt("Enter test score"));
total += score2;

const score3 = parseInt(prompt("Enter test score"));
total += score3;

const average = parseInt(total/3);

const html = `<p>Score 1 = ${score1}</p>
              <p>Score 2 = ${score2}</p>
              <p>Score 3 = ${score3}</p>
              <p>Average score = ${average}</p>`;
document.write(html);
```

Figure 2-17   The Test Scores application

Perspective

If you have programming experience, you can now see that JavaScript syntax is similar to other languages like Java and C#. As a result, you should have breezed through this chapter.

On the other hand, if you're new to programming and you understand all of the code in both of the applications in this chapter, you're off to a good start. Otherwise, you need to study the applications until you understand every line of code in each application. You should also do the exercises that follow.

Terms

external JavaScript file	empty string	modulus operator
embedded JavaScript	Boolean data type	order of precedence
JavaScript statement	Boolean value	compound assignment
whitespace	symbol data type	operator
strict mode	null data type	concatenate
identifier	undefined data type	join
reserved word	bigint data type	concatenation operator
keyword	variable	string expression
camel casing	declare a variable	template literal
snake casing	initialize a variable	escape sequence
comment	assignment statement	Unicode character
block comment	assignment operator	object
single-line comment	literal value	method
comment out	literal	property
uncomment	string literal	call a method
primitive data type	numeric literal	dot operator (dot)
number data type	constant	parameter
integer	hoisting	window object
decimal value	temporal dead zone	global object
floating-point number	(TDZ)	NaN
string data type	arithmetic expression	document object
string	arithmetic operator	

Summary

- The JavaScript for an HTML document page is commonly coded in an *external JavaScript file* that's identified by a script element. However, the JavaScript can also be *embedded* in a script element in the head or body of a document.

- A JavaScript *statement* has a *syntax* that's similar to Java's. When you write JavaScript code, you should use *strict mode* to help you write safer code.

- JavaScript's *identifiers* are case-sensitive and usually coded with either *camel casing* or *snake casing*. Its *comments* can be block or single-line.

- JavaScript provides seven *primitive data types*. The three most common are the *number data type*, which provides for both *integers* and *decimal values*; the *string data type*, which provides for character (*string*) data; and the *Boolean data type*, which provides for true and false values.

- After you *declare* a *variable* or *constant*, you *initialize* it by using the *assignment operator*.

- To assign a numeric value to a variable or constant, you can use *arithmetic expressions* that include *arithmetic operators*, variable and constant names, and *numeric literals*.

- To assign a string value to a variable or constant, you can use *string expressions* that include *concatenation operators*, variable and constant names, *string literals*, and *template literals*. Within a string literal or template literal, you can use *escape sequences* and *Unicode characters* to provide special characters and symbols.

- JavaScript provides many *objects* with *methods* and *properties* that you can *call* or refer to in your applications. Since the *window object* is the *global object* for JavaScript, you can omit it when referring to its methods or properties.

- The *document object* provides methods for working with the DOM, and the Number object provides methods for working with numeric data.

Before you do the exercises for this book...

If you haven't already done so, you should install the Chrome browser and the downloads for this book as described in appendix A (Windows) and appendix B (macOS).

Exercise 2-1   Test and modify the Miles Per Gallon application

In this exercise, you'll test the MPG application and then modify the JavaScript so it accepts and displays decimal values. When you're done, the browser window should look the one in figure 2-16, but it should work with decimal values:

The Miles Per Gallon Calculator

Miles driven = 247.93

Gallons of gas = 7.82

Miles per gallon = 31.70

Test the application

1. Open your text editor or IDE. Then, open the application in this folder:
   `javascript_jquery\exercises\ch02\mpg`

2.   Run the application by opening the index.html file in a browser. Then, enter decimal values for the miles and gallons, and note that these values are converted to integers.

3.   Run the application again by reloading the file in the browser. Then, enter invalid values like zeros or spaces, and note the result.

Modify the application

4.   Modify the JavaScript so it accepts and displays decimal values for the miles and gallons. Then, reload the file in the browser to run the application again, enter decimal values with two or more decimal places, and note the result.

5.   Modify the JavaScript so all of the values are rounded to two decimal places. Then, run the application one more time and note the result.

6.   If you have any problems when you test your exercises, please use Chrome's developer tools as shown in figure 1-17 of the last chapter.

Exercise 2-2   Test and modify the Test Scores application

In this exercise, you'll test the Test Scores application and then modify the JavaScript code so it uses concatenation operators instead of a template literal to display the output.

Test the application

1.   Open your text editor or IDE. Then, open the application in this folder:
`javascript_jquery\exercises\ch02\test_scores`

2.   Run the application by opening the index.html file in a browser, test it with valid entries, and note the result.

3.   Open the test_scores.js file, and note that it starts with the "use strict" directive.

4.   Delete the let keyword from the declaration for the total variable, save the file, and run the application again. This time, no dialog boxes will be displayed. That's because you can't declare a variable without using a keyword in strict mode. To see the error that JavaScript threw, open the developer tools and then display the Console panel. When you're done, add the let keyword back to the variable declaration.

Modify the application

5.   Modify this application so the value that's assigned to the html constant uses the concatenation operator (+) instead of a template literal.

6.   Save the changes and run the application one more time. The output should be displayed just as it was in figure 2-17.

Exercise 2-3   Create a simple application

Copying and modifying an existing application is often a good way to start a new application. So in this exercise, you'll modify the Miles Per Gallon application so it gets the length and width of a rectangle from the user, calculates the area and the perimeter of the rectangle, and displays the results in the browser like this:

The Area and Perimeter Calculator

Length: 25

Width: 10

Area: 250

Perimeter: 70

1. Open your text editor or IDE. Then, open the application in this folder: `javascript_jquery\exercises\ch02\rectangle`

2. Open the index.html file, and note that it contains the code for the Miles Per Gallon application.

3. Modify the code for this application so it works for the new application. (The area of a rectangle is length times width. The perimeter is 2 times length plus 2 times width.) Be sure to change the link element within the head element so it links to the correct CSS file.

3

The essential JavaScript statements

In the last chapter, you were introduced to the basics of JavaScript coding. Now, you'll learn how to code the JavaScript statements that drive the logic of an application.

How to code conditional expressions

Conditional expressions are expressions that evaluate to either true or false based on the result of a comparison between two or more values. You use these expressions in if statements as well as in looping statements.

How to use the relational operators

Figure 3-1 shows you how to code conditional expressions that use the six *relational operators*. To start, the table summarizes the six relational operators. Then, the examples of conditional expressions show how these operators work.

In the first expression, for example, if the value of lastName is equal to "Hopper", the expression will return true. Otherwise, it will return false. Similarly, in the second expression, if the value of the testScore variable is equal to 10, the expression returns true. Otherwise, it returns false.

The rest of the examples are similar, although they use the other operators. They also show that you can compare a variable with a literal or a variable with another variable. The last example shows that you can compare an arithmetic expression to a variable or another arithmetic expression.

In addition to using the relational operators to code a conditional expression, you can use the global isNaN() method. This method determines whether a string value is a valid numeric value, as illustrated by the next set of examples. To use this method, you pass a parameter that represents the string value that should be tested. Then, this method returns true if the value can't be converted to a number or false if it can be converted.

You should be aware that the Number object, which you'll learn more about in chapter 4, also has a static isNaN() method. However, that method works a little differently than the global isNaN() method, because it doesn't check if the value can be converted to a number. Instead, it only checks to see if the value it receives is the numeric NaN value. So, the statement

```
Number.isNaN("Hopper")
```

would return false, since the string "Hopper" is not the numeric NaN value.

When you use the equal to operator, you need to remember to use two equals signs, not one. That's because the one equals sign is the assignment operator, not the equal to operator. This is a common mistake when you're learning to program, and it causes a syntax error.

The relational operators

Operator	Name	Description
==	Equal to	Returns true if both operands are equal.
!=	Not equal to	Returns true if the operands are not equal.
>	Greater than	Returns true if the left operand is greater than the right operand.
<	Less than	Returns true if the left operand is less than the right operand.
>=	Greater than or equal to	Returns true if the left operand is greater than or equal to the right operand.
<=	Less than or equal to	Returns true if the left operand is less than or equal to the right operand.

Conditional expressions

```
lastName == "Hopper"
testScore == 10

firstName != "Grace"
months != 0

testScore > 100
age < 18

distance >= limit
stock <= reorder_point

rate / 100 >= 0.1
```

The syntax of the global isNaN() method

```
isNaN(expression)
```

Examples of the isNaN() method

```
isNaN("Hopper") // Returns true since "Hopper" is not a number
isNaN("123.45") // Returns false since "123.45" can be converted to a number
```

Description

- A *conditional expression* uses the *relational operators* to compare the results of two expressions and return a Boolean value.

- Because floating-point numbers aren't stored as exact values, you shouldn't use the equal to (==) or not equal to (!=) operators to compare them.

- The isNaN() method tests whether a string can be converted to a number. It returns true if the string is not a number and false if the string is a number.

Note

- Confusing the assignment operator (=) with the equal to operator (==) is a common programming error.

Figure 3-1   How to use the relational operators

How to use the logical operators

To code a *compound conditional expression*, you use the *logical operators* shown in figure 3-2 to combine two conditional expressions. If you use the AND operator (&&), the compound expression returns true if both expressions are true. If you use the OR operator (||), the compound expression returns true if either expression is true. If you use the NOT operator (!), the value returned by the expression is reversed. For instance, !isNaN() returns true if the parameter is a number, so isNaN(10) returns false, but !isNaN(10) returns true.

The examples in this figure show how these operators work. For instance, the first example uses the AND operator to combine two conditional expressions. As a result, it evaluates to true if the expression on its left *and* the expression on its right are both true. Similarly, the second example uses the OR operator to combine two conditional expressions. As a result, it evaluates to true if either the expression on its left *or* the expression on its right is true.

When you use the AND and OR operators, JavaScript evaluates the expressions from left to right, and the second expression is evaluated only if necessary. That's why these operators are known as *short-circuit operators*. If, for example, the first expression in an AND operation is false, the second expression isn't evaluated because the entire expression is going to be false. Similarly, if the first expression in an OR operation is true, the second expression isn't evaluated because the entire expression is going to be true.

The third example in this figure shows how to use the NOT operator to reverse the value of an expression. As a result, this expression evaluates to true if the age variable *is* equal to a number. In this case, using the NOT operator is okay, but often the NOT operator results in code that's difficult to read. In that case, it's a good practice to rewrite your code so it doesn't use the NOT operator.

This figure also shows the *order of precedence* for the logical operators. That is the order in which the operators are evaluated if more than one logical operator is used in a compound expression. This means that NOT operators are evaluated before AND operators, which are evaluated before OR operators. Although this is normally what you want, you can override this order by using parentheses.

In most cases, the conditional expressions that you use are relatively simple so coding them isn't much of a problem. In the rest of this chapter and book, you'll see some of the types of conditional expressions that are commonly used.

The logical operators

Operator	Name	Description
&&	AND	Returns a true value if both expressions are true. This operator only evaluates the second expression if necessary.
||	OR	Returns a true value if either expression is true. This operator only evaluates the second expression if necessary.
!	NOT	Reverses the value of the Boolean expression.

Conditional expressions that use logical operators

Example 1: The AND operator

```
age > 17 && score < 70
```

Example 2: The OR operator

```
isNaN(rate) || rate < 0
```

Example 3: The NOT operator

```
!isNaN(age)
```

The order of precedence for the logical operators

1. NOT operator
2. AND operator
3. OR operator

Description

- A *compound conditional expression* joins two or more conditional expressions using the *logical operators*.

- If logical operators are used to join two or more conditional expressions, the sequence in which the operations are performed is determined by the *order of precedence* of the operators. To clarify or change the order of precedence, you can use parentheses.

- The AND and OR operators only evaluate the second expression if necessary. As a result, they are known as *short-circuit operators*.

Figure 3-2   How to use the logical operators

How to code the basic control statements

Like all programming languages, JavaScript provides *control statements* that let you control how information is processed in an application. These statements include if statements as well as looping statements.

How to code if statements

An *if statement* lets you control the execution of statements based on the results of conditional expressions. In a syntax summary like the one in figure 3-3, the brackets [ ] indicate a portion of the syntax that is optional. As a result, this summary means that each if statement must start with an *if clause*. Then, it can have one or more *else if clauses*, but they are optional. Last, it can have an *else clause*, but that clause is also optional.

To code the if clause, you code the keyword *if* followed by a conditional expression in parentheses and a block of one or more statements inside braces. If the conditional expression is true, this block of code executes and any remaining clauses in the if statement are skipped. If the conditional expression is false, this block of code is skipped and any following clauses are evaluated.

To code an else if clause, you code the keywords *else if* followed by a conditional expression in parentheses and a block of one or more statements inside braces. If the conditional expression is true, its block of code executes and any remaining clauses in the if statement are skipped. This will continue until one of the else if expressions is true or they all are false.

To code an else clause, you code the keyword *else* followed by a block of one or more statements inside braces. This code only executes if all the conditional expressions in the if and else if clauses are false. If those expressions are false and there isn't an else clause, the if statement won't execute any code.

The first example in this figure shows an if statement with an else clause. Here, if age is greater than or equal to 18, the first message is displayed. Otherwise, the second message is displayed.

The second example shows an if statement with two else if clauses and an else clause. Here, if rate is not a number, the first message is displayed. If rate is less than zero, the second message is displayed. If rate is greater than 12, the third message is displayed. Otherwise, the message in the else clause is displayed.

The third example shows an if statement with a compound conditional expression that tests whether userEntry is not a number or whether it's less than or equal to zero. If either expression is true, a message is displayed. If both expressions are false, nothing is done because this if statement doesn't have else if clauses or an else clause.

The fourth set of examples shows two ways to test whether a Boolean value is true. Here, both statements are evaluated the same way. That's because a condition that is coded as just a Boolean variable or constant is tested to see

The syntax of the if statement

```
if ( condition-1 ) { statements }
[ else if ( condition-2 ) { statements }
  ...
  else if ( condition-n ) { statements } ]
[ else { statements } ]
```

An if statement with an else clause

```
if ( age >= 18 ) {
    alert ("You may vote.");
} else {
    alert ("You are not old enough to vote.");
}
```

An if statement with else if and else clauses

```
if ( isNaN(rate) ) {
    alert ("You did not provide a number for the rate.");
} else if ( rate < 0 ) {
    alert ("The rate may not be less than zero.");
} else if ( rate > 12 ) {
    alert ("The rate may not be greater than 12.");
} else {
    alert ("The rate is: " + rate + ".");
}
```

An if statement with a compound conditional expression

```
if ( isNaN(userEntry) || userEntry <= 0 ) {
    alert ("Please enter a valid number greater than zero.");
}
```

Two ways to test whether a Boolean value is true

```
if ( isValid == true ) { }
if ( isValid ) { }                      // same as isValid == true
```

Three ways to test whether a Boolean value is false

```
if ( isValid == false ) { }
if ( !isValid == true ) { }
if ( !isValid ) { }                     // same as !isValid == true
```

Description

- An *if statement* always has one *if clause*. It can also have one or more *else if clauses* and one *else clause* at the end. Because of that, it can also be referred to as an *if-else statement*.

- The statements in a clause are executed when its condition is true. Otherwise, control passes to the next clause. If none of the conditions in the preceding clauses are true, the statements in the else clause are executed.

- If necessary, you can code one if statement within the if, else if, or else clause of another if statement. This is referred to as *nesting if statements*.

Figure 3-3   How to code if statements

whether it is equal to true. In practice, this condition is usually coded the way it is in the second statement, with just the name of the variable or constant.

The fifth set of examples in figure 3-3 is similar. It shows three ways to test whether a Boolean value is false. Here again, the last statement illustrates the way this condition is usually coded: !isValid.

How to code while and do-while loops

Figure 3-4 starts by presenting the syntax of the *while statement* that is used to create *while loops*. This statement executes the block of code that's in the loop while its conditional expression is true.

The example that follows this syntax shows how a while loop can be used to add the numbers 1 through 5. Before the while statement starts, a variable named sum is set to zero and a variable named i is set to 1. Then, the condition for the while statement says that the loop should repeat as long as i is less than or equal to 5.

Within the while loop, the first statement adds the value of i to the sum variable. Then, the value of i is increased by 1. As a result, this loop is executed five times, one time each for the i values 1, 2, 3, 4, and 5. The loop ends when i is no longer less than or equal to 5, which is when its value equals 6.

Next is an example that uses a while loop to make sure that a user enters a positive number. Here, a variable named years is initialized with a value returned by the prompt() method and passed to the parseInt() method. Then, the while loop condition checks to see if the value is numeric and greater than zero. If not, the user is prompted again. This loop will run until the user enters a valid value.

This example is followed by the syntax for the *do-while statement* that is used to create *do-while loops*. This is like the while statement, but its condition is tested at the end of the loop instead of at the start. As a result, the statements in the loop always execute at least once.

To illustrate, the do-while loop shown here gets the same results as the second while loop. That is, it continues until a user enters a positive number. However, since the code within the do-while loop always runs at least once, this example only needs to code one prompt statement. The while version, on the other hand, prompts the user before the loop starts, and then again within the loop if the user enters invalid data.

This shows that, if coded correctly, you can get the same results with both while and do-while statements. However, if you know for sure that you want the code in the loop to run at least once, it can be more efficient to use a do-while loop.

If the condition for a while or do-while statement doesn't ever become false, the loop continues indefinitely. This is called an *infinite loop*. When you first start programming, it's common to code an infinite loop by mistake. If you do that, you can end the loop by closing the tab or browser for the application.

In general, you use a while or do-while loop when you don't know in advance how many times the loop needs to run. That's the case with the loops in this figure that run until the user enters a positive number. You'll see more examples like this later in this chapter.

The syntax of a while loop

```
while ( condition ) { statements }
```

A while loop that adds the numbers from 1 through 5

```
let sum = 0;
let i = 1;

while (i <= 5) {
    sum += i;                      // adds i to sum
    i++;
}
alert(sum);                        // displays 15
```

A while loop that makes sure a user enters a positive number

```
let years = parseInt(prompt("Enter number of years."));

while ( isNaN(years) || years <= 0 ) {
    years = parseInt(prompt("Years must be a valid positive number."));
}
```

The syntax of a do-while loop

```
do { statements } while ( condition );
```

A do-while loop that makes sure a user enters a positive number

```
let years = null;

do {
    years = parseInt(prompt("Enter number of years.\n" +
        "(Must be valid positive number)"));
}
while ( isNaN(years) || years <= 0 );
```

Description

- The *while statement* creates a *while loop* that contains a block of code that is executed while its condition is true. This condition is tested at the beginning of the loop, and the loop is skipped if the condition is false.

- The *do-while statement* creates a *do-while* loop that contains a block of code that is executed while its condition is true. However, its condition is tested at the end of the loop instead of the beginning, so the code in the loop will always be executed at least once.

- If the condition for a while or do-while loop never evaluates to false, the loop never ends. This is known as an *infinite loop*. You can end an infinite loop by closing the tab or browser window.

- If a condition includes a counter variable, a common coding practice is to name it *i* for *index*.

- You typically use a while or do-while loop when you don't know in advance how many times the loop will be executed.

Figure 3-4   How to code while and do-while loops

How to code for loops

Figure 3-5 shows how to use the *for statement* to create *for loops*. Within the parentheses of a for statement, you initialize a *counter* (or *index*) variable that will be used within the loop. Then, you code a condition that determines when the loop will end. Last, you code an expression that specifies how the counter should be incremented.

The first example in this figure shows how this works. Here, the first statement in the parentheses of the for statement declares a variable named i and initializes it to 1. Then, the condition in the parentheses determines that the loop will continue as long as i (the counter variable) is less than or equal to 5, and the expression that follows increments i by 1 each time through the loop. Within the loop, the value of i is added to the variable named sum.

If you compare this example to the while loop in figure 3-4 that adds the numbers 1 through 5, you can see that both get the same results. But with the for statement, you don't have to initialize the counter before the statement, and you don't have to increment the counter within the statement.

The next example shows a more realistic use of a for loop. This loop calculates the future value of an investment amount ($10,000) at a specific interest rate (7.0%) for a specific number of years (10). This time, the loop continues as long as the value of the counter variable i is less than or equal to the number of years. In other words, the statement in the loop is executed once for each of the 10 years.

Within the loop, this expression is used to calculate the interest for the year:

```
futureValue * annualRate / 100
```

Then, the += operator adds the interest to the futureValue variable. Note here that the annualRate needs to be divided by 100 for this calculation to work right (7.0 / 100 = .07). Note too in the statements after this example, that this statement could be coded in more than one way and still get the same results.

In the first two examples in this figure, the counter is incremented by 1 each time through the loop, which is usually the way this statement is coded. However, you can also increment or decrement the counter by other amounts. That just depends on what you're trying to do.

For instance, the third example shows how to increment the counter variable by 2 instead of by one. To do that, this code uses the compound assignment operator (+=). And the last example shows how to decrement rather than increment the counter variable. To do that, this code uses the decrement operator (--).

Unlike the while and do-while loops, you typically use a for loop when you know in advance how many times the loop needs to run. That's the case with the for loop in this figure that calculates the future value, which runs based on the years value entered by a user. That's also the case when you're processing arrays, which you'll learn how to do shortly.

The syntax of a for statement

```
for ( counterInitialization; condition; incrementExpression ) {
    statements
}
```

A for loop that adds the numbers 1 through 5

```
let sum = 0;
for ( let i = 1; i <= 5; i++ ) {
    sum += i;                              // adds i to sum
}
alert(sum);                                // displays 15
```

A for loop that calculates the future value of an investment

```
const investment = 10000;
const annualRate = 7.0;
const years = 10;

let futureValue = investment;
for ( let i = 1; i <= years; i++ ) {
    futureValue += futureValue * annualRate / 100;
}
alert(futureValue.toFixed(0));            // displays 19672
```

Other ways that the future value calculation could be coded

```
futureValue = futureValue + (futureValue * annualRate / 100);
futureValue = futureValue * (1 + (annualRate / 100));
```

A for loop that increments the counter by two

```
for ( let i = 0; i <= 10; i += 2 ) {
    document.write(i + " ");
}
// displays 0 2 4 6 8 10
```

A for loop that decrements the counter

```
for ( let i = 3; i > 0; i-- ) {
    document.write(i + "...");
}
document.write("Blast off!");
// displays 3...2...1...Blast off!
```

Description

- The *for statement* is used when you need to increment or decrement a counter that determines how many times the *for loop* is executed.

- Within the parentheses of a for statement, you code an expression that initializes a *counter* (or *index*) variable, a conditional expression that determines when the loop ends, and an increment expression that indicates how the counter should be incremented or decremented each time through the loop.

- The variable name *i* is commonly used for the counter in a for loop.

- You typically use a for loop when you know how many times the loop needs to execute.

Figure 3-5   How to code for loops

Three illustrative applications

The three applications that follow illustrate the use of the control statements that you just learned about. These still aren't realistic applications because they get the user entries from prompt statements instead of from controls on a form. But these applications should give you a better understanding of how the control statements work.

You should know that the JavaScript for all three of these applications is in strict mode. To save space, though, the "use strict" directive isn't shown.

The enhanced Miles Per Gallon application

Figure 3-6 presents an enhanced version of the Miles Per Gallon application that you reviewed in chapter 2. This application just gets user entries for miles driven and gallons of gas used and then calculates and displays the miles per gallon.

This time, though, this application lets the user do the calculation for more than one set of entries. It also checks the entries to make sure they are valid, and displays an error message if one or both aren't valid.

In the JavaScript, you can see how a do-while loop is used to let the user repeat the calculation. Before entering this loop, a variable named "again" is set to a value of "y". Then, the do-while loop is repeated until that value is changed by the user. The user can do that when the last statement in the loop displays the prompt dialog box shown at the top of this figure.

Within the do-while loop, you can see how an if-else statement is used to provide the data validation. Here, the condition for the if clause uses the AND (&&) operator to check whether the value entered for miles is greater than zero and also whether the value entered for gallons is greater than zero. If these conditions are true, the application calculates miles per gallon and displays the result on the page. If any one of the conditions isn't true, the application displays an error message in an alert dialog box.

In other words, this if-else statement tests to see whether both entries are valid. If so, it does the calculation and displays the result. If not, it displays an error message. Note that you could reverse this by testing to see whether one of the entries is invalid by using OR (||) operators. If so, you display the error message. If not, you do the calculation and display the result.

The prompt dialog for continuing the MPG application

```
This page says
Repeat entries? (y/n)

y

                              OK        Cancel
```

The MPG application in the browser after a user enters two calculations

The Miles Per Gallon Calculator

400 miles on 12 gallons = 33.33 MPG

350 miles on 9 gallons = 38.89 MPG

The body element in the HTML for the application

```html
<body>
    <main>
        <h1>The Miles Per Gallon Calculator</h1>
        <script src="mpg.js"></script>
    </main>
</body>
```

The mpg.js JavaScript file for the application

```javascript
let again = "y";

do {
    const miles = parseInt(prompt("Enter miles driven"));
    const gallons = parseInt(prompt("Enter gallons of gas used"));

    if (miles > 0 && gallons > 0) {
        const mpg = parseFloat(miles/gallons);

        const html = `<p>${miles} miles on ${gallons}
                       gallons = ${mpg.toFixed(2)} MPG</p>`;
        document.write(html);
    }
    else {
        alert("One or both entries are invalid");
    }

    again = prompt("Repeat entries? (y/n)", "y");
}
while (again == "y");
```

Figure 3-6   The enhanced Miles Per Gallon application

The Future Value application

Figure 3-7 presents a Future Value application that shows how a for loop can be used to calculate the future value of an investment amount. This application starts by using prompt statements to get the investment amount, interest rate, and number of years from the user. Note, however, that these prompt statements are coded within do-while loops that are executed until the user enters a numeric value. At the end of this chapter, you'll get a chance to improve this data validation code in one of the exercises.

Next, a for loop uses these entries to calculate the future value of the investment. To do that, it uses i as the name of the counter and increments it by 1 each time through the loop. It does that as long as the counter is less than or equal to the number of years entered by the user. This means that the loop will be run once for each year. If, for example, the user enters 10 for the number of years, the loop will be run 10 times.

Within the loop, the future value is calculated. To do that, the expression in the parentheses calculates the interest for the year. Then, the interest is added to the current value of the futureValue variable, and the result is stored in the futureValue variable. As figure 3-5 shows, this calculation could also be coded in other ways.

After the for loop finishes, this application uses four write() methods with template literals to display the values the user entered, as well as the calculated future value, in the browser. Here, the toFixed() method is called on the future-Value variable to round it to two decimal places.

As you can see, this application uses both do-while loops and for loops. It uses do-while loops to get data from the user because it doesn't know in advance how many times it will take for a user to enter valid data. Once it gets a valid number of years from the user, however, the application knows how many times the loop that calculates the future value needs to execute. Because of that, it uses a for loop to do the calculation.

The first of three prompt dialog boxes for the Future Value application

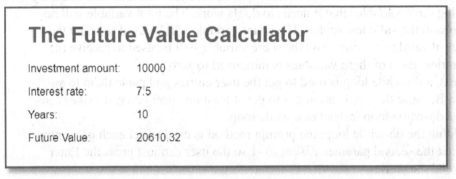

The results of the future value calculation in a browser

The Future Value Calculator

Investment amount: 10000

Interest rate: 7.5

Years: 10

Future Value: 20610.32

The future_value.js JavaScript file for the application

```javascript
let investment = 0;
do {
    investment = parseFloat(
        prompt("Enter investment amount as xxxxx.xx", 10000));
}
while ( isNaN(investment) );

let rate = 0;
do {
    rate = parseFloat(prompt("Enter interest rate as xx.x", 7.5));
}
while ( isNaN(rate) );

let years = 0;
do {
    years = parseInt(prompt("Enter number of years", 10));
}
while ( isNaN(years) );

let futureValue = investment;
for (let i = 1; i <= years; i++ ) {
    futureValue += futureValue * rate / 100;
}

document.write(`<p><label>Investment amount:</label> ${investment}</p>`);
document.write(`<p><label>Interest rate:</label> ${rate}</p>`);
document.write(`<p><label>Years:</label> ${years}</p>`);
document.write(`<p><label>Future Value:</label>
                ${futureValue.toFixed(2)}</p>`);
```

Figure 3-7   The Future Value application

The enhanced Test Scores application

Figure 3-8 presents an enhanced version of the Test Scores application that you reviewed in chapter 2. This time, the application uses a do-while loop to let the users enter as many scores as they want. Then, when a user enters -1 to end the entries, the application displays the average test score.

This version of the application also tests that each entry is a valid number from 0 through 100 before it is added to the test score total. If an entry isn't valid, the application displays an error message and issues another prompt statement so the user can either enter another score or -1 to end the entries.

If you look at the JavaScript for this application, you can see that it starts by declaring three variables that it needs to do its work. The total variable will be used to sum the valid test scores. The count variable will be used to count the number of valid test scores. And the score variable will be used to receive the user entries. Each of these variables is initialized to zero.

Next, a do-while loop is used to get the user entries and parse them to an integer. Because this application has to get at least one user entry, it makes sense to use a do-while loop instead of a while loop.

Within the do-while loop, the prompt method is used to get each user entry. Note that the second parameter is set to -1 so the user can just press the Enter key to end the entries.

After a user makes an entry, an if clause checks that the entry is between 0 and 100. If it is, the entry is valid so the entry value is added to the total variable and 1 is added to the count variable. Then, the score entered by the user is displayed in the browser.

If the entry isn't between 0 and 100, the else if clause that follows checks to see whether the entry is not equal to -1. If it isn't, an alert method displays an error message and the entry isn't processed. If the entry is -1, nothing is done.

When the statements in the loop are finished, the condition for the loop is tested. Then, if the entry value is -1, the loop ends. Otherwise, the loop is repeated for the next entry.

When the loop ends, the average test score is calculated by dividing the total variable by the count variable. Then, the parseInt method is used to convert the decimal value to an integer, and the average score is displayed in the browser.

The prompt dialog box for the Test Scores application

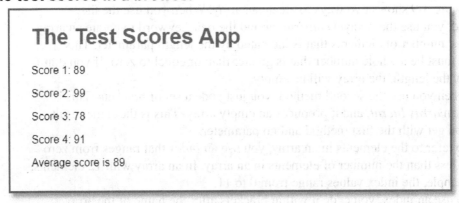

This page says

Enter a test score, or enter -1 to end scores.

-1

OK   Cancel

The test scores in a browser

The Test Scores App

Score 1: 89

Score 2: 99

Score 3: 78

Score 4: 91

Average score is 89

The test_scores.js JavaScript file

```
let total = 0;
let count = 0;
let score = 0;

do {
    // get a score from the user
    score = parseInt(
        prompt("Enter a test score, or enter -1 to end scores.", -1));

    // if it's valid, add to total, increment count, and display score
    if (score >= 0 && score <= 100) {
        total = total + score;
        count++;
        document.write(`<p>Score ${count}: ${score}</p>`);
    }
    // if user isn't ending scores, notify them of invalid data
    else if (score != -1){
        alert("Score must be a valid number from 0 through 100.");
    }
}
while(score != -1);

//calculate and display average score
const average = parseInt(total/count);
document.write(`<p>Average score is ${average}</p>`);
```

Figure 3-8   The enhanced Test Scores application

How to work with arrays

The figures that follow present the basic skills for working with arrays. As you will see, arrays are commonly used in JavaScript applications.

How to create and use arrays

An *array* is an object that contains one or more items called *elements*. Each of these elements can be a primitive data type or an object. The *length* of an array indicates the number of elements that it contains.

Figure 3-9 shows two ways to create an array. When you use the first method, you use the Array() *constructor* and the *new* keyword to create an array with the number of elements that is indicated by the length parameter. This length must be a whole number that is greater than or equal to zero. If you don't specify the length, the array will be empty.

When you use the second method, you just code a set of brackets. This is called an *array literal*, and it produces an empty array. This is the same result that you get with the first method and no parameter.

To refer to the elements in an array, you use an *index* that ranges from zero to one less than the number of elements in an array. In an array with 12 elements, for example, the index values range from 0 to 11.

To use an index, you code it within brackets after the name of the array. This is illustrated by the statements in the first example for adding values to an array. In this example, the first statement creates the array and the next three statements add values for the first three elements of the array. By contrast, the second example creates the array and assigns values to the first three elements in a single statement. To do that, it includes the values in a list within the brackets of an array literal. This is called *initializing an array*.

The next example in this figure shows how to refer to the elements in an array using indexes. Then, the last two examples show how to work with the array's length property. The length property returns the number of elements in an array. In the first example, the length property is stored in a variable for later use. In the second example, the length property is used as the index of a new element. Since this property will always be 1 more than the highest index used in the array, this adds the new element at the end of the array.

As shown in this figure, you can use either a literal value or a variable as an index for an array element. In either case, if you try to access an element that hasn't been assigned a value, the value of undefined will be returned.

In this figure, the arrays are all declared as constants. Although you might think that you'd have to define arrays as variables so you can add elements to them, that's not the case. However, you can't change the constant itself by assigning a new value to it. For example, you can't assign a null value or the value of another array to the array.

The syntax for creating an array

Using the Array() constructor and the new keyword

```
const arrayName = new Array(length);
```

Using an array literal

```
const arrayName = [];
```

The syntax for referring to an element of an array

```
arrayName[index]
```

The syntax for getting the length property of an array

```
arrayName.length
```

How to add values to an array

Using individual statements

```
const totals = [];
totals[0] = 141.95;
totals[1] = 212.25;
totals[2] = 411;
```

Using a single statement

```
const totals = [141.95, 212.25, 411];
```

How to refer to the elements in an array

```
totals[2]        // refers to the third element - 411
totals[1]        // refers to the second element - 212.25
```

How to determine how many elements are in an array

```
const count = totals.length;        // 3
```

How to add a value to the end of an array

```
totals[totals.length] = 135.75;       // adds a fourth element at index = 3
```

Description

- An *array* can store one or more *elements*. The *length* of an array is the number of elements in the array.
- One way to create an array is to use the *new* keyword, the name of the object (Array), and an optional length parameter. The other way to create an array is to code a set of brackets, called an *array literal*.
- When you use an array literal, you can also add values to the array by coding a list of elements within the brackets, separated by commas.
- To refer to the elements in an array, you use an *index* where 0 is the first element, 1 is the second element, and so on.
- One way to add an element to the end of an array is to use the length property as the index.

Figure 3-9   How to create and use arrays

How to use for loops to work with arrays

For loops are commonly used to process one array element at a time by incrementing an index variable. Figure 3-10 shows how this works.

The first example in this figure shows how to create an array and fill it with the numbers 1 through 10. First, this code creates an empty array named numbers. Then, it uses a for loop to add the numbers 1 through 10 to the array. In the body of this loop, one is added to the value in i and the result is stored in the array element. As a result, the element at index 0 stores a 1, the element at index 1 stores a 2, and so on.

Next, this example displays the values in the array. First, this code creates an empty string named displayString. Then, it uses a for loop to access the elements in the array. In the for loop, the length property of the array is used to control how many times the loop executes. This allows the same code to work with arrays of different lengths. Inside the for loop, the value in the element and a space are concatenated to the end of displayString. Finally, displayString is passed to the alert() method, which displays the ten numbers that were stored in the array.

The next example in this figure shows how to use for loops to add the totals in an array and to display those totals. First, the code puts four values into an array named totals. Then, a for loop adds the four totals in the array to a variable named sum. Last, a for loop concatenates the four totals in the array to a string variable that is displayed when the loop ends.

Code that puts the numbers 1 through 10 into an array

```
const numbers = [];
for (let i = 0; i < 10; i++) {
    numbers[i] = i + 1;
}
```

Code that displays the numbers in the array

```
let displayString = "";
for (let i = 0; i < numbers.length; i++) {
    displayString += numbers[i] + " ";
}
alert (displayString);     // displays 1 2 3 4 5 6 7 8 9 10
```

Code that puts four totals into an array

```
const totals = [];
totals[0] = 141.95;
totals[1] = 212.25;
totals[2] = 411;
totals[3] = 135.75;
```

Code that sums the totals in the array

```
let sum = 0;
for (var i = 0; i < totals.length; i++) {
    sum += totals[i];
}
```

Code that displays the totals and the sum

```
let totalsString = "";
for (let i = 0; i < totals.length; i++) {
    totalsString += totals[i] + "\n";
}
alert ("The totals are:\n" + totalsString + "\n" + "Sum: " + sum);
```

The message that's displayed

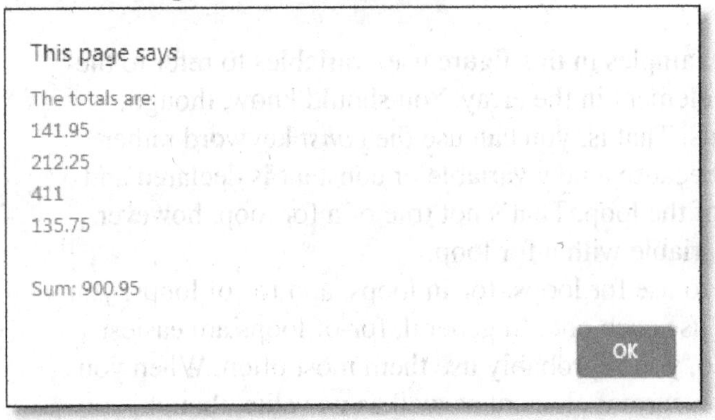

This page says

The totals are:

141.95
212.25
411
135.75

Sum: 900.95

OK

Description

- When you use a for loop to work with an array, you can use the counter for the loop as the index for the array.

Figure 3-10   How to use for loops to work with arrays

How to use for-in and for-of loops to work with arrays

In contrast to a for loop, a *for-in loop* or a *for-of loop* makes it easier to work with an array. Figure 3-11 shows how these types of loops work. All of the examples in this figure will work with the totals constant that's shown at the top of the figure. This constant holds an array that contains four numeric values.

As the syntax after the code for the totals constant shows, the for-in loop doesn't require separate expressions that initialize, test, and increment an index counter like a for loop does. Instead, you declare a variable that will be used to refer to the index of each element in the array. Then, within the loop, you can use this index to access each element in the array.

The example after the syntax shows how to use a for-in loop to sum the values in the totals array. Here, the variable i is declared to refer to the index of each element in the array. Then, within the loop, that index is used to get the value of the current element and add it to the sum variable.

One important difference between a for-in loop and a for loop is that the index value for a for-in loop is a string and the index value for a for loop is a number. This means that if you need to do any calculations with the index value in a for-in loop, you need to use the parseInt() method to convert it to a number first. Otherwise, you'll get unexpected results.

Next, this figure shows the syntax of the for-of loop. This syntax is similar to the for-in loop, except it uses the *of* keyword. With a for-of loop, however, the variable you declare refers to the value of the element itself rather than to the index of the element.

The example after the syntax shows how to use a for-of loop to sum the values in the totals array. Here, the variable val is declared to refer to the value of each element in the array. Then, within the loop, that value is added to the sum variable.

The code in both of the examples in this figure uses variables to refer to the index or value of the current element in the array. You should know, though, that you can also use constants. That is, you can use the *const* keyword rather than the *let* keyword. That's because a new variable or constant is declared and initialized for each iteration of the loop. That's not true of a for loop, however. As a result, you must use a variable with a for loop.

Now that you know how to use for loops, for-in loops, and for-of loops, you might be wondering when to use each one. In general, for-of loops are easiest to code and easiest to read. So, you'll probably use them most often. When you need access to the index of the current element as well as its value, though, you can use a for-in loop. And when you need to increment the counter by values other than 1, you need to decrement the counter, or you don't need to access all of the elements, you can use a for loop.

Code that puts four totals into an array

```
const totals = [];
totals[0] = 141.95;
totals[1] = 212.25;
totals[2] = 411;
totals[3] = 135.75;
```

The syntax of the for-in loop

```
for ( indexInitialization in array ) {
    statements
}
```

Code that totals the numbers in the array using a for-in loop

```
let sum = 0;
for (let i in totals) {     // variable i holds the current index
  sum += totals[i];         // use the index to get current value
}
alert(sum);                 // displays 900.95
```

The syntax of a for-of loop

```
for ( valueInitialization of array ) {
    statements
}
```

Code that totals the numbers in the array using a for-of loop

```
let sum = 0;
for (let val of totals) {   // variable val holds the current value
  sum += val;
}
alert(sum);                 // displays 900.95
```

Description

- The *for-in* and *for-of statements* are used to loop through the elements in an array without having to explicitly declare and increment a counter. They are used to create *for-in loops* and *for-of loops*.

- In a for-in loop, you declare a variable that stores the *index* of the current item in the array.

- In a for-of loop, you declare a variable that stores the *value* of the current item in the array.

- You can also use the *const* keyword to declare a constant instead of a variable for these statements. That's because a new variable or constant is initialized for each iteration of the loop.

- The index variable or constant in a for-in loop has a data type of string, not number. If you want to use that variable or constant in a calculation, then, you need to convert it to a number using the parseInt() method.

Figure 3-11   How to use for-in and for-of loops to work with arrays

The Test Scores application with an array

Figure 3-12 presents an enhanced version of the Test Scores application that stores the valid entries in an array. This will give you a better idea of how arrays and loops can be used.

The user interface

The user interface for this application works the same as the one in figure 3-8. It lets the users enter as many test scores as they want. Then, when a user enters -1 to end the series of entries, the application displays the scores the user entered and the average score.

The JavaScript

If you look at the JavaScript for this application, you can see that it starts by declaring an empty array named scores. Then, a do-while loop is used to get the user entries. This is like the do-while loop in figure 3-8.

Now, however, each valid entry is added to the scores array. Because of that, this application no longer needs to increment a counter variable.

When the do-while loop ends, an if statement is used to check that the array contains at least one element. If it does, processing continues. If it doesn't, it means that the user entered -1 for the first entry and processing ends.

If the array contains one or more elements, a for-in loop processes the scores in the array. This loop uses the length property of the scores array to determine how many times to execute the loop, and the loop's index variable (i) is used to retrieve the elements from the scores array.

Each time through the loop, the array element is added to the total variable and also displayed in the browser. The score number is also displayed so the user can see which score it is. To do that, the index value is incremented by 1 so the scores are displayed starting with 1 rather than with 0 ("Score 1", "Score 2", etc.). Because the variable for a for-in loop is a string, though, the parseint() method must be used to convert the string to an integer before 1 can be added to it.

When the for loop ends, the average test score is calculated and stored in the constant named average. This calculation simply divides the total variable by the length of the scores array, which is the number of scores in the array. This calculation is embedded within the parseInt method so the result is converted to an integer. Last, the average score is displayed in the browser.

The Test Scores application in a browser after a user enters four test scores

The Test Scores App

Score 1: 89

Score 2: 99

Score 3: 78

Score 4: 91

Average score is 89

The JavaScript for the enhanced Test Scores application

```javascript
// declare and initialize an array to hold test scores from user
const scores = [];

// use do-while loop to get scores from the user and store in array
let score = 0;
do {
    score = parseInt(
        prompt("Enter a test score, or enter -1 to end scores", -1));

    if (score >= 0 && score <= 100) {
        scores[scores.length] = score;
    }
    else if (score != -1){
        alert("Score must be a valid number from 0 through 100");
    }
}
while(score != -1);

if (scores.length > 0) {
    // use a for-in loop to add each score to total and display it
    let total = 0;
    for (let i in scores) {
        total = total + scores[i];
        document.write(`<p>Score ${parseInt(i) + 1}: ${scores[i]}</p>`);
    }

    //calculate and display the average
    const average = parseInt(total/scores.length);
    document.write(`<p>Average score is ${average}</p>`);
}
```

Figure 3-12   The Test Scores application with an array

Perspective

If you have programming experience, you can now see that the JavaScript control statements are similar to those in other languages like Java and C#. As a result, you probably skimmed your way through this chapter. You may also want to skip the exercises.

On the other hand, if you're new to programming and you understand all of the code in the applications in this chapter, you're off to a good start. Otherwise, you need to study the applications until you understand every line of code in each application. You should also do the exercises that follow.

Terms

conditional expression	else clause	array
relational operator	nested if statements	array element
compound conditional	while statement	array length
expression	while loop	array literal
logical operator	do-while statement	initialize an array
order of precedence	do-while loop	for-in statement
short-circuit operator	infinite loop	for-in loop
control statement	for statement	for-of statement
if statement	for loop	for-of loop
if clause	loop counter	
else if clause	loop index	

Summary

- When you code a *conditional expression*, you can use *relational operators*, the global isNaN() method, and *logical operators*.

- JavaScript provides *control statements* that let you control how information is processed in an application.

- An *if statement* lets you control the execution of statements based on the results of conditional expressions. An if statement always starts with an *if clause*. It can also have one or more *else if clauses* and a concluding *else clause*, but those clauses are optional.

- The *while* and *do-while* statements can be used to loop through a series of statements while a condition is true.

- The *for statement* can be used to loop through a series of statements once for each time a *counter* or *index* is incremented or decremented.

- An *array* can store one or more *elements* that you can refer to by the *indexes* of the elements. The *length* property of the array holds the number of elements in the array. To process the elements in an array, you can use a *for loop*.

- You can also use the *for-in* and *for-of loops* to process the elements in an array without having to explicitly declare and increment a counter. In a for-in loop, you declare a variable or constant that stores the *index* of the current item in the array. In a for-of loop, you declare a variable or constant that stores the *value* of the current item in the array.

Exercise 3-1   Enhance the Future Value application

This exercise will give you a chance to use if statements, do loops, and for loops as you enhance the Future Value application in figure 3-7. The eventual output of this application will be displayed in the browser and should look something like this:

```
The Future Value Calculator

Investment amount = 10000 Interest rate = 7.5 Years = 5
Year=1 Interest=750.00 Value=10750.00
Year=2 Interest=806.25 Value=11556.25
Year=3 Interest=866.72 Value=12422.97
Year=4 Interest=931.72 Value=13354.69
Year=5 Interest=1001.60 Value=14356.29

Investment amount = 10000 Interest rate = 8.5 Years = 6
Year=1 Interest=850.00 Value=10850.00
Year=2 Interest=922.25 Value=11772.25
Year=3 Interest=1000.64 Value=12772.89
Year=4 Interest=1085.70 Value=13858.59
Year=5 Interest=1177.98 Value=15036.57
Year=6 Interest=1278.11 Value=16314.68
```

If you have any problems when you're testing, remember to use Chrome's developer tools as shown in figure 1-17 of chapter 1.

Test the Future Value application

1. Open your text editor or IDE. Then, open the application in this folder:
   `javascript_jquery\exercises\ch03\future_value`

2. Run the application by opening the index.html file in a browser, and test it with valid entries. Then, test it with invalid entries.

Add a do-while statement for continuing the entries

3. Open the future_value.js file. Then, add a do-while statement to the application like the one for the MPG application in figure 3-6 so the user can repeat the calculation for another series of entries.

Improve the validation for the investment, rate, and year entries

4. Update the condition for the do-while statement for each user entry so the entry must also be a positive number.

5. For the interest rate entry, add code that makes sure the user enters a value that's greater than zero and less than 15.

Enhance the display of the results as shown above

6. Modify the for loop that calculates the future value so it displays the interest and future value for each year, as shown above. Use h4 elements for the user entries and <p> elements for the results. Note that you'll have to change the location of the existing write() methods to get the display the way it is above.

Exercise 3-2   Enhance the Test Scores application

In this exercise, you'll make an enhancement to the Test Scores application in figure 3-12 that uses an array. What you'll do is add a for loop that gets the highest score in the array and displays it below the average score in the browser:

The Test Scores App

Score 1: 85

Score 2: 96

Score 3: 72

Score 4: 98

Average score is 87

Highest score is 98

If you have any problems when you're testing, remember to use Chrome's developer tools as shown in figure 1-17 of chapter 1.

1. Open your text editor or IDE. Then, open the application in this folder:
   `javascript_jquery\exercises\ch03\scores_array`

2. Run the application by opening the index.html file in a browser, and test it with valid entries. Then, test it with invalid entries.

3. Declare a variable named highestScore at the start of the script that will be used to store the highest score. Its starting value should be zero.

4. Add a for-of loop at the end of the script that's executed once for each score in the array. Within the loop, an if statement should replace the value in the highestScore variable with the current score if that score is greater than the value in highestScore. That way, the highestScore variable will eventually store the highest score in the array.

5. Add a write() method after the for-of loop that displays the highest score as shown above.

6. When you've got that working, comment out the for-of loop that you just coded. Then, modify the other for loop so it not only sums the scores but also puts the highest score in the highestScore variable. After this change, the application should work the same as it did after step 5.

4

How to work with JavaScript objects, functions, and events

In the last two chapters, you learned how to code some simple, but unrealistic, applications using the prompt() method to get user entries. Now, in this chapter, you'll learn how to work with objects, like TextBox objects that let you get user entries, as well as objects that let you work with numbers, dates, and strings.

You'll also learn how to code blocks of statements called functions. And you'll learn how to respond to events that occur when users perform actions like clicking on a button, or when application events occur such as when a page is loaded. When you finish this chapter, you'll be able to start developing useful applications of your own.

How to use objects to work with data

In chapter 2, you learned the syntax for using the methods and properties of objects. You were also introduced to some of the methods and properties of the window object and document objects, as well as the toFixed() method of a Number object. Now, you'll learn more about these as well as other objects.

An introduction to JavaScript objects

As you learned in chapter 2, an *object* is a collection of *methods* that do actions and *properties* that contain data that relates to the object. As you've already seen, JavaScript provides objects that you can use in your code.

The objects that JavaScript provides are divided in to two main categories, which are presented in the tables in figure 4-1. The first category consists of *host objects*, which are part of the environment that JavaScript runs in. For example, when JavaScript runs in a browser, the browser is the host environment. Keep in mind, though, that JavaScript can also run outside a browser, such as when it runs in the Node.js runtime environment.

The window and document objects that you've already worked with are host objects, as are the navigator and history objects. If you look at the descriptions of these objects, you can see that they all provide for working with the browser in some way. Host objects aren't part of the ECMAScript specification.

The second category of objects consists of JavaScript *native*, or *built-in*, *objects*. These objects are provided by the JavaScript language and are part of the ECMAScript specification. Some of these objects, like the Object object and the Function object, are fundamental objects that other objects are based on. For instance, all JavaScript native objects inherit the base Object object, which means they have access to that object's properties and methods. You'll learn more about that in chapter 16.

The other native objects in this figure represent specific structures or data types. For instance, the Array object represents a collection of values, the Date object represents a date, and the Number object represents the numeric data type.

Finally, the Math object is a specific kind of object often called a *utility object*. This kind of object is a collection of useful properties and methods, often grouped together based on common functionality, like doing math. You'll learn more about the Math object in chapter 12.

Notice that the String, Number, and Boolean native objects correspond to the string, number, and boolean primitive data types. That's because these objects are *wrapper objects* for those types. A wrapper object is one that contains another object or data type and provides properties and methods for working with it.

Generally, you don't need to know the difference between the primitive data types and their wrappers or make decisions on when to use each one. Instead, JavaScript automatically converts a primitive type to its wrapper object when you call a method, and then discards the wrapper object when the call is done. You can see this in the example in this figure. Here, a numeric literal, which is a primitive data type, is assigned to the constant named pi. But you can still call the toFixed() method of the Number object with this constant.

Some of the host objects in a browser environment

Object	Description
window	Represents the open browser window. This is the *global object* for JavaScript.
document	Represents the HTML document in the browser window. Allows you to work with the Document Object Model (DOM).
navigator	Contains information about the browser.
history	Contains the URLs that a user has visited in the browser.

Some of the JavaScript native objects

Object	Description
Object	The base object that all other JavaScript objects inherit.
Array	An object that stores a collection of data.
Date	An object that stores a date.
Function	An object that stores a predefined collection of JavaScript statements.
Number	A wrapper object for working with the primitive number data type.
String	A wrapper object for working with the primitive string data type.
Boolean	A wrapper object for working with the primitive boolean data type.
Math	A utility object with static methods for working with numbers.

An example of how a Number object wraps a primitive number

A statement that creates a number variable

```
const pi = 3.14159;        // pi is a primitive number data type
```

A statement that uses a method of the Number object

```
alert(pi.toFixed(2));      // JavaScript converts pi to a Number object
                           // so it can call its toFixed() method
```

Description

- The JavaScript language provides many *objects* that you can use in your code. These objects have *properties* that contain data and *methods* that complete actions.

- *Host objects* are part of the environment that JavaScript runs in, such as a browser. These objects aren't part of the ECMAScript specification.

- JavaScript *native*, or *built-in*, *objects* are part of the ECMAScript specification.

- The String, Number, and Boolean native objects are *wrapper objects* that provide methods for the primitive string, number, and boolean data types.

- The Math object is a *utility object* that contains a collection of useful properties and methods related to mathematical calculations.

- JavaScript automatically converts a primitive type to its wrapper object when you call a method, and then discards the wrapper object when the call is done.

- Later in this book, you'll learn how to create your own objects.

Figure 4-1   An introduction to JavaScript objects

How to use the window object

In chapter 2, you were introduced to the prompt() and alert() methods of the *window object*. Now, the first table in figure 4-2 presents another method of the window object that can be used to confirm an action.

Then, the second table in this figure summarizes the parseInt() and parseFloat() methods that you learned about in chapter 2. They are also methods of the window object. These methods are needed because the values that are returned by the prompt() method and the values that the user enters into text boxes are treated as strings.

The use of the confirm() method is illustrated by the first example in this figure. Here, this method is used to confirm that an item should be deleted. As you can see, the dialog box that's displayed for this method includes OK and Cancel buttons. If the user clicks the OK button, the confirm() method returns true. If the user clicks the Cancel button, the method returns false. In either case, the statement that calls this method assigns the result to a constant. Then, the if statement that follows checks if the delete operation was confirmed. If so, the item is deleted.

The second example shows how to use the parseInt() and parseFloat() methods. For the statements in this example, assume that the default values in the prompt() methods aren't changed by the user. As a result, the first statement stores 12345.6789 as a string in a variable named entryA, and the second statement converts the string to an integer value of 12345. Similarly, the third statement stores 12345.6789 as a string in a variable named entryB, and the fourth statement converts the string to a decimal value of 12345.6789.

Note that the object name isn't coded before the method name in these examples. That's okay because the window object is the *global object* for JavaScript. Note too that the parseInt() method doesn't round the value. It just removes, or truncates, any decimal portion of the string.

Another method of the window object that displays a dialog box

Method	Description
confirm(*string*)	Displays a dialog box that contains the string in the parameter, an OK button, and a Cancel button. If the user clicks OK, true is returned. If the user clicks Cancel, false is returned.

Two methods of the window object for working with numbers

Method	Description
parseInt(*string*)	Converts the string that's passed to it to an integer data type and returns that value. If it can't convert the string to an integer, it returns NaN.
parseFloat(*string*)	Converts the string that's passed to it to a decimal data type and returns that value. If it can't convert the string to a decimal value, it returns NaN.

How to use a dialog box to confirm an operation

```
const confirmDelete = confirm("Are you sure you want to delete this item?");
if (confirmDelete) {
    // code that deletes the item
}
```

The dialog box that's displayed

How to convert strings to numbers

```
let entryA = prompt("Enter any value", 12345.6789);
entryA = parseInt(entryA);              // entryA = 12345

let entryB = prompt("Enter any value", 12345.6789);
entryB = parseFloat(entryB);            // entryB = 12345.6789
```

Description

- Because the window object is the *global object* for JavaScript, you can omit the object name and dot operator when referring to it.

Figure 4-2   How to use the window object

How to use the document object

The *document object* is the highest object in the DOM structure. It represents the HTML elements for the page, and you do need to code the object name (document) and the dot operator when you use one of its methods.

The table in this figure lists three methods of the document object. The querySelector() method returns an object that represents the first HTML element that matches the selector that's passed to it. The querySelectorAll() method returns an array of objects that represents all the HTML elements that match the selector that's passed to it. And the write() method writes a string to the document. Each of these methods accepts a string as a parameter.

To help you understand how the querySelector() and querySelectorAll() methods work, the first group of examples shows how to use different types of selectors with them. The first three statements show how to retrieve elements by id, type, and class. These types of selectors were presented in figure 1-14, but figure 4-3 shows how they work with the methods of the document object.

The first statement uses the querySelector() method to select an element by its id, in this case "rate". To do that, you precede the id with a pound sign (#). The second statement uses the querySelectorAll() method to return an array of elements by type. To do that, you simply code the type as the selector. Here, all <a> elements are returned. The third statement also uses the querySelectorAll() method, but it returns all elements assigned to a class, in this case, a class named error. To retrieve elements by class, you code a period before the class name.

The next three statements present selectors that weren't presented in chapter 1. The fourth statement uses a *descendant selector* with the querySelectorAll() method to get all h2 elements that are descendants of the element with an id of "faqs". To code a descendant selector, you code the selector for the parent element, followed by a space and the selector for the descendant element.

The fifth statement shows how to code a combination of selectors. In this case, the querySelectorAll() method is used to select all the div elements that have been assigned to the class named closed. To code a selector like this, you code the element type followed by a period and the class name.

The sixth statement shows that you can also pass multiple selectors to the querySelector() and querySelectorAll() methods. To do that, you simply separate the selectors with commas. In this case, all h2 elements that are descendants of the element with an id of "faqs" will be returned, along with any <p> elements that are descendants of div elements.

You should know that the document object also has some older methods for getting objects that represent HTML elements, such as getElementById(), getElementsByTagName(), and getElementsByClassName(). You may see these methods in legacy code or in online examples, and it's okay to use them. In fact, the getElementById() method performs slightly faster than the querySelector() method. However, most programmers prefer to use the query selector methods presented here because they're more flexible.

The last example in this figure uses the write() method that you learned about in chapter 2. The applications in the previous two chapters show some examples of this method.

Three methods of the document object

Method	Description
querySelector(*selector*)	Returns the first HTML element that matches the selector that's passed to it. The parameter is a string that must contain a valid CSS selector.
querySelectorAll(*selector*)	Returns all the HTML elements that match the selector that's passed to it. The parameter is a string that must contain a valid CSS selector.
write(*string*)	Writes the string parameter into the document.

Common ways to code selectors

Using an element id

```
// returns the object for the HTML element whose id is "rate"
const rate = document.querySelector("#rate");
```

Using an element type

```
// returns an array of objects for all the <a> elements in the document
const links = document.querySelectorAll("a");
```

Using a class

```
// returns an array of objects for all the elements assigned
// to the error class
const errors = document.querySelectorAll(".error");
```

Using a descendant selector

```
// returns an array of all the h2 elements that are descendants
// of the element whose id is "faqs".
const h2s = document.querySelectorAll("#faqs h2");
```

Using a combination of selectors

```
// returns an array of all the div elements assigned to the closed class
const minus = document.querySelectorAll("div.closed");
```

Using multiple selectors

```
// returns an array of elements specified by two descendant selectors
const elements = document.querySelectorAll("#faqs h2, div p");
```

How to write a line of HTML into the document

```
document.write("<b>Welcome to our website!</b>");
```

Description

- The document object is a property of the window object. It lets you work with the Document Object Model (DOM) that represents all of the HTML elements of the page.

- The querySelector() and querySelectorAll() methods of the document object are commonly used to get the object or objects for one or more HTML elements.

- Although the most common CSS selectors are shown above, you can use other types of selectors such as those that select adjacent sibling elements, general sibling elements, and child elements.

Figure 4-3   How to use the document object

How to use Textbox and Number objects

A Textbox object is one of the DOM objects. It represents a text box in the web page that is used to get input from the user or display output to the user. The first two tables in figure 4-4 summarize two of its methods and two of its properties. It also shows the HTML code for two text boxes that have "first_name" and "sales_amount" as their ids. These text boxes will be used by the examples that follow.

The first group of examples in this figure shows two ways to get the value from the text box with "first_name" as its id. To do that with two statements, the first statement uses the querySelector() method of the document object to get the Textbox object for that text box. Then, the second statement uses the value property of the Textbox object to get the value the user entered into the text box.

In practice, though, you would do that with just one statement by using *method chaining*, or just *chaining*. In that case, a single statement first uses the querySelector() method to get the Textbox object, and then uses the value property of the Textbox object to get the value from the text box. In other words, you combine the use of the two methods into a single statement. This also has the benefit of allowing you to use a constant instead of a variable, which is safer.

The second group of examples takes chaining to a third level. Without chaining, it takes three statements to get a valid number from a text box. First, the querySelector() method gets the Textbox object for the text box with "sales_amount" as its id. Second, the value property of the Textbox object gets the value that the user entered into the text box. Third, the parseFloat() method of the window object converts the string value to a decimal number. If the user entry is a valid number, this stores the number in the salesAmt variable, so it becomes a Number object.

With chaining, though, this requires only one statement. Code like this is sometimes called *fluent,* because it's more like a sentence and thus more readable to a human eye. It can also make your code shorter, and shorter code is usually easier to understand. You'll want to be careful with this, though. Like a run-on sentence in a book, if you get to the end of the statement and can't remember what the beginning was doing, you might have chained too much.

The third table in this figure summarizes the toFixed() method of the Number object, which you learned about in chapter 2. When a user enters a valid number in a text box and the parseInt() or parseFloat() method is used to parse it before it is stored in a variable or constant, the value that's stored is numeric. Then, you can use the properties and methods of the Number object to work with that value. For example, you can use the toFixed() method of a Number object to round the number to a specific number of decimal places.

This is illustrated by the first statement in the third group of examples, which adds the toFixed() method to the previous chain. As a result, the number that's stored in the salesAmount variable is rounded to two decimal places.

The last two statements in this group present two more examples of chaining. The first one shows how to assign a value to a text box. In this case, the value is an empty string, which in effect clears the text box of any data. The second statement shows how to move the focus to a text box.

Two methods of the Textbox object

Property	Description
focus()	Moves the cursor into the text box.
select()	Highlights all the text in the text box.

Two properties of the Textbox object

Property	Description
value	A string that represents the contents of the text box.
disabled	A Boolean value that controls whether the text box is disabled.

One method of the Number object

Method	Description
toFixed(*digits*)	Returns a string representation of the number after it has been rounded to the number of decimal places in the parameter.

HTML tags that define two text boxes

```
<input type="text" id="first_name">
<input type="text" id="sales_amount">
```

How to use the value property to get the value from a text box

Without chaining

```
let firstName = document.querySelector("#first_name");
firstName = firstName.value;
```

With chaining

```
const firstName = document.querySelector("#first_name").value;
```

How to use the parseFloat() method to get a number value from a text box

Without chaining

```
let salesAmt = document.querySelector("#sales_amount");
salesAmt = salesAmt.value;
salesAmt = parseFloat(salesAmt);
```

With chaining

```
const salesAmt = parseFloat(document.querySelector("#sales_amount").value);
```

Other examples of chaining

```
// convert text box value to number and then to string with 2 decimal places
const salesAmt =
    parseFloat(document.querySelector("#sales_amount").value).toFixed(2);
document.querySelector("#first_name").value = "";   // clear text box
document.querySelector("#first_name").focus();       // move focus to text box
```

Description

- When you use the querySelector() method to get a text box, the method returns a Textbox object. Then, you can use its value property to get the text in the box.

- You can use the properties and methods of the Number object to work with a variable or constant that contains a numeric value.

Figure 4-4   How to use Textbox and Number objects

How to use Date and String objects

When you store a numeric or string value in a variable or constant, it is automatically converted to a Number or String object when you use a property or method of those objects. This lets you use those properties and methods without having to explicitly create the objects.

However, there isn't a primitive data type for dates. As a result, you need to create a Date object before you can use its methods. To do that, you use the Date() *constructor* and the *new* keyword. You saw how to create an Array object using the *new* keyword and the Array() constructor in chapter 3. Now, the syntax for using a constructor is shown at the top of figure 4-5. This is followed by a statement that uses the Date() constructor to create a Date object. When you create a Date object, it is initialized with the current date and time, which is the date and time on the user's computer.

After you create a Date object, you can use the methods in the first table in this figure to work with it. These methods are illustrated by the first group of examples, assuming that the date is May 18, 2021. Here, the toDateString() method converts the date to a string. The getFullYear() method gets the four-digit year from the date. The getDate() method gets the day of the month. And the getMonth() method gets the month, counting from 0, not 1. As a result, the getMonth() method returns 4 for May, not 5.

The next two tables in this figure present one property and five methods of a String object. Then, the last group of examples presents some statements that show how these properties work. For example, the second statement uses the toUpperCase() method to convert a string to uppercase, and the third statement uses the length property to get the number of characters in a string.

The last two statements show how the indexOf() and substr() methods of a String object can be used to extract a substring from a string. Here, the indexOf() method is used to get the position (index) of the first space in the string, counting from zero. Since the space is in the sixth position, this method returns 5. Then, the substr() method gets the substring that starts at the first position and has a length of 5. As a result, this method returns "Grace".

It's important to note the difference between the substr() and substring() methods. If you start from the first position, as in the example, there is no difference. In that case, both methods will return "Grace". However, if you start anywhere else, you'll get different results depending on which method you use.

For example, if you start at the third position (with an index of 2), the substr() method will still return five characters, and you'll get the string "ace H". The substring() method, on the other hand, will stop at the sixth position (with an index of 5). This means it will only return 3 characters, the string "ace". (It doesn't return the character at the stop position.)

Incidentally, JavaScript provides many more methods and properties for Date and String objects, but these will get you started. You'll learn about more in chapter 12, and there is also extensive documentation on the properties and methods of these objects, and all the JavaScript native objects, online.

The syntax for using a constructor to create an object
```
const variableName = new ObjectType();
```

A statement that creates a Date object
```
const today = new Date();
```

A few of the methods of the Date object

Method	Description
toDateString()	Returns a string with the formatted date.
getFullYear()	Returns the four-digit year from the date.
getDate()	Returns the day of the month from the date.
getMonth()	Returns the month number from the date. The months are numbered starting with zero (January is 0 and December is 11).

Examples that use a Date object
```
const today = new Date();            // creates Date object with current date
alert( today.toDateString() );       // displays Tue May 18 2021 on 5/18/2021
alert( today.getFullYear() );        // displays 2021
alert( today.getDate() );            // displays 18
alert( today.getMonth() );           // displays 4, not 5 for May
```

One property of the String object

Property	Description
length	Returns the number of characters in the string.

A few of the methods of the String object

Method	Description
indexOf(*search, position*)	Searches for the first occurrence of the search string starting at the position specified or zero if position is omitted. If found, it returns the position of the first character, counting from 0. If not found, it returns -1.
substr(*start, length*)	Returns the substring that starts at the specified position (counting from zero) and contains the specified number of characters.
substring(*start, stop*)	Returns the substring that starts at the specified position (counting from zero) and stops at the specified position (counting from zero).
toLowerCase()	Returns a new string with the letters converted to lowercase.
toUpperCase()	Returns a new string with the letters converted to uppercase.

Examples that use properties and methods of the String object
```
const name = "Grace Hopper";
const nameUpper = name.toUpperCase();       // nameUpper = GRACE HOPPER
const nameLength = name.length;             // nameLength = 12
const index = name.indexOf(" ");            // index = 5
const firstName = name.substr(0, index);    // firstName = Grace
```

Description
- You use the Date() *constructor* and the *new* keyword to create a Date object and assign it to a variable or constant. You'll learn about constructors in chapter 16.
- You can use the properties and methods of the String object to work with a variable or constant that contains a string value.

Figure 4-5   How to use Date and String objects

How to use functions

When you develop JavaScript applications, you need to handle events like a user clicking on a button. To do that, you need to code and call functions that handle the events. As you will see, you can also use functions to organize related statements into a single block of code.

How to create and call a function declaration

A *function* is a block of statements that performs an action. It can receive *parameters* and return a value by issuing a *return statement*. Once you've defined a function, you can call it from other portions of your JavaScript code. In figure 4-6, you can see how to create and call a *function declaration*.

To code a function declaration, you start with the *function* keyword followed by an identifier that's the name of the function. After the function name, you code a list of parameters in parentheses and a block of code, often called the *function body*, in braces. Note that, even if a function won't accept parameters, the parentheses are required.

With one exception, we recommend you use function names that consist of verbs and nouns that indicate the type of processing the function will do. The exception is the $() function, which is always coded as in the second example in this figure.

To *call* a function declaration, you code the name of the function, followed by the parameters in parentheses. Then, the function uses the data that's passed to it in the parameters as it executes its block of code. Here again, the parentheses are required even if there are no parameters.

The first example in this figure creates a function named showYear(). This function doesn't require any parameters and doesn't return a value. When called, this function displays a dialog box that shows the current year.

The second example creates the $() function that you'll use in most applications. This function takes one parameter, which is a string that contains a CSS selector. This function returns an object that represents the first HTML element that matches the selector. In this example, the call statement gets the object for the HTML text box with "email_1" as its id. Then, it uses the value property of that object to get the value that the user entered.

The third example in this figure creates a function named calculateTax() that requires two numeric parameters and returns a value. It calculates sales tax, rounds it to two decimal places, and returns that rounded value.

To call this function, the statement passes two constants named subtotal and taxRate. In this case, the constant names are the same as the parameter names in the function, but that isn't necessary. What is required is that the calling statement must pass parameters in the same sequence as the parameters in the function.

Incidentally, some programmers treat *parameter* and *argument* as synonyms. Others use *parameter* to refer to a parameter in a function and *argument* to refer to the value that is passed to the function. In this section of the book, we use *parameter* for both purposes.

The syntax for a function declaration

```
function functionName (parameters) {
    // statements that run when the function is executed
}
```

A function declaration with no parameters that doesn't return a value

```
function showYear() {
    const today = new Date();
    alert( "The year is " + today.getFullYear() );
}
```

How to call the function

```
showYear();
```

A function declaration with one parameter that returns a DOM element

```
function $(selector) {
    return document.querySelector(selector);
}
```

How to call the function

```
const email1 = $("#email_1").value;
```

A function declaration with two parameters that returns a value

```
function calculateTax (subtotal, taxRate) {
    const tax = subtotal * taxRate;
    return tax.toFixed(2);
}
```

How to call the function

```
const subtotal = 85.00;
const taxRate = 0.05;
const salesTax = calculateTax(subtotal, taxRate); // calls the function
alert(salesTax);                                  // displays 4.25
```

Description

- A *function* contains a block of code that can be *called* (or *invoked*) by other statements in the program. When the function ends, the program continues with the statement that comes after the statement that called the function.

- A function can require that one or more *parameters* be passed to it when the function is called. In the calling statement, these parameters can also be referred to as *arguments*.

- To return a value to the statement that called it, a function uses a *return statement*. When the return statement is executed, the function returns the specified value and ends.

- To call a function declaration, you code its name, followed by any parameters in parentheses. If the function returns a value, you can assign it to a variable or constant.

- A *function declaration* is a function that is coded with a name. In the next two figures, you'll learn how to code functions without names.

- A function declaration is *hoisted* to the top of the file that contains it. Because of that, it doesn't have to be coded before any statements that call it.

Figure 4-6   How to create and call a function declaration

How to create and call a function expression

In the last figure, you learned how to code a function declaration. However, you can also assign a function to a variable or constant instead of giving it a name. Functions coded this way are called *function expressions* because they're assigned with the assignment operator. Incidentally, you'll usually want to assign a function expression to a constant so it can't be accidentally reassigned, so that's what we'll show in this chapter.

Figure 4-7 shows how to code a function expression. To start, you code the *const* keyword followed by the name of the constant that will store the function. Following the constant name, you code an assignment operator, the *function* keyword, a list of parameters in parentheses, and a block of code in braces. It's important to note that you must code a semicolon after the closing brace. That's because a function expression is coded as part of an assignment statement, so it must end with a semicolon like any other executable statement. A function declaration, by contrast, isn't an executable statement. Instead, it just declares the function.

After you code a function expression, you call it using techniques similar to the techniques you use to call function declarations. The only difference is that instead of referring to the function by its name, you refer to it by the name of the constant or variable it's assigned to. This is illustrated by the three examples in this figure.

These three function expressions perform the same actions as the function declarations shown in the previous figure. The showYear() function doesn't have any parameters and doesn't return a value. The $() function requires one string parameter that contains the value of a CSS selector and returns that element. And the calculateTax() function requires two numeric parameters and returns the sales tax value rounded to two decimal places.

These examples show that using function expressions is just another way to get the same results as using function declarations. Because of that, you may be wondering which one you should use. Mostly, it's a matter of personal preference.

When you use function declarations, though, you should know that they are *hoisted* when the script first runs, just like variables and constants. But, unlike variables and constants, the function definition is stored in memory. Because of that, function declarations can be coded after statements that call them. Even so, many programmers think that coding function declarations after they are called is a confusing practice that should be avoided.

In contrast to function declarations, function expressions aren't hoisted, and so must be coded before any statements that call them. In addition, function expressions are typically used to handle events. You'll see how this works later in this chapter.

The syntax for a function expression

```
const constantName = function(parameters) {
    // statements that run when the function is executed
};
```

A function expression with no parameters that doesn't return a value

```
const showYear = function() {
    const today = new Date();
    alert( "The year is " + today.getFullYear() );
};
```

How to call the function

```
showYear();
```

A function expression with one parameter that returns a DOM element

```
const $ = function(selector) {
    return document.querySelector(selector);
};
```

How to call the function

```
const email1 = $("#email_1").value;
```

A function expression with two parameters that returns a value

```
const calculateTax = function(subtotal, taxRate) {
    const tax = subtotal * taxRate;
    return tax.toFixed(2);
};
```

How to call the function

```
const subtotal = 85.00;
cont taxRate = 0.05;
const salesTax = calculateTax(subtotal, taxRate);  // calls the function
alert(salesTax);                                    // displays 4.25
```

Description

- A *function expression* is typically assigned to a constant and then referred to by the constant name. However, a function expression can also be assigned to a variable.

- Although a function expression isn't typically given a name, it technically can have one.

- You call a function expression using the same techniques you use to call a function declaration. The only difference is that you refer to a function expression using the name of the constant or variable it's assigned to.

- A function expression can be passed as an argument to another function. You'll see examples of that later in this chapter and throughout this book.

- In contrast to a function declaration, a function expression isn't hoisted. Because of that, a function expression must be coded before any statements that call it. Otherwise, an error will occur.

Figure 4-7   How to create and call a function expression

How to create and call an arrow function

ES6 introduced *arrow functions*, which provide a more concise way to code function expressions. Figure 4-8 shows how to code an arrow function.

To start, you code the *const* keyword followed by the name of the constant that will store the function. Then, you code an assignment operator just like you do when you assign any other function expression. After the assignment operator, though, you don't code the *function* keyword. Instead, you simply code a list of parameters in parentheses, followed by the *arrow operator* (=>) and the function body in braces. As before, you must code a semicolon after the closing brace.

This syntax simplifies function expressions by removing boilerplate code like the *function* keyword. In addition, you can simplify arrow functions even further in some cases.

The examples in this figure show how this works. The first example in the first group shows a regular function expression stored in a constant named calculateTax. The second example shows this expression rewritten as an arrow function. As you can see, the arrow function no longer has the *function* keyword, but it does have an arrow operator. You can think of this operator as pointing to the code that the function will execute.

The second example presents an arrow function with just one parameter. In that case, the parentheses around the parameter list can be omitted as shown here. Note that you're not required to omit the parentheses when an arrow function only has one parameter, but most programmers choose to omit them.

The third example shows that this function can be simplified even further. That's the case if the function body contains a single statement. Here, the two statements of the calculateTax() function have been combined into a single statement that calculates and rounds the tax. In this case, both the braces around the statement and the return keyword can be omitted. This is where you really see how an arrow function can simplify your code.

The fourth example presents an arrow function with no parameters. The important thing to note here is that when an arrow function has no parameters, you must include parentheses around the empty parameter list.

The last example in this figure shows how to call an arrow function. As you can see, you do that the same way you call any other function expression. That is, you code the name of the variable or constant that the function expression is assigned to, followed by the parameters, if any, in parentheses. Here again, the parentheses are required even if there are no parameters.

Since arrow functions make code more concise, this book uses them much of the time going forward. In addition to making code shorter, you should know that arrow functions also have slightly different behavior than "normal" functions in some situations. You'll learn more about that in chapter 17. For now, just know that this is unlikely to affect your code in most cases.

The syntax for an arrow function

```
const constantName = (parameters) => {
    // statements that run when the function is executed
};
```

A function expression rewritten as an arrow function

The function expression

```
const calculateTax = function(subtotal, taxRate) {
    const tax = subtotal * taxRate;
    return tax.toFixed(2);
};
```

How it looks as an arrow function

```
const calculateTax = (subtotal, taxRate) => {
    const tax = subtotal * taxRate;
    return tax.toFixed(2);
};
```

An arrow function with one parameter

```
const calculateTax = subtotal => {          // no parens around param list
    const tax = subtotal * 0.074;
    return tax.toFixed(2);
};
```

An arrow function with one parameter that executes one statement

```
const calculateTax = subtotal => (subtotal * 0.074).toFixed(2);
```

An arrow function with no parameters that executes one statement

```
const getCurrentUrl = () => document.location.href;          // empty parens
```

How to call an arrow function

```
const url = getCurrentUrl();
```

Description

- An *arrow function* provides a more concise way of coding a function expression.
- To code an arrow function, you omit the function keyword and then code an *arrow operator* (=>) preceding the braces and function body.
- If a function only has one parameter, you can simplify the code by omitting the parentheses around the parameter. If a function has no parameters, you must code the parentheses.
- If a function body consists of a single statement, you can omit the braces around that statement, as well as the return keyword if there is one.
- You call an arrow function the same way you call a function expression.
- Internally, arrow functions behave somewhat differently than "normal" functions, although most of the time this doesn't affect your code. You'll learn more about that in chapter 17.

Figure 4-8   How to create and call an arrow function

How to work with global, local, and block scope

Scope in a programming language refers to the visibility of your code. That is, it tells you where in your program you are allowed to use the variables, constants, and functions that you've defined. This topic focuses on the scope of variables and constants. You'll learn about the scope of functions in chapter 17.

In JavaScript, variables and constants that are defined outside of functions have *global scope*. This means they can be used by any function without passing them to the function as parameters. Additionally, if you declare a variable with the *var* keyword, it's added as a property of the window object. Variables and constants declared with *let* and *const*, on the other hand, are still global but aren't added to the window object. You can see this in the first example in figure 4-9.

The second example in this figure illustrates the use of global scope. Here, a function named calculateTax() uses the global taxRate variable to calculate a tax amount and store it in the global tax variable. As a result, the function doesn't have to return the tax variable. Instead, a statement outside of the function can refer to the variable because it's global.

Although it may seem easier to use global scope than to pass data to a function and return data from it, global scope often creates problems. That's because any function can modify a global variable, and it's all too easy to misspell a variable name or modify the wrong variable, especially in large applications. That in turn can create debugging problems. This problem is even worse if your code doesn't use strict mode.

By contrast, variables and constants that are defined within functions, either in the parameter list or the function body, have *local scope*. This means that they can only be used within the functions that define them.

The second example in this figure illustrates the use of local scope. Here, the calculateTax() function receives subtotal and taxRate values as parameters, and it calculates the sales tax and stores it in a constant named tax. Finally, it rounds the tax to two decimal places and returns it to the calling statement, where it's stored in another constant. Note, however, that a statement outside of the function can't refer to the tax constant. That's because it has local scope.

Local scope reduces the likelihood of naming conflicts. For instance, two different functions can use the same names for local variables or constants without causing conflicts. That of course means fewer errors and debugging problems. With just a few exceptions, then, all of the code in your applications should be in functions so all of the variables and constants are local.

When you work with local variables and constants, you should know that how you declare them makes a difference. If you use the *var* keyword to declare a variable, that variable has *function scope* and is available throughout the function. However, if you declare a variable or constant with *let* or *const*, it has *block scope* and is only available within the block of code where it's defined.

You can see this in the two loops of the function in the last example. In the first loop, the variable i is declared with *var*, so it's available after the loop ends. In the second loop, though, the variable j is declared with *let*, so you get an error when you try to access it after the loop ends. In general, you should use block scope instead of function scope because less code has access to it.

Two global variables

```
var taxRate = 0.074;      // adds taxRate property to window object
let tax = 0;              // doesn't add anything to window object

alert(window.taxRate);    // displays 0.074
alert(window.tax);        // displays undefined
```

A function that uses the global variables

```
const calculateTax = subtotal => {
    tax = subtotal * taxRate;
    tax = tax.toFixed(2);
};
calculateTax(100);
alert(tax);                   // displays 7.4
```

A function that uses local variables and constants

```
const calculateTax = (subtotal, taxRate) => {
    const tax = subtotal * taxRate;
    return tax.toFixed(2);
};
const tax = calculateTax(100, 0.074);
alert(tax);
```

A function with two loops

```
function local() {
    for(var i = 0; i < 5; i++) {...}    // function scope
    alert(i);                           // i still in scope - displays 5

    for(let j = 0; j < 5; j++) {...}    // block scope
    alert(j);                           // j not in scope - ReferenceError
}
```

Description

- The *scope* of a variable or constant determines what code has access to it.

- Variables and constants declared outside of functions are *global variables* and *global constants*, and the code in all functions has access to all global variables and constants.

- Global variables declared with the *var* keyword are added to the window object. Global variables declared with the *let* or *const* keyword aren't added to the window object.

- Variables and constants that are declared inside a function are *local variables* and *local constants*. Local variables and constants can only be referred to by the code within the function.

- Local variables declared with the *var* keyword have *function scope*. That means they can be seen throughout the entire function regardless of where they're coded.

- Local variables declared with the *let* keyword, as well as constants, have *block scope*. That means they can only be seen in the block they are coded in, such as the block for an if or for statement.

- In general, you should use local variables instead of global variables. And when you use local variables, you should use block variables instead of function variables. This will make your code easier to understand with less chance for errors.

Figure 4-9   How to work with global, local, and block scope

How to handle events

JavaScript applications commonly respond to user actions like clicking on a button. These actions are called *events*, and the functions that handle the events are called *event handlers*. To make this work, you attach the functions to the events.

How to attach an event handler to an event

The table in figure 4-10 summarizes some of the events that are commonly handled by JavaScript applications. For instance, the load event of the window object occurs when the browser has loaded the entire page, including external images and style sheets. The DOMContentLoaded event of the document object is similar but occurs earlier, when the HTML document is loaded and ready to be used. And the click event of a button object occurs when the user clicks on the button.

An event handler is a function that's executed when an event occurs. That is, it "handles" the event. You code an event handler just like any other function.

To attach an event handler, you use the addEventListener() method. The first parameter for this method is a string with the name of the event to listen for, and the second parameter is the function that handles the event when it occurs.

This first example in this figure shows how to attach an event handler named joinList that's coded as an arrow function and stored in a constant named joinList. This function simply displays an alert message, though you'll see more complex event handlers in a moment.

Next, a JavaScript statement attaches the joinList() function to the click event of a button that has "submit_button" as its id. To do that, this statement uses the $() function you saw earlier to get the object for that button. Then, the addEventListener() method is called and passed the string "click" and the name of the constant that stores the function that will handle the click event.

Note here that you don't code the parentheses after the name of the constant that stores the function. That's because you're attaching the event handler function, not calling it. That way, the function won't be called until the click event is fired. If you were to put parentheses after joinList, the function would be called right away, and the function wouldn't be attached to the event.

The next statement in this group attaches the joinList event handler to the double-click event of a text box that has "text_box_1" as its id. This means that the same event handler will be used for two different events.

Finally, this figure presents the syntax for the removeEventListener() method. You can use this method to remove an event handler. For it to work, it must have the same parameters as the addEventListener() method that attached the event handler.

Incidentally, there's another way to attach an event handler that you'll see in legacy code. With that technique, you assign the event handler function to object properties, such as the onclick or onchange properties. However, using the addEventListener() method is more flexible, and it's generally considered a better way to attach event handlers.

Common events

Object	Event	Occurs when...
`window`	`load`	The whole page has been loaded into the browser, including external style sheets and images.
`document`	`DOMContentLoaded`	The HTML document has been loaded into the browser and the DOM is ready.
`button`	`click`	The button is clicked.
`control` or `link`	`focus`	The control or link receives the focus.
	`blur`	The control or link loses the focus.
`control`	`change`	The user changes the value in the control.
	`select`	The user selects text in a text box or text area.
`element`	`click`	The user clicks on the element.
	`dblclick`	The user double-clicks on the element.
	`mouseover`	The user moves the mouse over the element.
	`mousein`	The user moves the mouse into the element.
	`mouseout`	The user moves the mouse out of the element.

The syntax for the addEventListener() method

```
eventTarget.addEventListener("eventName", eventHandlerFunction);
```

An event handler named joinList

```
const joinList = () => {
    alert("The statements for the function go here")
};
```

How to attach the event handler to the click event of a button

```
$("#submit_button").addEventListener("click", joinList);
```

How to attach the event handler to the double-click event of a text box

```
$("#text_box_1").addEventListener("dblclick", joinList);
```

The syntax for the removeEventListener() method

```
eventTarget.removeEventListener("eventName", eventHandlerFunction);
```

Description

- An *event handler* is a function that executes when an *event* occurs.
- To *attach* an event handler to an event, you call the addEventListener() method of the object that's the target for the event.
- The addEventListener() method accepts a string that's the name of the event that's being *listened* for, and the function that will handle that event.
- If you pass the constant or variable that stores a function to the addEventListener() method as the event handler, you don't code the parentheses after the constant or variable name. If you do, the function will be called rather than attached.
- The removeEventListener() method must have the same parameters as the addEventListener() method that attached the event handler, or it won't work.

Figure 4-10   How to attach an event handler to an event

How to use anonymous functions with event handlers

In the last figure, you saw how to attach event handlers to events by using function expressions for the event handlers. This is useful when you want to use the same function for more than one event, or when you later want to call the removeEventListener() method for an event. If you don't need to reuse or remove an event handler, though, you can code it using an *anonymous function* instead of a function expression. Figure 4-11 shows how this works.

Here, the two examples in the first group show the difference between using a function expression as an event handler and using an anonymous function as an event handler. The first example uses a function expression. This is similar to the example you saw in the previous figure, except that this event handler is attached to the DOMContentLoaded event of the document object.

The second example uses an anonymous function for the event handler. Here, you can see that instead of coding the name of the constant where the function is stored for the eventHandlerFunction parameter of the addEventListener() method, the code for the function itself is coded. This simplifies the code because all of the code for the event handler is contained within the addEventListener() method.

The second group of examples illustrates a more realistic use of anonymous functions. In the first example, you can see that a function expression is assigned to a constant named processEntries. Then, this function expression is attached to the click event of the element that has "calculate" as its id.

Note that this click event handler is coded within an anonymous function that attaches the event handler for the DOMContentLoaded event. This is where you'll typically attach event handlers like this. That way, they'll be available as soon as the HTML has been loaded into a user's browser and the DOM is ready. Occasionally, though, you may need to wait until the load event of the window occurs so the window is fully loaded.

The second example in this second group shows how to code one anonymous function within another. Here, the code from the processEntries function is coded as an anonymous function for the click event handler. Then, the click event handler is coded as an anonymous function for the DOMContentLoaded event handler as in the first example.

Incidentally, the event handler for the DOMContentLoaded or load event can do more than attach event handlers to events. In fact, it can do whatever needs to be done after the DOM is loaded, such as display messages or set the focus on a specific text box.

You should also know that when you embed your code within a script element at the end of the body element, it's executed when the DOM is ready. Because of that, you don't need to put event handlers in embedded code within the event handler for the DOMContentLoaded event. If your code is in a separate JavaScript file, though, you should. That way, you can be sure that the event handlers are attached when the DOM is ready, even if the file is included in the head element of the HTML document instead of at the end of the body.

Code that handles the DOMContentLoaded event

Using a function expression as the event handler

```
const showMessage = () => {
    const msg = "The DOM is ready!";
    alert(msg);
};

document.addEventListener("DOMContentLoaded", showMessage);
```

Using an anonymous function as the event handler

```
document.addEventListener("DOMContentLoaded", () => {
    const msg = "The DOM is ready!";
    alert(msg);
});
```

Code that attaches a click event handler for a button when the DOM is loaded

Using a function expression as the event handler

```
const processEntries = () => {
    // code that processes entries
};

document.addEventListener("DOMContentLoaded", () => {
    $("#calculate").addEventListener("click", processEntries);
});
```

Using an anonymous function as the event handler

```
document.addEventListener("DOMContentLoaded", () => {   // outer handler

    $("#calculate").addEventListener("click", () => {   // inner handler
        // code that processes entries
    });                                                 // end inner handler

});                                                     // end outer handler
```

Description

- If you want to use the same function as the event handler for more than one event, or if you want to be able to remove the event handler for an event, you can assign the event handler to a constant or variable.

- If you don't need to give the event handler a name, you can code the event handler as an anonymous function. An *anonymous function* is a function that doesn't have a name.

- To use an anonymous function, you code the function expression as the second parameter of the addEventListener() method.

- You can use the event handler for the DOMContentLoaded event of the document object or the load event of the window object to attach event handlers for other events after the DOM has been built.

Figure 4-11   How to use anonymous functions with event handlers

How to work with the Event object

When an event occurs, modern browsers automatically pass an Event object to the function that's handling the event. This object provides properties and methods that you can use to work with that event. One of those properties and one of those methods is presented at the top of figure 4-12

The currentTarget property contains an object that represents the HTML element that the event handler is attached to, such as the button that was clicked. You can use this property to work with that element.

The preventDefault() method stops the *default action* for the event from occurring. Not every event has a default action. For example, the default action of the click event for a button of type submit is to submit the form to the server, but a button of type button doesn't have a default action for its click event. Some of the common default actions are listed in the third table here.

The HTML in this figure shows a form element with two input elements. The type attribute of the first input element is set to "text", which means it's a text box. The type attribute of the second input element is set to "submit", which means it's a button whose default action is to submit the form to the server.

The JavaScript code below the HTML includes a function named joinList() that handles the click event of the submit button. Notice that this function has a single parameter named evt. That's all you need to do to access the Event object that the browser automatically passes to the event handler. Note that although you can give this parameter any name you want, e or evt are common.

Within the event handler function, the code checks the value the user entered in the text box. If it's an empty string, that means the user didn't enter anything. In that case, the code notifies the user that an email address is required. Then, the code uses the preventDefault() method of the Event object to stop the default action of the click event. Because of that, the form isn't submitted and the user has another chance to enter an email address. When the user does enter a valid email address, the preventDefault() method isn't executed and the default action of the click event takes place.

The Event object has other properties and methods besides those presented here. In addition, objects that inherit the Event object, such as the MouseEvent object, have even more properties and methods. You can learn more about them by searching online.

One property of the Event object

Property	Description
currentTarget	Contains the HTML element that the event is attached to.

One method of the Event object

Method	Description
preventDefault()	Stops the default action for the event from occurring.

Common HTML elements that have default actions for the click event

Element	Default action for the click event
<a>	Load the page or image in the href attribute.
<input>	Submit the form if the type attribute is set to submit.
<input>	Reset the form if the type attribute is set to reset.
<button>	Submit the form if the type attribute is set to submit.
<button>	Reset the form if the type attribute is set to reset.

An HTML form with a text box and a submit button

```
<form action="join.html" method="get">
    <input type="text" id="email_1" name="email_1">
    <input type="submit" id="join_list" value="Join List">
</form>
```

An event handler for the click event of the submit button

```
const joinList = evt => {               // has parameter that's an Event object
    if (document.querySelector("#email_1").value == "") {

        // notify user of error
        alert("Email is required.");

        // don't allow form to be submitted
        evt.preventDefault();
    }
};

document.addEventListener("DOMContentLoaded", () => {
    $("#join_list").addEventListener("click", joinList);
});
```

Description

- Modern browsers send an Event object to the event handler that's handling the event.
- You can use the currentTarget property to get the element that the event handler is attached to.
- If the event being listened for has a *default action*, you can use the preventDefault() method to stop that action from occurring.

Figure 4-12   How to work with the Event object

Two illustrative applications

To show you how the JavaScript you've just learned can be used to build applications, this chapter ends by presenting two of them.

The Miles Per Gallon application

Figure 4-13 presents the Miles Per Gallon application from chapter 2, but this time it uses text boxes rather than prompt dialog boxes to get the user entries, and it uses a button to process the entries. This version gets the user entries for miles and gallons. Then, it calculates miles per gallon, rounds it to two decimal places, and displays it in the third text box.

Note that the disabled attribute is set for the third text box in the HTML. This disables and shades this text box so the user can't enter data into it. Although the CSS isn't shown in this figure, you can see it in the downloaded application.

Finally, the script element for this application includes an external JavaScript file named mpg.js at the end of the body element. This means that any code in that file executes when the DOM is ready.

The Miles Per Gallon application in a browser

The Miles Per Gallon Calculator

Miles Driven: `400`

Gallons of Gas Used: `12`

Miles Per Gallon: `33.33`

[Calculate MPG]

The HTML

```
<!DOCTYPE html>
<html>
<head>
    <meta name="viewport" content="width=device-width, initial-scale=1">
    <title>Miles Per Gallon Calculator</title>
    <link rel="stylesheet" href="mpg.css">
</head>
<body>
    <main>
        <h1>The Miles Per Gallon Calculator</h1>

        <div>
            <label for="miles">Miles Driven:</label>
            <input type="text" id="miles">
        </div>

        <div>
            <label for="gallons">Gallons of Gas Used:</label>
            <input type="text" id="gallons">
        </div>

        <div>
            <label for="mpg">Miles Per Gallon:</label>
            <input type="text" id="mpg" disabled>
        </div>

        <div>
            <label> </label>
            <input type="button" id="calculate" value="Calculate MPG">
        </div>
    </main>
    <script src="mpg.js"></script>
</body>
</html>
```

Figure 4-13   The Miles Per Gallon application (part 1)

The second part of figure 4-13 presents the JavaScript for the Miles Per Gallon application. As you can see, except for the "use strict" directive and the addEventListener() method for the document object, all of the code is placed within four functions. As a result, nothing has global scope. Also, the event handler for the button is attached within the event handler for the DOMContentLoaded event to make sure it isn't attached before the DOM is ready. These are all best coding practices.

You should also note the sequence of the functions. Here, the first function is the $() function. The second function is the getErrorMsg() function, which returns an error message. The third function is the focusAndSelect() function, which calls the $() function. And the fourth function is the processEntries() function, which calls both the $() function and the focusAndSelect() function.

In short, each function only calls functions that precede it in the code. This is a logical sequence that makes your code easier to read and understand. It's also necessary because function expressions can't be called before they're defined.

In the processEntries() function, the user entries are retrieved using the $() function. Then, they're parsed into the miles and gallons constants. Finally, an if-else statement tests whether each entry is valid.

If the entries aren't valid, the getErrorMsg() function is called to create the error message that's displayed to the user. Then, the focusAndSelect() method is called. It receives the id of a text box, and it uses the $() function to get that textbox. After that, it moves the focus to that textbox and selects any text that it contains. This makes it easier for the user to correct an entry.

If both entries are valid, the code in the else clause calculates the miles per gallon by dividing miles by gallons. Then, it rounds the result to two decimal places and returns the result to the calling statement, which stores it in the value property of the text box with "mpg" as its id.

When the web page is loaded, the DOMContentLoaded event handler is executed first, even though it comes last in the script. It attaches the event handler for the click event of the Calculate MPG button. After that, the browser waits until the user clicks on that button. Then, the processEntries() function validates the entries and displays either an error message or the calculated value.

The JavaScript

```
"use strict";

const $ = selector => document.querySelector(selector);

const getErrorMsg = lbl =>
    `${lbl} must be a valid number greater than zero.`;

const focusAndSelect = selector => {
    const elem = $(selector);
    elem.focus();
    elem.select();
};

const processEntries = () => {
    const miles = parseFloat($("#miles").value);
    const gallons = parseFloat($("#gallons").value);

    if (isNaN(miles) || miles <= 0) {
        alert(getErrorMsg("Miles driven"));
        focusAndSelect("#miles");
    } else if (isNaN(gallons) || gallons <= 0) {
        alert(getErrorMsg("Gallons of gas used"));
        focusAndSelect("#gallons");
    } else {
        $("#mpg").value = (miles / gallons).toFixed(2);
    }
};

document.addEventListener("DOMContentLoaded", () => {
    $("#calculate").addEventListener("click", processEntries);
    $("#miles").focus();
});
```

Description

- The JavaScript for the Miles Per Gallon application uses arrow functions to streamline the code.

- The $(), getErrorMsg(), and focusAndSelect() functions are helper functions that reduce code duplication.

- The processEntries() function is an event handler that uses the helper functions to do its work.

- The addEventListener() method of the document object is used to attach an anonymous function as the event handler for the document's DOMContentLoaded event.

- Within the event handler for the DOMContentLoaded event, the code attaches the processEntries function as the event handler for the click event of the calculate button. Then, it sets the focus on the first textbox in the form.

- Since the code in this file runs in the DOMContentLoaded event, it's safe to use even if a programmer links to it in the head element. That's because putting code inside this event is the same as having your code at the bottom of the body element.

Figure 4-13   The Miles Per Gallon application (part 2)

The Email List application

Figure 4-14 presents an Email List application like the one that you were introduced to in chapter 1. In this application, the user enters the data for three text boxes and clicks the Join List button. Then, the JavaScript checks the data for validity. If any entries are invalid, a dialog box is displayed with an error message for each invalid entry. If all entries are valid, the data is submitted to the server for server-side processing.

The application also has a Clear Form button. When the user clicks this button, anything the user may have typed in any of the textboxes is cleared.

In the head section of the HTML, you can see that a link element is used to include a CSS file for this page. Here again, the CSS isn't shown because it's irrelevant to the operation of the application.

In the body of the HTML, you can see that the label and input elements for this page are coded within a form element. In addition, the type attribute of the Join List button is set to "submit". That way, when the user clicks the Join List button, the data in the text boxes will be submitted to the server if it's valid. In that case, a page named join.html is displayed, as you can see by the value of the action attribute of the form. You'll learn more about how this works in chapter 6.

You should also notice the id attributes for the form and text boxes. The id for the form is "email_form", and the ids for the text boxes are "email_1", "email_2", and "first_name". These are the ids that will be passed to the $() function in the JavaScript. You can also see a script element at the end of the body that includes the external JavaScript file for this page.

Note too that the values for the name attributes of the form and text boxes are the same as the values for their id attributes. The name attributes for the text boxes are used by the server-side code to get the user entries that are passed to it when the form data is submitted to the server.

The Email List application in a web browser

Please join our email list

Email Address: grace@yahoo.com

Confirm Email Address: grace@yahoo

First Name:

[Join List]   [Clear Form]

This page says

Both emails must match.
First name is required.

OK

The HTML

```html
<!DOCTYPE html>
<html>
<head>
    <meta name="viewport" content="width=device-width, initial-scale=1">
    <title>Join Email List</title>
    <link rel="stylesheet" href="email_list.css">
</head>
<body>
    <main>
        <h1>Please join our email list</h1>
        <form id="email_form" name="email_form"
              action="join.html" method="get">
            <div>
                <label for="email_1">Email Address:</label>
                <input type="text" id="email_1" name="email_1">
            </div>
            <div>
                <label for="email_2">Re-enter Email Address:</label>
                <input type="text" id="email_2" name="email_2">
            </div>
            <div>
                <label for="first_name">First Name:</label>
                <input type="text" id="first_name" name="first_name">
            </div>
            <div>
                <label> </label>
                <input type="submit" id="join_list" value="Join our List">
                <input type="button" id="clear_form" value="Clear form">
            </div>
        </form>
    </main>
    <script src="email_list.js"></script>
</body>
</html>
```

Figure 4-14   The Email List application (part 1)

The second part of figure 4-14 shows one way that the JavaScript for this application can be coded. This code includes three event handler functions: one for the DOMContentLoaded event, one for the click event of the Join List button, and one for the click event of the Clear Form button. Here, all of these event handlers are coded as anonymous functions. The only function that's stored in a constant is the $() function.

Within the event handler for the DOMContentLoaded event, the event handlers for the two buttons are attached. Then, this event handler ends by setting the focus on the first text box in the form. This makes the form easier for the user to use.

The event handler for the Join List button includes a parameter for an Event object. Then, its first three statements use the $() function to store the user's text box entries in constants named email1, email2, and firstName. Then, the fourth statement declares a variable named errorMessage and sets it to an empty string.

The if statements that follow validate the three entries. If any entry is invalid, an error message is added to the errorMessage variable. This data validation is typical of the client-side validation that's done for any form before its data is submitted to the server for processing.

After the three entries are checked for validity, another if statement tests the errorMessage variable to see if it's not empty. If it isn't, that means that one or more entries are invalid. In that case, the errorMessage variable is displayed and the preventDefault() method of the Event object is called to keep the form from being submitted to the server.

If you study this code, you can see that the first if statement checks the second email address entry for two types of validity. First, it checks that an entry has been made. Second, if an entry has been made, it checks that the second email address entry is equal to the first email address entry.

You might notice, though, that the code for this application doesn't provide all of the validity checking that you might want. For instance, it doesn't test whether the entries in the first two text boxes are valid email addresses. Later in this book, though, you'll learn how to provide more extensive data validation like this.

The event handler for the Clear Form button doesn't need to use the Event object. Therefore, it starts with an empty parameter list. You should know, though, that this event handler still receives an Event object from the browser. It just doesn't capture and use it by assigning it to a variable.

Within the function body, this event handler sets the value property of each text box to an empty string. This clears any values the user has entered. Finally, it sets the focus to the first text box.

The JavaScript

```javascript
const $ = selector => document.querySelector(selector);

document.addEventListener("DOMContentLoaded", () => {

    $("#join_list").addEventListener("click", evt => {
        // get values user entered in textboxes
        const email1 = $("#email_1").value;
        const email2 = $("#email_2").value;
        const firstName = $("#first_name").value;

        // create an error message and set it to an empty string
        let errorMessage = "";

        // check user entries - add to error message if invalid
        if (email1 == "") {
            errorMessage += "First email is required.\n";
        }

        if (email2 == "") {
            errorMessage += "Second email is required.\n";
        }

        if (email1 != email2) {
            errorMessage += "Both emails must match.\n";
        }

        if (firstName == "") {
            errorMessage += "First name is required.\n";
        }

        // prevent form submission if there's an error message
        if (errorMessage != "") {
            alert(errorMessage);
            evt.preventDefault();
        }
    });

    $("#clear_form").addEventListener("click", () => {
        $("#email_1").value = "";
        $("#email_2").value = "";
        $("#first_name").value = "";

        $("#email_1").focus();
    });

    $("#email_1").focus();
});
```

Description

- The event handler for the click event of the join_list submit button cancels the default action of submitting the form if the user's entries are invalid.

Figure 4-14   The Email List application (part 2)

Perspective

In this chapter, you've seen the way real-world JavaScript applications use objects and respond to events. Now, if you understand everything in this chapter, you should be ready to start developing useful applications of your own.

Terms

object
host object
native object (or built-in object)
utility object
wrapper object
window object
global object
document object
descendant selector
method chaining (or chaining)
fluent coding
constructor
function
call a function
parameter
argument
return statement
function declaration
function body

hoist a function
function expression
arrow function
arrow operator
scope
global variable
global constant
global scope
local variable
local constant
local scope
function scope
block scope
event
event handler
attach an event handler
anonymous function
default action

Summary

- JavaScript provides *objects* that have properties and methods that you can use in your code. *Host objects* are part of the environment that JavaScript runs in, and *native*, or *built-in*, *objects* are part of the ECMAScript specification.

- The Textbox, Number, Date, and String objects provide methods and properties for text boxes, number data types, dates, and string data types. When working with the methods and properties of these objects, you often use *method chaining*.

- A *function* consists of a block of code that is executed when the function is *called* (or *invoked*). The function can require one or more *parameters* that are passed to it by the calling statement.

- A *function expression* is stored in a constant or variable, and a *function declaration* is given a name but not stored in a constant or variable.

- An *arrow function* provides a more concise way of coding a function expression. To code an arrow function, you use the *arrow operator* (=>).

- *Local variables* and *local constants* are defined within a function and can only be accessed by statements within the function. *Global variables* and *global constants* are defined outside of all functions and can be accessed by any of the other code.

- Local variables can have *block scope*, in which case only the blocks where they're declared have access to them, or *function scope*, in which case they can be seen throughout the entire function. Constants always have block scope.

- An *event handler* is a function that is called when an *event* like clicking on a button occurs. To make this work, the function must be *attached* to the event.

- When you attach an event handler to an event, you can use an *anonymous function* for the event handler.

- When an event occurs, the browser sends an Event object to the event handler that handles the event. You can use the properties and methods of this object to work with it within the event handler. In particular, you can use it to cancel the *default action* of an object.

Exercise 4-1   Enhance the MPG application

In this exercise, you'll enhance the validation for the MPG application, and you'll provide for clearing the entries from the page.

If you have any problems when you're testing, remember to use Chrome's developer tools as shown in figure 1-17 of chapter 1.

Test the application

1. Open your text editor or IDE. Then, open the application in this folder:
   `javascript_jquery\exercises\ch04\mpg`

2. Open the mpg.js file, and review the JavaScript code to see that it's the same as in part 2 of figure 4-13.

3. Test this application with valid data to see how it works. When you click the Calculate MPG button, the correct result should be displayed.

4. Test the data validation routine. Note that one error message is displayed in an alert dialog box if the miles entry is nonnumeric or less than or equal to zero or if the gallons entry is nonnumeric or less than or equal to zero.

Enhance the data validation

5. Modify the if-else statement that provides the data validation so a different error message is displayed for each entry if it's nonnumeric or less than or equal to zero. To do that, you'll have to use two different functions that display different error messages.

6. Test this change to be sure that a different error message is displayed for a text box if it contains nonnumeric data versus if it contains a value less than or equal to zero.

Provide for clearing the entries from the form

7. Add a Clear Entries button below the Calculate MPG button. To do that, copy the HTML for the label and input elements for the Calculate button, and paste it after the input element for the Calculate button. Then, modify the HTML for the Clear Entries button so it has a unique id and an appropriate value attribute.

8. Add an arrow function named clearEntries() that clears the entries in the three text boxes and moves the focus to the first text box. Next, add a statement in the DOMContentLoaded event handler that attaches the clearEntries() function to the click event of the Clear Entries button. Then, test this change.

9. Add a statement to the DOMContentLoaded event handler that attaches the clearEntries() function to the double-click event of the miles text box. Then, test this change.

Exercise 4-2   Build a new Future Value application

In this exercise, you will build a new version of the Future Value application from chapter 3. Its user interface will look like this:

If you have any problems when you're testing, remember to use Chrome's developer tools as shown in figure 1-17 of chapter 1.

Open and review the starting files

1. Open your text editor or IDE, and open the HTML and JavaScript files in this folder:

    `javascript_jquery\exercises\ch04\future_value`

2. Open the HTML file in a browser to see that it provides the user interface, but nothing works.

3. Review the JavaScript file. Note that it contains just the "use strict" directive and the $() function.

Create a function for the Future Value calculation

4. Create an arrow function named calculateFV(). It should have three parameters that receive the user's entries: investment amount, interest rate, and number of years. It should calculate the future value based on these parameter values, round the result to two decimal places, and return the rounded result. If you need help with this calculation, you can refer back to the Future Value application in figure 3-7.

Create the event handler for the click event of the Calculate button

5. Create an arrow function named processEntries() that gets the user entries with no data validation. Start by declaring the constants that will hold the user's entries and assigning the user's entries to these variables.

6. Code a statement that calls the calculateFV() function and stores the result that's returned in the fourth text box.

7. Create an event handler for the DOMContentLoaded event. Code this event as an anonymous function that attaches the processEntries() function to the click event of the Calculate Future Value button. This event handler should also move the focus to the first text box.

8. Test this application with valid entries, and debug until this works correctly.

Add data validation

9. Declare a variable that will be used to store an error message right after the constant declarations in the processEntries() function.

10. Add an if-else statement that tests whether each entry is valid. If an entry is invalid, assign an error message to the variable you declared in step 9 and move the focus to the text box that contains the error. The values for the three entries should be as follows:

    Investment is a number that's greater than zero and less than or equal to 100,000.

    Interest rate is a number that's greater than zero and less than or equal to 15.

    Years is a number that's greater than zero and less than or equal to 50.

11. Add another if-else statement that tests whether any errors were detected. If not, the statement that you coded in step 6 should be executed. Otherwise, the error message should be displayed. Now, test this change.

Replace the processEntries() function with an anonymous function

12. Modify the statement that attaches the processEntries() function to the click event of the Calculate Future Value button so it uses an anonymous function instead. The easiest way to do that is to copy the code that's assigned to the processEntries constant, and then replace this constant in the addEventListener() method with its code.

13. Comment out the processEntries() function. Then, test the application one more time to be sure it works the same as it did before.

5

How to test and debug a JavaScript application

As you build a JavaScript application, you need to test it to make sure that it performs as expected. Then, if there are any problems, you need to debug your application to correct those problems. This chapter shows you how to do both.

An introduction to testing and debugging

When you *test* an application, you run it to make sure that it works correctly. As you test the application, you try every possible combination of input data and user actions to be certain that the application works in every case. In other words, the goal of testing is to make an application fail.

When you *debug* an application, you fix the errors (*bugs*) that you discover during testing. Each time you fix a bug, you test again to make sure that the change you made didn't affect any other aspect of the application.

The three types of errors that can occur

As you test an application, three types of errors can occur. These errors are described in figure 5-1.

Syntax errors violate the rules for coding JavaScript statements. These errors are detected by the JavaScript engine as a page is loaded into the browser. However, as you learned in chapter 1, some syntax errors are detected by IDEs and text editors like VS Code before the JavaScript is loaded into a browser. That's why syntax errors are easiest to fix.

A *runtime error* occurs after a page has been loaded into a browser and the application is running. Then, when a statement can't be executed, the JavaScript engine throws an *exception* (or *error*) that stops the execution of the application.

Logic errors are errors in the logic of the coding: an arithmetic expression that delivers the wrong result, using the wrong relational operator in a comparison, and so on. This type of error is often the most difficult to find and fix. For example, the Future Value application in this figure has a logic error that results in an incorrect result. In this case, though, it's hard to tell what the right future value should be. Later in this chapter, you'll learn one way to do that by tracing the execution of your code.

The Future Value application with a logic error

The Future Value Calculator

Total investment:	10000
Annual interest rate:	3.5
Number of years:	10
Future value:	10239964.20

Calculate Future Value

The goal of testing

- To find all errors before the application is put into production.

The goal of debugging

- To fix all errors before the application is put into production.

The three types of errors that can occur

- *Syntax errors* violate the rules for how JavaScript statements must be written. These errors are caught by the JavaScript engine as a page is loaded into the web browser.
- *Runtime errors* occur after a page is loaded and the application is being run. When a runtime error occurs, the JavaScript engine throws an error that stops the execution of the application.
- *Logic errors* are statements that don't cause syntax or runtime errors, but produce the wrong results.

Description

- To *test* a JavaScript application, you run it to make sure that it works properly no matter what data you enter or what events you initiate.
- When you *debug* an application, you find and fix all of the errors (*bugs*) that you find when you test the application.

Figure 5-1   The three types of errors that can occur

Common JavaScript errors

Figure 5-2 presents some of the coding errors that are commonly made as you write a JavaScript application. If you've been doing the exercises, you most likely have encountered several of these errors already. Now, if you study this figure, you'll have a better idea of what to watch out for.

If you're using a good text editor or IDE, you can avoid most of these errors by noting the error markers and warnings that are displayed as you enter the code. For instance, VS Code will help you avoid most of the syntax errors in the first group in this figure. However, it won't help you avoid the errors in the second and third groups.

The fourth group in this figure addresses the problem with floating-point arithmetic that was mentioned in chapter 2. In brief, JavaScript uses the IEEE 754 standard for floating-point numbers, and this standard can introduce inexact results, even for simple calculations. Although these results are extremely close to the exact results, they can cause problems, especially in comparisons. For instance, the number 7.495 is not equal to 7.495000000000001.

To get around this problem, you can round the result as shown by the examples. Here, the first statement rounds the salesTax value to two decimal places by using the toFixed() method of the Number object. In this case, the result is stored as a string because the toFixed() method returns a string.

By contrast, the second statement gets the rounded result and then uses the parseFloat() method to store it as a number. The approach you use depends on whether you need the result to be a string or a number.

The last group in this figure illustrates the type of problem that can occur when JavaScript assumes that a variable is global. In this example, the salesTax variable is declared properly by using the *let* keyword. But the next statement misspells salesTax as salestax when it tries to assign a rounded and parsed value to salesTax. As a result, salestax is treated as a global variable, and the rounded and parsed value goes into salestax, not salesTax, which of course causes a bug.

As you can imagine, typos like this are easy to make. Luckily, you can avoid that type of error by using strict mode for all of your JavaScript files. Then, the JavaScript engine will throw an error if you use a variable before it's declared so you'll have to fix the error. Otherwise, an error like this can be hard to find, which may lead to a difficult debugging problem.

Common syntax errors

- Misspelling keywords, like coding querySelecter() instead of querySelector().
- Omitting required parentheses, quotation marks, or braces.
- Not using the same opening and closing quotation mark.
- Omitting the semicolon at the end of a statement.
- Misspelling or incorrectly capitalizing an identifier, like defining a variable named salesTax and referring to it later as salestax.

Problems with HTML references

- Referring to an attribute value or other HTML component incorrectly, like referring to an id as "salesTax" when the id is "sales_tax".

Problems with data and comparisons

- Not making sure that a user entry is the right data type before processing it.
- Not using the parseInt() or parseFloat() method to convert a user entry into a numeric value before processing it.
- Using one equal sign instead of two when testing for equality.

Problems with floating-point arithmetic

- The number data type in JavaScript uses floating-point numbers, and that can lead to arithmetic results that are imprecise. For example,

```
var salesAmount = 74.95;
salesTax = salesAmount * .1;                    // result is 7.495000000000001
```

- One way to fix this potential problem is to round the result to the right number of decimal places. If necessary, you can also convert it back to a floating-point number:

```
salesTax = salesTax.toFixed(2)                  // result is 7.50 as a string
salesTax = parseFloat(salesTax.toFixed(2));     // result is 7.50 as a number
```

Problems with undeclared variables that are treated as global variables

- If you don't use strict mode and you assign a value to a variable that hasn't been declared, the JavaScript engine treats it as a global variable, as in this example:

```
const calculateTax = function(subtotal, taxRate) {
    let salesTax = subtotal * taxRate;              // salesTax is local
    salestax = parseFloat(salesTax.toFixed(2));     // salestax is global
    return salesTax;         // salesTax isn't rounded but salestax is
};
```

- The solution to this type of problem is to always use strict mode.

Description

- When the JavaScript engine in a browser comes to a JavaScript statement that it can't execute, it *throws an exception* (or *error*) and skips the rest of the JavaScript statements.

Figure 5-2   Common JavaScript errors

How to plan the test runs

When you test an application, you typically do so in at least two phases. In the first phase, you test the application with valid data. In the second phase, you test the application with invalid data. This is illustrated in figure 5-3.

As your applications become more complex, it helps to create a test plan for testing an application. This is simply a table or spreadsheet that shows what test data you're going to enter and what the results should be. Many programmers also use frameworks that allow them to automate testing, although that's beyond the scope of this book.

In the valid testing phase, you should start with test data that produces results that can be easily verified. This is illustrated by the Future Value application in this figure. Here, the first test data entries are for a $1000 investment at an annual interest rate of 10% for 1 year. The result should clearly be 1100, and it is.

Next, you should use test data that is more likely to produce an inaccurate result. That involves using a range of valid entries and verifying that the results are accurate. To do that, of course, you need to know what the results should be. For applications like the Calculate MPG application that perform simple calculations, that's not a problem. For applications like the Future Value application that perform more complex calculations, though, it can be difficult to determine what the results should be. In that case, you can use some of the debugging techniques that you'll learn about later in this chapter to determine if the result of a calculation is correct.

For the invalid testing phase, your test data should include all varieties of invalid entries. This is illustrated by the second example in this figure. This shows a test run of the Future Value application when the investment value is blank, the interest rate value is a negative number, and the years value is a positive number. As you can see, an error message is displayed showing that the investment and interest rate values are invalid.

When you create a test plan for invalid data, you try to make the program fail by testing every combination of valid data, invalid data, and user actions that you can think of. That should also include random actions like pressing the Enter key or clicking the mouse at the wrong time or place.

The Future Value application as it's tested with valid data

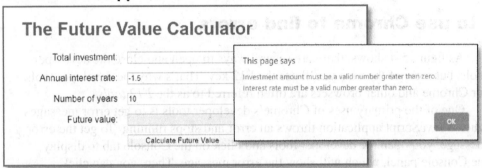

The Future Value application as it's tested with invalid data

The two critical test phases

1. Test the application with valid input data to make sure the results are correct.
2. Test the application with invalid data or unexpected user actions. Try everything you can think of to make the application fail.

How to make a test plan for the critical phases

1. List the valid entries that you're going to make and the correct results for each set of entries. Then, make sure that the results are correct when you test with these entries.
2. List the invalid entries that you're going to make. These should include entries that test the limits of the allowable values.

Two common testing problems

-   Not testing a wide enough range of entries.
-   Not knowing what the results of each set of entries should be and assuming that the results are correct because they look correct.

Description

-   It's easy to find and fix syntax and runtime errors because the application won't run correctly until you fix them.
-   Logic errors can slip through your test runs if you don't check that the results are correct, or if you don't test a wide enough range of entries.

Figure 5-3   How to plan the test runs

How to debug with Chrome's developer tools

In chapter 1, you were introduced to the Console panel of Chrome's *developer tools* as a way to find errors. Besides that, though, Chrome offers some excellent debugging features for more complicated problems.

Since Chrome's developer tools are relatively easy to use, the topics that follow don't present the procedures for using all of its features. Instead, they present the skills that you're going to use the most. Then, if you decide that you want to use some of the other features, you can experiment with them on your own.

How to use Chrome to find errors

As figure 5-4 shows, there are several ways to open and close the developer tools, but most of the time you'll use the F12 key. That's why the developer tools for Chrome and other browsers are often referred to as the *F12 tools*.

One of the primary uses of Chrome's developer tools is to get error messages when a JavaScript application throws an error and stops running. To get the error message, you open the developer tools and click on the Console tab to display the Console panel, which will show the error message. Then, you can click on the link to the right of the message to switch to the Sources panel with the JavaScript code for the error statement highlighted. In the Sources panel, you can hover your mouse over the error icon (an *X* in a red circle) to view more information about the error.

In the example in this figure, the problem is that the *isNaN()* function in the statement is spelled wrong. It is *isNan()* when it should be *isNaN()*. This shows how easy it can be to find an error. Often, the statement that's highlighted isn't the one that caused the error, but at least you have a clue that should help you find the actual error.

Incidentally, the error message that's displayed is for the first error that's detected, but there can be other errors in the code. To catch them, you have to correct the first error and run the application again. Then, if there are other errors, you repeat the process until they're all fixed and the application runs to completion.

Chrome with an open Console panel that shows an error

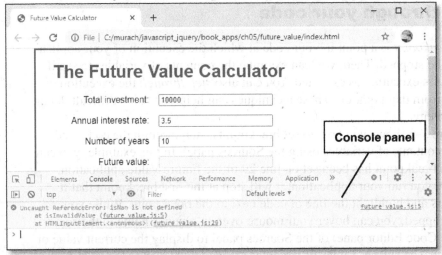

The Sources panel after the link in the Console panel has been clicked

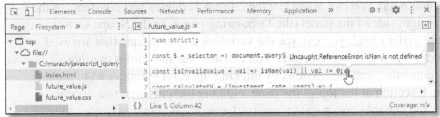

How to open or close Chrome's developer tools

- To open the developer tools, press F12 or Ctrl+Shift+I. Or, click on the Menu button in the upper right corner of the browser, and select More Tools→Developer Tools.

- To close the developer tools, click on the X in the upper right corner of the tools panel or press F12.

How to find the JavaScript statement that caused the error

- Open the Console panel by clicking on the Console tab. You should see an error message like the one above, along with the line of code that caused the error.

- Click on the link to the right of the error message that indicates the line of code. That will open the Sources panel and display the portion of JavaScript code that contains the statement with the statement highlighted.

- Hover your cursor over the red *x* to see more information about the error.

Description

- Chrome's *developer tools* provide some excellent debugging features, like identifying the JavaScript statement that caused an error.

- Because you usually start the developer tools by pressing the F12 key, these tools are often referred to as the *F12 tools*.

Figure 5-4   How to use Chrome to find errors

How to use breakpoints and step through your code

A *breakpoint* is a point in your code at which the execution of your application will be stopped. Then, you can examine the contents of variables to see if your code is executing as expected. You can also *step through* the execution of the code from that point on. These techniques can help you solve difficult debugging problems.

Figure 5-5 shows you how to set breakpoints, step through the code, and view the contents of variables using the Sources panel. In this example, you can see that a breakpoint has been set on line 29 of the Future Value application.

When you run your application, it will stop at the first breakpoint that it encounters and highlight the line of code next to the breakpoint. While your code is stopped, you can hover your mouse over an object's name in the center pane (the Code Editor pane) of the Sources panel to display the current value of that object. The current values of variables are also displayed to the right of the statements that declare them.

At a breakpoint, you can also view the current variables and constants in the pane at the right side of the panel (the Debugging pane). In the Scope section of that pane under Local, you can see the variables and constants that are used by the function that is being executed. You can also see the values of other variables, constants, and expressions by clicking the caret symbol (▶) to the left of the Watch section at the top of the pane, clicking the plus sign that appears, and typing the variable or constant name or the expression that you want to watch.

To step through the execution of an application after a breakpoint is reached, you can use the Step Into, Step Over, and Step Out buttons. These buttons are just above the Debugging pane. Or, you can press the key associated with these operations, as shown in the table in this figure.

If you repeatedly click or press Step Into, you will execute the code one line at a time and the next line to be executed will be highlighted. After each line of code is executed, you can use the Local or Watch section of the Debugging pane to observe any changes in the variables.

As you step through an application, you can use Step Over if you want to execute a called function without taking the time to step through it. Or, you can use Step Out to step out of a function that you don't want to step all the way through. When you want to return to normal execution, you can use Resume. Then, the application will run until the next breakpoint is reached.

These are powerful debugging features that can help you find the causes of serious debugging problems. Stepping through an application is also a good way to understand how the code in an existing application works. If, for example, you step through the for loop in the Future Value application, you'll get a better idea of how it works.

A breakpoint in the Sources panel

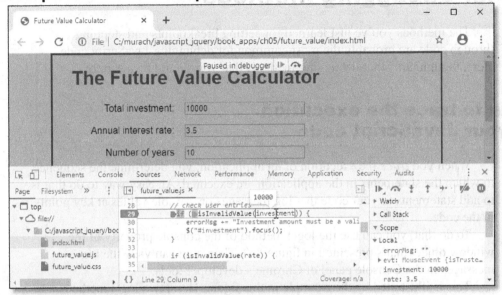

How to set or remove a breakpoint in the Sources panel

- Click on the Sources tab to display the Sources panel. Then, click on the JavaScript file in the left pane (the File Navigator pane) that you want to debug.
- In the center pane (the Code Editor pane), click on a line number in the bar to the left of a statement. This will either add a breakpoint or remove an existing one.

The buttons and keys for stepping through the JavaScript code

Button	Key	Description
Step Into	F11	Step through the code one line at a time.
Step Over	F10	Run any called functions without stepping through them.
Step Out	Shift+F11	Execute the rest of a function without stepping through it.
Resume	F8	Resume normal execution.

How to view the current data values at each step

- Hover the mouse pointer over a variable or constant name in the Code Editor pane.
- View the current values in the Local section of the right pane (the Debugging pane).
- Click the ▶ symbol in the Watch section of the Debugging pane, click the plus sign that appears, and type the variable or constant name or expression that you want to watch.
- The values are also displayed to the right of the declarations in the Code Editor pane.

Description

- You can set a *breakpoint* on any line except a blank line. When the JavaScript engine encounters a breakpoint, it stops before executing the statement with the breakpoint.
- A light blue arrow around the line number marks a breakpoint, and a light blue highlight marks the next statement to be executed as you *step through* your code.

Figure 5-5   How to use breakpoints and step through your code

Other debugging methods

The methods you've just learned for setting breakpoints and stepping through code are probably the most common for debugging JavaScript code. Here, though, are other debugging methods that you should be aware of.

How to trace the execution of your JavaScript code

When you *trace* the execution of an application, you determine the sequence in which the statements in the application are executed. An easy way to do that is to add statements to your code that log messages or variable values at key points in the code.

To do that, you can use the log() method of the console property of the window object that's presented in figure 5-6. Then, you can view the log messages in the Console panel of Chrome's developer tools.

This is illustrated by the example in this figure. Here, two log() methods are added to the calculateFV() function for the Future Value application. The first one is coded at the beginning of the function and lets you know that the calculateFV() function has been started. The second one is coded at the end of the for loop and displays the current value of the counter variable and the future value variable.

If you review the output from the log() methods, you should be able to tell why the result of the future value calculation is incorrect. Here, the loop is only executed nine times, but the Number of Years entry is 10. That means that the conditional expression that determines when the loop should end is incorrect. In this case, the loop should be executed until i is less than or equal to ten.

In this example, tracing helps you find a bug. However, you can also use tracing to make sure that the results are correct. For instance, you could easily assume that the future value result is correct without checking further. However, tracing the execution of the statements in the loop shows that the result can't possibly be correct.

When you use this technique, you usually start by adding just a few log() methods to the code. Then, if that doesn't help you solve the problem, you can add more. Often, this is all you need for solving simple debugging problems, and this is quicker than setting breakpoints and stepping through the code.

One way that tracing is better than stepping through code is when you're dealing with code that is executed many times. Say, for example, you've got an error that occurs somewhere inside a loop that performs a calculation on each element of an array with 1000 elements. Then, it would be daunting to step through the entire array to find the calculation that fails. With the console.log() method, though, you can send the loop's index and the element's value to the console on each iteration, and then look at the complete log when the script has stopped running.

You can also use the alert() method to trace the execution of an application.

One method of the console property of the window object

Method	Description
log(*string*)	Outputs a log message to the Console panel.

Code with two log() methods that trace its execution

```
const calculateFV = (investment, rate, years) => {
    console.log("calculateFV function has started");
    let futureValue = investment;
    for (let i = 1; i < years; i++ ) {
        futureValue += futureValue * rate / 100;
        console.log(`i = ${i}: future value = ${futureValue}`);
    }
    return futureValue;
};
```

The messages in the Console panel of Chrome's developer tools

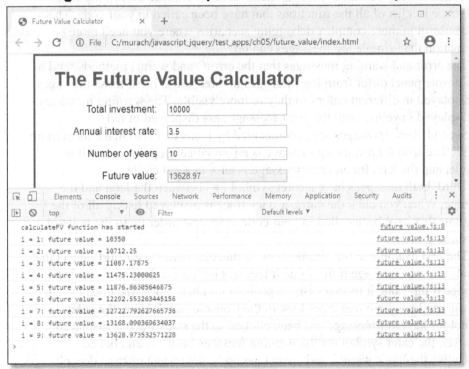

Description

- A simple way to *trace* the execution of a JavaScript application is to call the console.log() method at key points in the code. These methods can display messages in the Console panel that indicate what portion of the code is being executed or display the values of variables.

- You can also use the alert() method for tracing, but the resulting popups can be intrusive, especially if you're tracing something extensive like a loop.

Figure 5-6   How to trace the execution of your JavaScript code

This has the benefit of displaying the trace data directly in the browser rather than having to open the Console panel. When you use the alert() method, though, you can't see all of the generated messages at once, which makes it harder to use for tracing. In addition, it has the drawback of being intrusive.

In the example in figure 5-6, for instance, you would need to close an alert dialog box once when the calculateFV() function first starts and then once each time through the loop. That may not seem like much, but that can quickly become annoying, especially if you're tracing something extensive.

More methods for tracing execution

Figure 5-7 presents three more methods of the console property. Like the log() method, you can use these methods to send information about your code to the Console panel of Chrome's developer tools.

Unlike the log() method, though, these methods provide a *stack trace*. A stack trace is a list of all the functions that have been called in your code. This can be useful in more complex debugging scenarios where you need more information than simple log messages can provide.

The error and warning messages that the error() and warn() methods send to the Console panel differ from log messages in three ways. First, these messages are displayed in different colors so they're more visible. The warning messages are displayed in yellow, and the error messages are displayed in red.

Second, these messages are accompanied by icons that also make them more visible. The icon for a warning message is an exclamation point in a yellow triangle, and the icon for an error message is an *X* in a red circle.

Third, both messages have a caret symbol (▶) between the icon and the message. When you click the caret, a stack trace is displayed listing all of the functions that have been called in your code in reverse order up to the point of the warning or error.

The first example in this figure shows a function named isInvalidValue() that outputs an error message if the value it receives isn't a number, or a warning message if the value it receives isn't a positive number. Below the code example, you can see how these messages look in the Console panel. Here, the caret symbol for the error message has been clicked so the stack trace is displayed. However, the caret symbol for the warning message hasn't been clicked.

Unlike the log(), warn(), and error() methods, the trace() method doesn't send specific messages to the Console panel. Instead, it just displays the stack trace. The second example shows the calculateFV() function with calls to both the log() and trace() methods at the start of the code. Below this example, you can see how the stack trace looks in the Console panel. This shows that the calculateFV() function at line 9 was called by an anonymous function at line 50 of the JavaScript file named future_value.js.

Three more methods of the console property of the window object

Method	Description
warn (*string*)	Outputs a warning message in yellow to the Console panel, along with an icon of an exclamation point in a yellow triangle and a caret to display a stack trace.
error (*string*)	Outputs an error message in red to the Console panel, along with an icon of an X in a red circle and a caret to display a stack trace.
trace ()	Outputs a stack trace to the Console panel.

Code that sends error and warning messages to the Console panel

```
const isInvalidValue = val => {
    if (isNaN(val)) {
        console.error("Value is not a number");
    } else if (val <= 0) {
        console.warn(`Value ${val} is not greater than zero.`);
    }
    return isNaN(val) || val <= 0
};
```

How the messages look in the Console panel

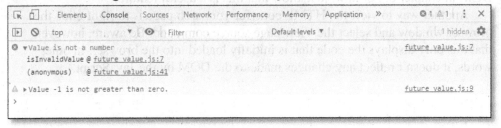

Code that sends a stack trace to the Console panel

```
const calculateFV = (investment, rate, years) => {
    console.log("calculateFV function has started");
    console.trace();
    // rest of code
};
```

How the stack trace looks when it's expanded in the Console panel

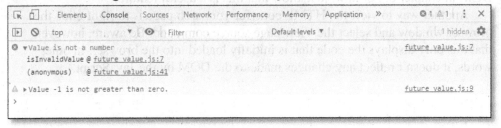

Description

- You can use three more methods of the console property of the window object to send warning and error messages and a stack trace to the Console panel.

- A *stack trace* lists all the functions that the code has called up to that point, listed in order from the most recent. You can click on the link for a function to go to its code.

Figure 5-7   More methods for tracing execution

How to view the HTML and CSS for a web page

Sometimes, it's useful to review the HTML and CSS for your web page. To do that, you can use the Elements panel of Chrome's developer tools that's shown in figure 5-8.

The Elements panel lets you drill down into the document's HTML. In this figure, for example, you can see that the body and main elements, as well as the first div element, have been expanded so you can see their content.

In the Styles pane at the right side of the Elements panel, you can also see the CSS that has been applied to the selected element. This pane shows all of the styles that have been applied from all of the style sheets that are attached to the web page. If a style in this pane has a line through it, that means it has been overridden by another style. This pane can be invaluable when you're trying to solve complicated formatting problems with cascading style sheets.

Another benefit of the Elements panel is that it shows you any changes to the HTML that your JavaScript code has made. For instance, if you've added any nodes to the DOM, they'll show here. You'll learn more about working with the DOM in chapter 6. For now, just know that this is a useful feature.

Another way to view the HTML code for your web page is to right-click the browser window and select the View page source command. Be aware, however, that this only displays the code that is initially loaded into the browser. In other words, it doesn't reflect any changes made to the DOM by the JavaScript.

The HTML and CSS for a web page in the Elements panel

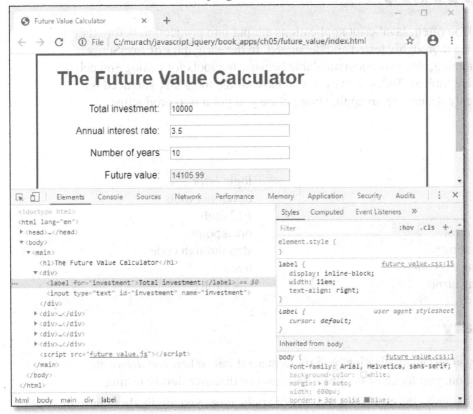

Description

- To see the Elements panel, open the developer tools and click on the Elements tab.

- The Elements panel displays the HTML nodes for a document. You can expand these nodes until you can see the HTML element you're looking for. You'll learn more about nodes in chapter 6.

- If your JavaScript code changes the DOM, such as by adding or removing nodes, the changes show in the Elements panel as well.

- To select a node, click on it. Then, you can see the CSS that's applied to the element in the Styles pane at the right side of the panel.

- You can also view the HTML for a web page by right-clicking the page and selecting the View page source command. Then, you can view the code in an external CSS file by clicking on the link for that file. However, when you view the HTML and CSS this way, you won't see any changes made by your JavaScript code.

Figure 5-8   How to view the HTML and CSS for a web page

Perspective

All too often, JavaScript applications are put into production before they have been thoroughly tested and debugged. In the early days of JavaScript programming, that was understandable because the tools for testing and debugging were limited. Today, however, you have all the tools that you need for thoroughly debugging an application before you put it into production.

Terms

test	logic error
debug	developer tools
bug	F12 tools
syntax error	breakpoint
runtime error	step through code
throw an exception	trace
throw an error	stack trace

Summary

- When you *test* an application, you try to make it fail. When you *debug* an application, you fix all of the problems that you discover during testing.

- When you write the code for a JavaScript application, you are likely to introduce three types of errors: *syntax errors*, *runtime errors*, and *logic errors*.

- Chrome's *developer tools* (or *F12 tools*) can help you debug an application when it stops running. First, the Console panel displays an error message. Then, the link in the message goes to the statement where the error occurred in the Sources panel.

- In the Sources panel of Chrome's developer tools, you can set *breakpoints* that stop the execution of code. Then, you can *step through* the code starting from a breakpoint and view the changes in the variables at each step.

- An easy way to *trace* the execution of an application is to call the console.log() method at key points in the JavaScript code. This method logs the specified data in Chrome's Console panel. You can also use the alert() method for tracing.

- In the Elements panel of Chrome's developer tools, you can view the HTML for a document, including any changes made to the DOM by the JavaScript code. You can also see the CSS that's applied to any element.

Exercise 5-1   Use Chrome's developer tools

In this exercise, you'll use Chrome's developer tools to find a syntax error and a logic error, set a breakpoint, and step through the Email List application.

1. Open the HTML and JavaScript files for the Email List application in this folder:

   `javascript_jquery\exercises\ch05\email_list`

2. Run the application in Chrome, enter valid values in all three text boxes, and click on the Join List button. Then, note that nothing happens.

3. Open the developer tools and use the Console panel to display the error that caused the problem, as shown in figure 5-4. Then, click the link for the error to see the statement that caused the error in the Sources panel.

4. Switch to your text editor or IDE and fix the code. The correction should be fairly obvious. Then, test the application again with valid values in all three text boxes. This time, an alert dialog box should be displayed with no message.

5. Click the OK button in the dialog box, and notice that there are no error messages in the Console panel. That's because a logic error has occurred.

6. Still in the developer tools, switch to the Sources panel. Then, if necessary, click on the email_list.js file in the File Navigator pane on the left to display the JavaScript code in the email_list.js file.

7. Set a breakpoint on the first statement in the event handler for the click event of the Join List button, as shown in figure 5-5. Then, with valid values still in the three text boxes, click the Join our List button again. The application should stop at the breakpoint.

8. Use the Step Into button or F11 key to step through the application. At each step, notice the values that are displayed for the local variables in the Debugging pane on the right. Also, hover the mouse over a variable in the JavaScript code to see what its value is.

9. Experiment with the Step Over and Step Out buttons as you step through the code. When you get to the second if-else statement in the event handler, watch carefully to see what statements are executed. That should help you determine the cause of the logic error.

10. Switch to your text editor or IDE and fix the code. Then, test the application with valid data one more time. When the breakpoint is reached, remove it and then continue execution. This time, the application should execute to completion.

Exercise 5-2   Use other debugging methods

In this exercise, you'll use the other debugging methods that you learned in this chapter.

1. Open this JavaScript file:

   `javascript_jquery\exercises\ch05\mpg\mpg.js`

   Review the code to see that it includes an isInvalidValue() function, as well as calls to console.log() methods for tracing the execution of the application.

2. Run this application in Chrome, don't enter anything into the text boxes, and click on the Calculate button. Note that error messages are displayed in an alert dialog box.

3. Close the dialog box. Then, open the developer tools, display the Console panel, and review the information in the log.

4. In the isInvalidValue() function, replace the two console.log() methods that check for errors with console.error() methods. Then, run the application again without making any entries.

5. Close the alert dialog box that's displayed, and review the messages in the Console panel. Then, expand the first error message to see that the stack trace indicates that the error occurred on line 7 in the isInvalidValue() function, which was called by line 33 in the processEntries() function.

6. Enter valid values in the two text boxes, and click on the Calculate button. Then, go to the Console panel to review the new information.

7. Display the Elements panel, and then select the body element and review its CSS in the Styles pane. Do the same for the main element and the h1 element.

8. Expand the last div element, and then select the input element to review its CSS. Continue experimenting if you want, and then close the browser.

6

How to script the DOM
with JavaScript

At this point, you have all of the JavaScript skills that you need for some
serious DOM scripting. You just need to learn how to use some of the properties and methods that are provided by the DOM specifications, as well as some
special skills for working with forms and controls.

DOM scripting properties and methods

To script the DOM, you use properties and methods of the objects that make up the DOM. These properties and methods are defined by the DOM Core specification that is implemented by all modern browsers, as well as by the DOM HTML specification.

DOM scripting concepts

Before you learn the properties and methods of the *DOM Core specification*, figure 6-1 presents the DOM scripting concepts that you should understand. First, the *Document Object Model*, or *DOM*, is built as an HTML page is loaded into the browser. It contains *nodes* that represent all of the HTML elements and attributes for the page. This is illustrated by the HTML and diagram in this figure.

Besides the *element nodes* that are represented by ovals in this diagram, the DOM includes *text nodes* that hold the data for the HTML elements. In this diagram, these text nodes are rectangles. For instance, the first text node contains the text for the title element in the head section: "Join Email List". The one to the right of that contains the text for the h1 element in the body: "Please join our email list". And so on.

For simplicity, this diagram only includes the element and text nodes, but the DOM also contains *attribute nodes*, and each attribute node can have a text node that holds the attribute value. Also, if the HTML includes comments, the DOM will include *comment nodes*.

If you study the table in this figure, you can see that an element node can have element, text, and comment nodes as child nodes. An attribute node can have a text node as a child node. And a text node can't have a child node. Even though an attribute node is attached to an element node, it isn't considered to be a child node of the element node.

The properties and methods for working with DOM nodes are defined by a specification called an *interface*. In the topics that follow, you'll learn how to work with the properties and methods of the Node, Document, and Element interfaces.

As you work with these interfaces, you'll come across terms like *parent*, *child*, *sibling*, and *descendant*. These terms are used just as they are in a family tree. In the diagram in this figure, for example, the form element is the parent of the label, input, and span elements, and the label, input, and span elements are children of the form element. The label, input, and span elements are also siblings because they have the same parent. Similarly, the h1 and form elements are children of the body element, and the h1, form, label, input, and span elements are all descendants of the body element.

You should also be able to see these relationships in the HTML for a web page. In the HTML in this figure, for example, the indentation clearly shows the children and descendants for each element.

The code for a web page

```html
<!DOCTYPE html>
<html>
<head>
    <title>Join Email List</title>
</head>
<body>
    <h1>Please join our email list</h1>
    <form id="email_form" name="email_form" action="join.html" method="get">
        <label for="email_address">Email Address:</label>
        <input type="text" id="email_address" name="email_address">
        <span id="email_error">*</span><br>
    </form>
</body>
</html>
```

The DOM for the web page

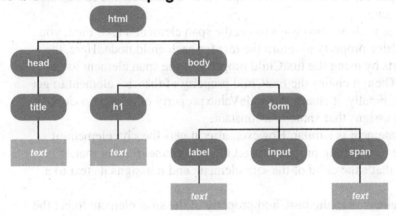

The DOM nodes that you commonly use

Type	Description
Document	Root node of the DOM. It can only have one Element node as a child node.
Element	An element in the web page. It can have Element, Text, and Comment nodes as child nodes.
Attr	An attribute of an element. Although it is attached to an Element node, it isn't considered a child node. It can have a Text node as a child node.
Text	The text for an element or attribute. It can't have a child node.

Description

- The *DOM* (*Document Object Model*) is a hierarchical collection of *nodes* in the web browser's memory that represents the current web page.

- The DOM for a web page is built as the page is loaded by the web browser.

- JavaScript can modify the web page in the browser by modifying the DOM. Whenever the DOM is changed, the web browser displays the results of the change.

- To modify the DOM, you can use the properties and methods that are defined by the *DOM Core specification*.

Figure 6-1   DOM scripting concepts

The properties of the Node interface

The table in figure 6-2 describes seven of the most useful properties for working with nodes. These properties are defined by the Node interface. The first five properties return nodes, and the last two properties get text from or write text to a Text, Comment, or Attribute node.

The first example in this figure shows an HTML span element with three child elements. The <b> element displays text in bold, the <u> element underlines text, and the <i> element displays text in italics. These three elements are siblings of each other and are children of the span element. Additionally, these three elements each have a child text node.

The second example uses the querySelector() method of the document object to get an Element object that represents the span element from the first example. This object is assigned to a constant named span, and it's used by the rest of the examples in this figure.

The third example shows two ways to get the span element's text. First, you can use the nodeValue property to return the text for each child node. Here, the first statement starts by using the firstChild property of the span element to get the <b> element. Then, it chains the firstChild property of the <b> element to get its child text node. Finally, it chains the nodeValue property of the text node to get the text, and it assigns that value to a constant.

The second statement is similar. However, after it gets the <b> element, it chains the nextElementSibling property to get the <u> element. After that, it gets the text node that's the child of the <u> element, and it assigns its text to a constant.

The third statement uses the lastChild property of the span element to get the <i> element. After that, it gets the text node for that element, and it assigns its text to a constant.

The last statement in this example uses the + operator to concatenate the string values stored in the three constants. Then, it passes that string to the log() method of the console object. This displays the string "Welcome Back!" in the console.

You can also get the same results using the textContent property. Unlike the nodeValue property, the textContent property returns all the text from all the child nodes of the span element. That means you don't have to navigate the child and sibling nodes, which makes the code simpler. If you need to retrieve all of the text for a node, then, you'll want to use the textContent property. Otherwise, you'll need to use the nodeValue property.

The fourth example shows how to use the textContent property to set the text for a child element of the span element. To do that, you have to navigate the child and sibling nodes just like you do when you get the text for a node. Then, you can assign a value to that node. In this example, the text for the first child node of the span element, the <b> element, is set to a new value.

The last example shows that you can also use the textContent property to set the node for the span element. When you do that, you should realize that all of the child nodes for the element are replaced by a single text node.

Some of the properties of the Node interface

Property	Description
parentNode	Returns the parent node of a node if one exists. Otherwise, this property returns a null value.
childNodes	Returns an array of Node objects representing the child nodes of a node. If the node doesn't have child nodes, the array contains no elements.
firstChild	Returns a Node object for the first child node of a node. If the node doesn't have child nodes, this property returns a null value.
lastChild	Returns a Node object for the last child node of a node. If the node doesn't have child nodes, this property returns a null value.
nextElementSibling	Returns a Node object for the next sibling of a node. If the node doesn't have a sibling element that follows it, this property returns a null value.
nodeValue	For a Text, Comment, or Attribute node, returns the text that's stored in the node. Otherwise, returns a null value. Can also be used to set the text for a node.
textContent	For a Text, Comment, or Attribute node, returns the text that's stored in the node and all descendant nodes. Otherwise, it returns a null value. Can also be used to set the text of a node and all descendant nodes.

An HTML span element with three child elements

```
<span><b>Welcome </b><u>Back</u><i>!</i></span>
```

How to get an Element object for the span element

```
const span = document.querySelector("span");
```

How to get the text from the span element

With the nodeValue property

```
const bElemText = span.firstChild.firstChild.nodeValue;
const uElemText = span.firstChild.nextElementSibling.firstChild.nodeValue;
const iElemText = span.lastChild.firstChild.nodeValue;
console.log(bElemText + uElemText + iElemText);   // displays Welcome Back!
```

With the textContent property

```
const spanText = span.textContent;
console.log(spanText);                             // displays Welcome Back!
```

How to set the text of the span element's first child element

```
span.firstChild.textContent = "Hurry ";
console.log(span.textContent);                     // displays Hurry Back!
```

How to set the text of the span element

```
span.textContent = "Hi";      // replaces all child elements with a text node
console.log(span.textContent);                     // displays "Hi"
```

Description

- An *interface* describes the properties and methods for an object.
- When DOM scripting, you often use the properties of the Node interface.

Figure 6-2   The properties of the Node interface

The methods of the Document and Element interfaces

The first table in figure 6-3 summarizes two methods that are in both the Document and Element interfaces. The first method returns an Element object that represents the first HTML element that matches the CSS selector it receives. For instance, if you pass it the selector "#my_element", it returns the HTML element whose id attribute has a value of "my_element". That's how you've seen this method used so far in this book.

However, you can also pass a selector that's an element name or a class name. In that case, the method returns the first element that matches that selector. For instance, if you pass the selector "a", it returns the first <a> element. Or, if you pass the selector ".small", it returns the first element that's assigned to the CSS class named "small".

The second method in the first table returns an array of Element objects. For instance, if you pass it the selector "a", it returns an array of all the <a> elements. Or, if you pass it the selector ".small", it returns an array of all the elements that are assigned to the CSS class named "small".

If these methods are used with the document object, they get the first element or all of the elements in the document. This is illustrated by the first example in this figure. It gets all of the <a> elements in the document and puts them in an array named links.

If these methods are used with an element as the object, however, they get the first element or all of the elements that are descendants of that element. For instance, the second example shows an HTML ul element with an id of "image_list" that has two child li elements. Then, the first statement in the third example uses the querySelector() method of the document object to get the ul element by its id, and it assigns that element to a constant named list. After that, the second statement uses the querySelectorAll() method to get an array of all of the li elements that are children of the ul element.

Note that if you don't need to refer to the ul element elsewhere in your code, you don't need to store it in a constant as shown here. Instead, you can retrieve the li elements using a descendant selector like this:

```
const items = document.querySelectorAll("#image_list li");
```

Or, if the $() function has been declared, you can get the li elements of the ul element using the Element interface like this:

```
const items = $("#image_list").querySelectorAll("li");
```

The second table in this figure summarizes some of the methods of the Element interface that work with attributes. For instance, the fourth example in this figure uses the hasAttribute() method to determine whether the ul element that was assigned to the list constant in the third example has a class attribute. If it does, it uses the getAttribute() method to get the value of that attribute.

The fifth example shows how to use the setAttribute() method to set the value of an attribute. It sets the class attribute of an element named list to "open". If the attribute doesn't already exist, this method adds the attribute to the

Common methods of the Document interface

Method	Description
`querySelector(selector)`	Returns the first HTML element that matches the selector that's passed to it. The parameter is a string that contains a valid CSS selector.
`querySelectorAll(selector)`	Returns all the HTML elements that match the selector that's passed to it. The parameter is a string that contains a valid CSS selector.

Common methods of the Element interface

Method	Description
`hasAttribute(name)`	Returns true if the Element has the attribute specified in name.
`getAttribute(name)`	Returns the value of the attribute specified in name or an empty string if an attribute of that name isn't set.
`setAttribute(name, value)`	Sets the attribute specified in name to the specified value. If the attribute doesn't already exist, it creates the attribute too.
`removeAttribute(name)`	Removes the attribute specified in name.

How to create an array of all <a> tags in a document

```
const links = document.querySelectorAll("a");
```

An HTML ul element

```
<ul id="image_list">
    <li><img src="images/lion.png"></li>
    <li><img src="images/tiger.png"></li>
</ul>
```

How to get an array of all li elements within the ul element

```
const list = document.querySelector("#image_list");
const items = list.querySelectorAll("li");
```

How to test for and get an attribute

```
if ( list.hasAttribute("class") ) {
    const classAttribute = list.getAttribute("class"));
}
```

How to set an attribute

```
list.setAttribute("class", "open");
```

How to remove an attribute

```
list.removeAttribute("class");
```

Description

- The methods of the Document and Element interfaces return objects that represent HTML elements.
- The methods of the Element interface also let you work with element attributes.

Figure 6-3   The methods of the Document and Element interfaces

element before setting its value. The last example in this figure uses the remove-Attribute() method to remove the class attribute from the list element.

The properties of the DOM HTML specification

The properties and methods that you've seen so far are part of the DOM Core specification. But there's also a *DOM HTML specification* that provides properties that make it easier to work with HTML elements. Figure 6-4 summarizes some of these properties and shows you how to use them.

When you work with the DOM HTML specification, you should remember that its properties don't provide new functionality. Instead, they provide shortcuts that make it easier to work with the DOM nodes of an HTML document.

The differences are illustrated by the first set of examples in this figure, which get and set the src attribute for an img element. With the DOM core specification, the getAttribute() and setAttribute() methods are used. With the DOM HTML specification, the src property is used, which shortens and simplifies the code.

The other examples in this figure show how to use some of the other properties of the DOM HTML specification. You'll also see some other properties used in the applications in this book. Usually, the property name is the same as the attribute name, but sometimes the property name is different. For instance, as one of the examples shows, the className property is used to get and set the class attribute.

Note that some of the examples here and in the figures that follow use the $() function. As you'll recall from other examples you've seen in this book, this function uses the document.querySelector() method to retrieve the first element that matches the CSS selector it receives.

If you want to use the online documentation for the DOM HTML specification, it helps to know that this specification is composed of several *interfaces* that describe the properties and methods of an object type. The base interface is HTMLElement, which describes a base HTML element. In addition, the HTMLElement interface *inherits* properties and methods from the DOM Core Element interface, which in turn inherits from the DOM Core Node interface. This means that all the Node, Element, and HTMLElement properties and methods are available to you when you work with HTML elements in JavaScript.

Beyond that, specific HTML elements use specific DOM HTML interfaces that inherit from the base HTMLElement interface. For example, an img element uses the HTMLImageElement interface, and an input element uses the HTMLInputElement interface.

Most of the time, you won't need to know which interface an element uses. Usually, you'll be able to use the element's attribute name as the DOM HTML property name in your code. But if that doesn't work, you can use the URL at the top of this figure to look up the correct property name. In the table of contents that you'll find there, you can find subheadings for the base HTMLElement interface, and for the more specific interfaces that inherit from HTMLElement, like HTMLLinkElement, HTMLImageElement, and HTMLInputElement.

The URL for the DOM HTML specification

www.w3.org/TR/DOM-Level-2-HTML/html.html

Typical properties available with the DOM HTML specification

Element	Property	Attribute
all	id	The id attribute
	title	The title attribute
	className	The class attribute. To set multiple class names, separate the names with spaces.
	tagName	The name of the tag, like div, h1, h2, a, or img.
<a>	href	The href attribute
img	src	The src attribute
	alt	The alt attribute
input	disabled	The disabled attribute

How the DOM HTML specification can simplify your code

How to get and set an img tag src attribute with the DOM core specification

```
const imageElement = $("#image");
alert(imageElement.getAttribute(src));      // displays the src attribute
imageElement.setAttribute(src, "lion.jpg"); // sets the src attribute
```

How to get and set the same attribute with the DOM HTML specification

```
alert(imageElement.src);                     // displays the src attribute
imageElement.src = "lion.jpg";               // sets the src attribute
```

Other examples of using the DOM HTML specification

How to get the id attribute of the first element in an array

```
const links = document.querySelectorAll("a");
const firstLinkId = links[0].id;
```

How to get the href attribute of an <a> element

```
const target = $("#first_link").href;
```

How to set and get the class attribute of an element with two class names

```
$("div").className = "open plus";
const classNames = $("div").className;      // classNames = "open plus"
```

How to get the tag attribute of the first element in an array

```
const links = document.querySelectorAll("a");
const tagName = links[0].tagName;           // tagName = "a"
```

How to disable and enable an element

```
$("#btnPlay").disabled = true;
$("#btnPlay").disabled = false;
```

Description

- The HTML specification provides shortcuts that make it easier to work with DOM nodes.

- The HTML specification is composed of *interfaces* that *inherit* properties and methods from other interfaces. The HTMLElement interface represents a base HTML element.

Figure 6-4   The properties of the DOM HTML specification

The classList property of the Element interface

In the preceding figures, you learned two ways that you can work with the class attribute of an element. First, you can use the setAttribute() and removeAttribute() methods of the DOM Core specification. Second, you can use the className property of the DOM HTML specification.

However, both of these ways of working with the class attribute are all-or-nothing. That is, you replace or remove the entire value of the attribute. But often, that's not what you want. For instance, suppose an element already has one or more class names and you want to add another. In that case, you need to get the existing attribute value, add the new class name to the string, and assign the updated string as the new value of the class attribute.

It's even more complicated if there are multiple class names in the class attribute and you want to remove some but not all of them. Then, you need to get the existing attribute value and use the methods of the String object you learned in chapter 4 to find the substring and remove it. This is called *string manipulation*, and it can be tedious and error-prone.

Fortunately, the Element interface has a classList property that makes it easier to work with the class attribute of an element. This property gets an object that contains the class names that are in that attribute, and it provides properties and methods for working with those names. The tables in figure 6-5 present some of these properties and methods.

Below the tables are several examples that show how to use the classList property. The first example presents an HTML h2 element with a class attribute whose value is a single CSS class named "first". Then, the second example selects that heading and assigns the object that represents it to a constant named hdg2. This object is used by the rest of the examples in this figure.

The third example uses the add() method of the classList property to add a CSS class named "blue" to the class attribute. Then, the fourth example uses the replace() method of the classList property to replace the CSS class named "blue" with a CSS class named "red". And the fifth example uses the remove() method of the classList property to remove the CSS class named "red" from the class attribute.

The statements in the sixth example use the toggle() method of the classList property to alternate between adding and removing the CSS class named "blue". Before the first statement executes, the value of the class attribute is "first". So, when the first statement calls the toggle() method, it adds the "blue" class to the attribute. Then, when the second statement executes the toggle() method again, it removes the "blue" class from the attribute value, and the third statement adds it again.

The last example uses the contains() method of the classList property to check if the CSS class named "blue" is already in the class attribute. If it is, the add() method adds the CSS class named "bold".

Another property of the Element interface

Property	Description
classList	Gets a DOMTokenList object, which contains the class names in the class attribute and provides properties and methods for working with them.

Common properties of the DOMTokenList object

Method	Description
length	Gets the number of class names in the class attribute.
value	Gets the class names in the class attribute in a single space-delimited string.

Common methods of the DOMTokenList object

Method	Description
contains(*className*)	Returns true if the specified class name is in the attribute.
add(*className*)	Adds the specified class name to the attribute.
remove(*className*)	Removes the specified class name from the attribute.
replace(*oldName*, *newName*)	Replaces the specified old class name with the new class name.
toggle(*className*)	Removes the specified class name if it's in the attribute, adds it if it isn't.

An HTML label element

```
<h2 class="first">Welcome to our website!</h2>
```

How to get an Element object for the label element

```
const hdg2 = document.querySelector("h2");
```

How to add a CSS class to the Element object

```
hdg2.classList.add("blue");                    // class attribute is "first blue"
```

How to replace a CSS class with another CSS class

```
hdg2.classList.replace("blue", "red");     // attribute is "first red"
```

How to remove a CSS class

```
hdg2.classList.remove("red");              // attribute is "first"
```

How to toggle a CSS class

```
hdg2.classList.toggle("blue");             // attribute is "first blue"
hdg2.classList.toggle("blue");             // attribute is "first"
hdg2.classList.toggle("blue");             // attribute is "first blue"
```

How to check for a CSS class before taking an action

```
if (hdg2.classList.contains("blue")) {
    hdg2.classList.add("bold");            // attribute is "first blue bold"
}
```

Description

- The classList property gets an object that contains the classes an element is assigned to. Then, you can use the properties and methods of that object to work with the classes.

Figure 6-5   The classList property of the Element interface

The FAQs application

Now, you'll see how the properties and methods of the Node, Document, and Element interfaces are used in a typical DOM scripting application. We call this the FAQs (Frequently Asked Questions) application, and you can see its user interface in figure 6-6.

Quite simply, if the user clicks on a heading with a plus sign before it, the text below it is displayed and the plus sign is changed to a minus sign. Similarly, if the user clicks on a heading with a minus sign before it, the text below it is hidden and the minus sign is changed to a plus sign. The user can display the text below all three headings at the same time, and the user can hide the text below all three headings at the same time.

The HTML

In the HTML in this figure, you can see that each of the questions is coded in an <a> element within an h2 element, and each h2 element is followed by a div element that contains the answer. Note that the href attributes in these elements are coded as # signs so these links don't go anywhere.

Because <a> elements are coded within the h2 elements, a user can tab from one heading to the next. Then, when a user tabs to a heading and presses the Enter key, the effect is the same as clicking on the heading. This makes this app easier to use for motor-impaired users who can't handle a mouse.

The HTML in this figure includes an external CSS style sheet in its head section, and an external JavaScript file at the end of its body. You'll see both of those files next. In particular, you'll see how the JavaScript adds and removes CSS classes to make this application work.

The FAQs application in a browser

> # jQuery FAQs
>
> ⊖ What is jQuery?
>
> jQuery is a library of the JavaScript functions that you're most likely to
> need as you develop websites.
>
> ⊕ **Why use jQuery?**
>
> ⊕ **Which is harder to learn: jQuery or JavaScript?**

The HTML

```html
<body>
    <main id="faqs">
        <h1>jQuery FAQs</h1>

        <h2><a href="#">What is jQuery?</a></h2>
        <div>
            <p>jQuery is a library of the JavaScript functions that you're
                most likely to need as you develop websites.</p>
        </div>

        <h2><a href="#">Why use jQuery?</a></h2>
        <div>
            <p>Three reasons:</p>
            <ul>
                <li>It's free.</li>
                <li>It lets you get more done in less time.</li>
                <li>It's cross-browser compatible.</li>
            </ul>
        </div>

        <h2><a href="#">Which is harder to learn: jQuery or
            JavaScript?</a></h2>
        <div>
            <p>For many things, jQuery is easier to learn than JavaScript.
                But remember that jQuery is JavaScript.</p>
        </div>
    </main>

    <script src="faqs.js"></script>
</body>
```

Figure 6-6   The FAQs application (part 1)

The CSS

In part 2 of figure 6-6, you can see that both the focus and hover pseudo-classes for <a> elements are set to the color blue. That way, they will look the same whether the user hovers the mouse over a link or tabs to the link.

Next, look at the two style rules for the h2 elements. The first one applies to all h2 elements, and it sets the cursor to a pointer when the user hovers the mouse over an h2 element. It also applies a background property that includes an image named plus.png. This image is displayed just once (no-repeat) to the left of the element and it is vertically centered.

The second style rule for the h2 elements applies to elements that have a class property set to "minus". This style rule applies a background property like the one for all h2 elements, but this time it uses an image named minus.png. That's the image that's used when the text below a heading is displayed.

Now, look at the two style rules for the div elements. The first one sets the display property to "none", which hides the contents of the div element. By contrast, the second style rule applies to div elements that have a class attribute set to "open". It sets the display property to block, which displays the contents.

The JavaScript

Part 2 of figure 6-6 also shows the JavaScript for this application. It consists of an event handler for the click event of each h2 element and an event handler for the DOM loaded event that attaches the click event handler.

The click event handler is coded as a toggle() function that receives an Event object. Its first statement assigns the currentTarget property of the Event object to a constant named h2Element. This is the element that triggered the event. Its second statement gets the div element that follows the h2 element.

The third statement uses the toggle() method of the classList property to modify the class attribute of the h2 element. If that attribute contains the "minus" CSS class, it's removed. If it doesn't, it's added. This changes the background image from a plus sign to a minus sign, or vice versa. The fourth statement does the same with the div element and the "open" CSS class. This changes the div from hidden to visible, or vice versa. The last statement calls the preventDefault() method of the Event object to cancel the default action for the click event of the <a> tag within the h2 element.

The toggle event handler is attached to the click event of each h2 element by the event handler for the DOMContentLoaded event. To do that, it uses a descendant selector to get an array of the h2 elements in the element that has "faqs" as its id, which is the main element in the HTML code. Then, it assigns that array to a constant named h2Elements. Finally, it uses a for-of loop to go through the elements in the h2Elements array and attach the toggle event handler to the click event of each h2 element.

The DOMContentLoaded event handler ends by setting the focus to the <a> tag in the first h2 element in the array of h2 elements. It does that by using an index of 0 to refer to the first element in the h2Elements array, and then using the firstChild property to refer to the first child of that element, which is its <a> tag.

The CSS

```css
a {
    color: black;
    text-decoration: none;
}
a:focus, a:hover {
    color: blue;
}
h2 {
    cursor: pointer;
    background: url(images/plus.png) no-repeat left center;
}
h2.minus {
    background: url(images/minus.png) no-repeat left center;
}
div {
    display: none;
}
div.open {
    display: block;
}
```

The JavaScript

```javascript
// the event handler for the click event of each h2 element
const toggle = evt => {
    const h2Element = evt.currentTarget;           // get the clicked h2
    const divElement = h2Element.nextElementSibling; // get h2's sibling div

    h2Element.classList.toggle("minus");
    divElement.classList.toggle("open");

    evt.preventDefault();           // cancel default action of h2's child <a>
};

document.addEventListener("DOMContentLoaded", () => {
    // get the h2 tags
    const h2Elements = document.querySelectorAll("#faqs h2");

    // attach event handler for each h2 tag
    for (let h2Element of h2Elements) {
        h2Element.addEventListener("click", toggle);
    }

    // set focus on first h2 tag's <a> tag
    h2Elements[0].firstChild.focus();
});
```

Description

- The first statement in the handler for the DOMContentLoaded event creates an array of the h2 elements in the main element that has "faqs" as its id.

- The for-of loop in that event handler is executed once for each of the h2 elements. It attaches the toggle event handler to the click event of each h2 element.

Figure 6-6   The FAQs application (part 2)

How to script forms and controls

A *form* contains one or more *controls* such as text boxes and buttons. The controls that accept user entries are also known as *fields*. In the topics that follow, you'll learn how to work with forms and controls.

How forms work

Figure 6-7 shows how to create a form that contains three controls: two text boxes and a button. To start, you code the form element. On the opening tag for this element, you code the action and method attributes. The action attribute specifies the file on the web server that will be used to process the data when the form is submitted. The method attribute specifies the HTTP method that will be used for sending the form to the web server.

In this example, the form will be submitted to the server using the HTTP "get" method when the user clicks the Join List button. Then, the data in the form will be processed on the server by the code in the file named join.php. That file will use PHP as the scripting language.

When you use the "get" method, the form data is sent as part of the URL for the HTTP request. That means that the data is visible in the address bar of the browser. This is illustrated by the URL in this figure. Here, the URL is followed by a question mark and name/value pairs separated by ampersands that present the name attributes and field values. In this case, two values are submitted: the email address and first name entries.

When you use the "post" method, by contrast, the form data is packaged as part of an HTTP request and isn't visible in the browser. Because of that, the submission is more secure than it is when you use the "get" method.

In addition to the action and method attributes, you can code id and name attributes in the opening tag, as the example in this figure shows. This is helpful if you need to select the form by id in your JavaScript. However, these attributes are optional. In fact, you'll often see form elements without them.

Within the opening and closing tags of the form element, you code the controls for the form. In this example, the first two input elements are for text boxes that receive an email address and first name. The third input element has "submit" as the value for its type attribute, which means it is a *submit button*. When it's clicked, the data in the form is automatically submitted to the server.

If the type attribute of an input element is "reset", the element is a *reset button*. When that type of button is clicked, all of the values in the controls of the form are reset to their starting HTML values.

When a form is submitted to the server, the data in the form should be completely validated on the server before the data is processed. Then, if any of the data isn't valid, the form is sent back to the browser with appropriate error messages so the entries can be corrected. This is referred to as *data validation*.

Usually, the form data is validated by the browser too before it is submitted to the server. Note, however, that the browser validation doesn't have to be as thorough as the server-side validation. If the browser validation catches 80 to 90% of the entry errors, it will save many round trips to the server.

A form in a web browser

The HTML for the form

```
<form id="email_form" name="email_form" action="join.php" method="get">
    <label for="email_address">Email Address:</label>
    <input type="text" id="email_address" name="email_address"><br>
    <label for="first_name">First Name:</label>
    <input type="text" id="first_name" name="first_name"><br>
    <label> </label>
    <input type="submit" id="join_list" value="Join our List"><br>
</form>
```

The URL that's sent when the form is submitted with the "get" method

```
join.php?email_address=grace%40yahoo.com&first_name=Grace
```

Attributes of the form element

Attribute	Description
name	A name that can be referred to by client-side or server-side code.
action	The URL of the file that will process the data in the form.
method	The HTTP method for submitting the form data. It can be set to either "get" or "post". The default value is "get".

Description

- A *form* contains one or more *controls* (or *fields*) like text boxes, radio buttons, lists, or check boxes that can receive data.

- When you click on a *submit button* for a form (type is "submit"), the form data is sent to the server as part of an HTTP request. When you click on a *reset button* for a form (type is "reset"), the form data is reset to its default values.

- When a form is submitted to the server for processing, the data in the controls is sent along with the HTTP request.

- When you use the "get" method to submit a form, the URL that requests the file is followed by a question mark and name/value pairs that are separated by ampersands. These pairs contain the name attributes and values of the data that is submitted. When you use the "post" method, the data is hidden.

- *Data validation* refers to checking the data collected by a form to make sure it's valid, and complete data validation is always done on the server. Then, if any invalid data is detected, the form is returned to the client so the user can correct the entries.

- To save round trips to the server when the data is invalid, some validation is usually done on the client before the data is sent to the server. However, this validation doesn't have to be as thorough as the validation that's done on the server.

Figure 6-7   How forms work

How to script Textbox, Textarea, and Select objects

Text boxes, text areas, and select lists are common controls that you should be familiar with. A Textbox object provides a single line for an entry, a Textarea object provides multiple lines for an entry, and a Select object provides a list of options that the user can select from, usually in a drop-down list.

The table in figure 6-8 shows the value property that's common to all three of these HTML objects. It returns a string containing either the entry that the user made or the option that the user selected from the list.

The HTML code in this figure uses these controls to get a user's name, comments, and country. Note that the select control's initial option has no display string and a value of an empty string. This is a common way to make the control appear as if no selection has been made when the page first loads. Another way to do this is to have the display string say something like "Select One" instead of being blank. If, however, you want to make sure that the user makes a selection, you can remove this blank option. This forces the user to either accept the default option or select a different one.

The first JavaScript example in this figure shows how to use the value property of these controls to get the values the user entered or selected. The first two statements use the $() function to store the text box and text area values in constants named name and comment. Then, because the value property returns strings, the next two lines use the length property to make sure the user entered a value. Of course, you could also check the value property for an empty string to make sure the user entered a value.

When doing this kind of check for a text area, you may need to think about how to handle line returns. For instance, if the user presses just the Enter key, a *hard return* is entered and becomes a character in the value property, even though the user didn't type any other text. If that's not what you want, you can use the replace() method of the String object to remove hard returns. For more information, see the online documentation.

In contrast to hard returns, *soft returns* are the automatic returns that occur when the line the user is entering overflows to the next line. These returns don't become characters in the value property, so you don't need to check for them.

The last portion of code in this example works with the select element. First, it uses the value property to retrieve the user's selection and store it in a constant named country. Then, it checks the value of the constant and performs different processing depending on which country was chosen, or it notifies the user if no country was chosen.

In addition to using the value property to retrieve the content of these controls, you can use it to set the content of the controls. The second JavaScript example in this figure shows how this works. In this case, each of the controls on the form has its value property set to an empty string. This is a common way to clear a form, but you can set the value property to any string.

When you set the value property for a Textbox or Textarea object, the value will replace the contents of the value property. But when you set the value of a Select object, it selects the option in the list with that value. For example, setting

Property of a Textbox, Textarea, or Select object

Property	Description
value	The content of the value attribute for the entered text or selected option. Returns a string.

HTML code for a text box, text area, and select list

```
<label for="name">First Name:</label>
<input type="text" name="name" id="name"><br>

<label for="comment">Comment:</label>
<textarea name="comment" id="comment" rows="5" cols="40"></textarea><br>

<label for="country">Country:</label>
<select name="country" id="country">
    <option value=""></option>
    <option value="usa">USA</option>
    <option value="can">Canada</option>
    <option value="mex">Mexico</option>
</select><br>
```

JavaScript code to get the text box, text area, and select list values

```
const name = $("#name").value;
const comment = $("#comment").value;

if (name.length == 0) { alert("Please enter a name."); }
if (comment.length == 0) { alert("Please enter a comment."); }

const country = $("#country").value;
if (country == "usa") { /* USA processing */ }
else if (country == "can") { /* Canada processing */ }
else if (country == "mex") { /* Mexico processing */ }
else { alert("Please select a country."); }
```

JavaScript code to set the text box, text area, and select list values

```
$("#country").value = "";
$("#name").value = "";
$("#comment").value = "";
```

Description

- The name and id attributes of these controls should be set to the same value.
- After you use the value property of one of these objects to get the value string, you can use the length property of the String object to get the number of characters in the string.
- Setting the value property of a Textbox or Textarea object replaces the text contents.
- Setting the value property of a Select object selects the option with the corresponding value.
- When the user presses the Enter key while typing in a text area, a *hard return* is entered into the text. Hard returns appear as characters in the value property.
- When the user types past the end of a line in a text area and a new line is automatically started, a *soft return* occurs. Soft returns do not appear as characters in the value property.

Figure 6-8   How to script Textbox, Textarea, and Select objects

the value property of the Select object to "can" will select the Canada option. If you set the value property to a value that isn't in the option list, nothing is selected, not even the Select object's default value. (The default value is the value of the first option in the list, or the option that has a selected attribute.)

How to script Radio and Checkbox objects

Two other types of controls that you should be familiar with are radio buttons and check boxes. Both of these controls let a user select an option. A group of radio buttons in a web page lets a user select one of several options. When the user clicks one button in a group, the other buttons in the group are deselected. By contrast, each check box on a page is independent. Selecting one check box has no effect on any other check box.

The table in figure 6-9 shows two of the properties common to these HTML objects. The value property returns a string containing the contents of the control's value attribute. The checked property returns a Boolean value indicating whether or not the radio button or check box is checked.

The HTML example in this figure contains two radio buttons and a check box. When you create a group of radio buttons, they must have the same name so the web browser knows they are in the same group. However, they must have different id values. In the example, both radio buttons have the name "contact", but one has an id of "text" and a value of "text" while the other has an id of "email" and a value of "email". Note that the id and value attributes don't have to be the same, but they often are.

Unlike radio buttons, when you create a check box, it must have a unique name and the name and id attributes must be set to the same value. In the example, the check box has a name and id of "accept".

The first JavaScript example in this figure shows how to get the user's choices from radio buttons and check boxes. First, it declares a variable named contact. Then, it checks if the radio button with an id of "text" is checked. If it is, it gets the contents of the radio button's value property and stores it in the contact variable.

Next, the code checks if the radio button with an id of "email" is checked. If it is, it gets the contents of the radio button's value property and stores it in the contact variable. Remember, though, that only one member of a radio button group can be checked. This means that only one of these radio buttons is going to have its checked property set to true.

Then, the code checks the value of the contact variable and does either text or email processing based on that value. If no radio button was selected, the code notifies the user to make a selection.

Finally, the code checks the value of the check box's checked property. If the value is true, the code processes the acceptance. If it isn't, the code notifies the user that the box needs to be checked.

The second JavaScript example in this figure shows how to set the checked property of radio buttons and check boxes. In this example, the radio buttons are unchecked and the check box is checked.

Two properties of a Radio or Checkbox object

Property	Description
value	The contents of the value attribute for the button or check box. Returns a string.
checked	If set to true, the button or check box is selected. If set to false, it isn't selected.

HTML code for two radio buttons and a check box

```
<label>Contact me by:</label>
<input type="radio" name="contact" id="text" value="text" checked>Text
<input type="radio" name="contact" id="email" value="email">Email<br>

<label>Terms of Service:</label>
<input type="checkbox" name="accept" id="accept" value="accept">I
accept<br>
```

JavaScript code to get the radio button and check box values

```
let contact = null;
if ($("#text").checked) {
    contact = $("#text").value;
}
if ($("#email").checked) {
    contact = $("#email").value;
}

if (contact == "text") { /*text processing*/ }
else if (contact == "email") { /*email processing*/ }
else { alert("You must select a contact method"); }

if ($("#accept").checked) { /*accept processing*/ }
else { alert("You must accept our terms of service."); }
```

JavaScript code to set the radio button and check box values

```
$("#text").checked = false;
$("#email").checked = false;
$("#accept").checked = true;
```

Description

- All radio buttons in a group must have the same name, but different ids. Only one button in a group may be checked at a time, but none of the buttons has to be checked.

- Each check box is independent of the other check boxes on the page. They aren't treated as a group. The name and id attributes of a check box should be set to the same value.

- To select a radio button, set its checked property to true. When you select a radio button, any other checked button in the same group will be cleared.

- To clear a radio button, set its checked property to false. When you clear a radio button, no other button will become checked.

- To select a check box, set its checked property to true. To clear a check box, set its checked property to false.

Figure 6-9   How to script Radio and Checkbox objects

How to use the methods and events for forms and controls

Figure 6-10 presents some of the common methods and events that you are likely to use with forms and controls. The first table summarizes two methods that are commonly used with forms.

The first method submits the form to the web server for processing. That's usually done after the user clicks a button to submit the form and all of the data is valid. The second method resets the data in the controls. That's usually done when the user clicks a button.

If you're familiar with HTML buttons, you know that input elements with their type attributes set to "submit" or "reset" call the submit() and reset() methods automatically with no JavaScript. If you want to validate the data in a form before you submit it to the server, though, you don't want that. In that case, you can use a regular input button.

The same is true for reset buttons. You may want to use a regular button as the reset button and issue the reset() method from your JavaScript. You'll see how to use JavaScript to both submit and reset a form in the application that follows.

The second table in this figure summarizes three methods that are commonly used with controls. In chapter 4, you learned how to use the focus() method to move the focus to a control, and you learned how to use the select() method to highlight any text in a control such as a text box or textarea. You can also use the blur() method to remove the focus from a control.

The third table summarizes six events that are commonly used with controls. In chapter 4, you learned how to use the addEventListener() method to add event handlers for click events. But you can also use other events to work with controls like text boxes, select lists, text areas, and links. For instance, you can write an event handler for the change event of a text box or the blur event of an <a> element.

The examples in this figure illustrate how these methods and events can be used. You code the reset() and submit() methods for forms, not controls. You write the event handlers for the controls. And you can use the event handler for the DOMContentLoaded event of the document object to attach the event handlers for the controls.

Two methods that are commonly used with forms

Method	Description
submit()	Submits the form and its data to the server.
reset()	Resets the controls in the form to their starting values.

Three methods that are commonly used with controls

Method	Description
focus()	Moves the focus to the control.
blur()	Removes the focus from the control.
select()	Selects all the text in a text box or text area.

Common control events

Event	Description
focus	The control receives the focus.
blur	The control loses the focus.
click	The user clicks the control.
dblclick	The user double-clicks the control.
change	The value of the control changes.
select	The user selects text in a text box or text area.

Statements that use the reset() and submit() methods

```
$("#registration_form").reset();
$("#registration_form").submit();
```

An event handler for the change event of a select list

```
const investmentChange = () => {
    calculateClick();            // call the calculateClick() function
    $("#investment").blur();  // remove the focus from the select list
};
```

An event handler for the dblclick event of a text box

```
const yearsDblclick = () => {
    $("#years").value = "";    // clear text box when double-clicked
};
```

A DOMContentLoaded event handler that attaches other event handlers

```
document.addEventListener("DOMContentLoaded", () => {
    $("#investment").addEventListener("change", investmentChange);
    $("#years").addEventListener("dblclick", yearsDblclick);
    $("#years").focus();
});
```

Description

- Input elements with the type attribute set to "submit" or "reset" automatically submit or reset a form. However, you can also use the JavaScript submit() or reset() method.

Figure 6-10   How to use the methods and events for forms and controls

The Register application

Figure 6-11 presents a Register application that consists of several controls on a form. If an entry is required, a red asterisk is displayed to the right of the control. Then, when the user clicks the Register button, the application checks the entries to make sure they're valid. If any of them aren't valid, the application displays error messages to the right of the fields. If all are valid, the application submits the form.

If the user clicks the Reset button somewhere along the way, the application resets the controls on the form to their starting values. That's done by issuing the reset() method for the form. But this application also clears any error messages and restores the starting asterisks, which isn't done by the reset() method.

The HTML

Part 1 of figure 6-11 shows some of the HTML for this application. Here, you can see that the form uses the "get" method to submit the values of the controls to a page named register_account.html. In practice, though, the form would use the "post" method because it's more secure, and it would send the form to a server page for processing.

Within the form, there are two text boxes named "email_address" and "phone", a select element named "country", a radio button group named "contact", and a check box named "terms". Within the radio button group are three radio buttons with ids of "text", "email", and "none". The first radio button has a checked attribute, which means that radio button is checked by default when the page loads.

Below these controls are two button elements named "register" and "reset_form". Notice that these buttons don't have type attributes of "submit" or "reset". This means that the form will be submitted or reset by the JavaScript code.

After some of the controls, you can see span elements. The starting values of these controls are asterisks (*) to indicate that these entries are required. These span elements are also where the error messages display if the user enters invalid data. The CSS for span elements in this application looks like this:

```
span { color: red; }
```

This means that both the starting asterisks and any error messages are displayed in red.

The Register application

The HTML for the form and controls

```html
<h1>Register for an Account</h1>

<form action="register_account.html" method="get">
    <div>
        <label for="email_address">E-Mail:</label>
        <input type="text" name="email_address" id="email_address">
        <span>*</span></div>
    <div>
        <label for="phone">Mobile Phone:</label>
        <input type="text" name="phone" id="phone">
        <span>*</span></div>
    <div>
        <label for="country">Country:</label>
        <select name="country" id="country">
            <option value="">Select a country</option>
            <option>USA</option>
            <option>Canada</option>
            <option>Mexico</option>
        </select>
        <span>*</span></div>
    <div>
        <label>Contact me by:</label>
        <input type="radio" name="contact" id="text"
            value="text" checked>Text
        <input type="radio" name="contact" id="email"
            value="email">Email
        <input type="radio" name="contact" id="none"
            value="none">Don't contact me</div>
    <div>
        <label>Terms of Service:</label>
        <input type="checkbox" name="terms" id="terms"
            value="yes">I accept
        <label> </label><span>*</span></div>
    <div>
        <label> </label>
        <input type="button" id="register" value="Register">
        <input type="button" id="reset_form" value="Reset"></div>
</form>
```

Figure 6-11   The Register application (part 1)

The JavaScript

Part 2 of figure 6-11 presents the JavaScript for this application, which consists of four functions starting with the $() function. Although the "use strict" directive isn't shown here, you can assume that this JavaScript is in strict mode.

The second function is an event handler named processEntries() that does the data validation for the controls and submits the form when all of the controls are valid. The third function is an event handler named resetForm() that resets the form. And the fourth function is the event handler for the DOMContentLoaded event of the document object that attaches the processEntries() and resetForm() event handlers to the click events of the Register and Reset buttons.

The processEntries() function is executed when the user clicks the Register button. It starts by assigning the objects that represent the email and phone text boxes, the country select list, and the terms checkbox to constants named email, phone, country, and terms. Note that this is different from the applications you saw in chapter 4 that stored the values of the controls in constants. That's because, as you'll see in a minute, this application needs to refer to the controls to work with the span elements that follow those controls.

After that, it declares a Boolean variable named isValid and initializes it with a starting value of true. Then, a series of if statements checks the values entered by the user. The first two if statements use the value property to check that the user entered values in the email address and phone number text boxes. The third if statement uses the value property to check that the user selected a value in the country select list. And the fourth if statement uses the checked property to be sure that the user checked the terms checkbox.

If any of the user entries is invalid, an error message is moved into the span element that follows the related control. It does that by using code like this:

```
email.nextElementSibling.textContent = "This field is required.";
```

This puts the message into the text node of the next sibling element after the control, which is the related span element. If the entry is valid, the code puts an empty string into the span element, which removes the asterisk or any previous error message. If an entry is invalid, the code also sets the isValid variable to false.

After the data validation, another if statement checks whether the isValid variable is true. If so, it submits the form to the server for processing. To do that, it uses the $() function to get the form and then calls the submit() method. If the isValid variable is false, the form isn't submitted. Then, the user can correct the entries.

The resetForm() function is executed when the user clicks the Reset button. It starts by calling the form's reset() method, which resets all of the values in the controls to their starting values. Then, the next four statements reset the values in the span elements to asterisks. Finally, the last statement moves the focus to the first text box.

The last function is the event handler for the DOMContentLoaded event of the document object. It just attaches the two event handlers to the Register and Reset buttons. Then, it moves the focus to the first text box.

The JavaScript

```javascript
const $ = selector => document.querySelector(selector);

const processEntries = () => {
    const email = $("#email_address");
    const phone = $("#phone");
    const country = $("#country");
    const terms = $("#terms");

    let isValid = true;
    if (email.value == "") {
        email.nextElementSibling.textContent = "This field is required.";
        isValid = false;
    } else {
        email.nextElementSibling.textContent = "";
    }

    if (phone.value == "") {
        phone.nextElementSibling.textContent = "This field is required.";
        isValid = false;
    } else {
        phone.nextElementSibling.textContent = "";
    }

    if (country.value == "") {
        country.nextElementSibling.textContent = "Please select a country.";
        isValid = false;
    } else {
        $("#country").nextElementSibling.textContent = "";
    }

    if (terms.checked == false) {
        terms.nextElementSibling.textContent = "This box must be checked.";
        isValid = false;
    } else {
        terms.nextElementSibling.textContent = "";
    }

    if (isValid == true) {
        $("form").submit();
    }
};

const resetForm = () => {
    $("form").reset();
    $("#email_address").nextElementSibling.textContent = "*";
    $("#phone").nextElementSibling.textContent = "*";
    $("#country").nextElementSibling.textContent = "*";
    $("#terms").nextElementSibling.textContent = "*";
    $("#email_address").focus();
};

document.addEventListener("DOMContentLoaded", () => {
    $("#register").addEventListener("click", processEntries);
    $("#reset_form").addEventListener("click", resetForm);
    $("#email_address").focus();
});
```

Figure 6-11   The Register application (part 2)

How to modify the DOM

Besides working with existing nodes, JavaScript lets you add nodes to and replace nodes in the DOM. You'll learn how to do that next. Then, you'll see a version of the Register application that uses some of these skills.

How to create, add, replace, and delete nodes

The first table in figure 6-12 presents two more methods of the Document interface. The first one, createElement(), creates a new HTML element based on the element name it receives. For instance, to create a new <a> element, you pass the string "a" as the parameter. The second one, createTextNode(), creates a new DOM text node and assigns the string it receives to that node's nodeValue property.

The second table in this figure presents five more methods of the Node interface. All of these methods except the last one work with the child nodes of the parent node that calls the method.

The appendChild() method receives a DOM node and adds it as a child of the parent node. For instance, to add a new li element as a child of a ul element, you call appendChild() on the ul element and pass the li element. When you use this method, the new node is added as the last child of the parent node. By contrast, when you use the insertBefore() method, the node that's passed as the first parameter is added before the existing child node that's passed as the second parameter.

Like the insertBefore() method, the replaceChild() method receives a new node and an existing node. Instead of inserting the new node, though, it replaces the existing node with the new node.

The last two methods let you remove a node. The removeChild() method removes the child node that's passed to it from the parent node. The remove() method, on the other hand, just removes the node that called the method.

The rest of this figure shows some of these methods in action. The HTML presented here consists of two <p> elements with text and an input element of type button. The first screen above the HTML shows how this looks. Then, when a user clicks the Add to DOM button, a new <p> element is added to the DOM between the two existing <p> elements. The second screen shows what the page looks like after the button is clicked.

The event handler for the button's click event starts by creating a new <p> element. Then, it creates a new text node, assigns the string "Middle paragraph" as its nodeValue, and adds the text node as a child of the new <p> element.

Next, the code gets the first existing <p> element from the document, as well as that element's parent. From this HTML, you can't tell what the parent element is. That's OK, though, because you don't need to know that to work with it.

Finally, the code inserts the new <p> element before the second <p> element. To do that, it passes the first <p> element's next sibling as the second parameter. Since the next sibling is the second <p> element, the new <p> element is inserted before that element.

Two more methods of the Document interface

Method	Description
`createElement(element)`	Creates a node for the specified element.
`createTextNode(value)`	Creates a Text node with the specified value.

Five more methods of the Node interface

Method	Description
`appendChild(node)`	Adds the specified node at the end of the child nodes for a parent node.
`insertBefore(new, existing)`	Adds the new node before the existing node of the child nodes for a parent node.
`replaceChild(new, existing)`	Replaces the existing node with the new node.
`removeChild(node)`	Removes the specified child node from a parent node.
`remove()`	Removes the node. Currently supported only by major browsers.

A button that adds a new <p> element to the DOM

Before button is clicked

First paragraph

Last paragraph

Add to DOM

After button is clicked

First paragraph

Middle paragraph

Last paragraph

Add to DOM

The HTML

```
<p>First paragraph</p>
<p>Last paragraph</p>
<input type="button" id="add" value="Add to DOM">
```

The click event handler for the button

```
$("#add").addEventListener("click", () => {
    // create a new <p> tag
    const newParagraph = document.createElement("p");

    // create a new text node and add it to the new <p> tag
    const text = document.createTextNode("Middle paragraph");
    newParagraph.appendChild(text);

    // get the first <p> tag in the document and its parent
    const firstParagraph = $("p");
    const parent = firstParagraph.parentNode;

    // insert the new <p> tag after the first <p> tag (that is,
    // before the element that comes after the first <p> tag)
    parent.insertBefore(newParagraph, firstParagraph.nextElementSibling);
});
```

Figure 6-12   How to create, add, replace, and delete nodes

The updated Register application

Figure 6-13 presents an updated Register application that displays a summary of error messages above the form instead of displaying those messages to the right of each control. This is a common way of displaying error messages that has the advantage of saving horizontal space, allowing for longer error messages, and allowing for more than one error message per control.

This figure also presents the CSS style rule for the "messages" class, which is used by the ul element that displays the error messages. This CSS class adds a red border around the element, sets the font color to red, adds padding of 2em on all sides, and adds a bottom margin of 2em. Although this figure doesn't present the HTML for the updated Register application, it's like the HTML in figure 6-11.

Next, this figure presents the updated JavaScript for this version of the application. Although the "use strict" directive and the $() function aren't shown, they're the same as what you've seen before.

By contrast, the displayErrorMsgs() function is new to this version of the Register application. This function receives a single parameter named msgs that contains an array of the error messages that should be displayed. This function starts by creating a new ul element. Then, it adds the CSS class named "messages" to that element's class attribute.

Next, a for-of loop processes each error message in the msgs array that's created by the processEntries() function on the next page. For each message, this loop creates a new li element and a new text node with the current message as the value of its nodeValue property. Then, it adds the text node as a child of the li element, and it adds the li element as a child of the ul element.

After that, this function checks if the DOM already has a ul element. That's necessary because when this application starts, the DOM doesn't contain a ul element. If the user clicked the Register button and errors were detected, though, a ul element has already been added to the DOM. As you'll see, the code that's executed depends on whether this element exists.

To check for a ul element, this code uses the $() function to select the first ul element and assign it to the constant named node. If the value of that constant is null, it means there's no ul element in the DOM. Otherwise, there is.

If there's no ul element in the DOM, this code uses the $() function to get an object that represents the form element. Then, it adds the new ul element to the parent of the form element, right before the form element. That way, the ul element with the error messages displays above the controls on the form.

If there is a ul element, the code doesn't add the new one it's created. If it did, the page would display both the old error messages and the new ones. Instead, it replaces the old ul element with the new one.

The updated Register application

Register for an Account

- Please enter an email address.
- Please enter a mobile phone number.
- Please select a country.
- You must agree to the terms of service.

E-Mail: [   ] *

Mobile Phone: [   ] *

Country: [Select a country ▼] *

Contact me by: ● Text ○ Email ○ Don't contact me

Terms of Service: ☐ I accept *

[Register] [Reset]

The CSS for the error messages

```css
.messages {
    border: 3px solid red;
    color: red;
    padding: 2em;
    margin-bottom: 2em;
}
```

The updated JavaScript

```javascript
const displayErrorMsgs = msgs => {
    // create new ul tag
    const ul = document.createElement("ul");
    ul.classList.add("messages");

    // create li tag for each error message and add to ul tag
    for (let msg of msgs) {
        const li = document.createElement("li");
        const text = document.createTextNode(msg);
        li.appendChild(text);
        ul.appendChild(li);
    }

    // if no ul element yet, add it before form tag. Otherwise, replace it.
    const node = $("ul");
    if (node == null) {
        const form = $("form");
        form.parentNode.insertBefore(ul, form);
    }
    else {
        node.parentNode.replaceChild(ul, node);
    }
}
```

Figure 6-13   The updated Register application (part 1)

Part 2 of figure 6-13 presents the processEntries() and resetForm() event handlers of the Register application. Both of these event handlers have significant changes from the ones you saw in part 2 of figure 6-11.

Like before, the processEntries() function starts by getting the user's entries for email address, phone number, country, and accepting the terms of service. After that, though, it creates an array named msgs. This array will hold the error messages for any invalid entries.

Next, the code checks each user entry just as it did before. This time, though, the code adds an error message to the msgs array if an entry is invalid. This provides for simpler data validation code.

Finally, this function checks the length property of the array. If the length is zero, that means there aren't any error messages in the array and the user's entries are valid. In that case, the code calls the submit() method of the form to submit the data to the server.

On the other hand, if there are error messages in the array, the code calls the displayErrorMsgs() function and passes the array as the parameter. As you saw in part 1 of this figure, this function either inserts a summary of error messages above the controls of the form if one doesn't already exist, or it replaces the summary if it does exist.

Like before, the resetForm() function starts by calling the reset() method of the form. This resets all the form controls to their starting values. It also removes the ul element that may have been added to display error messages. However, this function no longer needs to reset the text in the related span elements.

Finally, this figure shows the event handler for the DOMContentLoaded event of the document object. This event handler is unchanged from the one you saw in part 2 of figure 6-11.

The updated JavaScript (continued)

```javascript
const processEntries = () => {
    // get form controls to check for validity
    const email = $("#email_address");
    const phone = $("#phone");
    const country = $("#country");
    const terms = $("#terms");

    // create array for error messages
    const msgs = [];

    // check user entries for validity
    if (email.value == "") {
        msgs[msgs.length] = "Please enter an email address.";
    }
    if (phone.value == "") {
        msgs[msgs.length] = "Please enter a mobile phone number.";
    }
    if (country.value == "") {
        msgs[msgs.length] = "Please select a country.";
    }
    if (terms.checked == false) {
        msgs[msgs.length] = "You must agree to the terms of service.";
    }

    // submit the form or notify user of errors
    if (msgs.length == 0) {            // no error messages
        $("form").submit();
    } else {
        displayErrorMsgs(msgs);
    }
};

const resetForm = () => {
    $("form").reset();              // no longer need to clear span elements
    $("ul").remove();               // remove the error messages
    $("#email_address").focus();
};

document.addEventListener("DOMContentLoaded", () => {
    $("#register").addEventListener("click", processEntries);
    $("#reset_form").addEventListener("click", resetForm);
    $("#email_address").focus();
});
```

Figure 6-13   The updated Register application (part 2)

Perspective

The goal of this chapter has been to introduce you to some of the capabilities of DOM scripting with JavaScript. As a result, three different types of applications were presented. The FAQs application showed how you can use common properties and methods of the Document, Element, and Node interfaces. The Register application showed how JavaScript is commonly used for data validation. And the updated Register application showed how you can add HTML elements to the DOM.

Before you continue, you should know that there's a limit to how much DOM scripting you should do with JavaScript. That's because jQuery is a JavaScript library that is designed to make DOM scripting easier. As a result, most DOM scripting is done with a combination of JavaScript and jQuery. You'll learn more about jQuery in section 2.

Terms

DOM (Document Object Model)   form
DOM Core specification   control
DOM HTML specification   field
DOM node   submit button
element node   reset button
text node   data validation
attribute node   hard return
comment node   soft return
interface

Summary

- The *Document Object Model*, or *DOM*, is built when a page is loaded into a browser. It consists of various types of *nodes*.

- In the DOM, *element nodes* represent the elements in an HTML document and *text nodes* represent the text within those elements. The DOM can also contain *comment nodes*, and it can contain *attribute nodes* that have text nodes that store the attribute values.

- JavaScript provides properties and methods for the objects of the DOM that are described in the *DOM Core Specification*. These include the properties and methods that are described by the Node, Document, and Element *interfaces*.

- JavaScript also provides properties for the objects of the DOM that are described in the *DOM HTML Specification*. Although these properties don't provide new functionality, they do provide shortcuts that make it easier to work with the DOM nodes of an HTML document.

- A *form* contains one or more *controls* such as text boxes and buttons. The controls that accept user entries are also known as *fields*. Some common controls are text boxes, text areas, select lists, radio buttons, and check boxes.

- When you work with controls, you use properties like value and checked, methods like focus(), blur(), and select(), and events like focus, click, and blur.

- When you work with forms, you can use the submit() method to submit a form and the reset() method to reset the values in the controls of the form.

Exercise 6-1 Experiment with the FAQs application

This exercise will give you a chance to better understand the FAQs application as you work with its code. It will also give you a chance to use one of the properties of the DOM HTML specification.

If you have any problems when you're testing, remember to use Chrome's developer tools as shown in chapter 5.

Test and review the application

1. Use your text editor or IDE to open the HTML and JavaScript files that are in this folder:

   `javascript_jquery\exercises\ch06\faqs`

   Then, test this application to see how it works, and review its code.

Attach the event handlers to the <a> elements instead of the h2 elements

2. Change this application so the toggle() event handler is attached to the <a> elements within the h2 elements instead of to the h2 elements themselves. Then, change the toggle() event handler so it works with the <a> elements.

3. Test this change. When you do that, clicking on the headings should work, but clicking on the plus or minus signs before them shouldn't work.

Use the className property of the DOM HTML specification

4. Comment out the two statements in the toggle() event handler that call the toggle() method.

5. Below each commented out statement, code an if statement that uses the hasAttribute() method to check for a class attribute and then uses the removeAttribute() method to remove the appropriate class or the className property to add the appropriate class.

6. Test this change.

Exercise 6-2   Add controls to the Register application

In this exercise, you'll add another radio button and a text area to the form for the updated Register application, so the form looks like this:

If you have any problems when you're testing, remember to use Chrome's developer tools as shown in chapter 5.

1. Use your text editor or IDE to open the index.html and register.js files that are in this folder:

    `javascript_jquery\exercises\ch06\register_2.0`

2. Test this application with both invalid and valid data.

3. In the HTML file, add a radio button for Mobile phone and a text area for Comments, but watch out for duplicate id attributes. For the text area, you can use the example in figure 6-8 as your guide, but note that the height and width of the area will be set by the CSS. For the purposes of this exercise, assume that an entry is required in the text area.

4. In the JavaScript file, add the code that gets the text area. Then, modify the data validation code so an error message is displayed if no value is entered in this control.

5. Test the application to see that an error message is displayed if you click on the Register button without entering a comment.

6. Test the application again, but this time enter one or more hard returns in the comments area by pressing the Enter key. Then, note that no error message is displayed for the comments when you click the Register button.

7. Enter all valid data, and click the Register button to submit the form. Because the "get" method is used, the entries are added to the URL for the next page.

Exercise 6-3   Enhance the Email List application

In this exercise, you'll enhance an Email List application that's similar to the one you saw in chapter 4 by providing better data validation with error messages to the right of the entries:

Please join our email list

Email Address:	grace@yahoo.com
Confirm Email Address:	grace@yahoo Email addresses must match.
First Name:	First name is required.

Join List   Clear Form

If you have any problems when you're testing, remember to use Chrome's developer tools as shown in chapter 5.

Test the application

1. Use your text editor or IDE to open the index.html and email_list.js files that are in this folder:

   `javascript_jquery\exercises\ch06\email`

   Then, review the JavaScript code.

2. Test this application with valid data to see how it works. When you click the Join List button, another page should be displayed.

3. Click the back button in your browser, then test the application with invalid data. Note that the errors are displayed in an alert dialog box.

Enhance the data validation

4. Review the HTML and notice that span elements that contain asterisks have been added right after the first three input elements. Also notice that these span elements don't have ids.

5. Enhance the data validation so it displays the error messages in the span elements. Use a Boolean variable to keep track of whether any entries are invalid. Then, if all of the entries are valid, you can submit the form. If you need help, you can refer to the code for the Register application in figure 6-11.

6. Test the application with valid data to be sure it still works. If it does, click the back button in your browser to return to the previous page, and then click the Clear Form button to clear the text boxes.

7. Click the Join List button without entering any data. Then, use Chrome's developer tools to view the changes that have been made to the DOM to display the error messages. When you're done, close the developer tools.

7

How to work with images and timers

In the last chapter, you learned some of the most important DOM scripting skills. Now, this chapter presents some additional skills for working with images and timers. Because jQuery doesn't provide for all of the functionality that's presented here, it's important to know how to implement this functionality in JavaScript.

How to work with images

Many web applications manipulate the images that they display in a browser. To do that, you need to be able to work with the HTML img element and the HTMLImageElement object that represents an img element in JavaScript.

How to create an **HTMLImageElement** object

Figure 7-1 lists some of the attributes of the HTML img element, which displays an image in the browser. The src attribute tells the browser where to find the image to display, and it's required. The alt attribute should also be coded for img elements. You can use this attribute to provide information about the image in case it can't be displayed or the page is being accessed using a screen reader.

In most cases, you'll use imaging software to create images that are the right sizes for your web pages. Then, you can use the height and width attributes to tell the browser what the size is. That can help the browser lay out the page as the image is being loaded.

To work with an img element in JavaScript, you use an HTMLElementImage object. To create an instance of this object, you use the Image() constructor and the *new* keyword, as shown in the first example in this figure.

How to preload images

In JavaScript applications that load an image in response to a user event, the image isn't loaded into the browser until the JavaScript code changes the src attribute of the img tag. For large images or slow connections, this can cause a delay of a few seconds before the browser is able to display the image.

To solve this problem, an application can load the images before the user event occurs. This is known as *preloading images*. Then, the browser can display the images without delays. Although this may result in a page taking longer to load initially, the user won't encounter any delays when using the application.

The second example in figure 7-1 shows how to preload an image. First, you use the Image() constructor to create an HTMLImageElement object. Then, you set the src property to the URL of the image to be preloaded. This causes the web browser to preload the image. Note here that you don't need to use the object after setting the src property. The act of setting this property is what causes the browser to preload the image.

The last example in this figure shows how to preload the images for all the links on a page. This assumes that the href attribute in each link contains the URL of each image. First, the querySelectorAll() method gets an array of all the links and stores it in a variable named links. Then, a for-of loop is used to process each link in the array.

Within the loop, the first statement creates a new HTMLImageElement object. Then, the second statement sets the src property of the object to the href property of the link. This preloads the image. As a result, all of the images will be preloaded in the browser's cache when the loop finishes.

Some attributes of the HTML img element

Attribute	Description
src	The URL of the image to display.
alt	Alternate text to display in place of the image.
width	The width of the image in pixels.
height	The height of the image in pixels.

How to create an HTMLImageElement object

```
const image = new Image();
```

How to preload an image

```
const image = new Image();
image.src = "image_name.jpg";
```

How to preload all images referenced by the href attributes of <a> tags

```
const links = document.querySelectorAll("a");

for ( let link of links ) {
    const image = new Image();
    image.src = link.href;
}
```

Description

- The HTML img element is used to display an image that's identified by the src attribute.

- If an image can't be displayed, the text for the alt attribute is displayed instead. This text is also read aloud by screen readers for users with disabilities.

- The height and width attributes can be used to indicate the size of an image so the browser can allocate the correct amount of space on the page. These attributes can also be used to size an image, but it's usually better to use an image editor to do that.

- The JavaScript HTMLImageElement object represents an img element in code. It has properties that correspond to the attributes of the img element.

- To create an instance of the HTMLImageElement object you use the Image() constructor and the *new* keyword.

- When an application *preloads images*, it loads all of the images that it's going to need when the page loads, and it stores these images in the web browser's cache for future use.

- When the images are preloaded, the browser can display them whenever they're needed without any noticeable delay.

- To preload an image, you create a new HTMLImageElement object. Then, you set its src attribute to the URL for the image you want to preload.

Figure 7-1   How to create an HTMLImageElement object and preload images

The Image Swap application

Figure 7-2 shows an *image swap* application, which is a common type of JavaScript application. Here, the main image is swapped whenever the user clicks on one of the small (thumbnail) images. In this example, the user has clicked on the third thumbnail so the larger version of that image is displayed. In this application, the caption above the large image is also changed as part of the image swap, but that isn't always done in image swaps.

The HTML and CSS

In the HTML for this application, img elements are used to display the four thumbnail images. However, these elements are coded within <a> elements so the images are clickable and they can receive the focus. In the <a> elements, the href attributes identify the images to be swapped when the links are clicked, and the title attributes provide the text for the related captions. In this case, both the <a> elements and the img elements are coded within li elements of a ul element.

After the ul element, you can see the h2 element for the caption and the img element for the main image on the page. The contents of the h2 element provides the caption for the first image, and the src attribute of the img element provides the location for the first image. That way, when the application first starts, the first caption and image are displayed.

The three ids that are used by the JavaScript are highlighted here. First, the id of the ul element is set to "image_list" so the JavaScript can get its child <a> elements. Second, the id of the h2 element is set to "caption" so the JavaScript can change the caption. And third, the id of the main img element is set to "main_image" so the JavaScript can change the image.

For the motor-impaired, this HTML provides accessibility by coding the img elements for the thumbnails within <a> elements. Then, as you'll see in the next figure, the JavaScript sets the focus on the first <a> element. That way, the user can access the thumbnail links by pressing the Tab key, and the user can swap the main image by pressing the Enter key when a thumbnail has the focus, which starts the click event handler.

Of note in the CSS for this page is the rule set for the li elements. As this figure shows, their display properties are set to inline so the thumbnail images go from left to right instead of from top to bottom.

The Image Swap application

The HTML for the main element

```
<main>
    <h1>Fishing Images</h1>
    <p>Click on an image to enlarge.</p>
    <ul id="image_list">
        <li><a href="images/release.jpg" title="Catch and Release">
            <img src="thumbnails/release.jpg" alt="release fish"></a></li>
        <li><a href="images/deer.jpg" title="Deer at Play">
            <img src="thumbnails/deer.jpg" alt="deer"></a></li>
        <li><a href="images/hero.jpg" title="The Big One!">
            <img src="thumbnails/hero.jpg" alt="big fish"></a></li>
        <li><a href="images/bison.jpg" title="Roaming Bison">
            <img src="thumbnails/bison.jpg" alt="bison"></a></li>
    </ul>
    <h2 id="caption">Catch and Release</h2>
    <p><img id="main_image" src="images/release.jpg" alt="release fish"></p>
    <script src="image_swap.js"></script>
</main>
```

The CSS for the li elements

```
li { display: inline; }
```

Figure 7-2   The Image Swap application (part 1)

The JavaScript

The second part of figure 7-2 presents the JavaScript for this application. In the event handler for the DOMContentLoaded event, the first two statements get the objects for the h2 element for the caption and the img element that displays the enlarged image. Then, the third statement creates an array of the <a> elements within the ul element (image_list) and saves it in a variable named imageLinks. The code then uses a for-of loop to process each of the links in the array.

The for-of loop starts by preloading the image that will be swapped. Next, an event handler is attached to the click event of each link. Note here that the function for each event handler has an evt parameter that will receive the Event object for each link in a DOM-compliant browser.

Within the event handler, the first statement changes the src attribute of the image to the href attribute of the link. The second statement changes the alt attribute of the image to the title attribute of the link. And the third statement changes the value of the textContent property of the caption node to the title attribute of the link. When the application is run and the user clicks on a thumbnail, these statements will change the DOM so the image and caption are immediately changed in the display.

This event handler ends by cancelling the default action of the event for the link. Since the default action is to display the file identified by the href attribute, cancelling this action is essential. Otherwise, clicking on the link would open a new browser window or tab and display the image that's specified by the href attribute.

When the for loop ends, the code moves the focus to the first link. This allows the user to tab through the thumbnail images and press the Enter key to swap the main image, as described in the previous topic.

The JavaScript

```javascript
const $ = selector => document.querySelector(selector);

document.addEventListener("DOMContentLoaded", () => {

    const caption = $("#caption");            // the h2 element
    const mainImage = $("#main_image");       // the main img element

    // get all the <a> tags in the ul element
    const imageLinks = $("#image_list").querySelectorAll("a");

    // process image links
    for ( let link of imageLinks ) {

        // preload image
        const image = new Image();
        image.src = link.href;

        // attach event handler
        link.addEventListener("click", evt => {

            // set new image and caption
            mainImage.src = link.href;
            mainImage.alt = link.title;
            caption.textContent = link.title;

            // cancel the default action of the event
            evt.preventDefault();
        });
    }

    // set focus on first image link
    imageLinks[0].focus();
});
```

Figure 7-2   The Image Swap application (part 2)

How to use timers

A *timer* lets you execute a function after a specified period of time has elapsed. Timers are provided by web browsers rather than the DOM or ECMAScript standards. Timers are often useful in DOM scripting applications like the Slide Show application you'll see at the end of this chapter. Here, you'll learn about the two types of timers.

How to use a one-time timer

The first type of timer calls its function only once. To create this type of timer, you use the global setTimeout() method that's shown in figure 7-3. Its first parameter is the function that the timer calls. Its second parameter is the number of milliseconds to wait before calling that function.

When you use the setTimeout() method to create a timer, it returns a reference to the timer that's created. Then, if necessary, you can use this reference to cancel the timer. To do that, you pass this reference to the clearTimeout() method. If you don't need to use the reference to the timer, you can call the setTimeout() method without storing its return value in a variable.

The example in this figure is another version of the FAQs application that you saw in the last chapter. This application uses a one-time timer to take the user to the terms of service page after a delay of five seconds. The user can cancel the timer and accept the new terms without navigating to a new page by clicking the I Accept button before the five seconds have elapsed.

The HTML for this application includes a fieldset element that contains a legend element, a <p> element that explains what's going to happen, and a button to accept the new terms of service. Also, a CSS class named hidden has been added to the CSS file. It will be used to hide the fieldset element by setting its display property to none.

The JavaScript code starts by declaring a global variable for the timer. This is followed by functions named goToTerms() and acceptTerms(). The goToTerms() function simply navigates to the terms.html file that's in the root directory of the website.

The acceptTerms() function uses the clearTimeout() method to stop the timer that's started by the setTimeout() method. If this function is called before the timer calls the goToTerms() function, it will keep the code in the goToTerms() function from running. Then, this function hides the fieldset element by setting its class attribute to "hidden".

This is followed by the event hander for the DOMContentLoaded event. It uses the setTimeout() method to set the global timer variable to a timer that calls the goToTerms() function after a delay of 5 seconds (5000 milliseconds). Then, it attaches the acceptTerms() function to the I Accept button so the user can accept the terms before those 5 seconds elapse and stay on the current page.

Two methods for working with a timer that calls a function once

Method	Description
setTimeout(*function*,*delay*)	Creates a timer that calls the specified function once after the specified delay in milliseconds has elapsed.
clearTimeout(*timer*)	Cancels a timer created by the setTimeout() method.

An application that redirects after 5 seconds if a button isn't clicked

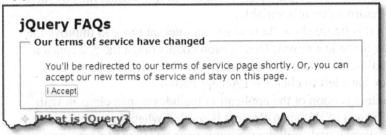

The HTML for the terms of service message

```
<fieldset id="terms">
    <legend>Our terms of service have changed</legend>
    <p>You'll be redirected to our terms of service page shortly.
    Or, you can accept our new terms of service and stay on this page.</p>
    <p><input type="button" id="accept" value="I Accept"></p>
</fieldset>
```

A CSS class to hide an element

```
.hidden { display: none; }
```

How to use a one-time timer to perform or cancel the redirection

```
// declare a variable to hold the reference to the timer;
// make it global so all the functions can access it
let timer = null;

const goToTerms = () => window.location.href = "terms.html";

const acceptTerms = () => {
    // code to accept terms goes here
    clearTimeout( timer );
    $("#terms").setAttribute("class", "hidden");
};

document.addEventListener("DOMContentLoaded", () => {
    ...
    timer = setTimeout( goToTerms, 5000 );
    $("#accept").addEventListener("click", acceptTerms);
    ...
});
```

Description

- The setTimeout() method returns a reference to the timer it creates. This timer can then can be used by the clearTimeout() method to cancel the timer.

Figure 7-3   How to use a one-time timer

How to use an interval timer

The second type of timer calls its function repeatedly. To create this type of timer, you use the global setInterval() method shown in figure 7-4. Its first parameter is the function to be called. Its second parameter is the time interval between function calls. To cancel this type of timer, you pass a reference to the timer to the clearInterval() method. As with the setTimeout() method, if you don't need to use the reference to the timer, you can call the setInterval() method without storing its return value in a variable.

The example in this figure shows how to use an interval timer to improve the application you saw in the last figure. This version counts down the 5 seconds it waits before redirecting to the terms of service page. That way, the user can see how much time they have left to click the I Accept button.

The HTML for this version of the application includes a span element with an id of seconds. The text of this span element is set to 5 when the page initially loads. Then, the JavaScript code will decrement it once per second. Here, you can see how the page looks when there are two seconds left before the page redirects.

The JavaScript code in this figure starts by declaring two global variables. The first one is for the timer, and the second one is for a counter. The counter variable is initialized with a value of 5, and it will be used to determine when five seconds have elapsed, as well as to display the remaining number of seconds.

The goToTerms() function is called each time the interval for the timer has elapsed. It starts by decrementing the value of the counter by 1. Then, it checks the value of the counter to see if it's equal to 0. If it is, the code redirects to the terms.html file. Otherwise, it updates the textContent property of the span element that has an id of "seconds" to display the number of seconds left in the countdown.

The acceptTerms() function is essentially the same as in the last figure. The only difference is that it passes the timer variable to the clearInterval() method rather than the clearTimeout() method.

The event handler for the DOMContentLoaded event is also much the same as it was before. This time, though, it uses the setInterval() method to start the timer so its function executes at intervals of 1 second (1000 milliseconds).

When you use the setInterval() method to create a timer, you should know that the timer waits for the specified interval to elapse before calling the function the first time. So, if you want the function to be called immediately, you need to call the function before you create the timer.

Two methods for working with a timer that calls a function repeatedly

Method	Description
`setInterval(function, interval)`	Creates a timer that calls a function each time the specified interval in milliseconds has elapsed.
`clearInterval(timer)`	Cancels a timer created by the setInterval() method.

The application updated to count down to the redirection

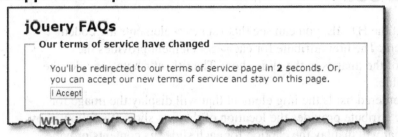

The updated HTML for the terms of service message

```
<p>You'll be redirected to our terms of service page in
<b><span id="seconds">5</span></b> seconds. Or...</p>
```

The updated code that uses an interval timer

```
// create global variables to hold the timer and the current count
let timer = null;
let counter = 5;

const goToTerms = () => {
    counter--;                                  // decrement counter
    if (counter == 0) {
        window.location.href = "terms.html";
    } else {
        $("#seconds").textContent = counter;    // update number of seconds
    }
};

const acceptTerms = () => {
    // code to accept terms goes here
    clearInterval( timer );
    $("#terms").setAttribute("class", "hidden");
};

document.addEventListener("DOMContentLoaded", () => {
    ...
    timer = setInterval( goToTerms, 1000 );
    $("#accept"). addEventListener("click", acceptTerms);
    ...
});
```

Description

- The setInterval() method returns a reference to the timer it creates. This timer can then be used by the clearInterval() method to cancel the timer.

- Although you can't modify an interval timer, you can cancel it and create a new one.

Figure 7-4   How to use an interval timer

The Slide Show application

Figure 7-5 illustrates a Slide Show application that requires the use of an interval timer. When the user starts this application, it displays a new caption and image every two seconds.

The HTML and CSS

If you look at the HTML, you can see that four <a> elements are coded within a ul element. The href attribute for each <a> element provides the location for one of the images in the slide show. The title attribute provides the caption for the slide.

After the unordered list is the img element that will display the image for each slide. Its src attribute provides the location of the first slide. It's followed by the h2 element that will display the caption for each slide. Its contents provide the caption for the first slide. That way, the first slide and caption are displayed when the application starts.

To keep this application simple, no controls are provided for stopping the slide show or moving through the slides manually. As a result, this slide show doesn't meet the best standards for usability or accessibility.

Of note in the CSS is the style rule for the ul element that contains the list. Since the purpose of this list is to provide the captions and images for the slide show, the list shouldn't be displayed. That's why its display property is set to none.

The Slide Show application

The HTML for the main element

```html
<main>
    <h1>Fishing Slide Show</h1>

    <ul id="image_list">
        <li><a href="images/release.jpg" title="Catch and Release"></a></li>
        <li><a href="images/deer.jpg" title="Deer at Play"></a></li>
        <li><a href="images/hero.jpg" title="The Big One!"></a></li>
        <li><a href="images/bison.jpg" title="Roaming Bison"></a></li>
    </ul>

    <p><img id="main_image" src="images/release.jpg"
            alt="Catch and Release"></p>
    <h2 id="caption">Catch and Release</h2>

    <script src="slide_show.js"></script>
</main>
```

The CSS for the ul element

```css
ul { display: none; }
```

Figure 7-5   The Slide Show application (part 1)

The JavaScript

The second part of figure 7-5 presents the JavaScript for this application. Here, you can see that the event handler for the DOMContentLoaded event starts by declaring constants that contain the nodes for the h2 element for the caption and the img element for the slide show. Then, the querySelectorAll() method is used to create an array named links that contains one object for each <a> element in the ul element.

Next, an array named imageCache and a variable named image are declared. The array will store all of the images to be displayed. The variable will store each image as it's preloaded, and it will store the current image to be displayed.

Each of the <a> elements in the links array is processed by the for-of loop that follows. This loop preloads the images and sets the alt property of each image to the title property of the current link. Then, it adds the HTMLImageElement object to the imageCache array so it can be used later.

At this point, the event handler starts the slide show by calling the setInterval() method. You should notice three things about this method call. First, because this code doesn't need to use the value returned by setInterval(), it doesn't store it in a variable. Second, it passes an anonymous function as the first parameter rather than assigning the function to a constant. This is a common way of coding the setInterval() method. Finally, it passes 2000 (2 seconds) as the second parameter.

The anonymous function that's passed to the setInterval() method displays the next slide when the interval time elapses. It starts by setting a variable named imageCounter to a value that determines which slide in the imageCache array will be displayed next. To do that, it adds one to imageCounter, which was initialized to a value of zero. Then, it uses the modulus operator (%) to get the remainder when the imageCounter property is divided by the length of the imageCache array. This means the imageCounter property will range from 0 through one less than the length of the array.

If, for example, the imageCache array contains 4 images, the counter values will range from 0 through 3 (1%4=1; 2%4=2; 3%4=3; 4%4=0). So, if the counter is used as the index of the imageCache array, the function will loop through the elements of the array and the index will never be greater than 3.

After the value of the imageCounter variable is set, the second statement in this function uses imageCounter as the index for the imageCache array and stores that image object in the image variable. The third statement sets the src attribute of the img node to the src attribute of the HTMLImageElement object. The fourth statement sets the alt attribute of the img node to the alt attribute of the HTMLImageElement object. And the last statement sets the text for the caption node to the alt attribute of the Image object. As soon as these changes are made to the DOM, the image and caption are changed in the browser display.

You might notice that this code doesn't set up any event handlers for user events. Instead, the slide show is driven by the interval timer, which issues timer events. Then, after each time interval passes, the function in the first parameter is executed again, which changes the src and alt attributes of the img element in the DOM and the text of the h2 element.

The JavaScript

```javascript
const $ = selector => document.querySelector(selector);

document.addEventListener("DOMContentLoaded", () => {

    const caption = $("#caption");          // the h2 element for the caption
    const mainImage = $("#main_image");     // the img element for the show

    // get all the <a> tags in the ul element
    const links = $("#image_list").querySelectorAll("a");

    // process image links
    const imageCache = [];
    let image = null;

    for ( let link of links ) {
        // preload image and copy title properties
        image = new Image();
        image.src = link.href;
        image.alt = link.title;

        // add image to array
        imageCache[imageCache.length] = image;
    }

    // start slide show
    let imageCounter = 0;

    setInterval( () => {
        // calculate the index for the current image
        imageCounter = (imageCounter + 1) % imageCache.length;

        // get image object from array
        image = imageCache[imageCounter];

        // set HTML img and h2 elements with values from image object
        mainImage.src = image.src;
        mainImage.alt = image.alt;
        caption.textContent = image.alt;
    },
    2000);  // 2 second interval

});
```

Figure 7-5   The Slide Show application (part 2)

Perspective

Now that you've completed this chapter, you should know how to use JavaScript to create simple applications that work with images and timers. When your applications get more complicated than the ones in this chapter, though, you should consider using jQuery instead of JavaScript. As you'll see in the next section of this book, jQuery makes it much easier to develop applications like the ones you've just seen.

Terms

preload an image
image swap
timer
one-time timer
interval timer

Summary

- To *preload* an image, you create a new HTMLImageElement object and set its src attribute to the URL for the image. When you preload images, the page may take longer to load, but the image changes will take place immediately.

- Browsers provide two types of *timers*. A *one-time timer* executes a function just once after the specified interval of time. An *interval timer* executes a function each time the specified time interval elapses.

- JavaScript provides methods to cancel a one-time timer before it executes for the first time, or to cancel an interval timer before the next scheduled execution.

Exercise 7-1   Develop a rollover application

In this exercise, you'll create an application with two images that change when you roll over them with the mouse.

Fishing Images

Move your mouse over an image to change it and back out of the image to restore the original image.

Open, test, and review the application

1. Use your text editor or IDE to open the files that are in this folder:
    `javascript_jquery\exercises\ch07\rollover`

2. Review the code in the index.html file, and note that each li element within the ul element contains an <a> element whose href attribute refers to one of the images used by this application. Also note that the <p> element at the bottom of the page contains two img elements with ids "image1" and "image2" whose src attributes determine the images that are currently displayed.

3. Review the code in the rollover.css file, and note that it contains a style rule that keeps the ul element in the index.html file from being displayed in the browser.

4. Review the code in the rollover.js file, and note that the images with ids "image1" and "image2" are stored in variables named image1 and image2. Also, the <a> elements in the ul element are stored in an array named links.

5. Use Chrome to test this application. Notice that the images shown above are displayed, but nothing happens when you move your mouse over them.

Add code to preload the images and implement the rollovers

6. In the DOMContentLoaded event handler, add code that uses the links array to preload the four images used by this application.

7. Add code to the mouseover and mouseout event handlers for the two image elements that are displayed on the page. The image element with id "image1" should display the release.jpg image when the mouse is over it and the hero.jpg image otherwise. The image element with id "image2" should display the deer.jpg image when the mouse is over it and the bison.jpg image otherwise.

8. Test the application to be sure that the rollovers are working and that the correct images are being displayed.

Exercise 7-2   Enhance the Slide Show application

In this exercise, you'll enhance the Slide Show application by adding buttons to start and pause the slide show.

Open and test the application

1. Use your text editor or IDE to open the HTML and JavaScript files that are in this folder:

    `javascript_jquery\exercises\ch07\slide_show`

2. Use Chrome to test this application. Notice that the slideshow isn't running, the Pause button is disabled, and nothing happens when you click on the Start button.

Add code to start the slide show when the Start button is clicked

3. Review the code in the index.html file, and notice that the disabled attribute of the Pause button is set to "true". That makes sense because the user shouldn't be able to click this button if the slide show isn't running.

4. Review the code in the slide_show.js file, and note that the code for running the slide show is coded in a function named runSlideShow(). Also note that some of the variables and constants are global so they can be accessed by the runSlideShow() function and the DOMContentLoaded() event handler.

5. Within the DOMContentLoaded() event handler, add code to the click event handler of the Start button that creates a timer that runs the slide show and changes the slide every 2 seconds. In addition, add code that disables the

Start button and enables the Pause button. To disable a button, you can set its disabled attribute to true. To enable a button, you can set its disabled attribute to false.

6. Test the application again and click the Start button to make sure the slide show is working. Notice that there's a delay of 2 seconds before the next slide is displayed.

7. Add code to the click event handler of the Start button that calls the runSlideShow() function before the timer is started. Then, test the application again to see that the next slide is displayed immediately when the Start button is clicked.

Add code to pause the slide show when the Pause button is clicked

8. Add code to the click event handler of the Pause button that cancels the timer. In addition, add code that enables the Start button and disables the Pause button.

9. Test the application again, click the Start button to start the slide show, and then click the Pause button to pause the slide show. Click the Start button again to restart the slide show. When you're done testing, close the browser.

Section 2

jQuery essentials

Now that you have some basic JavaScript skills, you're ready to learn jQuery. That's why chapter 8 presents a subset of jQuery that gets you off to a fast start. By the time you finish that chapter, you'll be able to use JavaScript and jQuery to build applications like image swaps and image rollovers.

Then, chapter 9 shows how to use the jQuery effects and animations that can bring a web page to life. Chapter 10 shows you how to use the jQuery features for working with forms. And chapter 11 shows how to use jQuery plugins and jQuery UI widgets to improve your productivity.

8

Get off to a fast start with jQuery

This chapter starts by showing how the jQuery library can make JavaScript programming easier. Then, this chapter presents a subset of jQuery that gets you off to a fast start. Along the way, this chapter presents four complete applications that show you how to apply jQuery in your JavaScript applications.

Introduction to jQuery

This introduction describes what jQuery is and describes how jQuery can simplify JavaScript development. After that, you'll be ready to start learning how to use jQuery with JavaScript.

What jQuery is

As figure 8-1 summarizes, *jQuery* is a free, open-source, JavaScript library that provides dozens of methods for common web features that make JavaScript programming easier. To provide these features, jQuery provides a lightweight, compressed library that loads quickly.

Beyond that, jQuery functions are coded and tested for cross-browser compatibility, so they work in all browsers. Back in 2015, browser support for JavaScript features was inconsistent. As a result, this was a big benefit that helped jQuery become extremely popular. Today, most modern browsers provide consistent support for JavaScript. As a result, cross-browser compatibility isn't as big of a benefit, and it's possible to use pure JavaScript instead of jQuery. Still, you may need to use jQuery to support older browsers. Or, you may need to maintain jQuery code on legacy websites.

Similarly, jQuery provides selectors that are compliant with CSS3. Back in 2015, CSS3-complicant selectors were a big benefit because JavaScript didn't provide a comparable feature. Now, however, JavaScript's querySelector() and querySelectorAll() methods provide a CSS3-compliant way to select HTML elements from the DOM.

Although the use of jQuery has been declining in recent years, as of Feb 2020, a W3Techs survey found that 74% of the top 10 million websites still use jQuery. So, although jQuery might not be as hot as it used to be, it's going to be around for a long time. In addition, for some tasks, jQuery is still more concise and easier to use than pure JavaScript.

As you learn jQuery, don't forget that it *is* JavaScript. In other words, when you use jQuery, you call JavaScript methods that are stored in the jQuery library. Also, you typically use JavaScript to call the jQuery methods. As a result, most applications that use jQuery also use JavaScript.

The jQuery website at jquery.com

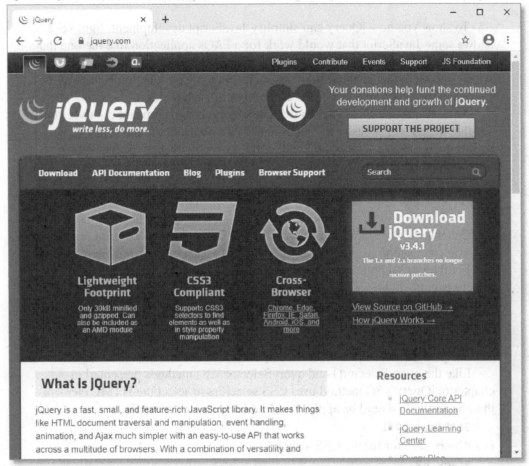

What jQuery offers

- Dozens of selectors, methods, and event methods that make it easier to add JavaScript features to your web pages
- A lightweight, compressed library that loads quickly so it doesn't degrade performance
- Cross-browser compatibility
- Selectors that are compliant with CSS3

Description

- *jQuery* is a free, open-source, JavaScript library that provides methods that make JavaScript programming easier.
- According to W3Techs, jQuery is used by 74.4% of the top 10 million websites as of Feb 2020.

Figure 8-1   What jQuery is

How jQuery can simplify JavaScript development

To show you how jQuery can simplify JavaScript development, figure 8-2 shows some JavaScript that would work for a FAQs application like the one that was presented in chapter 6. Note, however, that this JavaScript is different from what's shown in that chapter. In this case, an anonymous function is used as the event handler that's attached to the click event of each h2 tag.

Next, this figure shows the equivalent jQuery. If you compare the two, you'll see that the jQuery is easier to read. That's because jQuery's ready() method makes it easy to attach an event handler that's executed when the browser finishes loading the DOM. By contrast, JavaScript's addEventListener() method is longer and more unwieldy. Similarly, jQuery's click() event method makes it easy to attach an event handler that's executed when the user clicks an element.

In addition, jQuery's selectors make it possible to attach an event handler to all h2 elements without having to code a loop. By contrast, JavaScript requires that you code a loop to attach an event handler to each of the h2 elements.

For the FAQs application and the other applications presented in this chapter, jQuery is only slightly shorter and easier to read than the equivalent pure JavaScript. However, for applications that use animations and effects, jQuery can be much simpler than the equivalent JavaScript. For example, the applications presented in chapter 9 are significantly easier to code with jQuery than with JavaScript alone.

Like the querySelector() and querySelectorAll() methods presented in chapter 6, jQuery's $() method uses CSS selectors to select the HTML elements that the methods should be applied to. In this figure, for example,

```
$("#faqs h2")
```

is a jQuery selector for the CSS selector

```
#faqs h2
```

This selects all of the h2 elements in the element with "faqs" as its id. In fact, jQuery's $() method supports all of the CSS selectors including the CSS3 selectors, even in older browsers that don't support all of the CSS3 selectors. So, if you need to support older browsers, you probably want to use jQuery, not pure JavaScript.

The JavaScript for a FAQs application

```javascript
"use strict";
document.addEventListener("DOMContentLoaded", () => {

    // get the h2 tags
    const  h2s = document.querySelectorAll("#faqs h2");

    // loop through each h2 tag
    for (let  h2 of  h2s) {

        // attach an event handler for the h2 tag
        h2.addEventListener("click", evt => {

            h2.classList.toggle("minus");
            h2.nextElementSibling.classList.toggle("open");
            evt.preventDefault();
        });
    }

    // set focus on first h2 tag's <a> tag
    h2s[0].firstChild.focus();
});
```

The equivalent JavaScript and jQuery

```javascript
"use strict";
$(document).ready( () => {

    // attach event handler for all h2 tags
    $("#faqs h2").click( evt => {

        // get clicked h2 tag
        const h2 = evt.currentTarget;

        // toggle minus class for h2 tag and show or hide related div
        $(h2).toggleClass("minus");
        $(h2).next().toggleClass("open");
        evt.preventDefault();
    });

    // set focus on first h2 tag's <a> tag
    $("#faqs").find("a:first").focus();
});
```

Figure 8-2   How jQuery can simplify JavaScript development

The basics of jQuery

The figures that follow present the basics of jQuery. They show how to code jQuery selectors, call jQuery methods, and use jQuery event methods. But first, they show how to include jQuery in your web pages.

How to include jQuery in your web pages

If you go to the web page that's shown in figure 8-3, you'll see that it contains links that let you download various releases of the jQuery core library. At this writing, the most current release is jQuery 3.4.1, and it comes in four versions: uncompressed, compressed, slim uncompressed, and slim compressed.

The uncompressed versions allow programmers to study the JavaScript code that's used in the library. By contrast, all whitespace has been removed from the compressed versions. These versions are also known as *minified versions*, which is why they include "min" in their filenames. Although these versions are almost impossible for a human to read, they are much smaller, which improves performance. The slim version of jQuery was introduced with jQuery 3.0. It doesn't include the ajax or effects modules, so it's even smaller, which improves performance if you don't need these modules.

Once you've downloaded the jQuery library you want, you can include it in a web page by coding a script element like the first one in this figure. Then, if you store the file on your own computer or a local web server, you'll be able to develop jQuery applications without being connected to the Internet.

The other way to include the jQuery library in your web applications is to get the file from a *Content Delivery Network* (*CDN*). A CDN is a web server that hosts open-source software, and the download page shown here contains a link to the jQuery CDN. The next two examples in this figure show script elements that use the jQuery CDN with URLs that get the compressed and slim compressed version 3.4.1. Because using a CDN is a best practice, all the applications in this book use this technique.

Although you might think that you should always use the most current version of jQuery, that's not necessarily the case. In chapter 11, for example, you'll learn about some of the plugins that you can use with jQuery. One of these, the Box Slider plugin, only works with jQuery 3.3.1 or earlier. So if you use plugins, you'll need to use the appropriate release of jQuery.

Also, jQuery versions 1.9 and 3.0 dropped certain features that were included in earlier versions. So if you have old code that uses those features, you'll need to keep using the older versions of the library. Or, you can use the jQuery Migrate plugins to upgrade your application. To use these plugins, go to jquery.com/upgrade-guide, click on the upgrade you want, and then follow the step-by-step instructions.

Finally, you should know that jQuery recommends that you use *Subresource Integrity (SRI) checking* when you link to files on their CDN. This helps ensure that resources hosted on the CDN haven't been tampered with. The last example in this figure shows how this works. You can get more information on the jQuery

The download page for jQuery

```
https://jquery.com/download/
```

How to include jQuery 3.4.1 after you've downloaded it to your computer

```
<script src="jquery-3.4.1.min.js"></script>
```

How to include jQuery 3.4.1 from a CDN

```
<script src="https://code.jquery.com/jquery-3.4.1.min.js"></script>
```

How to include the slim version of jQuery 3.4.1 from a CDN

```
<script src="https://code.jquery.com/jquery-3.4.1.slim.min.js"></script>
```

The most important releases of jQuery

Version	Release date	Description
1.0	Aug 2006	First stable release.
1.9.1	Feb 2013	Deprecated interfaces removed.
1.12.4	May 2016	Last updated version of 1.x branch, which supports IE6-8.
2.0	April 2013	First version of 2.x branch. Dropped support for IE6-8.
2.2.4	May 2016	Last updated version of 2.x branch.
3.0	June 2016	First version of 3.x branch. A smaller, faster version of the 2.x branch, but with some breaking changes. Adds a slim version.
3.4.1	May 2019	Current version of jQuery.

Two jQuery migrate plugins

Version	Description
1.4.1	Restores features dropped by version 1.9.
3.0.0	Restores features dropped by version 3.0.

How to include SRI checking with the jQuery CDN

```
<script src="https://code.jquery.com/jquery-3.4.1.min.js"
integrity="sha256-hVVnYaiADRTO2PzUGmuLJr8BLUSjGIZsDYGmIJLv2b8="
crossorigin="anonymous"></script>
```

Description

- You can include jQuery by downloading its library and coding a script element for it or by coding a script element that gets the library from a *Content Delivery Network (CDN)*, which is a web server that hosts open-source software.

- jQuery recommends that you use *Subresource Integrity (SRI) checking* when you link to files on their CDN.

- The uncompressed versions of jQuery contain whitespace. This makes it possible for a human to study the JavaScript code that's used in the library.

- The compressed versions of jQuery don't contain whitespace. This makes it almost impossible for a human to read them, but it improves performance.

- The slim version of jQuery was introduced with jQuery 3.0. It doesn't include the ajax or effects modules, so it improves performance if you don't need these modules.

Figure 8-3   How to include jQuery in your web pages

CDN website and at https://www.srihash.org/. For brevity, the applications in this book don't use SRI checking.

How to code jQuery selectors

When you use jQuery, you start by selecting the element or elements that you want to apply a jQuery method to. To do that, you can use jQuery *selectors* as shown in figure 8-4.

To code a jQuery selector, you start by coding the dollar sign ($) followed by a set of parentheses that contains a set of quotation marks. Then, within the quotation marks, you code the CSS selector for the element or elements that you want to select. This is shown by the syntax summary at the top of this figure.

Note that the $ sign when used in this way is an alias for jQuery. In other words, instead of coding a selector like this:

```
$("#faqs")
```

you could code it like this:

```
jQuery("#faqs")
```

Because the dollar sign is shorter, though, you'll almost always see it used in place of jQuery.

The HTML and the examples that follow show how easy it is to select one or more elements with jQuery. In the first group of examples, for instance, the first selector selects all <p> elements within the entire document. The second selector selects the element with "faqs" as its id. And the third selector selects all elements with "minus" as the value of its class attribute.

In the second group of examples, other types of CSS selectors are coded with jQuery to get elements that are descendants, adjacent siblings, general siblings, and children. For instance, the first selector gets all <p> elements that are descendants of the element with "faqs" as its id. That includes all of the <p> elements in the HTML in this figure. By contrast, the second selector gets the div elements that are adjacent siblings to the h2 elements, which includes all of the div elements. The third selector gets all <p> elements that are siblings of ul elements, which selects the one <p> element in the second div element. And the fourth selector gets all ul elements that are children of div elements, which selects the ul element in the second div element.

The third group of examples shows how to code multiple selectors. To do that, you separate them with commas, just as you do with CSS.

The syntax for a jQuery selector

```
$("selector")
```

The HTML for the elements that are selected by the examples

```html
<main id="faqs">
    <h1>jQuery FAQs</h1>
    <h2 class="minus"><a href="#">What is jQuery?</a></h2>
    <div>
        <p>jQuery is a library of the JavaScript functions that you're most
            likely to need as you develop websites.
        </p>
    </div>
    <h2><a href="#">Why is jQuery so popular?</a></h2>
    <div>
        <p>Three reasons:</p>
        <ul>
            <li>It's free.</li>
            <li>It lets you get more done in less time.</li>
            <li>It's cross-browser compatible.</li>
        </ul>
    </div>
</main>
```

How to select elements by element, id, and class

By element type: All <p> elements in the entire document

```
$("p")
```

By id: The element with "faqs" as its id

```
$("#faqs")
```

By class: All elements with "minus" as a class

```
$(".minus")
```

How to select elements by relationship

Descendants: All <p> elements that are descendants of the main element

```
$("#faqs p")
```

Adjacent siblings: All div elements that are adjacent siblings of h2 elements

```
$("h2 + div")
```

General siblings: All <p> elements that are siblings of ul elements

```
$("ul ~ p")
```

Children: All ul elements that are children of div elements

```
$("div > ul")
```

How to code multiple selectors

```
$("#faqs li, div p")
$("p + ul, div ~ p")
```

Description

- When you use jQuery, you can use the dollar sign ($) to refer to the jQuery library.
  Then, you can code *selectors* by using the CSS syntax within quotation marks and
  parentheses.

Figure 8-4   How to code jQuery selectors

How to call jQuery methods

Once you've selected the element or elements that you want to apply a *method* to, you call the method using the syntax shown at the top of figure 8-5. This is the same way that you call a method of any object. You code the selector that gets the element or elements, the dot operator, the method name, and any parameters within parentheses.

To get you started fast, the table in this figure summarizes some common jQuery methods. For instance, the val() method without a parameter gets the value from a selected text box or other form control, and the val() method with a parameter sets the value in a selected text box or other form control. The first two examples after the table show how this works.

Similarly, the text() method without a parameter can be used to get the text of a selected element, and the text() method with a parameter can be used to set the text of a selected element. Methods like these are often referred to as *getter* and *setter* methods. In this figure, the third example shows the setter version of the text() method. This method sets the text of an element to "Email address is required".

The next() method gets the next (or adjacent) sibling of an element. This method is often followed by another method. To do that, you use *object chaining*. This works just as it does with JavaScript and is illustrated by the fourth example. Here, the next() method gets the next sibling after the element that has been selected, and the text() method sets the text for that sibling.

In most cases, you use the val(), text(), and next() methods with selectors that select a single control or element. However, you can also use them with selectors that select two or more controls or elements. In that case, the setter version of the val() and text() methods set the values of all the matching controls or elements. By contrast, the getter version of the val() method gets the value of just the first matching form control. The getter version of the text() method gets the combined text of all the matching elements. And the next() method gets the siblings of all the matched elements.

The submit() and focus() methods work like the JavaScript submit() and focus() methods. The submit() method submits the data for a selected form to the server, and the focus() method moves the focus to the selected form control or link.

In a moment, this chapter will show how these selectors and methods work together in an application. But first, you need to learn how to set up the event handlers for an application.

The syntax for calling a jQuery method

```
$("selector").methodName(parameters)
```

Some common jQuery methods

Method	Description
`val()`	Get the value of a text box or other form control.
`val(value)`	Set the value of a text box or other form control.
`text()`	Get the text of an element.
`text(value)`	Set the text of an element.
`next([type])`	Get the next sibling of an element or the next sibling of a specified type if the parameter is coded.
`submit()`	Submit the selected form.
`focus()`	Move the focus to the selected form control or link.

Examples

How to get the value from a text box

```
const gallons = $("#gallons").val();
```

How to set the value for an input element

```
$("#gallons").val("");
```

How to set the text in an element

```
$("#email_error").text("Email address is required");
```

How to set the text for the next sibling with object chaining

```
$("#last_name").next().text("Last name is required");
```

How to submit a form

```
$("#join_list").submit();
```

How to move the focus to a form control or link

```
$("#email").focus();
```

Description

- To call a jQuery *method*, you code a selector, the dot operator, the method name, and any parameters within parentheses. Then, that method is applied to the element or elements that are selected by the selector.

- When you use *object chaining* with jQuery, you code one method after the other. This works because each method returns the appropriate object.

- Although you'll typically use the val(), text(), and next() methods with selectors that select a single form control or element, you can also use them with selectors that select two or more form controls or elements. The result depends on the method you use.

Figure 8-5   How to call jQuery methods

How to use jQuery event methods

When you use jQuery, you use *event methods* to attach event handlers to events. To do that, you use the syntax shown at the top of figure 8-6. First, you code the selector for the element that initiates the event like a button that's clicked. Then, you code the name of the event method that represents the event that you want to use. Within the parentheses of the event method, you code a function that handles the event. This function is known as an event handler.

The table in this figure presents two of the most common event methods. The ready() event method is the jQuery alternative to the JavaScript DOMContentLoaded event. Because the DOM usually has to be built before you can use JavaScript or jQuery, you'll typically use the ready() event method in every jQuery application that you develop. The first example in this figure shows two ways to do that. In the long form, you use document as the selector for the web page followed by the dot operator, the method name, and the function that handles the event.

In the short form, you can omit the selector and event method name and just code the function in parentheses after the dollar sign. Although this form is often used by professional developers, all of the examples in this book use the long form. That way, it's easy to see where the ready() event method starts.

The second example shows how to attach an event handler to the click event of all h2 elements. To do that, you just use h2 as the selector and click() as the name of the event method.

The last example shows how to code an event method within the ready() event method. Here, the closing brace, parenthesis, and semicolon for each event method is critical. As you might guess, it's easy to accidentally omit one of these marks or to get them out of sequence, so this is a frequent source of errors. That's why some programmers code inline comments after the ending marks for each event method as shown in this example. This clearly shows how each ending mark matches up with each event method. However, it's generally considered a better practice to use indentation and vertical spacing to make this clear. That way, you don't have to worry about keeping the comments up to date as you modify your code.

As you review this figure, note that it uses arrow functions to define the event handler functions as described in chapter 4. This is a newer technique that has only been available since ES2015 (ES6). Of course, it's also possible to use standard function expressions to define event handler functions. For instance, the first example could be coded like this:

```
$(document).ready(function() {
    alert("The DOM is ready");
});
```

This technique was common prior to ES2015. However, since arrow functions are newer and more concise, all the applications in this chapter use them.

The syntax for a jQuery event method

```
$(selector).eventMethodName( () => {
    // the statements of the event handler
});
```

Two common jQuery event methods

Event method	Description
ready(handler)	The event handler runs when the DOM is ready.
click(handler)	The event handler runs when the selected element is clicked.

Two ways to code the jQuery ready() event method

The long way

```
$(document).ready( () => {
    alert("The DOM is ready");
});
```

The short way

```
$(() => {                          // (document).ready is assumed
    alert("The DOM is ready");
});
```

How to attach an event handler to the click event of all h2 elements

```
$("h2").click( () => {
    alert("This heading has been clicked");
});
```

The click() event method within the ready() event method

```
$(document).ready( () => {

    $("h2").click( () => {
        alert("This heading has been clicked");
    }); // end click()

}); // end ready()
```

Description

- To code a jQuery event handler, you code a selector, the dot operator, the name of the jQuery *event method*, and a set of parentheses. Within the parentheses, you code a function that handles the event. Although this is typically an anonymous function, it doesn't have to be.

- The event handler for the ready event runs any methods that it contains as soon as the DOM is ready, even if the browser is loading images and other content for the page. This works like the JavaScript DOMContentLoaded event.

- In this book, the ready() event method is always coded the long way that's shown above. In practice, though, many programmers use the short way.

- When coding one event handler within another, the use of the closing braces, parentheses, and semicolons is critical. To help get this right, many programmers code inline comments after these punctuation marks to identify the ends of the handlers.

Figure 8-6   How to use jQuery event methods

The Email List application

Now that you understand the basics of jQuery, you're ready to see how jQuery can be used in the Email List application that you studied in section 1.

The user interface and HTML

To refresh your memory, part 1 of figure 8-7 presents the user interface and HTML for the Email List application. To use the application, the user enters text into the first three text boxes and clicks the Join List button. Then, the JavaScript validates the entries and displays appropriate error messages if errors are found. If no errors are found, the data in the form is submitted to the web server for processing.

The HTML includes two script elements at the end of the body element. Here, the first script element loads the slim and minified version of the jQuery library from a CDN. Then, the second script element loads the JavaScript file (email_list.js) for the Email List application. That sequence is essential because the JavaScript file for the Email List application uses the jQuery library.

Within the form element, the span elements are adjacent siblings to the input elements for the text boxes, and the starting text for each of these span elements is an asterisk. This asterisk indicates that the text box entry is required. Later, if the JavaScript finds errors in the entries, it displays error messages in these span elements.

The user interface

Please join our email list

Email Address:	grace@yahoo.com
Confirm Email Address:	grace@yahoo The email addresses must match.
First Name:	This field is required.
	Join List Clear Form

The HTML

```html
<!DOCTYPE html>
<html>
<head>
    <meta charset="UTF-8">
    <meta name="viewport" content="width=device-width, initial-scale=1">
    <title>Join Email List</title>
    <link rel="stylesheet" href="email_list.css">
</head>
<body>
    <main>
        <h1>Please join our email list</h1>
        <form id="email_form" name="email_form"
              action="join.html" method="get">
            <div>
                <label for="email_1">Email Address:</label>
                <input type="text" id="email_1" name="email_1">
                <span>*</span>
            </div>
            <div>
                <label for="email_2">Confirm Email Address:</label>
                <input type="text" id="email_2" name="email_2">
                <span>*</span>
            </div>
            <div>
                <label for="first_name">First Name</label>
                <input type="text" id="first_name" name="first_name">
                <span>*</span>
            </div>
            <div>
                <label> </label>
                <input type="button" id="join_list" value="Join List">
                <input type="button" id="clear_form" value="Clear Form">
            </div>

        </form>
    </main>
    <script src="https://code.jquery.com/jquery-3.4.1.slim.min.js"></script>
    <script src="email_list.js"></script>
</body>
</html>
```

Figure 8-7   The Email List application (part 1)

The JavaScript and jQuery

Part 2 of figure 8-7 presents the JavaScript and jQuery for this application. This is the code in the email_list.js file that's included by the HTML. Here, all of the jQuery is highlighted. The rest of the code is JavaScript code.

To start, event handlers for the click event of the Join List and Clear Form buttons are coded within the event handler for the ready() event method. Within the event handler for the click event of the Join List button, the first two statements use jQuery selectors and the val() method to get the values from the first two text boxes. Then, the third statement declares a Boolean variable named isValid and initializes it to true. This variable is used to determine if all the user entries are valid.

In the first if statement, the code displays an error message if the user doesn't enter an email address in the first text box. Here, the next() method gets the adjacent sibling for the text box, which is the span element, and then the text() method sets an error message in that span element. This changes the DOM. As soon as this code changes the DOM, the browser displays the error message.

The next two if statements use the next(), text(), and val() methods in similar ways. Then, the fourth if statement checks whether the isValid variable is still true. If so, the data is valid. As a result, the code calls the submit() method of the form to send the data to the web server.

Within the event handler for the click event of the Clear Form button, the first three statements use the val() method to set the first three text boxes to empty strings. This clears these text boxes. Then, the next three statements use the next() and text() methods to set the text for the adjacent span element to an asterisk. This returns the form to its original state. Finally, the last statement moves the focus to the first text box, the one with "email_1" as its id.

The two event methods are followed by one more statement. It also moves the focus to the first text box. Because of that, the first text box is selected when you first load the page and the DOM becomes ready.

As you review this code, note that it doesn't require you to code the $() function like you typically do when you code pure JavaScript applications. That's because you can use the $ sign to code a selector that refers to jQuery, and that allows you to get one or more elements depending on the selector.

Although this jQuery code illustrates how jQuery can simplify a data validation application, it doesn't begin to show the power of jQuery. For that, you need to learn about more selectors, methods, and event methods. In addition, you need to see how they can be used in other types of applications like the ones shown later in this chapter.

The JavaScript and jQuery (email_list.js)

```javascript
$(document).ready( () => {

    // handle click on Join List button
    $("#join_list").click( () => {
        const email1 = $("#email_1").val();
        const email2 = $("#email_2").val();
        let isValid = true;

        if (email1 == "") {
            $("#email_1").next().text("This field is required.");
            isValid = false;
        } else {
            $("#email_1").next().text("");
        }

        if (email2 == "") {
            $("#email_2").next().text("This field is required.");
            isValid = false;
        } else if (email1 != email2) {
            $("#email_2").next().text("The email addresses must match.");
            isValid = false;
        } else {
            $("#email_2").next().text("");
        }

        if ($("#first_name").val() == "") {
            $("#first_name").next().text("This field is required.");
            isValid = false;
        }
        else {
            $("#first_name").next().text("");
        }

        // submit the form if all entries are valid
        if (isValid) {
            $("#email_form").submit();
        }
    });

    // handle click on Clear Form button
    $("#clear_form").click( () => {
        $("#email_1").val("");
        $("#email_2").val("");
        $("#first_name").val("");

        $("#email_1").next().text("*");
        $("#email_2").next().text("*");
        $("#first_name").next().text("*");

        $("#email_1").focus();
    });

    $("#email_1").focus();
});
```

Figure 8-7   The Email List application (part 2)

More skills for working with jQuery

The next three figures present more skills for working with the most useful jQuery selectors, methods, and event methods. Once you understand these skills, you'll be able to write significant jQuery applications of your own.

The most useful selectors

In figure 8-4, you were introduced to the basic selectors that you can use with jQuery. Now, figure 8-8 presents other useful selectors. The only selectors of significance that are missing are ones that you'll learn about in later chapters, like the animate selector that you use with animations and the form control selectors that you use with forms.

If this summary seems daunting, just read the list and realize that these selectors let you select just about any element that you need to select. Then, make sure that you understand the examples in this figure. Later, when you need to make a specific type of selection for an application, you can refer back to this summary and to figure 8-4.

To illustrate the use of these selectors, the first example shows how to use a selector to get the li elements that are the first children of their parent elements. If the HTML contains more than one list, this selects the first li element of each list.

The second example shows how to use a selector to get the even tr (table row) elements in an HTML table. Since the numbering for the rows starts at 0, the first tr element is even, the third tr element is even, and so on.

The third example shows how to use the :eq selector to get an element within an array of elements with the specified index. If, for example, there are four <p> elements that are descendants of the "faqs" element, the :eq(2) selector returns the <p> element that equals the index value of 2. Because the index values start with zero, this returns the third <p> element.

The last example shows a selector that gets all input elements with type attributes that have "text" as the value. In other words, this selector gets all text boxes. However, you can also get the text boxes by using this selector:

```
$("input[type=text]")
```

This shows that you can often select the elements that you want in more than one way.

A summary of the most useful jQuery selectors

Selector	Selects
[attribute]	All elements with the named attribute.
[attribute=value]	All elements with the named attribute and value.
:contains(text)	All elements that contain the specified text.
:empty	All elements with no children including text nodes.
:eq(n)	The element within the selected set where the index equals n.
:even	All elements with an even index within the selected set.
:first	The first element within the set.
:first-child	All elements that are first children of their parent elements.
:gt(n)	All elements within the selected set that have an index greater than n.
:has(selector)	All elements that contain the element specified by the selector.
:header	All elements that are headers (h1, h2, ...).
:hidden	All elements that are hidden.
:last	The last element within the selected set.
:last-child	All elements that are the last children of their parent elements.
:lt(n)	All elements within the selected set that have an index less than n.
:not(selector)	All elements that aren't selected by the selector.
:nth-child	All elements that are the nth children of their parent elements.
:odd	All elements with an odd index within the selected set.
:only-child	All elements that are the only children of their parent elements.
:parent	All elements that are parents of other elements, including text nodes.
:text	All input elements with the type attribute set to "text".
:visible	All elements that are visible.

Examples

How to select the li elements that are the first child of their parent element
```
$("li:first-child")
```

How to select the even tr elements of a table
```
$("table > tr:even")     // numbering starts at 0, so first tag is even
```

How to select the third descendant <p> element of an element
```
$("#faqs p:eq(2)")       // numbering starts at 0
```

How to select all input elements with "text" as the type attribute
```
$(":text")
```

Description

- Figure 8-4 and this figure summarize the selectors that you are most likely to need. However, this doesn't include some selectors such as six selectors that let you select attributes with attribute values that contain specific substrings.

- In chapter 9, you'll learn about a selector that's used with animation, and in chapter 10, you'll learn about other selectors that are used for form controls.

Figure 8-8   The most useful selectors

The most useful methods

The table in figure 8-9 represents a collection of methods that are taken from several jQuery categories. For instance, the prev(), next(), and find() methods are DOM traversal methods. The attr(), css(), addClass(), removeClass(), toggleClass(), and html() methods are DOM manipulation methods. The hide() and show() methods are effect methods. And the each() method is a miscellaneous method.

These are some of the most useful jQuery methods, and learning how to use them gets you off to a fast start with jQuery. Then, you can add other methods to your repertoire as you read the rest of the chapters in this section.

Again, if this table seems daunting, just read through these methods to see what's available. Then, study the examples until you understand how they work. Later, when you need a specific method for an application, you can refer back to this summary.

In the first example, the attr() method gets the src attribute of an element with "image" as its id. The second example uses the attr() method to add a src attribute to the selected element with the value that's stored in imageSource. If the element already has a src attribute, this method changes its value. The third example uses the css() method to change the color property of the selected elements to blue. And the fourth example uses the addClass() method to add a class to all of the h2 elements within the element that has "faqs" as its id.

In the fifth example, the html() method adds an h2 element to an aside element. To do that in JavaScript, you'd have to use methods of the Document and Node interfaces that you learned about in chapter 6.

In the last example, the each() method runs a function for each element in an array. In this case, the array contains all of the <a> elements within the element with "image_list" as its id. As a result, the each() method loops through these elements. This means that you don't need to code your own loop to process the array, which is one of the benefits of jQuery over JavaScript.

When you code the function for an each() method, you often need to access the current index and element of the loop. To do that, you can specify two parameters for the function that you pass to the each() method. In this example, these parameters are named index and elem. If you want, you can specify different names for these parameters, but the first parameter accesses the current index and the second accesses the current element. This works because the each() method passes these two arguments to the function.

In most cases, the jQuery methods operate on all of the selected elements. However, there are some exceptions. For example, if you use the attr() method to get the value of an attribute, it gets the value only for the first selected element. Similarly, the css() method gets the value of a property only for the first selected element.

A summary of the most useful jQuery methods

Method	Description
next([*selector*])	Get the next sibling of each selected element or the first sibling of a specified type if the parameter is coded.
prev([*selector*])	Get the previous sibling of each selected element or the previous sibling of a specified type if the parameter is coded.
find(*selector*)	Search the selected element and return descendant elements.
attr(*attrName*)	Get the value of the specified attribute from the first selected element.
attr(*attrName*, *value*)	Set the value of the specified attribute for each selected element.
css(*propName*)	Get the value of the specified property from the first selected element.
css(*propName*, *value*)	Set the value of the specified property for each selected element.
addClass(*className*)	Add one or more classes to the selected elements and, if necessary, create the class. If you use more than one class as the parameter, separate them with spaces.
removeClass([*className*])	Remove one or more classes. If you specify more than one class, separate them with spaces. If you omit the class, all classes are removed.
toggleClass(*className*)	If the class is present, remove it. Otherwise, add it.
html(*htmlString*)	Sets the HTML contents of each selected element to the specified HTML string.
hide([*duration*])	Hide the selected elements. The duration parameter can be "slow", "fast", or a number giving the time in milliseconds. By default, the duration is 400 milliseconds, "slow" is 600 milliseconds, and "fast" is 200 milliseconds.
show([*duration*])	Show the selected elements. The duration parameter is the same as for the hide() method.
each(*function*)	Run the specified function for each element in an array.

Get the value of the src attribute of an image

```
$("#image").attr("src");
```

Set the value of the src attribute of an image to the value of a variable

```
$("#image").attr("src", imageSource);
```

Set the value of the color property of the h2 elements to blue

```
$("h2").css("color", "blue");
```

Add a class to the h2 descendants of the "faqs" element

```
$("#faqs h2").addClass("minus");
```

Put an h2 element into an aside element

```
$("aside").html("<h2>Table of Contents</h2>");
```

Run a function for each <a> element within an "image_list" element

```
$("#image_list a").each( (index, elem) => {
    // the statements of the function
});
```

Figure 8-9   The most useful methods

The most useful event methods

Figure 8-10 summarizes some of the most useful event methods, including the ready() and click() event methods introduced in figure 8-6. Most of these event methods provide for a single event handler that runs when the event occurs. Those event methods work like the ready() and click() event methods, but they run when different events occur.

For instance, the first example works just like the click() event method that handles the click event, except that it uses the dblclick() event method to handle the double-click event. Here, the event handler that's passed to the dblclick() event method accesses the Event object by specifying a parameter named evt. This works because event methods always pass an Event object to the event handler. Then, the statement within the event handler uses the Event object's currentTarget property to get the HTML element that trigged the event and to set its value to an empty string. Since the jQuery selector selects text boxes, this clears the text box that the user double-clicked.

If you want to use jQuery instead of HTML to clear the text box, you can use a jQuery selector like this:

```
$(evt.currentTarget).val("");   // clear text box
```

This allows the event handler to use the jQuery val() method to set the value of the double-clicked text box instead of using the HTML value attribute as shown in the figure.

Unlike most of the event methods in this figure, the hover() event method provides for two event handlers: one for when the mouse pointer moves into an element and another for when the mouse pointer moves out of an element. The second example shows how this works. Here, the first event handler function is the first parameter of the hover() method, and it is followed by a comma. Then, the second event handler function is the second parameter of the hover() method. To end the parameters, the last line of code consists of a right parenthesis followed by a semicolon. In this example, both of the event handlers consist of a single statement. As a result, they don't need to include braces. However, if necessary, you can add braces and code multiple statements for each event handler.

The hover() method is typical of jQuery coding, which often requires the use of one or more functions within another function. That's why you need to code the functions with indentation that helps you keep the syntax correct.

The last example in this figure shows how to use the preventDefault() method of the Event object that's passed to the event handler to cancel the default action of the event. When you include the jQuery library, this jQuery method is executed in place of the preventDefault() method of the browser that you learned about in figure 4-12. Since the jQuery version of this method is cross-browser compatible, it works even with older browsers.

All three of these examples show that when a selector gets more than one element, the event method sets up the event handler for each of the selected elements. This makes it easy to set up multiple event handlers with jQuery.

A summary of the most useful jQuery event methods

Event method	Description
ready(*handler*)	The handler runs when the DOM is ready.
click(*handler*)	The handler runs when the selected element is clicked.
dblclick(*handler*)	The handler runs when the selected element is double-clicked.
mouseenter(*handler*)	The handler runs when the mouse pointer enters the selected element.
mouseover(*handler*)	The handler runs when the mouse pointer moves over the selected element.
mouseout(*handler*)	The handler runs when the mouse pointer moves out of the selected element.
hover(*handlerIn,handlerOut*)	The first event handler runs when the mouse pointer moves into an element. The second event handler runs when the mouse pointer moves out.

A property and a method of the Event object

Property/method	Description
currentTarget	Gets the HTML element that triggered the event.
preventDefault()	Prevents the default event handler from running.

A double-click() event method for all text boxes

```
$(":text").dblclick( evt => {
    evt.currentTarget.value = "";  // clear text box
});
```

A hover() event method for each img element within a list

```
$("#image_list img").hover(
    () => alert("The mouse pointer has moved into an img element"),
    () => alert("The mouse pointer has moved out of an img element")
);
```

A preventDefault() method that stops the default action of an event

```
$("#faqs a").click( evt => {        // the Event object is named evt
    evt.preventDefault();           // the method is run on the Event object
});
```

Description

- To get the Event object that's passed to a method, you can code a parameter for the event handler function. You can use whatever name you want for this parameter, but evt and event are common.
- This figure does not present all event methods. For example, it does not present the keydown(), keypress(), keyup(), mousedown(), mouseup(), mouseleave(), and mousemove() methods.

Figure 8-10   The most useful event methods

Other event methods that you should be aware of

In most cases, you'll use the event methods that have already been presented in this chapter, and you'll attach them as described earlier. Sometimes, though, you'll want to attach event handlers in other ways, remove an event handler, or trigger an event that starts an event handler. Then, you can use the methods that are presented in the table in figure 8-11.

The on() event method lets you attach an event handler to one or more events. In the first set of examples, it's used to attach an event handler to the click event of an element with "clear" as its id. You can also do this using the click() event method as shown here. A method like this is called a *shortcut method* because it actually uses the on() method internally. In a case like this where you're attaching a single event handler, you can use either the on() event method or the shortcut method.

One advantage of the on() event method is that you can use it to attach an event handler to multiple events. This is illustrated by the first example in the second set of examples. Here, two events (click and mouseover) are coded as the first parameter of the on() event method. As a result, the event handler is triggered whenever either of these events occurs on the selected elements.

By contrast, if you want to attach the same event handler to two different events of two different elements, you can use shortcut events. Because both event methods refer to the same event handler, you typically assign the event handler to a constant. Then, you can use the name of that constant as the parameter of the shortcut methods. In the second example in this set, the event handler is assigned to a constant named clearClick. Then, the click() event method is used to attach this event handler to an element with "clear" as its id, and the dblclick() event method is used to attach this event handler to all text boxes.

For some applications, you may want to remove an event handler when some condition occurs. To do that, you can use the off() event method as shown by the third example. If the event handler is assigned to a constant, you can also name the constant on the handler parameter of the off() event method.

If you want to remove an event handler after it runs just one time, you can use the one() event method. This is shown by the fourth example.

If you want to initiate an event from your jQuery code, you can use the trigger() event method in either the long or short form as shown by the fifth set of examples. Both of those examples trigger the click event of the element with "clear" as its id. This causes the event handler for that event to be run.

That provides another way to run the same event handler for two different events. All you have to do is trigger the event for one event handler from another event handler. That's shown by the last example in this figure. Here, the event handler for the double-click event of all text boxes triggers the click event of the element with "clear" as its id, and that starts the event handler.

Other event methods that you should be aware of

Event method	Description
on(*events,handler*)	Attach an event handler to one or more events.
off(*events,[handler]*)	Remove an event handler from one or more events.
one(*event,handler*)	Attach an event handler and remove it after it runs one time.
trigger(*event*)	Trigger the event for the selected element.

How to attach an event handler to an event

With the on() event method

```
$("#clear").on("click", () => {...});
```

With the shortcut method

```
$("#clear").click( () => {...});
```

How to attach an event handler to two different events

Of the same element

```
$("image_list img").on("click mouseover", () => {...});
```

Of two different elements

```
const clearClick = () => {...};
$("#clear").click(clearClick);
$(":text").dblclick(clearClick);
```

How to remove an event handler from an event

```
$("#clear").off("click");
```

How to attach and remove an event handler so it runs only once

```
$("#clear").one("click", () => {...});
```

How to trigger an event

With the trigger() method

```
$("#clear").trigger("click");
```

With the shortcut method

```
$("#clear").click();
```

How to trigger an event from an event handler

```
$(":text").dblclick( () => {
    $("#clear").click();
});
```

Description

- When you use a *shortcut method* to attach an event handler to an event, you're actually using the on() method.

- Event methods named bind() and unbind() were deprecated in jQuery 3.0. You may see them sometimes in older code examples online, but you shouldn't use them.

Figure 8-11   Other event methods that you should be aware of

Three illustrative applications

This chapter ends by presenting three typical JavaScript applications. These applications show how to use jQuery selectors, methods, and event methods in actual applications.

The FAQs application

Figure 8-12 presents a FAQs application similar to the one that you studied in chapter 6. However, this FAQs application uses jQuery.

Part 1 of this figure shows some of the HTML and CSS for this application. When this applications starts, the div elements after the h2 elements are hidden by the CSS, and the h2 elements are preceded by a plus sign. Then, if the user clicks an h2 element, the application displays the div element below the h2 element and changes the plus sign to a minus sign. Later, if the user clicks on the h2 element again, the application hides the div element and changes the minus sign to a plus sign.

The FAQs application in a browser

> ### jQuery FAQs
>
> − What is jQuery?
>
> jQuery is a library of the JavaScript functions that you're most likely to
> need as you develop websites.
>
> ⊕ **Why use jQuery?**
>
> ⊕ **Which is harder to learn: jQuery or JavaScript?**

Some of the HTML

```html
<main id="faqs">
    <h1>JavaScript FAQs</h1>
    <h2><a href="#">What is jQuery?</a></h2>
    <div>
        <p>jQuery is a library of the JavaScript functions that you're most
            likely to need as you develop websites.
        </p>
    </div>
    <h2><a href="#">Why use jQuery?</a></h2>
    <div>
        <p>Three reasons:</p>
        <ul>
            <li>It's free.</li>
            <li>It lets you get more done in less time.</li>
            <li>It's cross-browser compatible.</li>
        </ul>
    </div>
    <h2><a href="#">Which is harder to learn: jQuery or JavaScript?</a></h2>
    <div>
        <p>For many things, jQuery is easier to learn than JavaScript. But
            remember that jQuery is JavaScript.
        </p>
    </div>
</main>
<script src="https://code.jquery.com/jquery-3.4.1.slim.min.js"></script>
<script src="faqs.js"></script>
```

Some of the CSS

```css
h2 {
    background: url(images/plus.png) no-repeat left center;
}
h2.minus {
    background: url(images/minus.png) no-repeat left center;
}
div {
    display: none;
}
```

Figure 8-12   The FAQs application (part 1)

Part 2 of figure 8-12 shows the JavaScript and jQuery code for this application. It consists of a click() event method that's coded within the ready() event method. This click() event method sets up the event handlers for every h2 element within the section that has "faqs" as its id.

The event handler defines a parameter named evt that provides a way to access the Event object. Then, within the event handler, the first statement uses the currentTarget property of the Event object to get the h2 element that was clicked.

After getting the h2 element, the next statement uses the toggleClass() method to add a class named minus to the h2 element if it isn't present or to remove it if it is. The CSS that's shown in part 1 of this figure shows that the class named minus determines whether a plus or minus sign is displayed before the heading.

After toggling the minus class for the h2 element, this code uses an if statement to check the value of the class attribute of the h2 element. To do that, it uses the attr() method. If the class isn't equal to "minus", the div element that follows the h2 element shouldn't be displayed. That's why the statement within the if clause chains the next() and hide() methods to hide the div element that is a sibling to the h2 element.

However, if the class attribute of the h2 element is equal to "minus", the div element that follows the h2 element should be displayed. That's why the statement within the else clause uses the next() and show() methods to show the div element that is a sibling to the h2 element.

The click() event method ends by cancelling the default action of the <a> element that's within the h2 element. Since this application has loaded the jQuery library, this line of code works for older browsers that don't support the current ECMAScript standards.

After the click() event method, the ready() event method ends by using the find() method to get the <a> elements that are descendants of the element whose id is "faqs". Then, it uses the :first selector to get the first <a> element, and it sets the focus on that element.

Compared to the code presented in the second example in figure 8-2, the code in this figure is a little longer. That's because it uses an if statement to show or hide the div element that's related to the h2 element. This shows how you can use the show() and hide() methods to show or hide an element instead of using the toggleClass() method to perform the same task. The advantage of using the show() and hide() methods is that it allows an app to work without any extra CSS classes.

The JavaScript and jQuery

```
"use strict";
$(document).ready( () => {

    // attach event handlers for all h2 tags
    $("#faqs h2").click( evt => {

        // get clicked h2 tag
        const h2 = evt.currentTarget;

        // toggle minus class for h2 tag
        $(h2).toggleClass("minus");

        // show or hide related div
        if ($(h2).attr("class") !== "minus") {
            $(h2).next().hide();
        }
        else {
            $(h2).next().show();
        }

        evt.preventDefault();
    });

    // set focus on first h2 tag's <a> tag
    $("#faqs").find("a:first").focus();
});
```

Description

- When you attach an event handler to a link, you often need to cancel the default
  action of the link, which is to open the page or image that's identified by its href
  attribute. To do that, you can call the preventDefault() method of the event object
  that's passed to the event handler.

Figure 8-12   The FAQs application (part 2)

The Image Swap application

Figure 8-13 presents the jQuery version of the Image Swap application that was presented in chapter 7. In this application, when the user clicks on one of the thumbnail images at the top of the browser window, the application changes the caption and image below.

Part 1 of this figure shows some of the HTML and CSS for this application. The HTML uses img elements to display the four thumbnail images. However, this code nests these elements within <a> elements. That way, the images are clickable and can receive the focus. In each <a> element, the href attribute identifies the image to be swapped when the user clicks the link, and the title attribute provides the text for the related caption. In addition, this code nests each <a> and img element within a li element, and it nests the li elements within a ul element.

After the ul element, the HTML specifies the h2 element for the caption and the img element for the main image on the page. The ids of these elements are highlighted because jQuery uses those ids as it swaps captions and images into them.

By coding the img elements for the thumbnails within <a> elements, this HTML provides accessibility for the motor-impaired. That way, the user can access the thumbnail links by pressing the Tab key, and the user can swap the image by pressing the Enter key when a thumbnail has the focus, which starts the click event.

The CSS includes a style rule for the li elements. This style rule sets the display property of these elements to inline so the browser displays the images from left to right instead of from top to bottom.

The user interface for the Image Swap application

The HTML

```
<main>
    <h1>Fishing Images</h1>
    <p>Click on an image to enlarge.</p>
    <ul id="image_list">
        <li><a href="images/release.jpg" title="Catch and Release">
            <img src="thumbnails/release.jpg" alt=""></a></li>
        <li><a href="images/deer.jpg" title="Deer at Play">
            <img src="thumbnails/deer.jpg" alt=""></a></li>
        <li><a href="images/hero.jpg" title="The Big One!">
            <img src="thumbnails/hero.jpg" alt=""></a></li>
        <li><a href="images/bison.jpg" title="Grazing Bison">
            <img src="thumbnails/bison.jpg" alt=""></a></li>
    </ul>
    <h2 id="caption">Catch and Release</h2>
    <p><img id="main_image" src="images/release.jpg" alt=""></p>
</main>
<script src="https://code.jquery.com/jquery-3.4.1.slim.min.js"></script>
<script src="swap.js"></script>
```

The CSS for the li elements

```
li {
    display: inline;
}
```

Figure 8-13   The Image Swap application (part 1)

Part 2 of figure 8-13 presents the JavaScript and jQuery for this application. Within the ready() event method, the each() method runs a function for each <a> element in the image list. This function preloads the images for the app so they are in the browser cache when the user starts using the application. If an application uses many images, this can make the application run faster.

The function for each <a> element defines two parameters named index and link. Within this function, the first statement creates a new Image object. Then, the second statement uses the parameter named link to set the src attribute of the Image object to the value of the href attribute in the link. As soon as that statement completes, the image is loaded into the browser.

After preloading the images, this application attaches the event handlers for the click events of the <a> elements that contain the thumbnail images. The function for the click() event method defines a parameter named evt that provides a way to access the Event object that's passed to this function.

Within the event handler, the first statement uses the currentTarget property of the Event object to get the <a> element that was clicked. Then, the next statement swaps the image in the main portion of the browser window. To do that, it uses the attr() method to set the value of the src attribute of the main image element to the href attribute of the <a> element. As soon as that's done, the image is swapped in the browser.

The next statement works similarly. It swaps the caption of the image in the main portion of the browser window. This time, the caption is taken from the title attribute of the <a> element.

The last statement in the click() event method uses the preventDefault() method of the evt object that is passed to the event handler to cancel the default action of clicking on the link. This is the same statement presented in the FAQs application of the previous figure. However, it's more important here. If you don't cancel the default action of clicking on the <a> element in the FAQs application, the application stills work. It just reloads the page, which is less efficient. If the default action isn't cancelled when you click on a link in this application, though, the application displays the image that's referred to by the link in a new window or tab, which isn't what you want.

After the click() event method, the last statement in the ready() event method shows another way to set the focus to the first <a> element. Because that element contains the first thumbnail image, this makes it easier for the users to tab to the thumbnails that they want to swap. To identify the first <a> element, the :first-child selector gets the first li element of the unordered list. Then, a descendant selector gets the <a> element within the li element.

The JavaScript and jQuery

```
"use strict";
$(document).ready(() => {

    // preload images
    $("#image_list a").each( (index, link) => {
        const image = new Image();
        image.src = link.href;
    });

    // attach event handlers for links
    $("#image_list a").click( evt => {
        // get clicked <a> tag
        const link = evt.currentTarget;

        // swap image
        $("#main_image").attr("src", link.href);

        //swap caption
        $("#caption").text(link.title);

        // cancel the default action of the link
        evt.preventDefault();  // jQuery cross-browser method
    });

    // move focus to first thumbnail
    $("li:first-child a").focus();
});
```

Description

- When you use jQuery to work with images that aren't included in the HTML, preloading the images can improve the performance of the application because the user doesn't have to wait for a new image to be loaded into the browser.

- To preload an image, you can create a new Image object and assign the URL for the image to the Image object's src attribute.

Figure 8-13   The Image Swap application (part 2)

The Image Rollover application

Figure 8-14 presents the jQuery version of the Rollover application that's presented in the exercises for chapter 7. In this application, when the user hovers the mouse pointer over one of the starting images, the browser replaces the starting image with another image. Then, when the user moves the mouse pointer out of the image, the browser displays the starting image again.

The HTML for this application codes the img elements within the li elements of an unordered list. In these img elements, the src attribute identifies the image that's displayed when the browser loads the application, and the id attribute identifies the image that the browser should display when the mouse hovers over the img element.

In the JavaScript and jQuery shown here, the each() method runs a function that processes each occurrence of an img element within the ul element that has "image_rollovers" as its id. The function for the each() method starts by defining two parameters named index and img. Here, the img parameter provides a way to access each img element.

Within the function for the each() method, the first two statements use the img parameter to get the values of the src and id attributes of the current image and store them in constants named oldURL and newURL. Remember that these attributes hold the values that locate the starting image and its rollover image.

Note that the each() method applies the function to all img elements in the element with an id of "image_rollovers". That means that you can modify the HTML for this app to add more images to this element, and as long as the img elements have a src attribute with the original image and an id attribute with the new image, they will work as rollovers without modifying the jQuery.

The next two statements preload the rollover image by creating a new Image object and assigning the value of the newURL variable to its src attribute. As soon as the src attribute is set, the browser loads the image. Although preloading isn't essential, it can improve the user experience because the users won't have to wait for a rollover image to be loaded.

After preloading the images, the hover() event method attaches the event handlers for the current image. Remember, this event method has two event handlers as its parameters. The first event handler runs when the mouse pointer moves into the element, and the second runs when the mouse pointer moves out of the element.

In the function for the first event handler, a single statement uses the img parameter to set the src attribute of the image to the value of the newURL variable. That causes the rollover image to be displayed. Then, the function for the second event handler reverses this process by restoring the src attribute of the image to the value of the oldURL variable.

Of course, there's more than one way to code an application like this. For instance, you could implement this application by using the mouseover and mouseout events, similar to how the chapter 7 exercise worked. Then, you'd code the event handler for the mouseover event like the first event handler of the hover() event method, and you'd code the event handler for the mouseout event like the second event handler of the hover() event method.

Two images with the second image rolled over

The HTML

```
<main>
    <h1>Fishing Images</h1>
    <p>Move your mouse over an image to change it and back out of the
        image to restore the original image.</p>
    <ul id="image_rollovers">
        <li><img src="images/release.jpg" alt="" id="images/deer.jpg"></li>
        <li><img src="images/hero.jpg" alt="" id="images/bison.jpg"></li>
    </ul>
</main>
<script src="https://code.jquery.com/jquery-3.4.1.slim.min.js"></script>
<script src="rollover.js"></script>
```

The JavaScript and jQuery

```
"use strict";
$(document).ready(() => {

    // process each img tag
    $("#image_rollovers img").each( (index, img) => {
        const oldURL = img.src;        // gets the src attribute
        const newURL = img.id;         // gets the id attribute

        // preload rollover image
        const rolloverImage = new Image();
        rolloverImage.src = newURL;

        // set up event handlers for hovering over an image
        $(img).hover(    // use jQuery syntax to access hover() method
            () => img.src = newURL,   // hover over
            () => img.src = oldURL    // hover out
        );
    });

});
```

Figure 8-14   The Image Rollover application

Perspective

To get you off to a fast start, this chapter has presented the most useful jQuery selectors, methods, and event methods. That should give you a good idea of what you have to work with when you use jQuery. And you'll add to those selectors and methods as you read the next few chapters in this book.

The trick, of course, is figuring out how to apply the right selectors, methods, and event methods to the application that you're trying to develop. To get good at that, it helps to review many different types of jQuery applications. That's why this chapter has presented four applications, and that's why the rest of this book presents many more.

Terms

jQuery	getter method
CDN (Content Delivery Network)	setter method
Subresource Integrity (SRI) checking	object chaining
selector	event method
method	shortcut method

Summary

- *jQuery* is a JavaScript library that provides methods that make JavaScript programming easier. These methods have been tested for cross-browser compatibility.

- To use jQuery, you code a script element at the end of the body section that includes the file for the jQuery core library. This file can be downloaded and stored on your computer or server, or you can access it through a *Content Delivery Network (CDN)*.

- If you use the jQuery CDN, the jQuery website recommends that you use *Subresource Integrity (SRI) checking* to help ensure that resources from a third-party server aren't tampered with.

- When you code statements that use jQuery, you use *selectors* that are like those for CSS. You also use a dot syntax that consists of the selector for one or more elements, the dot, and the name of the *method* that should be executed.

- You can use *object chaining* to call a jQuery method on the object that's returned by another method.

- To set up event handlers in jQuery, you use *event methods*. Most of these methods have one parameter that is the event handler that runs when the event occurs. But some event methods like the hover() method take two event handler parameters.

Exercise 8-1   Add a Clear button to the Future Value application

In this exercise, you'll add a Clear button to a version of the Future Value application that uses jQuery instead of JavaScript. This should give you practice creating and attaching an event handler.

1. Use your text editor or IDE to open the application in this folder:
    `javascript_jquery\exercises\ch08\future_value`

2. Run the application to refresh your memory about how it works. Note that a Clear button has been added to the right of the Calculate button, but the button doesn't work.

3. Review the code in the future_value.js file. Note that it works similarly to the code for the Email List application except that it calculates and displays the future value if all the entries are valid.

4. Add an event handler for the click event of the Clear button that clears all of the text boxes by setting them to an empty string (""). This can be done in one statement. To select just the text boxes, you use a selector like the one in the last example in figure 8-8. To set the values to empty strings, you use the val() method like the second example in figure 8-5. Now, test this change.

5. This event handler should also put the asterisks back in the span elements that are displayed to the right of the text boxes to show that entries are required. That requires just one statement that uses the next() and the text() methods.

6. Add one more statement to this event handler that moves the focus to the first text box. Then, test this change.

7. Add another event handler to this application for the double-click event of any text box. This event handler should do the same thing that the event handler for the click event of the Clear button does. The easiest way to do that is to trigger the click event of the Clear button from the handler for the double-click event, as in the last example in figure 8-11. Test this change.

Exercise 8-2   Use different event methods for the Image Rollover application

This exercise asks you to modify the Image Rollover application of figure 8-14 so it uses different events for the event handlers.

1. Use your text editor or IDE to open the application in this folder:
    `javascript_jquery\exercises\ch08\rollover`

2. Run the application to refresh your memory about how it works.

3. Comment out the hover() event method in the rollover.js file, and rewrite the code so it uses the mouseover() and mouseout() event methods.

4. In the index.html file, add the two li elements that follow to the ul element whose id is image_rollovers:

    ```
    <li><img src="images/deer.jpg" alt="" id="images/release.jpg"></li>
    <li><img src="images/bison.jpg" alt="" id="images/hero.jpg"></li>
    ```

    This should display four rollover images on the web page.

Exercise 8-3   Develop a Book List application

In this exercise, you'll start with the HTML and CSS for the user interface that follows. Then, you'll develop the jQuery code that makes it work.

Development guidelines

1. You'll find the HTML, CSS, and image files for this application in this folder:

    `javascript_jquery\exercises\ch08\product_list`

    You'll also find a JavaScript file named product_list.js that contains just the "use strict" directive. You can add your code to this file.

2. This application works like the FAQs application you saw in this chapter, except that a list of book links is displayed below each heading. If the user clicks on one of these links, an image of the book is displayed to the right of the list. In addition, any time the user clicks on a heading with a plus or minus sign before it, the image should no longer be displayed.

3. The HTML for the links of this application is like the HTML for the Image Swap application. However, the links for this application don't require the title attribute since no caption is displayed for the image.

4. The images that are referred to by the href attributes of the links in this application should be preloaded. To do that, you can loop through all the links in the main element. Also, be sure to cancel the default actions of the links.

5. Feel free to copy and paste code from any of the applications that are available to you. That's the most efficient way to build a new application.

9

How to use effects and animations

Now that you know the basics of using jQuery, this chapter presents the methods for effects and animations. Many developers like these jQuery methods because effects and animations are fun to develop and can add interest to a page. As you study these methods, though, remember that the primary goal of a website is usability, so make sure that your effects and animations don't detract from that goal.

As you read this chapter, you may find it difficult to understand how some of these methods work until you see them in action. To help you with that, we've included most of the examples in this chapter in the downloadable source code. As a result, it should be easy for you to run these examples as you progress through this chapter to see how they work.

How to use effects

This chapter starts by presenting the basic methods for effects that are provided by jQuery. After you learn how to use them, you'll learn how to use what the jQuery documentation refers to as custom effects. In practice, though, any illusion of movement on a web page can be referred to as *animation*, so you can think of all the examples in this chapter as animation.

The jQuery methods for effects

Figure 9-1 summarizes the jQuery methods for *effects*. This summary includes the show() and hide() methods presented in chapter 8.

For all of the methods except the fadeTo() method, the primary parameter is the duration parameter that determines how long the effect takes. If, for example, the duration parameter for the fadeOut() method is 5000, the selected element or elements fades out over 5 seconds (5000 milliseconds). If the duration parameter is omitted, the effect takes place immediately so there is no animation.

By contrast, the fadeTo() method not only requires the duration parameter but also an opacity parameter. The opacity parameter must be a value from 0 through 1 where 1 is the full (normal) opacity and 0 is invisible.

The examples in this figure show how these methods work. Here, the first example uses the fadeOut() method to fade out a heading over 5 seconds. Then, the second example chains the fadeOut() and slideDown() methods to first fade out the heading over five seconds and then redisplay it by increasing its height over one second so it appears to slide down. As you'll see, method chaining is commonly used with effects to get the desired animation.

The third example chains two fadeTo() methods together. Here, the code fades the heading to an opacity of .2 over 5 seconds. Then, it fades the heading to an opacity of 1 over 1 second. This has the effect of the heading almost fading away completely and then being restored to its full opacity.

The fourth example shows how to use a *callback function* with any of these methods. To do that, you code a function as the last parameter of the method. Then, that function is called after the method finishes. In this example, the first fadeTo() method fades a heading to .2 opacity over 5 seconds. Then, the callback function fades the heading back to full opacity. Here, the callback function is coded as an arrow function. This function contains a single statement that uses the Event object to get the current target of the animation. In this example, the current target is the heading that's selected by the first fadeTo() method.

The third and fourth examples create the same animation. However, the code in the third example is shorter and easier to read. That's why most developers use method chaining, not callbacks, whenever possible.

Before going on, you may be interested to know that when you specify a duration with the hide() or show() method, the effect is implemented by changing the height, width, and opacity properties of the elements. To show an element, for example, its height, width, and opacity are increased so it appears to grow from its upper left corner. Conversely, to hide an element, its height, width, and opacity are decreased so it appears to shrink from its lower right corner.

The basic methods for jQuery effects

Method	Description
show()	Display the selected elements from the upper left to the lower right.
hide()	Hide the selected elements from the lower right to the upper left.
toggle()	Display or hide the selected elements.
slideDown()	Display the selected elements with a sliding motion.
slideUp()	Hide the selected elements with a sliding motion.
slideToggle()	Display or hide the selected elements with a sliding motion.
fadeIn()	Display the selected elements by fading them in to opaque.
fadeOut()	Hide the selected elements by fading them out to transparent.
fadeToggle()	Display or hide the selected elements by fading them in or out.
fadeTo()	Adjust the opacity property of the selected elements to the opacity set by the second parameter. The duration parameter must be specified with this method.

The basic syntax for all of the methods except the fadeTo() method

```
methodName([duration][, callback])
```

The basic syntax for the fadeTo() method

```
fadeTo(duration, opacity[, callback])
```

HTML for a heading that is animated after the web page is loaded

```
<h1 id="startup_message">Temporarily under construction!</h1>
```

jQuery that fades the heading out over 5 seconds

```
$("#startup_message").fadeOut(5000);
```

jQuery that uses chaining to fade the heading out and slide it back down

```
$("#startup_message").fadeOut(5000).slideDown(1000);
```

Chaining with fadeTo() methods

```
$("#startup_message").fadeTo(5000, .2).fadeTo(1000, 1);
```

jQuery with a callback function that gets the same result as the chaining

```
$("#startup_message").fadeTo(5000, .2,
    evt => $(evt.currentTarget).fadeTo(1000, 1)      // callback function
);
```

Description

- The duration parameter can be "slow", "fast", or a number giving the time in milliseconds. By default, the duration is 400 milliseconds, "slow" is 600 milliseconds, and "fast" is 200 milliseconds.

- The callback parameter is for a function that is called after the effect has finished. If more than one element is selected, the *callback function* is run once for each element.

- Chaining is commonly used with effects. This works because each effect method returns the object that it performed the effect on.

Figure 9-1   The jQuery methods for effects

The FAQs application with jQuery effects

Remember the FAQs application from the last chapter? That application used the show() and hide() methods without duration parameters to show and hide the answers to the questions in h2 elements. Now, figure 9-2 shows two ways that you can apply animation to that application.

The first example uses code similar to the code you saw in chapter 8. Here, when the user clicks on an h2 element, the event handler for the click event uses the toggleClass() method to add or remove a class named "minus". Then, the div element that's adjacent to the h2 element is displayed or hidden depending on whether the h2 element includes the "minus" class. In this case, though, the show() and hide() methods are replaced by slideDown() and fadeOut() methods with duration parameters to add animation to the application.

The second example shows another way to get the same results. Just as in the first example, the event handler for the click event starts by using the toggleClass() method to add or remove a class named "minus". Then, it uses the slideToggle() method to toggle the slideUp() and slideDown() methods on each click. This works much like the first example. However, it uses the slideUp() method instead of the fadeOut() method and also requires fewer lines of code.

The FAQs application as the text for a heading is displayed

jQuery FAQs

+ **What is jQuery?**

− **Why use jQuery?**

Three reasons:

• It's free.

• It lets you get more done in less time.

+ **Which is harder to learn: jQuery or JavaScript?**

The HTML

```
<main id="faqs">
    <h1>jQuery FAQs</h1>

    <h2><a href="#">What is jQuery?</a></h2>
    <div><!-- div content --></div>

    <h2><a href="#">Why use jQuery?</a></h2>
    <div><!-- div content --></div>

    <h2><a href="#">Which is harder to learn: jQuery or JavaScript?</a>
    <div><!-- div content --></div>
</main>
```

The JavaScript and jQuery with slideDown() and fadeOut() methods

```
"use strict";
$(document).ready( () => {

    $("#faqs h2").click( evt => {
        const target = evt.currentTarget;
        $(target).toggleClass("minus");
        if ($(target).attr("class") != "minus") {
            $(target).next().fadeOut(1000);
        }
        else {
            $(target).next().slideDown(1000);
        }
    });
});
```

The JavaScript and jQuery with the slideToggle() method

```
"use strict";
$(document).ready( () => {

    $("#faqs h2").click( evt => {
        $(evt.currentTarget).toggleClass("minus");
        $(evt.currentTarget).next().slideToggle(1000);
    });
});
```

Figure 9-2   The FAQs application with effects

A Slide Show application with effects

To give you a better idea of how effects can be used, this chapter now reviews two ways you can code a Slide Show application. Then, it shows how to stop and start a slide show.

The user interface, HTML, and CSS

Part 1 of figure 9-3 starts by showing the third slide in a slide show as it is being faded in. In the div element in the HTML, you can see that five img elements provide the slides for the show, and each of these has an alt attribute that provides the caption that's displayed above the slide.

The HTML uses an h2 element for the caption, an img element for the slide show, and a div element that contains the img elements for the slides. The id attributes for these elements are "caption", "slide", and "slides", and the "caption" and "slide" elements contain the caption and slide for the first slide in the show.

The CSS that's shown in this figure sets the height of the images to 250 pixels. In practice, all of the images for a slide show would usually be the same size, but setting the height for all of them ensures that the heights are the same, even if the widths aren't.

In addition, the CSS sets the display property of all of the img elements in the div element named "slides" to "none". That way, the browser doesn't display those img elements even if they're preloaded. Instead, it displays them one at a time as the jQuery code moves them into the "slide" img element.

The Slide Show application with fading out and fading in

Fishing Slide Show

Catch and Release on the Big Horn

The HTML

```
<main>
    <h1>Fishing Slide Show</h1>
    <h2 id="caption">Casting on the Upper Kings</h2>
    <img id="slide" src="images/casting1.jpg" alt="">
    <div id="slides">
        <img src="images/casting1.jpg" alt="Casting on the Upper Kings">
        <img src="images/casting2.jpg" alt="Casting on the Lower Kings">
        <img src="images/catchrelease.jpg"
            alt="Catch and Release on the Big Horn">
        <img src="images/fish.jpg" alt="Catching on the South Fork">
        <img src="images/lures.jpg" alt="The Lures for Catching">
    </div>
</main>
```

The critical CSS

```
img {
    height: 250px;
}
#slides img {
    display: none;
}
```

Description

- The images in the "slides" div element are used in the slide show.
- The caption for each image comes from its alt attribute.

Figure 9-3   The Slide Show application with effects (part 1)

Two ways to code the jQuery

By now, it should be obvious that you can code most jQuery applications in many different ways. In fact, one problem when learning jQuery is figuring out how to best apply jQuery to get the result that you want. That's why this book frequently shows more than one way to get a result, and that's why part 2 of figure 9-3 shows two possible ways to code the Slide Show application.

In the first example, the code starts by creating an array of Image objects that store the src and alt attributes of the five img elements in the "slides" div of the HTML. That's done by using the each() method to process each of the five elements. Within the processing loop, the code uses the attr() method to get the src and alt attributes from each img element and store them in the src and title properties of each Image object. Then, it adds the Image object to the array.

After the array has been created, this code uses the setInterval() method to perform its function (the first parameter) every 3000 milliseconds (the second parameter). Within that function, the first statement selects the caption and fades it out over 1000 milliseconds. Then, the second statement selects the slide and fades it out over 1000 milliseconds. In addition, this statement includes a callback function.

Within the callback function, the first statement gets a new value for the imageCounter variable, which was initially set to zero. To do that, it increases the counter value by 1 and uses the modulus operator to get the remainder that's left when the counter is divided by the length of the array. For the second slide in the show, that means the counter is increased to 1 and divided by 5 so the remainder is 1. For the fifth slide, the counter is increased to 5 and divided by 5 so the remainder is 0. Since this remainder is assigned back to the imageCounter variable, this means that variable ranges from 0 to 4 as the slide show progresses.

After setting the imageCounter value, the rest is easy. First, the code sets the nextImage constant to the next image in the array. Second, the code sets the src attribute for the "slide" img element to the src property of the next image object in the array and fades in that slide. Last, the code sets the text for the caption to the title property of the next image object in the array and fades in that caption.

In the second example, the code starts by setting the nextSlide variable to the first img element in the "slides" div. Then, the function for the setInterval timer fades out the starting slide and caption, just as it did in the first example. However, the code in the callback function for the fadeOut() method is completely different.

The callback function starts by testing whether the next img element in the "slides" div has a length of zero. If so, there isn't a next slide. In that case, this code sets the nextSlide variable to the first img element in that div. Otherwise, this code sets the next slide to the next img element in the "slides" div.

Once the next slide is established, the code sets constants for the next slide's src and alt attributes. Then, it uses the first constant to set the src attribute for the img element that is displaying the slide show and fades it in, and it uses the second constant to set the text for the next caption and fades it in.

This shows just two of the many ways that an application like this can be coded. When you develop any application, one of the goals is to write code that

One way to code the JavaScript and jQuery

```javascript
"use strict";
$(document).ready( () => {

    // create an array of the slide images
    let imageCache = [];
    $("#slides img").each( (index, img) => {
        const image = new Image();
        image.src = $(img).attr("src");
        image.title = $(img).attr("alt");
        imageCache[index] = image;
    });

    // start slide show
    let imageCounter = 0;
    setInterval( () => {
        $("#caption").fadeOut(1000);
        $("#slide").fadeOut(1000,
            () => {
                imageCounter = (imageCounter + 1) % imageCache.length;
                const nextImage = imageCache[imageCounter];
                $("#slide").attr("src", nextImage.src).fadeIn(1000);
                $("#caption").text(nextImage.title).fadeIn(1000);
            }); // end fadeOut() method
    },
    3000);         // end setInterval() method

});
```

Another way to code the JavaScript and jQuery

```javascript
"use strict";
$(document).ready( () => {
    let nextSlide = $("#slides img:first-child");

    // start slide show
    setInterval( () => {
        $("#caption").fadeOut(1000);
        $("#slide").fadeOut(1000,
            () => {
                if (nextSlide.next().length == 0) {
                    nextSlide = $("#slides img:first-child");
                }
                else {
                    nextSlide = nextSlide.next();
                }
                const nextSlideSource = nextSlide.attr("src");
                const nextCaption = nextSlide.attr("alt");
                $("#slide").attr("src", nextSlideSource).fadeIn(1000);
                $("#caption").text(nextCaption).fadeIn(1000);
            }); // end fadeOut() method
    },
    3000);         // end setInterval() method
});
```

Figure 9-3   The Slide Show application with effects (part 2)

is easy to read, maintain, and reuse in other web pages. The other is to write code that's efficient. Judging by those goals, the second example in figure 9-3 is better because its code is relatively straightforward, and it doesn't require an array of Image objects.

Regardless of how you code this application, when you run it, you'll notice that the captions and slides are faded out almost simultaneously, not one after the other. That's because the effects for two different elements run as soon as they're started. In this case, that means that one effect is started a few milliseconds after the other, so the fade out and in for the caption runs at almost the same time as the fade out and fade in for the slide.

How to stop and start a slide show

To improve the usability of a slide show, you usually provide some way for the user to stop and restart the show. Figure 9-4 shows one way to do that. It stops on the current slide when the user clicks on it, and it restarts when the user clicks on it again. Here are the points to note.

First, this code declares a constant named runSlideShow that stores an arrow function for running the slide show. The code in this function is the same as the code in the setInterval() function in the second example in the previous figure.

Second, this code executes a statement that creates a timer variable that calls the runSlideShow() function every 3 seconds. Note that this statement must be coded after the runSlideShow() function. Otherwise, the JavaScript engine would throw an error.

Third, this code defines an event handler for the click() event method that cancels and restores the timer on alternate clicks of the current slide. When a slide is clicked and the timer isn't null, the function uses the clearInterval() method to cancel the timer and stop the slide show. Otherwise, it calls the runSlideShow() method to restart the slide show. And it creates the timer for the slide show again.

When you run this application, you'll find that the slide show stops on a full image, not one that is fading out or fading in. That's because the clearInterval() method doesn't cancel the timer for the slide show until the current interval ends. Also, the slide show restarts with the next image in sequence. That's because this code declares the nextSlide variable outside of any functions. As a result, this code retains the value of the nextSlide variable even when the user cancels the timer.

Of course, there are many other ways that you can stop and restart a slide show. For instance, you could provide a stop/start button that works the same way that clicking on a slide works. You could also add next and previous buttons that would let the user manually move from one slide to the next while the slide show is stopped. Now that you know the basic code for running, stopping, and starting a slide show, you should be able to add these enhancements on your own.

The JavaScript and jQuery for stopping and restarting a slide show

```javascript
"use strict";
$(document).ready( () => {
    let nextSlide = $("#slides img:first-child");

    // the function for running the slide show
    const runSlideShow = () => {
        $("#caption").fadeOut(1000);
        $("#slide").fadeOut(1000,
            () => {
                if (nextSlide.next().length == 0) {
                    nextSlide = $("#slides img:first-child");
                }
                else {
                    nextSlide = nextSlide.next();
                }
                const nextSlideSource = nextSlide.attr("src");
                const nextCaption = nextSlide.attr("alt");
                $("#slide").attr("src", nextSlideSource).fadeIn(1000);
                $("#caption").text(nextCaption).fadeIn(1000);
            }
        ); // end fadeOut() method
    };          // end runSlideShow() arrow function

    // start slide show
    let timer1 = setInterval(runSlideShow, 3000);

    // starting and stopping the slide show
    $("#slide").click( () => {
        if (timer1 != null) {
            clearInterval(timer1);
            timer1 = null;                              // stop
        }
        else {
            runSlideShow();                             // start immediately
            timer1 = setInterval(runSlideShow, 3000); // change every 3 secs
        }
    });
});
```

Description

- With this code, the user can stop a slide show by clicking on a slide and restart the slide show by clicking on it again.

- So the code for the slide show doesn't have to be repeated, it is coded as an arrow function and stored in the constant named runSlideShow.

- Because the runSlideShow() function is an arrow function, it must be defined before the setInterval() method that calls it. Otherwise, the JavaScript engine will throw an error.

Figure 9-4   How to stop and start a slide show

How to use animation

Now that you know how to use the basic jQuery effects, you'll learn how to use what the jQuery website refers to as custom effects. We refer to these custom effects as animation, and that starts with the animate() method.

How to use the basic syntax of the animate() method

Figure 9-5 presents the basic syntax of the animate() method. Here, the first parameter is a *properties map* that's coded in braces. This map consists of name/value pairs. For instance, the second example in this figure sets the fontSize property to 275%, the opacity property to 1, and the left property to 0.

The second parameter is the duration for the animation. For instance, the second example sets the duration to 2 seconds (2000 milliseconds). When the animate() method is executed, it modifies the selected element or elements by changing their properties to the ones in the properties map over the duration specified. This provides the animation for the element.

The first example shows the starting CSS for the heading that is animated in this figure. Here, the heading starts with its font size at 75% of the browser default, its opacity at .2 (faded out), and its left position at -175 pixels, which is 175 pixels to the left of its normal position.

The second example uses the animate() method to increase the heading's font size to 275%, increase its opacity to 1, and change its left position to zero, which is its normal position. Since this is done over 2 seconds, the result is an animation that moves the heading from left to right and increases its size and opacity.

To make this work correctly, the position property for the heading must be set to relative. That means that the settings for the left and top properties are relative to the position the element would be in with normal flow. That position has left and top properties of 0.

The third example works like the second example, but it includes a callback function. Here, the callback function selects the h2 headings on the page and uses the next(), fadeIn(), and fadeOut() methods to fade in and out the div elements that follow the h2 headings. In addition, this example uses a slightly different properties map that specifies a left property of "+=175", instead of 0. This moves the heading 175 pixels to the right of where it started, which is another way to get the same results as the properties map in the second example.

When you code the properties map for a function, you must obey the rules that are described in this figure. For instance, you either use camel casing for the property names, like fontSize instead of font-size, or you code the property names in quotation marks. You code numeric values without quotation marks. Otherwise, you code the values in quotation marks. And when you code a numeric value for a property like left, pixels are assumed, unless you specify the unit of measurement and enclose the entire value in quotation marks.

For some properties, like width, height, and opacity, you can use "show", "hide", or "toggle" as the property values. If, for example, you code "hide" for

The basic syntax for the animate() method

```
animate({properties}[, duration][, callback])
```

An animated heading that is moving into the "faqs" section

The CSS for the h1 heading

```
#faqs h1 {
    position: relative;
    left: -175px;
    font-size: 75%;
    opacity: .2;
}
```

An animate() method for the h1 heading without a callback function

```
$("#faqs h1").animate(
    { fontSize: "275%", opacity: 1, left: 0 },    // the properties map
    2000                                          // duration
);
```

An animate() method for the h1 heading with a callback function

```
$("#faqs h1").animate(
    { fontSize: "275%", opacity: 1, left: "+=175" },
    2000,
    () => $("#faqs h2").next().fadeIn(1000).fadeOut(1000)  // callback
);
```

Description

- When the animate() method is run, the CSS properties for the selected elements are changed to the properties in the *properties map* that is coded as the first parameter of the method. The animation is done in a phased transition based on the duration parameter.

- To specify a property name in the properties map, you can use camel casing instead of the CSS hyphenation (as above) or you can enclose the property name in quotes.

- To specify a non-numeric property value, enclose the value in quotes.

- To specify a numeric property value, just code the value. For measurements, pixels are assumed. You can also use the += and -= operators with numeric values, but these expressions must be enclosed in quotes.

- For some properties, like width, height, and opacity, you can use "show", "hide", or "toggle" as the property values. These show, hide, or toggle the element by setting the property appropriately.

Figure 9-5   How to use the basic syntax of the animate() method

the width or opacity value, it is decreased to zero. If you code "show", the width is increased to its normal width or the opacity is increased to 1. And if you code "toggle", the values toggle between the show and hide values.

How to chain animate() methods

To chain animations, you use the same technique that you use for chaining effects or any other methods. You code a dot operator after the first animate() method and then code the second animate() method.

This is illustrated by the first example in figure 9-6, which chains two animate() methods in the click() event handler for a heading. Here, the indentation and alignment of the code shows that the two animate() methods are chained. The first method increases the font size and opacity and moves the heading 275 pixels to the right. Then, the second method reduces the font size and moves the heading 275 pixels to the left so it's back where it started.

When you chain effects or animations for a selected element, they are placed in the *queue* for that element. Then, the effects and animations are run in sequence. This makes it easy for you to create some interesting animations.

However, animations that are coded separately are also placed in queues. This is illustrated by the second example in this figure. Here, the first statement applies an animate() method to the h1 heading. Then, the second statement applies another animate() method to the same heading. When the user clicks this heading, jQuery places these animations in a queue and runs them in succession just as though they were chained. As a result, the code in this example works the same as the chained methods in the first example.

What happens if you click on the heading two or three times in quick succession? In that case, jQuery places the animate() methods in the queue for the heading and runs them two or three times in a row.

By contrast, the third example uses a callback function for the first animate() method to provide the second animate() method. Then, if the user clicks on the heading just once, it works the same as the other two examples. But if the user clicks on it twice in succession, the second click queues the second animate() method so it runs right after the first. But this may mean that the second animate() method starts before the callback method of the first animate() method finishes.

The concept of queuing is important for some applications, especially when you want to stop the methods in the queue from running. Also, it's important to know that there's a separate queue for each element. That's why the fading in and fading out of the captions and slides in the Slide Show application happen almost simultaneous.

A heading with two animations started by its click event

Chained animations

```
$("#faqs h1").click( evt => {
    $(evt.currentTarget)
        .animate({ fontSize: "650%", opacity: 1, left: "+=275" }, 2000)
        .animate({ fontSize: "175%", left: "-=275" }, 1000);
});
```

Queued animations

```
$("#faqs h1").click( evt => {
    $(evt.currentTarget).animate(
        { fontSize: "650%", opacity: 1, left: "+=275" }, 2000);
    $(evt.currentTarget).animate(
        { fontSize: "175%", left: "-=275" }, 1000);
});
```

An animation with a second animation in its callback function

```
$("#faqs h1").click( evt => {
    $(evt.currentTarget).animate(
        { fontSize: "650%", opacity: 1, left: "+=275" },
        2000,
        () => {
            $(evt.currentTarget).animate(
                { fontSize: "175%", left: "-=275" }, 1000
            );
        } // end callback
    );
});
```

Description

- When you chain the effects and animations for an element, they are placed in a *queue* for that element and run in sequence, not at the same time.

- When separate effects and animations are started for an element, they are also placed in a queue for that element and run in sequence.

- When you use a callback function with an animate() method, the callback function is run after the animation is finished.

- In some cases, a problem occurs if the user starts a second animation for an element before the callback function for the first animation finishes.

Figure 9-6   How to chain animate() methods

How to use the delay(), stop(), and finish() methods

Figure 9-7 shows how to use the delay(), stop(), and finish() methods for effects and animations. As the first example shows, the delay() method delays the start of the next animation in the queue for the number of milliseconds that are specified. Here, the fadeOut effect of the selected heading is delayed for five seconds.

By contrast, the stop() method stops the animations in the queue for the selected element. This is illustrated by the second example. Here, the code animates the hover event of the <a> elements in the HTML. This animation moves an <a> element down 15 pixels when the mouse pointer moves into the element and moves it back to its starting location when the mouse pointer moves out of the element.

But what if the second example didn't include the stop() method, and the user swipes the mouse pointer back and forth over the <a> elements several times in succession? As you've just learned, this would queue multiple animations for each <a> element, and it would run them in succession. This would cause a bouncing effect after the user stopped using the mouse, and that's not what you typically want.

That's why the second example uses the stop() method. As the summary shows, this method stops the current animation for the selected elements. In addition, since the code sets the first parameter to true, it clears the queues for the elements. As a result, all of the animations for the elements in the example are stopped and the queue is cleared before another animation is added to the queue. This stops the bouncing of the <a> elements, which is what you usually want.

If you set the second parameter for the stop() method to true, it stops the current animation immediately. For example, suppose an element is being faded in when the stop() method executes. In that case, the element remains at its current opacity. If that's not what you want, you can set the second parameter to true so the end result of the animation is displayed. In the case of the fadeIn() method, that means that the element is displayed with an opacity of 1.

The finish() method works like the stop() method with both of its parameters set to true. The difference is that the properties of *all* queued animations, not just the current animation, are immediately set to their end values when you use finish.

The delay(), stop(), and finish() methods

Method	Description
delay(*duration*)	Delay the start of the next animation in the queue.
stop([*clearQueue*] [,*jumpToEnd*])	Stop the current animation for the selected element. The two parameters are Boolean with false default values. If set to true, the first parameter clears the queue so no additional animations are run. The second parameter causes the current animation to be completed immediately.
finish()	Stop the current animation for the selected element, clear the queue, and complete all animations for the selected elements.

HTML for a heading that is displayed when the web page is loaded

```
<h1 id="startup_message">Temporarily under construction!</h1>
```

jQuery that fades the heading out after 5 seconds

```
$("#startup_message").delay(5000).fadeOut(1000);
```

An animation that moves thumbnail images down on mouse hover

The HTML for the thumbnail images

```
<ul id="image_list">
    <li><a href="images/h1.jpg" title="James Allison: 1-1">
        <img src="thumbnails/t1.jpg" alt=""></a></li>

    // four more li elements that contain thumbnail images

    <li><a href="images/h6.jpg" title="James Allison: 1-6">
        <img src="thumbnails/t6.jpg" alt=""></a></li>
</ul>
```

The CSS for the <a> elements

```
a {
    position: relative;
}
```

The jQuery that stops the bouncing effect

```
$("#image_list a").hover(
    evt => $(evt.currentTarget).stop(true).animate({ top: 15 }, "fast"),
    evt => $(evt.currentTarget).stop(true).animate({ top: 0 }, "fast")
);
```

Description

- The delay() method works as an alternative to the use of a one-time timer.
- The stop() method in the second example stops the bouncing effect that occurs if the user moves the mouse pointer rapidly back and forth over the thumbnails.

Figure 9-7   How to use the delay(), stop(), and finish() methods

How to use easings with effects and animations

Figure 9-8 shows how to use easings with effects and animations. An *easing* determines the way an animation is performed. For instance, an animation can start slowly and pick up speed as it goes. Or, an animation can start or end with a little bounce.

jQuery only provides two easings: linear and swing. As you might guess, the linear easing moves an animation at a uniform speed, but the swing easing varies the speed in a way that is more interesting. Fortunately, swing is the default, so you don't need to change that.

If you want to use other easings, you can use a plugin like the jQuery easing plugin shown in this figure. To use this plugin, you start by coding a script element for it. In the first example in this figure, the script element gets the jQuery easing plugin from the Cloudflare CDN. When you use this script element, you must code it after the script element for jQuery as shown in this figure. That's because the easing plugin uses jQuery.

To use one of the easings that this plugin provides, you code the easing parameter for an effect or animation. The location of this parameter varies depending on the method you use, as shown in the syntax summaries in this figure and by the two examples that follow. Here, the first example adds a little bounce to the animation, and the second example increases the speed of the animation exponentially.

Of course, to code an easing parameter, you need to know the name of the easing that you want to use. One good way to find the names of the available easings is to go to the URL that's specified at the bottom of this figure. This web page provides information about using the easing plugin, and it lets you test each easing so you can see how it works. That can help you select the easings you want to use for each type of animation.

A script element for getting the jQuery easing plugin from a CDN

```
<script src="https://code.jquery.com/jquery-3.4.1.min.js"></script>
<script src="https://cdnjs.cloudflare.com/ajax/libs/jquery-easing/1.3/
jquery.easing.min.js"></script>
```

The syntax for using easing with effects and animations

The syntax for all of the basic methods except the fadeTo() method

```
methodName([duration][, easing][, callback])
```

The syntax for the fadeTo() method

```
fadeTo(duration, opacity[, easing][, callback])
```

The syntax for the basic animate() method

```
animate({properties}[, duration][, easing][, callback])
```

Two easings used by the FAQs application

```
$("#faqs h2").click( evt => {
    const target = evt.currentTarget;
    $(target).toggleClass("minus");
    if ($(target).attr("class") == "minus") {
        $(target).next().slideDown(1000, "easeOutBounce");
    }
    else {
        $(target).next().slideUp(1000, "easeInBounce");
    }
});
```

Two easings for an animated heading

```
$("#faqs h1").click( evt => {
    $(evt.currentTarget)
        .animate({ fontSize: "650%", opacity: 1, left: "+=275" },
            2000, "easeInExpo")
        .animate({ fontSize: "175%", left: "-=275" },
            1000, "easeOutExpo");
});
```

A URL for a full list of jQuery easings with online demonstrations

http://gsgd.co.uk/sandbox/jquery/easing

Description

- *Easing* refers to the way an animation is performed. jQuery provides only two easings: swing and linear. Swing is the default, and it's the animation that you usually want.

- Plugins provide many other types of easings. Four of the easings in the jQuery easing plugin are shown in the examples above.

- To use an easing, you code a script element for the plugin library. Then, you code the easing parameter for a method with the name of any easing that the plugin supports.

- You'll learn more about using other plugins in chapter 11.

Figure 9-8   How to use easings with effects and animations

How to use the advanced animate syntax and the methods for working with queues

At this point, you've probably already learned all of the methods and skills that you're going to want to use for your effects and animations. However, if you ever need to build applications that require more control over the queues, figure 9-9 presents the advanced syntax of the animate() method and the methods for working with queues.

When you use the advanced syntax of the animate() method, you code two parameters within braces and separated by a comma. In the first set of braces, you code the properties map just as you do in the basic syntax. In the second set of braces, you code one or more of the options that are summarized in the first table in this figure.

The first example in this figure shows how this works with three options: duration, specialEasing, and complete. Here, the duration option is like the duration parameter in the basic syntax, and the complete option is like the callback parameter in the basic syntax. However, the special easing parameter lets you specify a different easing for each property that is being animated.

Although the use of special easings may be more than you need, you should know that you can also use them with the basic syntax. That is illustrated by the second example. Here, you just code each property and its easing within brackets within the properties map.

The step option of the advanced animate() method lets you run a function after each step of the animation. This makes you realize that an animation is actually broken down into small steps that give the illusion of continuous progress. If, for example, you code the step option with a function that displays an alert message after each step of the first example, you'll see how many steps this animation is broken down into.

The queue option of the advanced animate() method lets you execute an animation immediately without placing it in the queue. You can also use the methods in the second table in this figure to work with the animations in a queue. However, it's quite possible that you may never find the need for the advanced animate syntax or the methods for working with queues.

The advanced syntax for the animate() method

```
animate({properties}, {options})
```

Some of the options for the advanced syntax

Option	Description
duration	A string or number that specifies the duration of the animation.
easing	A string that specifies an easing.
complete	A callback function that runs when the animation is complete.
step	A function to call after each step that the animation is broken down into.
queue	A Boolean value. If true, the animation is placed in the queue. If false, the animation starts immediately.
specialEasing	A map of one or more of the properties in the properties map with their corresponding easings.

The methods for working with animation queues

Method	Description
queue([name])	Get the queue for the selected element.
queue([name],newQueue)	Replace the queue for the selected element with a new queue.
queue([name],callback)	Add a new function (callback) to the end of the queue for the selected element.
dequeue([name])	Run the next item in the queue for the selected element.
clearQueue([name])	Remove all items that haven't yet been run from the queue.

An animate() method that uses the advanced syntax

```
$("#faqs h1").animate(
    { fontSize: "650%", opacity: 1, left: "+=175" },
    { duration: 2000,
      specialEasing: { fontSize: "easeInExpo", left: "easeOutExpo" },
      complete: () => $("#faqs h2").next().fadeIn(1000).fadeOut(1000)
    }
);
```

How to provide easings by property with the basic syntax

```
$("#faqs h1").animate(
    { fontSize: ["650%", "easeInExpo"],
      opacity: [1, "swing"],
      left: ["+=275", "easeOutExpo"] }, 2000
);
```

Description

- The specialEasing option of the advanced syntax of the animate() method lets you specify easings by property, as shown by the first example. However, you can also do that with the basic syntax as shown by the second example.

- The name parameter in the methods for working with queues isn't needed for the default queue (fx). It's only needed for custom queues that you create.

Figure 9-9   How to use the advanced animate syntax and the methods for queues

A Carousel application with animation

This chapter ends by presenting a common application called a Carousel application. It makes use of a simple animate() method, but the setup for using that method is extensive.

The user interface, HTML, and CSS

Part 1 of figure 9-10 presents the user interface, HTML, and CSS for the Carousel application. Because carousels are so common, you've most likely used one on more than one website. If you click the button to the right of the three books in the carousel shown here, the books slide left and three more are shown. If you click the button to the left of the books, the books slide right to the previous three books.

The HTML consists of a div element for the entire carousel that contains three more div elements. The first of these div elements contains the left button; the second contains the nine books that are used in the carousel; and the third contains the right button.

The second of these three div elements contains a ul element that in turn contains nine li elements. Then, each li element contains an img element for each book within an <a> element. As a result, the user can click on each book to go to the page for that book. In this example, the values of all of the href attributes are coded as "newpage.html", but these values would refer to the actual pages for the books in a real-world application.

The critical CSS for this application begins by setting the width of the middle div element (id is "display_panel") to 300 pixels, which is the width of three list items. Also, its overflow property is set to hidden, which means that anything that goes beyond 300 pixels (the other books) is hidden.

Next, the CSS for the ul element (id is "image_list") sets the position property to relative, which means that any settings for the top or left properties are relative to the normal position of this element. The CSS for this element also sets the width to 900 pixels, and the list-style to "none", which removes the bullets from the list items.

The CSS for the list items floats them to the left. This displays the items in the ul element horizontally. When it does that, the 900 pixel width (100 pixels for each item) of these items exceeds the width of its div container by 600 pixels. Remember, though, that the CSS for the display panel hides this overflow.

The last CSS style rule sets the width of the img elements within the li elements to 95 pixels. That means that there should be 5 pixels to the right of each image within each of the li items.

Since there are nine images in total and each list item is set to a width of 100 pixels, nine images require 900 pixels and that's the width that the ul element has been set to. For this application to work properly, of course, the widths of the div, ul, and li elements have to be properly coordinated.

The Carousel application

The HTML

```
<main>
    <h1>View our Books</h1>
    <div id="carousel">
        <div id="left_button" class="button_panel">
            <img src="images/left.jpg" alt=""></div>
        <div id="display_panel">
            <ul id="image_list">
                <li><a href="newpage.html">
                    <img src="images/book1.jpg" alt=""></a></li>
                <li><a href="newpage.html">
                    <img src="images/book2.jpg" alt=""></a></li>
                // 7 more li elements that contain images
            </ul>
        </div>
        <div id="right_button" class="button_panel">
            <img src="images/right.jpg" alt=""></div>
    </div>
</main>
```

The critical CSS

```
#display_panel {
    width: 300px;
    overflow: hidden;
    float: left;
    height: 125px;
}
#image_list {
    position: relative;
    left: 0px;                  // required for IE
    width: 900px;
    list-style: none;
}
#image_list li {
    float: left;
    width: 100px;
}
#image_list li img {
    width: 95px;
}
```

Figure 9-10   The Carousel application (part 1)

The JavaScript and jQuery

The JavaScript and jQuery code for this application, shown in part 2 of figure 9-10, consists of two event handlers: one for the right button, and one for the left button. In each event handler, the last line uses the animate() method to change the left property of the slider to the value of the variable named newLeftProperty. Since the first statement in the ready() event handler sets the slider to the ul element, this moves the ul element right or left based on the value in the newLeftProperty variable.

The trick, then, is setting the value of the newLeftProperty variable each time the right or left button is clicked. That's what the code at the beginning of each event handler does. As you study this code, keep in mind that the ul element must move to the left to display the images in the li elements, so the left property is either zero (the starting position) or a negative number.

The event handler for the right button begins by getting the current value of the left property by using the css() method. Then, it uses the parseInt() method to convert that value to an integer. For instance, the first time the right button is clicked, the value is zero.

After getting the value of the left property, this code declares the newLeftProperty variable and initializes it to zero. Then, it checks if the current left property minus 300 (which is the width of three list items) is greater than -900. If so, this code subtracts 300 from the left property to get the new left property that the animate() method can use to move the slider three images to the left. Otherwise, this code leaves the new left property set at zero. This means that the last three images are already displayed, so the animate() method slides the images all the way back to the right to display the first three images.

The click event handler for the left button works similarly. This time, though, after it gets the current value of the left property and declares and initializes the newLeftProperty variable, it checks if the current left property is less than zero. If so, the new left property is increased by 300. This means that the animate() method moves the slider three images to the right. Otherwise, it leaves the new left property set at zero. This means that the first three images are already displayed and the animate() method doesn't need to move the slider.

The JavaScript and jQuery

```javascript
"use strict";
$(document).ready( () => {

    const slider = $("#image_list");                    // slider = ul element

    // the click event handler for the right button
    $("#right_button").click( () => {

        // get value of current left property
        const leftProperty = parseInt(slider.css("left"));

        // determine new value of left property
        let newLeftProperty = 0;
        if (leftProperty - 300 > -900) {
            newLeftProperty = leftProperty - 300;
        }

        // use the animate function to change the left property
        slider.animate({left: newLeftProperty}, 1000);
    });

    // the click event handler for the left button
    $("#left_button").click( () => {

        // get value of current left property
        const leftProperty = parseInt(slider.css("left"));

        // determine new value of left property
        let newLeftProperty = 0;
        if (leftProperty < 0) {
            newLeftProperty = leftProperty + 300;
        }

        // use the animate function to change the left property
        slider.animate({left: newLeftProperty}, 1000);
    });

});
```

Description

- To get the value of the left property of the ul element, this application uses the css() method.
- The value of the left property for the ul element ranges from 0 to -600.

Figure 9-10   The Carousel application (part 2)

Perspective

Now that you've completed this chapter, you should be able to add some common animations to your web pages, like a slide show or a carousel. In chapter 11, though, you'll learn how to use jQuery plugins to create these as well as other types of animations. Because plugins are typically easy to use and because they typically work better than code you could write yourself, you should use them whenever possible.

Terms

animation
effect
callback function
properties map
queue
easing

Summary

- jQuery provides methods for *effects*, like fading in and fading out, that let you add *animation* to your web pages.

- The jQuery animate() method lets you change the CSS properties for an element over a specific duration. This lets you create animations.

- To get the animation that you want, you often chain one effect after another. This places the effects in a *queue* so the effects are executed in sequence.

- If a user starts an effect for an element several times in quick succession, the effects are placed in a queue for that element. In some cases, you may want to use the stop() or finish() method to stop the effects and clear the queue.

- *Easings* refer to the ways that effects and animations are executed over time. Although jQuery provides for only two easings (linear and swing), the jQuery easing plugin provides for many more.

Exercise 9-1   Experiment with animation

In this exercise, you'll experiment with effects, animations, and easings.

Review the application

1. Use your text editor or IDE to open the application in this folder:
    `javascript_jquery\exercises\ch09\animation`

2. Run the application to see how it works. Note how the top-level heading is animated into view from off the page. Then, click on the FAQ headings to see what happens.

Experiment with the effects for the FAQ headings

3. In the JavaScript and jQuery code, change the effects for the FAQ headings so the answers fade in and fade out of view when the headings are clicked.

4. Now, change the effects for the FAQ headings so the answers slide down and slide up when the headings are clicked.

5. Experiment with the durations and effects to see which ones you think are best for usability.

Experiment with the h1 heading

6. Check the CSS for the h1 heading to see that it starts with its left property at minus 175 pixels. Then, check the JavaScript and jQuery code to see that it moves the left property 375 pixels to the right and then 200 pixels to the left, which means the left property ends at zero pixels.

7. Restart the application and note the animation as the h1 heading moves from off the page into its proper location. Then, click the heading to see that the animation is repeated, which moves the heading farther to the right. Click on it again to see that it's repeated, which moves the heading still farther.

8. Restart the application. Then, click on the top-level heading twice in rapid succession. This should run the animations twice in a row, which shows that the animations are queued.

9. Fix the animation for the top-level heading so it always returns to its proper location above the FAQs at the end of the animation. That way, it won't move across the page. To do that, set its ending left property to zero pixels.

Add jQuery UI easings to the application

10. Note that there's a script element for the jQuery easing plugin in the HTML for the page. Then, add the easings shown in figure 9-8 to the effects and animations. Does that improve them?

11. After you run the application to see how those easings work, click on the link at the bottom of the page to view information about using the jQuery easing plugin. Note that this opens a new page or tab in your browser. Then, try some of the other easings to see how you like them.

Exercise 9-2   Modify the Slide Show application

This is a simple exercise that has you experiment with the effects that can be used with the slide show in figure 9-3. It uses the second block of JavaScript and jQuery code that's shown in part 2 of that figure.

1. Use your text editor or IDE to open the application in this folder:
    `javascript_jquery\exercises\ch09\slide_show`
    Then, run the application to see how it works.

2. Modify the JavaScript and jQuery so the caption and the image slide up and then back down as the show moves from one slide to the next. Then, test to see how you like this.

3. Modify the JavaScript and jQuery so the caption is hidden by the hide() method and displayed by the show() method, both over an interval of one second. Also, increase the time for displaying and hiding the slide to two seconds, and increase the interval for the timer to five seconds. Then, test these changes.

4. If you're curious, experiment with effects, durations, and easings until you get the slide show to work in a way that you like.

Exercise 9-3   Modify the Carousel application

This is a simple exercise that tests whether you understand the code for the Carousel application in figure 9-10.

1. Use your text editor or IDE to open the application in this folder:
    `javascript_jquery\exercises\ch09\carousel`

2. The way it is now, nothing happens if you click on the left button when the first three books are displayed. Change this so the last three books are displayed when you click on the left button while the first three books are visible.

3. Modify the JavaScript and jQuery code so the carousel moves one book at a time when you click on one of the buttons instead of three books at a time. Now, what happens when you click on the right button when the last three books are displayed?

4. Modify the CSS and JavaScript and jQuery code so only one book is displayed. Otherwise, the application should work the same way.

10

How to work with forms and data validation

To get data from a user, you use HTML to create a form. Then, the user can enter data into the form and click on a button to submit that data to a web server for processing. Before the browser submits the data, though, it typically uses JavaScript to validate the data. In this chapter, you'll learn how to use jQuery to work with forms, and you'll learn some basic skills for using JavaScript and jQuery to validate the data in the browser.

Introduction to forms and controls

In chapter 6, you learned that a *form* contains one or more *controls* such as text boxes and buttons. The controls that accept user entries are also known as *fields*. The three figures that follow show how forms work and how to use the HTML5 features for working with forms.

How forms work

Figure 10-1 shows how to create a form that contains three controls: two text boxes and a button. To start, you code the form element. On the opening tag for this element, you code the action and method attributes. The action attribute specifies the file on the web server that processes the data when the form is submitted. The method attribute specifies the HTTP method that's used to send the form to the web server.

In the example in this figure, when the user clicks the Join our List button, the browser submits the form to the server using the HTTP GET method. Then, the server uses the code that's in the file named join.php to process the data. That file uses the PHP language to process the request.

When you use the HTTP GET method, the form data is included as part of the URL for the HTTP request. That means that the data is visible and the page can be bookmarked. This is illustrated by the URL in this figure. Here, the URL is followed by a question mark and name/value pairs separated by ampersands that present the name attributes and field values. In this case, two values are submitted: the email address and first name entries.

When you use the HTTP POST method, the form data is included as part of the HTTP request and isn't visible in the browser. This makes the submission more secure than when you use the HTTP GET method.

Within the opening and closing tags of the form element, you code the controls for the form. In this figure, the first two input elements are text boxes for getting the user's email address and first name. The third input element has "submit" as its type attribute, which means it is a *submit button*. When a user clicks it, the browser automatically submits the data in the form to the server.

If an input element has "reset" as its type attribute, the button is a *reset button*. When that type of button is clicked, the browser resets all of the values in the controls of the form to their starting HTML values.

When the browser submits a form to the server, code on the server should validate the data in the form before it processes that data. Then, if any of the data isn't valid, the server should send the form back to the browser with appropriate error messages so the entries can be corrected. This is referred to as *data validation*.

Usually, the browser also validates form data before it submits the data to the server. However, the validation done by the browser doesn't have to be as thorough as the server-side validation. If the browser validation catches 80 to 90% of the entry errors, it saves many round trips to the server.

A form in a web browser

The HTML for the form

```
<form id="email_form" name="email_form" action="join.php" method="get">
    <label for="email_address">Email Address:</label>
    <input type="text" id="email_address" name="email_address"><br>

    <label for="first_name">First Name:</label>
    <input type="text" id="first_name" name="first_name"><br>

    <label> </label>
    <input type="submit" id="join_list" value="Join our List"><br>
</form>
```

The URL when the form is submitted with the HTTP GET method

```
join.php?email_address=judy%40murach.com&first_name=Judy
```

Attributes of the form element

Attribute	Description
name	A name that can be referred to by client-side or server-side code.
action	A URL that maps to the file that processes the data in the form.
method	The HTTP method for submitting the form data. It is typically set to "get" or "post". The default value is "get".

Description

- A *form* contains one or more *controls* (or *fields*) like text boxes, radio buttons, lists, or check boxes that can receive data.

- When you click on a *submit button* for a form (type is "submit"), the form data is sent to the server as part of an HTTP request. When you click on a *reset button* for a form (type is "reset"), the form data is reset to its default values.

- When you use the "get" method to submit a form, the URL that requests the file is followed by a question mark and name/value pairs that are separated by ampersands. These pairs contain the name attributes and values of the data that is submitted. When you use the "post" method, the data is hidden.

- *Data validation* refers to checking the data collected by a form to make sure it is valid, and complete data validation is always done on the server. Then, if any invalid data is detected, the form is returned to the client so the user can correct the entries.

- To save round trips to the server when the data is invalid, some validation is usually done on the client before the data is sent to the server. However, this validation doesn't have to be as thorough as the validation that's done on the server.

Figure 10-1   How forms work

The HTML5 controls for working with forms

In case you aren't familiar with the HTML5 input controls, the first table in figure 10-2 summarizes some of the most common ones. When you use these controls, the type attribute indicates what type of data should be entered in the control. Then, in some cases, the browser validates the data that's entered into the text box that's displayed to be sure it's the right type. In other cases, the browser displays other types of controls to assist users in entering a valid value.

If, for example, you use "email" for the type attribute, all of the major browsers provide data validation for the email address that's entered into the text box. If you use "number" for the type attribute, all of the major browsers except Edge implement the control as a text box with up and down arrows that let the user increase or decrease the current value. And if you use "date" as the type attribute, most of the major browsers provide a good interface such as a popup calendar for allowing the user to select a date. However, this feature might not be supported in the same way by all browsers. For example, some versions of Safari use a text box with up and down arrows instead of a popup calendar. Still, these attributes indicate the type of data that the control is for, and that's good for semantic reasons.

HTML5 also provides attributes for working with controls, and two of the basic attributes are summarized in the second table in this figure. The autofocus attribute moves the focus to the control when the form is loaded. This means that you don't need to use JavaScript to do that. Also, you can use the placeholder attribute to put starting text in a control to help the user enter the data in the correct format. When the user starts to enter a value in the control, the browser removes the placeholder text.

The code example in this figure illustrates some of these controls and attributes. Here, the type attribute is set to "email" for the input control that accepts an email address. In addition, since this is the first input control in the form, the autofocus attribute is included so the control has the focus when the page is first displayed. The form in this figure shows the error message that's displayed in Chrome when an invalid entry is made in the email field.

The third input control in this example is for a telephone number and has its type attribute set to "tel". Although none of the current browsers provide data validation for this type, it's good to use it for semantic reasons. This control also uses the placeholder attribute to indicate the format of the phone number (999-999-9999). The form in this figure shows that this placeholder is displayed in a lighter color in Chrome.

Common HTML5 controls for input data

Control	Description
email	Gets an email address with validation done by the browser.
url	Gets a URL with validation done by the browser.
tel	Gets a telephone number with no validation done by the browser.
number	When supported, gets a numeric entry with min, max, and step attributes, browser validation, and up and down arrows.
range	When supported, gets a numeric entry with min, max, and step attributes, browser validation, and a slider control.
date	When supported, gets a date entry with min and max attributes and may include a popup calendar or up and down arrows.
time	When supported, gets a time entry with min and max attributes and may include up and down arrows.

The basic HTML5 attributes for working with forms

Attribute	Description
autofocus	A Boolean attribute that tells the browser to set the focus on the field when the page is loaded.
placeholder	A message in the field that is removed when an entry is made in the field.

The HTML for a form that uses some of these controls and attributes

```
<form id="email_form" name="email_form" action="join.php" method="get">
    <label for="email_address">Email Address:</label>
    <input type="email" id="email_address" name="email_address" autofocus><br>

    <label for="name">Name:</label>
    <input type="text" id="name" name="name"><br>

    <label for="phone">Phone Number:</label>
    <input type="tel" id="phone" name="phone" placeholder="999-999-9999"><br>

    <label> </label>
    <input type="submit" id="join_list" value="Join our List"><br>
</form>
```

The form in Chrome with an error message for the email address

Email Address: zak.modulemedia.com

Name:

Phone Number: 999-999-9999

Please include an '@' in the email address. 'zak.modulemedia.com' is missing an '@'.

Join

Description

- Many of the HTML5 input controls provide for basic data validation. You can also use the HTML5 attributes in figure 10-3 for data validation.

Figure 10-2   The HTML5 controls for working with forms

The HTML5 and CSS3 features for data validation

In addition to the HTML5 controls presented in the last figure, HTML5 and CSS3 provide some features specifically for data validation. These features are presented in figure 10-3.

For simple forms, you may be able to get by with just HTML5 controls and data validation attributes. For most forms, though, you are going to need JavaScript. That's because the HTML5 features don't provide for all of the types of validation that most forms need.

The table at the top of this figure summarizes the HTML5 attributes for data validation. To start, the required attribute causes the browser to check whether a field is empty before it submits the form for processing. If the field is empty, it displays a message and the form isn't submitted. The browser also highlights all of the other required fields that are empty when the submit button is clicked.

If you code a title attribute for a field, the value of that attribute is displayed when the mouse hovers over the field. It is also displayed at the end of the browser's standard error message for a field.

The pattern attribute provides for data validation through the use of regular expressions. A *regular expression* provides a way to match a user entry against a *pattern* of characters. As a result, regular expressions can be used for validating user entries like credit card numbers, zip codes, dates, or phone numbers. Regular expressions are supported by many programming languages including JavaScript, and now regular expressions are supported by HTML5. The trick of course is coding the regular expressions that you need, but chapter 13 shows how to do that.

If you want to stop a control from being validated, you can code the novalidate attribute for that control. And if you want to turn the auto-completion feature off for a control, you can set its autocomplete attribute to "off". By default, the *auto-completion feature* is on in all modern browsers. As a result, a browser displays a list of entry options when the user starts the entry for a field. These options are based on the entries the user has previously made for fields with similar names.

The code example in this figure shows how you can use some of these attributes. This form has the same fields as the form presented in the previous figure. However, it includes the required attribute for each input field. As a result, the user must make an entry for each field. In addition, it turns off the auto-completion feature for the email field, and it specifies a pattern and title for the phone field.

The form below the code example shows the error message that's displayed if the user enters a phone number with an invalid format. This error message includes the browser's standard error message as well as the text that's specified by the title attribute for this field.

This figure also presents three CSS3 pseudo-classes that you can use to format required, valid, and invalid fields. For instance, you can use the :required pseudo-class to format all required fields, and you can use the :invalid pseudo-class to format all invalid fields.

The HTML5 attributes for data validation

Attribute	Description
`required`	A Boolean attribute that indicates that a value is required for a field.
`title`	Text that is displayed in a tooltip when the mouse hovers over a field. This text is also displayed after the browser's default error message.
`pattern`	A regular expression that is used to validate the entry in a field.
`novalidate`	A Boolean attribute that tells the browser that it shouldn't validate the form or control that it is coded for.
`autocomplete`	Set this attribute to "off" to tell the browser to disable auto-completion. This can be coded for a form or a control.

CSS3 pseudo-classes for required, valid, and invalid fields

`:required`   `:valid`   `:invalid`

The HTML for a form that uses some of these attributes

```html
<form id="email_form" name="email_form" action="join.php" method="get">
    <label for="email_address">Email Address:</label>
    <input type="email" id="email_address" name="email_address"
        required autofocus autocomplete="off"><br>

    <label for="name">Name:</label>
    <input type="text" id="name" name="name" required><br>

    <label for="phone">Phone Number:</label>
    <input type="tel" id="phone" name="phone" required
        pattern="\d{3}[\-]\d{3}[\-]\d{4}"
        title="Must be 999-999-9999"><br>

    <label> </label>
    <input type="submit" id="join_list" value="Join our List"><br>
</form>
```

The form in Chrome with an error message for the phone field

Two of the reasons why you need JavaScript for data validation

- The HTML5 input controls and attributes for data validation may not be implemented the same way by all browsers.

- HTML5 is limited in the types of validation it can do. For instance, HTML5 can't check whether one field is equal to another, and it can't look up a state code in a table.

Figure 10-3   The HTML5 and CSS3 features for data validation

How to use jQuery to work with forms

jQuery provides selectors, methods, and event methods that make it easier to work with forms. However, as the next two figures show, jQuery doesn't provide specific features for data validation.

The jQuery selectors and methods for forms

The first table in figure 10-4 summarizes the jQuery selectors that you can use with forms. These selectors make it easy to select the various types of controls. They also make it easy to select disabled, enabled, checked, and selected controls.

The second table in this figure summarizes the val() methods that let you get and set the value in a control. For instance, the first example in this figure gets the entry in the control with "age" as its id and parses this entry into an integer before saving it in a constant named age.

The third table summarizes the jQuery trim() method that removes all spaces at the start and end of a string. The second example in this figure shows how to use this method to trim the entry in the control with "first_name" as its id before the entry is saved in the constant named firstName. The second statement in this example puts that trimmed entry back into the control.

The third example in this figure shows how to get the value of the checked radio button in a named group. Here, an attribute selector selects all of the input elements with a name attribute of "contact_by". That includes all the radio buttons in the group, since they all must have the same name. Then, it uses the :checked selector to get the radio button within that group with a checked attribute of true. This works because only one radio button in a named group can be selected. Finally, the val() method gets the selected radio button's value and saves that value in the constant named radioButton.

The fourth example shows how to get an array of the selected options from a select list that allows multiple selections. Here, the first statement creates an empty array named selectOptions. Then, the second statement uses the :selected selector to get all of the selected options in a select list with an id of "select_list", and it saves these options in the selectOptions variable.

In this example, there's a space between the id of the select list and the :selected selector. That's because a select list consists of a select element that contains option elements. So the selector in this example selects all the descendant option elements that are selected. Another way to code this statement would be like this:

```
selectOptions = $("#select_list option:selected");
```

By contrast, there's no space before the :checked selector in the third example. That's because a group of radio buttons consists of independent input elements with the same name attribute. So the selector in the third example selects the radio button that's checked in the group.

The jQuery selectors for form controls

Selector	Selects
:input	All input, select, textarea, and button elements.
:text	All text boxes: input elements with type equal to "text".
:radio	All radio buttons: input elements with type equal to "radio".
:checkbox	All check boxes: input elements with type equal to "checkbox".
:file	All file upload fields: input elements with type equal to "file".
:password	All password fields: input elements with type equal to "password".
:submit	All submit buttons and button elements: input elements with type equal to "submit" and button elements.
:reset	All reset buttons: input elements with type equal to "reset".
:image	All image buttons: input elements with type equal to "image".
:button	All buttons: button elements and input elements with type equal to "button".
:disabled	All disabled elements: elements that have the disabled attribute.
:enabled	All enabled elements: elements that don't have the disabled attribute.
:checked	All check boxes and radio buttons that are checked.
:selected	All options in select elements that are selected.

The jQuery methods for getting and setting control values

Method	Description
val()	Gets the value of a text box or other form control.
val(value)	Sets the value of a text box or other form control.

The jQuery method for trimming an entry

Method	Description
trim()	Removes all spaces at the start and end of the string.

How to get the value of a numeric entry from a text box

```
const age = parseInt($("#age").val());
```

How to trim the value of an entry and put it back into the same text box

```
const firstName = $("#first_name").val().trim();
$("#first_name").val(firstName);
```

How to get the value of the checked radio button in a group

```
const radioButton = $("input[name='contact_by']:checked").val();
```

How to get an array of the selected options from a list

```
let selectOptions = [];
selectOptions = $("#select_list :selected");
```

Description

- jQuery provides special selectors for selecting the controls on a form, the val() method for getting and setting the value in a control, and the trim() method for trimming an entry.

Figure 10-4   The jQuery selectors and methods for forms

The jQuery event methods for forms

The first table in figure 10-5 summarizes the jQuery event methods for working with forms, and you have already been introduced to some of these. For instance, the handler for the focus() event method runs when the focus moves to the selected element, and the handler for the change() event method runs when the value in the selected element is changed.

The last event method in this table runs when the submit event occurs. That event occurs when the user clicks on a submit button or when the user moves the focus to the submit button and presses the Enter key. But it also occurs when the jQuery for a page calls the submit() method to trigger the submit event.

The second table summarizes the jQuery methods for triggering (starting) events. If, for example, you write code that calls the focus() method of a text box, the browser moves the focus to that text box and triggers the focus event. However, if a handler hasn't been assigned to that event, that event isn't processed.

The names of these triggering methods are the same as the names of the event methods. However, the event methods accept an event handler, and the triggering methods don't accept any arguments.

The examples in this figure show how you can use these event methods. To start, the first example uses the change() event method to create an event handler for the change event of a check box with "contact_me" as its id. Then, the function within this handler checks whether the checked attribute of the box is checked. If so, the code turns off the disabled attribute of all of the radio buttons on the form. Otherwise, the code turns on the disabled attribute for all of the radio buttons.

Code like this is useful for an application where the radio buttons should only be enabled if the check box is checked. If, for example, the user checks the Contact Me box, the radio buttons should be enabled so the user can click the preferred method of contact. Otherwise, the radio buttons should be disabled.

The second example in this figure shows how to trigger the submit event at the end of an event handler for the click event of an input button with "button" as its type attribute. Here, the function for the event handler starts by validating the code in all of the entries. Then, if all the entries are valid, it uses the submit() method to trigger the submit event of the form that submits the form to the server.

Another way to provide for data validation is to use a submit button instead of a regular button. Then, you can code an event handler for the submit event of the form. Within that handler, you can test all of the entries for validity. If they are all valid, you can let the handler end so the form is submitted. However, if one or more entries are invalid, you can call the preventDefault() method of the event object to cancel the submission of the form. This is illustrated by the Validation application presented in figure 10-6.

The jQuery event methods for forms

Event method	Description
`focus(handler)`	The handler runs when the focus moves to the selected element.
`blur(handler)`	The handler runs when the focus leaves the selected element.
`change(handler)`	The handler runs when the value in the selected element is changed.
`select(handler)`	The handler runs when the user selects text in a text or textarea box.
`submit(handler)`	The handler runs when a submit button is clicked.

The jQuery methods for triggering events

Method	Description
`focus()`	Moves the focus to the selected element and triggers the focus event.
`blur()`	Removes the focus from the selected element and triggers the blur event.
`change()`	Triggers the change event.
`select()`	Triggers the select event.
`submit()`	Triggers the submit event for a form.

A handler that disables or enables radio buttons when a check box is checked or unchecked

```
$("#contact_me").change( () => {            // the change event for a check box
    if ($("#contact_me").attr("checked")) {
        $(":radio").attr("disabled", false)  // enable radio buttons
    } else {
        $(":radio").attr("disabled", true)   // disable radio buttons
    }
});
```

A handler that triggers the submit event after some data validation

```
$("#join_list").click( () => {  // a regular button, not a submit button

    // the data validation code goes here

    $("#email_form").submit();
});
```

Description

- You can use event handlers for the focus, blur, change, and select events to process data as the user works with individual controls.

- You can use an event handler for the click event of a regular button, not a submit button, to validate the data in a form. Then, if the data is valid, you can use the submit() method to submit the form.

- You can use an event handler for the submit event of a form to validate data before it is sent to the server. Then, if any of the data is invalid, you can issue the preventDefault() method of the event object to cancel the submission of the data to the server.

Figure 10-5   The jQuery event methods for forms

A Validation application

To show how you can use jQuery to work with forms, this chapter ends by presenting a simple Validation application. This application shows how easy it is to use jQuery to access user entries and display error messages. To test the validity of the user entries, though, you need to use JavaScript.

The user interface and HTML

Parts 1 and 2 of figure 10-6 present the user interface and HTML for the Validation application. To use the form, the user enters data into the text boxes. The user can also use the radio buttons to determine if the membership is for an individual or a company. By default, the Individual radio button is selected and the Company Name text box is disabled. If the user selects the Corporate radio button, though, the Company Name text box is enabled.

Once the form is complete, the user can click on the Submit button. Or, if the user wants to start over, she can click on the Reset button to return the fields to their original values.

In the HTML for this form, the id of the form is "member_form" and the Submit button at the bottom of the form is the "submit" type. This means that it automatically submits the form to the server when it is clicked. However, the JavaScript and jQuery for this form validate the entries before the form is actually submitted and cancels the submission if any entries are invalid.

Like the Email List application that you've seen in previous chapters, each text box in this application is followed by a span element. The application uses these span elements to display error messages to the right of the user entries as shown here. When the form is first loaded, the initial value of all but one of these span elements is an asterisk. This indicates that these fields are required. The exception is the span element for the Company Name text box. Because this text box is disabled by default, the span element that follows it has no initial value.

This HTML uses placeholder attributes for the password and phone number fields on this form. For the phone number field, this shows the user the entry format that should be used. For the password field, it's used to provide an entry hint. Remember, though, that as soon as the user starts entering a value into a field with a placeholder, the placeholder text disappears.

On the other hand, this HTML doesn't use the HTML5 type attributes for email, phone, and date entries. That way, you don't have to worry about getting some unexpected validation messages from the browser, like a message that indicates an invalid email address. Instead, the JavaScript and jQuery control the validation that's done.

The Validation application

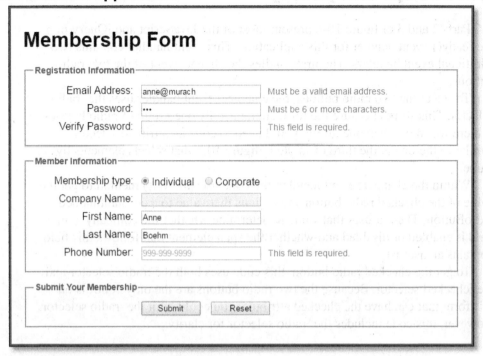

The HTML for the form

```html
<form action="register.html" method="get"
    name="member_form" id="member_form">
    <fieldset>
        <legend>Registration Information</legend>
        <div>
            <label for="email">Email Address:</label>
            <input type="text" id="email" name="email">
            <span>*</span>
        </div>
        <div>
            <label for="password">Password:</label>
            <input type="password" id="password" name="password"
                   placeholder="At least 6 characters" >
            <span>*</span>
        </div>
        <div>
            <label for="verify">Verify Password:</label>
            <input type="password" id="verify" name="verify">
            <span>*</span>
        </div>
    </fieldset>
```

Figure 10-6   The Validation application (part 1)

The JavaScript and jQuery

Parts 2 and 3 of figure 10-6 present most of the JavaScript and jQuery in the ready() event handler for this application. This event handler contains two additional event handlers. The first handles the change event of the two radio buttons.

To select the two radio buttons, the change() event handler uses the :radio selector. This works because the form contains only one group of radio buttons. If there was more than one group, you'd need to code an attribute selector similar to the one in the third example in figure 10-4 that selects elements by name.

Within the change() event handler, the code uses the val() method to get the value of the checked radio button and assigns that value to a constant named radioButton. Then, it uses that value to determine whether the company_name field is enabled or disabled and whether the span element that follows this field contains an asterisk.

To get the checked radio button, this code uses both the :radio selector and the :checked selector. Because the two radio buttons are the only controls on this form that can have the checked attribute, you could omit the :radio selector. However, this code includes the :radio selector for clarity.

The HTML for the form (continued)

```html
<fieldset>
    <legend>Member Information</legend>
    <div>
        <label>Membership type:</label>
        <input type="radio" name="type" id="individual"
               value="individual" checked>Individual
        <input type="radio" name="type" id="corporate"
               value="corporate">Corporate
    </div>
    <div>
        <label for="company_name">Company Name:</label>
        <input type="text" id="company_name" name="company_name" disabled>
        <span></span>
    </div>

    <!-- First and Last Name fields are omitted here -->

    <div>
        <label for="phone">Phone Number:</label>
        <input type="text" id="phone" name="phone"
               placeholder="999-999-9999">
        <span>*</span>
    </div>
</fieldset>
<fieldset id="buttons">
    <legend>Submit Your Membership</legend>
    <div>
        <label> </label>
        <input type="submit" id="submit" name="submit" value="Submit">
        <input type="reset" id="reset" name="reset" value="Reset">
    </div>
</fieldset>
</form>
```

The JavaScript and jQuery

```javascript
"use strict";
$(document).ready( () => {

    // move focus to first text box
    $("#email").focus();

    // the handler for the change event of the radio buttons
    $(":radio").change( () => {
        const radioButton = $(":radio:checked").val();
        if (radioButton == "corporate") {
            $("#company_name").attr("disabled", false);
            $("#company_name").next().text("*");
        } else {
            $("#company_name").attr("disabled", true);
            $("#company_name").next().text("");
        }
    });
});
```

Figure 10-6   The Validation application (part 2)

The event handler for the submit event of the form contains the validation routines for all of the text boxes on the form. This figure only presents the validation code for three of those fields. However, that should give you a good idea of how you can use JavaScript and jQuery for data validation.

The validation for the email entry shows how you can use a regular expression for validation. Chapter 13 presents regular expressions in more detail. For now, you just need to know that the test() method of a regular expression checks that a value has the specified pattern. In this case, the test() method checks that the user entry for the email field matches the pattern in the emailPattern constant. If it doesn't, the jQuery next() and text() methods are used to display an error message in the span element that follows the email field.

This figure also shows the validation for the password and company name. To validate the password, the code uses the length property of a string to check whether the length of the entry is less than 6. In a more realistic application, extensive string handling would be used to validate this entry. To validate the company name, the code checks the control to be sure it's enabled. If so, the code checks the user entry to make sure some data has been entered.

For all fields, the validation uses the jQuery trim() method to trim each entry before it checks whether the entry is equal to an empty string. That way, an entry of one or more spaces isn't treated as a valid entry. After the validation is complete, the val() method assigns the trimmed entry back to the field. That way, the code always displays the entry without any leading or trailing spaces.

After the validation code finishes, this event handler uses a final if statement to check whether the isValid variable is false. If so, one or more of the fields are invalid. In that case, the code calls the preventDefault() method of the Event object that's passed to the submit() event handler. This prevents the form from being submitted to the server. If you forget to call the preventDefault() method when one or more fields are invalid, the browser submits the form to the server, which isn't what you want for this application.

The JavaScript and jQuery (continued)

```javascript
    // the handler for the click event of the submit button
    $("#member_form").submit( event => {
        let isValid = true;

        // validate the email entry with a regular expression
        const emailPattern =
            /\b[A-Za-z0-9._%+-]+@[A-Za-z0-9.-]+\.[A-Za-z]{2,4}\b/;
        const email = $("#email").val().trim();
        if (email == "") {
            $("#email").next().text("This field is required.");
            isValid = false;
        } else if ( !emailPattern.test(email) ) {
            $("#email").next().text("Must be a valid email address.");
            isValid = false;
        } else {
            $("#email").next().text("");
        }
        $("#email").val(email);

        // validate the password entry
        const password = $("#password").val().trim();
        if ( password.length < 6) {
            $("#password").next().text("Must be 6 or more characters.");
            isValid = false;
        } else {
            $("#password").next().text("");
        }
        $("#password").val(password);

        // validate the verify password entry (not shown here)

        // validate the company name entry
        if ( !$("#company_name").attr("disabled")) {
            const companyName = $("#company_name").val().trim();
            if (companyName == "") {
                $("#company_name").next().text("This field is required.");
                isValid = false;
            } else {
                $("#company_name").next().text("");
            }
            $("#company_name").val(companyName);
        }

        // validate other text boxes (not shown here)

        // prevent the submission of the form if any entries are invalid
        if (isValid == false) {
            event.preventDefault();
        }
    });

}); // end ready() handler
```

Figure 10-6   The Validation application (part 3)

Perspective

At this point, you should be comfortable with the jQuery features for working with forms. You should also realize that you need both JavaScript and jQuery to validate the data on a form. In this chapter, you learned some of the basic JavaScript and jQuery skills for data validation, and you'll learn more in the chapters in section 3.

Terms

form	data validation
control	regular expression
field	pattern
submit button	auto-completion feature
reset button	

Summary

- A *form* contains one or more *controls* like text boxes, radio buttons, and check boxes that can receive data. These controls are also referred to as *fields*. When a form is submitted to the server for processing, the data in the controls is sent along with the HTTP request.

- A *submit button* submits the form data to the server when the button is clicked. A *reset button* resets all the data in the form when it is clicked.

- HTML5 introduces some input controls like the email, url, tel, and date controls that are good semantically because they indicate what types of data the controls are for. HTML5 also introduces some attributes for *data valida-tion*, and CSS3 introduces some pseudo-classes for formatting required, valid, and invalid fields.

- When a form is submitted to the server, the server should provide complete validation of the data in the form and return the form to the client if any errors are found.

- Before a form is submitted to the server, JavaScript should try to catch 80% or more of the entry errors. That reduces the number of trips to the server and back that are required to process the form.

- jQuery provides some selectors, methods, and event methods for working with forms, but nothing for data validation. So, to validate the entries that a user makes, many developers use JavaScript features like *regular expres-sions* and string methods.

Exercise 10-1   Validate with JavaScript

This exercise guides you through the process of making some enhancements to the Email List application. The form for this application looks like this:

Please join our email list

Email Address:	anne@murachcom	Must be a valid email address.
Confirm Email Address:	anne@murach.com	Must equal first email entry.
First Name:		This field is required.
Last Name:	Boehm	
State Code:	California	Use 2-character code.
Zip Code:	93722-1234	Use 99999 format.
Email me about:	☐ Web books ☐ Java books ☐ .NET books	Select at least one.

[Join List] [Reset]

1. Use your text editor or IDE to open the application in this folder:
   `javascript_jquery\exercises\ch10\email_list`

2. Test the application, and notice that the focus isn't in the first text box. Modify the JavaScript so it moves the focus to the first text box when the document is loaded, and then test again.

3. Review the code in the JavaScript file, and note that it contains validation routines for the first five fields. Then, test this form by clicking the Join List button before you enter any data in this form. Oops! The data is submitted even though no entries have been made.

4. To fix this, you must stop the default action of the submit button. To do that, code the preventDefault() method of the Event object in the if statement at the end of the file, as in figure 10-6. Remember that the name that you use for the Event object must be the same as the name of the parameter that's used for the submit() event handler. Now, test again with empty fields. This should display "This field is required." to the right of each field except the zip-code and email-me-about fields.

5. Enter four spaces in the first-name field and click the Join List button again. Note that the error message is removed, which means the four spaces have been accepted as a valid entry.

6. Fix this problem by trimming the first-name entry before it is validated, as in the code for the last-name entry. This trimmed value should also be placed in the text box whether or not the entry is valid. Test this enhancement by first entering just four spaces in this field and then by entering four spaces followed by a first name.

7. Add the code for validating the zip-code field. An entry is required, the entry must be numeric, and the entry must be five digits. Now, test this change.

8. Add the code for validating the check boxes. For this application, at least one check box must be selected. To perform this validation, you can create a variable that holds an array. Then, you can get all the check boxes that are selected. To do that, you can use the :checkbox and :checked selectors. If none of the check boxes are selected, display an error message in the span element that follows the last check box. Otherwise, clear that span element.

11

How to use jQuery plugins and UI widgets

One easy way to add common features like accordions, tabs, and carousels to your web pages is to use jQuery plugins and jQuery UI widgets. This chapter shows how to do that.

Introduction to jQuery plugins

In this introduction, you'll learn how to find and use jQuery plugins. A *jQuery plugin* is just a jQuery application that does one web task or a set of related web tasks. A plugin makes use of the jQuery library, and most plugins can be used with limited knowledge of JavaScript and jQuery.

How to find jQuery plugins

Figure 11-1 starts with a screen capture that shows the results of a Google search for "jquery rotator plugin". Often, searching the web like this is the best way to find what you're looking for. When you perform a search like this one, you should include the word *jquery* because there are other types of plugins.

Another way to find the type of plugin that you want is to go to the URLs for the websites shown this figure. The first one is for the jQuery Plugin Registry, which is part of the jQuery website. By contrast, the next three websites are repositories for many types of code, including jQuery plugins. As a result, you must search for jQuery plugins to find what you want on these sites.

In most cases, jQuery plugins are free or are available for a small price or donation. Besides that, jQuery plugins can often be used by non-programmers, and they can save you many hours of development time if you are a JavaScript programmer. For those reasons, it makes sense to look for a plugin whenever you need to add a common function to your website.

This figure also summarizes some of the most useful plugins for displaying images, creating slide shows and carousels, and performing data validation. In a moment, this chapter will show how to use three of these plugins to work with images, slide shows, and carousels.

A Google search for a jQuery plugin

Websites for finding jQuery plugins

Site name	URL
jQuery Plugin Registry	https://plugins.jquery.com
Google Code	https://code.google.com
GitHub	https://github.com
Sourceforge	https://sourceforge.net

Popular plugins for displaying images

Lightbox	https://lokeshdhakar.com/projects/lightbox2
Fancybox	https://fancyapps.com
ThickBox	http://codylindley.com/thickbox
ColorBox	https://www.jacklmoore.com/colorbox

Popular plugins for slide shows and carousels

bxSlider	https://bxslider.com
Malsup jQuery Cycle 2	http://jquery.malsup.com/cycle2
jCarousel	https://sorgalla.com/jcarousel

A popular plugin for data validation

jQuery Validation	https://jqueryvalidation.org/

Description

- jQuery *plugins* are JavaScript applications that extend the functionality of jQuery. These plugins require the use of the core jQuery library.

- Plugins are available for hundreds of web functions like slide shows, carousels, tabs, menus, text layout, data validation, and mobile application development.

- Some of the websites that provide jQuery plugins are listed above. Often, though, you can find what you're looking for by searching the Internet.

- In general, if you can find a plugin for doing what you want, that's better than writing the JavaScript code yourself.

Figure 11-1   How to find jQuery plugins

How to use any jQuery plugin

Figure 11-2 shows how to use any plugin after you find the one you want. First, you study the documentation for the plugin so you know what HTML and CSS it requires and what methods and options it provides. Usually, you can do this as you evaluate the plugin to determine if it does what you want and if its documentation tells you everything you need to know.

Second, you usually download the files for the plugin and save them on your web server. This download is often a zip file, and it always includes at least one JavaScript file. In addition, it may include any CSS or image files used by the plugin.

The download may also include two versions of the main JavaScript file for the plugin. If you want to review the code for the file, you can open the full version in your text editor. However, you should use the compressed version for your applications. That version usually has a name that ends with min.js.

For some plugins, the files are also available from a Content Delivery Network (CDN). If you want to access the files that way, you can use those URLs in the link and script elements for the files.

Third, if a plugin requires one or more CSS files, you code the link elements for them in the head element of the HTML. Then, at the end of the body element, you can code the script elements for the JavaScript files for the plugin. Usually, only one JavaScript file is required, but some plugins require more than one.

Fourth, if the download includes a folder for images, you need to make sure the folder has the right structural relationship with the CSS and JavaScript files for the plugin. Otherwise, you may have to adjust the CSS or JavaScript code so it can find the images folder (and you probably don't want to do that).

Fifth, you code the HTML and CSS for the plugin. And sixth, you code the JavaScript and jQuery for using the plugin. You can store this code in an external JavaScript file. Alternately, you can store this code in a script element within the HTML file. Since this code is typically short, this approach often makes sense.

The examples show how to apply this procedure to the bxSlider plugin. Here, the script elements show that the element for the plugin must come after the element for the jQuery library. That's because all jQuery plugins use the jQuery library. As this figure points out, not coding these script elements in this sequence is a common error.

The HTML shows the elements that the plugin requires. To start, this code sets the id attribute for the unordered list to "slider". That way, the jQuery code can select that element when it calls the bxSlider() method of the plugin. Also, the code sets the title attributes for the img elements to the captions for the slides.

The jQuery code for using this plugin calls the bxSlider() method as the first and only statement within the ready() event handler. Within the parentheses for the bxSlider() method, the code supplies a set of braces that contains the code for setting four options for this method.

Note that some plugins don't work with the latest version of jQuery. So if a plugin doesn't work, you can check its documentation to see what versions of jQuery it supports. For example, the documentation for the bxSlider plugin says it only supports jQuery 3.1.1 or earlier.

General steps for using a plugin within your web pages

1. Study the documentation for the plugin so you know what HTML and CSS it requires as well as what methods and options it provides.

2. If the plugin file or files are available via a Content Delivery Network (CDN) and you want to access them that way, get the URLs for them. Otherwise, download the file or files for the plugin, and save them in one of the folders of your website.

3. In the head element of the HTML, code the link elements for any CSS files that are required. Also, at the end of the body element, code the script elements for the JavaScript files that are required.

4. If the download for a plugin includes an images folder, make sure the folder has the right structural relationship with both the CSS and JavaScript files for the plugin.

5. Code the HTML and CSS for the page so it's appropriate for the plugin.

6. If necessary, write the JavaScript and jQuery code that uses the methods and options of the plugin.

The script elements for the jQuery library and the bxSlider plugin

```
<script src="https://code.jquery.com/jquery-3.1.1.min.js"></script>
<script src="js/jquery.bxSlider.min.js"></script>
```

The HTML for the bxSlider plugin

```
<ul id="slider">
    <li><img src="images/building_01.jpg" alt="" title="Front"></li>
    <li><img src="images/building_02.jpg" alt="" title="Left side"></li>
    ...
</ul>
```

The JavaScript and jQuery for using the bxSlider plugin

```
$(document).ready( ()=>
    $("#slider").bxSlider({
        minSlides: 2,
        maxSlides: 2,
        slideWidth: 250,
        slideMargin: 10
    })
)
```

Two cautions

- Make sure to include a script element for jQuery before the script element for the plugin.

- Some plugins don't work with the latest version of jQuery. So if you have problems with a plugin, check its documentation to see which versions of jQuery it supports.

Description

- Some plugins can be accessed via a CDN. Others must be downloaded and stored on your server.

Figure 11-2   How to use any jQuery plugin

How to use three of the most popular plugins

Now, this chapter shows how to work with three of the most useful plugins. This should introduce you to the power of plugins. It should also show you how to apply the procedure in the last figure to a specific plugin.

How to use the Lightbox plugin for images

Figure 11-3 presents the Lightbox plugin. This is a popular plugin that displays a larger version of a thumbnail image when the user clicks the thumbnail image. This image is displayed in a *modal dialog box*, which means that it must be closed before the user can continue. The image in this box has a thick white border, and it may have a caption below it. The part of the web page that's outside of the dialog box is darkened. To close the dialog box, the user clicks on the "X" in the bottom right corner.

If images are grouped in sets, this plugin not only displays the dialog box for the thumbnail, it also displays the image number and total number of images below the image, as in "Image 3 of 5". Also, when the mouse hovers over the left or right side of an image, the plugin displays previous and next icons. Then, if the user clicks on an icon, the plugin displays the previous or next image.

The link and script elements in this example show that this plugin requires both CSS and JavaScript files. These elements use the names of the downloaded files. Remember, though, that the script element for the plugin must come after the script element for the jQuery library.

The download also includes an images folder that contains the images used by the plugin. Here again, you must maintain the proper relationship between the images folder and the JavaScript and CSS files for this plugin.

Next, this figure shows the HTML for using this plugin. Here, img elements that represent the thumbnail images are coded within <a> elements. To make this work, each <a> element must have an href attribute that identifies the related large image and a data-lightbox attribute that activates the Lightbox plugin.

If you're using the Lightbox plugin with independent images, the value of the data-lightbox attribute should be unique for each <a> element. On the other hand, if you're using this plugin with a set of related images as shown here, the value of this attribute should be the same for all <a> elements. In addition, you can use the data-title attribute to provide a caption for each image.

With the Lightbox plugin, that's all you have to do. That's because you don't have to initiate the Lightbox plugin by calling one of its methods. In other words, no JavaScript code is required. It just works!

A Lightbox after the user has clicked on a thumbnail image to start it

Left side
Image 2 of 5

The URL for the Lightbox website

https://lokeshdhakar.com/projects/lightbox2/

The link and script elements for the Lightbox plugin

```
<link href="styles.css" rel="stylesheet">
<link href="css/lightbox.css" rel="stylesheet">
<script src="https://code.jquery.com/jquery-3.4.1.min.js"></script>
<script src="js/lightbox.min.js"></script>
```

The HTML for the images used by the Lightbox plugin

```
<a href="images/building_01.jpg" data-lightbox="vecta" data-title="Front">
    <img src="images/building_01_thumb.jpg" alt=""></a>
<a href="images/building_02.jpg" data-lightbox="vecta" data-title="Left side">
    <img src="images/building_02_thumb.jpg" alt=""></a>
...
```

Description

- The Lightbox plugin can be used to display larger versions of thumbnail images. The Lightbox starts when the user clicks one of the thumbnail images.

- When the user clicks on a thumbnail image within a set of images, the browser darkens the rest of the page and displays the image with a counter and a caption. Then, if the user moves the pointer over the image, the browser displays next or previous icons.

- The Lightbox download includes a CSS file, a plugin file, and an images folder that contains an image for loading and images for the close, next, and previous icons.

- The HTML for a Lightbox consists of img elements within <a> elements. The src attribute of each img element identifies the thumbnail image, and the href attribute of each <a> element identifies the larger image.

- The data-lightbox attribute of each <a> element activates the Lightbox plugin. This should be the same for a group of images but should be unique for an independent image.

- The data-title attribute of each <a> element sets the caption for the image.

Figure 11-3   How to use the Lightbox plugin for images

How to use the bxSlider plugin for carousels

Figure 11-4 shows how to use the bxSlider plugin for creating carousels. In this example, the bxSlider plugin displays two images at a time, it slides from one set of images to the next automatically, it provides captions for the slides, it provides controls below the carousel, and you can move to the next or previous image by clicking on the right or left icon that's displayed.

If you download the JavaScript file for this plugin, the script element can refer to it as shown in this figure. As part of this download, you also get a CSS file and an images folder that's used with this plugin.

This figure shows one way to set up the HTML for this plugin. Here, the HTML places img elements within the li elements of an unordered list. Then, the src attributes of the img elements identify the images to display, and the title attributes provide the captions.

To run the bxSlider plugin, you use the JavaScript and jQuery code shown here. Within the ready() event handler, the selector selects the ul element that contains the slides and executes the bxSlider() method.

Within the parentheses of that method, the code sets several options. The auto option makes the carousel run automatically, the autoControls option puts the controls below the carousel, the captions option causes the title attributes to be used for captions, the minSlides and maxSlides options set the carousel so it always displays 2 slides, and the slideWidth and slideMargin options set the size of the slides and the space between them.

These options show just some of the capabilities of this plugin. To learn more, you can go to the website for this plugin and review its demos and option summaries.

When you use this plugin, you may want to change the location of components like the left and right icons, the captions (which were adjusted for this example), and the controls below the carousel. To do that, you can adjust the styles in the CSS file for this plugin.

If, for example, you want to adjust the location of the left and right icons, like moving them outside of the slider, you can modify the CSS for the bx.next and bx.prev classes. These classes aren't in the HTML file, though, because the plugin adds them to the DOM. Usually, you can learn a lot by studying the code in the CSS files for plugins and by making adjustments to that code.

A web page that uses the bxSlider plugin for a carousel

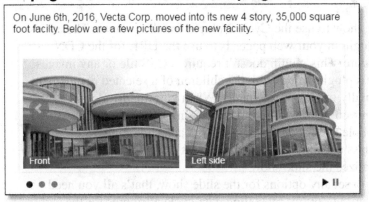

The URL for the bxSlider website

https://bxslider.com

The link and script elements for the bxSlider plugin

```
<link href="styles.css" rel="stylesheet">
<link href="jquery.bxslider.css" rel="stylesheet">
<script src="https://code.jquery.com/jquery-3.1.1.min.js"></script>
<script src="js/jquery.bxSlider.min.js">
```

The HTML for the bxSlider plugin

```
<ul id="slider">
    <li><img src="images/building_01.jpg" alt="" title="Front"></li>
    <li><img src="images/building_02.jpg" alt="" title="Left side"></li>
    ...
</ul>
```

The JavaScript and jQuery for using some of the bxSlider options

```
$(document).ready( () =>
    $("#slider").bxSlider({
        auto: true,
        autoControls: true,
        captions: true,
        minSlides: 2,
        maxSlides: 2,
        slideWidth: 250,
        slideMargin: 10
    })
)
```

Description

- The bxSlider plugin makes it easy to develop a carousel. The HTML specifies an unordered list with one list item for each slide that contains images or other HTML.
- The bxSlider website provides excellent examples and option summaries.
- If the slide images contain title attributes, the captions option makes them captions.
- The bxSlider download consists of a JavaScript file, a CSS file, and an images folder that contains the images used by the plugin.

Figure 11-4   How to use the bxSlider plugin for carousels

How to use the Cycle 2 plugin for slide shows

Figure 11-5 shows how to use the Cycle 2 plugin for slide shows. The easiest way to include this plugin in your web pages is to use the URL for the CDN that's shown in this figure. This plugin doesn't require a CSS file or any images.

The HTML for this plugin works with the children of a selected div element. These children are usually img or div elements. When you use div elements, you can code whatever you want within them, including headings, text, lists, and images. This example uses one img element for each slide in the show. The HTML sets the class attribute for the slide show's div element to "cycle-slideshow". This initializes the slide show.

If you don't want to set any options for the slide show, that's all you need to do. However, you can set options by coding data-cycle attributes for the slide show's div element. In this example, the code sets the options for the effect (fx) that's used to move from slide to slide as well as for how many milliseconds each slide should be displayed, where the captions should be displayed, and what caption template should be used. Here, the caption option points to the div element that's coded after the img elements.

If you prefer, you don't need to use the "cycle-slideshow" class to initialize a slide show and the data-cycle attributes to set options. Instead, you can call the cycle() method of the slide show's div element to initialize the slide show and code the options like you do for the bxSlider plugin. In general, though, most programmers prefer the approach in this figure.

The Cycle 2 website provides demos that show the many ways that you can use this plugin. In addition, it provides a complete summary of the options for this plugin.

A web page that uses the Cycle 2 plugin for slide shows

On June 6th, 2016, Vecta Corp. moved into its new 4 story, 35,000 square foot facilty. Below are a few pictures of the new facility.

Slide 2: Left side

The URL for the Cycle 2 website

http://jquery.malsup.com/cycle2/

The script elements for the Cycle 2 plugin

```
<script src="https://code.jquery.com/jquery-3.4.1.min.js"></script>
<script src="https://malsup.github.com/jquery.cycle2.js"></script>
```

The HTML for the Cycle 2 plugin

```
<div class="cycle-slideshow"
        data-cycle-fx="scrollHorz"
        data-cycle-timeout="2000"
        data-cycle-caption="#adv-custom-caption"
        data-cycle-caption-template="Slide {{slideNum}}: {{cycleTitle}}" >
    <img src="images/building_01.jpg" alt="" data-cycle-title="Front">
    <img src="images/building_02.jpg" alt="" data-cycle-title="Left side">
    ...
    <!-- empty element for caption -->
    <div id="adv-custom-caption"></div>
</div>
```

Description

- The Cycle 2 plugin treats the children of a div element as the slides. Those children are usually img elements, but they can be div elements that contain both text and images.
- The best way to include this plugin in your web pages is to use the GitHub CDN for it.
- The Cycle 2 website provides excellent demos and summaries that let you enhance a slide show in many ways.
- To set options for a slide show, you can code data-cycle attributes for the div element.
- To provide captions below the slides, you can code data-cycle-title attributes for the img elements, a data-cycle-caption attribute for the div element, and an empty div element for the captions below the slides.

Figure 11-5   How to use the Cycle 2 plugin for slide shows

Introduction to jQuery UI

To get you started with jQuery UI, the next few figures describe what it is, where to get it, how to download it, and how to add it to your web pages.

What jQuery UI is and where to get it

jQuery UI (User Interface) is a free, open-source, JavaScript library that extends the use of the jQuery library by providing higher-level features that you can use with a minimum of code. To provide those features, the jQuery UI library uses the jQuery library. In fact, you can think of jQuery UI as the official plugin library for jQuery.

Figure 11-6 shows the home page and the URL for the jQuery UI website. That's the site where you can download jQuery UI. The quickest way to do that is to click the Stable button in the Quick Downloads box on the right of the page.

This figure also summarizes the four types of features that jQuery UI provides. *Widgets* are controls like accordions, tabs, and date pickers. These are the jQuery features that developers use the most, and this chapter shows how to use five of them.

Themes provide the formatting for widgets, and they are implemented by a CSS style sheet that's part of the jQuery UI download. Interactions and effects are less-used features, so this book doesn't show how to use them.

The jQuery UI website

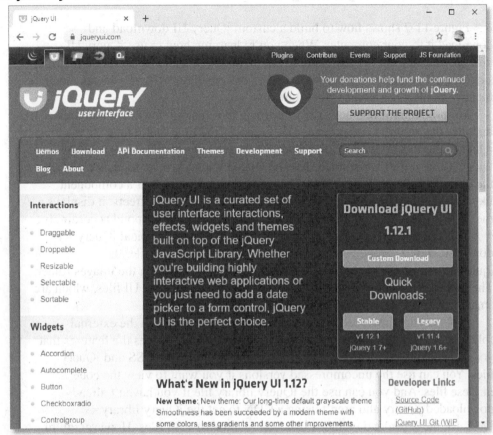

The URL for jQuery UI

https://jqueryui.com/

The four types of features provided by jQuery UI

Name	Description
Widgets	Accordions, tabs, date pickers, and more.
Themes	25 predefined themes as well as a ThemeRoller application that lets you create a custom theme. A theme is implemented by a CSS style sheet.
Interactions	Draggable, droppable, resizable, and more.
Effects	Color animations, class transitions, and more.

Description

- *jQuery UI* is a free, open-source, JavaScript library that extends the jQuery library by providing higher-level features. jQuery UI uses jQuery and can be thought of as the official plugin library for jQuery.

Figure 11-6   What jQuery UI is and where to get it

How to download jQuery UI

Figure 11-7 shows how to build a custom jQuery UI download and download it to your computer. When you're learning how to use jQuery UI, though, you can just click the Stable button under Quick Downloads on the right side of the home page that's shown in the previous figure. Then, you can experiment with all of the jQuery UI features.

For production websites, it's better to build a custom download that only includes the required components. That reduces the time that it takes to load jQuery UI into a browser. If, for example, you're only going to use a few of the widgets and you're not going to use the Dialog widget, you can uncheck all of the other widgets, the interactions, and the effects. However, if a component like a widget requires other components like interactions or effects, it displays a message that lets you know what you need. Then, you can respond accordingly.

This figure presents some of the folders and files for a typical jQuery UI download. For widgets, you only need the jquery-ui.min.css file, the jquery-ui.min.js file (the jQuery UI library), and the images in the images folder. The min files are compressed versions of the CSS and jQuery UI files, which are smaller than the uncompressed versions.

A jQuery UI download also includes the jQuery library in the external folder, an index.html file that displays a page that demonstrates the features that your download includes, and uncompressed versions of the CSS and jQuery files. You can use the uncompressed versions if you want to view the code in these files. And you can use the jQuery library file if you haven't already downloaded jQuery and aren't using a CDN to get the jQuery library.

Last, the download includes structure and theme CSS files. However, all of the style rules for these files are included in the core CSS file. As a result, you don't need these files unless you want to use only the structure or theme style rules.

How to include jQuery UI in your web pages

To include the jQuery UI CSS and JavaScript files in a web page, you use the link and script elements shown in this figure. Here, the link element points to the min version of the CSS file. Then, the first script element points to the CDN address for the jQuery library (it doesn't use the downloaded jQuery file). And the second script element points to the min version of the jQuery UI file. Here, the script element for the jQuery UI file must follow the script element for the jQuery file because jQuery UI uses jQuery.

The last script element either points to the developer's external JavaScript file or it contains the JavaScript code. If the code that's needed is short, it is often embedded within the script element in the HTML document. Otherwise, an external JavaScript file can be used.

The link and script elements in this example assume that the jQuery UI folders and files are kept in the top-level folder that's downloaded. But you can organize the downloaded files in the way that you think is best for your

The primary folders and files in a full jQuery UI download

Name	Type	Size	Date modified
external	File folder		12/8/2016 11:39 AM
images	File folder		12/8/2016 11:39 AM
index.html	Chrome HTML Document	32 KB	9/14/2016 6:34 PM
jquery-ui.css	Cascading Style Sheet Document	37 KB	9/14/2016 6:34 PM
jquery-ui.js	JScript Script File	509 KB	9/14/2016 6:34 PM
jquery-ui.min.css	Cascading Style Sheet Document	32 KB	9/14/2016 6:34 PM
jquery-ui.min.js	JScript Script File	248 KB	9/14/2016 6:34 PM

How to build a custom jQuery UI library and download its files

1. From the home page, click the Download link in the navigation bar or the Custom Download button. That should navigate to the Download Builder page.

2. Select or deselect the interactions, widgets, and effects until the checked boxes identify the components that you want in your download.

3. If you want to select a theme for the download, use the drop-down list at the bottom of the page. Or, if you want to build a custom theme, click on the link above the list.

4. After you select a theme or design a custom theme, click the Download button to download a zipped folder that contains the jQuery UI files.

How to include the downloaded files in your application

```
<!-- link elements for the jQuery UI stylesheets -->
<link rel="stylesheet" href="/jquery-ui-1.12.1/jquery-ui.min.css">

<!-- the script elements for the jQuery and jQuery UI libraries -->
<script src="https://code.jquery.com/jquery-3.4.1.min.js"></script>
<script src="/jquery-ui-1.12.1/jquery-ui.min.js"></script>

<!-- the script element for your external JavaScript file or your code -->
<script src="..."></script>
```

Description

- A jQuery UI download consists of a zip file that contains the CSS files, the images for the theme, the jQuery UI files, and an HTML document that demonstrates the components in the download.

- The only required folders and files are the images folder and the min (compressed) versions of the first CSS file and the jQuery UI file.

- The external folder in a download includes the jQuery library file.

- The download also includes full and compressed versions of structure and theme CSS files, but you don't need them because the jquery-ui.css and jquery-ui.min.css files include the style rules in both the structure and theme files.

- When you're building a download for a web page, you can keep the file sizes smaller by selecting just the widgets, interactions, and effects that the web page needs.

Figure 11-7   How to download jQuery UI and include it in your web pages

applications. For example, the download for this book organizes the folders so all applications for this chapter can share the same jQuery UI download.

How to use any jQuery UI widget

The next four figures show how to use five of the widgets in their basic forms. That may be all the information that you need for using these widgets in your own web pages. However, all of these widgets provide options, events, and methods that go beyond what these figures present. So, if you want to learn more about what these widgets can do, you can review the jQuery UI documentation for the widgets, which is excellent.

For instance, figure 11-8 shows how to use the documentation for the Accordion widget. A good way to start is to click on the names of the examples in the right side bar to see how the widget can be used. Then, you can click on the View Source link to see the source code that makes the example work. After that, you can review the options, methods, and events for the widget by clicking on the API Documentation link. (These two links aren't shown here, but they're right below the sample widget.)

After you're comfortable with the way a widget works, you're ready to implement it on a web page, which you do in three stages. First, you code the link and script elements for jQuery UI in the head and body elements of the HTML. Second, you code the required HTML for the widget. Third, you code the JavaScript and jQuery for running the widget.

Beyond that, though, you must make sure that the jQuery UI images folder and the jQuery CSS file have the relationship shown in this figure. Specifically, the images folder must be at the same level as the jQuery CSS file because that's where the CSS file looks to get the images that it requires.

The JavaScript and jQuery example in this figure shows the general structure for the jQuery code that's required for a widget. This is similar to the code for using a plugin. First, the ready() event handler contains the code for using the widget. Second, the code uses a jQuery selector to select the HTML element for the widget. Third, the code calls the method for running the widget. Fourth, the code passes any options for the widget to the method. To do that, it codes the options within a pair of braces.

The accordion documentation on the jQuery UI website

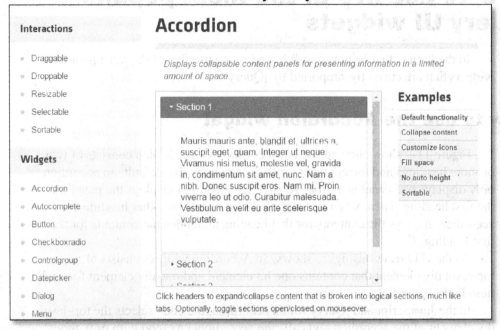

How to use the jQuery UI documentation

- In the left sidebar, click on a widget name to display its documentation.
- In the right sidebar, click on an example name to see a working example, then click on the View Source link to see the code for the example.
- Click the API Documentation link to display information about the widget's options, methods, and events.

The images folder and jquery-ui.min.css relationship that jQuery UI expects

The JavaScript and jQuery for using a widget

```
$(document).ready( () =>
    $("selector").widgetMethod({
        // option settings
    })
)
```

Description

- To use a jQuery UI *widget*, you code the HTML and the jQuery for the widget. In the jQuery, you code a selector, the method to be used, and the options.
- For a widget that requires images, jQuery UI expects the CSS file and the images folder to be at the same level.

Figure 11-8   How to use any jQuery UI widget

How to use five of the most popular jQuery UI widgets

In the figures that follow, you'll learn how to use five of the most popular widgets that are currently supported by jQuery UI.

How to use the Accordion widget

Figure 11-9 shows how to use an Accordion widget, which consists of two or more headings and the contents for those headings. By default, an accordion only displays one panel at a time. To start, an accordion displays the panel for the first heading. Then, when the user clicks on one of the other headings, the accordion displays the contents for that heading and hides the contents for the first heading.

As the HTML in this figure shows, an Accordion widget consists of a top-level div element that contains one h3 element and one div element for each item in the accordion.

In the JavaScript and jQuery for an accordion, the code selects the top-level div element of the accordion and calls the accordion() method with or without options. Because its defaults usually work the way you want them to, it's common to use this method without options.

However, the example in this figure sets three options. First, the event option changes the event that causes the contents of a heading to be displayed from "click" to "mouseover" (hover). Second, the heightStyle option is set to "content" so the height of an open panel is based on the height of its content. Third, the collapsible option is set to true so all of the panels can be closed at the same time.

Although the basic formatting for an accordion is done by the CSS style sheet for jQuery UI, you can use your own style sheet to format the contents of a panel. In fact, you usually need to do that when the panel consists of several different types of HTML elements.

The JavaScript and jQuery code in this example is typical of the code for all widgets. As a result, take a moment to make sure you understand it. As you can see, this code uses parentheses, braces, commas, and colons in a way that can be confusing to new programmers, and every punctuation mark is required for this code to work.

For that reason, it's usually easiest to copy a block of code like this into your script and modify it for whatever widget you're going to use. In general, you just change the selector for the widget, the method name, and the options. For the options, you code the name of the option before the colon and the value after it, with a comma after every option except the last one.

An Accordion widget

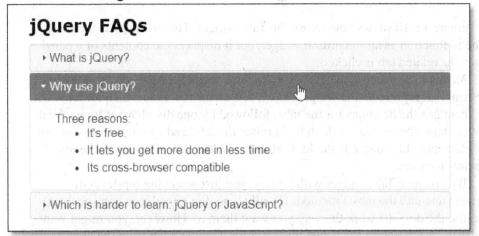

The HTML for the accordion

```
<div id="accordion">
    <h3>What is jQuery?</h3>
    <div><!-- the content for the panel --></div>

    <h3>Why use jQuery?</h3>
    <div><!-- the content for the panel --></div>

    <h3>Which is harder to learn: jQuery or JavaScript?</h3>
    <div><!-- the content for the panel --></div>
</div>
```

The JavaScript and jQuery for the accordion

```
$(document).ready( () =>
    $("#accordion").accordion({
        event: "mouseover",
        heightStyle: "content",
        collapsible: true
    })
)
```

Description

- The HTML consists of h3 elements that provide the headers for the panels, followed by div elements that contain the contents for the panels. These elements should be within an outer div element that represents the accordion.

- The JavaScript and jQuery code uses the accordion() method to implement the accordion widget for the div element with an id of "accordion".

- By default, a panel is opened when its header is clicked, one panel always has to be open, and all the panels open to the same size. However, you can change this behavior by setting options for the accordion() method.

- The CSS file for jQuery UI provides the basic formatting for the accordion, but you can use your style sheet to format the contents within the panels, and you can modify the jQuery UI style sheet to change the appearance of the accordion.

Figure 11-9   How to use the Accordion widget

How to use the Tabs widget

Figure 11-10 shows how to use the Tabs widget. This widget has the same general function as an Accordion widget, but it displays the contents of a panel when the related tab is clicked.

As this figure shows, the HTML for a Tabs widget consists of a top-level div element that represents the widget. Then, this element contains an unordered list that contains the headings for the tabs, followed by one div element for each tab that contains the content of the tab. To relate the tab headings to their respective div elements, this code sets the href attributes of the <a> elements to the ids of the div elements.

To activate a Tabs widget with jQuery, you just select the top-level div element and call the tabs() method. Usually, you don't need to set any options because the defaults work the way you want them to. However, you might want to use the event option to change the event for opening a tab from the click event to the mouseover event because that can work well with tabs.

Here again, the CSS style sheet for jQuery UI does the basic formatting for a Tabs widget. However, you can use your own style sheet to format the contents of a panel. In fact, you usually need to do that when the panel consists of several different types of HTML elements. You can also use your style sheet to override the other jQuery UI formatting.

A Tabs widget

Murach's HTML5 and CSS3 4th Edition

Book description	About the author	Who this book is for

With this book, you can teach yourself how to design web pages the way the professionals do, by using HTML and CSS in tandem to structure and format the page content. It begins with a crash course that teaches you more about HTML and CSS than you can learn from most full books. That includes a chapter on Responsive Web Design that shows you how to build responsive websites that will look and work right on all devices, from phones to tablets to desktop computers.

From that point, you can go to any other chapter to learn what you want to know next, like how to work with Flexible Box Layout and Grid Layout, images, tables, forms, audio and video, transitions and animations, and website design and deployment. You can get an overview of using JavaScript and jQuery or third-party tools like Bootstrap and Node.js. And you can turn to the book for answers whenever you need them on the job.

The HTML for the tabs

```
<div id="tabs">
    <ul>
        <li><a href="#tabs-1">Book description</a></li>
        <li><a href="#tabs-2">About the author</a></li>
        <li><a href="#tabs-3">Who this book is for</a></li>
    </ul>
    <div id="tabs-1"><!-- the content --></div>
    <div id="tabs-2"><!-- the content --></div>
    <div id="tabs-3"><!-- the content --></div>
</div>
```

The JavaScript and jQuery for the tabs

```
$(document).ready( () =>
    $("#tabs").tabs()
)
```

Description

- The HTML should consist of a div element that contains an unordered list that represents the tabs, followed by div elements that contain the contents for the tabs.

- The heading for each tab should be in an <a> element within an li element of the list. The value of the href attribute for each tab should be set to the id of the div element that contains the contents for the tab.

- The JavaScript and jQuery code uses the tabs() method to implement the Tabs widget. By default, you can switch to a tab by clicking on its header.

- The CSS for jQuery UI provides the basic formatting of the tabs, but you can use your own CSS to format the contents within the panels or override the UI formatting.

Figure 11-10   How to use the Tabs widget

How to use the Button and Dialog widgets

Figure 11-11 shows how the Button and Dialog widgets work. The HTML for a Button widget is often an input element of the "button" type, but this widget also works with the "submit", "reset", "radio", and "checkbox" types. In addition, it works with <a> elements.

When the jQuery button() method activates a Button widget, it converts the HTML into a button that uses the jQuery UI theme. Other than that, the button works normally. The example in this figure codes the Button widget as an <a> element that contains an img element for a book, but jQuery UI changes its appearance by adding an outline that makes it look more like a button. When the user clicks on this book, the code opens the Dialog widget.

The HTML for a Dialog widget consists of a div element. Here, the title attribute of this div element specifies the heading for the dialog box. And the body of this div element contains the contents for the dialog box, which can be any HTML elements.

By default, when the dialog box is displayed, it is both draggable and resizable. This means that you can drag the box by its title bar and resize it by dragging the resize handle in the lower right corner. You can also close the box by clicking on the "X" icon in the upper right corner.

To display a Dialog widget with jQuery, you call its dialog() method. If, for example, you want to display a dialog box right when a page is ready, you add code to the ready() event handler to select the div element for the dialog box and call its dialog() method. If you want the user to have to close the dialog box before continuing, you can also set the modal option to true.

Usually, though, you want to open a dialog box when some event occurs, like clicking on a Button widget. To do that, you can use the JavaScript and jQuery code that's shown in this figure. First, this code calls the button() method to convert the HTML for the button to a Button widget. Then, it adds an event handler for the click event of the button. Within this event handler, the code calls the dialog() method of the dialog widget to display the box. This method call sets the modal option to true so the user has to close the dialog box before proceeding. That's why the page behind the dialog box in this figure is dimmed.

You may also need to use some of the other options for a Dialog widget. If, for example, you want to change the height or width of the dialog box, you can set the height or width option. If you don't want the dialog box to be draggable and resizable, you can set those options to false. And you can use the title option to set the title for a dialog box if you don't want to use the title attribute for that purpose.

Incidentally, the Dialog widget is generally considered to be a nice improvement over the JavaScript technique for opening another window and using it as a dialog box. That's especially true because most browsers have built-in features for blocking popup windows.

A Button widget that activates a Dialog widget

The HTML for the Button and Dialog widgets

```
<a id="book"><img src="images/4HTM.jpg" alt="HTML5 and CSS3 book"/></a>
<div id="dialog" title="HTML5 and CSS3" style="display:none;">
    <!-- the contents for the dialog box -->
</div>
```

The JavaScript and jQuery for the Button and Dialog widgets

```
$(document).ready( () => {
    $("#book").button();
    $("#book").click( () =>
        $("#dialog").dialog({ modal:true })
    );
})
```

Description

- The HTML for a Button widget can be an input element with any of these type attributes: button, submit, reset, radio, or checkbox. It can also be an <a> element. When activated, jQuery UI styles a Button widget so it looks like a button.

- The HTML for a Dialog widget consists of a div element that contains the contents for the dialog box. The title attribute can be used to provide the heading for the dialog box.

- To prevent the Dialog widget from appearing when the page loads, set its display property to "none".

- The JavaScript and jQuery uses the button() method to activate the Button widget. Then, the click() event handler for the button uses the dialog() method to display the Dialog widget.

- jQuery UI provides many options for Dialog widgets. For instance, if you set the modal option to true, the box must be closed before the user can proceed. And you can use the width option to change the width of the box from its default of 300 pixels.

- By default, a dialog box is resizable and draggable, but you can change those options by setting them to false.

Figure 11-11   How to use the Button and Dialog widgets

How to use the Datepicker widget

Figure 11-12 shows how to use a Datepicker widget that's associated with a text box. When the user clicks in this text box, the widget displays a calendar that can be used to select a date. After the user selects a date, the widget hides the calendar and displays the selected date in the text box.

To implement a Datepicker widget, you code a text box in the HTML. Then, you write JavaScript and jQuery code that selects that text box and calls the datepicker() method as shown by the first JavaScript and jQuery example. By default, the calendar looks like the one in this figure with the currently selected date displayed in mm/dd/yyyy format. But many options are available for customizing the date format, language, selectable date ranges, and more.

The second JavaScript and jQuery example sets three options. The first option sets the minimum date to the current date. To do that, it assigns a new Date object to the option. The second option sets the maximum date that the widget accepts to 45 days after the current date. And the third option displays a panel beneath the calendar that contains Today and Done buttons. If the user clicks the Today button after moving to another month, the calendar returns to the month that contains the current date. If the user clicks the Done button, the widget closes the calendar.

A Datepicker widget with no options set

The HTML for the Datepicker widget

```
<label>Arrival date:</label>
<label><input type="text" id="datepicker"></label>
```

The JavaScript and jQuery for the Datepicker widget with no options

```
$(document).ready( () =>
    $("#datepicker").datepicker()
)
```

The JavaScript and jQuery for the Datepicker widget with three options

```
$(document).ready( () =>
    $("#datepicker").datepicker({
        minDate: new Date(),
        maxDate: +45,
        showButtonPanel: true
    })
)
```

Description

- The HTML for a Datepicker widget specifies a text box.
- The JavaScript and jQuery implements a Datepicker widget by calling the datepicker() method on the appropriate text box.
- By default, when the user moves the focus into the text box, the browser displays the Datepicker widget and selects the current date.
- jQuery UI provides many options for the Datepicker widget. For instance, minDate sets the minimum date that the user can select, maxDate sets the maximum date that the user can select, and showButtonPanel displays a bar at the bottom of the widget with Today and Done buttons.

Figure 11-12   How to use the Datepicker widget

Perspective

Now that you've completed this chapter, you should be able to use some of the most popular jQuery plugins and jQuery UI widgets. That's an easy way to add features like slide shows, carousels, tabs, and accordions to your web pages. In addition, because you've learned the basic skills for working with any type of plugin, you should be able to use plugins that aren't presented in this chapter, such as the popular jQuery Validation plugin.

Terms

jQuery plugin	widget
modal dialog box	theme
jQuery UI (User Interface)	

Summary

- If you need a common function for a web page, chances are that a *jQuery plugin* is already available for it. By using a plugin, you can often save hours of work and do the job even better than you would have done it on your own.

- To access a plugin, you code a script element for it at the end of the body element of the HTML document. This script element must come after the script element for the jQuery library, because all jQuery plugins use that library.

- To use a plugin, you often need to use JavaScript and jQuery code to call its method within the ready() event handler for a page. Then, if the plugin requires options, you code the options as part of the method call. For some plugins, though, you just need to code the HTML and the required attributes correctly.

- *jQuery UI (User Interface)* is a JavaScript library that extends the jQuery library. Since the jQuery UI library uses the jQuery library, the script element for jQuery UI must come after the script element for jQuery.

- As you build a jQuery UI download, you can select the components for the features that you're going to use, including widgets, interactions, and effects. As you would expect, the fewer components you select, the smaller the jQuery UI file that has to be loaded into the user's browser.

- You can also select a *theme* to include with a jQuery UI download that provides the styles for the jQuery UI components. You can also create a custom theme.

- The most widely-used jQuery UI components are the *widgets*. To use a widget, you code the prescribed HTML for it. Then, in the JavaScript and jQuery, you select the widget and run its primary method, often with one or more options.

Exercise 11-1   Experiment with the Cycle 2 plugin

In this exercise, you'll experiment with the Cycle 2 plugin and the slide show that's in figure 11-5. You'll also review the documentation for this plugin. This should give you a better idea of how you can use plugins.

Review the application

1. Use your text editor or IDE to open the HTML file in this folder:

   `javascript_jquery\exercises\ch11\cycle2`

2. Note that the options for using the Cycle 2 plugin are coded as attributes in the HTML for the slide show. Then, run the application to see how it works.

Experiment with the options

3. Change the value of the data-cycle-fx option to "fadeout". Then, add a data-cycle-speed option with a value of "1000". Test the application to see how this changes the way it works.

4. Go to the website for the Cycle 2 plugin, which is at this URL:

   `http://jquery.malsup.com/cycle2/`

   Click on the Demos link on the home page, then review any of the demos to see the information they present.

5. Go back to the home page of the website. Then, click on the API link to learn more about the options you can use with this plugin.

6. If you're interested, try using one or more of these options.

Check out the download

7. Go back to the Home page one more time and click on the Download link. Then, click on the Download button for the production version of the plugin. In most browsers, this displays the JavaScript for the plugin. Although this isn't the way most downloads work, this is relatively common with plugins.

8. If the code for the plugin is displayed, download it by right-clicking in the code, selecting Save As from the menu that's displayed, and saving the file in a new folder named "js" in your website. Otherwise, use the standard technique to download the code.

9. Change the script element for the Cycle 2 plugin so it refers to the file you just downloaded. Then, make sure the application still works.

Exercise 11-2   Experiment with the Accordion widget

In this exercise, you'll review the jQuery UI demos and documentation for the Accordion widget. Then, you'll make some minor modifications to the application that uses this widget.

Review the demos and documentation for the widget

1.   Go to the jQuery UI website at this URL:

     `https://jqueryui.com/`

     Then, click on the link for the Accordion widget in the left sidebar.

2.   Use the accordion at the top of the page to see how it works. Then, click the View Source link below the accordion to display the code that implements it, and review this code. In particular, notice that the accordion() method doesn't use any options.

3.   Select one or more of the examples to the right of the accordion to see how they change the way the accordion works, and review the jQuery code to see what options are used.

4.   Click the API Documentation link and review the options on the page that's displayed.

Review the application

5.   Use your text editor or IDE to open the accordion application in this folder:

     `javascript_jquery\exercises\ch11\accordion`

     Then, run the application to see how it works.

6.   Modify the JavaScript and jQuery code for the accordion in the HTML file so the panels are displayed when the user double-clicks on them rather than when the mouse moves over them. Test this change.

7.   Modify the JavaScript and jQuery code so all of the panels are closed when the application starts. To do that, use the active option. Then, test this change.

Section 3

Advanced JavaScript skills

If you've read section 2, you know that you use jQuery for DOM scripting and you use JavaScript for everything else that an application has to do. That's why section 3 presents the other JavaScript skills that you're going to need as you build client-side applications.

In chapter 12, you'll learn more about working with numbers, strings, and dates. In chapter 13, you'll learn more about using control structures as well as how to handle exceptions and how to use regular expressions. In chapter 14, you'll learn how to work with the web browser, including how to use cookies and web storage. In chapter 15, you'll learn more about working with arrays, and you'll learn how to work with sets and maps. And in chapter 16, you'll learn how to create and use your own objects, including how to work with iterator and generator functions.

What's interesting about the chapters in this section is that all of the applications show how to apply the JavaScript skills that you learn as well as the jQuery skills that you learned in section 2. In other words, the applications are coded as they would be in the real world.

12

How to work with numbers, strings, and dates

In chapters 2 and 4, you learned some basic skills for working with numbers, strings, and dates. Now, you'll learn the other essential skills for working with data in your JavaScript applications.

How to work with numbers

In chapter 2, you learned how to declare numeric variables, perform common arithmetic operations, and convert a decimal value to a string, rounded to a fixed number of decimal places. Now, you'll build on those skills.

How to use the properties of the Number object

Figure 12-1 starts with a table that summarizes several properties of the Number object that you can use to represent special values. These properties are *static properties*. That is, they're not properties on individual constants or variables. This means that you must include the name of the Number object when you use them, as shown in the table.

Number.MAX_VALUE represents the largest positive value that can be represented by JavaScript. Curiously, each language has a maximum value that it can represent, and JavaScript's is approximately 1798 followed by 305 zeros (an extremely large number). Similarly, Number.MIN_VALUE is an extremely small number.

Number.MAX_SAFE_INTEGER and Number.MIN_SAFE_INTEGER are similar. They represent the maximum and minimum integer values that JavaScript can accurately represent.

Number.POSITIVE_INFINITY is any number greater than the maximum value, Number.NEGATIVE_INFINITY is any number smaller than the minimum value, and Number.EPSILON is the difference between 1 and the minimum value. This last property is sometimes used to correct for imprecision when checking floating-point numbers for equality.

The last property in this table stands for "not a number", which represents any non-numeric value. Because NaN can represent around 9 quadrillion different values, the equality test NaN == NaN will always return false. That's why you must use the global isNaN() or the Number.isNaN method to test whether a value is not a number. You'll learn about the Number.isNaN method in the next figure.

The first example in this figure shows how to test a result for Number.POSITIVE_INFINITY, Number.NEGATIVE_INFINITY, and Number.NaN. Notice, however, that this example uses the shortcut names for these properties: Infinity, -Infinity, and NaN.

The second example shows how JavaScript handles division by zero, which in most other languages results in a runtime error. When you divide 0 by 0 in JavaScript, the result is NaN. However, when you divide a non-zero number by zero, the result is either Infinity or -Infinity depending on the sign of the non-zero number.

The last example shows the difference between safe and unsafe integers. Here, the first two integers are safe but the next two are bigger than Number. MAX_SAFE_INTEGER and so are unsafe. Because of this, JavaScript is able to accurately compare the first two integers but not the next two.

Static properties of the Number object

Property	Shortcut	Description
Number.MAX_VALUE		The largest numeric value that can be represented.
Number.MIN_VALUE		The smallest numeric value that can be represented.
Number.MAX_SAFE_INTEGER		The largest integer that can be stored accurately.
Number.MIN_SAFE_INTEGER		The smallest integer that can be stored accurately.
Number.POSITIVE_INFINITY	Infinity	Represents positive infinity.
Number.NEGATIVE_INFINITY	-Infinity	Represents negative infinity.
Number.EPSILON		The difference between 1 and Number.MIN_VALUE.
Number.NaN	NaN	Represents a value that isn't a number.

Example 1: Testing for Infinity, -Infinity, and NaN

```
if ( result == Infinity ) {
    alert( "The result is greater than " + Number.MAX_VALUE );
} else if ( result == -Infinity ) {
    alert( "The result is less than " + Number.MIN_VALUE );
} else if ( isNaN(result) ) {
    alert( "The result is not a number" );
} else {
    alert( "The result is " + result );
}
```

Example 2: Division by zero

```
alert( 0 / 0 );      // displays NaN
alert( 10 / 0 );     // displays Infinity
alert( -1 / 0 );     // displays -Infinity
```

Example 3: Safe and unsafe integers

```
const safe1 = Number.MAX_SAFE_INTEGER - 1;
const safe2 = Number.MAX_SAFE_INTEGER - 2;
const tooBig1 = Number.MAX_SAFE_INTEGER + 1;
const tooBig2 = Number.MAX_SAFE_INTEGER + 2;
alert( safe1 == safe2 );      // displays false
alert( tooBig1 == tooBig2 );  // displays true; ints not stored accurately
```

Description

- Any numerical operation that results in a number greater than Number.MAX_VALUE will return the value Infinity, and any operation that results in a number less than Number.MIN_VALUE will return the value -Infinity.

- Any numerical operation with a non-numeric operand will return NaN.

- You can't test for equality with the NaN property. Instead, you must use the global isNaN() or the Number.isNaN() method (see figure 12-2).

- Division of zero by zero results in NaN, but division of a non-zero number by zero results in either Infinity or -Infinity.

- To work with integers bigger or smaller than Number.MAX_SAFE_INTEGER and Number.MIN_SAFE_INTEGER, you can use the BigInt data type (ES2020).

Figure 12-1   How to use the properties of the Number object

How to use the methods of the Number object

Figure 12-2 starts with a table that summarizes several methods of the Number object. The first two methods are *instance methods*. That means that you call them on individual constants or variables that store numeric values. Remember, JavaScript automatically creates a Number object when you call an instance method on such a constant or variable.

By contrast, the four methods in the second table are *static methods*. This means that you must include the name of the Number object when you call them.

The first example in this figure shows how to use the toFixed() method. Here, the third statement rounds the number 1.49925 to two decimal places, or 1.50.

The second example shows how the toString() method is used implicitly by JavaScript. Here, the integer value in age is automatically converted to a string by the toString() method when age is concatenated with a string literal. This implicit conversion is done whenever a number is used in an expression that mixes string and number values. Occasionally, though, you may want to use the toString() method explicitly, especially if you want to change a number from the default base 10.

The third example shows how to use the Number.isNaN() method, and also how that method is different from the global isNaN() method. When the global isNaN() method checks a value, it attempts to convert that value to a number first. If the value can't be converted to a number, it's converted to NaN. That's why the first three statements in this example all return true.

By contrast, when the Number.isNaN() method checks a value, it doesn't convert the value. Instead, it checks whether the value is of the number data type, as well as checking that the value is NaN. That's why the next two statements in this example return false. For instance, the string "four" clearly isn't a number, but it also isn't the numeric value NaN, so Number.isNaN() returns false. On the other hand, the third statement checks the value NaN, which also isn't a number. However, it is equal to NaN, so the method returns true.

The fourth example shows how to use the Number.isFinite() method to test for values of Infinity and -Infinity. Like the Number.isNaN() method, this method checks that the value is both numeric and finite. That is, it doesn't convert the value to a number before checking it.

You should know that there's also a global isFinite() method that, like the global isNaN() method, converts the value to a number before checking it. That means that

```
isFinite("4")
```

returns true, while

```
Number.isFinite("4")
```

returns false.

Finally, the last example shows how to use the Number.isInteger() method to check whether a value is an integer, and the Number.isSafeInteger() method to check whether a value is an integer within the range of safe integers. Like the

Instance methods of a Number object

Method	Description
`toFixed(digits)`	Returns a string with the number rounded to the given decimal places.
`toString([base])`	Returns a string with the number in the given base, or base 10.

Example 1: Using the toFixed() method

```
const subtotal = 19.99, rate = 0.075;
const tax = subtotal * rate;          // tax is 1.49925
alert( tax.toFixed(2) );              // displays 1.50
```

Example 2: Implicit use of the toString() method for base 10 conversions

```
const age = parseInt( prompt("Please enter your age.") );
alert( "Your age is " + age );
```

Static methods of a Number object

Method	Description
`Number.isNaN(value)`	Returns a Boolean that indicates whether a value is NaN and has the Number type.
`Number.isFinite(value)`	Returns a Boolean that indicates whether a value is finite.
`Number.isInteger(value)`	Returns a Boolean that indicates whether a value is an integer.
`Number.isSafeInteger(value)`	Returns a Boolean that indicates whether a value is a safe integer.

Example 3: isNaN() vs Number.isNaN()

```
alert( isNaN("four") );               // displays true
alert( isNaN([1,2,3]) );              // displays true
alert( isNaN(NaN) );                  // displays true

alert( Number.isNaN("four") );        // displays false
alert( Number.isNaN([1,2,3]) );       // displays false
alert( Number.isNaN(NaN) );           // displays true
```

Example 4: Using the isFinite() method

```
alert( Number.isFinite( 10 / 0 ) );   // displays false
alert( Number.isFinite( -1 / 0 ) );   // displays false
alert( Number.isFinite(200) );        // displays true
```

Example 5: Using the isInteger() and isSafeInteger() methods

```
const tooBig = Number.MAX_SAFE_INTEGER + 1;

alert( Number.isInteger(tooBig) );         // displays true
alert( Number.isSafeInteger(tooBig) );     // displays false
alert( Number.isSafeInteger(tooBig - 1) ); // displays true
```

Description

- The toString() method with no parameters is used implicitly whenever JavaScript needs to convert a number to a string.

- The global isNaN() method tries to convert a value to the number data type and then checks if it is NaN. The Number.isNaN() method checks if a value is of the number data type and if it is NaN.

Figure 12-2   How to use the methods of the Number object

other two static methods presented here, these two methods don't convert the value to a number before checking it. That means that

```
Number.isInteger("4")
```

returns false.

How to use the properties and methods of the Math object

Figure 12-3 shows how to use one of the properties and some of the common methods of the Math object. All of the properties and methods of the Math object are static. This means that you must include the name of the Math object when you use them, as shown in the tables in this figure.

The first example shows how to use the Math.PI property, which returns the value of π. In this example, the Math.PI property is used to calculate the area of a circle whose radius is 3.

The second example shows how to use the Math.abs(), or absolute value, method. When given a negative number, it returns that number as a positive value.

The third example shows how to use the Math.round() method. Note that in the third statement, -3.5 rounds up to -3. It does not round down to -4.

The fourth example shows how to use the ceil() (ceiling), floor(), and trunc() (truncate) methods. The ceil() method always rounds a fractional value towards positive infinity. The floor() method always rounds a fractional value towards negative infinity. And the trunc() method doesn't do any rounding at all. Instead, it returns the integer part of the value with the fractional value truncated.

The fifth example shows how to use the pow() method to raise a value to a power and the sqrt() method to get the square root of a value. Note that the power parameter of the pow() method can be a fractional value. In the second statement, for example, 125 is raised to the 1/3rd power. This is the equivalent of taking the cube root of 125.

The sixth example shows you how to use the min() and max() methods. These methods are not limited to two parameters, so you can supply as many parameters as needed. Then, these methods will find the minimum or maximum value in the list of parameters.

Finally, this figure presents the exponentiation operator, which can be used as an alternative to the Math.pow() method. Here, 2 is raised to the power of 3. Whether you use the exponentiation operator or the Math.pow() method is mostly a matter of personal preference.

The Math object also provides many trigonometric and logarithmic methods. If you have the appropriate mathematical background, you should be able to use these methods with no problem. If you use them, though, one point to remember is that the trigonometric methods use radians to measure angles, not degrees.

One static property of the Math object

Property	Description
Math.PI	Returns 3.141592653589793, which is the ratio of the circumference of a circle to its diameter.

Example 1: The PI property
```
const area = Math.PI * 3 * 3;          // area is 28.274333882308138
```

Common static methods of the Math object

Method	Description
Math.abs(*x*)	Returns the absolute value of x.
Math.round(*x*)	Returns the value of x rounded up or down to the closest integer value.
Math.ceil(*x*)	Returns the value of x rounded up to the next higher integer value.
Math.floor(*x*)	Returns the value of x rounded down to the next lower integer value.
Math.trunc(*x*)	Returns the integer value of x with no rounding.
Math.pow(*x, power*)	Returns the value of x raised to the given power (integer or decimal).
Math.sqrt(*x*)	Returns the square root of x.
Math.min(*x1, x2, ...*)	Returns the smallest value from its parameters.
Math.max(*x1, x2, ...*)	Returns the largest value from its parameters.

Example 2: The abs() method
```
const result_2a = Math.abs(-3.4);          // result_2a is 3.4
```

Example 3: The round() method
```
const result_3a = Math.round(12.5);     // result_3a is 13
const result_3b = Math.round(-3.4);     // result_3b is -3
const result_3c = Math.round(-3.5);     // result_3c is -3
const result_3d = Math.round(-3.51);    // result_3d is -4
```

Example 4: The floor(), ceil(), and trunc() methods
```
const result_4a = Math.floor(12.5);     // result_4a is 12
const result_4b = Math.ceil(12.5);      // result_4b is 13
const result_4c = Math.trunc(12.5);     // result_4c is 12
const result_4d = Math.floor(-3.4);     // result_4d is -4
const result_4e = Math.ceil(-3.4);      // result_4e is -3
const result_4f = Math.trunc(-3.4);     // result_4f is -3
```

Example 5: The pow() and sqrt() methods
```
const result_5a = Math.pow(2,3);        // result_5a is 8 (the cube of 2)
const result_5b = Math.pow(125, 1/3);   // result_5b is 5 (cube root of 125)
const result_5c = Math.sqrt(16);        // result_5c is 4
```

Example 6: The min() and max() methods
```
const result_6a = Math.max(12.5, -3.4); // result_6a is 12.5
const result_6b = Math.min(12.5, -3.4); // result_6b is -3.4
```

How to use the exponentiation operator instead of Math.pow()
```
const result_7a = 2 ** 3;               // same as Math.pow(2,3)
```

Figure 12-3   How to use the properties and methods of the Math object

How to generate a random number

The random() method of the Math object generates a random number that is equal to or greater than zero but less than one. To use this method, you code a statement like the one in the first example in figure 12-4. Often, though, you want a random number that's in a different range than that.

The second example presents a function that will generate a random number in a range between 1 and a specified maximum. The getRandomNumber() function takes a single parameter, which is the maximum value for the range of random numbers that the function should generate.

This function first declares a variable named random. This variable will hold the random number that's generated by the function. Next, the function validates the max parameter to ensure it's a number. If it fails the isNaN() test, the function simply returns the random variable declared at the beginning of the function. Since this variable was initialized to null, that means if the max parameter is not a number, the getRandomNumber() function returns null.

If the max parameter is a number, the function computes a whole number between 1 and max. To do this, the function gets a value from the Math.random() method and multiplies it by the value of max. It then uses the Math.floor() method to round the number down to the nearest integer and adds 1 to this result.

For example, if max is 6, then 6 times a random number between 0 and 1 returns a value from 0 to just less than 6. Then, using the Math.floor() method rounds the number down to an integer that ranges from 0 to 5, and adding 1 to it returns a random number in the requested range.

The getRandomNumber() function in this figure is a simple one, but you could easily improve it. For example, you could make it so you can pass in the minimum value for the range as well as the maximum value. Or, you could make it allow a range of decimals as well as a range of whole numbers. You'll find many online examples of random number generation that you can use as guides for these and other improvements.

The random() method of the Math object

Method	Description
`Math.random()`	Returns a random decimal number >= 0.0 but < 1.0.

How to generate a random number

```
const result = Math.random();
```

A function that generates a random number

```
const getRandomNumber = max => {
    let random = null;

    if (!isNaN(max)) {
        // value >= 0.0 and < 1.0
        random = Math.random();

        // value is an integer between 0 and max - 1
        random = Math.floor(random * max);

        // value is an integer between 1 and max
        random = random + 1;
    }
    // if max is not a number, will return null
    return random;
};
```

A statement that calls the getRandomNumber() function

```
// returns an integer that ranges from 1 through 100
const randomNumber = getRandomNumber(100);
```

Description

- You can use the getRandomNumber() function to generate a random number between 1 and the specified maximum value.

- Random numbers can be used for testing and are often used in games or applications that provide animation.

- There are many ways to use the Math.random() function to create a random number generator. If you do an Internet search, you will find many examples, some with more extensive functionality than the simple generator shown here.

Figure 12-4   How to generate a random number

The PIG application

Figure 12-5 shows the user interface for a dice game called PIG. This application requires the use of just one die and illustrates the use of a random number generator.

When the application starts, the two bottom rows of the game are hidden. Then, the user enters names in the Player 1 and Player 2 text boxes and clicks the New Game button to start the game. This displays the bottom two rows of the interface with the first player's name shown in red.

From that point on, the players take turns until one of them reaches 50 and wins. For each turn, a player can click the Roll button to roll the die one or more times. If the player rolls a 2 or higher, that number is added to the player's points for that turn. Then, the player can click the Hold button to keep the points that they've earned during that turn. If the player rolls a 1 before clicking the Hold button, though, the turn ends and the player gets zero points for that turn.

The CSS

Part 1 of figure 12-5 presents some of the CSS for this application. This is in addition to the basic CSS you saw in chapter 2 for the applications presented in this book.

The first two style rules use type selectors to apply CSS to the HTML label and input elements. You've seen code like this before, so you shouldn't have any trouble understanding how it works.

The third style rule uses a descendant selector to select the div element within the element whose id is "turn". This is the element that contains the current player's name, and this CSS makes that player's name appear in red.

The fourth style rule uses id selectors to apply CSS to the HTML elements whose ids are "score1", "score2", "die", and "total". It sets the width of the disabled input elements for the player scores and the die and total amounts for the current turn.

Finally, the last style rule uses a class selector to apply CSS to any HTML element that's assigned to the CSS class named "hide". This style rule hides any element assigned to that class.

The user interface

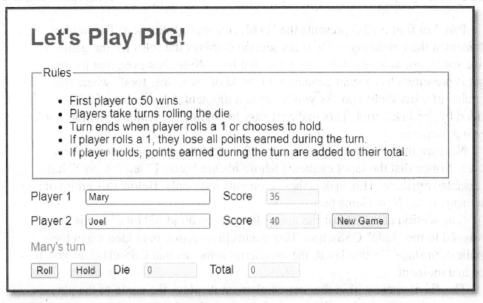

The CSS

```
label {
    display: inline-block;
    margin-right: 1em;
}

input {
    margin-top: 1em;
    margin-right: 1em;
}

#turn div {
    color: red;
    margin-top: 1em;
}

#score1, #score2, #die, #total {
    width: 5em;
}

.hide {
    display: none;
}
```

Figure 12-5   The PIG application (part 1)

The HTML

Part 2 of figure 12-5 presents the HTML for this application. The fieldset element at the beginning of the main section displays the rules for the game. To save space, not all of the rules are presented here. Note, however, that the one that is presented has a span element with an id of "winning_total" where the number of wins should go. As you'll see in a moment, the number of wins is added by the JavaScript. This makes it easy to change the winning number for testing purposes.

Next are the label and input elements for each player's name and current score. Notice that the input elements whose ids are "score1" and "score2" have a disabled attribute. This makes these elements read-only. Below this group of elements is the New Game button.

The section at the end of the main element has an id of "turn" and is assigned to the "hide" CSS class. This means this section is hidden when the application starts. To display it, the JavaScript removes that CSS class, as you'll see in a moment.

The div element within the section element displays the name of the player whose turn it is. To do that, the JavaScript inserts the player name in the span element with an id of "current". You'll see that in a moment, too. The rest of the section element consists of the buttons the players use while taking a turn and the labels and text boxes that display the current roll and the total for the turn.

Finally, the script elements for the JavaScript files are at the end of the body element. Like all the applications in this section of the book, this one uses jQuery for DOM scripting, so the first script element identifies the jQuery library. Then, the second script element identifies the JavaScript file for this application.

The JavaScript

Part 2 of figure 12-5 also presents the beginning of the JavaScript for this application. Like all of the applications in this book, this one starts with the "use strict" directive so the JavaScript is in strict mode.

Next is the declaration for a constant named winningTotal that's initialized with a value of 50. This is the value that's used to determine when there's a winner. It's also the value that's displayed in the first rule for the game. If you want to change the number a player needs to win, you can change it here. For instance, it can be helpful to to reduce this number during testing.

Next is a function named getRandomNumber(). This is the same function that you saw in figure 12-4. The application uses this function to simulate the roll of a die.

The HTML

```
<body>
    <main>
        <h1>Let's Play PIG!</h1>
        <fieldset>
            <legend>Rules</legend>
            <ul>
                <li>First player to <span id="winning_total"></span>
                    wins.</li>
                    ...
            </ul>
        </fieldset>

        <label for="player1">Player 1</label>
        <input type="text" id="player1" >
        <label for="score1">Score</label>
        <input type="text" id="score1" value="0" disabled><br>

        <label for="player2">Player 2</label>
        <input type="text" id="player2">
        <label for="score2">Score</label>
        <input type="text" id="score2" value="0" disabled>

        <input type="button" id="new_game" value="New Game"><br>

        <section id="turn" class="hide">
            <div><span id="current"></span>'s turn</div>

            <input type="button" id="roll" value="Roll">
            <input type="button" id="hold" value="Hold">

            <label for="die">Die</label>
            <input type="text" id="die" disabled>

            <label for="total">Total</label>
            <input type="text" id="total" disabled>
        </section>
    </main>
    <script src="https://code.jquery.com/jquery-3.4.1.slim.min.js"></script>
    <script src="pig.js"></script>
</body>
```

The JavaScript

```
"use strict";
const winningTotal = 50;

const getRandomNumber = max => {
    let rand = null;
    if (!isNaN(max)) {
        rand = Math.random();
        rand = Math.floor(rand * max);
        rand = rand + 1;
    }
    return rand;
};
```

Figure 12-5   The PIG application (part 2)

Part 3 of figure 12-5 presents the rest of the JavaScript for this application. The changePlayer() function is a helper function that's called when a new game starts and when the turn for a player ends. The if statement in this function changes the name in the "current" span element to the name that's in the text box for the other player. Because the "current" span element is empty when the first game starts, player 1 is always set as the first player for that game. Then, this function sets the values of the Die and Total text boxes to zero, and it moves the focus to the Roll button.

Next is the jQuery ready() event handler, which fires when the DOM is ready. It contains three event handlers for the click events of the New Game, Roll, and Hold buttons.

The event handler for the click event of the New Game button starts by resetting the scores for the players to zero. Then, the if statement checks if the name in the text box for either player is an empty space (blank). If it is, this function displays a message that says the two player names must be entered. Otherwise, the else clause of the if statement removes the "hide" CSS class to display the "turn" section, and then calls the changePlayer() function.

Note that to remove the CSS class, this code uses the jQuery removeClass() method. However, it could just as easily use the remove() method of the JavaScript classList property. The method you use is mostly a matter of personal preference.

The event handler for the click event of the Roll button starts by getting the total value for that turn from the Total text box. Then, it calls the getRandomNumber() function to get the result of one roll of the die. It passes the value 6 to the getRandomNumber() function so the range of possible return values is between 1 and 6, just like a physical die.

If the result is 1, the total is reset to zero and the changePlayer() function is called. Otherwise, the result of the roll is added to the total value, and the die and total values are displayed in their text boxes so the player can decide whether to roll or hold.

The event handler for the click event of the Hold button starts by declaring a variable named score and initializing it to zero. Then, it declares a constant named total and assigns the value from the Total text box to it. Next, an if statement tests whether the current player is player 1. If so, the code gets the "score1" Textbox object and stores it in the score variable. Otherwise, it gets the "score2" Textbox object and stores it in the score variable. Then, it sets the new value of the score Textbox object to the value of the score Textbox object plus the total value. Finally, if the score value is greater than or equal to the value in the winningTotal constant, an alert dialog box is displayed that declares the winner. Otherwise, the changePlayer() function is called so the other player can take another turn.

The ready() event handler ends with two additional statements. The first one sets the text of the span element whose id is "winning_total" to the value of the winningTotal constant. And the second one moves the focus to the Player 1 text box, which is the first text box on the page.

The JavaScript (continued)

```javascript
const changePlayer = () => {
    if ( $("#current").text() == $("#player1").val() ) {
        $("#current").text( $("#player2").val() );
    } else {
        $("#current").text( $("#player1").val() );
    }
    $("#die").val("0");
    $("#total").val("0");
    $("#roll").focus();
};

$( document ).ready( () => {
    $("#new_game").click( () => {
        $("#score1").val("0");
        $("#score2").val("0");

        if ( $("#player1").val() == "" || $("#player2").val() == "" ) {
            alert("Please enter two player names.");
        } else {
            $("#turn").removeClass("hide");
            changePlayer();
        }
    });
    $("#roll").click( () => {
        let total = parseInt( $("#total").val() );
        const die = getRandomNumber(6);

        if (die == 1) {
            total = 0;
            changePlayer();
        } else {
            total = total + die;
        }
        $("#die").val(die);
        $("#total").val(total);
    });
    $("#hold").click( () => {
        let score = 0;
        const total = parseInt( $("#total").val() );

        if ( $("#current").text() == $("#player1").val() ) {
            score = $("#score1");
        } else {
            score = $("#score2");
        }

        score.val( parseInt( score.val() ) + total );
        if (score.val() >= winningTotal) {
            alert( $("#current").text() + " WINS!" );
        } else {
            changePlayer();
        }
    });
    $("#winning_total").text(winningTotal);
    $("#player1").focus();
});
```

Figure 12-5   The PIG application (part 3)

How to work with strings

In chapter 2, you learned how to create and work with simple strings. Then, in chapter 4, you learned one property and a few of the methods of the String object. Now, you'll review this property and these methods and you'll learn about some other methods.

How to use the properties and methods of the String object

Figure 12-6 describes one property and several methods of String objects. All of them are instance properties or methods. That means that you call them on constants or variables that store string values. Remember, JavaScript automatically creates a String object when you refer to an instance property or call an instance method on such a constant or variable.

The length property lets you find out how many characters are in a string. Because the positions in a string are numbered from zero, not 1, the last character in a string is at the position identified by the length minus 1.

The first statement in this figure declares and initializes a string constant that's used by the examples that follow. Then, the first example uses that constant to illustrate the length property.

Example 2 shows how to use the charAt() method. Here, the J in JavaScript is the character at position 0, and the character at position 4 is S.

Example 3 shows how to use the concat() method. If you specify more than one parameter, the strings are concatenated in order. This is another way to concatenate strings, in addition to using the + operator and the template literal techniques you learned in chapter 2.

Example 4 shows the use of the indexOf() method. If you omit the position parameter, the search is performed from the start of the string. If the search string isn't found, the method returns -1.

Example 5 shows the use of the substr() and substring() methods. Note that the character specified in the end parameter for the substring() method is *not* included in the result. If start is greater than end, the two values are swapped. If either value is less than 0, it is replaced with 0. If either value is greater than the length of the string, it is replaced with the length of the string.

Example 6 shows how to use the toUpperCase() and toLowerCase() methods. These methods have no parameters, but don't forget to include the empty set of parentheses after the method name.

This example also shows a common use of these methods, which is to perform a case insensitive test for equality between two strings. This is useful because the == operator is case sensitive when used with strings. This example uses the toLowerCase() function to convert each string to lowercase before doing the comparison. You could also use the toUpperCase() function for this comparison. You just need to make sure that both strings call the same function.

One property of a String object

Property	Description
length	The number of characters in the string.

Constant used by the following examples

```
const message = "JavaScript";
```

Example 1: The length property

```
const result_1 = message.length;            // result_1 is 10
```

Methods of a String object

Method	Description
charAt(*position*)	Returns the character at the specified position in the string.
concat(*string1,string2,...*)	Returns a new string that is the concatenation of this string with each of the strings specified in the parameter list.
indexOf(*search[,start]*)	Searches the string for the first occurrence of the search string starting at the position specified or the beginning if the position is omitted. If the search string is found, it returns the position in the string. If not found, it returns -1.
substr(*start,length*)	Returns the substring from the start position through the number of characters specified by the length parameter.
substring(*start*)	Returns the substring from the start position to the end of the string.
substring(*start,end*)	Returns the substring from the start position to, but not including, the end position.
toLowerCase()	Returns the string with all letters converted to lowercase.
toUpperCase()	Returns the string with all letters converted to uppercase.

Example 2: The charAt() method

```
const letter = message.charAt(4);           // letter is "S"
```

Example 3: The concat() method

```
const result_3 = message.concat(" rules"); // result_3 is "JavaScript rules"
```

Example 4: The indexOf() method

```
const result_4a = message.indexOf("a");     // result_4a is 1
const result_4b = message.indexOf("a", 2); // result_4b is 3
const result_4c = message.indexOf("s");     // result_4c is -1
```

Example 5: The substr() and substring() methods

```
const result_5a = message.substr(4, 5);     // result_5a is "Scrip"
const result_5b = message.substring(4);     // result_5b is "Script"
const result_5c = message.substring(0, 4); // result_5c is "Java"
```

Example 6: The toLowerCase() and toUpperCase() methods

```
const result_6a = message.toLowerCase();    // result_6a is "javascript"
const result_6b = message.toUpperCase();    // result_6b is "JAVASCRIPT"
// compare two strings ignoring case
alert( result_6a.toLowerCase() == result_6b.toLowerCase() ) // displays true
```

Figure 12-6   How to use the properties and methods of the String object

More methods of the String object

Figure 12-7 presents even more methods of the String object. Then, it declares and initializes two constants that are used by most of the examples in this figure. The first constant contains a string, and the second contains the length of that string.

Example 1 shows how to use the startsWith(), endsWith(), and includes() methods. Each of these methods has a required first parameter that's the string to search for, which is case sensitive. Each method also has an optional second parameter. For the startsWith() and includes() method, this parameter is the index where you want to start the search. If you omit this parameter, the search is performed from index zero. For the endsWith() method, this parameter is the length of the string to search, starting at the first character. If you omit this parameter, the entire length is searched.

Example 2 shows how to use the padStart() and padEnd() methods. Each method has a required first parameter that's the length the new string should be after the padding is done. Each method also has an optional second parameter that indicates the character to use for the padding. If you omit this parameter, a space is used. In this example, the first statement adds three spaces to the beginning of the string, and the second statement adds three dots to the end of the string.

Example 3 shows how to use the trimStart(), trimEnd(), and trim() methods to remove whitespace (spaces, tabs, and line breaks). First, though, this example uses the padStart() and padEnd() methods to add three blank spaces to the beginning and end of the string. Notice that the call to padEnd() adds 6 to the original length of the string. That's because the string returned by the padStart() method is already three characters longer than the original string, so this method call needs to add three more than that.

Example 4 shows how to use the repeat() method. This method accepts an integer between 0 and Infinity and then returns a new string that is a result of concatenating the original string the specified number of times. Here, you can see that the string "Hey " is repeated three times. This example also shows that you can call the methods of the String object on a string literal.

More methods of a String object

Method	Description
startsWith(*string*[,*start*])	Returns a Boolean that indicates whether the string starts with the specified string. Searches from the specified position or the start of the string if a position isn't specified.
endsWith(*string*[,*length*])	Returns a Boolean value that indicates whether the string ends with the specified string. Searches from the start of the string for the specified length or the entire sting if a length isn't specified.
includes(*string*[,*start*])	Returns a Boolean that indicates whether the string contains the specified string. Searches from the specified position or the start of the string if a position isn't specified.
trimStart()	Returns a string with whitespace removed from the beginning.
trimEnd()	Returns a string with whitespace removed from the end.
trim()	Returns a string with whitespace removed from the beginning and the end.
padStart(*length*[,*string*])	Returns the string with the specified string added to the beginning until the string is the specified length. If a string isn't specified, a space is used.
padEnd(*length*[,*string*])	Returns the string with the specified string added to the end until the string is the specified length. If a string isn't specified, a space is used.
repeat(*times*)	Returns the string repeated the specified number of times.

Constants used by the following examples

```
const str = "jQuery";
const len = str.length;
```

Example 1: The startsWith(), endsWith(), and includes() methods

```
const result_1a = str.startsWith("j");        // result_1a is true
const result_1b = str.startsWith("j", 2);      // result_1b is false
const result_1c = str.endsWith("ry");          // result_1c is true
const result_1d = str.endsWith("ry", 2);       // result_1d is false
const result_1e = str.includes("Que");         // result_1e is true
const result_1f = str.includes("Que", 2);      // result_1f is false
```

Example 2: The padStart() and padEnd() methods

```
const result_2a = str.padStart(len + 3);        // result_2a is "   jQuery"
const result_2b = str.padEnd(len + 3, ".");     // result_2b is "jQuery..."
```

Example 3: The trimStart(), trimEnd(), and trim() methods

```
const str_2 = str.padStart(len + 3).padEnd(len + 6);
                                                // str_2 is "   jQuery   "
const result_3a = str_2.trimStart();            // result_3a is "jQuery   "
const result_3b = str_2.trimEnd();              // result_3b is "   jQuery"
const result_3c = str_2.trim();                 // result_3c is "jQuery"
```

Example 4: The repeat() method

```
const result_4a = "Hey ".repeat(3);             // result_4a is "Hey Hey Hey "
```

Figure 12-7   More methods of the String object

How to create an array from a string

Figure 12-8 presents one more method of the String object. The split() method can be used to divide a string into multiple substrings based on a separator character that's coded as the first parameter. It then creates a new array with each of the substrings as an element. If you code a second parameter, it's used to limit the number of elements that can be included in the new array. Note that the separator character itself isn't added to the substrings in the array.

The first example in this figure declares and initializes two constants. The first one, named fullName, stores a string that consists of a first name, a middle initial, and a last name. The second one, named date, contains a date string whose date parts are separated by hyphens. The examples that follow use these two constants.

The second example shows how to split the fullName string into an array named words using a space as the separator. This results in an array that contains the elements "Grace", "M", and "Hopper". Next, it gets the length of the new array and stores it in a constant named len. Then, it assigns the last element at the last index in the array (len - 1) to a constant named lastName.

Similarly, the third example shows how to split the date string into an array named dateParts using a hyphen as the separator. Then, the fourth example shows how to split the fullName string into individual characters. This happens when you call the split() method with an empty string as its parameter.

The fifth example shows how to limit the number of substrings that are copied into the new array. Here, the split() method uses a space as the separator to split the firstName string, but it limits the number of substrings to one. The result is an array that contains just the first name in one element. Note that the code in the last statement in this example is able to use that single-element array in a template literal just like a regular string.

The sixth example shows what happens if the separator character isn't in the string. Here, the date constant contains a string that has hyphens, but the split() method is called with a slash as the separator. In this case, the resulting array only has one element with the same value as the original string.

The last example shows what happens if the separator character is the first or last character in the string. Here, a constant named path contains a string with a slash character as its first and last characters. Then, the split() method is called with a slash as the separator. In this case, the resulting array has an empty string element at the beginning and at the end of the array.

A String method that creates an array

Method	Description
`split(separator[, limit])`	Splits a string into an array based on the value of the separator parameter and returns the array. The optional limit parameter specifies the maximum number of elements in the new array.

Two constants that are used by the following examples

```
const fullName = "Grace M Hopper";
const date = "7-4-2021";
```

How to split a string that's separated by spaces into an array

```
const words = fullName.split(" ");      // words is ["Grace", "M", "Hopper"]
const len = words.length;               // len is 3
const lastName = words[len - 1];        // lastName is "Hopper"
```

How to split a string that's separated by hyphens into an array

```
const dateParts = date.split("-");      // dateParts is ["7", "4", "2021"]
const month = dateParts[0];             // month is "7"
const year = dateParts[2];              // year is "2021"
```

How to split a string into an array of characters

```
const characters = fullName.split("");
// ["G", "r", "a", "c", "e", " ", "M", " ", "H", "o", "p", "p", "e", "r"]
```

How to get just one element from a string

```
const firstName = fullName.split(" ", 1);   // firstName is ["Grace"]
const len = firstName.length;               // len is 1
```

A statement that uses the firstName constant like a regular string

```
const greeting = `Hello, ${firstName}!`;    // greeting is "Hello, Grace!"
```

How it works if the string doesn't contain the separator

```
const dateParts = date.split("/");      // dateParts is ["7-4-2021"]
len = dateParts.length;                 // len is 1
```

How it works if the string contains the separator at the beginning or end

```
const path = "/directory/";
const pathParts = path.split("/"); // pathParts is ["", "directory", ""]
```

Description

- The split() method of a String object breaks a string into substrings and returns those substrings as elements in an array.
- If a string doesn't include the separator that's specified in the parameter of the split() method, the entire string is returned as the first element in a one-element array.
- If the separator that's specified by the parameter is an empty string, each character in the string becomes an element in the array that's returned by the method.
- If the string includes the separator at the beginning or end of the string, an empty string is included as an element at the beginning or end of the array.

Figure 12-8   How to create an array from a string

How to work with dates and times

In chapter 4, you learned how to create Date objects and how to use four methods for working with them. In this topic, you'll learn more about creating Date objects and using the methods of those objects.

In JavaScript, dates are represented by the number of milliseconds since midnight, January 1, 1970. Positive values come after this date while negative values come before. Internally, the dates are stored in universal time, or Greenwich Mean Time (GMT). However, JavaScript has access to the time zone on the client's computer and adjusts the dates to the local time.

How to create Date objects

Figure 12-9 starts by summarizing how the Date() constructor works. Here, you can see that you can use several techniques to create a Date object.

The first example shows how to create a Date object that represents the local time on the user's computer. This is done by specifying the Date constructor with no parameters. This is the method that you learned in chapter 4.

The second example shows how to create a Date object by specifying a date and time in a string parameter. In this case, the hours must be specified in 24-hour (or military) time. For example, 3:15pm is 15:15 on a 24-hour clock. If you omit the time, midnight is used. Additionally, to make sure the date is created correctly, the year should be 4 digits.

The third example shows how to create a Date object by specifying numeric values for the parts of the date. Here, year and month are required. Then, if day is omitted, 1 is used. And if any of the remaining date parts are omitted, 0 is used.

When you use this method, remember that the months are numbered from 0 through 11 where 0 is January and 11 is December. As a result, 3 is April and 10 is November. This makes it easier to use the month numbers with arrays, which are also numbered starting with 0.

The fourth example shows how to create a Date object by copying another Date object. This lets you manipulate the copy without affecting the original. You'll learn more about that in the next two figures.

The fifth example shows what happens if you pass invalid values to the Date constructor. In that case, a Date object is still created, but its value is set to the string "Invalid Date". Here, the date is February 29, 2021, which isn't a valid date because 2021 isn't a leap year.

The two statements in the sixth example show some unexpected results you may get in some browsers if you use a string parameter with dashes or with a 2-digit year. Not all browsers produce these results, but some do, so you should keep this in mind when working with the Date object. If, for example, you're accepting dates from users, you'll want to validate them to make sure they're in a correct format before passing them as an argument to the Date object.

In the next figure, you'll learn about some of the methods for working with dates. Before you use these methods, you may want to check that a constant or variable contains a date. To do that, you can use the instanceof operator as shown in the last example in this figure.

Summary of how the Date constructor works

Parameters	Description
None	Creates a new Date object set to the current date and time.
String value	Creates a new Date object set to the date and time of the string.
Numeric values	Creates a new Date object set to the year, month, day, hours, minutes, seconds, and milliseconds of the numbers. Year and month are required.
Date object	Creates a new Date object that's a copy of the Date object it received.
Invalid values	Creates a new Date object that contains "Invalid Date".

How to create a Date object that represents the current date and time

```
const now = new Date();
```

How to create a Date object by specifying a date string

```
const electionDay = new Date("11/3/2020");
const grandOpening = new Date("2/16/2021 8:00");
const departureTime = new Date("4/6/2021 18:30:00");
```

How to create a Date object by specifying numeric values

Syntax of the constructor for the Date object

```
new Date( year, month, day, hours, minutes, seconds, milliseconds )
```

Examples

```
const electionDay = new Date(2020, 10, 3);        // 10 is November
const grandOpening = new Date(2021, 1, 16, 8);     // 1 is February
const departureTime = new Date(2021, 3, 6, 18, 30); // 3 is April
```

How to create a Date object by copying another Date object

```
const invoiceDate = new Date("8/8/2021");
const dueDate = new Date( invoiceDate );
// You can then add a number of days to due_date. See figure 12-11.
```

What happens when an invalid date is passed to the Date Constructor

```
const leapDate = new Date("2/29/2021");           // Invalid Date
```

Date strings that can lead to unexpected results in some browsers

```
const electionDay = new Date("11-3-2020");        // Invalid Date
const electionDay = new Date("11/3/20");          // 11/3/1920
```

How to check whether an object is a Date object

```
if (electionDay instanceof Date) { ... }
```

Description

- In JavaScript, dates are represented by the number of milliseconds since midnight, January 1, 1970.

- When you create a Date object, the date and times are specified as local time. Local time is in the time zone specified on the computer that's running the user's web browser.

- Month numbers start with 0, so January is 0 and December is 11. This allows these values to be used with arrays.

- You can use the instanceof operator to test whether an object is a Date object.

Figure 12-9   How to create Date objects

How to use the methods of the Date object

Figure 12-10 describes several methods that are provided by the Date object. The first group of methods creates a formatted string from a date. However, as the examples show, you can't control the format used by these methods. In the next figure, though, you'll learn how to create your own formats for date and time strings. And at the end of this chapter, you'll learn how to use another feature of JavaScript to format dates based on different locales.

The methods in the second group are used to extract the parts from a Date object. Here, all of the methods except the getTime() method return the date part from the local time. By contrast, the getTime() method uses universal time, which is the number of milliseconds since midnight, January 1, 1970. There is also a getYear() method that returns a two-digit year, but its use is not recommended.

The methods in the third group are used to set new values for the parts in a Date object. These methods let you use values that are outside the allowed range. Then, any value over or under the allowed range will cause the next most significant date part to roll over.

For example, if you set the hours of a date to 25, the time will be set to 1 and one day will be added to the day of the month. Or, if you set the day of the month to 0, the month will be rolled back one and the day will be set to the last day of that month. By letting you use values that are out of the normal range, JavaScript provides a mechanism to perform date math using any of the parts of the date or time. You'll see examples of this in the next figure.

The formatting methods of a Date object

Method	Description
toString()	Returns a string containing the date and time in local time using the client's time zone.
toDateString()	Returns a string representing just the date in local time.
toTimeString()	Returns a string representing just the time in local time.

Examples of the formatting methods

```
const birthday = new Date( 2001, 0, 7, 8, 25); // Jan 7, 2001 8:25am
alert( birthday.toString() );       // "Sun Jan 07 2001 08:25:00 GMT-0800"
alert( birthday.toDateString() );   // "Sun Jan 07 2001"
alert( birthday.toTimeString() );   // "08:25:00 GMT-0800"
```

The get methods of a Date object

Method	Description
getTime()	Returns the number of milliseconds since midnight, January 1, 1970 in universal time (GMT).
getFullYear()	Returns the four-digit year in local time.
getMonth()	Returns the month in local time, starting with 0 for January.
getDate()	Returns the day of the month in local time.
getDay()	Returns the day of the week (1=Sunday, 2=Monday, and so on).
getHours()	Returns the hour in 24-hour format in local time.
getMinutes()	Returns the minutes in local time.
getSeconds()	Returns the seconds in local time.
getMilliseconds()	Returns the milliseconds in local time.

The set methods of a Date object

Method	Description
setFullYear(year)	Sets the four-digit year in local time.
setMonth(month)	Sets the month in local time.
setDate(day)	Sets the day of the month in local time.
setHours(hour)	Sets the hour in 24-hour format in local time.
setMinutes(minute)	Sets the minutes in local time.
setSeconds(second)	Sets the seconds in local time.
setMilliseconds(ms)	Sets the milliseconds in local time.

Description

- Except for the getTime() method, the get and set methods use the time zone specified on the user's computer to work with local time.
- There are complementary get and set methods that start with getUTC and setUTC that work with the Date object in universal time (GMT). For example, the getUTCHours() method returns the hour in 24-hour format in universal time.

Figure 12-10   How to use the methods of the Date object

Examples of working with dates

Figure 12-11 shows how you can apply the methods of the last figure. The first example shows you how to format a date. The last three examples show you how to perform calculations with dates. This should give you some ideas for how you can use Date objects in your own applications.

Example 1 shows how to format a date. To do that, the JavaScript code first creates a new Date object that contains a date and time. Next, it extracts the year, month, and date parts, and it adds 1 to the month number. Then, it builds a text string using these values. As the string is built, the month and date numbers are padded with a leading zero if they are one digit.

Example 2 shows how to calculate the number of days from the current date until the New Year. First, the current date is retrieved in a Date object and a copy of this object is made. Then, the month and day in the copy are set to January 1st, and 1 is added to the year. At this point, the now constant contains the current date and the newYear constant contains the January 1st date of the following year.

Next, the number of milliseconds between the two dates is calculated by subtracting the dates that are extracted by the getTime() method. After that, the number of milliseconds in a day is calculated by multiplying the number of hours in a day (24) by the number of minutes in an hour (60) by the number of seconds in a minute (60) by the number of milliseconds in a second (1000).

Then, the number of days is calculated by dividing the number of milliseconds between the two dates by the number of milliseconds in one day and rounding that value up using the ceil() method. Last, a message is displayed that indicates the number of days remaining. To do that, an if-else statement is used to alter the message when there is only one day left.

Example 3 shows how to calculate a due date. Here, the invoiceDate constant contains a Date object with the current date. Then, a dueDate constant is created that contains a Date object with the same date as the one in the invoiceDate constant. Last, 21 is added to the date in the dueDate object so the due date is 21 days after the invoice date.

Example 4 shows how to determine the last day of the current month. Here, the endOfMonth constant starts at today's date. Then, 1 is added to the month, and the day is set to zero. This rolls the date back one day, which causes 1 to be subtracted from the month and the day of the month to be set to the last day of the month. If, for example, the current date is December 2, adding 1 to the month number rolls it over to month 0, or January. Then, when the date is set to zero, the date and month roll back to December 31.

Example 1: How to display the date in your own format

```
const departTime = new Date(2021, 3, 16, 18, 30); // April 16, 2021 6:30pm
const year = departTime.getFullYear();
const month = departTime.getMonth() + 1;  // add 1 since months start at 0
const day = departTime.getDate();

let dateText = year + "-";
dateText += month.toString().padStart(2, "0") + "-"; // pad month if 1 digit
dateText += day.toString().padStart(2, "0");         // pad day if 1 digit

// final dateText is "2021-04-16"
```

Example 2: How to calculate the days until the New Year

```
const now = new Date();            // get the current date and time
const newYear = new Date(now);     // copy the current date and time
newYear.setMonth(0);               // set the month to January
newYear.setDate(1);                // set the day to the 1st
newYear.setFullYear( newYear.getFullYear() + 1 );  // add 1 to the year

// time in milliseconds
const timeLeft = newYear.getTime() - now.getTime();

// milliseconds in a day: hrs * mins * secs * milliseconds
const msInOneDay = 24 * 60 * 60 * 1000;

// convert milliseconds to days
const daysLeft = Math.ceil( timeLeft / msInOneDay );

let message = "There ";
if (daysLeft == 1) {
    message += "is one day";
}
else {
    message += "are " + daysLeft + " days";
}
message += " left until the New Year.";

// If today is November 3, 2020, message is
// "There are 59 days left until the New Year."
```

Example 3: How to calculate a due date

```
const invoiceDate = new Date();
const dueDate = new Date( invoiceDate );
dueDate.setDate( dueDate.getDate() + 21 );  // due date is 3 weeks later
```

Example 4: How to find the end of the month

```
const endOfMonth = new Date();

// Set the month to next month
endOfMonth.setMonth( endOfMonth.getMonth() + 1 );

// Set the date to one day before the start of the month
endOfMonth.setDate( 0 );
```

Figure 12-11   Examples of working with dates

The Count Down application

To illustrate the use of strings and dates, figure 12-12 presents a Count Down application. This application accepts an event name and event date from a user and calculates the number of days between the current date and that event.

The application displays a different message if the date is in the future, in the past, or is today's date. In addition, it makes sure the user enters the date in an expected format. To do this work, this application uses a Date object for the calculation. And, it uses a String object to create the message that's displayed.

The HTML and CSS

In part 1 of figure 12-12, you can see the HTML and some of the CSS for this application. The HTML in the main element includes two text boxes and a button. When the user enters data into the text boxes and clicks the Countdown! button, a message is displayed in the label element below the button. As before, the id attributes for these elements are the ones that are used in the JavaScript.

At the end of the body element of the HTML, you can see the two script elements for the JavaScript files. The first one identifies the jQuery library. The second one identifies the JavaScript file that's shown in the next figure.

In the CSS in this figure, you can see the style rule for the label element that has "message" as its id attribute. This sets the font color to red and the font weight to bold.

The user interface for the Count Down application

Countdown To...

Event Name: [Earth Day]

Event Date: [04/22/2021]

[Countdown!]

276 day(s) until Earth Day! (Thu Apr 22 2021)

The HTML for the application

```html
<!DOCTYPE html>
<html lang="en">
<head>
    <meta charset="UTF-8">
    <meta name="viewport" content="width=device-width, initial-scale=1">
    <title>Count Down</title>
    <link rel="stylesheet" href="count_down.css">
</head>

<body>
    <main>
        <h1>Countdown To...</h1>
        <div>
            <label for="event">Event Name:</label>
            <input type="text" name="event" id="event">
        </div>
        <div>
            <label for="date">Event Date:</label>
            <input type="text" name="date" id="date"><br>
        </div>
        <div>
            <label> </label>
            <input type="button" name="countdown" id="countdown"
                value="Countdown!">
        </div>
        <div><label id="message"></label></div>
    </main>

    <script src="https://code.jquery.com/jquery-3.4.1.slim.min.js"></script>
    <script src="count_down.js"></script>
</body>
</html>
```

The CSS style rule for the label element

```css
#message {
    color: red;
    font-weight: bold;
}
```

Figure 12-12   The Count Down application (part 1)

The JavaScript

Parts 2 and 3 of figure 12-12 show the JavaScript for this application. All of this JavaScript except for the "use strict" directive is coded within the ready() event handler. This event handler consists of the click() event handler for the Countdown button, as well as a final statement that moves the focus to the Event Name text box.

The click() event handler starts by getting the values the user entered for the event name and date. Then, it retrieves the label element with an id of "message" and stores it in a constant named messageLbl. This element is the one that will be used to display messages to the user.

Next, this event handler starts a series of data validation checks using if statements. First, it uses the length property of the String object to make sure that the user entered something for the event name and the event date.

Second, it uses the split() method of the String object to make sure the date has been entered with two slashes. This works because if the user has done that, there should be three elements in the resulting array when the string is split on the slash character. If there aren't three elements, then there aren't two slashes in the string.

Third, it uses the substring() method of the String object to get the last four characters of the date string, and then uses the global isNaN() method to make sure those characters are a number. This works because, if the last 4 characters contain a character like "-" or a "/", the isNaN() method returns true.

Fourth, it uses the date string entered by the user to create a new Date object. Then, it checks if the new Date object contains "Invalid Date".

If any of these data validation checks fail, they use the text() method of the label element that's in the messageLbl constant to display an appropriate error message and then return. This means that as soon as a check fails, the message is displayed and the event handler stops running.

If all the data validation checks pass, the code formats the event name so the first letter in each word of the name is capitalized and the rest of the letters are lowercase. To do that, it starts by declaring a variable named formattedName that will store the event name as it's formatted. Then, it uses the split() method to break the event name into words by passing it a space.

Next, the code loops through the words. For each word, the loop uses the substring() method to get the first letter of the word, and the toUppercase() method to capitalize it. After that, it uses the substring() method again to get the rest of the letters in the word. Then, it uses the toLowercase() method to convert them to lower case, and it adds them to the capitalized first letter. Finally, it adds the word to the formattedName variable, padding the end with a space to replace the space removed by the split() method.

When the loop ends, the code calls the trimEnd() method of the formattedName variable. This removes the trailing space that was added to the last word.

The JavaScript

```javascript
"use strict";

$( document ).ready( () => {

    $("#countdown").click( () => {
        const eventName = $("#event").val();
        const eventDate = $("#date").val();
        const messageLbl = $("#message");

        // make sure user enters an event name and date
        if (eventName.length == 0 || eventDate.length == 0) {
            messageLbl.text( "Please enter both a name and a date." );
            return;
        }

        // make sure event date string has two slashes
        const dateParts = eventDate.split("/");
        if (dateParts.length != 3) {
            messageLbl.text( "Please enter the date in MM/DD/YYYY format." );
            return;
        }

        // make sure event date string has a 4-digit year
        const year = eventDate.substring(eventDate.length - 4);
        if (isNaN(year)) {
            messageLbl.text( "Please enter the date in MM/DD/YYYY format." );
            return;
        }

        // convert event date string to Date object and check for validity
        let date = new Date(eventDate);
        if (date == "Invalid Date") {
            messageLbl.text( "Please enter the date in MM/DD/YYYY format." );
            return;
        }

        // capitalize each word of event name
        let formattedName = "";
        const words = eventName.split(" ");
        for (const i in words) {
            const firstLetter = words[i].substring(0,1).toUpperCase();
            const word = firstLetter + words[i].substring(1).toLowerCase();
            formattedName += word.padEnd(word.length + 1);
        }
        formattedName = formattedName.trimEnd();
```

Figure 12-12   The Count Down application (part 2)

Next, the code calculates the number of days between the current date and the event date. To do that, it creates a new Date object with the current date and stores it in the today constant. Then, it uses the getTime() method of the Date object to subtract the today value from the event date value, which are both in milliseconds, and stores the resulting value in the msFromToday constant.

After that, it calculates the number of milliseconds in a day and stores that value in the msForOneDay constant. Finally, it divides the msFromToday value by the msForOneDay value and rounds up the resulting value using the Math. ceil() method. This value is then assigned to the daysToDate variable.

Last, this event handler declares a variable named msg that will hold the message to be displayed and formats the date as a string. Then, it checks the daysToDate variable. If it's zero, the date entered by the user is today. If it's greater than zero, the date is in the future. And if it's less than zero, the date is in the past. For each result, this function constructs a different message using a template literal, and then uses the text() method of the label element to display that message.

The JavaScript (continued)

```javascript
        // calculate days
        const today = new Date();
        const msFromToday = date.getTime() - today.getTime();
        const msForOneDay = 24 * 60 * 60 * 1000;
        let daysToDate = Math.ceil( msFromToday / msForOneDay );

        // create and display message
        let msg = "";
        date = date.toDateString();
        if (daysToDate == 0) {
            msg = `Hooray! Today is ${formattedName}! (${date})`;
        }
        else if (daysToDate > 0) {
            msg = `${daysToDate} day(s) until ${formattedName}! (${date})`;
        }
        else if (daysToDate < 0) {
            daysToDate = Math.abs(daysToDate);
            msg = `${formattedName} happened ${daysToDate} day(s) ago.
                (${date})`;
        }
        messageLbl.text(msg);
    });

    $("#event").focus();
});
```

Figure 12-12   The Count Down application (part 3)

The Internationalization API

The *ECMAScript Internationalization API Specification* is sometimes included in lists of the features of the ECMAScript specification. However, it's actually a separate specification that's a complement to the ECMAScript Specification.

The Internationalization API has a single object named Intl. This object, in turn, has constructors, two of which are presented in the table in figure 12-13. You can use these constructors to create objects that perform language-sensitive formatting on numbers and dates.

However, there's more to the Internationalization API than what's presented here. To learn more, you can go to the URL at the bottom of this figure.

How to format numbers

The first example in figure 12-13 shows how to use the NumberFormat() constructor to format numbers for two different locales. Here, the locales are coded using a language and a country. The first statement creates a NumberFormat object for the English language in the United States, and the second statement creates a NumberFormat object for the German language (Deutsch) in Germany. Note that the two parts of each locale are separated by a hyphen.

The next two statements show the results of calling the format() method of each NumberFormat object on a decimal value. Here, you can see that commas and a period are used as the separators for the first locale. By contrast, periods and a comma are used for the second locale.

The second example shows how to use the NumberFormat constructor to format numbers using a currency format. The first three statements create NumberFormat objects for three different locales: English in the United States, English in Great Britain, and German in Germany. In addition to the locale parameter, an options parameter is included with two options. The first option, style, indicates that the numbers should be formatted as currency. The second option, currency, indicates the currency format to be used.

The next three statements show the result of calling the format() method on these objects. As you can see, the first number is formatted using U.S. dollars, the second number is formatted using British pounds, and the third number is formatted using euros.

How to format dates

The third example in figure 12-13 shows how to use the DateTimeFormat constructor to format dates for different locales. In this example, the first two statements create DateTimeFormat objects using the English, United States and German, Germany locales. Then, the next two statements call the format() method on these objects, which produce different date formats for the different locales.

Two of the constructors of the Intl object

Constructor	Description
`NumberFormat(locale[,options])`	Creates a new NumberFormat object for the specified locale with the specified formatting options.
`DateTimeFormat(locale[,options])`	Creates a new DateTimeFormat object for the specified locale with the specified formatting options.

A method of the NumberFormat and DateTimeFormat objects

Method	Description
`format(object)`	Formats the specified NumberFormat or DateTimeFormat object according to its locale and formatting options.

How to use NumberFormat objects to format numbers

```
const us = new Intl.NumberFormat( "en-US" );
const de = new Intl.NumberFormat( "de-DE" );

const result_1a = us.format(1234567.89);      // result_1a is 1,234,567.89
const result_1b = de.format(1234567.89);      // result_1b is 1.234.567,89
```

How to use NumberFormat objects to format currency

```
const us = new Intl.NumberFormat( "en-US",
                                  {style:"currency", currency:"USD"} );
const gb = new Intl.NumberFormat( "en-GB",
                                  {style:"currency", currency:"GBP"} );
const de = new Intl.NumberFormat( "de-DE",
                                  {style:"currency", currency:"EUR"} );

const result_2a = us.format(100200300.40);  // result_2a is $100,200,300.40
const result_2b = gb.format(100200300.40);  // result_2b is £100,200,300.40
const result_2c = de.format(100200300.40);  // result_2c is 100.200.300,40 €
```

How to use DateTimeFormat objects to format dates

```
const dt = new Date("7/4/2021");

const us = new Intl.DateTimeFormat( "en-US" );
const de = new Intl.DateTimeFormat( "de-DE" );

const result_3a = us.format(dt);              // result_3a is 7/4/2021
const result_3b = de.format(dt);              // result_3b is 4.7.2021
```

A URL with more information about the Internationalization API

https://developer.mozilla.org/en-US/docs/Web/JavaScript/Reference/
Global_Objects/Intl

Description

- The *ECMAScript Internationalization API specification* allows you to format numbers and dates in language-sensitive ways.

- The Internationalization API has a single object, Intl, with constructors that allow you to create objects that have format() methods to do the formatting.

- You can use the URL shown above to learn more about the Internationalization API.

Figure 12-13   How to work with the Internationalization API

Perspective

This chapter has presented the essential skills for working with numbers, strings, and dates. To add to this skillset, you can read chapter 15, which shows how to use the string methods for working with arrays.

Terms

instance method
static property
static method
ECMAScript Internationalization API specification

Summary

- To work with numeric data, you can use the *static properties* and *static methods* of the Number and Math objects, as well as the *instance methods* of the Number object. This includes the random() method of the Math object, which generates a random number from 0 to 1.

- The length property of a String object returns the number of characters in the string, and the methods of a String object let you work with the characters in the string.

- In JavaScript, dates are stored in Date objects, and they are represented by the number of milliseconds since midnight, January 1, 1970.

- The constructors of the Date object let you create a Date object in four different ways. Then you can use the methods of the Date object to work with the date in the object.

- The *ECMAScript Internationalization API specification* allows you to format numbers and dates in language-sensitive ways.

Exercise 12-1   Enhance the Future Value application

In this exercise, you'll enhance a Future Value application that looks like the one that follows. Along the way, you'll work with large numbers, use a random number generator, work with dates, and work with strings.

The Future Value Calculator

Investment amount: 11275

Interest rate: 4

Years: 34

Future value: $42,780.92

Calculate

Today is 06/02/2020 at 14:47.

Open, review, and test the application

1. Use your text editor or IDE to open the application in this folder:

    `javascript_jquery\exercises\ch12\future_value`

    Then, test this application with valid values to see how it works.

2. Review the JavaScript code for this application, and note that it includes the getRandomNumber() function of figure 12-4 so you can use it later on.

Work with large numbers

3. Test this application with these values: 10000 for investment amount, 15 for interest rate, and 1000 for number of years. This should return the future value with e notation and as many significant digits as JavaScript provides for.

4. Change the entry for the number of years to 10000 and test the application again. This time, it should return Infinity for the future value. That's because the future value is larger than the maximum value that JavaScript can represent.

5. Modify the JavaScript by adding an if statement to the for loop that calculates the future value. This if statement should test whether the future value is equal to infinity. If it is, the if statement should use the alert() method to display a message like this, where i is the counter for the loop:

    ```
    Future value = Infinity
    i = 4995
    ```

    This if statement should also set the value of i to the value of years so the loop will end.

6. Add an alert() method that displays the maximum value of a JavaScript number after the for loop finishes, since this has nothing to do with the calculation. Then, test the application to see the alert messages that are displayed.

Use a random number generator

7. Comment out the three statements that get investment, rate, and years from the text boxes. Then, use the getRandomNumber() function to get random values for investment, rate, and years. The maximum values for these variables should be 50000, 15, and 50. The application should get these random values each time the user clicks the Calculate button, display these values in the first three text boxes, and calculate the future value using these values.

8. Comment out the alert() method that you added in step 6. Then, test this application by clicking on the Calculate button several times to see how the values are varied. This illustrates how a random number generator can be used to quickly test an application with a wide range of values.

Format the future value with a dollar sign and commas

9. Create a new function named formatFutureValue() that gets the future value after it has been calculated and returns a formatted version of that value like the one shown above.

    To do this, you need to use the indexOf() method to get the location of the decimal point and the substring() method to extract the cents, hundreds, thousands, and millions digits from the future value. Then, you can concatenate the parts with a dollar sign, commas, and decimal point. The trick is that some future values won't have millions digits, so you need to provide for that with if statements.

10. Modify the click event handler for the Calculate button so it calls this method to format the future value after it has been calculated and then displays it in the future value text box.

11. Comment out the statement you added in step 10 that calls the formatFutureValue() function. Then, add code that formats the future value using the NumberFormat object of the Internationalization API.

Add the current date to the <p> element below the button

12. Start by creating a new function named getDate() that gets the current date and formats it like this:
    Today is 04/15/2021 at 14:29.

    To do that, you need to get a Date object that contains the current date. Then, you need to use the Date methods to extract the appropriate date and time parts so you can format them as shown above. Note that 24-hour format is used.

13. Modify the ready event handler so it calls the getDate() function to get the formatted date and then displays it in the <p> element below the button in the HTML.

13

How to work with control structures, exceptions, and regular expressions

In chapter 3, you were introduced to conditional expressions and the if, while, do-while, and for statements. Now, you'll learn more about coding these expressions and statements, including how to use the conditional operator, the switch, break, and continue statements, and how to work with non-Boolean values in conditional statements.

After that, you'll learn how to handle any exceptions that might be thrown by an application, and how to use regular expressions. Both of these skills are useful when validating user input.

What else you need to know about control structures

In chapter 3, you learned how to code conditional expressions and how to use them in if, for, and while statements. Now, you'll learn more about using these structures.

How to use the equality and identity operators

In chapter 3, you learned how to use the *equality operators* that are shown at the top of figure 13-1. For simple comparisons, these operators work fine. But when the tests are more complex, unexpected results may occur for two reasons.

First, the equality operators perform *type coercion*. This means that if different types of data are being compared, the values will be converted to the same data type before the comparison takes place. For example, in the test 3 == "3", the string "3" is converted to the number 3 and then the comparison is done.

Second, the type conversion that's done for type coercion is different from the type conversion that's done by the parseInt() and parseFloat() methods. For instance, an empty string is converted to 0 during type coercion, but the parse-Float() method converts an empty string to NaN.

These problems can be avoided by using the *identity operators* presented in the second table in this figure. That's because the identity operators don't perform type coercion. Then, if two values of different types are compared, the result will always be false. For this reason, some IDEs consider the use of the identity operators a best practice, and warn you when you use equality operators.

How to use the break and continue statements

The break and continue statements give you additional control over how loops work. The *break statement* skips to the end of the current loop, while the *continue statement* skips to the start of the next iteration of the loop.

The first example in figure 13-1 shows how the break statement can be used in a while statement that will loop forever because its condition is set to true. However, this loop will only run until the user enters a valid number in the prompt dialog box. Then, a break statement ends the loop so the entry can be processed.

The second example shows how the continue statement can be used in a while loop. Here, the loop runs while a number ranges from 1 to 40. Then, within the loop, the number is divided by 5 and the remainder is tested to see whether it is zero. If so, the continue statement skips to the start of the loop. If it isn't, the number is added to the sum variable. When the loop ends, that sum is displayed in an alert dialog box.

The equality operators

Operator	Description	Example
==	Equal	`lastName == "Hopper"`
!=	Not equal	`months != 0`

The identity operators

Operator	Description	Example
===	Equal	`lastName === "Hopper"`
!==	Not equal	`months !== 0`

Example 1: The break statement in a while loop

```
let number = 0;
while (true) {
    number = parseInt( prompt("Enter a number from 1 to 10.") );
    if ( isNaN(number) || number < 1 || number > 10 ) {
        alert("Invalid entry. Try again.");
    } else {
        break;
    }
}
alert(number);
```

Example 2: The continue statement in a while loop

```
let sum = 0;
let number = 0;
while ( number <= 40 ) {
    number++;
    if ( number % 5 !== 0 ) {
        continue;                          // if number isn't divisible by 5
    }
    sum += number;
}
alert(sum);         // displays sum of 5, 10, 15, 20, 25, 30, 35, 40
```

Description

- The *equality operators* perform *type coercion* whenever that's necessary. That means they convert data from one type to another. For example, they often convert strings to numbers before the comparisons.

- However, the type conversion that's done by the equality operators is different from that done by the parseInt() or parseFloat() methods.

- The *identity operators* do not perform type coercion. If the two operands are of different types, the result will always be false.

- The *break statement* ends a loop. In other words, it jumps out of the loop.

- The *continue statement* ends the current iteration of a loop, but allows the next iteration to proceed. In other words, it jumps to the start of the loop.

- When you're working with nested loops, the break and continue statements apply only to the loop that they're in.

Figure 13-1   The equality and identity operators and the break and continue statements

How to use the switch statement

A *switch statement* is a convenient way to express a certain form of if state-ment. Specifically, it can be used in place of an if statement with multiple else if clauses in which one expression is tested for equality with several values. This is illustrated by the statements in figure 13-2.

The switch statement starts with the keyword *switch* followed by a *switch expression* inside of parentheses. This expression is not a conditional expres-sion. It is an expression that returns a single value that will be used to determine which *case* to execute. The expression is often as simple as a single constant as shown in the examples in this figure.

When the switch statement is executed, it checks each of the values in the *case labels*. If it finds one that's equal to the result of the expression, it executes the code that follows that case label. It continues executing until it reaches either a *break statement*, a *return statement*, or the end of the switch statement.

If no case labels match the value in the switch expression, the switch state-ment starts executing the code that follows the default label. But this default case is optional. If it is omitted and no case labels match the expression, the switch statement won't execute any code. A switch statement can only have one default case. It's usually the last case in the statement, but it can be anywhere.

In the first example in this figure, the expression is just a constant named letterGrade that should contain a letter. Then, each case label is checked against the value of this constant. If, for example, letterGrade is "B", the switch state-ment starts executing the code after the label for that case and sets the message variable to "above average". It then encounters a break statement and no further code is executed by the switch statement. If letterGrade had been "Z", however, the code after the default label would have been executed and the message would have been set to "invalid grade".

In the second example, the case labels are coded in a way that provides *fall through*. This occurs when code starts executing at one case label but doesn't encounter a break or return statement, so it continues by executing the code for the next case label. Although this is often discouraged because it can be confusing, this example shows one case where fall through is useful.

In this example, the same code should be executed when letterGrade is "A" or "B". Instead of repeating the code, two case labels are placed before the code. Then, if letterGrade is "A", the switch statement will fall through and execute the code after the case for "B". Likewise, if letterGrade is "D", the switch statement will fall through and execute the code after the case for "F". Except for simple cases like this, though, you should avoid using fall through in your switch state-ments because that can lead to unexpected errors and be hard to debug.

The last example shows how to use return statements rather than break state-ments to stop the execution of a switch statement. This is common in functions that use switch statements to determine the value to return.

When you use a switch statement, you can nest if statements within the cases. You can also nest switch statements within the cases of another switch statement. As always, you need to use caution with nesting since it can make your code confusing and hard to maintain.

A switch statement with a default case

```
switch ( letterGrade ) {
    case "A":
        message = "well above average";
        break;
    case "B":
        message = "above average";
        break;
    case "C":
        message = "average";
        break;
    case "D":
        message = "below average";
        break;
    case "F":
        message = "failing";
        break;
    default:
        message = "invalid grade";
        break;
}
```

A switch statement with fall through

```
switch ( letterGrade ) {
    case "A":
    case "B":
        message = "Scholarship approved.";
        break;
    case "C":
        message = "Application requires review.";
        break;
    case "D":
    case "F":
        message = "Scholarship not approved.";
        break;
}
```

A function that uses a switch statement to return a value

```
const getTimeOfDay = ampm => {
    switch( ampm.toUpperCase() ) {
        case "AM":
            return "morning";
        case "PM":
            return "evening";
        default:
            return "invalid";
    }
};
```

Description

- The *switch statement* evaluates the *switch expression* in the parentheses and then executes the code in the *case label* whose value matches that expression.

- Execution stops when it reaches a *break statement* or a *return statement*.

- If a case doesn't contain a break or return statement, execution will *fall through* to the next label.

Figure 13-2   How to use the switch statement

How to use the conditional operator

Figure 13-3 shows how to use JavaScript's *conditional operator*. This is JavaScript's only *ternary operator*, which means it has three operands. By contrast, a *unary operator*, such as ++, has one operand (the value being incremented) and a *binary operator*, such as *, has two operands (the two values being multiplied).

Since the conditional operator has three operands (the conditional expression, the value to return if true, and the value to return if false), it needs two symbols to separate them. As the syntax at the top of this figure shows, the question mark and colon are used as the separators.

When executed, the conditional operator first evaluates the conditional expression to get a true or false result. Then, if the conditional expression is true, the result of the expression in the middle operand is used as the result of the conditional operator. If the conditional expression is false, the result of the expression in the last operand is used as the result of the conditional operator.

The first example in this figure shows how to use the conditional operator to set a constant to one of two values based on the comparison. If the age is 18 or more, message will contain "Can vote". If the age is less than 18, message will contain "Cannot vote".

The second example shows how to use an expression in one of the operands. If hours is over 40, overtime will contain 1.5 times the pay rate for the hours over 40. If hours is not over 40, overtime will be zero.

The third example shows how to select between a singular or plural ending for use in a message to the user. If error_count is 1, the ending will be empty. Otherwise, "s" will be used for the ending.

The fourth example shows how to add one to a value or set it back to 1 depending on whether the value is at its maximum. For example, if max_value is 10 and value is 6, the test will be false and value will become the value plus 1. However, when value reaches 10, it will be set to 1.

If you need to perform this kind of rollover of a variable but the starting value is 0 instead of 1, you don't have to use the conditional operator. Instead, you can use the % operator. For example, if you execute this statement repeatedly with a starting value of 9

```
value = (value + 1) % 10
```

the values will range from 0 to 9 and then back to 0.

The fifth example shows how to combine the conditional operator with the return keyword so the result is returned by a function. Here, if number is greater than highest, highest is returned. Otherwise, the number is returned.

For clarity, it is often better to use if statements than conditional operators. This is illustrated by the last two examples in this figure. Nevertheless, many JavaScript programmers like to use conditional operators because they require less code.

Syntax of the conditional operator

```
( conditional_expression ) ? value_if_true : value_if_false
```

Examples of using the conditional operator

Example 1: Setting a string based on a comparison

```
const message = ( age >= 18 ) ? "Can vote" : "Cannot vote";
```

Example 2: Calculating overtime pay

```
const overtime = ( hours > 40 ) ? ( hours - 40 ) * rate * 1.5 : 0;
```

Example 3: Selecting a singular or plural ending based on a value

```
const ending = ( errorCount == 1 ) ? "" : "s".
const message = "Found " + error_count + " error" + ending + ".";
```

Example 4: Setting a value to 1 if it's at a maximum value

```
let value = ( value == maxValue ) ? 1 : value + 1;
```

Example 5: Returning one of two values based on a comparison

```
return ( number > highest ) ? highest : number;
```

How conditional operators can be rewritten with if statements

Example 1 rewritten with an if statement

```
let message;
if ( age >= 18 ) {
    message = "Can vote";
} else {
    message = "Cannot vote";
}
```

Example 4 rewritten with an if statement

```
if ( value == maxValue ) {
    value = 1;
}
else {
    value = value + 1;
}
```

Description

- The *conditional operator* first evaluates the conditional expression. Then, if the expression is true, the value that results from the middle operand is returned. But if the expression is false, the value that results from the third operand is returned.

- Although the use of the conditional operator can lead to cryptic code, JavaScript programmers commonly use this operator. For clarity, though, conditional operators can be rewritten with if statements.

Figure 13-3   How to use the conditional operator

How to use non-Boolean values in conditions

So far in this book, you've seen conditions that use relational and logical operators to return Boolean values of true or false. However, non-Boolean values such as numbers or strings also evaluate to either true or false in JavaScript. Because of that, they can be used as conditions. When used as a condition, these values can be called *truthy* or *falsey* to indicate that they aren't actually Boolean values, even though they can evaluate to true or false.

Figure 13-4 shows how you can use non-Boolean values in conditions. To start, it presents the non-Boolean values that JavaScript evaluates as false (falsey values) and true (truthy values). The values that it evaluates as false are the number 0, an empty string, the null data type, the undefined data type, and an empty array (that is, an array with no elements). The values that it evaluates as true are any number that isn't zero, any string or array that isn't empty, any object, and any symbol.

This figure also shows three examples of how to use a non-Boolean value as the condition for an if statement. The first example declares a variable named val but doesn't initialize it. Because of that, the value is undefined. Then, an if statement tests whether the val variable is false. In this case, because the value of val is undefined, it will evaluate as false and the code in the if block will execute.

The second example uses the prompt() method to get a value from the user, and that value is assigned to the name constant. Then, an if statement tests the name constant to determine if the user entered a value. If so, name will evaluate as true and the if block will execute. If not, name will contain an empty string, which evaluates as false. In that case, the code in the else block will execute.

The if statement in the third example uses the geolocation property of the navigator property of the window object as its condition. If the geolocation property doesn't exist, the value of the condition is undefined and evaluates to false. That means that the code in the if block only executes if the property exists. This is a good way to avoid errors by making sure a property exists before you use it.

Non-Boolean values that JavaScript evaluates as false

- 0
- `""` (Empty string)
- `null`
- `undefined`
- an empty array

Non-Boolean values that JavaScript evaluates as true

- any number other than zero
- any string that isn't empty
- any array that isn't empty
- any object
- any symbol

Example 1: An if statement that checks if a variable is initialized

```
let val;
if (!val) {
    alert("Variable 'val' is not initialized");
}
```

Example 2: An if-else statement that checks for an empty string

```
const name = prompt("Please enter a name");
if (name) {
    alert(name);
} else {
    alert("You did not enter a name");
}
```

Example 3: An if statement that checks for the existence of a property

```
if (window.navigator.geolocation) {
    // code that uses the geolocation property of the window object's
    // Navigator object
}
```

Description

- JavaScript allows you to use non-Boolean as well as Boolean values in conditions.
- Non-Boolean values that are used in this way are called *truthy* or *falsey* to indicate that they aren't actual Boolean values but can still be used in conditions.
- You can use non-Boolean values to test for a number of conditions like uninitialized variables, strings that are empty, and properties that are nonexistent.

Figure 13-4   How to use non-Boolean values in conditions

Additional techniques
for using the logical operators

As you learned in chapter 3, the logical OR and AND operators are short-circuit operators. That is, they evaluate from left to right and stop as soon as the value of a condition is enough to determine the value of the entire condition. Then, these operators return the value of the last condition they evaluated. As a result, you can use them to assign values to constants and variables as shown in the first two examples in figure 13-5.

In the first example, both operands use identity operators to return a Boolean value. This means that the OR operator will return a Boolean value. If, for example, the state is equal to "CA", the entire expression is going to be true, the evaluation stops, and true is stored in the constant. But if the state isn't equal to "CA", the evaluation continues and either true or false is returned based on the evaluation of the next operand. The second example is similar except that it uses the AND operator to determine if a true or false value is stored in the constant.

You can also use this *short-circuit evaluation* with non-Boolean values. For instance, the third example shows how you can use the OR operator to provide a default value. Here, a prompt() method prompts the user for a value. If the user enters a value, this method returns a non-empty string. Then, the OR operator evaluates it as true, short-circuits, and returns the value. But if the user doesn't enter a value, the prompt() method returns an empty string. Then, the OR operator evaluates it as false, evaluates the second operand as true, and returns the value of the second operand. As a result, the name constant will be assigned either the value entered by the user or the default value "N/A".

The fourth example shows how you can achieve the same effect using the *nullish coalescing operator* (??) that was introduced with ES2020. As you can see, this statement is identical to the first one except for the operator that's used.

You can use a similar technique with the AND operator to make sure that a property exists. For instance, the third example in the last figure checked that the geolocation property exists using this conditional expression:

```
if (window.navigator.geolocation)
```

However, this assumes that the navigator property also exists. That's probably a safe assumption for the window object, but it may not be for other objects.

The fifth example in this figure shows how to use the AND operator to make sure that the window, navigator, and geolocation properties exist. This works because if any of these properties is undefined, it evaluates to false, so the whole expression is false.

The sixth example shows how you can achieve the same result with the *optional chaining operator* (?.). Like the nullish coalescing operator, this operator was introduced with ES2020.

The last two examples show how to combine these two tasks. Here, the seventh example uses the AND and OR operators to check that a chained property exists and provide a default value if it doesn't. The second statement accomplishes the same thing using the nullish coalescing and optional chaining operators.

Statements that store a true or false value in a constant

Example 1: Using the OR operator

```
const selected = state === "CA" || state === "NC";
```

Example 2: Using the AND operator

```
const canVote = age >= 18 && citizen;
```

Statements that store a value and provide a default value

Example 3: Using the OR operator

```
const name = prompt("Please enter a name") || "N/A";
```

Example 4: Using the nullish coalescing operator

```
const name = prompt("Please enter a name") ?? "N/A";
```

Statements that check for the existence of a property

Example 5: Using the AND operator

```
if (window && window.navigator && window.navigator.geolocation) { ... }
```

Example 6: Using the optional chaining operator

```
if (window?.navigator?.geolocation) { ... }
```

Statements that store the value of a property or a default value if the property doesn't exist

Example 7: Using the AND and OR operators

```
const initial = book && book.author && book.author.middleInitial ||
              "No Middle Initial";
```

Example 8: Using the nullish coalescing and optional chaining operators

```
const initial = book?.author?.middleInitial ?? "No Middle Initial";
```

Description

- When the AND and OR logical operators are used to create a compound condition, the result of the last condition that was evaluated is returned.

- The logical operators use *short-circuit evaluation* to determine the result that's returned by both Boolean and non-Boolean values. The result can then be stored in a constant or variable. If the result is a Boolean value, it can also be used as a condition in a control statement.

- The OR operator is commonly used with non-Boolean values to return a default value if a value isn't provided.

- The AND operator is commonly used with non-Boolean values to make sure that a property exists.

- ES2020 provides a *nullish coalescing operator* (??) that can be used in place of the OR operator and an *optional chaining operator* (?) that can be used in place of the AND operator. Both of these features are supported by all of the major browsers.

Figure 13-5   Additional techniques for using the logical operators

The Invoice application

Figure 13-6 shows a web application that calculates a discount amount and total for an invoice. This application uses some of the conditional expressions and selection structures described in this chapter to determine the discount percent.

The user interface for this application, shown in part 1 of this figure, consists of a drop-down list, four text boxes, and a button. The drop-down list is used to select the type of customer: Regular, Loyalty Program, or Honored Citizen. The first text box accepts an invoice subtotal amount from the user. And the next three text boxes are used to display the results of the calculation.

By the way, to save space, not all of the HTML for this application is shown. But, like the other applications in this book, the script elements that include the jQuery library and the JavaScript file are at the end of the body element. Similarly, the "use strict" directive isn't shown in the JavaScript. But, like the other applications in this book, the JavaScript is in strict mode.

The HTML

Part 1 of figure 13-6 also shows some of the HTML for this application. Here, you can see that a select element is used for the drop-down list, and the values that it returns are "reg" for Regular, "loyal" for Loyalty Program, and "honored" for Honored Citizen. You'll see these values used by the JavaScript code in the next figure.

Otherwise, this code is similar to what you've seen before. Of interest are the id attributes because they're used by the JavaScript code. Also, note that the last three text boxes include a disabled attribute. This means that the user can't enter data into them and their backgrounds are shaded.

The user interface

Invoice Total Calculator

Enter the two values that follow and click "Calculate".

Customer Type: [Honored Citizen ▾]

Invoice Subtotal: [120.00]

Discount Percent: [40.00]   %

Discount Amount: [48.00]

Invoice Total: [72.00]

[Calculate]

The HTML

```
<main>
    <h1>Invoice Total Calculator</h1>
    <p>Enter the two values that follow and click "Calculate".</p>
    <div>
        <label for="type">Customer Type:</label>
        <select id="type">
            <option value="reg">Regular</option>
            <option value="loyal">Loyalty Program</option>
            <option value="honored">Honored Citizen</option>
        </select>
    </div>
    <div>
        <label for="subtotal">Invoice Subtotal:</label>
        <input type="text" id="subtotal">
    </div>
    <hr>
    <div>
        <label for="percent">Discount Percent:</label>
        <input type="text" id="percent" disabled>%
    </div>
    <div>
        <label for="discount">Discount Amount:</label>
        <input type="text" id="discount" disabled>
    </div>
    <div>
        <label for="total">Invoice Total:</label>
        <input type="text" id="total" disabled><br>
    </div>
    <div>
        <label> </label>
        <input type="button" id="calculate" value="Calculate">
    </div>
</main>
```

Figure 13-6   The Invoice application (part 1)

The JavaScript

The JavaScript code in part 2 of figure 13-6 starts with the calculateDiscount() function. This function receives the value of the customer type and the amount of the invoice subtotal. Then, it uses a switch statement to check the customer type.

The code that follows the first case label is executed if the customer type is Regular. This code consists of an if-else statement that checks the value of the subtotal parameter for various ranges and returns a discount amount of .1 (10%) for a subtotal between 100 and 250, .25 (25%) for a subtotal between 250 and 500, and .3 (30%) for a subtotal greater than or equal to 500. If the subtotal amount doesn't meet any of these conditions, a discount amount of zero is returned.

This shows how you can nest an if statement within a case label of a switch statement. Although you could also use another switch statement to test the value of the subtotal parameter, this would be more difficult and produce less readable code than using an if-else statement because you're checking for ranges of values. So, the statement you use depends on the testing you need to do.

The code after the second case label is executed if the customer type is Loyalty Program. This code simply returns a discount of .3 (30%).

The code after the third case label is executed if the customer type is Honored Citizen. Here, the code uses the conditional operator to return a discount of .4 (40%) if the subtotal amount is less than 500, or .5 (50%) otherwise.

Notice that this switch statement doesn't have a default label. That's because the value of the customer parameter that's passed to the function is determined by the selection the user makes from the drop-down list. And, since all of the possible values of this list are accounted for by the case labels, it isn't necessary to have a default label.

After the calculateDiscount() function is the jQuery ready() event handler, which contains the event handler for the click event of the Calculate button. That handler starts by getting the values that the user entered for customer type and invoice subtotal. Note that it provides a default value of zero for the subtotal if the user doesn't enter a value. It also calls the parseFloat() method to convert the subtotal amount to a decimal.

Next, the code calls the calculateDiscount() function and passes it the customer type and subtotal values. The code then uses the discountPercent value returned by that function to calculate the discount amount and the total amount for the invoice.

After that, the code reloads the subtotal text box so the subtotal entry will be displayed with two decimal digits. Then, the code uses jQuery to display the discount percent, discount amount, and invoice total in the related text boxes.

The click() event handler ends by setting the focus on the Customer Type drop-down list so the user can perform another calculation. The last line of the ready() event handler also sets the focus on this drop-down list.

The JavaScript

```javascript
const calculateDiscount = (customer, subtotal) => {
    switch(customer) {
        case "reg":
            if (subtotal >= 100 && subtotal < 250) {
                return .1;
            } else if (subtotal >= 250 && subtotal < 500) {
                return  .25;
            } else if (subtotal >= 500) {
                return .3;
            } else {
                return 0;
            }
        case "loyal":
            return .3;
        case "honored":
            return (subtotal < 500) ? .4 : .5;
    }
};

$( document ).ready( () => {

    $("#calculate").click( () => {

        const customerType = $("#type").val();
        let subtotal = $("#subtotal").val() || 0;  // default value of zero
        subtotal = parseFloat(subtotal);

        const discountPercent = calculateDiscount(customerType, subtotal);
        const discountAmount = subtotal * discountPercent;
        const invoiceTotal = subtotal - discountAmount;

        $("#subtotal").val( subtotal.toFixed(2) );
        $("#percent").val( (discountPercent * 100).toFixed(2) );
        $("#discount").val( discountAmount.toFixed(2) );
        $("#total").val(  invoiceTotal.toFixed(2) );

        // set focus on type drop-down when done
        $("#type").focus();
    });

    // set focus on type drop-down on initial load
    $("#type").focus();
});
```

Figure 13-6   The Invoice application (part 2)

How to handle exceptions

Runtime errors can also be referred to as *exceptions*. Because exceptions shouldn't occur in real-world applications, most programming languages provide a way to handle the exceptions that are *thrown* by an application so the applications don't crash. This programming process is referred to as *exception handling*. In this topic, you'll learn how to handle exceptions in your JavaScript applications.

How to use try-catch statements

To handle exceptions in JavaScript, you use a *try-catch statement* as shown in figure 13-7. First, you code a *try block* around the statement or statements that may throw an exception. Then, you code a *catch block* that contains the statements that will be executed if an exception is thrown by any statement in the try block. If necessary, you can also code a *finally block* that is executed whether or not an exception is thrown, but that block is optional.

The first example in this figure shows how you can use a try-catch statement to catch any exceptions that are thrown in the try block. Then, if an exception is thrown by one of the statements in that block, the execution of the program jumps to the first statement in the catch block. In this example, the catch block contains just one alert() method that displays an error message.

When an exception is thrown, an Error object is created that contains information about the exception. To access the Error object, you code a variable name in the parentheses after the catch keyword. Then, you can use the name and message properties of the Error object in that variable to display the error information. This is illustrated by the catch block in the first example. Here, the variable name for the Error object is error, but it could be any valid name.

Of course, you don't have to use the Error object in the catch block. This is illustrated by the catch block in the second example in this figure. In this case, a custom message is displayed by the alert() method.

If you know for sure that you don't need to use the Error object in your catch block, you can omit it as shown in the last example. This is a new feature of ES2019. Before that, you had to code a name for the Error object even if you didn't use it.

You should also know that if an exception is thrown in a function like the one in this figure and it isn't caught by a try-catch statement, the exception is passed to the calling function. This passing of the exception continues until the exception is caught or the application ends with a runtime error. When this happens, you can open the Console panel of the developer tools to see information about the error.

An interesting feature of JavaScript is that it throws fewer exceptions than other languages. For example, because JavaScript has an Infinity value, it doesn't throw an error when an arithmetic expression divides by zero. JavaScript also has a NaN value, so it doesn't throw an error when you pass a string to the parseInt() function. As a result, you need to do less exception handling when you use JavaScript than you do with other languages.

The syntax for a try-catch statement

```
try { statements }
catch([errorName]) { statements }
[ finally { statements } ]         // the finally block is optional
```

Two properties of Error objects

Property	Description
name	The type of error.
message	The message that describes the error.

A try-catch statement for a calculateFV() function

```
const calculateFV = (investment, rate, years) => {
    try {
        let futureValue = investment;
        for (let i = 1; i <= years; i++ ) {
            futureValue += futureValue * rate / 100;
        }
        return futureValue.toFixed(2);
    }
    catch(error) {
        alert (error.name + ": " + error.message)
    }
};
```

A catch block that displays a custom message

```
catch(error) {
    alert("The calculateFV function has thrown an error." );
};
```

A catch block with no error parameter

```
catch {
    alert("The calculateFV function has thrown an error." );
};
```

Description

- You can use a *try-catch statement* to process any errors that are thrown by an application. These errors are referred to as *exceptions*, and this process is known as *exception handling*.

- In a try-catch statement, you code a *try block* that contains the statements that may throw exceptions. Then, you code a *catch block* that contains the statements that are executed when an exception is thrown in the try block.

- The optional *finally block* is executed whether or not the statements in the catch block are executed.

- The errorName parameter in the catch block gives you access to the Error object. This object has two properties that you can use to display the error type and message.

- If you don't need to use the Error object, you can omit the errorName parameter.

Figure 13-7   How to use try-catch statements to handle exceptions

How to create and throw Error objects

In some cases, you will want to *throw* your own exceptions. If, for example, you're creating a utility library that will be used by other programmers, you can throw exceptions to alert those using the library that something is wrong.

To throw an exception, you first create a new Error object. Then, you use the *throw statement* to throw it. The throw statement can throw an Error object that already exists, or it can create and throw an Error object in one statement. This is illustrated by figure 13-8.

To create a new Error object, you call the Error() constructor and pass one parameter to it that contains a message. If that parameter isn't a string, it's converted to one. This message is then stored in the Error object's message property. In general, it's best to make your message as specific as possible about what the error is and where in the code it occurred.

After you create an Error object, you can use the throw statement to throw it. This is illustrated by the first example in this figure. Here, a function that calculates the future value throws an exception if one of the values it receives is invalid. The error message includes information about which function experienced the problem. When the exception is thrown, the function ends and control is passed to the code that called it.

Then, the code that calls that function can catch the exception and display its message property. Or, the programmer who is using the function can fix the code so appropriate values are passed to the function. In this example, the exception is caught by a try-catch statement in the code that called it. This example also illustrates the use of a finally block that sets the focus on the text box for the investment entry.

This use of try-catch statements makes sense when you're calling functions that somebody else has written and you're not sure what the arguments should be. Then, if the called functions throw exceptions with clear error messages, you can find out what you're doing wrong and debug your code.

Another use for the throw statement is to test that errors are caught and handled appropriately. To do that, you can code the throw statement in a try block to be sure the catch block works the way you want.

In some cases, you may want to perform some processing when an error occurs and then throw it again. To do that, you simply catch the error, perform the necessary processing, and then rethrow the error. When you do that, the error is passed up to the calling function.

As the table in this figure shows, JavaScript also provides a hierarchy of Error objects that it throws. For instance, a RangeError object is thrown when a numeric value has exceeded an allowable range. A ReferenceError object is thrown when the JavaScript code refers to a variable that hasn't been defined. And a SyntaxError object is thrown when the syntax of a statement is invalid.

As the example below this table shows, you can also create and throw any of these object types. Then, that object type is displayed by the name property of the Error object. If, for example, you create and throw a RangeError object, its name property is set to "RangeError".

The syntax for creating a new Error object

```
new Error(message)
```

The syntax for the throw statement

```
throw errorObject;
```

A calculateFV() method that throws a new Error object

```
const calculateFV = ( investment, rate, years ) => {
    if ( isNaN(investment) || investment <= 0 ) {
        throw new Error("calculateFV requires investment greater than 0.");
    }
    if ( isNaN(rate) || rate <= 0 ) {
        throw new Error("calculateFV requires annual rate greater than 0.");
    }
    let futureValue = investment;
    for (let i = 1; i <= years; i++ ) {
        futureValue += futureValue * rate / 100;
    }
    return futureValue.toFixed(2);
};
```

A try-catch statement that catches the Error object that has been thrown

```
try {
    $("future_value").text = calculateFV(investment, rate, years);
}
catch(error) {
    alert (error.name + ": " + error.message);
}
finally {
    $("investment").focus();
}
```

Some of the error types in the Error hierarchy

Type	Thrown when
RangeError	A numeric value has exceeded the allowable range
ReferenceError	A variable is read that hasn't been defined
SyntaxError	A runtime syntax error is encountered
TypeError	The type of a value is different from what was expected

A statement that throws a RangeError object

```
throw new RangeError("Annual rate is invalid."); // throws RangeError
```

Three reasons for using throw statements

- To test the operation of a try-catch statement
- To throw an error from a function that lets the calling code know that one or more of the arguments that were passed are invalid
- To perform some processing after catching an error and then throw the error again.

Description

- To create a new Error object, you use its constructor with a string as the parameter.
- To trigger a runtime error, you use the *throw statement*.

Figure 13-8   How to create and throw Error objects

How to use regular expressions

Regular expressions are coded patterns that can be used to search for matching patterns in strings. These expressions are commonly used to validate the data that is entered by users. In the topics that follow, you'll learn the basic skills for using regular expressions for this purpose.

You should know, though, that JavaScript has more regular expression functionality than what's presented here. In particular, the more recent versions of the ECMAScript specification added many advanced features. There are many good tutorials online for using these features.

How to create and use regular expressions

Figure 13-9 shows how regular expressions work. To start, you create a *regular expression object* that contains the *pattern* that will be used. To do that, you can use either syntax that's shown at the top of this figure.

With the first technique, you use the new keyword with the RegExp() constructor, and you code the pattern in quotation marks as the parameter. With the second technique, you code a *regular expression literal* that consists of the pattern between slashes. In either case, this creates a new RegExp object that contains the pattern. In the two statements in the first example, that pattern is simply "Babbage".

Once you've created a regular expression object, you can use it to find pattern matches in a string. To do that, you can use the test() method of the regular expression object. This is illustrated by the two statements in the second example that use this method.

In the first statement, the test() method searches for the pattern "Babbage" in the constant named inventor. Since that constant contains "Charles Babbage", the pattern is found and the method returns true. In the second statement, the constant named programmer contains "Ada Lovelace", so the pattern isn't found and the method returns false.

In addition to the pattern that you code when you create a regular expression object, you can code one or more *flags* to set one or more properties of the object to true. To do that when you use the RegExp() constructor, you code a string for the second parameter that includes the flags you want to use. To do that when you code a regular expression literal, you code the flags after the slash that follows the expression.

The third example illustrates how this works. Here, both statements create a regular expression object with the pattern "lovelace". Both statements also include the *i* flag, which sets the ignoreCase property of the object to true. That changes the test that's done from the default of case-sensitive to case-insensitive. Because of that, the test in the fourth example will return a value of true when the programmer constant, which contains the string "Lovelace", is checked for the pattern.

Two ways to create a regular expression object

By using the RegExp() constructor
```
const constantName = new RegExp("expression"[, "flags"]);
```

By coding a regular expression literal
```
const constantName = /expression/[flags];
```

One method of a regular expression

Method	Description
test(*string*)	Searches for the regular expression in the string. It returns true if the pattern is found and false if it's not found.

Two statements that create a regular expression that will find "Babbage"
```
const pattern = new RegExp("Babbage");
const pattern = /Babbage/;
```

How to use the test() method of a regular expression

Two strings to test
```
const inventor = "Charles Babbage";
const programmer = "Ada Lovelace";
```

How to use the test() method to search for the pattern
```
alert( pattern.test(inventor) );        // displays true
alert( pattern.test(programmer) );      // displays false
```

Two statements that create a case-insensitive regular expression
```
const pattern = new RegExp("lovelace", "i");
const pattern = /lovelace/i;
```

How to use a case-insensitive regular expression
```
alert( pattern.test(programmer) );      // displays true
```

Description

- A *regular expression* defines a *pattern* that can be searched for in a string. This pattern is stored in a *regular expression object*.

- To create a regular expression object, you can use the RegExp() constructor. Then, the pattern is coded within quotation marks as the first parameter.

- Another way to create a regular expression object is to code a *regular expression literal*. To do that, you code a pattern within two forward slashes.

- You can use the test() method of a regular expression object to search for the pattern in the string parameter.

- You can use *flags* to set one or more properties of a regular expression object to true. You can code flags within quotation marks as the second parameter of the RegExp() constructor or on a regular expression literal following the second slash.

- You can use the i flag to change the ignoreCase property to true so the regular expression pattern is case-insensitive rather than case-sensitive.

Figure 13-9   How to create and use regular expressions

How to match special characters and types of characters

The trick to using regular expressions is coding the patterns, and that can get complicated. That's why the next two figures move from the simple to the complex as they show you how to create patterns. To start, though, remember that all letters and numbers represent themselves in a pattern.

The first table in figure 13-10 shows you how to include special characters in a pattern. To do that, you start with the *escape character*, which is the backslash. For instance, \\ is equivalent to one backslash; \/ is equivalent to one forward slash; and \xA9 is equivalent to \u00A9, which is equivalent to the copyright symbol.

Note, however, that this table doesn't include all of the special characters that you need to precede with backslashes. For instance, the second table points out that you need to use \. to represent a period, and the first table on the next page points out that you need to use \$ to match a dollar sign.

The examples after the first table show how these special characters can be used in regular expression patterns. Here, the second and third statements use a regular expression literal followed by .test to call the test() method for that expression object. The second statement looks for one slash in the constant named string and finds it. The third statement looks for the copyright symbol and finds it.

Then, the fourth statement uses the first technique in figure 13-9 to create a RegExp object. But when you use the RegExp() constructor to create a regular expression object, you have to code two backslashes in the pattern for every one that you use in a regular expression literal. That's because the RegExp() constructor takes a string parameter, and the backslash is also the escape character for strings. For this reason, it's easier to use regular expression literals. In this example, the pattern is equivalent to one backslash, but the fifth statement doesn't find it because the string constant contains the escape sequence for a new line (\n), not a backslash.

The second table shows how to match types of characters instead of specific characters. If, for example, the literal is /MB\d/, the pattern will match the letters MB followed by any digit. Or, if the literal is /MB.../, the pattern will match MB followed by any three characters.

The examples after this table show how this works. Here, the second statement looks for MB followed by any character and finds it. The third statement looks for MB followed by either T or F and finds it. And the fourth statement looks for MBT- followed by any character that's not a letter, number or the underscore. It doesn't find a match, though, because the string contains MBT-3.

How to match special characters

Pattern	Matches
\\	Backslash character
\/	Forward slash
\t	Tab
\n	Newline
\r	Carriage return
\f	Form feed
\v	Vertical tab
[\b]	Backspace (the only special character that must be inside brackets)
\u*dddd*	The Unicode character whose value is the four hexadecimal digits.
\x*dd*	The Latin-1 character whose value is the two hexadecimal digits. Equivalent to \u00*dd*.

Examples

```
const string = "©2020 MMA Inc.\nAll rights reserved (8/2020).";
alert( /\//.test(string) );          // matches / and displays true
alert( /\xA9/.test(string) );        // matches © and displays true

const pattern = new RegExp("\\\\");  // same as /\\/
alert( pattern.test(string) );       // displays false since there's no \
```

How to match types of characters

Pattern	Matches
.	Any character except a newline (use \ . to match a period)
[ ]	Any character in the brackets (use \[or \] to match a bracket)
[^]	Any character not in the brackets
[a-z]	Any character in the range of characters when used inside brackets
\w	Any letter, number, or the underscore
\W	Any character that's not a letter, number, or the underscore
\d	Any digit
\D	Any character that's not a digit
\s	Any whitespace character (space, tab, newline, carriage return, form feed, or vertical tab)
\S	Any character that's not whitespace

Examples

```
const string = "The product code is MBT-3461.";
alert( /MB./.test(string) );       // displays true
alert( /MB[TF]/.test(string) );    // displays true
alert( /MBT-\W/.test(string) );    // displays false
```

Description

- The backslash is used as the *escape character* in regular expressions.
- When you use the RegExp() constructor, any backslash in your pattern must be preceded by another backslash. That's because the backslash is also the escape character in strings.

Figure 13-10   How to match special characters and types of characters

How to match string positions, subpatterns, and repeating patterns

Figure 13-11 presents some additional skills for creating regular expressions. The first table in this figure shows how to match characters at specific positions in a string. For instance, the pattern /^com/ will find the letters "com" at the start of a string. And the pattern /com$/ will find the letters "com" at the end of a string. This is illustrated by the examples after this table.

Here, the last statement displays false because "Ad" is followed by another word character. To say that another way, "Ad" is found at the beginning of a word but not at the end of a word (the first word in the string is "Ada"). One use of the \b pattern is to find whole words.

The second table shows how to group and match a *subpattern* that is coded in parentheses. This is illustrated by the examples after this table. Here, the second statement will match a subpattern of either "Rob" or "Bob".

If you code more than one subpattern in a pattern, the patterns are numbered from left to right. Then, if you want to repeat the subpattern in the pattern, you can specify the number of the pattern that you want to repeat. This is illustrated by the third statement after the table. Here, the \1 indicates that the first pattern, which matches any three letters, numbers, or underscores, should be used again. This returns true because that pattern is repeated. It would also return true if the pattern were /(Rob) \1/ because "Rob" is repeated.

The third table shows how to use a *quantifier* that's coded in braces to match a repeating pattern. For instance, /\d{3}/ will match any three digits in succession, and /\${1,3}/ will match from one to three occurrences of a dollar sign. Here again, this is illustrated by the examples that follow the table. The third statement matches three digits at the start of a string, a hyphen, three more digits, another hyphen, and four digits at the end of the string. And the fourth statement matches a left parenthesis at the start of the string, three digits, a right parenthesis, zero or one space (as indicated by the question mark quantifier after the space), three more digits followed by a hyphen, and four digits at the end of the string. Both of these patterns can be used to validate phone numbers.

Then, the pattern in the fifth statement combines the patterns of the third and fourth statements so a phone number can start with either three digits in parentheses or three digits followed by a hyphen. Here again, the question mark after the space means that zero or one space can be used after an area code in parentheses, so this pattern will find telephone numbers like 559-555-1234, (559)555-1234, and (559) 555-1234.

These tables and examples should get you started coding patterns of your own. And you'll get more proficient with them as you study the examples in the rest of this chapter. Before you take on a complex pattern, though, you might want to do an Internet search for "regular expressions" or "regular expression library". You'll probably find that someone else has already written the pattern you need.

How to match string positions

Pattern	Matches
^	The beginning of the string (use \^ to match a caret)
$	The end of the string (use \$ to match a dollar sign)
\b	Word characters that aren't followed or preceded by a word character
\B	Word characters that are followed or preceded by a word character

Examples

```
const inventor = "Charles Babbage";
alert( /^Charles/.test(inventor) );        // displays true
alert( /Babbage$/.test(inventor) );        // displays true
alert( /^Babbage/.test(inventor) );        // displays false

const programmer = "Ada Lovelace";
alert( /Ad/.test(programmer) );            // displays true
alert( /Ad\b/.test(programmer) );          // displays false
```

How to group and match subpatterns

Pattern	Matches
(subpattern)	Creates a subpattern (use \(and \) to match a parenthesis)
|	Matches either the left or right subpattern (use \\| to match a vertical bar)
\n	Matches the subpattern in the specified position

Examples

```
const name = "Rob Robertson";
alert( /^(Rob)|(Bob)\b/.test(name) );  // displays true
alert( /^(\w\w\w) \1/.test(name) );      // displays true
```

How to match a repeating pattern

Pattern	Matches
{n}	Pattern must repeat exactly *n* times (use \{ and \} to match a brace)
{n,}	Pattern must repeat *n* or more times
{n,m}	Subpattern must repeat from *n* to *m* times
?	Zero or one of the previous subpattern (same as {0,1})
+	One or more of the previous subpattern (same as {1,})
*	Zero or more of the previous subpattern (same as {0,})

Examples

```
const phone = "559-555-6627";
const fax   = "(559) 555-6635";
alert( /^\d{3}-\d{3}-\d{4}$/.test(phone) );       // displays true
alert( /^\(\d{3}\) ?\d{3}-\d{4}$/.test(fax) );   // displays true

const phonePattern = /^(\d{3}-)|(\(\d{3}\) ?)\d{3}-\d{4}$/;
alert( phonePattern.test(phone) );                 // displays true
alert( phonePattern.test(fax) );                   // displays true
```

Figure 13-11   How to match string positions, subpatterns, and repeating patterns

Regular expressions for data validation

Figure 13-12 starts with some patterns that are commonly used for data validation. For instance, the first pattern is for phone numbers, so it matches 3 digits at the start of the string, a hyphen, 3 more digits, another hyphen, and 4 digits at the end of the string. Similarly, the second one is for credit card numbers, so it matches four groups of 4 digits separated by hyphens.

The third pattern is for 5- or 9-digit zip codes. It requires 5 digits at the start of the string. Then, it uses the ? quantifier with a subpattern that contains a hyphen followed by four digits. As a result, this subpattern is optional.

The fourth pattern is for email addresses. It makes sure there's an @ sign and a period, allows letters, numbers, underscores, dashes, and periods before and after the @ sign, but only allows letters after the period. It uses the + quantifier to ensure at least one character before and after the @ sign and after the period.

The fifth pattern is for dates in the mm/dd/yyyy format, but it also accepts a date in the m/dd/yyyy format. To start, this pattern uses the ? quantifier to show that the string can start with zero or one occurrences of 0 or 1. This means that the month in the date can be coded like 03/19/1940 or 3/19/1940. But if two digits are used for the month, the first digit has to be either 0 or 1.

Then, the pattern calls for one digit, a slash, either 0, 1, 2, or 3, another digit, another slash, and four more digits. As a result, this pattern doesn't match a string if its first month digit is greater than 1 or if its first day digit is greater than 3. But this will still match invalid dates like 19/21/2020 or 9/39/2021, so additional data validation is required. You'll see the additional validation later.

The examples that follow these patterns show how they can be used in your code. The first example uses the phone number pattern with the test() method and displays an error message if a match isn't found. The second example works the same way, but it uses the date pattern. Remember, though, that this pattern will match some invalid date formats.

This figure ends by presenting a function named isEmail() that is based on the SMTP specification for how an email address may be formed. This function is a more complete validation of an email address than just a regular expression.

In brief, this isEmail() function splits the address into the parts before and after the @ symbol and returns false if there aren't two parts or if either part has too many characters. Next, this function builds a regular expression pattern named localPart by combining two subpatterns with the | character, which means that the string can match either subpattern. Then, it searches for the pattern in the part of the address before the @ symbol. If it doesn't find the pattern, it returns false.

Similarly, the last part of this function builds a regular expression pattern named domainPart by combining two subpatterns. Then, it searches for the pattern in the part of the address after the @ symbol. If it doesn't find the pattern, it returns false. Otherwise, it returns true because the email address is valid.

Of course, it is the patterns in this function that are the most difficult to understand. The good news is that you don't need to understand this pattern to use it. In fact, many programmers find complex patterns like this online and use them without completely understanding them.

Regular expressions for testing validity

A pattern for testing phone numbers in this format: 999-999-9999

```
/^\d{3}-\d{3}-\d{4}$/
```

A pattern for testing credit card numbers in this format: 9999-9999-9999-9999

```
/^\d{4}-\d{4}-\d{4}-\d{4}$/
```

A pattern for testing zip codes in either of these formats: 99999 or 99999-9999

```
/^\d{5}(-\d{4})?$/
```

A pattern for testing emails in this format: username@mailserver.domain

```
/^[\w\.\-]+@[\w\.\-]+\.[a-zA-Z]+$/
```

A pattern for testing dates in this format: mm/dd/yyyy

```
/^[01]?\d\/[0-3]\d\/\d{4}$/
```

Examples that use these expressions

Testing a phone number for validity

```
const phone = "559-555-6624";                  // valid phone number
const phonePattern = /^\d{3}-\d{3}-\d{4}$/;
if ( !phonePattern.test(phone) ) {
    alert("Invalid phone number");             // not displayed
}
```

Testing a date for a valid format, but not for a valid month, day, and year

```
const startDate = "8/10/220";                  // invalid date
const datePattern = /^[01]?\d\/[0-3]\d\/\d{4}$/;
// this pattern will match dates like 19/21/2020 and 9/39/2021
if ( !datePattern.test(startDate) ) {
    alert("Invalid start date");               // displays error message
}
```

A function that does more complete validation of an email address

```
const isEmail = email => {
    if (email.length === 0) { return false; }
    const parts = email.split("@");
    if (parts.length !== 2) { return false; }
    if (parts[0].length > 64) { return false; }
    if (parts[1].length > 255) { return false; }

    const address =
        "(^[\\w!#$%&'*+/=?^`{|}~-]+(\\.[\\w!#$%&'*+/=?^`{|}~-]+)*$)";
    const quotedText = "(^\"(([^\\\\\"])|(\\\\[\\\\\"]))+\"$)";
    const localPart = new RegExp( address + "|" + quotedText );
    if ( !localPart.test(parts[0]) ) { return false; }

    const hostnames =
        "(([a-zA-Z0-9]\\.)|([a-zA-Z0-9][-a-zA-Z0-9]{0,62}[a-zA-Z0-9]\\.))+";
    const tld = "[a-zA-Z0-9]{2,6}";
    const domainPart = new RegExp("^" + hostnames + tld + "$");
    if ( !domainPart.test(parts[1]) ) { return false; }

    return true;
};
alert( isEmail("grace@yahoo.com") );           // displays true
alert( isEmail("grace@yahoocom") );            // displays false
```

Figure 13-12   Regular expressions for data validation

The Account Profile application

Now, to show you how you can use regular expressions for data validation, figure 13-13 presents an Account Profile application. This application represents a simplified version of a web page that stores the data the users enter when they register.

Part 1 of this figure shows the user interface for this application. After the user enters data and clicks the Save button, the JavaScript code checks the data for validity. Then, if the data isn't valid, the application displays error messages to the right of input text boxes. Remember, though, that JavaScript validation like this is just a convenience for the user, to prevent the delay of a round trip to the server. Your application should repeat this validation on the server as well.

As before, not all of the HTML for this application is shown. But the script elements that include the jQuery library and the JavaScript file are at the end of the body element. Similarly, the "use strict" directive isn't shown in the JavaScript, but the JavaScript is in strict mode.

The HTML

Part 1 of figure 13-13 also shows some of the HTML for this application. Here, you can see that the main element includes an h1 element and four input elements for the text boxes. After each of these input elements is a span element where the error message for that entry will be displayed. These input elements are followed by one last input element for a button with an id of "save". It is used to start the validation of the data that's been entered.

The Account Profile application with error messages

My Account Profile

E-Mail:	grace@yahoo	Please enter a valid email.
Mobile phone:	555-123-456	Please enter a phone number in NNN-NNN-NNNN format.
ZIP Code:	1234	Please enter a valid zip code.
Date of Birth:	15/18/1980	Please enter a valid date in MM/DD/YYYY format.

Save

The HTML

```
<main>
    <h1>My Account Profile</h1>

    <div>
        <label for="email">E-Mail:</label>
        <input type="text" name="email" id="email">
        <span></span>
    </div>

    <div>
        <label for="phone">Mobile phone:</label>
        <input type="text" name="phone" id="phone">
        <span></span>
    </div>

    <div>
        <label for="zip">ZIP Code:</label>
        <input type="text" name="zip" id="zip">
        <span></span>
    </div>

    <div>
        <label for="dob">Date of Birth:</label>
        <input type="text" name="dob" id="dob">
        <span></span>
    </div>

    <div>
        <label></label>
        <input type="button" id="save" value="Save">
    </div>
</main>
```

Figure 13-13   The Account Profile application (part 1)

The JavaScript

Part 2 of figure 13-13 presents the JavaScript code for this application. It starts with a function named isDate(). This function receives a date and a regular expression object. The reason this code is in a function is because, as you saw in figure 13-12, a regular expression by itself can't fully validate a date.

As a result, this function first tests the value that it receives to see if it passes the regular expression check. If it doesn't, the isDate() function returns false. But if it does, the function gets the month and day parts of the date and makes sure the month is between 1 and 12 and the day isn't greater than 31. In real life, of course, you would refine this code to handle months that have fewer than 31 days and to handle leap years. But this gives you an idea of what you can do.

This function is followed by the jQuery ready() event handler, which contains the click() event handler for the Save button. This event handler starts by using jQuery to set the text of all the span elements in the page to empty strings. This clears any error messages that might have been displayed previously.

Next, the code uses jQuery to retrieve the values entered by the user for email address, mobile phone, zip code, and date of birth. After that, it creates a regular expression object to check each value.

Then, this code declares a Boolean variable named isValid and initializes it to true. This variable will be used to keep track of whether the data entered by the user is valid. After that, the code issues a series of if statements to check the user's entries.

The first three if statements check the email, phone, and zip code values. First, they check to see if the user entered values. Then, they use the test() method of the regular expression object to see if the value is valid. If either of these checks fails, the isValid variable is set to false and an error message is displayed. Note that this code uses the jQuery next() method to find the span element that's the sibling of the text box with the invalid value and set its text.

The fourth if statement checks the date of birth value. It starts by checking if the user entered a date of birth. After that, it passes the date of birth and the date regular expression object to the isDate() function to check if it's valid. If either of these checks fails, the isValid variable is set to false and an error message is displayed.

The last if statement checks the value of the isValid variable. If it's still true, all of the data entered by the user is valid. Then, the JavaScript code (not shown) saves the profile information to the server, where it's validated again.

This event handler ends by setting the focus on the Email text box. This makes it easier for the user to either enter new profile information or correct any invalid entries. The last line of the ready() event handler also sets the focus on the Email text box.

The JavaScript

```javascript
const isDate = (date, datePattern) => {
    if (!datePattern.test(date)) { return false; }

    const dateParts = date.split("/");
    const month = parseInt( dateParts[0] );
    const day = parseInt( dateParts[1] );

    if ( month < 1 || month > 12 ) { return false; }
    if ( day > 31 ) { return false; }
    return true;
};

$( document ).ready( () => {
    $( "#save" ).click( () => {
        $("span").text("");    // clear any previous error messages

        // get values entered by user
        const email = $("#email").val();
        const phone = $("#phone").val();
        const zip = $("#zip").val();
        const dob = $("#dob").val();

        // regular expressions for validity testing
        const emailPattern = /^[\w\.\-]+@[\w\.\-]+\.[a-zA-Z]+$/;
        const phonePattern = /^\d{3}-\d{3}-\d{4}$/;
        const zipPattern = /^\d{5}(-\d{4})?$/;
        const datePattern = /^[01]?\d\/[0-3]\d\/\d{4}$/;

        // check user entries for validity
        let isValid = true;
        if ( email === "" || !emailPattern.test(email) ) {
            isValid = false;
            $("#email").next().text("Please enter a valid email.");
        }
        if ( phone === "" || !phonePattern.test(phone) ) {
            isValid = false;
            $("#phone").next().text(
                "Please enter a phone number in NNN-NNN-NNNN format.");
        }
        if ( zip === "" || !zipPattern.test(zip) ) {
            isValid = false;
            $("#zip").next().text("Please enter a valid zip code.");
        }
        if ( dob === "" || !isDate(dob, datePattern) ) {
            isValid = false;
            $("#dob").next().text(
                "Please enter a valid date in MM/DD/YYYY format.");
        }
        if ( isValid ) {
            // code that saves profile info goes here
        }
        $("#email").focus();
    });

    $("#email").focus();        // set focus on initial load
});
```

Figure 13-13   The Account Profile application (part 2)

Perspective

Now that you've finished this chapter, you should know how to use the identity operators, the break and continue statements, the switch statement, and the conditional operator, as well as how to use non-Boolean values in conditional expressions. You should also know when and how to handle exceptions and how to create and use regular expressions for data validation.

Terms

equality operator	optional chaining operator
type coercion	exception
identity operator	throw an exception
break statement	exception handling
continue statement	try-catch statement
switch statement	try block
switch expression	catch block
case label	finally block
return statement	throw statement
fall through	regular expression
conditional operator	regular expression object
ternary operator	pattern
unary operator	regular expression literal
binary operator	flag
truthy value	escape character
falsey value	subpattern
short-circuit evaluation	quantifier
nullish coalescing operator	

Summary

- Unlike the *equality operators*, the *identity operators* don't use *type coercion* in their comparisons. If an identity operator is used to compare two variables that aren't of the same type, the result is always false.

- The *break statement* jumps out of a loop and ends the loop. The *continue statement* jumps to the start of the loop but lets the loop continue.

- The *switch statement* lets you code the statements for *cases* that are based on the value of a single expression. If the result of the expression matches the value of a *case label*, the switch statement executes the code for that case until it reaches a break or return statement or the switch statement ends.

- The *conditional operator* returns one value if a condition is true and another if it is false. This is an alternative to a simple if-else statement.

- Non-Boolean values that are used in conditions are called *truthy* or *falsey* to indicate that they aren't Boolean values but can still evaluate to true or false.

- Because the AND and OR logical operators are short-circuit operators, they can be used to assign the result of an expression that includes Boolean or non-Boolean values to a constant or variable. The AND operator can also be used to test for the existence of a property.

- ES2020 provides a *nullish coalescing operator* that can be used in place of the OR operator and an *optional chaining operator* that can be used in place of the AND operator.

- An *exception* is a runtime error that is *thrown* when an error condition occurs. To catch an exception, you use a *try-catch statement*, which consists of a *try block*, a *catch block*, and an optional *finally block*.

- You can also create and throw your own exceptions in the form of Error objects. This can be useful when you're writing functions that are going to be used by others.

- A *regular expression* defines a *pattern* that can be searched for in a string. This pattern is stored in a *regular expression object*.

- The test() method of a regular expression object is commonly used to test the validity of user entries.

Exercise 13-1   Enhance the Prime Number application

This exercise will give you a chance to practice some of the skills that you learned for working with control structures. In its initial form, this application determines whether the number that's entered is a prime number, which is one that can only be divided by one and itself.

Find Prime Numbers

Enter Number: [17]

[Calculate]

17 is a prime number.

Test the application and review the code

1. Use your text editor or IDE to open the application in this folder:
   `javascript_jquery\exercises\ch13\prime`

2. Run the application and test it with a prime number like 11 and a non-prime number like 10.

3. Review the JavaScript file, noting how the isPrimeNumber() function uses the conditional operator and the break statement.

Change the code to display all the prime numbers up to the one entered

Now, you'll enhance the application so it displays all the prime numbers up to and including the one that's entered. When you're done, it will look like this:

Find Prime Numbers

Enter Number: `31`

[Calculate]

2 3 5 7 11 13 17 19 23 29 31

4. In the click() event handler, comment out the code that calls the isPrimeNumber() function and the code that displays the message about whether the number is prime.

5. Still in the handler, add code that clears any previous text from the message label. Then, code a loop that iterates through the numbers from 1 to the number entered by the user. Within the loop, call the isPrimeNumber() function for each number. Then, if the number is prime, add it to the text that will be displayed in the message label. If it isn't prime, continue with the next iteration of the loop.

Exercise 13-2   Add exception handling to the Future Value application

In this exercise, you'll add exception handling to a Future Value application. Here's what the application looks like when an error message is displayed.

The Future Value Calculator

Investment amount: [|]

Interest rate: [   ]

Years: [   ]

Future value: [   ]

[Calculate] [Clear]

RangeError: All entries must be numbers greater than zero.

1. Open and review the HTML and JavaScript files in this folder:
   `javascript_jquery\exercises\ch13\future_value`

2. Test the application with valid entries. Then, try to make the application throw an exception by clicking the Calculate button with no entries in the text boxes or with string entries like "one" or "two". Either way, the application displays a future value of NaN without throwing an exception. This shows how difficult it is to make a JavaScript application throw an exception.

3. In the JavaScript file, add exception handling to the click() event handler for the Calculate button. Put all of the statements in this handler except the last two in the try block, and display an error message like the one shown above in the catch block. The message should include both the name and message properties of the Error object. Now, put the last two statements in a finally block.

4. Add a throw statement after the if statement in the calculateFutureValue() function. It should throw a RangeError object with the message shown above. A throw statement like this can be used to test the exception handling of an application. Now, test this change.

5. To see how this might work in a real application, move the throw statement into the if statement above it. Then, test the application to see that the message above is displayed when any of the arguments are invalid. This type of coding is often included in a function that's used by other programs. It forces the user to pass valid arguments to the function.

Exercise 13-3   Enhance the Account Profile application

This exercise asks you to enhance the Account Profile application for this chapter by adding validation for two new fields:

My Account Profile

E-Mail:	grace@yahoo.com
Mobile phone:	555-123-4567
ZIP Code:	12345
Date of Birth:	5/18/80	Please enter a valid date in MM/DD/YYYY format.
Credit Card #:	111222333444	Please enter a credit card in NNNN-NNNN-NNNN-NNNN format.
Expire Date:	11/20	Please enter a valid date in MM/YYYY format

    Save

Open and test the application

1. Open the application in this folder:
    `javascript_jquery\exercises\ch13\account_profile`

2. Test the application and notice that two fields have been added for a credit card number and an expiration date. Because no validation is provided for these fields, though, you can enter any values in them.

Validate the credit card field

3. In the JavaScript file, find the click() event handler for the Save button and add a line of code that gets the value entered for the credit card. Add another line of code that defines a regular expression pattern for a credit card number as shown in the error message above.

4. Add an if statement that checks whether the user entered something for the credit card. If there's an entry, use the regular expression to make sure the credit card number is in the correct format.

5. If either of these checks fails, set the isValid variable to false and display an error message in the span element after the input element for the credit card number. Then, test the application.

Validate the expiration date field

6. Add two more statements to the click() event handler for the Save button that get the value entered for the expiration date and define a regular expression pattern for the date as shown in the error message above.

7. Modify the isDate() function so it accepts a third parameter that will indicate the type of date that's passed to it. The two types are a full date in the MM/DD/YYYY format and a credit card date in the MM/YYYY format. Then, modify the code that validates the date of birth so it uses this type.

8. Add code to the isDate() function that validates a credit card date using the code that validates a full date as a guide.

9. Add an if statement to the click() event handler for the Save button that checks whether the user entered something for the expiration date. If so, call the isDate() function to make sure the date is in the correct format.

10. If either of these checks fails, set the isValid variable to false and display an error message. Test the application one more time.

14

How to work with browser objects, cookies, and web storage

This chapter shows how to use browser objects to navigate browser pages and to get information about the browser. Then, it shows how to use JavaScript to put cookies in a user's web browser and how to read and use those cookies. Last, it shows how to use web storage, which is another way to store information in the user's browser.

How to script browser objects

This chapter starts by showing how to use the location and history objects of the browser. The location object lets you work with the URL for a web page. It also lets you control the reloading of the current web page and the loading of new web pages. The history object lets you work with the pages that are stored in a browser's history.

With the rise of JavaScript frameworks that handle these types of processing, you're less likely to use the location and history objects in your own applications. For instance, many of the frameworks for single page applications (SPAs) handle page navigation and history for you. Still, it's good to have a basic understanding of how these objects work.

How to use the location object

The location object has properties and methods that parse the URL that's in the address bar of the browser. Figure 14-1 shows how these properties and methods work. To start, this figure shows a URL that contains the six parts of a URL that can be parsed.

This URL includes two parameters. These parameters start after the question mark that follows the URL address. They consist of *name/value pairs* that are connected by equals signs. If the URL includes multiple parameters, it separates them with ampersands. In this figure, the URL sends two parameters named first and last to the server.

After the parameters, this URL contains a placeholder name that starts with the pound sign (#). It represents a placeholder on the page that has been created by an <a> tag. Then, when a browser loads the page, it scrolls to the placeholder.

With that as background, you can better understand the eight location properties presented in this figure. For example, the href property stores the entire URL. The host property stores a combination of the hostname and port properties. And the other six properties store other parts of the URL.

This figure also summarizes two methods of the location object. The reload() method lets you reload the current page either from cache memory or from the server if the force parameter is set to true. The replace() method lets you load a new page while replacing the current page in the browser's history.

The first example shows two ways to use the location object to load a new page in the browser. Then, the second example shows how to reload pages.

The third example shows how to use the replace() method to load a new page. When you use this technique, it overwrites the current page in the URL history. To illustrate, suppose the user first visits page1 and then visits page2 so both pages are in the browser's history list. Then, if page2 uses the replace() method to load page3, page3 replaces page2 in the history list. At that point, if the user clicks the browser's Back button, the browser navigates to page1, not page2.

A URL with search parameters

```
http://www.murach.com:8181/javascript/location.html?first=G&last=Hopper#result
```

Properties of the location object

Property	Description	Value in the URL above
href	The complete URL of the web page	Complete URL
protocol	The protocol portion of the URL including the colon	http:
hostname	The host name portion of the URL	www.murach.com
port	The port number of the web server	8181
host	The host name and port number	www.murach.com:8181
path	The path to the web page	/javascript/location.html
search	The query string from the URL	?first=G&last=Hopper
hash	The anchor name from the URL	#result

Methods of the location object

Method	Description
reload(*force*)	Reloads the current webpage. If the parameter is set to true, the browser loads the page from the server rather than from cache memory.
replace(*url*)	Loads a new page in the browser and replaces the current page in the history list.

How to load a new web page

```
location.href = "https://www.murach.com";
location = "https://www.murach.com";
```

How to reload a web page

```
location.reload();       // reloads the current page from the cache
location.reload(true);   // reloads the current page from the server
```

How to load a new page and overwrite the current history page

```
location.replace("https://www.murach.com");
```

Description

- The properties of the location object let you examine different parts of the current URL.
- The methods of the location object give you greater control over how the current page is reloaded and how a new page is loaded into the browser.

Figure 14-1   How to use the location object

How to use the history object

The history object represents the browser's history of viewed web pages. However, because of privacy concerns, the amount of information you can get from the history object is limited. As a result, the properties and methods of the history object are limited as shown by figure 14-2.

For instance, the length property tells how many URLs there are in the history list. However, you can't use the history object to determine the position of the current page in the list. As a result, you can't determine whether the current page is first, last, or somewhere in the middle of the history list.

Similarly, the methods shown in this figure are limited. Here, the back() method is equivalent to clicking the Back button in the browser. The forward() method is equivalent to clicking the Forward button. The go() method with a numeric parameter simulates multiple clicks of the Forward or Back button. And the go() method with a substring parameter goes to the most recent URL in the history list that contains that substring.

Beyond the methods shown in this figure, the history object also includes two more methods: pushState() and replaceState(). These methods are generally used with Ajax calls to mimic the way that the history object works with traditional round trips to the server.

One property of the history object

Property	Description
length	The number of URLs in the history object

Methods of the history object

Method	Description
back()	Goes back one step in the URL history
forward()	Goes forward one step in the URL history
go(position)	Goes forward or back the specified number of steps in the URL history
go(substring)	Goes to the most recent URL in the history that contains the substring

How to use the back() method

```
history.back();
```

How to use the forward() method

```
history.forward();
```

How to use the go() method

Go forward two URLs

```
history.go(2);
```

Go back three URLs

```
history.go(-3);
```

Go to the most recent URL that contains "google"

```
history.go("google");
```

Description

- The history object is an array that holds a history of the pages that have been loaded.
- There is no way to determine what the URLs in the history object are. You can only get the URL of the current page from the location object.
- Since there is no way to determine the position of the current URL in the history object, you can't find out if there are pages to go back or forward to.
- HTML5 introduced two more methods to the history object: pushState() and replaceState(). These methods let you add specific information to the history stack.

Figure 14-2   How to use the history object

The Tutorial application

Figure 14-3 presents the Tutorial application. In this application, the tutorial pages replace the currently displayed page in the history object. This controls how the history object works and determines what page the browser displays when the user clicks the Back button in the browser.

On the starting page for this application, the Enter and Tutorial buttons let users choose to go straight to the main page (not shown) or to take a tutorial first. If users click the Tutorial button, they navigate through three tutorial pages before going to the main page. To make that navigation work, the first tutorial page has a Next button, the second tutorial page has Prev and Next buttons, and the third tutorial page has Prev and Finish buttons.

After users navigate through the tutorial pages, the application displays the main page of the application, not the starting page. Then, if users click the Back button in the browser, the application displays the starting page. This is true whether they clicked the Enter button to go to the main page or navigated through the tutorial before getting to the main page. That's because the JavaScript for each tutorial page replaces that page in the browser's history when the next page is displayed.

The HTML

Part 1 of figure 14-3 presents some of the HTML used by the files in the Tutorial application. More specifically, it presents the HTML for the main element of each page. This HTML consists of h1, <p>, and input elements for buttons. Each button has an id attribute that's used by embedded JavaScript to provide the navigation.

In the tutorial3.html file, the id of the second button is "next", even though the text for that button is "Finish". This is just to keep the code consistent. However, you could change the id of that button to "finish" if you thought that would make the code clearer.

The web pages of the tutorial

The main element for each HTML file

index.html

```
<h1>Welcome to our site!</h1>
<p>If you're an old hand here, just click on Enter and go on in!</p>
<p>If you haven't been here before, though, check out our Tutorial.</p>
<input type="button" id="enter" value="Enter">
<input type="button" id="tutorial" value="Tutorial">
```

tutorial1.html

```
<h1>Tutorial - page 1</h1>
<p>Here's the first thing you need to know about our site.</p>
<input type="button" id="next" value="Next">
```

tutorial2.html

```
<h1>Tutorial - page 2</h1>
<p>Here's the second thing you need to know about our site.</p>
<input type="button" id="prev" value="Prev">
<input type="button" id="next" value="Next">
```

tutorial3.html

```
<h1>Tutorial - page 3</h1>
<p>Here's the third thing you need to know about our site.</p>
<input type="button" id="prev" value="Prev">
<input type="button" id="next" value="Finish">
```

Figure 14-3   The Tutorial application (part 1)

The JavaScript

Part 2 of figure 14-3 presents the JavaScript for the four pages presented in the previous figure. The first thing to notice is that this JavaScript isn't coded within ready() event handlers. That's because it's coded at the end of the body section of the HTML, so it won't be executed until the DOM is ready.

When the application starts, the index.html page is added to the browser's history. This page handles the click events of the Enter and Tutorial buttons. These event handlers set the value of the location object to navigate to the main page of the application or the first page of the tutorial. Since this code sets the value of the location object, the page that's displayed is added to the browser's history. For example, if the user clicks the Tutorial button, the history list will include the index.html and tutorial1.html pages.

The tutorial1.html page handles the click event of the Next button. This event handler uses the replace() method of the location object to navigate to the second page of the tutorial. Because of that, the code replaces the tutorial1.html page in the browser's history with the tutorial2.html page.

The tutorial2.html page handles the click events for the Prev and Next buttons. These event handlers use the replace() method of the location object to navigate either back to the first page of the tutorial or forward to the third page of the tutorial. Because of that, this code replaces the tutorial2.html page in the browser's history with the new page.

The tutorial3.html page works like the tutorial2.html page, except that it handles the click events of the Prev and Finish buttons. Like the tutorial2.html page, the JavaScript in the tutorial3.html page replaces the tutorial3.html page in the browser's history with the next page that's displayed. If the user clicks the Finish button, for example, this code replaces the tutorial3.html page with the main.html page. At that point, only the index.html and the main.html pages are in the browser's history.

This code allows a user to navigate the tutorial pages without permanently storing those pages in the browser's history. As a result, a user can navigate through this tutorial without accidentally navigating back to its pages later in the application.

The JavaScript for each HTML file

index.html

```
<script>
    $("#enter").click( () => location = "main.html");
    $("#tutorial").click( () => location = "tutorial1.html");
</script>
```

tutorial1.html

```
<script>
    $("#next").click( () => location.replace("tutorial2.html"));
</script>
```

tutorial2.html

```
<script>
    $("#prev").click( () => location.replace("tutorial1.html"));
    $("#next").click( () => location.replace("tutorial3.html"));
</script>
```

tutorial3.html

```
<script>
    $("#prev").click( () => location.replace("tutorial2.html"));
    $("#next").click( () => location.replace("main.html"));
</script>
```

Description

- The JavaScript on the index.html page sets the value of the location object to navigate to another page. This adds the new page to the browser's history.

- The three tutorial html pages use the replace() method of the location object to navigate to another page. This replaces the current page in the browser's history with the new page.

- Because the JavaScript is coded at the end of the body element in each HTML file, it isn't necessary to place it within ready() event handlers.

Figure 14-3   The Tutorial application (part 2)

How to use cookies

Cookies let a web server or web page store information in a user's browser and retrieve it when the user requests a new page. This concerns some web users because they've heard rumors that cookies can transmit viruses, steal passwords, and copy files from their hard drive. Although those rumors aren't true, some developers abuse the use of cookies. For example, advertisers sometimes use cookies to track the websites you have visited. These cookies are called *third-party cookies* because an ad on a website, not the website itself, sends these cookies to your browser. To combat this abuse, modern web browsers let you block third-party cookies by changing browser options.

This topic shows how to use cookies in a way that makes a web application work better for the user. In particular, it shows how to use cookies to save user data so your users don't have to re-enter that data the next time they use the application.

An introduction to cookies

A *cookie* is a short text string that's stored by the browser as a *name/value pair*. When you request a web page, the server can return a cookie as part of the HTTP response. If it does and the browser has cookies enabled, the web browser stores the cookie. Then, when you load another page from the server, the browser sends the cookie back to the server as part of the HTTP request. Figure 14-4 shows how this works.

At the least, a cookie must start with a name/value pair that's connected by an equals sign. For instance, the first example in this figure specifies a name/value pair that has a name of email and a value of grace@yahoo.com. This pair can be followed by any of the attributes listed in the table. In the cookie string, these name/value pairs must be separated by semicolons and spaces.

If a cookie doesn't include a max-age attribute, it's called a *session cookie*. The browser deletes this type of cookie when the user closes the browser or the tab for the web application. For instance, the first example creates a session cookie since it doesn't specify the max-age attribute.

However, if a cookie includes a max-age attribute with a positive value, it's called a *persistent cookie*. The web browser stores this type of cookie on the user's hard drive until the number of seconds in this attribute elapses. For instance, the second example creates a persistent cookie by setting the max-age attribute to 21 days (21 days * 24 hours * 60 minutes * 60 seconds = 1,814,400 seconds).

Typically, the path attribute for a cookie is set to the root folder of the website as shown in both examples. That way, every page in the website has access to the cookie.

The next few figures show how JavaScript objects and methods make it easy to create, read, and delete cookies. When you use JavaScript to create cookies, the browser treats them the same as cookies received from the web server.

A browser usually gets a cookie as part of an HTTP response

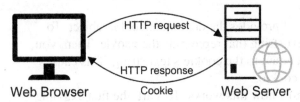

A browser sends the cookie back to the server with each HTTP request

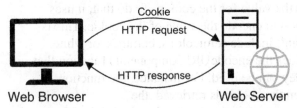

Attributes of a cookie

Attribute	Description
max-age	The lifetime of the cookie in seconds
path	The path on the web server that can see the cookie
domain	The domain names that can see the cookie
secure	If present, the cookie must be encrypted when it is transmitted, and it can only be transmitted when the browser and server are connected by HTTPS or another secure protocol.

Cookie examples

```
email=grace@yahoo.com; path=/
username=ghopper; max-age=1814400; path=/
```

Description

- A *cookie* is a small text string that is stored by a web browser. A cookie consists of name/value pairs, and it must start with a name/value pair that names the cookie and provides a value for the cookie.

- The browser usually gets a cookie from a web server as part of an HTTP response. Then, the browser sends the cookie back to the server as part of each HTTP request.

- A *session cookie* is deleted by the web browser when the browser is closed.

- A *persistent cookie* is saved by the web browser and remains available even after the browser is closed. This type of cookie has an expiration date that is after the current date.

- JavaScript can create, read, and delete cookies.

Figure 14-4   An introduction to cookies

How to create cookies

To work with cookies, JavaScript provides the document.cookie object. To create a cookie, you can create a text string that represents the cookie. Then, you can set the document.cookie object equal to the cookie's text string. This causes the browser to create and store the cookie.

The examples in figure 14-5 show how this works. To start, the first example creates a session cookie. Here, the first statement stores the name of the cookie (tasks) and an equals sign in a variable named cookie.

The second statement appends the value for the cookie. To do that, it uses the encodeURIComponent() function to encode the value of the cookie. This is necessary because cookie values can't include semicolons, commas, or white space. That's why JavaScript provides the encodeURIComponent() function that encodes the illegal characters so they can be used. For instance, the function converts spaces to %20. Later, when the cookie is retrieved, the decodeURIComponent() function can convert the data back to its original form.

The third statement appends a path to the cookie string. Then, the fourth statement assigns the cookie string to the document.cookie object. This stores the cookie in the browser. Because this is a session cookie, the browser deletes it when the browser closes.

The second example in this figure creates a persistent cookie. This works like the first example, but it adds a max-age attribute to the cookie. As a result, the browser stores this cookie on the user's hard drive after the browser is closed. However, it deletes the cookie after 21 days. To get the number of seconds for 21 days, this code multiplies 21 days by 24 hours, 60 minutes, and 60 seconds.

When you add a cookie with a new name to the document.cookie object, it doesn't replace existing cookies. Instead, the new cookie is added to the end of the existing text string. In other words, you can store more than one cookie in the browser as long as each cookie has a unique name.

The third example shows how this works. Here, the first statement adds a cookie named email to the browser. The second statement adds a cookie named username. And the third statement replaces the value in the email cookie since that cookie already exists.

The fourth example shows a function that creates a session cookie or a persistent cookie. It accepts three parameters called name, value, and days. Within the function, the first statement concatenates the cookie name with an equals sign and an encoded cookie value. Then, it checks whether the days parameter has a value. If so, the function appends a max-age attribute to the cookie, using the days value to calculate the number of seconds. Finally, it appends the root path to the cookie and assigns the cookie to document.cookie.

In a production application, you would probably want to add some data validation to this function. For instance, you might want to make sure the days parameter contains a numeric value and that the name parameter doesn't contain any illegal characters. Still, the code for this function should give you a good starting point.

Two functions for working with cookies

Function	Description
`encodeURIComponent(value)`	Encodes values that contain semicolons, commas, or whitespace
`decodeURIComponent(value)`	Decodes values that have been encoded

How to create a session cookie

```
let cookie = "tasks=";                          // create the cookie name
cookie +=                                        // encode and add the data
    encodeURIComponent("Feed dog\nWater plants");
cookie += "; path=/";                            // add the path
document.cookie = cookie;                         // store the cookie
```

How to create a persistent cookie

```
let cookie = "tasks=";                          // create the cookie name
cookie +=                                        // encode and add the data
    encodeURIComponent("Feed dog\nWater plants");
cookie += "; max-age=" + 21 * 24 * 60 * 60;      // add the max-age attribute
cookie += "; path=/";                            // add the path
document.cookie = cookie;                         // store the cookie
```

How to add multiple cookies to the document.cookie object

```
document.cookie = "email=john@doe.com; path=/"
document.cookie = "username=ghopper; max-age=1814400; path=/"
document.cookie = "email=grace@yahoo.com; path=/"
```

The cookies that are added to the document.cookie object

```
email=grace@yahoo.com; username=ghopper
```

A setCookie() function that creates a session or persistent cookie

```
const setCookie = (name, value, days) => {
    // concatenate cookie name and encoded value
    let cookie = name + "=" + encodeURIComponent(value);

    // if there's a value for days, add max-age to cookie
    if (days) {
        cookie += "; max-age=" + days * 24 * 60 * 60;
    }
    // add the path and then store the cookie
    cookie += "; path=/";
    document.cookie = cookie;
};
```

How to use the setCookie() function to create a persistent cookie

```
setCookie("tasks", "Water plants", 21);
```

Description

- Although cookie values can't include semicolons, commas, or whitespace, you can use the encodeURIComponent() function to encode those values. Then, you must use the decodeURIComponent() function to decode the values when the cookies are retrieved.

- To add multiple cookies to the cookie object, you assign multiple name/value pairs. Unlike other JavaScript objects, each assignment doesn't overwrite the previous one.

Figure 14-5   How to create cookies

How to read cookies

Figure 14-6 shows how to read cookies that have been stored in a browser. Remember that more than one cookie can be stored in a browser, and these cookies are stored in a single document.cookie object. The easiest way to retrieve these cookies is to store the value of document.cookie in a constant. When you do that, the value in the constant is a string. Then, you can use the methods of the String object to retrieve the data you want.

This figure presents a function named getCookieByName() that allows you to retrieve the cookie with the specified name from the document.cookie object. Within this function, the first statement gets the string from the document.cookie object and stores it in a constant named cookies.

The second statement uses the indexOf() method of this string to locate the starting index of the name of the cookie. To do that, this code appends an equals sign to the name it's looking for, which increases the chances that the indexOf() method will return the correct index. For instance, suppose the cookie string contains both "email=grace@yahoo.com" and "tasks=send%20email". If you pass "email" to the indexOf() function, you might get the wrong index. But if you pass "email=", you'll get the correct index.

The if statement checks the start variable to see what value the indexOf() method returned. If the value is -1, there's no cookie with that name in the cookie string. In that case, the function returns an empty string and ends.

Otherwise, the code continues processing the cookie string. First, it adjusts the start variable to make sure that the cookie name and the equals sign aren't included in the string that the function returns. To do that, it increments the start variable by the length of the cookie name, plus 1 for the equals sign. Then, the code calls the indexOf() method of the cookie string again to get the index of the semi-colon at the end of the cookie. This code passes the start variable as the second parameter of the indexOf() method, so it starts looking for the semi-colon at the start of the specified cookie value rather than at the beginning of the cookie string.

If the indexOf() method returns -1, the cookie is the last cookie in the string. That's because the last cookie in the string doesn't have an ending semicolon. In this case, the end position of the cookie is the same as the end positon of the cookie string. As a result, this code sets the end variable to the value of the length of the cookie string.

At this point, the code has the starting index and the ending index of the cookie value to retrieve. This allows it to use the substring() method of the cookie string to retrieve the value of the cookie. Then, it calls the decodeURIComponent() function and returns the decoded value of the cookie.

The last example shows how to use the getCookieByName() function. Here, the code retrieves the value of the tasks cookie from the cookie string at the top of the figure, and it stores this value in a variable named tasks.

Chapter 14   How to work with browser objects, cookies, and web storage   **445**

Three cookies in the document.cookie object

```
username=ghopper; status=active; tasks=Water%20plants
```

A getCookieByName() function that gets a cookie by name

```
const getCookieByName = name => {
    const cookies = document.cookie;

    // get the starting index of the cookie name followed by an equals sign
    let start = cookies.indexOf(name + "=");

    if (start === -1) { // no cookie with that name
        return "";          // return empty string
    }
    else {                      // get cookie value
        // adjust so the name and equals sign aren't included in the result
        start = start + (name.length + 1);

        // get the index of the semi-colon at the end of the cookie value
        let end = cookies.indexOf(";", start);
        if (end === -1) {        // if no semi-colon - last cookie
            end = cookies.length;
        }

        // use the start and end indexes to get the cookie value
        const cookieValue = cookies.substring(start, end);

        // return the decoded cookie value
        return decodeURIComponent(cookieValue);
    }
};
```

How to use the getCookieByName() function to read a cookie

```
const tasks = getCookieByName("tasks");          // tasks = "Water plants"
```

Description

- When you assign the document.cookie object to a constant or variable, its value is stored as a String object. Then you can use the methods of the String object to locate the cookie value you want. You learned how to use many of these methods in chapter 12.

- The split() method of the String object is often used with cookies because it provides a way to split the cookie string into an array of cookies.

- The cookie string follows a predictable pattern that makes it easy to manipulate with methods of the String object.

Figure 14-6   How to read cookies

How to delete cookies

To delete a cookie, you store the cookie a second time, but with no value and with a max-age attribute that has a value of zero. In addition, the other parts of the cookie such as the path and domain must be set to the same values as when the cookie was first created. If you try to change the path or domain of the cookie, the browser ignores your attempt to delete the cookie.

Figure 14-7 shows how to delete a cookie. Here, the first example is the cookie to be deleted, and the second example presents the code for deleting it. This code is similar to the code for creating a persistent cookie, but with two differences. First, it doesn't supply a value for the cookie. Second, it sets the max-age attribute to zero. As a result, when the code stores the updated cookie in the document.cookie object, the browser deletes the cookie named tasks.

The third example in this figure shows a deleteCookie() function that deletes a cookie. It uses the name parameter to create a cookie with no value and a max-age value of 0. This deletes the cookie. Here, the arrow method only contains a single statement. As a result, you could make this code more concise by removing the braces and the ending semicolon.

The fourth example shows how you can use the deleteCookie() function to delete the cookie named tasks. This performs the same task as the second example, but it's much shorter since it uses the deleteCookie() function defined in the third example.

The cookie to delete

```
tasks=Feed dog; max-age=1814400; path=/
```

How to delete a cookie

```
let cookie = "tasks=";              // set the name and data
cookie += "; max-age=" + 0;         // set max-age to 0
cookie += "; path=/";               // set the path
document.cookie = cookie;           // delete the cookie
```

A deleteCookie() function that deletes a cookie

```
const deleteCookie = name => {
    document.cookie = name + "=''; max-age=0; path=/";
};
```

How to use the deleteCookie() function to delete a cookie

```
deleteCookie("tasks");
```

Description

- To delete a cookie, you set its max-age attribute to 0.

- When you delete a cookie, the data must be empty, but the equals sign is still required. Also, the path and domain must match the path and domain that were used when the cookie was created.

- JavaScript can't determine the path and domain for a cookie after it has been created. However, you can use the Applications panel of the Chrome browser to get this information as described later in this chapter.

Figure 14-7   How to delete cookies

The Task List application

To show you how you can use cookies to make an application more useful, figure 14-8 presents a Task List application. This application saves the items in the task list in a persistent cookie. That way, the task list is available to the user each time the user accesses the page, until the cookie expires. However, because the user's current browser stores the task list, this list isn't available if the user switches to a different browser.

Another thing you should know is that if you run this application from the file system, it doesn't work in Chrome. That's because Chrome disables cookies in websites that are run from the file system. In other words, it disables cookies from URLs that begin with file:///. Although you can use another browser like Firefox to get this to work, Firefox will only save the cookies for the current session. Because of that, they aren't displayed if you return to the page later.

To fix these problems, you can deploy this application to a web server. That can be a remote web server or a local one that's running on your computer. One way to do that is to run this application from a Node.js web server like the http-server module that's presented in chapter 19. Then, you can use Chrome to run the application from that web server by specifying its URL.

The HTML and CSS

Part 1 of figure 14-8 presents the user interface for this application. The text box and two buttons let the user add and delete tasks, and the text area on the right side of the page displays the task list. In the HTML, the script elements at the end of the body element show that this application uses one JavaScript file in addition to the jQuery library.

In the main element of the HTML, the first div element contains the text area that displays the list of tasks. Then, the CSS uses the id of this div element, which is "tasks", to float the div element to the right of the div elements that contain the text box and buttons. In addition, the text area has an id of "task_list" and the Add Task and Clear Tasks button have ids of "add_task" and "clear_task". As usual, JavaScript uses these ids to refer to these elements.

The Task List application

```
Task List

Task
|

        Add Task

        Clear Tasks
```
```
Task List
Finish current project
Meet with Mike
Get specs for new project
```

The HTML file

```html
<!DOCTYPE html>
<html>
<head>
  <meta charset="UTF-8">
  <meta name="viewport" content="width=device-width, initial-scale=1">
  <title>Task List</title>
  <link rel="stylesheet" href="task_list.css">
</head>
<body>
  <main>
    <h1>Task List</h1>
    <div id="tasks">
      <label for="task_list">Task List</label><br>
      <textarea id="task_list" rows="6" cols="50"></textarea>
    </div>
    <div>
      <label for="task">Task</label><br>
      <input type="text" name="task" id="task">
    </div>
    <div>
      <input type="button" name="add_task" id="add_task" value="Add Task"><br>
      <input type="button" name="clear_tasks" id="clear_tasks"
        value="Clear Tasks">
    </div>
  </main>
  <script src="https://code.jquery.com/jquery-3.4.1.min.js"></script>
  <script src="task_list.js"></script>
</body>
</html>
```

The CSS for the div element with "tasks" as its id

```css
#tasks {
    margin-top: 0;
    float: right;
}
```

Description

- The Task List application lets the user build a list of tasks and displays the tasks in the textarea element.
- The user can add new tasks to the list or clear all of the tasks.
- This application stores tasks in a persistent cookie in the user's browser.

Figure 14-8   The Task List application (part 1)

The JavaScript

Part 2 of figure 14-8 presents the JavaScript file for this application. It starts with the three helper functions that work with cookies named setCookie(), getCookieByName(), and deleteCookie(). These functions work like the functions presented earlier in this chapter.

To review, the setCookie() function accepts a name, a value, and an optional number of days and creates either a session or persistent cookie. The getCookieByName() function accepts a name and returns either an empty string or the value of the cookie with that name. And the deleteCookie() function accepts a name and deletes the cookie with that name.

After these helper functions is the ready() event handler. Within this event handler, the code defines the event handlers for the click events of the Add Task and Clear Tasks buttons.

The handler for the Add Task button starts by getting the task input element and storing it in a variable named textbox. Then, it uses the jQuery val() method to retrieve the text the user has entered in the textbox. After that, it checks whether the text is equal to an empty string. If so, the code displays an error message and sets the focus on the text box so the user can make another entry.

If the user has entered a task, this handler uses the getCookieByName() function to retrieve a cookie named tasks. Remember, this function returns a string, even if there's no such cookie in the browser. Because of that, this code can use the concat() method of the tasks string to append the task entered by the user. It also appends a new line character to display each task on its own line in the text area.

Next, this handler calls the setCookie() function to create a cookie named tasks to store the value in the current tasks variable. Since this code passes a value of 21 for the days parameter, this code creates a persistent cookie that expires in 21 days. If this tasks cookie doesn't exist yet, the setCookie() function creates it. However, if the tasks cookie already exists, the setCookie() function updates its value.

Finally, the event handler clears the tasks text box. Then, it re-displays the tasks by calling the getCookieByName() function and passing the value it returns to the val() method of the text area. Finally, it sets the focus back on the task input element, so the application is ready for the user to enter another task.

The event handler for the click event of the Clear Tasks button uses the deleteCookie() function to delete the cookie named tasks. Then, it clears all the tasks displayed in the text area and sets the focus on the text box. At this point, the application is ready for the user to enter another task.

The ready() event handler ends by calling the getCookieByName() function and passing the value it returns to the val() method of the text area. Then, it sets the focus on the text box. As a result, when the application first loads, it displays any tasks that are already stored in the persistent cookie in the user's browser and is ready for the user to enter another task.

The JavaScript

```javascript
const setCookie = (name, value, days) => {
    let cookie = name + "=" + encodeURIComponent(value);
    if (days) {
        cookie += "; max-age=" + days * 24 * 60 * 60;
    }
    cookie += "; path=/";
    document.cookie = cookie;
};

const getCookieByName = name => {
    const cookies = document.cookie;
    let start = cookies.indexOf(name + "=");
    if (start === -1) {  // no cookie with that name
        return "";
    } else {
        start = start + (name.length + 1);
        let end = cookies.indexOf(";", start);
        if (end === -1) {  // if no semicolon - last cookie
            end = cookies.length;
        }
        const cookieValue = cookies.substring(start, end);
        return decodeURIComponent(cookieValue);
    }
};

const deleteCookie = name =>
    document.cookie = name + "=''; max-age=0; path=/";

$(document).ready( () => {

    $("#add_task").click( () => {
        const textbox = $("#task");
        const task = textbox.val();
        if (task === "") {
            alert("Please enter a task.");
            textbox.focus();
        } else {
            let tasks = getCookieByName("tasks");
            tasks = tasks.concat(task, "\n");
            setCookie("tasks", tasks, 21); // 21 day persistent cookie

            textbox.val("");
            $("#task_list").val(getCookieByName("tasks"));
            textbox.focus();
        }
    });

    $("#clear_tasks").click( () => {
        deleteCookie("tasks");
        $("#task_list").val("");
        $("#task").focus();
    });

    $("#task_list").val(getCookieByName("tasks"));  // initial load
    $("#task").focus();
});
```

Figure 14-8   The Task List application (part 2)

How to use web storage

In the old days, cookies were the only option for storing data on the user's system. But cookies have some downsides. They are passed to the server with every HTTP request. In addition, they can only store about 4,000 bytes.

Fortunately, modern browsers now offer *web storage* that can be processed by JavaScript on the browser. Web storage provides several advantages over cookies. First, the data isn't passed to the server with every HTTP request. Second, web storage can store more data, approximately 5MB. Third, the code for working with them is shorter and easier to understand.

Web storage includes both *local storage* and *session storage*. The difference is that items in local storage persist between browser sessions, like a persistent cookie. But items in session storage are removed when the browser session ends, like a session cookie.

How to use local and session storage

Figure 14-9 shows how to work with local and session storage. To do that, you use the localStorage and sessionStorage objects. These objects store their items in *key/value pairs* and provide setItem(), getItem(), removeItem(), and clear() methods to work with the items.

For instance, the setItem() method requires two parameters that provide the key and value for an item. So, to add two items, you can use code like this:

```
localStorage.setItem("email", "grace@yahoo.com");
localStorage.setItem("phone", "555-555-1212");
```

Then, to get the value for an item, you can pass the item key to the getItem() method like this:

```
const phone = localStorage.getItem("phone");
```

To make this code more concise, you can use the shortcut syntax shown in this figure. For instance, you can save the email and phone items like this:

```
localStorage.email = "grace@yahoo.com";
localStorage.phone = "555-555-1212";
```

And you can retrieve the value of the phone item like this:

```
var phone = localStorage.phone;
```

The example in this figure uses the shortcut syntax. Here, if statements check whether the hits item exists in local storage and session storage. If so, it converts the value in that item to a number and adds 1 to it. Otherwise, it saves a new item named hits with a value of 1. After that, the code displays the value of the hits item in both local and session storage in the Console panel. This figure shows the message that's displayed if the user views the page three times, closes the browser, and views the page two more times.

When you use web storage to store data, it stores the data as a string. Then, when you get the original data, you must be able to convert the string back to the original data type. In figure 14-9, the example automatically converts a number

The syntax for working with local storage

```
localStorage.setItem("key", "value")   // saves the data in the item
localStorage.getItem("key")            // gets the data in the item
localStorage.removeItem("key")         // removes the item
localStorage.clear()                   // removes all items
```

The syntax for working with session storage

```
sessionStorage.setItem("key", "value") // saves the data in the item
sessionStorage.getItem("key")          // gets the data in the item
sessionStorage.removeItem("key")       // removes the item
sessionStorage.clear()                 // removes all items
```

The shortcut syntax for getting or saving an item

```
localStorage.key                       // saves or gets the data in the item
sessionStorage.key                     // saves or gets the data in the item
```

JavaScript that uses local and session storage for hit counters

```javascript
$(document).ready( () => {

    if (localStorage.hits) {
        localStorage.hits = parseInt(localStorage.hits) + 1;
    } else {
        localStorage.hits = 1;
    }

    if (sessionStorage.hits) {
        sessionStorage.hits = parseInt(sessionStorage.hits) + 1;
    } else {
        sessionStorage.hits = 1;
    }

    console.log("Hits for this browser: " + localStorage.hits + "\n" +
                "Hits for this session: " + sessionStorage.hits)
});
```

A console message that shows the current values of both hits items

```
Hits for this browser: 5
Hits for this session: 2
```

Description

- *Web storage* lets the web page use JavaScript to store data in *key/value pairs*. This feature is currently supported by every modern browser.

- Of the two types of web storage, *local storage* is retained indefinitely, and *session storage* is lost when the user ends the session by closing the browser.

- Unlike cookies, web storage is designed to be accessed by JavaScript, not server-side code. As a result, web storage isn't passed to the server with each HTTP request.

- You can store more data in web storage than you can in cookies. However, the HTML5 specification recommends a storage limit of 5MB.

Figure 14-9   How to use web storage

to a string when it saves the number. Then, it uses the ParseInt() function to convert the string back to a number when it retrieves the number.

When working with simple objects like Number and Date objects, you can often write the code that performs the data type conversion yourself. However, if you want to work with more complex objects, including custom objects like the ones presented in chapter 16, you can use the JSON.stringify() method to convert the object to a string. This uses JavaScript Object Notation (JSON) to store the object as a string. Then, you can use the JSON.parse() method to convert that JSON string back to an object. In figure 15-13 of the next chapter, you can see examples of how this works.

The Task List application with web storage

Figure 14-10 presents the JavaScript for a Task List application that's been updated to use local storage instead of a persistent cookie. This works better than persistent cookies for several reasons.

First, the code is shorter because it no longer needs helper functions to create, retrieve, and delete cookies. Instead, it just uses the methods of the localStorage object.

Second, it works with all web browsers even if you run the application from the file system. Remember, cookies only work with Chrome when you run the application from a web server, not when you run the application from the file system.

Third, it stores the task list in the browser indefinitely instead of just for 21 days. That's because local storage doesn't have an expiration date. Of course, you may sometimes want to remove something from local storage after a set amount of time has elapsed. In those cases, you can set another key/value pair with an expiration date for the item, and use that date to trigger the deletion of the item.

Because the shortcut syntax is more concise and easier to read than using the setItem() and getItem() methods, the code in this figure uses the shortcut syntax to save and get the item named myTasks. In addition, it uses the removeItem() method to remove this item.

In this code, the statement that retrieves the tasks from local storage uses the OR operator (| |) to set a default value. As a result, if the shortcut syntax doesn't return any tasks, this statement sets the tasks variable to an empty string. That way, the value of myTasks is always a string. Without this default value, the call to the concat() method in the next statement would throw an exception when there are no tasks in local storage.

The Task List application

```
Task List

Task
[                              ]

[        Add Task        ]

[        Clear Tasks       ]

Task List
Finish current project
Meet with Mike
Get specs for new project
```

The JavaScript

```javascript
$(document).ready( () => {

    $("#add_task").click( () => {
        const textbox = $("#task");
        const task = textbox.val();
        if (task === "") {
            alert("Please enter a task.");
            textbox.focus();
        } else {
            let tasks = localStorage.myTasks || "";   // "" is default
            localStorage.myTasks = tasks.concat(task, "\n");

            textbox.val("");
            $("#task_list").val(localStorage.myTasks);
            textbox.focus();
        }
    });

    $("#clear_tasks").click( () => {
        localStorage.removeItem("myTasks");
        $("#task_list").val("");
        $("#task").focus();
    });

    // display tasks on initial load
    $("#task_list").val(localStorage.myTasks);
    $("#task").focus();
});
```

Description

- This version of the Task List application stores tasks in local storage on the user's browser rather than in a cookie.
- The HTML for this application is the same as it is in figure 14-8.

Figure 14-10   The Task List application with web storage

How to use Chrome
with cookies and web storage

As you test and debug an application that uses cookies or web storage, it can sometimes be helpful to view the values that are currently stored. That's why this chapter finishes by showing how to use the Application panel of the Chrome browser to do just that.

This can be useful not only for testing your own applications, but for seeing what items other websites are storing in your browser. For example, you can navigate to google.com and open the Application panel to view what Google is storing on your computer, which can be an interesting exercise. The Application panel also shows you what's in the browser-based databases that most modern browsers support.

In addition to viewing cookies and web storage, the Application panel lets you delete and edit items. This can be useful when testing and debugging your own applications. But take care when doing this for other websites, since you might delete something that affects the way the website works for you.

How to work with cookies

You can use the procedure presented in figure 14-11 to view the cookies that your application has stored in the browser. For each cookie, the Application panel displays information like its name, value, path, and expiration date. In addition, you can use this panel to delete and edit cookies. This can be handy during the development of an application.

How to work with web storage

You can also use the procedure in this figure to view the web storage items that your application has stored in the browser. For these items, the Application panel displays the key and value fields for the items that are stored in local or session storage.

As with cookies, you can use the Application panel to delete and edit items in web storage. This can be useful when you're developing an application.

The cookies for an application in the Application panel

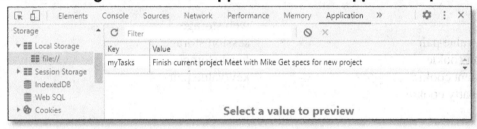

The local storage items for an application in the Application panel

How to view cookies and stored items

1. Press F12 to open the developer tools.
2. Click on the Application tab at the top of the tools window, and then look for the Storage section in the pane on the left-hand side.
3. Expand an appropriate storage type such as Cookies, Local Storage, or Session Storage.
4. Click on the appropriate URL to display the stored values in a grid. For cookie storage, you may want to filter the cookies by entering the name of the cookie you want to view.

How to delete or edit cookies or stored items

-   To delete an item, right-click the item and select Delete.
-   To edit an item, right-click the item and select Edit Value. Then, edit the text for the value.
-   To apply the edit or deletion to the application, make sure to refresh the page.

Description

-   You can use the Application panel in Chrome's developer tools to work with cookies and items in local and session storage.

Figure 14-11   How to use Chrome with items in the browser

Perspective

Now that you've finished this chapter, you should have the skills you need to work with the location object, the history object, cookies, and web storage. Because anyone can view the values of cookies and web storage, they aren't secure. As a result, you shouldn't store sensitive personal information such as passwords in them.

Terms

cookie	web storage
name/value pair	session storage
session cookie	local storage
persistent cookie	key/value pair
third-party cookie	

Summary

- The properties of the location object let you examine different parts of the current URL. The methods of this object give you greater control over how a new page is loaded into the browser.

- The history object stores a history of the pages that a user has visited. The methods of this object allow you to control what's stored in the history object and how the navigation between pages works.

- A *cookie* is a text string that is stored in a user's browser. A cookie consists of a *name/value pair*. A *session cookie* is removed when the browser closes, but a *persistent cookie* is removed after a specified amount of time has elapsed.

- Cookies are passed between the browser and the server on each HTTP request and response. They can be created, read, and deleted with JavaScript.

- *Web storage* provides another way to store data in a user's browser. Web storage items are stored in *key/value pairs*. Unlike cookies, these items aren't passed between the browser and the server with each request.

- There are two types of web storage. *Local storage* remains indefinitely, and *session storage* is lost when the browser session ends.

- You can use Chrome's developer tools to view, edit, and delete cookies and items in web storage.

Exercise 14-1   Test the Tutorial application

In this exercise, you'll test the Tutorial application that was presented in this chapter. Then you'll make a few changes to better illustrate how it uses the location and history objects.

Open and test the Tutorial application

1. Use your text editor or IDE to open the application in this folder:
   `javascript_jquery\exercises\ch14\tutorial`

2. Review the main.html file. Notice that there is a script element at the bottom of the page that uses the document.write() method to display the value in the length property of the history object.

3. Review and run the index.html file. First, click on the Enter button to go directly to the main page. Then, look at the bottom of the page and see that there are two pages in history.

4. Use the Back button on the page or the browser's back button to go back to the initial page, which is the index.html page.

5. Click on the Tutorial button and click through all the pages of the tutorial. When you get to the main page, note that there are still only two pages in history. This shows that the tutorial pages were replaced in the history object when the next page was displayed.

6. Use the Back button on the page or the browser's back button to go back to the initial page. Once again, because the tutorial pages are replaced when the next page is displayed, this takes you back to the index.html page.

Adjust the application so the pages of the tutorial are kept in history

7. Change the JavaScript code in the script element of the tutorial1.html file so it sets the value of the location object rather than calling the replace() method. Do the same for the tutorial2.html and tutorial3.html files.

8. Save your changes, run the application, and repeat steps 3 through 6 to see how the application works now. This time, when you get to the main page after clicking through the tutorial pages, it says that there are 5 pages in history. And when you click the back button, you go back to the last page of the tutorial, not to the initial page of the application. This shows that the tutorial pages are now stored in the history object.

Exercise 14-2   Enhance the Task List application

In this exercise, you'll adjust the Task List application that uses web storage so the tasks in local storage have an expiration date. That way, they'll behave more like a persistent cookie rather than staying in local storage indefinitely.

Open and test the Task List application

1. Use your text editor or IDE to open the application in this folder:
    `javascript_jquery\exercises\ch14\task_list`

2. Run the application in Chrome and enter a task or two. Then click on the F12 button to open the developer tools, and navigate to the Application panel. In the Storage pane, expand the Local Storage node and then select the URL for the website to view the tasks storage item named E14tasks.

3. Click on the Clear Tasks button to clear the tasks and then close the browser.

Enhance the task storage to include an expiration date

4. Display the task_list.js file. Then, find the line of code in the event handler for the click event of the Add Task button that adds the updated tasks to local storage.

5. After that code, create a new Date object for today's date and add 21 days to that date. Then, call the toDateString() method of the Date object and store the resulting value in local storage in a property named expiration.

6. Repeat step 2. Notice that this time there's a tasks storage item and an expiration storage item.

7. In the event handler for the click event of the Clear Tasks button, add code that removes the expiration item from local storage.

8. Comment out the line of code near the end of the ready() event handler that sets the value of the task_list text area. Then, write code that retrieves the expiration value from local storage and converts it to a Date object. After that, create a Date object for today's date.

9. Code an if statement that checks whether the expiration date is in the past. To do that, compare the values returned by the getTime() method of each Date object. Then, if the expiration date is in the past, remove both the tasks and expiration items from local storage. If not, retrieve the tasks from local storage and display them as before.

10. Run the application and enter a task or two if none are already there. Next, open the Application panel and edit the expiration date so it's in the past. Then, refresh the application. Notice that the tasks are cleared from both the application display and from local storage.

15

How to work with arrays, sets, and maps

Chapter 3 introduced arrays. Now, this chapter presents more skills for working with arrays, which are an important part of many JavaScript applications. For example, you can use an array to store a list of tasks that you can update and display. In addition, this chapter presents some basic skills for working with sets and maps. Like arrays, sets and maps provide a way to work with a collection of elements.

How to create and use an array

To start, this chapter reviews some of the skills presented in chapter 3. Then, it presents some additional skills for creating and using arrays.

How to create an array

An *array* is an object that contains zero or more items called *elements*. Each element can be a native data type or an object. For instance, you can store numbers, strings, and Date objects in the same array. The *length* of an array indicates the number of elements that it contains.

Figure 15-1 shows three ways to create an array. To use the first method, you use the *new* keyword with the Array() constructor. If you don't code an optional length parameter, the array is empty. If you do, the specified number of elements are added to the array, each with a value of undefined. The length parameter must be a whole number that is greater than or equal to zero.

To use the second method, you call the static Array.of() method. To use the third method, you just code a set of brackets, also called an *array literal*. Both of these methods produce an empty array.

After the three ways to create an array, this figure shows the syntax for assigning values to an array when you create it. To do that, you code the values separated by commas and pass them to the Array() constructor or Array.of() method. Or, you code the values between the brackets of the array literal.

When you use the Array() constructor to create an array and assign a list of values, the list must not contain a single number. If it does, it's treated as the length of the array rather than as a value in the array. By contrast, because the Array.of() method doesn't accept a length parameter, it adds all the values it receives, including a single number, as elements of the array. For this reason, some programmers prefer the Array.of() method to the Array() constructor.

After the two syntax summaries, the first example in this figure shows how to create a new array and assign values to its elements in a single statement. The first statement uses the Array() constructor to create an array named rates with four elements. The second statement uses the Array.of() method to create an array named dice with six elements. And the third statement uses an array literal to create an array named names with three elements.

To refer to the elements in an array, you use an *index* that ranges from zero to one less than the number of elements in an array. In an array with 12 elements, for example, the index values range from 0 to 11. This is why the getMonth() method of a Date object numbers the months from 0 to 11 instead of 1 to 12.

To use an index, you code it within brackets after the name of the array. In this figure, all of the examples use literal values for the indexes, but you can also use a constant or variable that contains an index value. If you access an element that hasn't been assigned a value, the array returns a value of undefined.

The last example shows how to assign values to an empty array. To do that, you refer to the elements by using indexes, and you assign values to those elements.

The syntax for creating an array

Using the *new* keyword with the Array() constructor
```
const arrayName = new Array(length);
```

Using the static Array.of() method
```
const arrayName = Array.of();
```

Using an array literal
```
const arrayName = [];
```

The syntax for creating an array and assigning values in one statement

Using the *new* keyword with the Array() constructor
```
const arrayName = new Array(arrayList);
```

Using the static Array.of() method
```
const arrayName = Array.of(arrayList);
```

Using an array literal
```
const arrayName = [arrayList];
```

Examples that create an array and assign values in one statement
```
const rates = new Array(14.95, 12.95, 11.95, 9.95);   // Array() constructor
const dice = Array.of(1, 2, 3, 4, 5, 6);              // Array.of() method
const names = ["Grace", "Charles", "Ada"];            // array literal
```

The syntax for referring to an element of an array
```
arrayName[index]
```

Code that refers to the elements in an array
```
rates[2]        // Refers to the third element in the rates array
names[1]        // Refers to the second element in the names array
```

How to assign values to an array by accessing each element

How to assign numbers to an array that starts with four undefined elements
```
const rates = new Array(4);
rates[0] = 14.95;
rates[1] = 12.95;
rates[2] = 11.95;
rates[3] = 9.95;
```

How to assign strings to an array that starts with no elements
```
const names = [];
names[0] = "Grace";
names[1] = "Charles";
names[2] = "Ada";
```

Description

- An *array* can store one or more *elements*. Its *length* is the number of elements in the array.

- If you create an array without specifying the length, the array doesn't contain any elements.

- When you create an array of one or more elements without assigning values to them, each element is set to undefined.

- To refer to the elements in an array, you use an *index* where 0 is the first element, 1 is the second element, and so on.

Figure 15-1   How to create an array

How to add and delete array elements

JavaScript provides one property and one operator that can help you modify an array. Figure 15-2 shows how to use them.

To add an element to the end of an array, you can use the length property of the array as the index of the new element. This is illustrated by the first example in this figure. Since the length property is always one more than the highest index used in the array, this adds the new element to the end of the array.

To add an element at a specific index, you use its index to refer to the element and assign a value to it. This is illustrated by the second example. If you use an index that's greater than the length of the array, JavaScript creates the elements that you skipped over and assigns a value of undefined to them.

To delete an element from an array, you can use the delete operator. This is illustrated by the third example. When you do this, JavaScript leaves the deleted element in the array with a value of undefined. In other words, JavaScript doesn't shift the elements in the array to fill in this gap. To delete elements without leaving a gap in the array, you can use the splice() method of an array as described later in this chapter.

To remove all elements in an array, you can set the length property of the array to zero. This is illustrated by the fourth example. This is different from using the delete operator because JavaScript doesn't leave the elements in the array with a value of undefined. Instead, it removes the elements completely, leaving an array with no elements.

In JavaScript, a *sparse array* is an array with a large number of elements but with few assigned values. This is illustrated by the fifth example. Here, the array has 1001 elements, but only two of these elements have assigned values. For an array like this, some programming languages would reserve space for all 1001 elements in the computer's memory. However, JavaScript only reserves space for the elements that have assigned values.

One property of an array and the delete operator

Property	Description
`length`	The number of elements in an array.

Operator	Description
`delete`	Deletes the contents of an element and sets the element to undefined, but doesn't remove the element from the array.

How to add an element to the end of an array

```
const numbers = [1, 2, 3];        // array is 1, 2, 3
numbers[numbers.length] = 4;      // array is 1, 2, 3, 4
```

How to add an element at a specific index

```
const numbers = [1, 2, 3];        // array is 1, 2, 3
numbers[5] = 6;                   // array is 1, 2, 3, undefined, undefined, 6
```

How to delete a number at a specific index

```
const numbers = [1, 2, 3];        // array is 1, 2, 3
delete numbers[1];                // array is 1, undefined, 3
```

How to remove all elements

```
const numbers = [1, 2, 3];        // array contains three elements
numbers.length = 0;               // removes all elements from array
```

A sparse array that contains 999 undefined elements

```
const numbers = [1];              // array contains 1
numbers[1000] = 1001;             // array contains 1 and 1001 with 999
                                  // undefined elements in between
```

Description

- You can add an element to the end of an array by using the length property as the index.

- If you add an element at a specific index that isn't the next one in sequence, JavaScript adds undefined elements to the array between the new element and the end of the original array.

- When you use the delete operator to delete an element, JavaScript deletes the element's value but keeps the element in the array with a value of undefined.

- To remove all the elements from an array, you can set the array's length property to zero. Unlike the delete operator, this removes all the elements, not just the elements' values.

- A *sparse array* is a large array with few defined elements. For efficiency, though, JavaScript only reserves space for the elements that are assigned values.

- As you progress through this chapter, you'll learn more ways that you can add and remove elements from an array.

Figure 15-2   How to add and delete array elements

How to use for, for-in, and for-of loops with arrays

This book has already shown how to use for, for-in, and for-of loops to process the elements in an array. Now, figure 15-3 reviews these skills.

The first example begins with a statement that creates an array named names that's used by all the examples in this figure. Because three string values are coded between the brackets, JavaScript adds three elements with these values to the array. Then, the second statement adds a string element at index 5. This adds two undefined elements between the third element and this new element.

The second example shows how to use a for loop with the names array. This for loop initializes the counter variable to 0, loops as long as the counter is less than the number of elements in the array, and increments the counter by 1. Then, within the loop, the code uses the counter variable to access the value of the current array element. Note that this loop processes the undefined elements in the array.

Note also that you don't have to process all the elements in an array when you use a for loop. For example, you could skip the first element in the array by initializing the counter to 1, or skip every other element by incrementing the counter by two. In other words, a for loop gives you a lot of control over how it processes the elements in an array.

The third example shows how to use a for-in loop with the names array. This requires less code than a for loop. That's because a for-in loop automatically processes all the elements in the array. As a result, you don't need to initialize and update the counter variable or code a stop condition.

To code a for-in loop, you start by declaring a constant or variable that represents the index of the current array element. Then, you can use this constant or variable to get the value of the current element, as the example below the syntax shows. Unlike a for loop, a for-in loop does *not* process the undefined elements in the array.

The fourth example shows how to use a for-of loop with the names array. This works similarly to the for-in loop, but the constant or variable that you declare in the loop represents the value of the current array element, not its index. Because of that, you don't need to use an index to get the element value. Like a for loop, a for-of loop processes the undefined elements in the array.

Since the for, for-in, and for-of loops work somewhat differently, the type of loop you should use depends on what you need to do. If you need to process all the values in an array, the for-of loop yields code that's short and easy to read. However, if you need to work with the index value, or if you want to skip undefined elements, a for-in loop probably works best. Or, if you need more control over which elements are processed, you should probably use a for loop.

An array that's used by the following examples

```
const names = ["Grace", "Charles", "Ada"];
names[5] = "Alan";   // adds two undefined elements between "Ada" and "Alan"
```

How to use a for loop with an array

The syntax for processing all the elements

```
for (let index = 0; index < arrayName.length; index++) {
    // statements that use the index to access the array element value
}
```

Code that uses a for loop

```
let displayString = "";
for (let i = 0; i < names.length; i++) {
    displayString += names[i] + " ";
}
// displayString is Grace Charles Ada undefined undefined Alan
```

How to use a for-in loop with an array

The syntax

```
for (const|let index in arrayName) {
    // statements that use the index to access the array element value
}
```

Code that uses a for-in loop

```
let displayString = "";
for (const i in names) {
    displayString += names[i] + " ";
}
// displayString is Grace Charles Ada Alan
```

How to use a for-of loop with an array

The syntax

```
for (const|let value of arrayName) {
    // statements that use the array element value
}
```

Code that uses a for-of loop

```
let displayString = "";
for (const val of names) {
    displayString += val + " ";
}
// displayString is Grace Charles Ada undefined undefined Alan
```

Description

- You can use a *for loop*, a *for-in loop*, or a *for-of loop* to iterate the elements of an array.

- You can use a constant or variable with a for-in or for-of statement to refer to an element index or value. By contrast, the counter in a for statement must be a variable.

- The constant or variable that's declared in a for-in statement is the index of the current element, and the constant or variable that's declared in a for-of statement is the value of the current element.

- A for-in loop doesn't process undefined elements, but for and for-of loops do.

Figure 15-3   How to use for, for-in, and for-of loops with arrays

How to destructure an array

So far, this chapter has shown how to use indexes to assign the individual elements in an array to constants or variables. However, JavaScript also allows you to assign multiple array elements to multiple constants or variables in a single statement without using indexes. This is called *destructuring* an array.

To start, figure 15-4 presents the syntax for destructuring an array. To do that, you code the const or let keyword depending on whether you want to assign the elements of the array to constants or variables. Then, you code the names of the constants or variables within brackets. Next, you code the assignment operator followed by the name of the array whose elements are being destructured.

The examples show how this syntax works. After two arrays are defined, the first example assigns the first three elements in the totals array to constants named total1, total2, and total3. This is equivalent to these statements:

```
const total1 = totals[0];
const total2 = totals[1];
const total3 = totals[2];
```

The second example shows how you can skip the assignment of an element. To do that, you use a comma as a placeholder.

The third example shows how you can code a default value that's assigned if the corresponding element in an array doesn't exist. In this case, the fullName array only has three elements. As a result, this code assigns the default value to the fourth constant.

The fourth example shows how to use the *rest operator* (...) to assign elements in an array to a new array. To use the rest operator, you prepend it to the name of the new array. Then, after assigning any other elements, JavaScript assigns the *rest* of the elements to the new array. In this example, JavaScript assigns the first two elements to the total1 and total2 constants, and it assigns the rest of the elements to an array named remainingTotals.

If you use the rest operator, you can only use it once per destructuring statement. In addition, you can only use it with the last constant or variable in the list.

The last example shows that you can also destructure strings. This makes sense because a string works much like an array of characters. When you destructure a string, JavaScript assigns the individual characters of the string to the variables or constants within the brackets. As with arrays, you can use commas to skip characters, you can provide default character values, and you can use the rest operator to create an array of characters.

The syntax for destructuring an array

```
const|let [identifier1, identifier2, ...] = arrayName;
```

Two arrays that are used by the following examples

```
const totals = [141.95, 212.25, 411, 135.75];
const fullName = ["Grace", "M", "Hopper"];
```

Example 1: Assign the first three elements in an array

```
const [total1, total2, total3] = totals;
// total1 is 141.95, total2 is 212.25, total3 is 411
```

Example 2: Skip an array element

```
const [firstName, , lastName] = fullName;
// firstName is "Grace", lastName is "Hopper"
```

Example 3: Use a default value

```
const [first, middle, last, suffix = "none"] = fullName;
// first is "Grace", middle is "M", last is "Hopper", suffix is "none"
```

Example 4: Use the rest operator to assign some elements to a new array

```
const [total1, total2, ...remainingTotals] = totals;
// total1 is 141.95, total2 is 212.25, remainingTotals is [411, 135.75]
```

Example 5: Destructure a string

```
const [first, second, third] = "USA";
// first is "U", second is "S", third is "A"
```

Description

- You can assign the elements in an array to individual constants or variables by coding the *const* or *let* keyword, followed by a list of variable or constant names enclosed in brackets ([]), an equals sign, and the name of the array. This is called *destructuring* an array.

- When you destructure an array, you can skip elements by coding commas as placeholders. You can also specify default values that are assigned if an element doesn't exist.

- When you destructure an array, you can use the *rest operator* (...) to assign the rest of the elements in an array to another array. *Destructuring* and the rest operator were introduced with ECMAScript 2015 and can't be used with older browsers.

- You can also destructure the individual characters of a string.

- When you destructure an array or a string, the original array or string isn't changed.

Figure 15-4   How to destructure an array

How to use the methods of the Array type

The Array object type includes several methods that you can use to work with the elements in an array. The topics that follow show how to use some of these methods.

Methods that add, modify, remove, and copy elements

Figure 15-5 summarizes some of the methods of the Array type that you can use to add, modify, remove, or copy elements. Except for the slice() method, these methods change the original array in some way. The slice() method, on the other hand, copies some or all of an array's elements into a new array and doesn't change the original array.

The first two methods, push() and pop(), add elements to and remove elements from the end of an array. This lets you use an array as a data structure known as a stack. In a stack, the last element added to collection is the first element removed (last-in, first-out). This works much like adding a plate to a stack of plates where the last plate added is the first plate removed. The first example in this figure illustrates these methods.

The next two methods, unshift() and shift(), add elements to and remove elements from the beginning of an array. The second example illustrates how these methods work.

The splice() method lets you remove, replace, or add elements in an array. To remove elements, you call the splice() method with the index of the first element to remove and the number of elements to remove. To replace elements, you call the splice() method with the index of the first element to replace, the number of elements to be replaced, and a list of the replacement values. To add elements, you call the splice() method with the index where you want the first element added, zero for the number of elements, and a list of the values to add.

The third example shows how to use the splice() method to replace elements. Here, the first parameter indicates that the elements starting at index 1 should be replaced. The second parameter indicates that two elements should be replaced. And the third and fourth parameters list those two elements.

The slice() method lets you create a new array from part or all of an array without modifying the original array. The first parameter indicates the index of the element where the copy starts, and the second parameter indicates the index up to which the elements are copied. In other words, the element at the index specified by the second parameter isn't copied. The fourth example shows how this works. Here, the code copies the elements with indexes 1 and 2 into a new array.

You can also use the slice() method to copy all of the elements of an array to a new array. To do that, you omit the parameters of this method as shown in the last example.

Methods of the Array type that add, modify, remove, and copy elements

Method	Description
push(*element_list*)	Adds one or more elements to the end of the array and returns the new length of the array.
pop()	Removes the last element in the array, decrements the length, and returns the element that it removed.
unshift(*element_list*)	Adds one or more elements to the beginning of the array, shifts other elements to the right, and returns the new length.
shift()	Removes the first element, shifts all elements one index to the left, decrements the length, and returns the removed element.
splice(*start,number*)	Removes the number of elements given by the second parameter starting with the index given by the first parameter. It returns the elements that were removed.
splice(*start,number, element_list*)	Removes the number of elements given by the second parameter starting with the index given by the first parameter, and replaces those elements with the ones given by the third parameter. If the second parameter is 0, the elements are added at the start index instead of being replaced. It returns the elements that were removed.
slice([*start*][,*end*])	Returns a new array that starts with the index given by the first parameter and ends with the element before the index given by the second parameter. It doesn't change the original array.

An array that's used by the following examples

```
const names = ["Grace", "Charles", "Ada"];
```

Example 1: Add elements to and remove an element from the end of the array

```
names.push("Alan", "Linus");
// names is ["Grace", "Charles", "Ada", "Alan", "Linus"]
let removedName = names.pop();          // removedName is Linus
// names is ["Grace", "Charles", "Ada", "Alan"]
```

Example 2: Add and remove an element from the beginning of the array

```
names.unshift("Linus");
// names is ["Linus", "Grace", "Charles", "Ada", "Alan"]
removedName = names.shift();           // removedName is Linus
// names is ["Grace", "Charles", "Ada", "Alan"]
```

Example 3: Replace elements from a specific index

```
names.splice(1, 2, "Mary", "Linus");
// names is ["Grace", "Mary", "Linus", "Alan"]
```

Example 4: Copy some of the elements of the array to a new array

```
const partialCopy = names.slice(1, 3);
// partialCopy is ["Mary", "Linus"] - names array is unchanged
```

Example 5: Copy all the elements of the array to a new array

```
const fullCopy = names.slice();
// fullCopy is ["Grace", "Mary", "Linus", "Alan"] - names is unchanged
```

Figure 15-5   Methods of the Array type that add, modify, remove, and copy elements

Methods that inspect an array or its elements

Figure 15-6 summarizes some of the methods of the Array type that inspect the elements of an array. For example, the indexOf() and lastIndexOf() methods let you search for a specific value in the array from either the beginning or end of the array. Each of these methods has a second optional parameter that allows you to indicate the index where the search starts. Both methods return the index of the value being searched for, or -1 if the value isn't found in the array.

The includes() method also searches for a value in the array and has an optional second parameter that allows you to indicate the index where the search starts. However, this method returns true if the value is found, not an index value. Otherwise, it returns false, not -1. This method can make your code easier to read if you just need to know whether the value is in the array. To illustrate, the first example in this figure shows that an if statement that uses the includes() method is easier to read than an if statement that uses the indexOf() method.

The next five methods accept a function as the parameter. A function that's passed to a method like this is known as a *callback function*. A callback function is called by the method that receives it to complete its task. For an Array object, the methods call the callback function for each element in the array.

Like the indexOf(), lastIndexOf(), and includes() methods, the find() and findIndex() methods search for elements in the array. However, rather than searching for a specific value, these methods search for elements that meet the condition tested by the callback function. The find() method returns the value of the first element that meets the condition, or undefined if no element meets the condition. The findIndex() method returns the index of the first element that meets the condition, or -1 if no element meets the condition.

The filter() method also searches for elements that meet the condition tested by the function it receives. However, rather than returning the first value or index it finds, it returns an array that contains all the elements that meet the condition. The second example shows how this works. Here, the code creates an array that contains all numbers that are less than 10.

The some() and every() methods check whether the elements in the array meet the condition tested by the callback function. The some() method returns true if one or more of the elements meet the condition. Otherwise, it returns false. By contrast, the every() method returns true only if all the elements in the array meet the criteria. The third example shows how this works. Here, the code checks that all the numbers are positive.

The entries(), values(), and keys() methods return iterator objects. In the next chapter, you'll learn how iterator objects work. For now, just know that you can use an iterator object with for-of loops as shown by the fourth example. Here, the entries() method returns an array whose elements are arrays that consist of a key and a value. Then, the for-of loop displays the key and value from each element.

The static Array.isArray() method checks that the object that's passed to it is an array. Developers typically use this method to check that an object is an array before trying to call methods from that Array object.

Methods of the Array type that inspect an array or its elements

Method	Description
`indexOf(value[,start])`	Returns the first index at which the first parameter is found, or -1 if the value isn't found. The optional second parameter specifies the index to start searching from.
`lastIndexOf(value[,start])`	Returns the last index at which the first parameter is found, or -1 if the value isn't found. The optional second parameter specifies the index to start searching from.
`includes(value[,start])`	Returns a Boolean value that indicates whether the specified value is in the array. The optional second parameter specifies the index to start searching from.
`find(function)`	Returns the value of the first element that meets the condition of the function, or undefined if no element meets the condition.
`findIndex(function)`	Returns the index of the first element that meets the condition of the function, or -1 if no element meets the condition.
`filter(function)`	Returns an array containing all the elements that meet the condition of the function.
`every(function)`	Returns a Boolean value that indicates whether all elements meet the condition of the function.
`some(function)`	Returns a Boolean value that indicates whether at least one element meets the condition of the function.
`entries()`	Returns an iterator that contains a [key, value] array for each element. The key is the index of the element.
`values()`	Returns an iterator that contains the value of each element.
`keys()`	Returns an iterator that contains a key for each element.
`isArray(object)`	A static method that returns a Boolean value that indicates whether the specified object is an array.

An array that's used by the following examples

```
const numbers = [1,2,3,4,5,6,7,8,9,10,11,12,13,14,15,16,17,18,19,20];
```

Example 1: Two ways to check if a specific value is in the array

```
if(numbers.indexOf(5) != -1) { ... }
if(numbers.includes(5)) { ... }
```

Example 2: Filter the numbers in the array to get all the values less than 10

```
const lessThanTen = numbers.filter( value => value < 10 );
// lessThanTen is [1, 2, 3, 4, 5, 6, 7, 8, 9] – numbers array is unchanged
```

Example 3: Check if all the numbers in the array are positive

```
const isAllPos = numbers.every( value => value > 0 );   // isAllPos is true
```

Example 4: Use a for-of loop with the entries() method

```
for(let [key, val] of numbers.entries()) {
    console.log(`key: ${key}, val: ${val}`);
}
// displays "key: 0, val: 1", "key: 1, val: 2", etc.
```

Figure 15-6   Methods of the Array type that inspect an array or its elements

Methods that transform the elements

Figure 15-7 summarizes some of the methods of the Array type that transform the elements in an array. To start, the forEach() method accepts a function and applies it to every element in the array.

The join() and toString() methods create a string that lists the array's elements. However, the join() method lets you specify the separator for the elements, and the toString() method always specifies a comma as the separator. The first example shows how this works.

The sort() method sorts the elements in the array. By default, it treats all elements as strings and sorts any undefined elements last. This means it sorts strings in alphabetic sequence, but it might not sort numbers in numeric sequence. For instance, if you sorted the numbers array shown in the second example, the number 12 would appear before the other numbers. To fix this, the second example passes a callback function to the sort() method.

This callback function should receive two parameters and return a positive, zero, or negative value based on a comparison of these two values. In the second example, the callback function defines parameters named x and y that returns the value of x minus y. So, if x is greater than y, it returns a positive value, if x and y are equal, it returns zero, and if x is less than y, it returns a negative value. This causes the numbers in the array to be sorted in ascending numeric sequence. You can use this same technique to perform other types of sorts.

The reverse() method reverses the order of the elements in the array, and the map() method creates a new array that contains the results of executing a function on each item of the original array. The third example shows how to use the map() method to create a new array that contains each element of the original array after it has been multiplied by 2. This doesn't change the original array.

The reduce() method returns all the elements in the array, reduced to a single value. It accepts a callback function and an optional second parameter that sets the initial value that's returned by the function. Here, the callback function should define two parameters. The first parameter specifies the value returned by the previous function call. This is how the reduce() method keeps track of the value that the array elements are reduced to. The second parameter specifies the value of the current element. This method is illustrated by the fourth example.

The flat() and flatMap() methods flatten nested arrays into a single array. The flat() method lets you specify how many layers to flatten, and the flatMap() method applies a callback function to each element and then flattens the array. In a moment, this chapter describes nested arrays in more detail.

For now, just know that it's possible to add an array as an element of another array. For example, the fifth example begins by creating an array that contains a nested array. In turn, this nested array contains another nested array. So, the array is nested two layers deep. To flatten it, the code passes a value of 2 to the flat() method. This converts the nested array to a single array with all the same elements of the nested arrays.

Methods of the Array type that transform elements

Method	Description
forEach(*function*)	Executes the function once for each element and returns a value of undefined.
join([*separator*])	Converts all the elements of the array to strings and concatenates them separated by commas or by the string value of the parameter if one is specified.
toString()	Same as the join() method without any parameter passed to it.
sort([*comparison_function*])	Sorts the elements into ascending alphanumeric sequence, converting numeric elements to strings if necessary. Accepts an optional function to change the default sort order.
reverse()	Reverses the order of the elements.
map(*function*)	Executes the function once for each element and returns an array that contains the results of each function call.
reduce(*function*[,*init*])	Executes a function that returns all the elements reduced to one value, processed in ascending sequence. The optional second parameter sets the initial value for the function.
flat([*depth*])	Returns an array with any nested array elements included. The optional parameter is the number of levels to flatten. The default is 1.
flatMap(*function*)	Returns an array with the results of the function call, flattened to one level. Equivalent to calling flat() after calling map().

Example 1: Convert the elements in an array to a single string

```
const names = ["Grace", "Charles", "Ada", "Alan"];
let str = names.join();              // str is "Grace,Charles,Ada,Alan"
str = names.join(", ");              // str is "Grace, Charles, Ada, Alan"
str = names.toString();              // str is "Grace,Charles,Ada,Alan"
```

Example 2: Sort numeric values in ascending sequence

```
const numbers = [5, 12, 8, 6, 9, 2];
numbers.sort( (x, y) => x - y );     // numbers is [2, 5, 6, 8, 9, 12]
```

Example 3: Create a new array with each element multiplied by 2

```
const doubled = numbers.map( value => value * 2 );
// doubled is [4, 10, 12, 16, 18, 24] - numbers is unchanged
```

Example 4: Transform the elements and then convert to a single string

```
const names = ["Grace", "Charles", "Ada", "Alan"];
let str = names.reduce( (prev, current) =>
    prev + " " + current.toLowerCase(), "Names:" );
// str is "Names: grace charles ada alan"
```

Example 5: Flatten an array that's nested two levels deep

```
const nested = [5, 12, 8, 6, 9, [4, [0, 7], 1], 2];
const flattened = nested.flat(2);
// flattened is [5, 12, 8, 6, 9, 4, 0, 7, 1, 2]
```

Figure 15-7   Methods of the Array type that transform elements

The Test Scores application

The next two figures present another version of the Test Scores application that was first presented in chapter 3. This version of the application shows how to use some of the skills presented in this chapter to work with an array. To start, it allows users to enter a score into the text box. Then, when the user clicks the Add Score button, the application adds the score to an array and displays all of the scores as well as the average score. In addition, it displays a list of the last three scores in the reverse sequence from which they were entered.

The HTML

Part 1 of figure 15-8 shows the HTML for this application. Because this book has presented other applications that work similarly, you shouldn't have any trouble understanding this HTML. However, unlike some earlier applications, this HTML uses labels, not disabled text boxes, to display score values.

The Test Scores application

My Test Scores

All scores:	92, 89, 82, 97
Average score:	90.00
Last 3 scores:	97, 82, 89
Enter new score:	[ ] [Add Score]

The HTML

```
<body>
    <main>
        <h1>My Test Scores</h1>
        <div>
            <label>All scores:</label>
            <label id="all"></label>
        </div>
        <div>
            <label>Average score:</label>
            <label id="avg"></label>
        </div>
        <div>
            <label>Last 3 scores:</label>
            <label id="last"></label>
        </div>
        <div>
            <label for="score">Enter new score:</label>
            <input type="text" id="score">
            <input type="button" id="add_score" value="Add Score">
            <span></span>
        </div>
    </main>

    <script src="https://code.jquery.com/jquery-3.4.1.slim.min.js"></script>
    <script src="test_scores.js"></script>
</body>
```

Figure 15-8   The Test Scores application (part 1)

The JavaScript

Part 2 of figure 15-8 presents the JavaScript for this application. It starts with the "use strict" directive, followed by the jQuery ready() event handler. Within this event handler, the first statement creates an array named scores to hold the scores entered by the user. After this statement, the code adds a click() event handler for the Add Score button. This event handler contains most of the code for this application. After the click() event handler, the ready() event handler ends by setting the focus on the score text box.

The click() event handler starts by getting the value the user entered in the score text box and converting it to a decimal value. Then, it validates that value by checking that it's a number from 0 to 100. If it isn't, it displays an error message in the span element that follows the Add Score button.

However, if the score is valid, the click() event handler continues by removing any error message that may have been previously displayed. Then, it uses the push() method to add the score to the end of the scores array, and it uses the join() method to format the elements as a string of numbers separated by a comma and a space. Next, it assigns the formatted string to the label that has an id of "all".

After displaying all scores, this code calculates the total of all scores. To do that, it starts by using the reduce() method to get the total of the scores in the array. Here, the callback function for this method defines two parameters. The parameter named tot represents the total of the elements that have already been processed, and the parameter named val represents the value of the current element. Then, the function adds the value of the current element to the total. Since this code passes an initial value of 0 to the reduce function(), this code initializes the value of the tot parameter to zero, which is usually what you want.

After calculating the total, this code calculates and displays the average score. To calculate the average score, this code divides the total by the length of the array. Then, it rounds the average to two decimal places and displays it in the label that has an id of "avg".

After displaying the average score, this code displays the last three scores that were entered in the reverse order in which they were entered. To do that, it starts by getting the length of the array. Then, it uses the conditional operator to check if the length is less than or equal to three. If so, the code uses the slice() method to copy all scores in the array to a new array named lastScores. Otherwise, the code uses the slice() method to store the last three elements of the array in the array. To do that, it uses the length of the array minus three as the starting index and the length as the ending index. This works because the slice() method doesn't return the element at the ending index.

After getting an array that stores the last three scores, this code uses the reverse() method to reverse the order of the elements in that array. Then, it uses the join() method to format those scores, and it displays them in the label that has an id of "last".

The last two statements prepare for the next user entry. The first statement sets the value of the text box to an empty string, and the second statement moves the focus to that text box.

The JavaScript

```javascript
"use strict";

$(document).ready( () => {

    const scores = [];

    $("#add_score").click( () => {

        const score = parseFloat($("#score").val());

        if (isNaN(score) || score < 0 || score > 100) {
            $("#add_score").next().text("Score must be from 0 to 100.");
        }
        else {
            $("#add_score").next().text("");   // remove any previous message

            // add score to scores array
            scores.push(score);

            // display all scores
            $("#all").text(scores.join(", "));

            // calculate and display average score
            const total = scores.reduce( (tot, val) => tot + val, 0 );
            const avg = total/scores.length;
            $("#avg").text(avg.toFixed(2));

            // display last 3 scores
            const len = scores.length;
            const lastScores = (len <= 3) ? scores.slice() :
                scores.slice(len - 3, len); // copy last three
            lastScores.reverse();
            $("#last").text(lastScores.join(", "));
        }

        // get text box ready for next entry
        $("#score").val("");
        $("#score").focus();
    });

    // set focus on initial load
    $("#score").focus();
});
```

Figure 15-8   The Test Scores application (part 2)

More skills for working with arrays

Now that you've learned the basic skills for creating and working with arrays, you're ready to learn some more skills for working with arrays.

How to split a string into an array

Figure 15-9 presents the split() method of a String object. You can use this method to split a string into multiple substrings based on a separator character that's coded as the first parameter. This creates a new array with each of the substrings as elements. If you supply a second parameter, the split() method uses it to limit the number of elements that can be included in the new array.

The first example in this figure shows how this works. To start, it splits a string that's separated by spaces into an array named nameParts. Then, it displays the length of the new array and the elements in the array. Next, it assigns the element at the last index in the array (length - 1) to a constant named lastName and displays that constant.

The second example works similarly. However, it shows how to split a string that's separated by hyphens into an array.

The third example shows how to split a string into individual characters. To do that, this example calls the split() method and passes it an empty string.

Note how the first three examples display the array. Here, the first example uses the toString() method of the array to display the elements separated by commas. The second example uses the join() method of the array and specifies a front slash as the separator, which produces the string "1/2/2021". The third example calls the join() method but doesn't specify a separator. As a result, JavaScript uses the default separator of a comma. This works like the first example.

The fourth example shows what happens if the string doesn't contains the separator character specified by the split() method. Here, the example begins by creating a date string that has hyphens. Then, it calls the split() method with a slash as the separator. In this case, the resulting array only has one element and it is a copy of the original date string.

The fifth example shows how to limit the number of substrings that are copied into the new array. Here, the split() method uses a space as the separator, but it limits the number of substrings to one. This returns an array that contains a single element that contains the first name.

A String method that creates an array

Method	Description
`split(separator[, limit])`	Splits a string into an array based on the value of the separator parameter and returns the array. The optional limit parameter specifies the maximum number of elements in the new array.

How to split a string that's separated by spaces into an array

```
const fullName = "Grace M Hopper";
const nameParts = fullName.split(" ");  // creates an array

console.log(nameParts.length);          // displays 3
console.log(nameParts.toString());      // displays Grace,M,Hopper

const lastName = nameParts[nameParts.length - 1];
console.log(lastName);                   // displays Hopper
```

How to split a string that's separated by hyphens into an array

```
const date = "1-2-2021";
const dateParts = date.split("-");      // creates an array

console.log(dateParts.length);          // displays 3
console.log(dateParts.join("/"));       // displays 1/2/2021
```

How to split a string into an array of characters

```
const fullName = "Grace Hopper";
const nameCharacters = fullName.split("");

console.log(nameCharacters.length);     // displays 12
console.log(nameCharacters.join());     // displays G,r,a,c,e, ,H,o,p,p,e,r
```

How it works if the string doesn't contain the separator

```
const date = "1-2-2021";
const dateParts = date.split("/");

console.log(dateParts.length);          // displays 1
console.log(dateParts.join());          // displays 1-2-2021
```

How to get just one element from a string

```
const fullName = "Grace M Hopper";
const firstName = fullName.split(" ", 1);

console.log(firstName.length);          // displays 1
console.log(firstName[0]);              // displays Grace
```

Description

- The split() method of a String object can split a string into an array.

- If a string doesn't include the separator specified by the split() method, the split() method returns the entire string as the first element in a one-element array.

- If the separator specified by the split() method is an empty string, the split() method returns an array where each character in the string is an element in the array.

Figure 15-9   How to split a string into an array

How to make a copy of an array

Sometimes you need to make a copy of an array. You might think that you could do this by assigning an existing array to another constant or variable like this:

```
const newArray = existingArray;
```

However, this doesn't work. In this case, both constants refer to the same array. So, if you change the value of an element in newArray, it's changed in existingArray as well. Usually, this isn't what you want.

To copy an array, you need to create a new Array object and copy the value of each element from the original array to the new array. You can use a loop to do that, but JavaScript provides several other ways to copy an array that are less verbose than using a loop.

Figure 15-10 presents four techniques you can use to make a copy of an array. The first technique uses the slice() method of the Array type. If you don't pass any values to this method, it creates a new array and copies all the elements of the original array to it as shown in the second example. Here, the statement makes a copy of the names array that's defined in the first example.

The second technique uses the static Array.from() method. This method accepts an array and returns a copy of that array. The third example shows how this works. Like the second example, it makes a copy of the names array that's defined in the first example.

The third technique uses the destructuring syntax presented earlier in this chapter. Remember, when you destructure an array, you can use the rest operator to collect some of the elements of the array into a new array. However, if there's only one constant or variable within the brackets of a destructuring statement, and that constant or variable is prepended with the rest operator, JavaScript copies all the elements of the original array to the new array. The fourth example shows how this works.

Finally, the fourth technique uses the *spread operator* (. . .) to make a copy of an array. This operator takes the elements of an array and *spreads* them out into a comma separated list. As a result, you can use it to create a list of values that can be passed to a new array. The fifth example shows how this works. Here, the spread operator spreads the elements in the names array into a list that's passed to the array literal that creates a new array. This is functionally the same as the following code:

```
const namesCopy = [names[0], names[1], names[2]];
```

The technique you use to copy an array is mostly a matter of personal preference. However, the slice() method of the Array type has been around since ECMAScript 1. As a result, if you want to support older browsers, you might want to use the slice() method. However, you can also add JavaScript libraries called polyfill libraries to your application to make the Array.from() method work with older browsers. By contrast, the rest and spread operators only work with modern browsers.

A static method of the Array type

Method	Description
`from(array)`	Returns a copy of the array that it receives.

Four ways to make a copy of an existing array

- Call the slice() method of the array.
- Pass the array to the static from() method of the Array type.
- Destructure the array with a rest operator.
- Use an array literal with a spread operator and the array.

An array that's used by the following examples

```
const names = ["Grace", "Charles", "Ada"];
```

Use the slice() method

```
const namesCopy = names.slice();
```

Use the Array.from() method

```
const namesCopy = Array.from(names);
```

Use destructuring and the rest operator

```
const [...namesCopy] = names;
```

Use an array literal and the spread operator

```
const namesCopy = [...names];
```

Description

- JavaScript provides several ways to make a copy of an existing array.
- Because the slice() method has been available since ECMAScript 1, it will work with older browsers.
- The Array.from() method wasn't introduced until ECMAScript 2015, so it doesn't work with older browsers. However, JavaScript libraries called polyfill libraries are available that allow the Array.from() method to be used with older browsers.
- You use the *spread operator* (. . .) to spread out the elements of an array into a list separated by commas. Then, you can use that list in an array literal that assigns values to the elements of a new array.
- Like the rest operator, the spread operator was introduced with ECMAScript 2015 and can't be used with older browsers.

Figure 15-10   How to make a copy of an array

How to create and use an associative array

So far, the arrays presented in this chapter have used integer values as indexes. By contrast, an *associative array* uses strings as the indexes. In some cases, using an associative array can make your code easier to read and understand than using an indexed array. Figure 15-11 shows how to create and use associative arrays.

The first example creates an associative array with four elements. First, it creates an empty array. Then, it stores four values in the array using strings for the indexes. Finally, it displays the length of the associative array. However, because the length property of an array only counts elements with numeric indexes, the length is zero.

Fortunately, you can use the static keys() method of the Object type to return an array that contains the names of the associative array's string indexes. Then, you can use that array's length property to get the length of the associative array. The last statement in this example shows how that works.

The second example adds an element to the array with a string index of "lineCost". To start, the code for this element uses an expression to calculate the line cost by multiplying cost by quantity. Then, it uses the toFixed() method to round the result to two decimal places.

The third example displays a formatted string that's built from the elements in the array. The dialog box that follows the code example shows that the array now contains five elements.

The fourth example shows how to use the for-in loop with an associative array. This for-in loop builds a string that contains the element indexes and values. In this case, though, the index is the string associated with the value rather than a numeric index.

Although it's technically possible to mix numeric and string indexes within a single array, it's generally considered a best practice to avoid doing that. That's because mixed arrays present some unnecessary complications. For example, the length property indicates only the number of elements with numeric indexes. Also, if you process a mixed array with a for loop, the associative elements aren't included in the processing. But if you process a mixed array with a for-in loop, all of the elements are processed.

How to create an associative array with four elements

```
const item = [];
item["code"] = 123;
item["name"] = "HTML5";
item["cost"] = 54.5;
item["quantity"] = 5;

console.log(item.length);                    // Displays 0
console.log(Object.keys(item).length);       // Displays 4
```

How to add an element to the associative array

```
item["lineCost"] = (item["cost"] * item["quantity"]).toFixed(2);
```

How to retrieve and display the elements in the associative array

```
alert("Item elements:\n" +
      "\nCode = " + item["code"] +
      "\nName = " + item["name"] +
      "\nCost = " + item["cost"] +
      "\nQuantity = " + item["quantity"] +
      "\nLine Cost = " + item["lineCost"]);
```

The message displayed by the alert statement

```
Item elements:

Code = 123
Name = HTML5
Cost = 54.5
Quantity = 5
Line Cost = 272.50

                                    OK
```

How to use a for-in loop with the associative array

```
let result = "";
for (let i in item) {
    result += i + "=" + item[i] + " ";
}
// result is "code=123 name=HTML5 cost=54.5 quantity=5 lineCost=272.50 "
```

Description

- When you create an *associative array*, you use strings as the indexes instead of numbers.

- If you mix numeric and string indexes in an array, the length will indicate only the number of elements with numeric indexes and a for loop will only process the elements with numeric indexes. However, a for-in loop will process all the elements.

- To get the number of elements with string indexes, you can use the static keys() method of the Object type to get an array of all string indexes.

- Because elements with string indexes are actually object properties, some of the array properties and methods don't work as expected with associative arrays. For instance, the length property returns 0 and the pop() method returns undefined.

Figure 15-11   How to create and use an associative array

How to create and use an array of arrays

Although JavaScript doesn't let you create multi-dimensional arrays, you can get the same effect by creating an *array of arrays*. To do that, you store arrays in each element of another array. These arrays don't have to be the same length, and it's common to nest an associative array inside a numerically indexed array.

The first example in figure 15-12 shows how to create and use an array of arrays. First, it creates an empty array named students. Then, it stores an array of test scores in each of the first four elements of the students array. This array represents four students and their test scores.

The next two statements show how to access the elements in this array. Here, the first statement displays the value that's at index 0 of the students array and index 1 of the test scores array. In other words, it displays the first student's second test score. The second statement displays the value that's at index 2 of the students array and index 3 of the test scores array. In other words, the third student's fourth test score.

The second example shows how to nest two associative arrays in a numerically indexed array. Here, the first statement creates an array named invoice that's numerically indexed. Then, this example stores an empty array as the first element in the invoice array. After that, it adds four elements to the empty array using strings as indexes. This creates an associative array nested within a numeric array.

After nesting the first associative array, the second example uses another technique to nest another associative array. To start, this code begins by creating a new array named item. Then, it adds four elements with string indexes to the item array. Next, it uses the push() method to add the item array to the end of the invoice array.

After nesting the two associative arrays, the second example finishes by showing how to access the elements of the nested array. Here, the first statement displays the code of the first invoice. This displays "123". Then, the second statement displays the name of the second invoice. This displays "jQuery".

If you use the second technique to nest the item array in the invoice array, you can't re-use the item array for the next array you want to add. That's because the push() method stores a reference to the item array, not a copy of the item array. As a result, you need to declare a separate array variable for each array you want to add. If this doesn't make complete sense right now, don't worry. It should make more sense when you learn more about object references in the next chapter.

How to create and use an array of arrays

Code that creates an array of arrays

```
const students = [];
students[0] = [80, 82, 90, 87, 85];
students[1] = [79, 80, 74];
students[2] = [93, 95, 89, 100];
students[3] = [60, 72, 65, 71];
```

Code that refers to elements in the array of arrays

```
console.log(students[0][1]);        // displays 82
console.log(students[2][3]);        // displays 100
```

How to create and use an array of associative arrays

Code that creates an array

```
const invoice = [];                 // create an empty invoice array
```

Code that adds an associative array to the invoice array directly

```
invoice[0] = [];
invoice[0]["code"] = 123;
invoice[0]["name"] = "HTML5";
invoice[0]["cost"] = 54.5;
invoice[0]["quantity"] = 5;
```

Code that creates an associative array and then adds it to the invoice array

```
const item = [];
item["code"] = 456;
item["name"] = "jQuery";
item["cost"] = 52.5;
item["quantity"] = 2;
invoice.push(item);  // add the item array to the end of the invoice array
```

Code that refers to the elements in the array of associative arrays

```
console.log(invoice[0]["code"]);    // displays 123
console.log(invoice[1]["name"]);    // displays jQuery
```

Description

- Although JavaScript doesn't provide for multi-dimensional arrays, you can get the same effect by creating an *array of arrays*. In an array of arrays, each element in the first array is another array.

- The arrays within an array can be regular arrays or associative arrays.

- To refer to the elements in an array of arrays, you use two index values for each element. The first value is for an element in the primary array. The second value is for an element in the nested array.

- If necessary, you can nest arrays beyond the two dimensions that are illustrated here. In other words, you can create an array of arrays of arrays, and so on. As usual, be careful with this as your code can become hard to read and maintain if it's too complex.

Figure 15-12   How to create and use an array of arrays

How to convert an array to JSON and back

When working with an array, you may sometimes need to convert it to a string to store it or to share it with another application. For example, before you can store an array in web storage, you need to convert it to a string. Later, you can get this string from web storage and convert it back into an array so you can work with its data.

In the old days of JavaScript programming, developers typically had to write their own code to perform these types of conversions. Fortunately, modern JavaScript provides ways to perform these conversions automatically. In particular, it provides the two static methods of the JSON type that are shown in figure 15-13. The JSON.stringify() method allows you to convert an object such as an array into *JSON (JavaScript Object Notation)*, a format that uses a string to store the data for an object. And the JSON.parse() method allows you to convert the JSON back into an object.

Although the JS in JSON stands for JavaScript, most modern programming languages provide a way to convert objects to JSON and back. As a result, it's a useful data format for sharing object data across languages and applications.

The first example in this figure shows how to use the JSON.stringify() method to convert an Array object to a JSON string and store that string in web storage. To start, this code creates an array named tasks that stores two nested arrays. Here, each of the nested arrays contains the data for a task. In each nested array, the first element is a description of the task, and the second element is a Date object for the due date. For example, the first nested array stores a string of "Finish current project" as its first element and a Date object for 11/20/2020 as its second element.

After creating the array of arrays, this example uses the JSON.stringify() method to convert the array named tasks to a JSON string. Then, it stores that string in local web storage.

The second example shows the JSON that's stored in web storage. To start, the outermost brackets identify the Array object for the tasks array. Then, the inner brackets identify the arrays for the two nested tasks. Here, commas separate each element.

The third example shows how to use the JSON.parse() method to convert the JSON string back into an array of arrays. To start, this code gets the JSON string for the tasks array from local web storage. Then, it uses the JSON.parse() method to convert the JSON string back into an array. This works because the JSON.parse() method is able to convert the JSON string to an Array object.

However, the JSON.parse() method isn't able to convert the strings for the dates back into Date objects. Instead, each nested array stores a string for the date. If necessary, you can convert the date string to a Date object by using the *new* keyword to call the Date() constructor as shown by the last two statements.

Although this figure shows how to use the JSON methods to work with Array and Date objects, you can use these methods with most types of native JavaScript objects. In addition, you can use these methods with user-defined objects like the ones presented in the next chapter.

Two static methods of the JSON type

Method	Description
`stringify(object)`	Returns a JSON string for the specified object or array.
`parse(json)`	Returns an object or array that contains the data in the specified JSON string.

How to convert an Array object to JSON

```
// create an array of arrays that stores 2 tasks
const tasks = [];
tasks.push(["Finish current project", new Date("11/20/2020")]);
tasks.push(["Get specs for next project", new Date("12/01/2020")]);

const json = JSON.stringify(tasks);   // convert array to JSON
localStorage.tasks = json;            // save JSON to web storage
```

The JSON for the Array object

```
[["Finish current project","2020-11-20T08:00:00.000Z"],
 ["Get specs for next project","2020-12-01T08:00:00.000Z"]]
```

How to convert JSON to an Array object

```
const json = localStorage.tasks;      // get JSON from web storage
const tasks = JSON.parse(json);       // convert JSON to array
console.log(tasks[0][0]);             // displays "Finish current project"
console.log(tasks[1][1]);             // displays "2020-12-01T08:00:00.000Z"

const date = new Date(tasks[1][1]);   // convert JSON string to Date object
console.log(date.toDateString());     // displays "Tue Dec 1 2020"
```

Description

- *JSON (JavaScript Object Notation)* is a format that uses text to store and transmit the data for an object such as an array.

- The JSON format was originally based on the notation for objects that was used by JavaScript, but most programming languages now provide a way to generate and parse JSON. As a result, it's a useful data format for sharing object data across languages and applications.

- When using the JSON.parse() method to convert a JSON string back into objects, you may need to call the constructor of the object again. For example, to convert a JSON string back to a Date object, you need to use the *new* keyword and the Date() constructor to create the Date object from the JSON string.

- You can use the JSON.stringify() and JSON.parse() methods to work with most types of native JavaScript objects as well as user-defined objects like the ones presented in the next chapter.

Figure 15-13   How to convert an array to JSON and back

The Task List application

To show how some of the skills you've just learned can be used in an application, this chapter now presents another version of the Task List application presented in the previous chapter. This version uses an array of arrays for the task list, and it stores the task list in a JSON string in local web storage.

As before, this application displays the tasks in a textarea element on the right side of the page. Now, though, the tasks include a due date and are sorted by this date in ascending order.

The HTML

The HTML for this application is shown in part 1 of figure 15-14. This HTML is mostly the same as the Task List application presented in the previous chapter. However, the main element now includes a label and an input element for the due date as well as for the task description. Then, when the user clicks the Add Task button, the application adds a nested task array that includes the description and due date to the array of tasks. In addition, it converts the array of tasks to a JSON string and stores the JSON string in web storage.

The Task List application

The HTML

```html
<body>
    <main>
        <h1>Task List</h1>
        <div id="tasks">
            <label for="task_list">Task List</label><br>
            <textarea id="task_list" rows="6" cols="50"></textarea>
        </div>
        <div>
            <label for="task">Task:</label><br>
            <input type="text" name="task" id="task">
        </div>
        <div>
            <label for="due_date">Due Date:</label><br>
            <input type="text" name="due_date" id="due_date">
        </div>
        <div>
            <input type="button" id="add_task" value="Add Task"><br>
            <input type="button" id="clear_tasks" value="Clear Tasks">
        </div>
    </main>

    <script src="https://code.jquery.com/jquery-3.4.1.slim.min.js"></script>
    <script src="task_list.js"></script>
</body>
```

Figure 15-14   The Task List application (part 1)

The JavaScript

Part 2 of figure 15-14 presents the JavaScript for this application. It starts with a function named displayTaskList() that accepts an array of tasks and formats and displays those tasks in the Task List text area. To do that, this function starts by declaring a variable named taskString and initializing it to an empty string. Then, it checks if the tasks array contains at least one element. If so, it passes a callback function to the map() method of the tasks array that converts the date string for each element to a Date object.

After the conversion, this function sorts the array of arrays by due date. It does this by passing a callback function to the sort() method of the tasks array. Since this is an array of arrays, that means the two elements being compared are arrays. So, the callback function gets the Date object from each array and returns -1, 1, or 0, depending on whether the first date is less than, greater than, or equal to the second date. This sorts the dates in ascending order.

After the sort, this function uses the reduce() method of the tasks array to create a single string to display all tasks. Remember that the callback function for the reduce() method accepts the previous value returned by the function, plus the current value in the array. Since this is an array of arrays, that means the current value is an array. So, the callback function formats the Date object as a string, concatenates that value with the task description separated by a dash, and ends with a newline character. The call to the reduce() method also sets the initial value of the prev parameter to an empty string so the concatenation works properly. After creating this string, the code displays it in the Task List text area. However, if the tasks array doesn't contain any elements, this code displays an empty string in that text area. Either way, the last statement moves the focus to the Task text box.

The ready() event handler starts by attempting to retrieve the JSON string of tasks from local storage. Then, if this code retrieves a string, the parse() method of the JSON type converts that string to an array and stores it in the tasks constant. Otherwise, it stores an empty array in that constant.

The click() event handler for the Add Task button starts by getting the two values the user entered and converting the date string to a Date object. Then, it checks that the user entered a task and date and that the date is valid. If so, this code creates a new task from the user entries. Next, it adds that task to the tasks array, converts the array to a JSON string, and stores that JSON string in local storage. After that, it clears the Task and Due Date text boxes to prepare for the next entry and passes the tasks array to the displayTaskList() function so the new task is displayed in the list. If the user doesn't make valid entries for both text boxes, the application displays an error message. Then, it selects the Task text box so the user can change it if necessary.

The click() event handler for the Clear Tasks button clears all tasks. To do that, this event handler sets the length of the tasks array to zero, removes the tasks from local storage, clears the text area, and sets the focus on the text box to prepare for the next entry.

After both click() event handlers, the ready() event handler passes the tasks array to the displayTaskList() function. This formats and displays the tasks in the Task List text area when the application initially loads.

The JavaScript

```javascript
const displayTaskList = tasks => {
    let taskString = "";
    if (tasks.length > 0) {
        // convert stored date string to Date object
        tasks = tasks.map( task => [task[0], new Date(task[1])] );

        tasks.sort( (task1, task2) => {    // sort by date
            const date1 = task1[1]; // get Date object from task1
            const date2 = task2[1]; // get Date object from task2
            if (date1 < date2) { return -1; }
            else if (date1 > date2) { return 1; }
            else { return 0; }
        });

        taskString = tasks.reduce( (prev, curr) => {
            return prev + curr[1].toDateString() + " - " + curr[0] + "\n";
        }, ""); // pass initial value for prev parameter
    }

    $("#task_list").val(taskString);
    $("#task").focus();
};

$(document).ready( () => {
    const taskString = localStorage.tasks;
    const tasks = (taskString) ? JSON.parse(taskString) : [];

    $("#add_task").click( () => {
        const task = $("#task").val();
        const dateString = $("#due_date").val();
        const dueDate = new Date(dateString);

        if (task && dateString && dueDate != "Invalid Date") {
            const newTask = [task, dateString];  // store dateString
            tasks.push(newTask);
            localStorage.tasks = JSON.stringify(tasks);

            $("#task").val("");
            $("#due_date").val("");
            displayTaskList(tasks);
        } else {
            alert("Please enter a task and valid due date.");
            $("#task").select();
        }
    });

    $("#clear_tasks").click( () => {
        tasks.length = 0;
        localStorage.removeItem("tasks");
        $("#task_list").val("");
        $("#task").focus();
    });

    displayTaskList(tasks);
});
```

Figure 15-14   The Task List application (part 2)

How to work with sets and maps

So far, this chapter has shown how to use the Array type to work with collections of data. This data type is optimal when you want to keep elements in sequential order and use indexes to quickly access and modify those elements. However, it isn't the optimal data type for all situations. That's why ECMAScript 2015 added two more data types that you can use to work with collections of data: Set and Map. These data types are often optimal if you need to work with a set of unique values or if you want to use unique keys to access values.

How to create and use a set

Like an array, a *set* is an object that contains zero or more elements. Also, for both arrays and sets, each element can be a native data type or an object. The difference is that the elements of a set must have unique values.

Figure 15-15 presents the basic skills for creating and using a set. To start, you create a set by using the *new* keyword and the Set() constructor. If you don't pass a parameter to this constructor, it creates an empty set as in the first example in this figure. Then, you can use the add() method to add values to the set. You can also pass an array to the Set() constructor as shown by the second example. This statement creates a set named names from an array with three elements.

The table in this figure presents one property and some of the methods of the Set type. You shouldn't have any trouble understanding how to use the property and the first four methods. And the last four methods work like they do for an array. When you use a set, though, the key and the value for each element are the same. That means that the values() and keys() methods both return an iterator with the values in the elements, and the entries() method returns an iterator that contains an array for each element where the key and value are the same.

After the table, the first example shows how to use the has() method to check if the set contains a value. Here, both statements use the names set created by the second example above the table. So, when the first statement checks if the set has a value of "Grace", this statement returns true. But when the second statement checks if the set has a value of "Linus", the statement returns false.

The second example after the table shows how to add values to a set. It starts by using the size property to get the number of elements in the names set, which has three elements. Then, it uses the add() method to add an element to the set. Next, it calls the size property again to show that the set now has four elements.

After that, this example uses the add() method to add an element with a value that already exists in the set. However, because the values in a set must be unique, this code doesn't add this element, and the size of the set remains at four.

Because arrays provide more functionality and generally work faster than sets, it's a good practice to only use sets when they provide functionality that isn't available for an array. And sometimes, you can convert between sets and arrays to get the best of both worlds. If, for example, you need unique values *and* the functionality of an array, you can use a set to remove duplicate values from

How to create a set

The syntax for creating a set

```
const setName = new Set([array]);
```

A statement that creates an empty set

```
const emptySet = new Set();
```

A statement that creates a set from an array

```
const names = new Set(["Grace", "Charles", "Ada"]);
```

A property and some of the methods of the Set type

Property	Description
size	The number of elements in the set.

Method	Description
add(value)	Adds the value to the end of the set if it isn't already in the set.
delete(value)	Removes the value from the set.
clear()	Removes all the values from the set.
has(value)	Returns a Boolean that indicates whether the value is in the set.
forEach(function)	Calls the function once for each value in the set.
entries()	Returns an iterator with a [key, value] array for each element in the set. For a set, key and value are the same.
values()	Returns an iterator with the value of each element in the set.
keys()	Returns an iterator with the key value of each element in the set.

How to check for values in a set

```
let hasName = names.has("Grace");    // hasName is true
hasName = names.has("Linus");        // hasName is false
```

How to add values to a set

```
let size = names.size;               // size is 3
names.add("Linus");                  // adds new value to set
size = names.size;                   // size is 4

names.add("Grace");                  // already in set so not added
size = names.size;                   // size is 4
```

How to use a set to remove duplicate values from an array

```
const dupeArray = [4, 6, 2, 3, 2, 3, 4, 7, 6, 8, 9, 2, 8, 2];
const set = new Set(dupeArray);
const noDupes = Array.from(set);   // noDupes is [4, 6, 2, 3, 7, 8, 9]
```

Description

- A *set* can store zero or more elements where each element has a unique value.
- To create a set, you must use the Set() constructor. This constructor accepts an optional array value. If the array contains duplicate values, the constructor removes them when it assigns the array elements to the set.
- A set has less functionality than an array, but you can easily convert a set to an array.

Figure 15-15   How to create and use a set

an array as shown by the last example. To do that, this example creates a new set from an array that contains duplicate values, which removes the duplicates. Then, it converts the set back to an array.

How to create and use a map

Unlike the elements of a set, where each value must be unique, the elements of a *map* are pairs of keys and values, where each key must be unique. For example, you might use a map to store a collection of products that can be accessed by product codes that uniquely identify each product.

Figure 15-16 presents some of the basic skills for creating and using maps. To start, you create a map using the *new* keyword and the Map() constructor. If you don't pass a parameter to this constructor, it creates an empty map as shown by the first example. You can also pass an array of arrays to this constructor as shown by the second example. This statement creates a map named names with two elements. Here, the first element has a key of "Grace" that accesses a value of "Hopper". Similarly, the second element has a key of "Ada" that accesses a value of "Lovelace".

The table in this figure presents one property and some of the methods of the Map type. Many of these are the same as the Set type described in the previous figure. However, because the elements of a map are key/value pairs, the entries() method returns an iterator with a key/value array for each element, the values() method returns an iterator that contains the value of each element, and the keys() method returns an iterator that contains the key of each element.

After the table, the first example shows how to use two of these methods. It starts by using the has() method to check if the names map contains an element with a key value of "Grace". If so, it uses the get() method to get the value of that element. In this case, it gets a value of "Hopper".

The next example shows how to add elements to a map. It starts by using the size property to get the number of elements in the map. Then, it uses the set() method to add a key/value pair with a key of "Charles" and a value of "Babbage". Next, it calls the size property again to show that the map now contains three elements.

After that, this example calls the set() method again to add another element to the map. This time, though, an element with the key value already exists in the map. Because of that, this code doesn't add the element to the map. Instead, it replaces the value of the existing element with the new value.

The last example shows how to get an array of keys and key/value pairs from the map. Here, the first statement uses the Array.from() method to convert the map to an array of arrays. The second statement works similarly, but it uses the keys() method of the map to get just the keys of the elements in the map. Then, it uses the Array.from() method to convert those keys to an array.

How to create a map
The syntax for creating a map
```
const mapName = new Map([arrayOfArrays]);
```

A statement that creates an empty map
```
const map = new Map();
```

A statement that creates a map from an array of arrays
```
const names = new Map([ ["Grace", "Hopper"], ["Ada", "Lovelace"] ]);
```

A property and some of the methods of the Map type

Property	Description
size	The number of elements in the map.

Method	Description
set(key,value)	Adds an element to the end of the map if the key isn't already in the map.
get(key)	Returns the value associated with the key, or undefined if the key isn't found.
delete(key)	Removes the element with the key from the map.
clear()	Removes all the elements from the map.
has(key)	Returns a Boolean that indicates whether an element with the key exists.
forEach(function)	Calls the function once for each element in the map.
entries()	Returns an iterator with a [key, value] array for each element in the map.
values()	Returns an iterator with the value of each element in the map.
keys()	Returns an iterator with the key of each element in the map.

How to check for a key in the map and retrieve its associated value
```
if (names.has("Grace")) {
    console.log(names.get("Grace"));         // displays "Hopper"
}
```

How to add key/value pairs to the map
```
let size = names.size;                  // size is 2
names.set("Charles", "Babbage");        // adds new key/value pair to map
size = names.size;                      // size is 3
names.set("Grace", "Slick");            // replaces value associated with key
size = names.size;                      // size is 3
```

How to get arrays of the keys and key/value pairs of the map
```
const full = Array.from(names);
// full is [["Grace", "Slick"], ["Ada", "Lovelace"], ["Charles", "Babbage"]]
const firstNames = Array.from(names.keys());
// firstNames is ["Grace", "Ada", "Charles"]
```

Description
- A *map* can store one or more elements consisting of key/value pairs. The key for each pair must be unique.

- To create a map, you must use the Map() constructor. This constructor accepts an optional array of arrays. If the nested arrays contain duplicate keys, the constructor replaces the value for each duplicate key when it assigns the element to the map.

Figure 15-16   How to create and use a map

Perspective

Arrays are an optimal data structure if you want to keep a collection of elements in sequential order and use indexes to quickly access and modify those elements. In most cases, that's what you want to do, and JavaScript provides some excellent methods for performing these operations. That's why this chapter focuses on working with arrays.

However, this chapter also presents some of the basic skills for working with sets and maps. These data structures can be useful when you need to work with a set of unique values or if you need to store key/value pairs that you can access with a unique key.

Terms

array	rest operator
element	stack
length	callback function
array literal	spread operator
index	associative array
destructuring an array	array of arrays
for loop	JSON (JavaScript Object Notation)
for-of loop	set
for-in loop	map
sparse array	

Summary

- An *array* can store zero or more *elements*. The *length* of an array is the number of elements in the array. To refer to the elements in an array, you use an *index* where 0 is the index of the first element in the array.

- To code an *array literal*, you can code a set of brackets.

- You can use a *for loop*, a *for-in loop,* or a *for-of loop* to iterate the elements of an array. A for-in loop doesn't process undefined elements, but for loops and for-of loops do.

- In JavaScript, a *sparse array* is an array with a large number of elements but few with assigned values.

- *Destructuring* allows you to assign two or more array elements to constants or variables in a single statement without using indexes.

- You can use the *rest operator* to create a new array that contains the *rest* of the elements in the array that's being destructured.

- You can use the *spread operator* to take the elements of an array and *spread* them out into a comma-separated list.

- In a *stack*, the last element added to collection is the first element removed (last-in, first-out).

- A *callback function* is a function that's called by the method that receives it to complete its task.

- An *associative array* uses strings for the indexes instead of integers.

- In an *array of arrays*, each element in the first array is another array.

- *JSON* (*JavaScript Object Notation*) is a format that uses a string to store the data for an object.

- A *set* can store zero or more elements, but each value must be unique.

- A *map* can store zero or more elements consisting of key/value pairs, but the key for each pair must be unique.

Exercise 15-1   Enhance the Test Scores application

This exercise gives you a chance to work with arrays as you enhance the Test Scores application. The enhanced version has a new Delete Score button:

My Test Scores

All scores:	94, 87, 95, 92
Average score:	92.00
Last 3 scores:	92, 95, 87
Enter new score:	[ ] [Add Score]
Enter index:	[3] [Delete Score]

Open, test, and review this application

1. Use your text editor or IDE to open the application in this folder:
    `javascript_jquery\exercises\ch15\test_scores`

2. Test this application in Chrome by using the Add Score button to add scores to the two lists. Then, click on the Delete Score button to see that it doesn't do anything yet.

3. Review the JavaScript file for this application to see that the ready() event handler contains a click() event handler for the Delete Score button.

Code the Delete Score event handler

4. Code the click() event handler for the Delete Score button. It should start by getting the index entry as an integer. Then, it should use the splice() method to delete the element and redisplay the list of all the scores. For now, don't worry about updating the average score or the list of the last three scores.

5. Run the application, add one or more scores, and test the Delete Score button. Notice that if you enter an index value that isn't in the array or a value that isn't a number, nothing happens.

6. Add data validation to the click() event handler for the Delete Score button so the user's entry has to be a number and has to be an index value that's in the array. If either data validation check fails, display a message to the user in the span element that follows the Delete Score button. Then, test this change.

7. Move the code that calculates the average score to a helper function outside of the ready() event handler. Then, call this function from the click() event handlers for the Add Score and Delete Score buttons to display the average score.

8. Repeat the previous step for the code that gets the last three scores.

9. Repeat step 7 for the code that updates the DOM with all scores, the average score, and the last three scores.

10. Add code to the click() event handler for the Delete Score button that clears the Index text box and moves the focus to the Score text box. Then, test the application one more time to be sure everything is working properly.

Exercise 15-2   Enhance the Task List application

This exercise gives you a chance to work with an array of arrays as you enhance the Task List application in this chapter. The enhanced version has a Filter button that lets you filter tasks by a search term. In the example that follows, the application displays only the first and third tasks when the user clicks the OK button in the dialog box:

Task List

Task:

Due Date:

Add Task

Clear Tasks

Filter

Task List
```
Fri Nov 20 2020 - Finish current project
Wed Nov 25 2020 - Meet with Ben
Tue Dec 01 2020 - Get specs for new project
```

This page says

Enter text to filter tasks by, or leave blank to see all tasks.

Project

OK   Cancel

Open, test, and review this application

1. Use your text editor or IDE to open the application in this folder:
    `javascript_jquery\exercises\ch15\task_list`

2. Test this application in Chrome by using the Add Task button to add a few tasks to the list. Then, click on the Filter button to see that it doesn't do anything yet.

3. Review the JavaScript file for this application. Note that the ready() event handler contains an empty click() event handler for the Filter button.

Code the Filter event handler

4. In the click() event handler for the Filter button, use the prompt() method to ask the user for the text to search for. This prompt should inform the user that all tasks are displayed if nothing is entered. Then, store the value that's returned by the prompt() method in a variable named searchTerm.

5. Code an if-else statement that tests whether the search term is an empty string. If so, the code should call the displayTaskList() function to display all tasks.

6. If the value of the searchTerm variable isn't an empty string, the else clause should use the toLowerCase() method to set the value of the searchTerm variable to all lowercase characters.

7. Still in the else clause, the code should call the filter() method of the tasks array to filter the tasks based on the searchTerm variable. This method returns an array of the items that have been filtered. The callback function that's passed to the filter() method should return true if the element should be included in the filtered array or false if it shouldn't be.

    However, you need to filter an array of arrays. As a result, the parameter for the callback function is a task array with two elements: the text string for the task and the date string. When you code this function, you want to include any task arrays for which the search term is found in either the date or the text element. In addition, you want to use lowercase text values for the comparisons so they aren't case sensitive.

    The last statement of the else clause should use the displayTaskList() function to display the array of filtered tasks.

8. Test the application by clicking the Filter button and entering a search term. This should display the filtered list of tasks. Then, click the Filter button again and leave the text box blank. This should display all tasks.

16

How to work with objects

So far, the code in this book has been using native JavaScript object types like the Number, String, Date, and Array types. Now, this chapter shows how to create and use your own object types. This provides a way to group related data and functions, and that makes it easier to maintain and reuse the code that you create.

Basic skills for working with objects

This topic presents the basic skills for creating and using objects. That includes how to create and use libraries that store your objects.

How to create object literals

The simplest way to create your own object is by coding an *object literal*. To do that, you code a pair of braces. Then, within the braces, you code the *properties* and *methods* for the object as shown in figure 16-1. When you create an object literal, you are actually creating an instance of the Object type that's described later in this chapter.

The first example in this figure uses an empty set of braces to create an object that has no properties or methods. That's sometimes useful if you plan to add properties and methods later as described later in this chapter.

The second example creates an object literal that has one property and one method. The property is named named taxRate and has a value of 0.0875. For this to work, the code must separate the property name and value with a colon.

The method is named getTotal(). It works much like a function declaration, except that it doesn't include the *function* keyword. To start, it defines a parameter named subtotal. Within the braces for the function, the code calculates the sales tax by multiplying the subtotal by the tax rate. Then, it returns the total for the object, which is the subtotal plus the sales tax. To do that, the getTotal() method uses the *this* keyword to get the value of the taxRate property. This works because the *this* keyword in the method of an object usually refers to the object itself.

When you code the properties and methods for an object, you must separate them with commas. For instance, the second example uses a comma to separate the taxRate property from the getTotal() method.

After you create the properties and methods for an object, you can use them just as you use the properties and methods of native objects. That means you can use the dot operator to refer to the properties and methods as shown by the third example. Here, the first statement displays the value of the taxRate property, and the second statement calls the getTotal() method and passes it a subtotal of 100.

The fourth example shows how to *nest* one object within another. Here, a terms object is nested within an invoice object. To do that, the invoice object is initialized with one property named terms, and the terms property is itself an object that is initialized with two properties named dueDays and description.

The fifth example shows how to use the dot operator to access nested properties. Here, the first statement displays the value of the dueDays property, and the second statement displays the value of the description property.

How to initialize a new object with an object literal

```
const invoice = {};
```

How to initialize a new object with properties and methods

```
const invoice = {
    taxRate: 0.0875,                                // property
    getTotal(subtotal) {                            // method
        const salesTax = subtotal * this.taxRate;   // this = the object
        return subtotal + salesTax;
    }
};
```

How to use dot notation to refer to an object's properties and methods

```
console.log(invoice.taxRate);              // displays 0.0875
const total = invoice.getTotal(100);       // total is 108.75
```

How to nest objects

```
const invoice = {
    terms: {
        dueDays: 30,
        description: "Net due 30 days"
    }
};
```

How to use dot notation to refer to nested objects

```
console.log(invoice.terms.dueDays);        // displays 30
console.log(invoice.terms.description);    // displays 'Net due 30 days'
```

Description

- You can create a new object by coding a literal value ({}). Then, the object that's created is known as an *object literal*.

- When you create an object literal, you can add a *property* by coding the property name, a colon, and the property value.

- When you code an object literal, you can add a *method* by coding a method name followed by a set of parentheses and a set of braces. Within the parentheses, you can code the parameters for the method. Within the braces, you code the statements for the method.

- Inside a method, the value of the *this* keyword is usually the object itself.

- To access a property or method, you can use the dot operator.

- To *nest* one object inside another, make the inner object a property of the outer object.

Figure 16-1   How to create object literals

More skills for coding methods and properties

Figure 16-2 presents more skills for coding the methods and properties of an object. To start, the first example shows two syntaxes for coding a method.

With the traditional syntax, you begin by coding the name of the method, a colon, the *function* keyword, and a set of parentheses. Then, within the parentheses, you code the parameters for the function. This shows that a method is just a function that's stored as a property of an object.

With the concise syntax, you begin by coding the name of the function and a set of parentheses. Then, within the parentheses, you code the parameters for the function. Since this syntax makes your code shorter and easier to read, it's generally considered a best practice to use the concise syntax for new development. However, if you need to maintain legacy code, you may want to continue using the traditional syntax, and you may see this syntax used in examples on the web.

In some cases, you may want to initialize a property of an object literal with a variable or constant of the same name. The second example shows two syntaxes for doing that.

With the traditional syntax, you code the variable or constant as the value for the property. In this figure, for example, the code for the person object begins by specifying the name property, a colon, and the name variable that contains a value of "Grace". Similarly, it specifies the year property, a colon, and the year variable that contains a value of 2021.

However, if you want to write the same code more concisely, you can use the *shorthand property notation*. To do that, you just code the name of the property. In other words, you don't need to code the colon and the name of the constant or variable. Instead, you let JavaScript take care of this for you automatically. Keep in mind, though, that this only works if the constants and variables have the same names as the properties of the object.

Two ways to code a method

Using traditional syntax

```
const invoice = {
    getTotal: function(subtotal, taxRate) {
        return subtotal + (subtotal * taxRate);
    }
};
```

Using concise method syntax

```
const invoice = {
    getTotal(subtotal, taxRate) {
        return subtotal + (subtotal * taxRate);
    }
};
```

Two ways to initialize a property to a variable or constant

Two variables

```
let name = "Grace";
let year = 2021;
```

Using traditional syntax

```
const person = {
    name: name,
    year: year
};
```

Using shorthand properties

```
const person = {
    name,
    year
};
```

Description

- Newer versions of JavaScript have improvements that remove repetitive syntax, making it easier to code objects.

- The *concise method syntax* removes boilerplate code like the colon and *function* keyword from the traditional syntax.

- If you want to initialize a property with a variable or constant of the same name, the *shorthand property notation* provides a more concise way to do that than the traditional syntax.

Figure 16-2   More skills for coding methods and properties

How to extend or modify an object

After you create an object, you can extend the object by adding new properties and methods to it. The first example in figure 16-3 shows how this works. To add a property, you assign a new property to an object and give it a value. To add a method, you assign a new property and code a function expression as its value.

Once a property has been created, you can modify it by assigning a new value to it as shown by the second example in this figure. You can also change a method by assigning a new function expression to it.

To remove a property from an object, you can use the *delete operator* as shown in the third example. In this example, the delete operator removes the taxRate property from the invoice object. Once deleted, the property has a value of undefined, just as if it had never been created.

When you create an object and store it in a constant or variable, JavaScript stores a *reference* to the object in the constant or variable. The diagram in this figure shows how this works. In this case, both the today and now constants refer to the same Date object. As a result, if you change the Date object that the today constant refers to, the change also applies to the now constant.

In this example, the code uses the setFullYear() method of the today constant to set the year to 1968. Since the now constant refers to the same Date object, that causes the getFullYear() method of the now constant to return 1968. When you pass an object to a function or method as an argument, you are passing a reference to the object.

How to add properties and methods to an object

```
const invoice = {};                         // create an object
invoice.taxRate = 0.0875;                   // add a property
invoice.getSalesTax(subtotal) {             // add a method
    return (subtotal * this.taxRate);
};
```

How to modify the value of a property

```
invoice.taxRate = 0.095;
```

How to remove a property from an object

```
delete invoice.taxRate;
console.log(invoice.taxRate);               // displays undefined
```

Two constants that refer to the same object

```
const today = new Date();
const now = today;

today.setFullYear(1968);
console.log(now.getFullYear());             // displays 1968
```

A diagram that illustrates these references

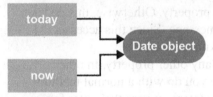

Description

- Once an object is created, you can add new properties and methods to it. This is true for object literals and the object types presented later in this chapter.

- You can also change the value of an existing property by assigning a new value to it, and you can change a method by assigning a new function expression to it.

- To remove a property or method from an object, you can use the *delete operator*.

- A variable or property holds a *reference* to an object, not the object itself. When you pass an object to a function or method as an argument, you are passing a reference to the object.

Figure 16-3   How to modify an existing object

How to work with accessor properties

So far, this chapter has shown how to work with *data properties*, which are properties that store a specific item of data in memory. Now, figure 16-4 shows how to use *accessor properties*, which are properties that don't store any data in memory. Instead, an accessor property can refer to data that's stored in another property, constant, or variable. Or, it can refer to a computed value.

The first example shows how this works. Here, the person object contains data properties that store the first and last names of the person. Then, the code uses the *get* keyword to define a property that gets the full name of the person. To do that, the *get* keyword is followed by a method that's coded with the concise syntax. This method computes the value of the full name by concatenating the first name, a space, and the last name. Since this accessor property uses the *get* keyword to get a value, it's known as a *getter*.

After the getter, the code uses the *set* keyword to define a property that sets the full name of the person. To do that, the *set* keyword is followed by a method that uses the concise syntax. Within the method, the first statement uses the split() method to split the full name value that's passed to the method into an array of names using the space as the delimiter. Then, the code checks whether the array has 2 elements. If so, it stores the first element in the firstName property and the second element in the lastName property. Otherwise, this code throws a TypeError that includes an appropriate message. Since this accessor property uses the *set* keyword to set a value, it's known as a *setter*.

To call an accessor property, you code it like any other property. In other words, you don't need to include parentheses like you do with a normal method call. In the second example, for instance, the first statement uses the getter for the fullName property to display the full name that's stored in the person object. Then, the second statement uses the setter for the fullName property to set the full name to "Ada Lovelace". Since this string contains a first and last name separated by a space, it successfully sets the firstName and lastName properties as shown by the last three statements.

Accessor properties can make your code easier to call. For example, you could code a regular method named getFullName() to get the full name from the person object. However, coding a getter for the fullName() property makes the calling code shorter since you don't need to code "get" or the parentheses after the method name.

Accessor properties allow you to perform tasks like transforming a value before returning it or validating a value before storing it. For example, the getter for the fullName property transforms the full name by returning the first and last names separated by a space. And the setter for the fullName property validates the value that's passed to it by checking to make sure that it's a string that contains two names separated by a space. Here, both the transformation and the validation could be expanded to perform more complex tasks.

Although the fullName property in this figure has a getter and a setter, you can create a *read-only property* by only coding a getter. Conversely, you can code a *write-only property* by only coding a setter.

An object with an accessor property named fullName

```
const person = {
    firstName: "Grace",
    lastName: "Hopper",
    get fullName() {
        return `${this.firstName} ${this.lastName}`;
    },
    set fullName(val) {
        const names = val.split(" ");
        if(names && names.length === 2) {
            this.firstName = names[0];
            this.lastName = names[1];
        }
        else {
            throw new TypeError(
                "fullName must include first and last name.");
        }
    }
};
```

Code that uses the accessor property

```
console.log(person.fullName);            // displays "Grace Hopper"

person.fullName = "Ada Lovelace";
console.log(person.firstName);           // displays "Ada"
console.log(person.lastName);            // displays "Lovelace"
console.log(person.fullName);            // displays "Ada Lovelace"
```

Description

- A *data property* stores a specific item of data in memory.
- An *accessor property* doesn't store data in memory. Instead, it refers to data that's stored in another property, constant, variable. Or, it refers to a computed value.
- To code an accessor property, you code the *get* or *set* keyword followed by a method. The resulting properties are called *getters* and *setters*.
- An accessor property that only gets data is known as a *read-only property*, and an accessor property that only sets data is known as a *write-only property*.
- To call an accessor property, you code it like any other property. In other words, you don't need to include parentheses like you do with a normal method call.
- Accessor properties can make your code easier to call and they allow you to perform tasks like transforming a value before returning it or validating a value before storing it.

Figure 16-4   How to work with accessor properties

How to create and use JavaScript libraries

A *library* is a file that contains a group of related functions, objects, or classes. Often, you'll write your own libraries, but you can also use third-party libraries like jQuery and jQuery UI. Figure 16-5 begins by listing some of the benefits of organizing your code in libraries.

One of the main benefits of libraries is code re-use. This is because you can write a function or object once and then use it from several different places in your code.

Another benefit of libraries is that they help you keep your JavaScript files smaller, which makes them easier to understand and easier to reuse. For example, you can write a library that provides functionality for working with web storage. Since that's all it does, it should be small. Then, you can include that file with any applications that need to use web storage.

Finally, organizing your JavaScript code in libraries encourages you to group code that has similar functionality. This, in turn, encourages *separation of concerns*. For example, one library might focus on web storage, another might focus on data validation, and another might focus on working with dates and times. When you group your code in libraries like this, your application becomes easier to maintain and the code becomes easier to re-use in other applications.

The first example in this figure shows a simple library file named lib_mpg.js. As its name suggests, it contains an object named mpg with properties and methods for calculating miles per gallon.

The second example shows how to include this JavaScript library in an application and use it. Since a JavaScript library is just a JavaScript file, you use a script element to include a library as shown throughout this book. In the index.html file shown here, the first script element refers to the jQuery library, the second refers to the mpg library, and the third refers to the main JavaScript file for the application that uses both of these libraries.

When you include library files in this way, the JavaScript works as if all of the code is in the same file. However, you need to think about the sequence in which you include the files. Specifically, if one file depends on the functionality in another file, you need to include the files in the proper sequence. For example, the jQuery UI library uses the functionality in the jQuery library. So when you use jQuery UI, you need to make sure that the script element for jQuery UI comes after the script element for jQuery.

The same goes for working with your own libraries. In this figure, for instance, the main JavaScript file depends on both the mpg library and the jQuery library. As a result, its script element needs to be coded after the script elements for both of those libraries. However, the mpg library doesn't depend on any other libraries, so its script element could be coded either before or after the jQuery library.

The benefits of JavaScript libraries

- They let you group similar functionality in a single file.
- They make your code easier to understand, maintain, and reuse.
- They encourage the separation of concerns.

The lib_mpg.js file

```
const mpg = {
    miles: 0,
    gallons: 0,
    calculate() {
        return this.miles / this.gallons;
    }
};
```

How to include and use JavaScript libraries in your application

In the index.html file

```
<body>
    ...
    <script src="https://code.jquery.com/jquery-3.4.1.min.js"></script>
    <script src="lib_mpg.js"></script>
    <script src="main.js"></script>
</body>
```

In the main.js file

```
$(document).ready( () => {
    $("#calculate").click( () => {
        mpg.miles = parseFloat($("#miles").val());
        mpg.gallons = parseFloat($("#gallons").val());
        $("#mpg").val(mpg.calculate().toFixed(1));
    });
});
```

Description

- A JavaScript *library* is an external file that contains related functions, objects, or classes.
- JavaScript libraries range from simple collections of functions and objects that you write yourself to extensive third-party libraries like jQuery.
- A JavaScript library is normal JavaScript, so you create a library by grouping related functions, objects, and classes in a single file. You should also name your JavaScript libraries so it's clear what they do.
- You include JavaScript libraries in your applications by using script elements. If a JavaScript file depends on a library, you must make sure that the script element for the required library precedes the one for the file that depends on it.

Figure 16-5   How to create and use JavaScript libraries

The Miles Per Gallon application

Figure 16-6 presents another version of the Miles Per Gallon application first presented in chapter 4. However, this version uses an object and a library file to organize its code. This makes it easier to understand the code that works with miles per gallon. In addition, it makes it easier to reuse this code on other pages or in other applications.

The HTML

The first two script elements at the end of the body section identify the two JavaScript libraries used by this application: the jQuery library and the mpg library. Then, the third script element identifies the main JavaScript file that uses both of these libraries.

The HTML for the main element contains two text box elements. These text boxes allow the user to enter the number of miles driven and the number of gallons used. Then, the main element contains a text box that displays the calculated miles per gallon. This text box includes the disabled attribute. That way, it can display the calculated value, but the user can't change this value. Finally, the HTML defines two buttons: one that calculates the miles per gallon and one that clears all the text boxes.

The Miles Per Gallon application

```
Calculate Miles Per Gallon

Miles Driven:           033

Gallons of Gas Used:    9.5

Miles Per Gallon        35.1

              Calculate MPG    Clear
```

The HTML

```
<body>
    <main>
        <h1>Calculate Miles Per Gallon</h1>
        <div>
            <label for="miles">Miles Driven:</label>
            <input type="text" id="miles">
        </div>
        <div>
            <label for="gallons">Gallons of Gas Used:</label>
            <input type="text" id="gallons">
        </div>
        <div>
            <label for="mpg">Miles Per Gallon</label>
            <input type="text" id="mpg" disabled>
        </div>
        <div>
            <label></label>
            <input type="button" id="calculate" value="Calculate MPG">
            <input type="button" id="clear" value="Clear">
        </div>
    </main>

    <script src="https://code.jquery.com/jquery-3.4.1.slim.min.js"></script>
    <script src="lib_mpg.js"></script>
    <script src="mpg.js"></script>
</body>
</html>
```

Description

- This application is an updated version of the application presented in chapter 4. It accepts number of miles driven and number of gallons used from the user, and it calculates the miles per gallon.

- This application links to the jQuery library and to a library file that contains an object with properties and methods for calculating miles per gallon. Then, it has a main JavaScript file that uses these libraries.

- Since the main JavaScript file (mpg.js) depends on the jQuery library and the mpg library (lib_mpg.js), its script element is coded after the script elements for those libraries.

Figure 16-6   The Miles Per Gallon application (part 1)

The JavaScript

Part 2 of figure 16-6 presents two files. The lib_mpg.js file is a library file that contains code for working with miles per gallon. It contains an object literal named mpg with two data properties, a read-only property, and a method. The miles and gallons data properties have initial values of zero. The read-only isValid property checks whether the values in the miles and gallons properties are valid. And the calculate() method uses the two data properties to calculate the miles per gallon. Note that both the read-only isValid property and the calculate() method use the *this* keyword to access the data properties.

The second file is the mpg.js file. This is the main JavaScript file, and it contains the jQuery ready() event handler. This event handler starts by attaching a click() event handler to the Calculate MPG button. This handler begins by setting the miles and gallons properties of the mpg object to the values entered by the user. Then, it calls the isValid property of the mpg object to check if the user entered valid data. If not, the code alerts the user.

If the user did enter valid data, the event handler calls the calculate() method of the mpg object to get the value for the miles per gallon. Then, it sets that value as the value of the Miles Per Gallon text box. In this case, since the calculate() method returns a number, the code can call the toFixed() method of a Number object to display the number with just one decimal place.

After displaying the miles per gallon, this event handler calls the select() method of the Miles Driven text box. This method works like the focus() method, but it also selects the text in the text box as shown in part 1 of this figure. That makes it easier for the user to enter another value.

After the click() event handler of the Calculate MPG button, the ready() event handler attaches a click() event handler to the Clear button. This event handler sets the values of all the text boxes to empty strings and sets the focus on the Miles Driven text box. Finally, the ready() event handler sets the focus on the Miles Driven text box when the application first loads.

In this application, the main JavaScript file can use the mpg object without needing to create it. That's because the script element for the library file comes before the script element for the main file in the index.html file. As a result, the main file can use the mpg object in the library file just as if it were coded at the start of the main file.

Often, object literals like this are all you need for what you want to do. Sometimes, though, you need to create more than one instance of an object. Then, you can use classes to define an object type, and you can create multiple instances of the object from the class as described in the next figure.

The lib_mpg.js file

```javascript
"use strict";

const mpg = {
    miles: 0,
    gallons: 0,
    get isValid() {
        if (isNaN(this.miles) || isNaN(this.gallons)) {
            return false;
        } else if (this.miles <= 0 || this.gallons <= 0) {
            return false;
        } else {
            return true;
        }
    },
    calculate() {
        return this.miles / this.gallons;
    }
};
```

The mpg.js file

```javascript
"use strict";

$(document).ready( () => {
    $("#calculate").click( () => {
        mpg.miles = parseFloat($("#miles").val());
        mpg.gallons = parseFloat($("#gallons").val());

        if (mpg.isValid) {
            $("#mpg").val(mpg.calculate().toFixed(1));
            $("#miles").select();
        } else {
            alert("Both entries must be numeric and greater than zero.");
            $("#miles").focus();
        }
    });

    $("#clear").click( () => {
        $("#miles").val("");
        $("#gallons").val("");
        $("#mpg").val("");

        $("#miles").focus();
    });

    $("#miles").focus();
});
```

Description

- The lib_mpg.js file contains an object literal named mpg. This object has two data properties, one read-only accessor property, and one method.

- The isValid accessor property and the calculate() method use the *this* keyword to refer to the miles and gallons properties.

- The main JavaScript file uses the properties and methods of the mpg object.

Figure 16-6 The Miles Per Gallon application (part 2)

How to work with classes

If you've worked in other programming languages, you're probably familiar with classes. You can think of a *class* as a template that defines the properties and methods of an object but isn't an object itself. Instead, you can create an object from the class. Languages that use classes to define and create objects are called *class-based* or *classical languages*.

In contrast, JavaScript is a *prototypal language* that uses prototypes to create objects. Nevertheless, modern JavaScript provides a syntax that's similar to class-based languages. This syntax is more concise than the syntax for working with prototypes. In addition, it's familiar to programmers who have experience with class-based languages. As a result, it's generally considered a best practice to use this syntax for new development.

How to use a class to define an object type

Figure 16-7 shows how to use a class to define an object type. By convention, class names start with an uppercase letter, and object names start with a lowercase letter. That's why this figure uses Invoice as the name of the class and invoice or something similar for the objects created from the class.

In the first example, the Invoice class begins by defining the *constructor* that creates, or constructs, an invoice object. To do that, this class defines the constructor() function. Within the constructor, the code defines the properties for the class. Here, the code uses the *this* keyword to define properties named subtotal and taxRate, and it initializes both properties to null. After the constructor, this class defines a method named getTotal() that gets the total for the invoice based on the values of the subtotal and taxRate properties.

After defining the Invoice object, the code in the first example uses the *new* keyword to create a new Invoice object named invoice. Then, this code sets the subtotal and taxRate properties of the Invoice object. This is necessary because they're set to null for a new Invoice object. Next, this code calls the getTotal() method of the Invoice object to get the total for the invoice. Note that when you create the Invoice object, you must use the *new* keyword to call the constructor. If you don't, JavaScript throws a TypeError exception.

In the second example, the constructor for the Invoice class includes two parameters that provide the values for its two properties. As a result, the code that uses this class can use a single statement to create an Invoice object and set its two properties. This makes it easier to create multiple Invoice objects. In this example, for instance, the code creates Invoice objects named invoice, invoice1, and invoice2. This is also known as creating an *instance* of the class.

When you code an object literal, you must separate properties and methods with commas. But when you define classes, you don't include those commas. Instead, you code the data properties within the constructor, and you use braces to specify the start and end of each accessor property or method.

The Invoice class

```
class Invoice {
    constructor() {
        this.subtotal = null;
        this.taxRate = null;
    }
    getTotal() {
        const salesTax = this.subtotal * this.taxRate
        return this.subtotal + salesTax;
    }
}
```

How to create and use an Invoice object

```
const invoice = new Invoice();
invoice.subtotal = 100;
invoice.taxRate = 0.0875;
total = invoice.getTotal();              // total is 108.75
```

Code that attempts to create an Invoice object without the *new* keyword

```
const invoice = Invoice();               // throws a TypeError exception
```

How to add parameters to the constructor for the Invoice type

```
class Invoice {
    constructor(subtotal, taxRate) {
        this.subtotal = subtotal;
        this.taxRate = taxRate;
    }
    getTotal() { /* same as before */ }
}
```

How to pass arguments to the constructor

```
const invoice = new Invoice(100, 0.0875);
total = invoice.getTotal();              // total is 108.75
```

How to create two Invoice objects that hold different data

```
const invoice1 = new Invoice(100, 0.0875);
const invoice2 = new Invoice(1000, 0.07);

const total1 = invoice1.getTotal();      // total1 is 108.75
const total2 = invoice2.getTotal();      // total2 is 1070
```

Description

- You can use a JavaScript *class* to define a *constructor* that allows you to create, or construct, an object from the class. This is also known as creating an *instance* of the class. To do that, you must use the *new* keyword.

- You code the data properties for your class inside the constructor() function.

- You code the accessor properties and methods for your class outside the constructor() function. All instances of the object type share these accessor properties and methods.

- By convention, class names start with an uppercase letter.

Figure 16-7   How to use a class to define an object type

How to use inheritance

JavaScript has a hierarchy of *native object types* that's shown by the chart in figure 16-8. The first level consists of the Object type. The second level consists of other native object types like the String, Number, Boolean, Date, and Array types that you've already learned about. In addition, this hierarchy shows the Function type that's used to store functions.

This hierarchy means that all of the object types at the second level *inherit* the properties and methods of the Object type. This also means that every object type can use the properties and methods of the Object type. For instance, the Object type defines a toString() method that converts an object to a string.

When you define a class, it inherits the Object type by default. For instance, the Person class in the first example inherits the Object type. As a result, you can call the toString() method from an object created from the Person class. In addition, you can call the firstName, lastName, and fullName properties defined by this class. Here, the last two statements use the instanceof operator to show that the Person object is an instance of both the Object type and the Person type.

When working with classes, you may sometimes want to use *inheritance* to create a new class based on an existing class. Then, the new class inherits the properties and methods of the existing class. For instance, the second example defines a class named Employee that uses the *extends* keyword to inherit the Person class. As a result, you can call all of the properties and methods of the Person class from an object created from the Employee class. In addition, you can call the hireDate property that's added to the Employee class as shown by the code below the Employee class.

In this figure, the Employee class is a *subclass* of the Person class. Conversely, the Person class is the *superclass* of the Employee class. For a subclass to work correctly, it sometimes needs to call constructors or methods of the superclass. To do that, it can use the *super* keyword. In this figure, the constructor of the Employee class uses the *super* keyword to pass the first and last name to the constructor of the Person class, which is necessary for the Employee class to work correctly.

The JavaScript object hierarchy

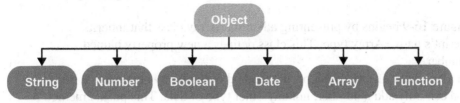

The Person class

```
class Person {
    constructor(fname, lname) {
        this.firstName = fname;
        this.lastName = lname;
    }
    get fullName() {
        return `${this.firstName} ${this.lastName}`;
    }
}
```

How to create and use a Person object

```
const p = new Person("Grace", "Hopper");       // create Person object
console.log(p.fullName);                        // displays "Grace Hopper"
console.log(p instanceof Object);               // displays true
console.log(p instanceof Person);               // displays true
```

An Employee class that inherits the Person class

```
class Employee extends Person {
    constructor(fname, lname, hireDate) {
        super(fname, lname);
        this.hireDate = hireDate;
    }
}
```

How to create and use an Employee object

```
const emp = new Employee("Bjarne", "Stroustrup", new Date("1/1/1979"));
console.log(emp.fullName);                       // displays "Bjarne Stroustrup"
console.log(emp.hireDate.toDateString());        // displays "Mon Jan 01 1979"
console.log(emp instanceof Person);              // displays true
console.log(emp instanceof Employee);            // displays true
```

Description

- JavaScript provides a two-level hierarchy of *native object types*. The first level consists of the Object type. The second level consists of other types that inherit the Object type.

- *Inheritance* lets you create a new class based on an existing class. Then, the new class *inherits* the properties and methods of the existing class.

- When you define a class, you can use the *extends* keyword to inherit the specified class.

- A *subclass* is a class that inherits another class that's known as a *superclass*.

- When defining a class that uses the concise method syntax, you can use the *super* keyword to call constructors or methods of the superclass.

- When working with objects, you can use the instanceof operator to check whether an object is an instance of the specified class.

Figure 16-8   How to use inheritance

When to use inheritance

Figure 16-9 begins by presenting a NumberArray class that inherits JavaScript's native Array type. This class defines a new property named lastNumber.

In addition, it *overrides* the push() method of the Array class so that this method can only add a number, not any other type of data. This push() method begins by using the typeof operator to check whether the parameter value named num is of the Number type. If so, this code calls the push() method of the Array superclass to add the number to the array, and it sets the lastNumber property to the new number. Otherwise, this code throws an exception with an appropriate error message.

The code below the NumberArray class shows how to create and use a NumberArray object. Here, the first statement creates a NumberArray object. Then, the next three statements use the push() method to add three numbers. A fifth statement is commented out because it attempts to add a string, which would throw an exception. The next three statements show how to call the lastNumber property, the length property, and the toString() method from the NumberArray object. This shows that the NumberArray object can access properties and methods from the Object, Array, and NumberArray types. Finally, the last statement shows that you can use the unshift() method to add a string to a NumberArray object, which you probably don't want to allow.

Below the code example, this figure lists three guidelines for when it makes sense to use inheritance in your programs. First, it makes sense to use inheritance when the subclass *is a* type of the superclass. In this case, the NumberArray object that *is a* type of Array object, just a more specialized type of array.

Second, it makes sense to use inheritance when both classes are part of the same logical domain. For example, the Person and Employee objects shown in this chapter are both in the same domain. In other words, they're both part of a domain that's attempting to define the different types of people for a system. Similarly, the NumberArray object is in the same domain as the Array object since they're both attempting to define a general-purpose array, though the NumberArray object is more specialized than the Array object.

Third, it makes sense to use inheritance when the subclass primarily adds features to the superclass. In other words, it makes sense when a subclass adds new properties or methods to the superclass that are only needed in the subclass. For example, the NumberArray object adds the lastNumber property and could add a getTotal() method that gets the total of all numbers in the array. In addition, a subclass may override some properties and methods to change the behavior of the subclass. However, if the subclass needs to override many properties and methods, you may be better off using object composition as described in the next figure.

A NumberArray class that uses inheritance

```
class NumberArray extends Array {
    constructor() {
        super();
        this.lastNumber = null;                  // defines a new property
    }
    push(num) {                                  // overrides an existing method
        if(typeof num === "number") {
            super.push(num);
            this.lastNumber = num;
        } else {
            throw new TypeError("NumberArray can only store numbers");
        }
    }
}
```

How to create a NumberArray object and use it

```
const arr = new NumberArray();
arr.push(1.07);
arr.push(2.21);
arr.push(3.14);
// arr.push("Grace");                   // Would throw TypeError
console.log(arr.lastNumber);            // displays 3.14
console.log(arr.length);               // displays 3
console.log(arr.toString());           // displays 1.07,2.21,3.14
arr.unshift("Grace");                  // PROBLEM! stores invalid value
```

It makes sense to use inheritance when...

- One object *is a* type of another object.
- Both classes are part of the same logical domain.
- The subclass primarily adds features to the superclass.

A problem with the NumberArray class

- Not all inherited methods that add elements to the array check to make sure the element is a number. As a result, it's possible to add invalid data to the NumberArray object.

Description

- When working with objects, you can use the typeof operator to check whether an object is an instance of the specified type.

Figure 16-9   When to use inheritance

When to use object composition

Figure 16-10 shows when and how to use *object composition*, which is a technique for combining simple objects into more complex data structures. Often, object composition is a good alternative to inheritance. That's why this figure shows the NumberArray class from the previous figure after it has been coded to use object composition instead of inheritance.

The constructor for the NumberArray class begins by defining a property named _numbers that stores an array. Then, it defines the lastNumber property.

In other languages, you would use *encapsulation* to hide the _numbers property from other code that uses the object. However, JavaScript doesn't provide an easy way to encapsulate properties or methods. As a result, it's a common convention to code an underscore at the beginning of any property or method names that shouldn't be called from outside code. This doesn't provide true encapsulation, but it lets other programmers know that they shouldn't access this property directly.

After the constructor, the NumberArray class defines a read-only length property that returns the length of the _numbers array. Then, it defines push() and toString() methods that use the push() and toString() methods of the _ numbers array. As a result, a NumberArray object only provides the lastNumber and length properties along with the push() and toString() methods.

This limits the options that other programmers have for working with a NumberArray object, which can make it easier to understand and use. For example, you can't use the unshift() method to add an element to a NumberArray object because this object doesn't define the unshift() method.

Below the code example, this figure lists two guidelines for when it makes sense to use object composition in your programs. First, it makes sense when one object *has a* type of another object. For example, the NumberArray object *has an* Array object as one of its properties, although you shouldn't access this property from outside code.

Second, it makes sense to use object composition when the subclass primarily restricts access to features of the superclass. In other words, if you want to create a subclass that provides fewer properties and methods than the superclass, you should use object composition. For example, this figure shows how to use object composition to code a NumberArray class that provides far fewer properties and methods than are available from the Array class.

A NumberArray class that uses object composition

```
class NumberArray {
    constructor() {
        this._numbers = [];                // defines a 'private' property
        this.lastNumber = null;
    }
    get length() {                         // defines a read-only property
        return this._numbers.length;
    }
    push(num) {                            // defines a method
        if(typeof num === "number") {
            this._numbers.push(num);
            this.lastNumber = num;
        } else {
            throw new TypeError("NumberArray can only store numbers");
        }
    }
    toString() {                           // defines a method
        return this._numbers.toString();
    }
}
```

How to create a NumberArray object and use it

```
const arr = new NumberArray();
arr.push(1.07);
arr.push(2.21);
arr.push(3.14);
// arr.push("Grace");                 // Would throw TypeError
console.log(arr.lastNumber);          // displays 3.14
console.log(arr.length);              // displays 3
console.log(arr.toString());          // displays 1.07,2.21,3.14
// arr.unshift("Grace");              // Would throw TypeError
                                      // because method isn't defined
```

It makes sense to use object composition when...

- One object *has a* type of another object.
- The subclass restricts access to features of the superclass.

Description

- *Object composition* is a way to combine simple objects into more complex ones.
- *Encapsulation* allows you to hide the properties or methods of an object from other code that uses the object. This is also known as *data hiding*.
- JavaScript doesn't provide an easy way to encapsulate properties or methods, but it's a common convention to code an underscore at the beginning of any property or method name that shouldn't be called from outside code.
- If you need to provide encapsulation for some properties or methods, you can use closures or modules to provide private state as described in chapter 17.

Figure 16-10   When to use object composition

The Trips application

The Trips application presented in figure 16-11 logs the destination, miles driven, and miles per gallon for several trips rather than calculating miles per gallon for a single trip. Because of that, this application uses a separate Trip object for each trip, and it uses a Trips object to store multiple Trips objects. As a result, it's a good example of object composition.

The HTML and CSS

Like the Miles Per Gallon application, the Trips applications includes several script elements at the end of the body section that identify the jQuery library, a custom trips library, and the main JavaScript file that uses these libraries. Since the main JavaScript file depends on both the jQuery library and the trips library, it's coded last.

As before, the HTML in the main element contains text boxes for user input about a trip. It also contains a button that calculates miles per gallon and adds that trip to the display. The HTML also contains a div element with an id of "trips" that contains a textarea element that displays data about each trip as well as the MPG calculation for all trips.

The CSS snippet below the HTML shows the style rule for the "trips" element. This style rule floats the div element that contains the text area to the right of the div elements that get the data for each trip.

The Trips application

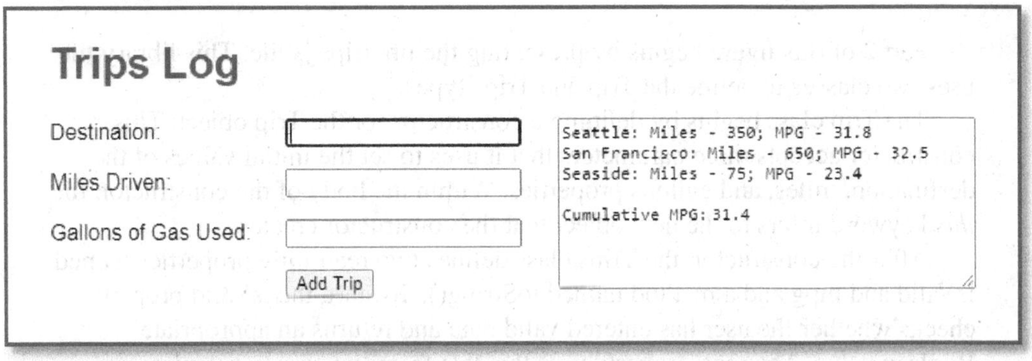

Trips Log

Destination:

Miles Driven:

Gallons of Gas Used:

[Add Trip]

```
Seattle: Miles - 350; MPG - 31.8
San Francisco: Miles - 650; MPG - 32.5
Seaside: Miles - 75; MPG - 23.4

Cumulative MPG: 31.4
```

The HTML

```html
<body>
    <main>
        <h1>Trips Log</h1>
        <div id="trips">
            <textarea id="trip_list" rows="8" cols="42"></textarea>
        </div>
        <div>
            <label for="destination">Destination:</label>
            <input type="text" id="destination">
        </div>
        <div>
            <label for="miles">Miles Driven:</label>
            <input type="text" id="miles">
        </div>
        <div>
            <label for="gallons">Gallons of Gas Used:</label>
            <input type="text" id="gallons">
        </div>
        <div>
            <label></label>
            <input type="button" id="add_trip" value="Add Trip">
        </div>
    </main>
    <script src="https://code.jquery.com/jquery-3.4.1.slim.min.js"></script>
    <script src="lib_trips.js"></script>
    <script src="trips.js"></script>
</body>
```

Some of the CSS for the application

```css
#trips {
    float: right;
}
```

Description

- This application calculates and stores the miles per gallon for one or more trips.

Figure 16-11   The Trips application (part 1)

The JavaScript

Part 2 of this figure begins by presenting the lib_trips.js file. This library file uses two classes to define the Trip and Trips types.

The Trip class begins by defining a constructor for the Trip object. This constructor accepts three parameters that it uses to set the initial values of the destination, miles, and gallons properties. Within the body of the constructor, the *this* keyword refers to the new object that the constructor creates.

After the constructor, the Trips class defines two read-only properties named isValid and mpg and a method named toString(). To start, the isValid property checks whether the user has entered valid data and returns an appropriate Boolean value. The mpg property uses the data from the user to calculate and return the miles per gallon. And the toString() method creates a string that contains data about the trip. This shows how you can override a method of the Object type. Here, the toString() method replaces the toString() method that was inherited from the Object type.

The Trips class begins by defining a constructor for the Trips object. This constructor doesn't accept any arguments. Within its body, it initializes the _trips property to an empty array. Here, the _trips property begins with an underscore to indicate that it shouldn't be called by code that's outside of the Trips class. After the constructor, the Trips class defines two methods and a read-only property.

The push() method adds a Trip object to the _trips array. To start, this method checks whether the trip parameter is a Trip object. If so, this method adds the Trip object to the _trips array. Otherwise, it doesn't do anything, which is adequate for a simple application like this one. Another option would be to throw an exception to indicate that the operation didn't complete successfully.

The read-only property named totalMpg gets the total miles and total gallons for all trips. To do that, it loops through all Trip objects stored in the _trips array. Then, it calculates and returns the total MPG for all trips.

The lib_trips.js file

```
"use strict";

class Trip {
    constructor(destination, miles, gallons) {
        this.destination = destination;
        this.miles = parseFloat(miles);
        this.gallons = parseFloat(gallons);
    }

    get isValid() {                    // a read-only property
        if (this.destination == "" || isNaN(this.miles) ||
                                       isNaN(this.gallons)) {
            return false;
        } else if (this.miles <= 0 || this.gallons <= 0){
            return false;
        } else {
            return true;
        }
    }

    get mpg() {                        // a read-only property
        return this.miles / this.gallons;
    }

    toString() {
        const mpg = this.mpg.toFixed(1);
        return `${this.destination}: Miles - ${this.miles}; MPG - ${mpg}`;
    }
}

class Trips {
    constructor() {
        this._trips = [];
    }

    push(trip) {
        // only allow Trip objects to be added to array
        if (trip instanceof Trip) {
            this._trips.push(trip);
        }
    }

    get totalMpg() {                   // a read-only property
        let totalMiles = 0;
        let totalGallons = 0;
        for (let trip of this._trips) {
            totalMiles += trip.miles;
            totalGallons += trip.gallons;
        }
        return totalMiles / totalGallons;
    }
```

Figure 16-11   The Trips application (part 2)

The toString() method of the Trips class returns a string that contains data that summarizes all trips. To do that, it loops through all Trip objects stored in the _trips array. Within that loop, the code calls the toString() method of the trips object to get a string that contains the data for each trip, and it appends that string to a variable named str. After the loop, the code appends a string that contains the total miles per gallon for the trip to the variable named str, and it returns that variable. Note that the loop adds a newline character at the end of the data for each trip so each trip is displayed on its own line.

After the lib_trips.js file, this figure presents the trips.js file that contains the jQuery ready() event handler that's executed when the page is first loaded. This event handler starts by creating a Trips object.

Next, it adds a click() event handler to the Add Trip button. This handler creates a new instance of a Trip object by passing the values entered by the user to its constructor. Then, it uses the isValid property of the Trip object to check whether the user entered valid data. If not, the code alerts the user.

However, if the data is valid, this code adds the Trip object to the Trips object. Then, it uses the toString() method of the Trips object as the value of the textarea element. This displays the data for all trips in the textarea element. Next, the code clears all three text boxes and moves the focus to the text box for the destination. This makes it easy for the user to start entering another trip.

After adding the click() event handler to the Add Trip button, the ready() function ends by moving the focus to the text box for the destination. Again, this makes it easy for the user to start entering another trip.

When you work with the toString() method, you should know that JavaScript calls it automatically in situations where it expects a string. As a result, you can often omit the call to the toString() method. For example, you don't need to call the toString() method like this:

```
$("#trip_list").val(trips.toString());
```

Instead, you can omit the toString() call like this:

```
$("#trip_list").val(trips);
```

The advantage of this approach is that it yields code that's more concise. The disadvantage is that some JavaScript programmers might not realize that JavaScript is automatically calling the toString() method.

The lib_trips.js file (continued)

```
    toString() {
        let str = "";
        for (let trip of this._trips) {
            str += trip.toString() + "\n";
        }
        str += "\nCumulative MPG: " + this.totalMpg.toFixed(1);
        return str;
    }
}
```

The trips.js flle

```
"use strict";

$(document).ready( () => {
    const trips = new Trips();

    $("#add_trip").click( () => {
        const trip = new Trip(
            $("#destination").val(), $("#miles").val(), $("#gallons").val());

        if (trip.isValid) {
            trips.push(trip);
            $("#trip_list").val(trips.toString());

            $("#destination").val("");
            $("#miles").val("");
            $("#gallons").val("");

            $("#destination").focus();
        }
        else {
            alert("Please complete all fields.\nMiles and gallons "
                + "must be numeric and greater than zero.");
            $("#destination").select();
        }
    });

    $("#destination").focus();
});
```

Figure 16-11   The Trips application (part 3)

How to work with prototypes

As mentioned earlier in this chapter, even if you use classes to define objects, JavaScript still uses prototypes to create objects. Unlike a class, a *prototype* is an object, and it's *cloned* to create a new object.

An introduction to prototypes

A new object that's created by cloning a prototype object has references to the methods of that prototype, rather than actual copies of those methods. For example, an object literal has a reference to the toString() method on the prototype of the Object object. Thus, all object literals refer to the same toString() method of the Object object. This keeps duplicate copies of the toString() method out of memory.

The first example in figure 16-12 shows how this works. Here, the first two statements create two instances of the Date type and each stores a different date. However, each object also has access to the toDateString() method as shown by the third and fourth statements. That's because the toDateString() method is available from the prototype object of the Date type.

This works even if a method is added to the prototype object after you've created an instance of an object type. The second example shows how this works. Here, the first statement adds a method named toNumericDateString() to the prototype object of the Date type. To do that, it uses the dot operator to access the prototype object of the Date type. As the second and third statements show, the two Date objects created in the previous example can access this method. This shows that it's possible to add methods to the prototype objects of the native data types.

The third example shows that this works differently when you add a property or method to an object. In that case, a new property or method is added for that object only. In this example, the first statement adds a property named hasExtension to the Date object named taxDay. But as the second and third statements show, this property is only available to the Date object named taxDay, not to the Date object named xmas.

A property that's added to an object is known as an *own property*, and it can be used to *override* a prototype property as shown by the fourth example. Here, the first statement adds a method named toDateString() to the Date object named xmas. This adds a new method to memory for that object. Since it has the same name as a method of the prototype object, it overrides (replaces) that method. But as the third and fourth statements show, it only overrides it for this instance of the Date object, not for the prototype object.

Code that creates two instances of the Date type

```
const taxDay = new Date("4/15/2021");
const xmas = new Date("12/25/2021");

console.log(taxDay.toDateString());          // displays Thu Apr 15 2021
console.log(xmas.toDateString());            // displays Sat Dec 25 2021
```

Code that adds a method to the prototype object of the Date type

```
Date.prototype.toNumericDateString = function() {
    const m = this.getMonth() + 1;           // month is zero based
    const d = this.getDate();
    const y = this.getFullYear();
    return m + "/" + d + "/" + y;
};

console.log(taxDay.toNumericDateString());   // displays 4/15/2021
console.log(xmas.toNumericDateString());     // displays 12/25/2021
```

Code that adds an own property to one instance of the Date type

```
taxDay.hasExtension = true;

console.log(taxDay.hasExtension);            // displays true
console.log(xmas.hasExtension);              // displays undefined
```

Code that uses an own property to override a prototype property

```
xmas.toDateString = function() {
    return "It's Christmas Day";
};

console.log(taxDay.toDateString());          // displays Thu Apr 15 2021
console.log(xmas.toDateString());            // displays It's Christmas Day
```

Description

- Even though you can use the *class* keyword to define objects, JavaScript doesn't actually use classes to create objects. Instead, it uses *prototype objects* that are cloned to create new objects. That's why JavaScript is known as a *prototypal language*.

- When you create a new object, it's *cloned* from the prototype object of its object type and it inherits all of the methods of that prototype. For example, a Date object is cloned from the prototype of the Date type.

- When you add a method to the prototype object of an object type, it's available to all instances of that object type. Those instances have a reference to the method, not a copy of the method. This keeps duplicate function definitions out of memory.

- When you add a property or method to an instance of an object type, it's created directly on the instance, not on the prototype. Because of that, it's only available to that instance. This kind of property is called a *direct property* or *own property*.

- You can use an own property to *override* a method on a prototype object, but the property only overrides the method for that instance of the object.

Figure 16-12   An introduction to prototypes

Legacy code for creating objects

As mentioned earlier, for new development, it's generally considered a best practice to use the *class* keyword to define object types. However, prior to the introduction of class-based syntax, it was a common practice to use a *constructor function* to create multiple instances of an object type. As a result, you should be aware of how constructor functions work in case you come across them when maintaining legacy code or reviewing online examples.

Figure 16-13 shows how to code constructors that can be used to create multiple instances of an object type. Here, the first example shows how to code a constructor named Invoice that can create multiple Invoice objects. By convention, the name of a constructor function starts with a capital letter. Within the body of this constructor, the *this* keyword refers to the new object that the constructor creates. As a result, this code sets the initial values of the subtotal and taxRate properties to the values in the subtotal and taxRate parameters. Here, the parameter and property names don't have to be the same. However, that's a common coding practice.

After you code a constructor, you can add methods to it. To do that, you add each method to the constructor's prototype object. For each method, you code the name of the Object type, a dot operator, the *prototype* keyword, another dot operator, and the name of the method. Then, you assign a function expression to the method. When you do, the method becomes available to all Invoice objects that are created by the constructor.

To create a new object from a constructor, you use the *new* keyword to call the constructor. This returns a new object of the constructor type. In this example, the code creates two Invoice objects from the constructor, each with its own subtotal and tax rate values, and it assigns these objects to constants named invoice1 and invoice2. After the objects have been created, you can refer to their properties and methods just as you refer to the properties and methods of any other object as shown by the last two statements in this example.

Since JavaScript isn't a class-based language, some programmers prefer to create new objects in a way that makes the prototypal nature of JavaScript more obvious. To address this, the Object type provides a static Object.create() method that creates an object from the prototype that's supplied as the first parameter.

The second example shows how to use this method in a *factory function*, which is a function that creates, initializes, and returns objects. In this example, the factory function begins by defining an object literal for the prototype of an invoice object. This object literal contains a single getTotal() method. Since this method uses the subtotal and taxRate properties of the object, the factory function must define these properties for the invoice object after it creates the object from the object literal for its prototype.

The code that follows the factory function shows how you can use the factory function to create two invoice objects. This code works like the code that uses the constructor function except that this code doesn't use the *new* keyword to create an object. Instead, it calls the factory function and passes it values for the subtotal and taxRate parameters. This creates two objects of the Object type, not the Invoice type.

A constructor function that creates Invoice objects

```
const Invoice = function(subtotal, taxRate) {
    this.subtotal = subtotal;
    this.taxRate = taxRate;
};
```

Code that adds a method to the Invoice object prototype

```
Invoice.prototype.getTotal = function() {
    const salesTax = this.subtotal * this.taxRate
    return this.subtotal + salesTax;
};
```

Code that uses the constructor function to create two Invoice objects

```
const invoice1 = new Invoice(100, 0.0875);
const invoice2 = new Invoice(1000, 0.07);
const total1 = invoice1.getTotal();     // total1 is 108.75
const total2 = invoice2.getTotal();     // total2 is 1070
```

A factory function that creates Invoice objects

```
const getInvoice = function(subtotal, taxRate) {
    const invoicePrototype = {    // define prototype methods
        getTotal: function() {
            const salesTax = this.subtotal * this.taxRate
            return this.subtotal + salesTax;
        }
    };
    const invoice = Object.create(invoicePrototype);
    invoice.subtotal = subtotal;
    invoice.taxRate = taxRate;
    return invoice;
};
```

Code that uses a factory function to create two Object types

```
const invoice1 = getInvoice(100, 0.0875);
const invoice2 = getInvoice(1000, 0.07);
const total1 = invoice1.getTotal();     // total1 is 108.75
const total2 = invoice2.getTotal();     // total2 is 1070
```

Description

- Prior to the *class* keyword, it was common to code a *constructor function* to create multiple instances of a custom object type. In fact, that's what the *class* keyword does under the covers.

- By convention, constructor names start with an uppercase letter.

- When using constructor functions to define objects, you can add the methods to the prototype object.

- To create a new object from a constructor, you should use the *new* keyword.

- You can use the static create() method of the Object type to create a new object that's based on a prototype. Then, you can add any properties that the prototype object needs.

- A *factory function* can use the create() method to create and return new objects.

- Some programmers prefer to use factory functions because they make the prototypal nature of JavaScript clear.

Figure 16-13   Legacy code for creating objects

More skills for working with objects

At this point, you have the basic skills you need for working with objects. Now, this chapter presents more skills that you may need from time to time. Although you probably won't use these skills in every application, you should at least be aware of them so you can use them when they're appropriate.

How to use a symbol as a computed property or method name

Although you typically use the dot operator to refer to the properties and methods of an object, you can use brackets to accomplish the same task as shown in the first example in figure 16-14. Since using the dot operator results in code that's shorter and easier to read, you typically only use brackets if you need to use a computed value as a name.

One reason to use a computed value as a name is to prevent name collisions. In the first example, for instance, the invoice object defines a method named getTotal(). Then, later in the example, the code adds a getTotal() method that calculates the total differently. The name of this new getTotal() method *collides* with the name for the original getTotal() causing the new method to override, or replace, the original one. In many cases, this isn't what you want.

As a result, if you have a property or method that you want to protect against name collisions, you can compute a unique name for the property or method. One easy way to do that is to use the Symbol() function to create a *symbol*, which is a native data type that represents a unique value. Although the Symbol() function begins with a capital letter, it isn't a constructor. As a result, JavaScript throws an error if you call it with the *new* keyword.

When you call the Symbol() function, it always returns a symbol that has a unique value, even if you don't pass a string to it. However, to make debugging easier, you can also pass a descriptive string to the Symbol() function as shown by the second example. Here, the code passes a string of "taxRate" to the Symbol() function and stores the symbol that's returned in the constant named taxRate. Then, the invoice object uses the symbol as the name for the property that stores the taxRate. To do that, this code must use brackets, not the dot operator. This makes this property somewhat hidden, but doesn't make it completely private. To do that, you can use closures or modules as described in chapter 17.

The third example shows how you could use a symbol to make the array from the Trips application presented earlier in this chapter somewhat private. To start, the code stores a symbol in the constant named trips. Then, within the constructor for this class, the code uses brackets to assign an empty array to the computed property name. After that, the other methods in the Trips class can use the brackets to access the trips array instead of the dot operator syntax that's used by the Trips class presented earlier in this chapter.

How to use brackets to refer to properties and methods of an object

```
const invoice = {
    taxRate: 0.0875,                                  // property
    getTotal(subtotal) {                              // method
        return subtotal + subtotal * this.taxRate;
    }
};

console.log(invoice.taxRate);                         // displays 0.0875
console.log(invoice["taxRate"]);                      // displays 0.0875

const total1 = invoice.getTotal(100);                 // total1 is 108.75
const total2 = invoice["getTotal"](100);              // total2 is 108.75

invoice.getTotal = function(subtotal) {    // collides with getTotal()
    return subtotal + subtotal * 0.10;
};
const total3 = invoice.getTotal(100);                 // total3 is 110.00
console.log(total3);
```

How to use a symbol as a computed property name in an object

```
const taxRate = Symbol("taxRate");
const invoice = {
    [taxRate]: 0.0875
};

invoice.taxRate = 0.07;               // doesn't collide with taxRate symbol
console.log(invoice[taxRate]);        // displays 0.0875
console.log(invoice.taxRate);         // displays 0.07
```

How to use a symbol as a computed property name in a class

```
const trips = Symbol("trips");
class Trips {
    constructor() {
        this[trips] = [];
    }
    // other methods that use the symbol named trips go here
}
```

Description

- You can use brackets to refer to the properties and methods of an object.

- A *symbol* is a native data type that represents a unique value.

- To create a symbol, call the Symbol() function. Since this function is not a constructor, JavaScript throws an error if you call it with the *new* keyword.

- The Symbol() function always returns a symbol that has a unique value. However, to make debugging easier, you can also pass a descriptive string to the Symbol() function.

- You can use a symbol as a computed name for a property or method. That way, the name is unique and doesn't *collide* with other property or method names.

- When you use a symbol as a computed name for a property or method, the property or method is somewhat hidden. However, this doesn't make it completely private. To do that, you can use closures or modules as described in chapter 17.

Figure 16-14   How to use a symbol as a computed property or method name

How to work with iterators

JavaScript provides several ways to loop through, or *iterate*, the items in a collection such as an array or a string. For instance, you can use a for-of loop. Or, you can use the spread operator as described in the next chapter.

When you define a custom object that contains a collection of items, you will often want to provide a way to iterate through the items. In other words, you want to make your object *iterable*. To do that, you can use the skills presented in figure 16-15 to add a method to your object that returns an *iterator*, which is an object that can be used to iterate the items in a collection.

The example in this figure begins by defining an object literal named taskList that stores multiple task objects. The taskList object begins by defining a property named tasks that uses an array to store each task. Then, it defines the method that returns an object literal for an iterator.

After defining the properties, the taskList object defines the @@iterator() method whose name is the *well-known symbol,* Symbol.iterator. To do that, this code places the Symbol.iterator within brackets and follows it with a set of parentheses. This protects the @@iterator() method from name collisions with other methods.

Within the body of the @@iterator() method, the code returns an object literal for the iterator. This iterator object must include the next() method, and this method must return an object with a done property and a value property. This object is often called an IteratorResult object.

In this example, the iterator object begins by defining a property named tasks that stores the value of the tasks property for the taskList object, and a property named index that stores the index for the array. The tasks property is necessary to keep the array of tasks in scope for the iterator object. (For now, don't worry if you don't understand why this property is necessary.)

After the properties, this code defines the next() method. Within this method, an if statement checks whether the index property is equal to the length of the tasks property. If so, the iteration is complete. In that case, the next() method returns an IteratorResult object with a done property that has been set to true. Otherwise, the code returns an IteratorResult object with the done property set to false. But first, it sets the value property of the IteratorResult object to the task that's at the current index. In addition, it increments the index by 1.

The second example shows how to use a for-of loop to *consume* the iterator for the taskList object. This code loops through each task in the taskList object. Within the loop, a single statement displays the description for the task. This code assumes that the task object has a description property that stores that description.

Two of the well-known symbols

Symbol	Method Name	Method Description
`Symbol.hasInstance`	`@@hasInstance()`	Defines how an object behaves when used with the instanceof operator.
`Symbol.iterator`	`@@iterator()`	Defines how an object behaves when used with a for-of loop or with a spread operator that's described in the next chapter.

One method required by an iterator object

Method	Description
`next()`	Executes the specified code and returns an IteratorResult object.

Two properties of the IteratorResult object

Property	Description
`done`	A Boolean value that indicates whether the iteration is done.
`value`	The value of the current item in the sequence. Can be omitted when done is true.

An object literal that's iterable

```
const taskList = {
    tasks: [],
    // methods of the taskList object go here
    [Symbol.iterator]() {          // define the iterator() method
        return {                   // return the Iterator object
            tasks: this.tasks,
            index: 0,
            next() {               // required method of the Iterator object
                if (this.index == this.tasks.length) {
                    return {done: true};           // return IteratorResult
                } else {
                    let value = this.tasks[this.index];
                    this.index++;
                    return {value, done: false};  // return IteratorResult
                }
            }
        };
    }
};
```

A for-of loop that consumes the object

```
for (const task of taskList) {
    console.log(task.description)
}
```

Description

- The *well-known symbols* are used as keys for methods of the Object type. You can change how an object behaves by coding a custom method for a well-known symbol.

- Symbol.iterator is a well-known symbol that's often used with generator functions to make an object iterable, as shown in the next figure.

Figure 16-15   How to work with iterators

How to work with generator functions

Iterators are useful, but they require a fair amount of work. Fortunately, JavaScript provides *generator functions* to automate much of this work for you as shown by figure 16-16.

To start, you can use the * operator to define a generator function. To do that, you can code the * operator at the beginning of the function name as shown in the first example. You can code it immediately after the *function* keyword as shown in the third example. Or, you can code it by itself with a space between the *function* keyword and the function name.

When a generator function is called, the code in the body doesn't execute. Instead, it returns an iterator object that's of the Generator type. When the next() method of a Generator object is called, the code in the body of the generator function executes. Although you can write code that explicitly calls this method, you typically use a for-of loop to automatically call this method. In this figure, for instance, the second example uses a for-of loop to call the next() method.

When the code in the body of a generator function executes, it runs until it reaches a *yield statement*, which is a statement that begins with the *yield* keyword. At that point, the code returns an IteratorResult object and pauses execution. Like a return statement, a yield statement can return a value. If it does, that value is assigned to the value property of the IteratorResult object. Otherwise, the value property is undefined. In addition, the done property is set to false.

When next() is called again, the code executes from where execution was paused and continues until it reaches another yield statement. Then, it executes the yield statement and pauses execution again. This continues until the code returns an IteratorResult object whose done property has been set to true.

The third example shows how you can use a generator function to define a Date object that's iterable. Here, the code adds a generator function to the prototype for Date objects. This generated function returns a different part of the Date object each time it's called. For example, the first call returns the full year, the second call returns the month, and the third call returns the day.

Below this generator method, the fourth example creates an iterable Date object for the current date and time. Then, it uses a for-of loop to display each of the six of the date parts on its own line.

When working with generator functions, there are two things you should know. First, a generator function must be a regular function, not an arrow function. Second, the *yield* keyword can't be used outside of a generator function.

A keyword that's used with generator functions

Keyword	Description
`yield`	Returns an IteratorResult object and pauses execution.

An object literal that's iterable

```
const taskList = {
    tasks: [],
    // methods of the taskList object go here
    *[Symbol.iterator]() {                    // define the iterator() method
        for (let task of this.tasks) {
            yield task;
        }
    }
};
```

A for-of loop that consumes the object

```
for (const task of taskList) {
    console.log(task.description)
}
```

A Date object that's iterable

```
Date.prototype[Symbol.iterator] = function*() {
    yield this.getFullYear();
    yield this.getMonth();
    yield this.getDate();
    yield this.getHours();
    yield this.getMinutes();
    yield this.getSeconds();
};
```

A for-of loop that consumes an iterable Date object

```
const now = new Date();
for (const part of now) {
    console.log(part);    // displays 6 date parts
}
```

Description

- A *generator function* makes it easier to create an iterator object that's iterable.
- You can use the * operator to identify a generator function.
- When you call a generator function, it doesn't execute the code in its body. Instead, it returns an iterator object of the Generator type.
- The code in the body of a generator function executes when the iterator's next() method is called. Typically, this method is called automatically by a for-of statement or by the spread operator that's described in the next chapter.
- When the next() method is called, the code executes until it comes to a *yield statement*. Then, that statement returns an IteratorResult object and pauses execution. If there are no more yield statements, the generator returns an IteratorResult object and the code execution ends.
- A generator function must be a regular function, not an arrow function.

Figure 16-16   How to work with generator functions

How to create cascading methods

A *cascading method* is a method of an object that can be chained with other methods. To do that, the method must return a reference to the original object as shown in figure 16-17. Typically, a method can use the *this* keyword to return a reference to the original object.

Code that uses cascading methods is sometimes called *fluent*. That's because a line of code like

```
taskList.load().add(task);
```

reads like a sentence. This type of code is also known as *method chaining*. That's because the method calls are chained together.

The first example presents a taskList object with two methods: load() and add(). Since neither of these methods returns a reference to the taskList object, they can't be chained. If you try to chain the methods, a runtime error occurs because the load() method doesn't return an object that has an add() method. Thus, you must use separate statements to call these methods.

The second example presents these same methods, but now they each end with this statement:

```
return this;
```

This returns a reference to the taskList object so the methods can be chained.

Since method chaining is common, it's a good practice to provide for chaining by returning the object at the end of a method. Of course, if you're returning something else, like a Boolean value or a string, you can't return the object too. But whenever you can return the object, you should.

Two methods that modify an object but don't return the object

Two methods of the taskList object

```
const taskList = {
    load() {
        // load code goes here
    },
    add(task) {
        // add code goes here
    }
};
```

Chaining these method calls doesn't work

```
taskList.load().add(task);
// TypeError: Cannot read property 'add' of undefined
```

The methods must be called one at a time

```
taskList.load();
taskList.add(task);
```

Two methods that modify an object and then return the object

Two methods of the taskList object

```
const taskList = {
    load() {
        // load code goes here
        return this;
    },
    add(task) {
        // add code goes here
        return this;
    }
};
```

Chaining these method calls works

```
taskList.load().add(task);
```

Description

- A *cascading method* is a method of an object that can be chained with other methods of that object. This style of coding is sometimes called *fluent* because of the way the code reads. This is also known as *method chaining*.

- To support cascading methods, a method must return the object represented by the *this* keyword.

Figure 16-17   How to create cascading methods

How to destructure an object

Figure 16-18 shows how to use the *destructuring* syntax to assign the values of object properties to individual constants or variables in a single statement. To start, the first example defines a person object that has firstName, lastName, and dob properties with values of "Grace", "Hopper", and null.

To destructure this object, you can use the same syntax as defining an object literal to specify the constants or variables that should store the values of the object properties. Then, you can assign the property values of the object to the constants or variables as shown in the second example.

Here, the first statement specifies two constants (firstName and lastName) that have the same names as the property names of the person object. As a result, this code assigns "Grace" to the firstName constant and "Hopper" to the lastName constant.

Then, the second statement specifies two constant names that are different than the property names of the person object, but it specifies how these constant names map to the property names. As a result, this code assigns "Grace" to the fname constant and "Hopper" to the lname constant.

The third example shows how to provide a default value for a property. To do that, you just code the name of the property followed by an equals sign and the default value. Here, the first statement provides a default value of "unknown" for the property named age. As a result, this code assigns "Grace" to the first-Name constant, null to the dob constant, and "unknown" to the age constant. That's because the person object in this figure doesn't define a property named age.

The fourth example shows how to destructure an object in the parameter list of a function. Here, the code defines a function named displayGreeting() that uses destructuring to assign values to the firstName and lastName parameters. As a result, when the first statement calls this function and passes it the person object, it displays a greeting of "Hello, Grace Hopper". However, when the second statement calls this function without passing a person object, it causes a type error.

The fifth and sixth examples show how to work with the properties of a nested object. To start, the fifth example defines an invoice object that has a subtotal property of 100 and a nested terms object that has taxRate and dueDays properties of 0.0875 and 30. Then, the sixth example shows how to use destructuring syntax to assign a property value of this nested object to a constant or variable. Here, the statement specifies a constant named subtotal for the subtotal property and a constant named taxRate for the taxRate property of the nested terms object. As a result, this code assigns 100 to the subtotal constant and 0.0875 to the taxRate property.

A person object with three properties that have values

```
const person = {
    firstName: "Grace", lastName: "Hopper", dob: null
};
```

How to assign property values to variables or constants

Using the same names

```
const {firstName, lastName} = person;
```

Using different names

```
const {firstName: fname, lastName: lname} = person;
```

How to provide a default value for an assignment

```
const {firstName, dob, age = "unknown"} = person;

console.log(dob);    // displays null
console.log(age);    // displays "unknown"
```

How to destructure an object in the parameter list of a function

```
const displayGreeting = ({firstName, lastName}) => {
    console.log("Hello, " + firstName + " " + lastName);
};
```

Code that calls the function

```
displayGreeting(person);    // displays "Hello, Grace Hopper"
displayGreeting();          // TypeError: Cannot destructure property
```

An object that has a nested object that has two properties

```
const invoice = {
    subtotal: 100,
    terms: {taxRate: 0.0875, dueDays: 30}  // nested object
};
```

How to assign property values of a nested object

```
const {subtotal, terms: {taxRate}} = invoice;
```

Description

- The *destructuring* syntax provides a way to assign the values of object properties to multiple constants or variables in a single statement.
- To destructure an object, you use the same syntax as defining an object literal to specify the constants or variables that should store the values of the object properties.
- You can specify the same names as the object property names, or you can specify new names.
- You can include default values for the individual constants or variables.
- You can destructure an object in the parameter list of a function.

Figure 16-18   How to destructure an object

An introduction to the static methods of the Object type

Figure 16-19 introduces some of the static methods of the Object type. If necessary, you can use these methods to gain more control over how the properties of an object work. Or, you may want to use them to inspect the properties of an object. In addition, this figure presents the for-in statement that you can use to loop through the properties of an object as well as the in operator that you can use to check whether a property is in an object.

The example in this figure shows how this works. To start, this example defines an object literal and stores it in a constant named pet. Within this object literal, the code uses standard syntax to define a property named name. When you use code like this, JavaScript sets the configurable, enumerable, and writeable attributes of the property to true. In most cases, that's what you want.

However, if you want to gain control over these attributes, you can use the defineProperties() method to add one or more properties. To do that, you pass two values to this method. First, you pass the object that you want to work with. Second, you pass a descriptor object that specifies the names and attributes for the property or properties you want to define. By default, this method sets the configurable, writable, and enumerable attributes of a property to false. As a result, if you want these attributes to be true, you have to set them to true.

The example continues by creating a descriptor object that defines three properties named id, species, and adoptionDate. Here, the id property only speci-fies a value attribute of "1234". As a result, this property has a value of "1234" that can't be changed since its writable attribute is left at its default value of false. The adoptionDate property doesn't specify a value attribute, but it sets the writable attribute to true, so a value can be set for this property later. Similarly, the species attribute sets the writable and enumerable attributes to true. As a result, a value can be set for this property later, and this property can be enumer-ated by a for-in loop.

After adding the three properties, the example uses for-in loop to display the names of all enumerable properties of the pet object. This displays the name and species properties because these two properties are enumerable. Next, the code uses the in operator to check whether the adoptionDate and id properties are in the pet object. This code shows that these properties are in the object, even though they aren't enumerated by a for-in loop.

The last four statements in this example show how you can use the static methods of the Object type to inspect the object. Here, the keys() method returns all enumerable properties of the pet object. The getOwnPropertyNames() method returns all properties of the pet object, except any property that uses a symbol as its name. The getOwnPropertySymbols() method returns all symbol properties of the pet object. In this case, the pet object doesn't have any symbol properties. And the getOwnPropertyDescriptors() method returns the descriptor object for each property.

Static methods of the Object type

Method	Description
defineProperties(*obj*,*desc*)	Define one or more properties on the object it receives. Sets the property attributes based on a descriptor object.
keys(*obj*)	An array of the names of the enumerable properties of the specified object, not including symbol properties.
getOwnPropertyNames(*obj*)	An array of the names of the enumerable and non-enumerable properties of the specified object, not including symbol properties.
getOwnPropertySymbols(*obj*)	An array of the symbol properties of the specified object.
getOwnPropertyDescriptors(*obj*)	A descriptor object for all the properties in the specified object, including symbol properties.

A statement and an operator for working with properties

Name	Description
for-in	A statement that loops through the properties of an object, not including non-enumerable and symbol properties.
in	An operator that returns a Boolean value that indicates if the specified property is in the object, including non-enumerable and symbol properties.

An example that works with properties

```
const pet = {
    name: "Maisie"              // configurable, writable, and enumerable
};

// add three properties to the object
Object.defineProperties(pet, {
    id: {value: "1234"},    // NOT configurable, writable, or enumerable
    adoptionDate: {writable: true},
    species: {writable: true, enumerable: true}
});

// inspect the object with a for-in loop and the in operator
for (let propName in pet) {
    console.log(propName);  // only displays "name" and "species"
}
console.log("adoptionDate" in pet);             // displays true
console.log("id" in pet);                       // displays true

// get information about the object
Object.keys(pet);                       // ["name","species"]
Object.getOwnPropertyNames(pet);        // ["name","id","adoptionDate","species"]
Object.getOwnPropertySymbols(pet); // []
Object.getOwnPropertyDescriptors(pet);  // descriptor for each property
```

Description

- When you use the defineProperties() method to add a property to an object, the property's configurable, enumerable, and writeable attributes are set to false by default.

Figure 16-19   An introduction to the static methods of the Object type

The Task List application

The Task List application presented in figure 16-20 is another version of the application presented in earlier chapters. This version has a due date, a task name, adds links to delete individual tasks, and uses objects and object libraries.

The HTML and CSS

The script elements at the end of the body element identify the libraries used by this application: jQuery, a storage library, a task library, and a task list library. The last script element is for the main JavaScript file that uses these libraries. The script elements are in this order because the storage library depends on the task library, the task list library depends on both the storage and task libraries, and the main JavaScript file depends on the task list and task libraries, as well as on jQuery.

The HTML in the main element contains a div element with an id attribute of "tasks". The individual tasks, as well as the links the user can use to delete them, are added directly to this div element by the JavaScript code. There's also a second div element with no id attribute but a class attribute of "clear".

The CSS snippet below the HTML shows the style rules for the div element with the id of "tasks" and the "clear" class. Here, the tasks style rule floats the tasks div to the right. It also sets the div's width, margins, and padding, and it puts a border around it. Finally, it sets a minimum height so that when there are no tasks in local storage, the bordered area is roughly the same height as the text box and buttons.

This is followed by the CSS style rule for the <a> elements within the tasks div. It contains only one declaration that adds some space to the right of the <a> elements.

Last, the style rule for the div with the "clear" class sets the CSS clear property to "both". This clears the floating of the elements that precede it. If you omit this style rule, the border of the tasks div element doesn't expand as tasks are added to the task list.

The Task List application

The HTML

```
<body>
    <main>
        <h1>Task List</h1>
        <div id="tasks"></div>
        <div>
            <label for="task">Task:</label>
            <input type="text" name="task" id="task">
        </div>
        <div>
            <label for="due_date">Due Date:</label>
            <input type="text" name="due_date" id="due_date">
        </div>
        <div>
            <input type="button" id="add_task" value="Add Task">
            <input type="button" id="clear_tasks" value="Clear Tasks">
        </div>
        <div class="clear"></div>
    </main>
    <script src="https://code.jquery.com/jquery-3.4.1.slim.min.js"></script>
    <script src="lib_task.js"></script>
    <script src="lib_storage.js"></script>
    <script src="lib_task_list.js"></script>
    <script src="task_list.js"></script>
</body>
```

Some of the CSS for the application

```
#tasks {
    float: right;
    width: 25em;
    margin: 0 0 .5em;
    padding: 1em;
    border: 2px solid black;
    min-height: 5em;
}
#tasks a { margin-right: 0.5em; }
.clear { clear: both; }
```

Figure 16-20   The Task List application (part 1)

The JavaScript

Part 2 of figure 16-20 presents two library files. The lib_task.js file is the library for working with individual tasks. It contains a class named Task that defines a constructor that accepts an object and uses destructuring to get the description and dueDate properties from this object.

Within the constructor, the first statement assigns the description property of the object parameter to the description property of the current object. Then, the constructor checks whether the object parameter has a dueDate property. If so, it converts the value in that parameter to a Date object and assigns it to a property named dueDate. Otherwise, it assigns a new Date object with a default value of one month from the current date to the dueDate property. Because of that, you can create a Task object from an object that doesn't have a dueDate property. In other words, this dueDate property is optional.

After the constructor, the code defines a read-only isValid property and a toString() method. The isValid property checks whether the description property has been set and whether the dueDate property is a date in the future. Then, the toString() method returns a string that displays the description and dueDate properties.

After the lib_task.js file, the lib_storage.js file defines an object literal named storage that provides a way to get Task objects in and out of local web storage. To start, the storage object defines a retrieve() method that gets a JSON string from local storage and converts it into an array of zero or more Task objects. Then, it defines a store() method that accepts an array of Task objects, converts that array to a JSON string, and stores that string in local storage. Finally, it defines a clear() method that clears all Task objects from local storage.

Here, the retrieve() method uses a for-of loop to loop through each object in the array of tasks. Within that loop, the code creates a Task object by passing the object to the constructor of the Task class. This works because the constructor of the Task class uses destructuring to get the description and dueDate values from the object.

The lib_task.js file

```javascript
"use strict";

class Task {
    constructor({description, dueDate}) {  // uses destructuring
        this.description = description;
        if (dueDate) {
            this.dueDate = new Date(dueDate);
        } else {
            this.dueDate = new Date();
            this.dueDate.setMonth(this.dueDate.getMonth() + 1);
        }
    }

    get isValid() {
        if (this.description === "") {    // description is required
            return false;
        }
        const today = new Date();         // due date must be in future
        if (this.dueDate.getTime() <= today.getTime() ) {
            return false;
        }
        return true;
    }

    toString() {
        return `${this.description}<br>
                Due Date: ${this.dueDate.toDateString()}`;
    }
}
```

The lib_storage.js file

```javascript
"use strict";

const storage = {
    retrieve() {
        const tasks = [];
        const json = localStorage.tasks;
        if(json) {
            const taskArray = JSON.parse(json);
            for(let obj of taskArray) {
                tasks.push(new Task(obj)); // uses destructuring
            }
        }
        return tasks;
    },
    store(tasks) {
        localStorage.tasks = JSON.stringify(tasks);
    },
    clear() {
        localStorage.tasks = "";
    }
};
```

Figure 16-20   The Task List application (part 2)

Part 3 of figure 16-20 shows the library for working with the task list. It contains an object named taskList that holds, edits, and displays tasks. Because the application only needs one instance of this object, it's coded as an object literal that has one property and seven methods. Also, the first six methods return the *this* keyword, so they support method chaining.

The tasks property contains an array that holds the Task objects. Since this property shouldn't be accessed by outside code, it uses a symbol as a computed name. As a result, this property is somewhat hidden from outside code. However, if you want to hide this property completely, you can use a closure or a module to give it private state as described in chapter 17.

The load() method calls the retrieve() method of the storage object to retrieve the tasks from local storage as an array of Task objects. This stores an array of Task objects in the tasks property.

The save() method calls the store() method of the storage object and passes it the array of Tasks objects. This stores the array of Tasks in local storage.

The sort() method calls the sort() method of the tasks array. It passes that method a function that sorts the Task objects in the array by due date.

The add() method accepts a Task object as a parameter. Then, it uses the push() method of the tasks array to add the Task object to the array.

The delete() method accepts an index parameter. It starts by calling the sort() method to sort the tasks. It does this to make sure the tasks are in the same sort order as those displayed in the browser. Then, it removes the task at the specified index in the tasks array using the splice() method of that array.

This delete() method works adequately for this application, but it would be better if it accepted an id that uniquely identified the Task object. Then, this code could find the matching Task object in the array and remove it. However, for that approach to work, the Task object needs to have a unique identifier, and the Task object defined by this application doesn't have such an identifier.

The clear() method calls the clear() method of the storage object. This removes all task data from local storage.

The seventh method returns the iterator for the taskList object. The * at the beginning of this method indicates that it uses a generator function to generate the iterator object that's returned. Within this method, the code uses a for-of loop to loop through all Task objects in the tasks array. Within the loop, a yield statement returns the current Task object and pauses execution until the next() method of the iterator object is called again.

The lib_task_list.js file

```javascript
"use strict";

const tasks = Symbol("tasks");

const taskList = {
    [tasks]: [],
    load() {
        this[tasks] = storage.retrieve();
        return this;
    },
    save() {
        storage.store(this[tasks]);
        return this;
    },
    sort() {
        this[tasks].sort( (task1, task2) => {
            if (task1.dueDate < task2.dueDate) {
                return -1;
            } else if (task1.dueDate > task2.dueDate) {
                return 1;
            } else {
                return 0;
            }
        });
        return this;
    },
    add(task) {
        this[tasks].push(task);
        return this;
    },
    delete(i) {
        this.sort();
        this[tasks].splice(i, 1);
        return this;
    },
    clear() {
        storage.clear();
        return this;
    },
    *[Symbol.iterator]() {
        for (let task of this[tasks]) {
            yield task;
        }
    }
};
```

Figure 16-20   The Task List application (part 3)

Part 4 of figure 16-20 shows the main JavaScript file for this application. It begins by defining a function that displays the array of tasks that are stored in the taskList object. To start, this method calls the sort() method of the taskList object to sort the tasks by due date. This is possible because the taskList object is coded as an object literal. As a result, it's available as soon as its file is loaded. Here, sorting the tasks is necessary to make sure they're in the same order as the delete() method of the taskList object.

After sorting the tasks, this code loops through each task and constructs an HTML string. To do that, it uses a for-of loop. This is possible because the taskList object provides an iterator method. The HTML string that's generated uses an <a> element to define a Delete link for each task. Here, each href attribute has a placeholder value of "#". After the <a> element, this code uses the toString() method of the Task object to display its description and due date.

After the loop, this code displays the tasks. To do that, it passes the HTML string to the jQuery html() method of the div element that displays the tasks. Then, it adds a click() event handler to each of the <a> elements that it just added. To do this, it chains the jQuery find() and each() methods, which finds each <a> element and then loops through them.

The event handler for each <a> element is an arrow function that specifies parameters for the index of each <a> element as well as the <a> element itself. Within this function, the first statement uses the methods of the taskList object to load the tasks, delete the task at the specified index, and save the updated list of tasks to local storage. Since these three method calls are chained, they are coded on a single line. This works because these methods of the taskList object all return the taskList object. Then, the second statement displays the tasks. The third statement prevents the default action of the link. And the fourth statement sets the focus on the first text box on the page.

After the displayTasks() function, this code defines the ready() event handler. This event handler begins by defining the click() event handler for the Add Task button. To start, this click() event handler creates an object literal for a task object from the values in the two text boxes. Then, it creates a Task object by passing the object literal to the constructor of the Task class. This works because the constructor of the Task class uses destructuring to get the values of the description and dueDate properties from this object literal.

After creating the Task object, this code uses its isValid property to check whether the user entered valid data. If so, the code uses method chaining to call three methods of the taskList object to load the tasks from local storage, add the new task, and save the updated tasks array back to local storage. Then, the function displays the new list of tasks and clears both text boxes. However, if the task isn't valid, this event handler notifies the user. Regardless, the function ends by selecting the Task text box.

The click() event handler for the Clear Tasks button starts by calling the clear() method of the taskList object to remove all tasks from local storage. Then, it clears the text from the div element that displays the tasks as well as the two text boxes. Next, it sets the focus on the Task text box.

After the click() event handlers, this code loads and displays any tasks that are in local storage when the page loads. It also sets the focus on the Task text box.

The task_list.js file

```javascript
"use strict";

const displayTasks = () => {
    taskList.sort();

    let html = "";
    for (const task of taskList) {
        html += "<p><a href='#'>Delete</a>" + task.toString() + "</p>";
    }
    $("#tasks").html(html);

    // add click() event handler to each <a> element
    $("#tasks").find("a").each( (index, a) => {
        $(a).click( evt => {
            taskList.load().delete(index).save();
            displayTasks();
            evt.preventDefault();
            $("input:first").focus();
        });
    });
}

$(document).ready( () => {
    $("#add_task").click( () => {
        const taskObj = {                      // object literal
            description: $("#task").val(),
            dueDate: $("#due_date").val()
        };
        const newTask = new Task(taskObj);   // Task object

        if (newTask.isValid) {
            taskList.load().add(newTask).save();
            displayTasks();
            $("#task").val("");
            $("#due_date").val("");
        } else {
            alert("Please enter a task and/or " +
                "a due date that's in the future.");
        }
        $("#task").select();
    });

    $("#clear_tasks").click( () => {
        taskList.clear();
        $("#tasks").html("");
        $("#task").val("");
        $("#due_date").val("");
        $("#task").focus();
    });

    taskList.load()
    displayTasks();
    $("#task").focus();
});
```

Figure 16-20   The Task List application (part 4)

Perspective

Now that you've finished this chapter, you should be able to define custom objects that you can use in your applications. That should make your applications easier to maintain and your code easier to reuse. That's especially true for applications that are large or complex.

Terms

object literal	subclass
property	superclass
method	object composition
nested object	encapsulation
concise method syntax	data hiding
shorthand property notation	prototypal language
delete operator	prototype object
object reference	direct property
data property	own property
accessor property	constructor function
getter	factory function
setter	symbol
read-only property	well-known symbol
write-only property	collision
library	iterator
class	generator function
constructor	yield statement
instance	cascading method
class-based language	fluent coding
native object types	method chaining.
inheritance	destructuring

Summary

- You can create an object by coding an *object literal* with *properties* and *methods*. Within a method, the *this* keyword usually refers to the object itself.

- To *nest* one object inside another, make the inner object a property of the outer object.

- The *concise method syntax* removes boilerplate code from the traditional syntax.

- If you want to initialize a property with a variable or constant of the same name, the *shorthand property notation* provides a more concise way to do that than the traditional syntax.

- To remove a property or method from an object, you can use the *delete operator*.

- A variable or property holds a *reference* to an object, not the object itself. When you pass an object to a function, you are passing a reference to the object.

- A *data property* stores a specific item of data in memory, but an *accessor property* doesn't store data in memory. Instead, it refers to data that's stored in another property, constant, or variable. Or, it refers to a computed value.

- To code an accessor property, you code the *get* or *set* keyword followed by a method. The resulting properties are called *getters* and *setters*.

- An accessor property that only gets data is known as a *read-only property*, and an accessor property that only sets data is known as a *write-only property*.

- A JavaScript *library* is an external file that may contain related functions, objects, and classes.

- You can use a JavaScript *class* to define a *constructor* that allows you to construct an object from the class. This is also known as creating an *instance* of the class. To do that, you must use the *new* keyword.

- JavaScript provides a two-level hierarchy of *native object types*. The first level consists of the Object type. The second level consists of other types that inherit the Object type.

- *Inheritance* lets you create a new class based on an existing class. Then, the new class *inherits* the properties and methods of the existing class.

- A *subclass* is a class that inherits another class that's known as a *superclass*.

- *Object composition* is a way to combine simple objects into more complex ones.

- *Encapsulation* allows you to hide the properties or methods of an object from other code that uses the object. This is also known as *data hiding*.

- Languages that use classes to define and create objects are called *class-based* or *classical languages*.

- JavaScript is a *prototypal language* that creates objects by *cloning* them from a *prototype object*. That's true even when objects are created from classes.

- When you add a property or method to an instance of an object type, it's created directly on the instance, not on the prototype. Because of that, it's only available to that instance. This kind of property is called a *direct property* or *own property*.

- You can use an own property to *override* a method on a prototype object, but the property only overrides the method for that instance of the object.

- Prior to the *class* keyword, it was common to code a *constructor function* to create multiple instances of a custom object type.

- You can use the create() method of the Object object to create a new object that's based on a custom prototype object. You can do this within a *factory function* to create instances of the prototype object without using constructors.

- A *symbol* is a native data type that represents a unique value.

- You can use a symbol as a computed name for a property or method. That way, the name is unique and doesn't *collide* with other property or method names.

- The *well-known symbols* are used as keys for methods of the Object type. You can change how an object behaves by overriding a method for a well-known symbol.

  - An *iterator* is an object that allows you to loop through, or *iterate*, a sequence of items. An *iterable* object can be consumed by a for-of loop or by the spread operator described in the next chapter.

  - A *generator function* uses a *yield statement* to make it easier to create an object that's iterable.

  - A *cascading method* is a method of an object that can be chained with other methods of that object. This style of coding is sometimes called *fluent* because of the way it reads. It's also known as *method chaining*.

  - The *destructuring* syntax provides a way to assign the values of object properties to multiple constants or variables in a single statement.

Exercise 16-1   Enhance the Countdown application to use classes and libraries

This exercise guides you through the process of changing a procedural Countdown application that uses functions to organize its code to an object-oriented application that uses classes and objects to organize its code.

Countdown To...

Event Name: New Year's Day

Event Date: 1/1/2021

Countdown!

189 day(s) until New Year's Day! (Fri Jan 01 2021)

Open, test, and review the application

1. Use your text editor or IDE to open the application in this folder:
   `\javascript_jquery\exercises\ch16\countdown\`

2. Run the application in Chrome and test it. To do that, enter an event name, enter an event date, and click the Countdown button.

3. Review the code in the click() event handler for the Countdown button. Note that the click() event handler contains most of the code for this application. As a result, the only way to reuse this code is to copy it, which isn't a good practice.

Add two JavaScript library files

4. Add two JavaScript files to the application. Name them lib_event.js and lib_validation.js.

5. In the index.html file, add script elements to include these new files. Since the main JavaScript file will use these files, make sure to code the script elements for the library files before the script element for the main file.

Use an Event class to define an Event object

6. In the event library file, code a class named Event that has a constructor that accepts two parameters: name and dateString. Store the values of these parameters in properties of the same name.

7. Add another property named date. Set this property to a new Date object that's created from the dateString parameter.

8. Switch to the click() event handler for the Countdown button. Then, find the code that gets the event name and date from the user and modify this code so it creates an Event object from the Event class. To do that, pass the event name and date string entered by the user to the constructor of the Event class.

9. Replace the code in the click() event handler that uses the name, dateString, or date variables with code that uses the name, dateString, or date properties of the Event object.

10. Test the application to make sure it still works correctly.

11. In the Event class, add a read-only accessor property named days. Then, move the code that calculates the number of days from the click() event handler to this property, and make sure the property returns the calculated number of days.

12. In the click() event handler, modify the code so it uses the days property of the Event object instead of the days variable.

13. Test the application to make sure it still works correctly.

14. In the Event class, add a method named getCountdownMessage(). Then, move the code that displays the countdown message from the click() event handler into this method. Make sure to return a string that contains the countdown message.

15. In the click() event handler, modify the code so it uses the getCoundownMessage() property of the Event object to get the countdown message. Then, display the countdown message on the web page.

16. Test the application to make sure these changes work correctly.

Move the validation code to the validation library file

17. In the validation library file, code an object literal named validation with four methods named isEmpty(), hasNoSlashes(), isInvalidYear(), and isInvalid-Date(). Each method should accept one parameter named val.

18. Code the isEmpty() method so it returns true if the string argument it receives is empty. Otherwise, return false.

19. In the click() event handler, find the code that checks the length of the event name and date string, and replace that code with calls to the isEmpty() method of the validation object.

20. Test the application to make sure it still works correctly.

21. Repeat the previous three steps for the hasNoSlashes(), isInvalidYear(), and isInvalidDate() methods of the validation object. When you're done, the click() event handler should use these methods to check for slashes, a 4-digit year, and an invalid date.

Exercise 16-2 Enhance the Test Scores application to use an object literal

This exercise guides you through the process of changing a procedural Test Scores application to an object-oriented application that uses an object literal to organize its code.

Open, test, and review the application

1. Use your text editor or IDE to open the application in this folder:
   `\javascript_jquery\exercises\ch16\test_scores\`

2. Run the application in Chrome and test it. To do that, enter four or more scores and note that the application displays the scores, the average score, and the last three scores in reverse order.

3. Review the code in the click() event handler for the Add Score button. Note that it contains most of the code for this application. As a result, the only way to reuse this code is to copy it, which isn't a good practice.

Add a JavaScript library file

4. Add a JavaScript file named lib_test_scores.js to the application.

5. In the index.html file, add a script element that includes this new file. Since the main JavaScript file will use this file, make sure to code the script element for the library file before the script element for the main file.

Use an object literal to define a testScores object

6. In the test scores library file, code an object literal and assign it to a constant named testStores.

7. In the object literal, add a property named _scores and initialize it to an empty array.

8. In the object literal, add a method named add() that accepts a score and adds it to the _scores array if it is a number from 0 to 100. Otherwise, throw an exception with an appropriate message. To do this, you can copy some code from the click() event handler for the Add Score button.

9. In the object literal, add read-only properties named total, length, avg, and lastThree. These properties should get the total of all test scores, the length of the _scores property, the average test score, and the last three test scores.

10. In the object literal, add a method named toString() that displays all test scores, separating each score with a comma and a space.

11. In the main application file, delete the statement that creates the array named scores. Then, replace all code that uses the scores array with code that uses the testScores object literal. Note how this makes the code in the ready() event handler shorter and easier to understand.

12. Test the application to make sure it still works correctly.

13. In the click() event handler, remove the if statement that validates the test score that's entered by the user.

14. Test the application by entering an invalid test score such as "x" or 200. Since the add() method of the testScore object doesn't add invalid scores, this should not add the test score. Instead, it should display the exception that's thrown by the add() method on the console.

15. Restore the if statement that validates the user entry. This prevents the add() method of the testScores object from throwing an exception, which is usually what you want.

16. Test the application to make sure it still works correctly.

Add an iterator to the testScores object

17. At the end of the click() event handler, add a for-of statement that attempts to display each score in the testScores object on the console like this:

```
for (const score of testScores) {
    console.log(score);
}
```

18. Test the application by adding a valid score. The console should display an error message that indicates that the testScores object is not iterable.

19. In the testScores object, add a generator function that defines the iterator() method. Within this method, the code can use a yield statement within a for-of loop to return each score in the _scores property.

20. Test the application again by adding one or more valid scores. This time, the console should display each valid score on the console.

Section 4

Take it to the next level

The first three sections of this book have presented all the essential skills
that you need for building client-side JavaScript applications. Now, section
4 presents skills that will take your JavaScript coding to the next level.

To start, chapter 17 presents more skills for working with functions.
It also shows how to use closures and modules to provide private state for
your objects.

Then, chapter 18 shows how to build asynchronous JavaScript
applications that let you update your web pages without reloading the
entire page. This is known as Ajax (Asynchronous JavaScript and XML),
and it's used by the biggest and most popular websites.

Last, chapter 19 shows you how to use Node.js to write JavaScript
code that runs on a server. In other words, it shows how to use JavaScript to
write server-side applications. This works because many server-side tasks
should be executed asynchronously, and JavaScript and Node.js provide
many features that support that.

17

How to work with functions, closures, and modules

Chapter 4 presented the basics of working with functions. Now, this chapter reviews those basics and expands on them. In addition, it describes how to use closures and modules to provide private state for your objects.

When coding functions, you should know that there are some subtle differences in how functions work that depend on whether the code uses regular mode or strict mode. Since it's generally considered a best practice to use strict mode, the examples in this chapter assume that you're using strict mode.

Basic skills for working with functions

This topic begins by reviewing the skills for creating functions that were presented in chapter 4. Then, it adds a few more basic skills.

How to create a function

A *function* is a block of statements that performs an action. It can define *parameters* and return a value by issuing a *return statement*. Once you've defined a function, you can call it from other portions of your JavaScript code.

Chapter 4 showed how to code function declarations, function expressions, and arrow functions. Figure 17-1 reviews the syntax for each type of function.

To code a *function declaration*, you start with the *function* keyword followed by the name of the function. After the function name, you code a list of parameters in parentheses and the function body in braces.

To code a *function expression*, you start with the *const* keyword followed by the name of the constant that stores the function. Then, you code an assignment operator, the *function* keyword, a list of parameters in parentheses, the function body in braces, and a semicolon after the closing brace.

To code an *arrow function*, you start with the *const* keyword followed by the name of the constant that stores the function. Then, you code an assignment operator, a list of parameters in parentheses, the *arrow operator* (=>), the function body in braces, and a semicolon after the closing brace.

With an arrow function, you can sometimes omit some elements of the full syntax. For example, when an arrow function has only one parameter, you can omit the parentheses around the parameter list. And when it has only one statement in the function body, you can omit the braces and the return statement (if any).

After you code a function, you call it with code that's similar for a function declaration, a function expression, or an arrow function. In this figure, the first three examples all define a function named $() that works much like the jQuery $() function. As a result, the fourth example can be used to call any of the $() functions defined by the previous examples.

Function declarations are *hoisted* when the script first runs, and the function definition is stored in memory. Because of that, function declarations can be coded after statements that call them. Even so, this is generally considered to be a bad practice. Function expressions and arrow functions, by contrast, aren't hoisted. As a result, they must be coded before any statements that call them.

Functions can break a large block of code into many smaller blocks of code. This has several benefits. First, a smaller block of code can be easier to read and understand. Second, you can break out general-purpose functions that can be re-used in many projects. For example, you can have a function that retrieves a value from any text box, or a function that displays any error message. And third, if you name your functions well, they can make the code that uses them easier to understand. This should become clear as you progress through this chapter.

A function declaration

The syntax

```
function functionName(parameters) {
    // statements that run when the function is executed
}
```

An example

```
function $(selector) {
    return document.querySelector(selector);
}
```

A function expression

The syntax

```
const constantName = function(parameters) {
    // statements that run when the function is executed
};
```

An example

```
const $ = function(selector) {
    return document.querySelector(selector);
};
```

An arrow function

The full syntax

```
const constantName = (parameterList) => {
    // statements that run when the function is executed
};
```

An example of the full syntax

```
const $ = (selector) => {
    return document.querySelector(selector);
};
```

An abbreviated syntax for one parameter and one statement

```
const constantName = parameter => statement;
```

An example of the abbreviated syntax

```
const $ = selector => document.querySelector(selector);
```

How to call these functions

```
const email1 = $("#email_1").value;
```

Description

- A *function* contains a block of code that can be *called* (or *invoked*) by other statements in the program.

- A *function declaration* is a function that starts with the *function* keyword.

- A *function expression* uses the *function* keyword to create a function that can be assigned to a constant.

- An *arrow function* uses the *arrow operator* (=>) to create a function.

Figure 17-1   How to create a function

How to work with default parameters

So far, this book has presented functions that require the calling statement to pass one value for each parameter. But what if you omit a parameter when you call a function? In that case, the value of the parameter is undefined, which isn't usually what you want.

To make sure a parameter value isn't undefined, you can code your functions to check for undefined parameters before they're used. To do that, you can check for falsey values as described in chapter 13. Or, if you want to check specifically for the undefined value, you can use the typeof operator, like this:

```
if(typeof parameterName == "undefined") { ... }
```

However, you often know that you want to use a default value when the calling code doesn't supply a parameter value. To do that, you can assign that default value when you code the parameter as shown in figure 17-2.

The first example presents an arrow function named calculateTax() that provides a default value of 0.074 for its taxRate parameter. As a result, if the calling code doesn't pass a value to the taxRate parameter, the function uses the default tax rate of 0.074. On the other hand, if the calling code passes a value to this parameter, the function uses that value. This is shown by the first two statements that call this function.

The third and fourth statements show what happens if you pass null or undefined as a parameter. Because JavaScript considers null to be a valid value, the calculateTax() function doesn't use the default value when the calling code passes null. Instead, it uses null in the calculation and returns a value of 0. On the other hand, JavaScript considers undefined to be an invalid value. Because of that, the fourth statement causes the function to use the default value.

A default value can be a literal value, a constant, a variable, or an expression. In addition, you can use an earlier parameter as a default value for a later parameter. In an arrow function, if you provide a default value for a single parameter, you must enclose that parameter in parentheses as shown by the second example.

The third example shows that a function can have more than one default parameter in a parameter list. To pass a value for a parameter that's later in the parameter list, though, you must provide values for the parameters that come before it. For instance, the fourth call to the toPlaces() function returns a value of NaN because it assigns a value of "floor" to the places parameter, which expects a number. To pass "floor" so it's assigned to the type parameter, the code needs to pass a value to the places parameter. That's why the fifth call to this function passes a value of undefined. This causes the function to use the default value of 2 for the places parameter.

Unlike many other programming languages, JavaScript doesn't require you to code the default parameters at the end of the parameter list. However, it's generally considered a good practice to do that. That way, you don't need to pass a value of undefined to optional parameters before you pass values to the required parameters.

A function with a default parameter

```
const calculateTax = (subtotal, taxRate = 0.074) => {
    const tax = subtotal * taxRate;
    return tax.toFixed(2);
}
```

Code that calls the function

```
const tax1 = calculateTax(100);                    // tax1 is 7.40
const tax2 = calculateTax(100, 0.087);             // tax2 is 8.70
const tax3 = calculateTax(100, null);              // tax3 is 0.00
const tax4 = calculateTax(100, undefined);         // tax4 is 7.40
```

An arrow function with a single parameter and a default value

```
const getPI = (places = 15) => {
    return Math.round(Math.PI * (10 ** places) ) / (10 ** places);
};
```

Code that calls the function

```
const pi = getPI();                   // pi is 3.141592653589793
const pi2 = getPI(4);                 // pi2 is 3.1416
```

A function with two parameters that have default values

```
const toPlaces = (num, places = 2, type = "round") => {
    if (type == "floor") {
        return Math.floor(num * (10 ** places) ) / (10 ** places);
    } else if (type == "ceil") {
        return Math.ceil(num * (10 ** places) ) / (10 ** places);
    } else {
        return Math.round(num * (10 ** places) ) / (10 ** places);
    }
};
```

Code that calls the function

```
const num1 = toPlaces(5.22873);                    // num1 is 5.23
const num2 = toPlaces(5.22873, 4);                 // num2 is 5.2287
const num3 = toPlaces(5.22873, 4, "ceil");         // num3 is 5.2288
const num4 = toPlaces(5.22873, "floor");           // num4 is NaN
const num5 = toPlaces(5.22873, undefined, "floor"); // num5 is 5.22
```

Description

- You can assign a default value to a function parameter. Then, if the code that calls the function doesn't provide a value for that parameter, the function uses the default value.

- The default value can be a literal value or an expression. Parameters that come later in the parameter list can use the value of earlier parameters as their default value.

- If you pass a null value to a function, it is used instead of the default value. By contrast, if you pass an undefined value, it isn't used instead of the default value.

- In an arrow function, a single parameter with a default value must be in parentheses.

- A function can define multiple parameters with default values. These parameters aren't required to be coded at the end of the parameter list, though they usually are.

- To preserve the default values of earlier parameters, you can pass undefined.

Figure 17-2   How to work with default parameters

How to use the rest and spread operators

In chapter 15 you learned how to use the *rest operator* (. . .) with arrays. Now, figure 17-3 shows how to use the rest operator in a function to define a *rest parameter* that collects one or more values into an array. This provides a nice syntax for defining a function that accepts a varying number of parameters, which is known as a *variadic function*.

The first example in this figure defines a calculateTaxAll() function. This function has a taxRate parameter and a subtotals parameter that's prepended with the rest operator. Because of the rest operator, any parameters coded after the taxRate parameter are collected in the subtotals parameter as elements in an array. In the body of the function, the code loops through this array to calculate the tax for each subtotal amount and adds it to the overall tax amount.

When you code a rest parameter, you can only code one, and it must be the last parameter in the list. In other words, a rest parameter collects the *rest* of the values that are passed to the function.

The second example shows how to call the calculateTaxAll() function. Here, the first three statements call the function with varying numbers of parameters. Then, the fourth and fifth statements show how to use the *spread operator* (. . .) to call a variadic function. The fourth statement creates a new array named taxRateAndAmounts and initializes it with five values. Then, the fifth statement passes this array to the calculateTaxAll() function. However, since this array is prepended with the spread operator, JavaScript passes the array elements as individual parameters. In other words, the elements in the array are *spread* out into individual parameters.

The next three statements show how to use multiple spread operators when you call a function. Note that these spread operators don't need to come at the end of the parameter list. In addition, they can be mixed with literal values. Here, the code that calls the calculateTaxAll() function prepends the two arrays with the spread operator and passes a final parameter that's a numeric literal. This produces the same result as passing the values individually.

Although these examples use the spread operator with variadic functions, the spread operator can also be used with non-variadic functions. For example, this code calls the toPlaces() function that's in the previous figure:

```
const argsArray = [5.22873, 4, "ceil"];
const num6 = toPlaces(...argsArray);          // num6 is 5.2288
```

The third example shows the definition for a function expression that performs the same task as the arrow function in the first example. To do that, the function expression uses its arguments property. This arguments property is similar to an array. However, it isn't a true Array object. As a result, you can't use all of the properties and methods of an array that are presented in chapter 15.

In the past, developers commonly used the arguments property to create variadic functions and set default values. However, now that modern JavaScript supports rest parameters and default values, it's generally considered a better practice to use them instead of the arguments property. In fact, some browsers are deprecating the arguments property. Still, it's often used in legacy code and online examples.

An arrow function with a rest parameter

```
const calculateTaxAll = (taxRate, ...subtotals) => {
    let tax = 0;
    for (let subtotal of subtotals) {    // rest parameter provides an array
        tax += subtotal * taxRate;
    }
    return tax.toFixed(2);
}
```

How to call this function

With a list of parameters

```
const tax1 = calculateTaxAll(0.074, 100);                     // tax1 is 7.40
const tax2 = calculateTaxAll(0.074, 100, 200);                // tax2 is 22.20
const tax3 = calculateTaxAll(0.074, 100, 200, 400, 500);   // tax3 is 88.80
```

With a single spread operator

```
const taxRateAndAmounts = [0.074, 100, 200, 400, 500];
const tax4 = calculateTaxAll(...taxRateAndAmounts);        // tax4 is 88.80
```

With multiple spread operators

```
const rateAndAmounts = [0.074, 100];
const moreAmounts = [200, 400];
const tax5 = calculateTaxAll(...rateAndAmounts, ...moreAmounts, 500);
// tax5 is 88.80
```

A regular function that uses the arguments property (not recommended)

```
const calculateTaxAll = function() {
    const taxRate = arguments[0];
    let tax = 0;
    for (let i = 1; i < arguments.length; i++) {
        const subtotal = arguments[i];
        tax += subtotal * taxRate;
    }
    return tax.toFixed(2);
}
```

Description

- You can use the *rest operator* (...) to accept a variable number of parameters and put them in an array. The parameter with the rest operator is called a *rest parameter*.

- A function can only define one rest parameter, and it must be the last parameter in the parameter list.

- You can use the *spread operator* (...) to pass the elements in an array to a variadic function as individual parameters. A function call can use more than one spread operator, and the spread operator doesn't need to be the last argument.

- Regular functions (function declarations or function expressions) have an arguments property that stores the arguments passed to a function in an array-like object. Legacy code sometimes uses this arguments property to create variadic functions.

Figure 17-3   How to use the rest and spread operators

How to work with the *this* keyword

So far, this book has shown how to use the *this* keyword within the methods of an object to refer to that object. However, in a regular function (a function declaration or function expression), the value of *this* depends on how the function is called. This works differently than many other programming languages and has caused a lot of confusion over the years. Because of that, recent versions of the EMCAScript specification attempt to make working with the *this* keyword easier.

To start, the *this* keyword works differently for arrow functions than it does for regular functions. That's because an arrow function doesn't have its own *this* keyword. Instead, it always uses *this* to refer to its containing environment.

Regular functions, by contrast, each store their own value for the *this* keyword. Further, as figure 17-4 shows, the value for the *this* keyword depends on how it's called. For example, if you code a regular function as a method of an object and call it from that object, *this* stores the current object. However, if you code a regular function as an event handler and call it by raising an event, *this* stores the object that raised the event.

In JavaScript, a regular function has methods that work with the *this* keyword, including the three methods shown in this figure. When you use one of these methods, you use the first argument to specify the value of *this* for the function. These methods also let you pass any other arguments that the function might need.

In general, though, it's a better practice to use arrow functions as shown later in this chapter. However, if you're maintaining legacy code and you encounter the call(), apply(), or bind() method, please read on.

One traditional use of the call() and apply() methods is to "borrow" functionality from other objects. For instance, the first example shows how to use the call() method to borrow the join() method of the Array object to work with the function's arguments property. This is necessary because the arguments property isn't an array and doesn't provide its own join() method.

The second example shows how to use the apply() method to work with the Math.max() method. Here, the code passes null for the first parameter because the value of *this* doesn't matter for the max() method, and the second parameter passes an array of numbers. This works even though the max() method expects individual numbers, not an array. These days, you can accomplish the same task more simply by using a spread operator.

The bind() method of a function lets you specify the value of *this* at the time that the function is defined or assigned, rather than when it's called. One traditional use of the bind() method is to work with closures.

The value of the *this* keyword in a regular function

How function is called	Value of the *this* keyword
Normal function call	Undefined in strict mode. Otherwise, the window object.
As a method of an object	The object that contains the function.
As an event handler	The object that raised the event such as a button that was clicked.

Methods of a function for specifying the value of *this*

Method	Description
call(*thisArg*[,*arg1*]...)	Calls a function, sets the value of *this* for the function, and passes zero or more values to the function.
apply(*thisArg*,*argArray*)	Calls a function, sets the value of *this* for the function, and passes an array of values to the function.
bind(*thisArg*[,*arg1*]...)	Binds the value of *this* to a function. Then, the value of *this* can't be changed later.

How to use the call() method to "borrow" a method from the Array object

```
const displayArguments = function() {
    const display = Array.prototype.join.call(arguments, " ");
    console.log(display);
};
displayArguments("Michael", "R", "Murach");  // Displays "Michael R Murach"
```

How to use the apply() method to pass an array to the Math.max() method

```
const scores = [89,78,99,92,87];
const highScore = Math.max.apply(null, scores);  // highScore is 99
```

Description

- An arrow function doesn't have its own *this* keyword. Instead, it always uses *this* to refer to its containing environment.

- A regular function stores its own value for the *this* keyword and that value depends on how the function is called.

- In legacy code, regular functions sometimes use the call(), apply(), and bind() methods to control the value of the *this* keyword. For new code, it's generally considered a better practice to use newer JavaScript features such as arrow functions and rest parameters.

- With regular functions, the call() and apply() methods can be used to "borrow" methods from another object such as the Array object.

Figure 17-4   How to use the *this* keyword

The Test Scores application

The Test Scores application presented in this chapter is an update of the application presented in chapter 15. It accepts a variable number of scores from the user and displays the average score, high score, low score, last three scores, and all scores.

The HTML and CSS

Part 1 of figure 17-5 shows the HTML for the main element of the Test Scores application. It contains label elements to display scores, a text box that allows the user to enter a score, and a button that adds the score. When the user adds a new score, the application recalculates and redisplays the information about the scores.

After the button, this HTML includes a <p> element that's used to display any error messages. This application uses a <p> element rather than a span element because a paragraph automatically starts on a new line with spacing between it and the previous element. Additionally, this <p> element doesn't have an id attribute because the jQuery code can find it based on its sibling relationship with the button element.

The CSS snippet below the HTML in this figure shows the style rule for the <p> element. This style rule displays the text for the <p> element in red.

The Test Scores application

> # My Test Scores
>
> Average score: 90.00
>
> High score: 98
>
> Low score: 77
>
> Last 3 scores: 98, 94, 77
>
> All scores: 90, 89, 93, 91, 91, 87, 77, 94, 98
>
> Enter new score: [   ]   [Add Score]

The HTML

```html
<main>
    <h1>My Test Scores</h1>
    <div>
        <label>Average score:</label>
        <label id="avg"></label>
    </div>
    <div>
        <label>High score:</label>
        <label id="high"></label>
    </div>
    <div>
        <label>Low score:</label>
        <label id="low"></label>
    </div>
    <div>
        <label>Last 3 scores:</label>
        <label id="last"></label>
    </div>
    <div>
        <label>All scores:</label>
        <span id="all"></span>
    </div>
    <div>
        <label for="score">Enter new score:</label>
        <input type="text" id="score">
        <input type="button" id="add_score" value="Add Score">
        <p></p>
    </div>
</main>
```

Some of the CSS

```css
p {
    color: red;
}
```

Figure 17-5   The Test Scores application (part 1)

The JavaScript

Part 2 of figure 17-5 presents the JavaScript for the Test Scores application. After the "use strict" declaration, this code defines three helper functions for the application. These functions are all arrow functions.

The isInvalid() function accepts a score and returns true if that score is a number from 1 to 100. If you wanted, you could make this function more general purpose by passing the minimum and maximum values as parameters and setting default values for them.

The getAverage() function accepts an array of scores and uses the reduce() method of the array to get a total. Then, it divides the total value by the number of scores in the array and returns the resulting value. This function is general purpose and could be used with any array of numeric values.

The getLast() function accepts an array of scores and a parameter named num that specifies how many scores to return. Here, the num parameter has a default value of 3. The body of the function starts by using the spread operator to make a copy of the array of scores. Then, it uses the reverse() method to reverse the order of the elements in the array. As a result, the last score entered by the user is now the first score in the array, the second to last is now second, and so on. Finally, the code uses the slice() method to return an array that contains elements in the scores array from the first element to the number in the num parameter. Again, this function is general purpose and could be used with any array.

After the three helper functions, the jQuery ready() event handler starts by declaring an array named scores. Then, it adds a click() event handler to the Add Score button. This event handler is a regular function, not an arrow function. As a result, the *this* keyword refers to the element that raised the event. In this case, that element is the Add Score button.

Within the event handler, the code starts by getting the value entered by the user and uses the isInvalid() function to check whether the score is invalid. If so, the code displays an error message. Otherwise, the code removes any previous error messages. To do that, it uses the *this* keyword to get the Add Score button. Remember, this works because the event handler is a regular function. Then, it passes the *this* keyword to the jQuery $() function, so the code can use the next() method to get the <p> element that follows the button.

If the score is valid, the code adds the new score to the scores array and updates the calculations. For the high and low scores, it uses the spread operator to pass the scores array to the Math.max() and Math.min() methods. For the average score, it passes the scores array to the getAverage() function. For the last three scores, it passes the scores array to the getLast() function but doesn't pass a value for the second parameter. As a result, the function uses the default value of 3. Finally to display all the scores, it calls the join() method. Note how the helper functions make this code short and readable.

The click() event handler ends by clearing any previous score from the text box and setting the focus on the text box. Then, the ready() event handler ends by also setting the focus on the text box.

The JavaScript

```
"use strict";

const isInvalid = score => isNaN(score) || score < 1 || score > 100;

const getAverage = arr => {
    const total = arr.reduce( (tot, val) => tot + val, 0 );
    return total/arr.length;
};

const getLast = (arr, num = 3) => {
    const copy = [...arr];
    copy.reverse();
    return copy.slice(0, num);
};

$(document).ready( () => {

    const scores = [];

    $("#add_score").click( function() {

        const score = parseFloat($("#score").val());

        if (isInvalid(score)) {
            $(this).next().text("Score must be between 1 and 100.");
        }
        else {
            $(this).next().text("");    // remove any previous error message

            // add to array and update calculations
            scores.push(score);

            $("#high").text(Math.max(...scores));
            $("#low").text(Math.min(...scores));
            $("#last").text(getLast(scores).join(", "));
            $("#avg").text(getAverage(scores).toFixed(2));
            $("#all").text(scores.join(", "));
        }

        // get text box ready for next entry
        $("#score").val("");
        $("#score").focus();
    });

    // set focus on initial load
    $("#score").focus();
});
```

Description

- The click() event handler for the Add Score button is a regular function, so its *this* keyword holds a reference to the Add Score button.

- The spread operator passes the values in the scores array as individual parameter values to the variadic max() and min() methods of the Math object.

Figure 17-5   The Test Scores application (part 2)

How to work with closures

Closures are a powerful feature of the JavaScript language. Unfortunately, they can be hard to understand. The figures that follow describe what closures are and how to use them.

An introduction to closures

In chapter 4, you learned about *scope*, which refers to the visibility of JavaScript objects. In brief, a variable, constant, or function that's created outside a function has *global scope*, so it can be seen and used by any other JavaScript object. In contrast, a variable, constant, or function that's created inside a function has *local scope*, so it can only be seen and used inside its function.

To understand closures, you need to understand two more things about scope. First, an object has access to its own scope as well as to the scope of the object that contains it. This is called the *scope chain*.

Second, if an object in the scope chain has something that refers to it, it stays *in scope* even if the object that contains it is *out of scope*. The most common way to create such a reference is to create a *closure*, which is when an outer function returns an inner function that refers to something in the outer function's scope.

Figure 17-6 shows how this works. To start, an outer function named createClickCounter() contains a variable named count that's set to zero. It also contains an inner function named clickCounter() that increments the outer count variable by one. In addition, this inner function logs the id of the element that was clicked and the current value of the count variable. After that, the outer createClickCounter() function returns the definition of the inner clickCounter() function. To do that, it specifies the name of the function, but not the parentheses that come after the function.

To understand this code, it's important to note that the count variable is in the outer function, not the inner function. As a result, when the outer function returns the definition of the inner function, the count variable stays "alive". That's because the inner function has a reference to the count variable.

After the function definitions, the ready() event handler assigns click() event handlers to two buttons. However, these event handlers work a little differently than what you're used to. That's because they call the createClickCounter() function by including parentheses after it.

When the createClickCounter() function is called, JavaScript creates its count variable and initializes it to zero. Then, it creates its inner clickCounter() function definition and assigns it to the button's event handler. At that point, the createClickCounter() function finishes and goes out of scope. However, the inner function refers to the outer function's count variable, and the button refers to the inner function. As a result, the count variable stays in scope, even though the createClickCounter() function that contains it goes out of scope.

In addition, each button has a separate version of the count variable in its scope chain. That's because the createClickCounter() function is called twice, once for each button. So, each button has access to a different internal count variable that keeps track of how many times it has been clicked.

An example that illustrates a closure

```
const createClickCounter = () => {  // outer function
    let count = 0;                    // local variable

    const clickCounter = evt => {    // inner function
        count++;
        console.log(evt.currentTarget.id + " count is " + count);
    };
    return clickCounter;
};

$(document).ready( () => {
    $("#first_button").click(createClickCounter());
    $("#second_button").click(createClickCounter());
});
```

The Console panel after clicking the two buttons several times

```
first_button count is 1
second_button count is 1
second_button count is 2
second_button count is 3
first_button count is 2
```

Description

- The *scope chain* in JavaScript refers to what is *in scope*, or what can be seen and used by an object.

- An object that is created within another object has access to its own scope as well as the scope of the object that contains it.

- An object in the scope chain is available, or "alive", as long as something is referring to it. This is true even if the object that contains it has finished executing and is *out of scope*.

- A *closure* is created when an inner function refers to one or more objects in the scope of the outer function that contains it.

Figure 17-6   An introduction to closures

This also means that each count variable is available in the scope chain of the button that it's attached to but nowhere else. So, if you try to access it directly, JavaScript throws an exception. This protects each internal count variable from being changed or deleted by other code.

The screen in figure 17-6 shows Chrome's Console panel after the two buttons named first_button and second_button have been clicked a few times each. Note that clicking one button doesn't affect the count of the other.

How to use closures to create private state

Chapter 7 presented a slide show application with all of its code in the DOMContentLoaded event handler. In the real world, most of that code would be in a separate JavaScript file. In that case, though, if you use standard functions or objects in the file, they are global and can be called and even overwritten or deleted by other code. That can be a problem if you're creating a library that you intend to use with other JavaScript libraries. One way to get around that problem is to use closures to create *private state* to protect these objects.

To illustrate, the first example in figure 17-7 presents a function named createSlideShow() that contains several variables, constants, and functions and returns an object with three methods. For now, the code in the functions and methods isn't shown. This allows the figure to focus on where the variables, constants, functions, and methods are placed in the code.

To start, this function declares several variables and constants that hold values that the slide show needs. Then, this code creates two inner functions that perform actions that the slide show needs. Because these variables, constants, and functions are coded inside the outer function, they have local scope. This means that they are available to the other objects within the outer function, but they can't be called by code outside that outer function. In other words, they are private.

After defining the private variables, constants, and functions, this code creates and returns an object literal that contains three methods. These methods are inner functions that refer to the variables, constants, and functions of the outer function. In other words, they are closures. Returning an object with methods like this is a common way to return more than one inner function from an outer function.

The second example calls the createSlideShow() function and stores the object it returns in a constant named slideShow. Then, it calls the loadImages() method and passes it an array of slides. As long as the slideShow constant is alive, the variables, constants, and functions in the createSlideShow() function are also alive, even though the createSlideShow() function has completed and is out of scope. In addition, there's no way to directly access the private variables, constants, and functions of this function. You can only access them indirectly by calling the public methods from the object that's returned by this function.

A function that creates a closure with private state

```
const createSlideShow = () => {
    // private variables and constants
    let timer = null;
    let play = true;
    let speed = 2000;
    const nodes = { image: null, caption: null };
    const img = { cache: [], counter: 0 };

    // private functions
    const stopSlideShow = () => { ... };
    const displayNextImage = () => { ... };

    return {                                    // a public object
        loadImages(slides) { ... },             // public method #1
        startSlideShow(image, caption) { ... }, // public method #2
        getToggleHandler(){ ... }               // public method #3
    };
};
```

Code that creates and uses the slide show object returned by the function

```
const slideShow = createSlideShow();   // create the slideShow object
slideShow.loadImages(slides);          // call a public method from it
```

Description

- All variables, constants, and functions in global scope are publically available.

- All the properties and methods of a JavaScript object that's in global scope are publically available. That means that critical objects can be overwritten or deleted.

- To protect the variables, constants, and functions of an object, you can use closures to create *private state*.

- You can create a closure by returning an inner function that refers to objects in the outer function.

- To return multiple inner functions, you can return an object that contains the inner functions as its methods.

Figure 17-7 How to use closures to create private state in objects

How to work with the *this* keyword in closures

As you've seen, an inner function has access to the scope of the outer function that contains it. However, with regular functions, this doesn't apply to the value of an outer function's *this* keyword. That's because the outer function and the inner function each has its own *this* keyword. This can cause problems when the inner function needs to refer to the value of *this* in the outer function.

The easiest way to fix this problem is to use an arrow function for the inner function. Remember, an arrow function doesn't have its own *this* value. So, it uses the value of *this* from the function that contains it, which is the outer function.

The first example in figure 17-8 shows how this works. Here, an object literal named item has a method named displayFullPrice() that returns a function definition that needs to access the current object and the event target. Since this function is an arrow function, the *this* keyword refers to the containing environment. In this case, that's the item object. As a result, the function can call the calc() method from *this*. In addition, this function uses the currentTarget property of its Event object to get the id of the target of the event. In this case, that's the button that's clicked.

In general, using an arrow function is considered the best practice for writing this type of code. That's because the *this* keyword works consistently by always referring to the containing environment. In addition, using the currentTarget property of the Event object makes the code easy to understand.

If you attempted to use a regular function for the inner function, the *this* keyword would refer to the button that was clicked, not the item object. As a result, there would be no way to access the current object.

Before arrow functions, though, some programmers would solve this problem by calling the bind() method of the inner function to make sure that the value of *this* in the inner function was the same as the outer function. Other programmers would solve this problem by storing the value of *this* in the outer function in a constant or variable. Then, because the inner function has access to the outer function's scope, it has access to the constant or variable containing the value of *this* and to its own *this* value.

The second example shows how this second approach works. Here, the outer function stores the value of *this* in a constant named me. This adheres to a programming convention that says that when you store the value of *this* in a constant or variable, it should be named *that*, *self*, or *me*. However, since the window object has a global property named *self*, it's usually better to use a name of *that* or *me*.

You should also know that the arguments property of a function works similarly. That's because a regular function has its own arguments property. So, you can't access the outer function's arguments property from the inner function. However, you can store the outer function's arguments property in a constant or variable if an inner regular function needs to use it.

An arrow function that accesses the current object and the event target

```
const item = {
    rate: 0.075,
    calc(subtotal) {
        return (subtotal + (subtotal * this.rate)).toFixed(2);
    },
    displayFullPrice(subtotal) {
        return evt => {
            console.log(
                `Full price for ${evt.currentTarget.id} = ${
                    this.calc(subtotal)}`);
        };
    }
};
```

A regular function that performs the same task (not recommended)

```
const item = {
    rate: 0.075,
    calc(subtotal) {
        return (subtotal + (subtotal * this.rate)).toFixed(2);
    },
    displayFullPrice(subtotal) {
        const me = this;      // store the current object as 'me'
        return function() {
            console.log(       // use 'this' to access current event target
                `Full price for ${this.id} = ${me.calc(subtotal)}`);
        };
    }
};
```

Code that attaches the inner function as an event handler for a button

```
$("#camera").click(item.displayFullPrice(125));
```

The text that's displayed when you click the button

```
Full price for camera = 134.38
```

Description

- An arrow function doesn't have its own *this* keyword. Because of that, the value of *this* for an inner arrow function is the value of the outer function's *this* keyword.

- By contrast, a regular function does have its own *this* keyword. Because of that, an inner regular function can't access the outer function's *this* keyword.

- One way to make the outer function's *this* keyword available to an inner regular function is to pass it to that inner function's bind() method. In most cases, though, it's better to just use an arrow function.

- Another way to make the outer function's *this* keyword available to an inner regular function is to store it in a constant or variable that's traditionally named *that*, *self*, or *me*. In most cases, though, it's better to just use an arrow function.

Figure 17-8   How to work with the *this* keyword in closures

The Slide Show application

Now that you know how closures work, this chapter shows a version of the Slide Show application of chapter 7 after it has been rewritten to use closures. This protects the variables, constants, and functions the application needs for its internal operations.

The HTML

Figure 17-9 begins by showing the HTML for this version of the Slide Show application. In the main element, you can see an img element whose id is "image" and a span element whose id is "caption". These elements display the image and caption for the current slide.

In addition, this HTML includes a button element whose id is "play_pause". As its name suggests, this button allows a user to play a slide show that's paused and to pause a slide show that's playing.

Unlike the application in chapter 7, this one doesn't code the images of the slide show in the HTML. Instead, this application uses JavaScript to load information about the images in the slide show as shown by part 3 of this figure.

The Slide Show application in the browser

The HTML

```
<main>
    <h1>Fishing Slide Show</h1>
    <p><img id="image"></p>
    <h2 id="caption"></h2>
    <p><input type="button" id="play_pause" value="Pause"></p>
</main>
```

Description

- This Slide Show application is an updated version of the one you saw in chapter 7.
- This version has a Pause button that allows the user to stop the slide show on the image currently in the browser. Then, the button's text changes from "Pause" to "Resume", and the user can click the Resume button to start the slide show again.
- This version has been rewritten to use closures. This provides private state for its internal variables, constants, and functions, which protects them from being overwritten by outside code.

Figure 17-9   The Slide Show application (part 1)

The JavaScript

Part 2 of figure 17-9 presents the JavaScript in the lib_slide_show.js file. This code starts with a function named createSlideShow(). This function declares a timer variable, a Boolean play variable, a numeric speed variable, a nodes constant that's an object literal, and an img constant that's an object literal. Because these variables and constants are inside the outer createSlideShow() function, they have local scope. That means they can't be accessed by code outside the function, so they can't be changed or deleted by outside code.

After declaring the private variables and constants, this code defines the stopSlideShow() and displayNextImage() functions. These functions contain code similar to the code presented in chapter 7. Like the variables and constants above them, these functions are private because they are inside the createSlide-Show() function. However, they have access to the outer function's scope, so they can still use all the private variables and constants.

After creating the private variables, constants, and functions the slide show needs for its internal operations, the outer function creates and returns an object literal that has three methods: loadImages(), startSlideShow(), and getToggle-Handler(). Each of these methods refers to the private variables, constants, and functions defined earlier, so those variables and functions stay alive as long as the object returned by the createSlideShow() function stays alive. The first two methods also use the *this* keyword to return the current object. This allows these methods to be chained.

The loadImages() method has code that is similar to code presented in chapter 7. However, this version gets information about the images in the slide show from the slides parameter rather than from an element in the page.

The startSlideShow() method starts by checking if any arguments were sent to it. If so, the method stores information from those arguments in its private constants and variables. This is how the slide show gets information about the img and span elements that it displays the slides in. After that, this method calls the displayNextImage() function to start the slide show. Then, it passes the definition of the displayNextImage() function and the speed variable to the setInterval() function to show the next image at the specified interval and stores the timer object in the private timer variable.

The getToggleHandler() method returns a function definition. That's because it's meant to attach an event handler to the Pause/Resume button. This method begins by checking whether the private play variable is true. If so, it calls the private stopSlideShow() function to stop the slide show. Otherwise, it calls the startSlideShow() method to start the slide show. However, because startSlide-Show() is a method of the object literal, not a private function, the code calls this method from the *this* keyword that contains a reference to the object.

After starting or stopping the slide show, the getToggleHandler() method sets the value of the button based on the value of the private play variable. After it stops or starts the slide show, this code uses the currentTarget property of the Event object to get a reference to the button. Then, it sets the appropriate text on the button. Finally, it toggles the value of the private play variable by setting it to the opposite of its current value.

The lib_slide_show.js file

```javascript
"use strict";

const createSlideShow = () => {
    // private variables and constants
    let timer = null;
    let play = true;
    let speed = 2000;
    const nodes = { image: null, caption: null };
    const img = { cache: [], counter: 0 };

    // private methods
    const stopSlideShow = () => clearInterval(timer);

    const displayNextImage = () => {
        img.counter = ++img.counter % img.cache.length;
        const image = img.cache[img.counter];
        nodes.image.attr("src", image.src);
        nodes.image.attr("alt", image.alt);
        nodes.caption.text(image.alt);
    };

    // public methods that access private state
    return {
        loadImages(slides) {
            for (let slide of slides) {
                const image = new Image();
                image.src = "images/" + slide.href;
                image.alt = slide.title;
                img.cache.push(image);
            }
            return this;  // returns object for slide show
        },
        startSlideShow(image, caption) {
            if(image && caption) {
                nodes.image = image;
                nodes.caption = caption;
            }
            displayNextImage();
            timer = setInterval(displayNextImage, speed);
            return this;  // returns object for slide show
        },
        getToggleHandler() {
            return evt => {
                if (play) {
                    stopSlideShow();
                } else {
                    this.startSlideShow();  // call method from object
                }
                const button = evt.currentTarget;
                button.value = (play) ? "Resume" : "Pause";
                play = !play;    // toggle play flag
            };
        }
    };
};
```

Figure 17-9   The Slide Show application (part 2)

Part 3 of figure 17-9 presents the JavaScript in the slide_show.js file. Here, the ready() event handler starts by calling the global createSlideShow() function to create the slideShow object. This object provides the three methods that are needed to run the slide show.

After getting the slideShow object, the ready() event handler creates an array of slide objects with information about the images for the slide show. Then, it calls the getToggleHandler() method of the slideShow object to get the function that it uses as the click() event handler for the Play/Pause button.

After setting the click() event handler for the Play/Pause button, the ready() event handler chains two of the slideShow object's methods. First, it calls the loadImages() method and passes it the array of slide objects. Then, it calls the startSlideShow() method and passes it the image and span elements that the slideShow object uses to display the slide show.

Below the code, this figure shows the slideShow object in the Watch pane of the Sources panel in Chrome's developer tools. Here, the Watch pane only displays the three public methods, plus the object's prototype object. This shows that outside code can't access variables like speed, constants like nodes, or functions like stopSlideShow() or displayNextImage(). This means that the users of the slide show library can't overwrite or delete the private variables, constants, and functions that the slideShow object needs to function properly.

The slide_show.js file

```
"use strict";

$(document).ready( () => {
    // create the slideShow object
    const slideShow = createSlideShow();

    const slides = [
        {href:"release.jpg", title:"Catch and Release"},
        {href:"deer.jpg", title:"Deer at Play"},
        {href:"hero.jpg", title:"The Big One!"},
        {href:"bison.jpg", title:"Roaming Bison"}
    ];

    $("#play_pause").click(slideShow.getToggleHandler());

    slideShow.loadImages(slides)
        .startSlideShow($("#image"), $("#caption"));
});
```

The slideShow object in the Watch pane of the Chrome developer tools

```
▼ Watch                                          +  C
▼ slideShow: Object
  ▶ getToggleHandler: getToggleHandler() { return evt => {…}
  ▶ loadImages: ƒ loadImages(slides)
  ▶ startSlideShow: ƒ startSlideShow(image, caption)
  ▶ __proto__: Object
```

Description

- In the lib_slide_show.js file, the code consists of an outer function named createSlideShow() that contains several private variables, constants, and functions. This createSlideShow() function returns an object literal with three public methods that refer to the private state of the outer function.

- In the slide_show.js file, the code calls the createSlideShow() function and stores the object it returns in a constant named slideShow. Then, it uses the methods of that object to attach an event handler for the Play/Pause button, set up the slide show, and start the slide show.

- You can examine the slideShow object in Chrome's developer tools to verify that only the three methods returned by the createSlideShow() function are available to outside code. As a result, there's no way to overwrite any of the slideShow object's private state.

Figure 17-9   The Slide Show application (part 3)

How to work with the module pattern

Many developers and third-party libraries use the *module pattern* to create a single object that has private state. To do that, you use an *immediately invoked function expression (IIFE)* to define a function expression and immediately call, or *invoke*, it. In conversation, an IIFE is commonly referred to as an "iffy."

How to code an IIFE

In most cases, you use one statement to define a function expression and a second statement to invoke it as shown by the first example in figure 17-10. With an IIFE, you use a single statement to define a function expression and invoke it. This is illustrated by the second example. Here, the code places the function expression inside parentheses and places parentheses after the expression to invoke it immediately. As a result, this code doesn't need to store the function expression in a constant as in the first example.

The term *IIFE* was coined before arrow functions were added to JavaScript. However, you can use the same technique with arrow functions as shown by the third example. That makes sense because an arrow function is a concise way to code an expression that defines a function.

You can code the parentheses of an IIFE in one of the two ways shown in the fourth example. Although some programmers have strong opinions about which one is best, both styles work, so you can choose the style that's easiest for you to understand and use. This book uses the first style.

You should also know that if an IIFE is coded after the start of a line of code, the JavaScript engine doesn't require the outside parentheses. Still, it's considered a best practice to use them because it's a programming convention that helps other programmers recognize the code as an IIFE.

IIFEs can be used to keep variables, constants, and functions out of global scope and to prevent name conflicts. For instance, the fifth example begins with an IIFE that defines a variable named message that's used to store a string. Since this variable is coded within an IIFE, it doesn't conflict with the variable named message that's coded after the IIFE.

Like any other function, you can code a parameter list for an IIFE. Then, you pass arguments to the IIFE by coding them within the parentheses that invoke the IIFE. In this chapter, the code doesn't pass any arguments to the IIFE. However, this is a useful technique if you need to extend an object that uses the module pattern. For example, you can extend the slideShow object presented in figure 17-11 by passing it to an IIFE that adds a method or accessor property to the slideShow object.

A function expression that is defined and then invoked

```
const sayHello = function() { // define function
    console.log("Hello");
};
sayHello();                               // invoke function
```

An immediately invoked function expression (IIFE)

```
(function() {                    // define and invoke function
    console.log("Hello");
})();
```

An immediately invoked arrow function

```
( () => {                    // define and invoke function
    console.log("Hello");
})();
```

Two ways to code the parentheses of an IIFE

```
(function() { console.log ("Hello"); } ) ();
(function() { console.log ("Hello"); } () );
```

An IIFE...

- Helps keep variables, constants, and functions out of global scope.
- Helps prevent name conflicts.
- Can be used to create private state for an object.

An IIFE that prevents name conflicts

```
const result = ( () => {
    const message = "Thanks!";
    return message;
})();
console.log(result);                          // displays "Thanks!"

const message = "Have a great weekend!"; // no name conflict
console.log(message);                     // displays "Have a great weekend!"
```

Description

- An *immediately invoked function expression (IIFE)* is a function that is defined and invoked in a single statement.
- To define the function that's immediately invoked, you can use a function expression or an arrow function.
- If an IIFE is coded within a statement, you don't need to code parentheses around it. Still, it's generally considered a best practice to code an IIFE within parentheses to help other programmers recognize that the code is using an IIFE.
- Like a regular function call, an IIFE ends with opening and closing parentheses that can include arguments.

Figure 17-10   How to code an IIFE

How to use the module pattern and namespaces

A *singleton* is a pattern that creates a single instance of an object. In JavaScript, the easiest way to create a singleton is to use an object literal. For example, the taskList object presented in chapter 16 is a single object that contains all the operations of working with tasks in the Task List application. It's created when the file that contains it loads, and there's no way to create a second one, which is often what you want.

With an object literal, there's no easy way to create private state for its variables, constants, and methods. You can overcome this problem by using a function to create a closure with private state. However, this allows you to create multiple instances of the object by making multiple calls to the function that creates it.

Sometimes, having more than one instance of the object is what you want. For example, you want the createClickCounter() function described earlier in this chapter to be able to create multiple clickCounter objects. Other times, this may cause problems. For example, if you create two slideShow objects that hold references to different images, the Slide Show application might not work correctly.

The *module pattern* allows you to combine the benefits of object literals and closures. It uses an IIFE to create a single instance of the object that's returned by the function that creates the closure. That way, you get a single instance of an object that has private state. This object can be referred to as a *module*.

The first example in figure 17-11 shows how this works. Here, the code uses an IIFE with a closure to return a slideShow object that has private state. Since this function is immediately invoked, it doesn't need to be called to create the object. Instead, the global slideShow constant refers to the object returned by the IIFE as soon as the library file loads.

When working with the module pattern, it's common to also use a *namespace*, which is a way to keep your objects out of the global namespace. This helps you avoid name conflicts with other libraries. The namespace examples show how to create and use a namespace.

To create a namespace, you assign an object literal to a constant or variable as shown by the first statement. Here, the code creates a namespace named myapp. However, it's common to use a namespace that uniquely identifies you or your company. For example, a programmer named Mike Murach might use a namespace named murach.

If you want to prevent yourself from overwriting an existing namespace, you can check whether the namespace exists. If so, you can use that namespace. Otherwise, you can create a new namespace. This is shown by the second statement. For this code to work correctly, it must use the older *var* keyword.

Once you've created a namespace, you can add the object created by the IIFE to the namespace as shown by the third statement. Then, you can use the namespace to access the object created by the IIFE whenever you need to as shown by the fourth statement.

The pros and cons of object literals vs closures

Type	Pros and cons
Object literal	Pros: The library creates the object so the programmer can use it.
	Cons: All of the object's properties and methods are public.
Closure	Cons: The programmer must call a function to create an object before being able to use it.
	Pros: The objects created by calling the function can have private state.

A module pattern that creates an object with private state

```
const slideShow = ( () => {
    // private variables and constants
    let timer = null;
    let play = true;
    let speed = 2000;
    const nodes = { image: null, caption: null };
    const img = { cache: [], counter: 0 };

    // private methods
    const stopSlideShow = () => { ... };
    const displayNextImage = () => { ... };

    // public methods
    return {
        loadImages(slides) { ... },
        startSlideShow(image, caption) { ... },
        getToggleHandler(){ ... }
    };
})(); // Invoke the IIFE to create the object
```

How to create and use a namespace

An object literal that's used as a namespace

```
const myapp = {};
```

How to make sure you don't overwrite an existing namespace

```
var myapp = myapp || {};  // must use var, not let or const
```

Code that adds a slideShow object to the myapp namespace

```
myapp.slideShow = ( () => {
    ...
})(); // Invoke the IIFE to create the object
```

A statement that uses the slideshow object of the myapp namespace

```
myapp.slideShow.loadImages(slides);
```

Description

- The *module pattern* uses an IIFE to create a single instance of the object, or *module*, that's returned by the function. That way, you get the benefits of an object literal while still having the private state of a closure.

- The module pattern is often used with a *namespace*, which provides a way to keep your objects out of the global namespace.

Figure 17-11   How to use the module pattern and namespaces

How to work with ES modules

Closures and the module pattern provide a way to give private state to multiple objects or to a single object. However, they are cumbersome and result in code that's often difficult to understand. To solve these and other problems, JavaScript introduced its own module system in 2015. This system is known as *ES modules*, or *ECMAScript modules*, and it provides many advantages over using closures and the module pattern for creating private state.

How to import and export module items

ES modules allow you to use the *import* and *export* keywords to import and export items from a module. These items include variables, constants, functions, and classes. Figure 17-12 shows how to import and export items from a module.

The first example uses the *export* keyword to export three functions from a module file for working with a slide show. This file begins by defining three variables and two constants. Then, it defines five functions. Of these five functions, the code uses the *export* keyword to export the last three functions. As a result, these three functions are public and can be imported by other modules. However, the first two functions aren't exported. As a result, they're private and can't be imported by other modules. Similarly, this code doesn't export any of the variables and constants, so these items have private state.

As you review the code for the first example, note how much easier it is to understand than the code that uses a closure. This code simply defines the top-level variables, constants, and functions needed to create a slide show.

Coding the *export* keyword before an item as shown by the first example is one way to export an item. However, it's sometimes more convenient to code a single export statement that specifies which items to export as shown by the second example.

Once you've exported items from a module, you can use the import statement to import them into another module as shown by the third example. Here, the import statement imports the functions named loadImages() and startSlide-Show() from the file named lib_slide_show.js. To specify a path to this file that's relative to the root directory for the application, this code starts the string for the path with ./.

After the import statement, the code in the module defines the ready() event handler. This event handler calls the two imported functions to load the images for the slide show and to start it.

When you import items, they are available in the file as read-only views of the exported item. Because of that, you can't change the value of a variable that's imported, but you can modify its properties. This is similar to how a constant works. For example, if you exported the speed variable, you wouldn't be able to change its value directly. However, you would be able to view its value. To change the value of the speed variable, you would need to code and export a setSpeed() function. Then, you could import that function and use it to change the speed variable.

A module file that exports three functions

```
// variables and constants
let timer = null;
let play = true;
let speed = 2000;
const nodes = { image: null, caption: null };
const img = { cache: [], counter: 0 };

// functions
const stopSlideShow = () => { ... };
const displayNextImage = () => { ... };
export const loadImages = (slides) => { ... };
export const startSlideShow = (image, caption) => { ... };
export const getToggleHandler = () => { ... };
```

Another way to export the three functions

```
export { loadImages, startSlideShow, getToggleHandler };
```

A module that imports and uses two functions

```
import { loadImages, startSlideShow } from './lib_slide_show.js';

$(document).ready( () => {
    ...
    // load the images and start the slide show
    loadImages(slides);
    startSlideShow($("#image"), $("#caption"));

    // speed = 200;          // Error: speed is not defined
    // stopSlideShow();       // Error: stopSlideShow is not defined
});
```

Description

- *ES modules*, or *ECMAScript modules*, provide a way to define a module that has private state. They have many advantages over using closures and the module pattern to create private state.

- To export a single item, code the *export* keyword before the declaration for the item.

- To export a list of items for a file, code a single export statement followed by a set of braces. Within the braces, code a comma-separated list of the items you want to export.

- You can't code an export statement inside a function. As a result, you can only export top-level items.

- To import items, code an import statement at the beginning of a JavaScript file. After the *import* keyword, code braces that contain a comma-separated list of items to import, the *from* keyword, and a path to the module file.

- In an import statement, you can code a path that's relative to the root directory for the application by starting the path with ./.

- When you import items, they are available in the file as read-only views of the exported item. Because of that, you can't change the value of a variable that's imported, but you can modify its properties. This is similar to how a constant works.

Figure 17-12   How to import and export module items

How to declare a script as a module

To be able to import or export items, you must declare the script as a module. That way, JavaScript can use the ES module system to work with the script.

To declare a script as a module, you can modify the HTML for an application so the script element has a type attribute that's set to "module" as shown in figure 17-13. Here, the first example begins by using the first script element to set the type attribute for the lib_slide_show.js file that exports the functions for working with a slide show. Then, the second script element sets the type attribute for the slide_show.js file that imports two of these functions.

The second example works like the first example, but it shows that you can also declare inline JavaScript as a module. Here, the second script element contains inline JavaScript that uses an import statement to import two functions.

When you use ES modules, you should know that the ES module system provides many features beyond creating private state. Many of these features provide for better security and performance, and they impact the way you develop the code.

To start, code that uses ES modules must be run from a server. If you try to run a module from the file system, JavaScript throws errors due to module security requirements. In addition, ES modules use strict mode and the defer attribute automatically. As a result, you don't need to code the "use strict" declaration at the top of a module or to code the defer attribute when loading a module. Similarly, an ES module is only executed once. That's true even if it has been referenced by multiple script elements.

Finally, an ES module is imported into the scope of a single script. In other words, it isn't imported into global scope. As a result, you can only access imported items in the script they are imported into. For example, you can't access these items from the JavaScript console or view them in all debugging tools.

The ES module examples in this book use files that have a .js extension to indicate that they are JavaScript files. Then, these examples use the type attribute of the script element to indicate that these files are ES modules. This works well on most servers because they're typically configured to work with .js files.

However, it's also possible for a module file to have an .mjs extension to indicate that it's a JavaScript module. This allows some servers to automatically treat the file as a JavaScript module without having to code the script element's type attribute. Unfortunately, many servers don't yet work correctly with .mjs files. That's why this book uses .js files for ES modules.

Script elements that declare the modules

```
<script src="lib_slide_show.js" type="module"></script>
<script src="slide_show.js" type="module"></script>
```

A script element that declares inline JavaScript as a module

```
<script src="lib_slide_show.js" type="module"></script>
<script type="module">
    import { loadImages, startSlideShow } from './lib_slide_show.js';

    // load the images and start the slide show
    loadImages(slides);
    startSlideShow($("#image"), $("#caption"));
</script>
```

A module...

- **Must be run from a server.** If you try to run a module from the file system, JavaScript throws errors due to module security requirements.
- **Uses strict mode automatically.** As a result, you don't need to code the "use strict" declaration at the top of a module.
- **Uses the defer attribute of the script element automatically.** As a result, there's no need to code this attribute when loading a module.
- **Is only executed once.** That's true even if it has been referenced by multiple script elements.
- **Is imported into the scope of a single script.** In other words, it isn't imported into global scope. As a result, you can only access imported items in the script they are imported into.

Description

- To declare JavaScript as an ES module, you can set the type attribute of its script element to "module". Otherwise, the JavaScript is not treated as an ES module.
- A file for an ES module can have a .js or .mjs extension. The .mjs extension makes it clear that the file is a module and allows some servers and build tools to automatically treat the file as a module. However, many servers don't yet work correctly with .mjs files. As a result, it's still common to use .js for module files.

Figure 17-13   How to declare a script as a module

More skills for working with modules

The previous two figures presented the basic skills that you need to get started with ES modules. Now, figure 17-14 presents more skills for working with ES modules. In particular, you can rename a module item, import all module items into a module object, or use a class as a module. These techniques are sometimes helpful for avoiding name conflicts.

The first example shows how to rename an item in a module. To do that, you can code the item's name in the import or export statement followed by the *as* keyword and a new name for the item. For instance, the import statement in this example renames two imported functions so that they both start with "slide-Show". That way, it's clear that both of these functions are for working with a slide show, and it reduces the chance that these function names will conflict with any other function names defined later in the script.

Conversely, the export statement renames functions in the module so that they're shorter. This may increase the chances of these function names conflicting with other function names. However, you can minimize this chance by importing these functions into a module object as shown in the second example.

The second example shows how to import all items of a module into a module object. To do that, you code the * character to indicate that you want to import all items. Then, you code the *as* keyword and the name of the module object. In this example, the code imports the load(), start(), and getToggle() functions as the methods of a module object named slideShow.

After importing items into a module object, you can use the module object to access the items of the module. In this example, the code uses the slideShow object to call its load() and start() methods.

So far, the ES modules presented in this chapter work with procedural code that only uses variables, constants, and functions. However, you can also use ES modules with object-oriented code that uses classes to define objects. In the third example, the export statement exports the two classes named Trip and Trips that are stored in the lib_trips.js file. Then, the import statement imports these two classes into the trips.js file so the code in this file can create Trips and Trip objects. Finally, the two script elements use the type attribute to identify both JavaScript files as modules.

When you use the ES module system with classes, it doesn't create private state for the objects created from the classes. To do that, you can use a closure to return objects that have private state. Or, if you only need one instance of the object, you can use the module pattern to return a single object.

How to rename imports and exports

Code that renames two imported items

```
import { loadImages as slideShowLoadImages,
        startSlideShow as slideShowStart } from './lib_slide_show.js';
```

Code that renames three exported items

```
export { loadImages as load,
         startSlideShow as start,
         getToggleHandler as getToggle };
```

How to create and use a module object

```
import * as slideShow from './lib_slide_show.js';

$(document).ready( () => {
    const slides = [...];

    slideShow.load(slides);
    slideShow.start($("#image"), $("#caption"));
});
```

How to use imports and exports with classes

Code that exports two classes

```
export { Trip, Trips };

class Trip {...}
class Trips {...}
```

Code that imports two classes

```
import { Trip, Trips } from './lib_trips.js';

$(document).ready( () => {
    const trips = new Trips();
    const trip = new Trip("Seattle", 100, 3.5);
});
```

Code that declares the two files that use the classes as modules

```
<script src="lib_trips.js" type="module"></script>
<script src="trips.js" type="module"></script>
```

Description

- You can rename a module item, import all module items into a module object, or use a class as a module. These techniques are sometimes helpful for avoiding name conflicts.

- To rename an item, code the item's name in the import or export statement followed by the *as* keyword and a new name for the item.

- To import all items of a module into a module object, use the * character to indicate that you want to import all items followed by the *as* keyword and the name of the module object. Then, you can use the module object to access the items of the module.

- To import or export a class, code the name of the class or classes within the braces of an import or export statement.

Figure 17-14   More skills for working with modules

The Slide Show 2.0 application

Figure 17-15 shows another version of the Slide Show application that was presented earlier in this chapter. This version works like the one presented earlier. However, it uses ES modules to protect its private state. Because of that, this application doesn't work correctly if you run it from the file system. As a result, to get this application to work correctly, you must deploy it to a web server and run it from that server. One way to do that is to run this application from a Node.js web server like the http-server module described in chapter 19.

The HTML

The HTML for this version of the Slide Show application uses the type attribute of its script elements to identify the lib_slide_show.js and slide_show.js files as ES modules. This is necessary because the lib_slide_show.js file uses an export statement, and the slide_show.js file uses an import statement. As a result, JavaScript needs to use the ES module system to process these files.

The JavaScript

The lib_slide_show.js file begins with an export statement that exports three functions. Then, it defines some private variables and constants and a couple private functions before defining the three public functions that are exported. Note that the syntax for this code is cleaner and easier to understand than the syntax for using a closure to create private state.

The HTML

```
<body>
    <main>
        <h1>Fishing Slide Show</h1>
        <p><img id="image"></p>
        <h2 id="caption"></h2>
        <p><input type="button" id="play_pause" value="Pause"></p>
    </main>
    <script src="https://code.jquery.com/jquery-3.4.1.slim.min.js"></script>
    <script src="lib_slide_show.js" type="module"></script>
    <script src="slide_show.js" type="module"></script>
</body>
```

The lib_slide_show.js file

```
export { loadImages, startSlideShow, getToggleHandler };

// private variables and constants
let timer = null;
let play = true;
let speed = 2000;
const nodes = { image: null, caption: null };
const img = { cache: [], counter: 0 };

// private functions
const stopSlideShow = () => clearInterval(timer);

const displayNextImage = () => {
    img.counter = ++img.counter % img.cache.length;
    const image = img.cache[img.counter];
    nodes.image.attr("src", image.src);
    nodes.image.attr("alt", image.alt);
    nodes.caption.text(image.alt);
};

// public functions
const loadImages = (slides) => {
    for (let slide of slides) {
        const image = new Image();
        image.src = "images/" + slide.href;
        image.alt = slide.title;
        img.cache.push(image);
    }
}

const startSlideShow = (image, caption) => {
    if(image && caption) {
        nodes.image = image;
        nodes.caption = caption;
    }
    displayNextImage();
    timer = setInterval(displayNextImage, speed);
}
```

Figure 17-15   The Slide Show 2.0 application (part 1)

The slide_show.js file begins with an import statement that imports all items from the lib_slide_show.js file into an object named slideShow. In other words, it imports the three functions exported from that file as methods of the slideShow object. Then, the slide_show.js file defines the ready() event handler.

Within this event handler, the code uses the slideShow object to call all three imported functions. First, it calls its getToggleHandler() method to set the click() event handler for the Play/Pause button. Second, it calls its loadImages() method to load the images for the slides. Third, it calls its startSlideShow() method to start the slide show.

If you run the Slide Show application from a server, you can examine the slideShow object in Chrome's developer tools to verify that only the three functions exported by the lib_slide_show.js module are available to outside code. In this example, the Watch window shows that Chrome's debugger can only access these three methods from the slideShow object. As a result, there's no way to overwrite any of the slideShow object's private state.

The lib_slide_show.js file (continued)

```
const getToggleHandler = () => {
    return evt => {
        if (play) {
            stopSlideShow();
        } else {
            startSlideShow();
        }
        const button = evt.currentTarget;
        button.value = (play) ? "Resume" : "Pause";
        play = !play;      // toggle play flag
    };
}
```

The slide_show.js file

```
import * as slideShow from './lib_slide_show.js';

$(document).ready( () => {
    // define the slides
    const slides = [
        {href:"release.jpg", title:"Catch and Release"},
        {href:"deer.jpg", title:"Deer at Play"},
        {href:"hero.jpg", title:"The Big One!"},
        {href:"bison.jpg", title:"Roaming Bison"}
    ];

    // attach the event handler for the Play/Pause button
    $("#play_pause").click(slideShow.getToggleHandler());

    // load the images and start the slide show
    slideShow.loadImages(slides);
    slideShow.startSlideShow($("#image"), $("#caption"));
});
```

The slideShow object in the Watch pane of the Chrome developer tools

```
▼ Watch                                               +  ↻
▼slideShow: Module
  getToggleHandler: (...)
  loadImages: (...)
  startSlideShow: (...)
  Symbol(Symbol.toStringTag): "Module"
```

Description

- This version of the Slide Show application works like the one presented earlier in this chapter, except that it uses ES modules to protect its private state.

- You can examine the slideShow object in Chrome's developer tools to verify that only the three methods exported by the lib_slide_show.js module are available to outside code. As a result, there's no way to overwrite any of the slideShow object's private state.

Figure 17-15   The Slide Show 2.0 application (part 2)

Perspective

This chapter has presented skills that you need to work with functions. It has focused on the best practices for developing new code such as using rest parameters and arrow functions. But it also presents some techniques that were commonly used with older versions of JavaScript such as using the *this* keyword with regular functions. Some of the old techniques are unique to JavaScript programming and difficult to understand. In most cases, though, you only need to use these techniques if you're maintaining legacy code.

This chapter also showed how to use closures and the module pattern to create one or more objects that have private state. These techniques have been around for a long time and are still commonly used. As a result, you should be familiar with them. However, for new development, the ES module system described in this chapter provides several advantages over using closures or the module pattern.

Terms

function	in scope
call a function	out of scope
function declaration	closure
function expression	private state
arrow function	immediately invoked function
variadic function	expression (IIFE)
rest operator	singleton
rest parameter	module pattern
spread operator	module
global scope	namespace
local scope	ECMAScript modules (ES modules)
scope chain	

Summary

- A *function* defines a block of code that can be *called* (or *invoked*) by other statements.

- A *function declaration* is a function that starts with the *function* keyword and the name of the function.

- A *function expression* uses the *function* keyword to create a function that can be assigned to a constant.

- An *arrow function* uses the arrow operator (=>) to create a function.

- A *variadic function* accepts a variable number of arguments.

- You can use the *rest operator* (. . .) to define a *rest parameter.* This parameter must be coded as the last parameter of the function, and it collects the *rest* of the values that are passed to the function into an array.

- You can use the *spread operator* (. . .) to *spread* an array into individual values.
- Regular functions (function declarations and function expressions) have a *this* keyword whose value depends on how the function is called.
- Arrow functions can use the *this* keyword to access the environment that contains the function such as an object or outer function.
- You can use the call() and apply() methods of a function to set the value of *this* when a function is invoked. These methods can be used to "borrow" methods from another object.
- In JavaScript, the *scope chain* refers to what is *in scope*. An object in the scope chain is available, or "alive", as long as something is referring to it. This is true even if the object that contains it has finished executing and is *out of scope*.
- A *closure* is created when an inner function refers to one or more objects in the scope of the outer function. As long as a reference to the inner function is alive, the outer function's variables and constants stay in scope.
- Closures can be used to create *private state* that protects an object's internal variables, constants, and functions from outside code.
- An *immediately invoked function expression (IIFE)* defines a function expression and immediately calls it.
- A *singleton* is a design pattern that creates a single instance of an object.
- Many developers and third-party libraries use the *module pattern* to create a single object that has private state.
- The module pattern is often used in conjunction with *namespaces*. This provides a way to keep your objects out of the global namespace.
- In 2015, JavaScript introduced a module system known as *ECMAScript modules*, or *ES modules,* that provides many advantages over using closures and the module pattern.

Exercise 17-1 Experiment with the functions of the Test Scores application

This exercise guides you through the process of experimenting with some of the functions used by the Test Scores application presented in this chapter.

Test the application

1. Use your text editor or IDE to open the application in this folder:
   `\javascript_jquery\exercises\ch17\test_scores`

2. Run the application and test it to make sure it works as described in this chapter.

Use function declarations for the helper methods

3. Modify the isInvalid(), getAverage(), and getLast() functions so they use a function declaration instead of an arrow function. Note that this uses a simple and consistent syntax that identifies these functions as functions, not constants.

4. Test the application to make sure it still works correctly.

Use an arrow function for the click() event handler

5. Modify the click() event handler so it uses an arrow function instead of a function expression. To do that, you'll need to modify the code within the event handler, so it doesn't use the *this* keyword to access the Add Score button. This makes the code a little longer, but it also makes it easier to read since you don't have to wonder what the *this* keyword refers to.

6. Test the application to make sure it still works correctly.

Modify the getAverage() function so it uses a default value

7. Modify the getAverage() function so it returns a string for the average that displays 2 decimal places.

8. Modify the code that calls the getAverage() function so it no longer uses the toFixed() method to round the average to 2 decimal places.

9. Test the application to make sure it still works correctly.

10. Add a second parameter to the getAverage() function that specifies the number of decimal places to display. This parameter should specify a default value of 2. Within the function, modify the code so it uses the parameter to set the number of decimal places for the average.

11. Test the application to make sure it still works correctly.

12. Modify the code that calls the getAverage() function so it overrides the default value by passing a value of 1 to the second parameter.

13. Test the application to make sure it still works correctly. Now, it should round the average to 1 decimal place.

Exercise 17-2   Update the Task List application to use the module pattern

This exercise guides you through the process of implementing the module pattern for the Task List application presented in chapter 16.

Test and break the Task List application

1. Use your text editor or IDE to open the application in this folder:
   `\javascript_jquery\exercises\ch17\task_list`

2. Run the application and add a few tasks. Then, close the browser.

3. In the task_list.js file, at the beginning of the displayTasks() function, add this line of code:
   `taskList.tasks = [];`

4. Test this change in Chrome, and note that the tasks you entered in step 2 don't display when the page loads. That's because the line of code from step 3 has set the tasks property to an empty array. The taskList object shouldn't allow this because its tasks property should be private.

5. Delete the statement that you added in step 3, and test the application to make sure it's working correctly again.

Update the Task List application to use the module pattern

6. In the lib_task_list.js file, change the code that assigns an object to the taskList constant so it assigns an object that's returned by an IIFE rather than an object literal. To do that, code an empty IIFE. Then, copy and paste the current object literal so it's returned by the IIFE.

7. In the body of the IIFE, before the return statement, code a tasks variable that holds an empty array. Then, delete the tasks property and adjust the code in the methods so they refer to the private tasks constant (tasks), not the tasks property (this.tasks).

8. Test the application to make sure it still works correctly.

Try to break the Task List application again

9. In the task_list.js file, at the beginning of the displayTasks() function, add this line of code again:
   `taskList.tasks = [];`

10. Test this change and note that the application still works correctly. That's because this code adds a new property named tasks to the taskList object, but it doesn't change the array that's stored by the private tasks variable.

18

How to work with Ajax

This chapter shows how to use Ajax to update a web page without loading a new web page into the browser. Since Ajax is commonly used to get data from web services, this chapter also shows how to work with two web services that provide data that you can use for development and testing.

Introduction to Ajax

This chapter begins by describing how Ajax works. Then, it describes two data formats commonly used with Ajax.

How Ajax works

Ajax (Asynchronous JavaScript and XML) allows a web browser to update a web page with data from a web server without reloading the entire page. Figure 18-1 begins by showing Google's Auto Suggest feature because it's an example of a typical Ajax application. As you type the start of a search entry, Google uses Ajax to get the terms and links of items that match the characters that you have typed so far. Ajax does this without refreshing the page so the user doesn't experience any delays. This is sometimes called a "partial page refresh."

Modern browsers provide two ways to send an Ajax request to the web server and to process the data in the response that's returned from the server: the *XMLHttpRequest (XHR) object* and the *Fetch API*. This chapter describes both of these techniques.

When working with Ajax, the browser uses JavaScript to send the request, parse the returned data, and modify the DOM so the page reflects the returned data. In many cases, a request includes data that tells the server what data to return.

On the web server, an application or script that's written in a server-side language like PHP typically returns the data that is requested. Often, these applications or scripts are part of a *web service* that provides an *Application Programming Interface (API)* that developers can use to get data from a website. Then, you can use that data to enhance your own web pages. For instance, many of the biggest and most popular websites provide APIs that let you make Ajax requests for data from their sites.

The two diagrams in this figure show how a normal HTTP request compares to an Ajax request. For a normal HTTP request, the browser makes an HTTP request for an entire page, the server returns an HTTP response for the page, and the browser loads the entire page. In contrast, with an Ajax request, the browser uses JavaScript to send an asynchronous request to the server, the server returns the requested data in the response, and the web page uses JavaScript to update the DOM with the new data. As a result, the browser doesn't need to reload the entire page.

Because Ajax is so powerful, it's used by many of the biggest and most popular websites. For instance, when you post a comment to Facebook, the comment just appears. And when you drag within a Google Map, the map is automatically adjusted. In neither case is the entire page reloaded.

Google's Auto Suggest is an Ajax application

How a normal HTTP request is processed

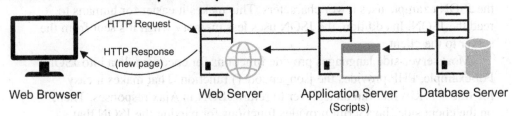

How an Ajax request is processed

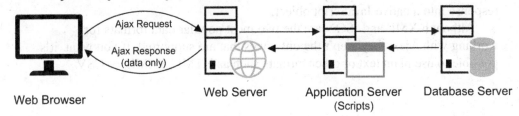

Description

- Unlike normal HTTP requests, *Ajax* (*Asynchronous JavaScript and XML*) requests update a page with data from a web server without needing to reload the entire page. This is sometimes known as a "partial page refresh."

- When working with Ajax, JavaScript sends the request, processes the response, and updates the DOM with the new data. As a result, the browser doesn't need to reload the entire page.

- To send an Ajax request, JavaScript can use a browser object known as the *XMLHttpRequest (XHR) object*, or it can use the *Fetch API*.

- Ajax requests are often made to *web services* that provide *Application Programming Interfaces* (*APIs*) that developers can use to get data from a website.

- Many popular websites provide APIs that let you use Ajax to get data from their sites.

- Many popular websites use Ajax to improve the way they function.

Figure 18-1   How Ajax works

Two common data formats for Ajax

Figure 18-2 presents the two most common data formats for Ajax applications: XML and JSON. Ajax was originally designed to be used with *XML (Extensible Markup Language)*. That's why XML is part of the Ajax name.

XML is a format that works well for exchanging data across the Internet. In addition, XML is a markup language that works much like HTML. As a result, it's easy for programmers who have experience with HTML to understand. Because of that, XML was commonly used in the early days of Ajax.

Today, *JSON (JavaScript Object Notation)* is the most popular format for working with Ajax. JSON, pronounced "Jason", is similar to XML in that it's a format that works well for exchanging data across the Internet. However, it's less verbose than XML.

In this figure, the XML and JSON examples store the same data. However, the JSON example uses fewer characters. This makes it easier for humans to read the JSON. In addition, the JSON uses less memory when it's sent from the server to the client.

Most server-side languages provide functions for encoding data into JSON. For example, PHP provides the json_encode() function. That makes it easy for web services that run on a server to return JSON in Ajax responses. Then, on the client side, JavaScript provides functions for parsing the JSON that's returned from the client into a JavaScript object. For example, the json() function described later in this chapter parses the JSON that's returned in an Ajax response into a native JavaScript object.

Although XML and JSON are the two most popular data formats for working with Ajax, they aren't the only ones that are supported. If you want, it's possible to use plain text or other formats such as HTML, YAML, or CSV.

Two common data formats for Ajax

Format	Description	File extension
XML	Extensible Markup Language	xml
JSON	JavaScript Object Notation	json

XML data

```xml
<?xml version="1.0" encoding="utf-8"?>
<management>
    <teammember>
        <name>Agnes</name>
        <title>Vice President of Accounting</title>
        <bio>With over 14 years of public accounting ... </bio>
    </teammember>
    <teammember>
        <name>Wilbur</name>
        <title>Founder and CEO</title>
        <bio>While Wilbur is the founder and CEO ... </bio>
    </teammember>
</management>
```

JSON data

```json
{"teammembers":[
    {
        "name":"Agnes",
        "title":"Vice President of Accounting",
        "bio":"With over 14 years of public accounting... "
    },
    {
        "name":"Wilbur",
        "title":"Founder and CEO",
        "bio":"While Wilbur is the founder and CEO ... "
    }
]}
```

Description

- The two most common data formats for working with Ajax are XML and JSON.
- Both *XML* (*Extensible Markup Language*) and *JSON* (*JavaScript Object Notation*) are formats that use text to store and transmit data.
- Most server-side languages provide methods for encoding data into JSON.
- JavaScript provides methods for parsing the JSON that's returned from a web service into a JavaScript object.
- JSON is less verbose than XML, so it uses less memory when being sent from the server to the client.

Figure 18-2   Two common data formats for Ajax

The JSON Placeholder API

Ajax requests typically get data from a web service. That's why figure 18-3 begins by presenting some information about a web service named JSON Placeholder. This web service provides an API that accesses fake data that's in JSON format. This data mimics the kind of data that's typically returned by real web services. Using an API like this allows you to practice making Ajax calls without having to set up accounts or worry about other implementation details.

The table in this figure describes the type of data you can request from the JSON Placeholder web service. This data includes information about users, blog posts, comments, and so on. Most of the data is related to other data. For example, comments are related to a blog post, and photos are related to an album.

To make a GET request with the JSON Placeholder API, you use the URL for the web service with the desired resource added to the end. For example, to get data for all users, you use the URL like the one shown in the first example. This returns the JSON data shown in the second example. However, if you want to get the data for a single user, you can add the id for the user to the end of the URL like this:

```
https://jsonplaceholder.typicode.com/users/1
```

You can use this API to simulate other kinds of HTTP requests such as POST, PUT, and DELETE requests. This chapter doesn't show how to make those types of requests, but the documentation for this web service does.

The JSON Placeholder web service

`https://jsonplaceholder.typicode.com`

The fake data that's available from this web service

Resource	Description
/users	10 users with data such as name, username, and email address.
/posts	100 blog posts with each one related to a specific user.
/comments	500 comments with each one related to a specific blog post.
/albums	100 photo albums with each one related to a specific user.
/photos	5000 simple photos of various colors with each one related to a specific album. This includes one photo that's 600x600 pixels and a thumbnail that's 150x150 pixels.
/todos	200 tasks with each one related to a specific user.

A URL that returns data

`https://jsonplaceholder.typicode.com/users`

Some of the JSON that's returned

```
[
    {
        "id": 1,
        "name": "Leanne Graham",
        "username": "Bret",
        "email": "Sincere@april.biz",
        ...
    }
},
...
    {
        "id": 10,
        "name": "Clementina DuBuque",
        "username": "Moriah.Stanton",
        "email": "Rey.Padberg@karina.biz",
        ...
    }
}
]
```

Description

- The JSON Placeholder web service provides an API that accesses fake data that's in JSON format. This data mimics the kind of data that's typically returned by real web services.
- Using the JSON Placeholder API allows you to practice making Ajax calls without having to set up accounts or worry about other implementation details.
- Much of the data returned by the JSON Placeholder API uses Latin text that's been used in printing and typesetting since the 1500s.

Figure 18-3   The JSON Placeholder API

How to make a single Ajax request

This chapter continues by showing two techniques for making a single Ajax request. First, this chapter shows how to use the XMLHttpRequest object. Then, it shows how to use the Fetch API. Although using the XMLHttpRequest object was common in the early days of Ajax, it has some drawbacks that have led to the rise of the newer Fetch API.

How to use the XMLHttpRequest object

Figure 18-4 presents some of the *members* (methods, properties, and events) of the XMLHttpRequest object. To start, every Ajax request uses the open() and send() methods. The open() method opens a connection for a request. Its first parameter specifies whether the request is a GET or POST request, and the second parameter provides the URL for the request. In a production application, the URL typically specifies a web service.

After the open() method opens a connection, the send() method sends the request. If necessary, the first parameter of this method can specify any data that's sent to the server along with the request. Typically, the server uses this data to filter the data that it returns.

The responseType property specifies the format for the data that's returned by the server, and the response property gets that data in the specified format. Then, the readyState property indicates the state of the request, and the status property provides the status code that's returned by the server.

The two events determine what happens when the Ajax request completes. The onreadystatechange event can be used to processes the data that's returned, and the onerror event can be used to handle any errors that might occur.

To work with these events, you assign *callback functions* to them. This is similar to assigning an event handler function by passing it to the addEventListener() method. Callback functions are essential to asynchronous JavaScript. That's because asynchronous code can't return a value or throw an exception the way synchronous code can. Instead, you must define a callback function that runs when the return value is ready or the error occurs.

The example in this figure shows how to use the XMLHttpRequest object to request data from the JSON Placeholder API. To start, this code creates a new XMLHttpRequest object. Then, it assigns a string of "json" to the responseType property to specify that the response should be in JSON format.

After setting the response type, this code assigns a callback function to the onreadystatechange event. This callback function begins by checking whether the readyState property is 4 (DONE) and the status property is 200 (SUCCESS). If so, it displays the JSON data in the response in the console. In a more realistic application, this code would parse the response data and update the DOM. For now, though, this simple code shows how the XMLHttpRequest object works.

After assigning the first callback function, this code assigns a callback function to the onerror event. This callback function displays an error message in the console. Again, though, in a more realistic application it would typically log the error or update the DOM to notify the user of the error.

Common members of the XMLHttpRequest object

Method	Description
open(*method*, *url*)	Opens a connection for a request. The parameters let you set the method to GET or POST and set the URL for the request.
send([*data*])	Starts the request. This method can include data that gets sent with the request. This method must be called after a request connection has been opened.

Property	Description
responseType	A string that indicates the format of data the response contains. Common values are "text", "json", "document", and "blob".
response	The content that's returned from the server. The format of the response depends on the value of the responseType property.
readyState	A numeric value that indicates the state of the current request: 0 is UNSENT, 1 is OPENED, 2 is HEADERS_RECEIVED, 3 is LOADING, and 4 is DONE.
status	The status code returned from the server in numeric format. Common values include 200 for SUCCESS and 404 for NOT FOUND.

Event	Description
onreadystatechange	An event that occurs when the state of the request changes.
onerror	An event that occurs when an error occurs.

Code that uses the XMLHttpRequest object to get and display user data

```
const xhr = new XMLHttpRequest();
xhr.responseType = "json";

xhr.onreadystatechange = () => {
    if (xhr.readyState == 4 && xhr.status == 200) {
        console.log(xhr.response);
    }
};
xhr.onerror = e => console.log(e.message);

xhr.open("GET", "https://jsonplaceholder.typicode.com/users");
xhr.send();
```

The data displayed in the console

```
▼(10) [{…}, {…}, {…}, {…}, {…}, {…}, {…}, {…}, {…}, {…}]
 ▶0: {id: 1, name: "Leanne Graham", username: "Bret", email: "Sincere@april.biz", address: {…}, …}
 ▶1: {id: 2, name: "Ervin Howell", username: "Antonette", email: "Shanna@melissa.tv", address: {…}, …}
 ▶2: {id: 3, name: "Clementine Bauch", username: "Samantha", email: "Nathan@yesenia.net", address: {…}, …}
 ▶3: {id: 4, name: "Patricia Lebsack", username: "Karianne", email: "Julianne.OConner@kory.org", address: {…}…
```

Description

- A *member* of an object is one of its methods, properties, or events.

- To handle the events raised by the XMLHttpRequest object, you can assign a *callback function* to the event. Then, the callback function runs when the event occurs. Callback functions are essential to asynchronous JavaScript.

Figure 18-4   How to make an Ajax request using the XMLHttpRequest object

At this point, the code has set up the callback functions for the request, but it hasn't sent the request. To do that, this code uses the open() method to open the connection for the request. This statement sets the method for the request to GET and provides the URL for the JSON data. Then, the last statement uses the send() method to send the request.

How to use the Fetch API

The Fetch API provides methods and objects for making Ajax requests. For new development, it's generally considered a best practice to use the Fetch API, not the older XMLHttpRequest object.

The first table in figure 18-5 summarizes the fetch() method of the Fetch API. It accepts the URL for a GET request and returns a Promise object, which represents the eventual return value of the asynchronous request. In this case, that eventual return value is a Response object, which represents an HTTP response.

A Promise object (or *promise*) has three states. When a Promise object is first created, it's *pending*. When the request returns its value, the promise is *fulfilled*. However, if an error occurs during the request, the promise is *rejected*.

There are two more terms you need to understand to work with Promise objects. First, a promise that is no longer pending is considered *settled*. This is true whether the promise is fulfilled or rejected. Second, a promise can be *resolved* without being fulfilled. For example, if a promise returns another promise, the original promise is resolved, even though the requested data isn't returned yet and so the promise isn't fulfilled.

The tables in this figure present the methods that you can use to make an Ajax request with the Fetch API. Because each of these methods returns a Promise object, they can be chained with each other. Of these methods, the then() method is the most difficult to understand because it accepts a callback function that executes when the promise is resolved. The parameter that's passed to this callback function is the eventual return value of that promise. The catch() method works similarly, but it executes when the promise is rejected.

The example below the tables shows how to use these methods. To start, this code passes a URL for a GET request to the fetch() method, which returns a promise that resolves when the status and headers of the HTTP response are received. However, at this point, the data of the HTTP response isn't received yet. So, this first promise is resolved because it has returned a Response object, but it isn't fulfilled, because the requested data isn't received yet.

The first then() method accepts a callback that executes when the promise from the fetch() method resolves. This callback accepts the Response object and calls its json() method, which returns a promise that resolves to a JavaScript object that's created from the JSON stored in the response. At that point, the original promise is fulfilled.

The second then() method accepts a callback that executes when the promise from the json() method resolves. This callback accepts a JavaScript object named json and displays that object in the console.

The catch() method accepts a callback that executes when the promise is rejected. This callback function displays an error message in the console.

One method of the Fetch API

Method	Description
fetch(url)	Makes an asynchronous GET request to the specified URL. Returns a Promise object that eventually returns a Response object.

Two methods of the Promise object

Method	Description
then(callback)	Registers the callback function to execute when the promise is resolved. The callback function receives a single parameter, which is the eventual return value of the asynchronous request. Returns a Promise object.
catch(callback)	Registers the callback function to execute when the promise is rejected. The callback function receives a single parameter, which is usually an Error object. Returns a Promise object.

One method of the Response object

Method	Description
json()	Returns a Promise object that eventually resolves to a JavaScript object that's created from the JSON that's returned by the asynchronous request.

Code that uses the Fetch API to get and display user data

```
fetch("https://jsonplaceholder.typicode.com/users")
    .then( response => response.json() )
    .then( json => console.log(json) )
    .catch( e => console.log(e.message) );
```

The data displayed in the console

```
▼(10) [{…}, {…}, {…}, {…}, {…}, {…}, {…}, {…}, {…}, {…}]
  ▶0: {id: 1, name: "Leanne Graham", username: "Bret", email: "Sincere@april.biz", address: {…}, …}
  ▶1: {id: 2, name: "Ervin Howell", username: "Antonette", email: "Shanna@melissa.tv", address: {…}, …}
  ▶2: {id: 3, name: "Clementine Bauch", username: "Samantha", email: "Nathan@yesenia.net", address: {…}, …}
  ▶3: {id: 4, name: "Patricia Lebsack", username: "Karianne", email: "Julianne.OConner@kory.org", address: {…}…
```

Description

- For new development, it's generally considered a best practice to use the Fetch API, not the older XMLHttpRequest object.

Figure 18-5 How to make an Ajax request with the Fetch API

The Astronomy Picture
Of the Day application

Figure 18-6 presents an Astronomy Picture of the Day (APOD) application that displays an image or video for any date between June 16, 1995 and today. In addition, it displays some related data such as title, date, copyright, and explanation. To make this possible, the APOD application gets its data from the API that's available from NASA's APOD web service.

The Astronomy Picture Of the Day application

Astronomy Picture Of the Day

Enter date: 2020-7-9   [View]

Noctilucent Clouds and Comet NEOWISE

2020-07-09   © Emmanuel Paoly

These silvery blue waves washing over a tree-lined horizon in the eastern French Alps are noctilucent clouds. From high in planet Earth's mesosphere, they reflect sunlight in this predawn skyscape taken on July 8. This summer, the night-shining clouds are not new to the northern high-latitudes. Comet NEOWISE is though. Also known as C/2020 F3, the comet was discovered in March by the Earth-orbiting Near Earth Object Wide-field Infrared Survey Explorer (NEOWISE) satellite. It's now emerging in morning twilight only just visible to the unaided eye from a clear location above the northeastern horizon.

Description

- The Astronomy Picture of the Day (APOD) application allows the user to enter a date and click the View button. Then, it displays an image or video for the specified date. In addition, it displays some related data such as title, date, copyright, and explanation.

- The APOD application gets its data from the API that's available from NASA's APOD web service.

- When it loads, the APOD application displays the current date in the "Enter date" text box.

Figure 18-6   The Astronomy Picture Of the Day application (part 1)

The HTML and CSS

Part 2 of figure 18-6 begins by presenting some of the HTML and CSS for the application. To start, the HTML displays the title of the application as well as a text box and a View button that allow the user to enter a date. Here, the text box has an id of "date", and the View button has an id of "view_button". Below the View button, this HTML includes a div element with an id of "display". This is where the application displays the picture and its related data if the Ajax request is fulfilled. It's also where the application displays any error messages.

The CSS aligns the label and input elements. In addition, it provides the classes named error and right. The application uses the error class to display error messages in red, and it uses the right class to align the copyright data with the right side of its container element.

The NASA APOD API

After the CSS, this figure shows the URL for NASA's APOD API. To use this API, you need to supply an api_key parameter as described in the table and shown by the example URL.

When you're first getting started, the api_key parameter can specify a value of DEMO_KEY. However, this key only supports 30 requests per hour or 50 requests per day. As a result, if you need to make more requests than that, you should get your own API key. To do that, you can visit this URL:

`https://api.nasa.gov/`

This URL also provides information about using the APOD API and other similar NASA APIs.

If you don't supply a date parameter, the APOD API returns the JSON data for the current date. However, the APOD application presented in this figure allows the user to specify a date. As a result, it must supply a date parameter as shown by the example URL.

The HTML

```html
<body>
    <main>
        <h1>Astronomy Picture Of the Day</h1>
        <div>
            <label for="date">Enter date:</label>
            <input type="text" name="date" id="date">
            <input type="button" id="view_button" value="View">
        </div>
        <div id="display"></div>
    </main>
    <script src="https://code.jquery.com/jquery-3.4.1.min.js"></script>
    <script src="apod.js"></script>
</body>
```

Some of the CSS

```css
div {
    margin-bottom: 1em;
}
label {
    display: inline-block;
    width: 5em;
}
input {
    margin-right: 0.5em;
}
.error {
    color: red;
}
.right {
    float: right;
}
```

The URL for NASA's Astronomy Picture of the Day (APOD) API

https://api.nasa.gov/planetary/apod

Parameters

Parameter	Description
api_key	The API key for the web service. You can specify a value of DEMO_KEY to explore the API. However, this key only supports 30 requests per IP address per hour or 50 requests per day. As a result, you should sign up for your own API key if you plan to use the API extensively.
date	The date of the APOD data to retrieve. This date must be in YYYY-MM-DD format. If you don't specify this parameter, the API retrieves the data for today's date.

Example URL

https://api.nasa.gov/planetary/apod?api_key=DEMO_KEY&date=2020-07-22

Figure 18-6   The Astronomy Picture Of the Day application (part 2)

The JavaScript

Part 3 of figure 18-6 shows the JavaScript for the APOD application. To start, this JavaScript defines a helper function named getDateString(). This function accepts a Date object and returns a corresponding date string in the YYYY-MM-DD format that's required by the APOD API.

After the getDateString() function, this code defines a function named displayPicture(). This function displays the JSON data that's returned by an Ajax call to the APOD API. To start, this code defines a variable to store the HTML that's displayed. Then, it checks whether the data object that's passed to this function has an error property. If so, an error occurred. As a result, this code notifies the user by setting the HTML to a span element that displays the message that's stored in the error property.

After checking the error property, this code checks whether the data object has a code property. If so, the request succeeded but there's a problem with the data. As a result, the JavaScript notifies the user by setting the HTML to a span element that displays the message that's stored in the code property.

If the data object doesn't contain an error property or a code property, the Ajax request succeeded. In that case, the JavaScript gets data from the data object to set the HTML so it displays the title for the image or video, the image or video itself, the date, the copyright (if one exists), and the explanation.

After the if statement, the last statement in this function displays the HTML in the div element that has the id of "display". If the HTML contains an error message, this displays the error message. Otherwise, it displays the image or video and its related data.

After the displayPicture() function, this code defines a function named displayError(). This function accepts an Error object and sets the HTML to a span element that displays the message that's stored in the Error object. Then, it displays this span element in the div element that has the id of "display".

The JavaScript

```javascript
"use strict";

// returns date string in YYYY-MM-DD format
const getDateString = date =>
    `${date.getFullYear()}-${date.getMonth() + 1}-${date.getDate()}`;

const displayPicture = data => {
    let html = "";
    if(data.error) {            // error - display message
        html += `<span class="error">${data.error.message}</span>`;
    }
    else if (data.code) {   // problem - display message
        html += `<span class="error">${data.msg}</span>`;
    }
    else {                          // success - display image/video data
        html += `<h3>${data.title}</h3>`;
        const width = 700;
        switch (data.media_type) {
            case "image":
                html += `<img src="${data.url}" width="${width}"
                        alt="NASA photo">`;
                break;
            case "video":
                html += `<iframe src="${data.url}"
                        frameborder="0"
                            allowfullscreen></iframe>`;
                break;
            default:
                html += `<img src="images/notavailable.png"
                        width="${width}" alt="NASA photo">`;
        }

        // date and copyright
        html += `<div>${data.date}`;
        if (data.copyright) {
            html += `<span class="right">&copy; ${data.copyright}</span>`;
        }
        html += "</div>";

        // explanation
        html += `<p>${data.explanation}</p>`;
    }

    // display HTML
    $("#display").html(html);
};

const displayError = error => {
    let html = `<span class="error">${error.message}</span>`;
    $("#display").html(html);
};
```

Figure 18-6   The Astronomy Picture Of the Day application (part 3)

Part 4 of figure 18-6 shows the ready() event handler for the application. To start, this event handler gets today's date and converts it to a date string in the YYYY-MM-DD format. Then, it sets that date string in the "Enter date" text box and moves the focus to that text box. As a result, when the application loads, it displays the current date in the "Enter date" text box.

After setting up the "Enter date" text box, this code assigns a click() event handler to the View button. Within this event handler, the code begins by getting the date string from the text box. This date string may be today's date or it may be any other date entered by the user. Then, it converts this date string to a Date object.

After creating a Date object from the string, the code checks whether the Date object is invalid. If so, it displays a message that indicates that the date is invalid. Otherwise, it continues by using the getDateString() function to make sure the Date object is in the YYYY-MM-DD format. This is necessary because it's possible for a user to enter a date that's in another format such as MM/DD/YY.

After making sure the date string is in the necessary format, this code builds the URL for the Ajax request. In this figure, the code uses an API key value of DEMO_KEY. This key is appropriate for testing, but a production application should have its own key, which would be a long string of letters and numbers. In addition, this code sets the date parameter of the request to the date string.

After building the URL for the API request, this code uses the methods of the Fetch API to make the Ajax request. If this request is successful, the second then() method displays the picture by passing the JavaScript object that's returned by the json() method to the displayPicture() function defined in part 3. This JavaScript object is created from the JSON stored in the Ajax response. Otherwise, the catch() method displays an error by passing an Error object to the displayError() function defined in part 3.

The last statement of the click() event handler moves the focus to the "Enter date" text box. As a result, after the user clicks the View button, the focus is always moved to this text box, regardless of whether the application displays an error or the picture.

The JavaScript (continued)

```javascript
$(document).ready( () => {

    // on load, get today's date in YYYY-MM-DD format
    const today = new Date();
    let dateStr = getDateString(today);

    // set today's date in textbox
    const dateTextbox = $("#date");
    dateTextbox.val(dateStr);
    dateTextbox.focus();

    $("#view_button").click( () => {

        // get date from textbox
        dateStr = $("#date").val();
        const dateObj = new Date(dateStr);

        if (dateObj == "Invalid Date") {
            const msg = "Please enter valid date in YYYY-MM-DD format.";
            $("#display").html(`<span class="error">${msg}</span>`);
        }
        else {
            // make sure date string is in proper format
            dateStr = getDateString(dateObj);

            // build URL for API request
            const domain = `https://api.nasa.gov/planetary/apod`;
            const request = `?api_key=DEMO_KEY&date=${dateStr}`;
            const url = domain + request;

            fetch(url)
                .then( response => response.json() )
                .then( json => displayPicture(json) )
                .catch( e => displayError(e) );
        }
        $("#date").focus();
    });
});
```

Figure 18-6   The Astronomy Picture Of the Day application (part 4)

How to make multiple Ajax requests

Making a single Ajax request as shown so far in this chapter allows you to add all sorts of nifty functionality to your websites. However, if you need to make additional Ajax requests based on the data that's returned by a previous Ajax response, your code becomes more complicated.

That's especially true if you're using the XMLHttpRequest object. In that case, you need to nest those additional requests within the callback function for the initial request. This can lead to repetitive code that includes callback functions nested several layers deep, a situation some developers refer to as "callback hell". Fortunately, the Fetch API provides several ways to solve "callback hell".

The XMLHttpRequest object and "callback hell"

The code example in figure 18-7 illustrates the problem that occurs if you use the XMLHttpRequest object to make nested Ajax requests. Here, the code starts by making an Ajax request for the photo with the id of 1. Then, the callback function for that request makes a second Ajax request. This request uses the photo object that's returned by the first Ajax request to get data for the album the photo is in. To do that, it uses the albumId property of the photo object.

In turn, the callback function for the second Ajax request makes a third Ajax request. This request uses the album object returned by the second request to get data for the user that created the album. To do that, it uses the userId property of the album object. Then, when these objects are ready, the code in the callback function uses them to add HMTL elements to the DOM.

In this figure, the nested callbacks and repetitive code makes the example difficult to read and maintain. Also, each XMLHttpRequest object should have its own callback function for its onerror event, which would make this code even harder to read and maintain.

The jQuery library has an $.ajax() method that can reduce some of the repetitive code shown in this example. However, that method uses callback functions in a similar way, so it doesn't help with "callback hell". Fortunately, the new Fetch API provides a way to make Ajax requests that solves most of these drawbacks.

Code that uses the XMLHttpRequest object to get related data

```
const xhr1 = new XMLHttpRequest();
xhr1.responseType = "json";

const domain = "https://jsonplaceholder.typicode.com";
let url = `${domain}/photos/1`;

xhr1.onreadystatechange = () => {
    if (xhr1.readyState == 4 && xhr1.status == 200) {
        const photo = xhr1.response;

        const xhr2 = new XMLHttpRequest();
        xhr2.responseType = "json";
        url = `${domain}/albums/${photo.albumId}`;

        xhr2.onreadystatechange = () => {
            if (xhr2.readyState == 4 && xhr2.status == 200) {
                const album = xhr2.response;

                const xhr3 = new XMLHttpRequest();
                xhr3.responseType = "json";
                url = `${domain}/users/${album.userId}`;

                xhr3.onreadystatechange = () => {
                    if (xhr3.readyState == 4 && xhr3.status == 200) {
                        const user = xhr3.response;

                        let html = `<img src="${photo.url}"
                            alt="${photo.title}">`;
                        html += `<h4>In album ${album.title}</h4>`;
                        html += `Posted by ${user.username}`;
                        $("#photo").html(html);
                    }
                };
                xhr3.open("GET", url);
                xhr3.send();
            }
        };
        xhr2.open("GET", url);
        xhr2.send();
    }
};
xhr1.open("GET", url);
xhr1.send();
```

Description

- If you need to use the data from an asynchronous call to make another asynchronous call for related data, and you're using the XMLHttpRequest object, you can nest one callback function within another callback function.

- Some developers call nested callback functions "callback hell" because they can be difficult to read and maintain.

Figure 18-7   The XMLHttpRequest object and "callback hell"

How the Fetch API solves "callback hell"

The example in figure 18-8 shows the "callback hell" example from the previous figure after it has been rewritten to use the Fetch API. Instead of nesting callbacks, this example chains promises. This removes much of the repetitive code and indentation, which makes the code easier to read and maintain.

However, because this example no longer nests the callback functions, they don't have access to the local constants or variables of the other callbacks like the "callback hell" example. That's why each callback must retrieve and update the HTML element with the id of "photo".

One way to fix this issue is to use the *async* and *await* keywords as described later in this chapter. Another way to fix this issue is to use named callback functions as shown next.

Code that uses the Fetch API to get related data

```
const domain = "https://jsonplaceholder.typicode.com";
fetch(`${domain}/photos/1`)
    .then( response => response.json() )
    .then( photo => {
        $("#photo").html(`<img src="${photo.url}" alt="${photo.title}">`);
        return fetch(`${domain}/albums/${photo.albumId}`)
    })
    .then( response => response.json() )
    .then( album => {
        let html = $("#photo").html();
        html += `<h4>In album ${album.title}</h4>`;
        $("#photo").html(html);
        return fetch(`${domain}/users/${album.userId}`)
    })
    .then( response => response.json() )
    .then( user => {
        let html = $("#photo").html();
        html += `Posted by ${user.username}`;
        $("#photo").html(html);
    });
```

Description

- Because the methods of the Fetch API return Promise objects, they can be chained. This solves the "callback hell" problem that's common when you use the XMLHttpRequest object.

Figure 18-8   How the Fetch API solves "callback hell"

How to use named callback functions

The code in the previous figure is more readable that the code in the figure that came before it. However, the code in the previous figure can't use earlier return values in later callback functions. To fix this issue, you can use named callback functions rather than anonymous ones as shown by figure 18-9. This makes your code easier to read and maintain. In fact, if you name your callbacks well, a chain of named callback functions can like a sentence.

The first example in this figure presents four named functions. To start, the getPhoto() function returns a promise that resolves to the photo object that's created from the JSON stored in the Ajax response.

The getPhotoAlbum() function accepts a photo object as a parameter. Then, the first then() method gets a promise that resolves to the album object that's related to the photo parameter. However, rather than return that promise, it chains a second then() method. This registers a callback that accepts the album object and adds it to the photo object as a property named album. Then, it returns a promise that resolves to the updated photo object.

This works because the then() method returns a Promise object. So, when the callback you register returns a JavaScript object, the then() method wraps it in a Promise object that eventually resolves to the specified object.

The getPhotoAlbumUser() function works like the getPhotoAlbum() function. However, it uses the album property of the photo object to get the related user object, and it adds the user object to the photo object as a nested property.

The displayPhotoData() function also defines a photo object as a parameter. Then, it uses the data stored in this object to update the DOM. To do that, this code uses the album and nested album.user properties set by the previous two methods.

The second example uses these callback functions in a chain of promises. This code is concise and reads like a sentence.

The third example shows an even more concise way to code the second example that reads even more like a sentence. This works because you can omit the arrow function and just code the name of the callback function if that callback function only has a single parameter that's the same as the value that the promise resolves to.

Named callback functions that get related data

```
const getPhoto = () =>
    fetch(`${domain}/photos/1`)
        .then( response => response.json() );   // resolves to photo object

const getPhotoAlbum = photo => {
    return fetch(`${domain}/albums/${photo.albumId}`)
        .then( response => response.json() )      // resolves to album object
        .then( album => {
            photo.album = album;                  // add album property
            return photo;                         // resolves to photo object
        });
};

const getPhotoAlbumUser = photo => {
    return fetch(`${domain}/users/${photo.album.userId}`)
        .then( response => response.json() )      // resolves to user object
        .then( user => {
            photo.album.user = user;              // add album.user property
            return photo;                         // resolves to photo object
        });
};

const displayPhotoData = photo => {
    let html = `<img src="${photo.url}" alt="${photo.title}">`;
    html    += `<h4>In album ${photo.album.title}</h4>`;
    html    += `Posted by ${photo.album.user.username}`;
    $("#photo").html(html);
};
```

A promise chain that uses the named callback functions

```
getPhoto()
    .then( photo => getPhotoAlbum(photo) )
    .then( photo => getPhotoAlbumUser(photo) )
    .then( photo => displayPhotoData(photo) );
```

A more concise way to code the same promise chain

```
getPhoto()
    .then(getPhotoAlbum)
    .then(getPhotoAlbumUser)
    .then(displayPhotoData);
```

Description

- You can use named callback functions to make a promise chain easier to read, understand, and maintain.

- If a callback function only has a single parameter that's the same as the value that the promise resolves to, you can omit the arrow function and just code the name of the callback function.

Figure 18-9   How to use named callback functions

How to handle errors

Figure 18-10 shows some more techniques for handling errors that are often useful if you have a chain of promises. To start, the table in figure 18-10 presents the finally() method of the Promise object that you can use to handle errors. This method works much like the finally clause of a try-catch-finally statement.

The finally() method registers a callback function that's executed when the promise is settled. Remember, a promise is settled when it is either fulfilled or rejected. For a finally() method, the callback doesn't receive any parameters. Typically, this callback is used for cleanup operations like closing files or clearing messages that notify the user that an action is pending.

The first example in this figure shows how the catch() method is typically used. Here, the code only supplies a single catch() method at the end of a chain of promises. This catch() method handles any errors that occur in any of the callback functions registered with the then() methods in the chain. This catch() method displays an error message on the console.

The second example shows how to use the catch() method to recover from an error. To start, the getMyPhoto() function begins by checking whether its id parameter is greater than zero. If so, it returns a promise from the fetch() method. Otherwise, it returns a rejected promise. To do that, this code uses the static Promise.reject() method that's described later in this chapter.

After defining the getMyPhoto() function, this example defines three more functions named getGenericPhoto(), displayPhoto(), and logError(). Then, it begins a chain of promises by calling the getMyPhoto() function, and it calls the catch() method to register the getGenericPhoto() function as the callback to execute if the getMyPhoto() function returns a rejected promise. This works because the catch() method automatically wraps the object literal that's returned by getGenericPhoto() in a promise that resolves to that object literal.

After the first catch() method, the then() method registers the displayPhoto() function as the callback to execute when the earlier promise resolves. As a result, if there's an error, displayPhoto() executes when the promise returned by the catch() method resolves to the generic photo. Otherwise, the catch() method is skipped and displayPhoto() executes when the promise returned by the getMy-Photo() function resolves to the photo for the specified id.

The third example shows how to use the finally() method to execute cleanup code. Here, the finally() method registers a function named closeFile() as the callback to execute when all the promises in the chain are settled. This callback function makes sure that the file that's opened by the readFile() function at the start of this code is always closed, whether an error occurs or not. To focus on the catch() and finally() methods, this example doesn't show the code for the readFile(), displayContents(), logError(), or closeFile() functions.

One more method of the Promise type

Method	Description
`finally(callback)`	Registers the callback function to execute when a promise is settled. The callback function doesn't receive a parameter. Returns a Promise object.

A catch() method for general errors

```
getPhoto()
    .then(getPhotoAlbum)
    .then(getPhotoAlbumUser)
    .then(displayPhotoData)
    .catch( e => console.log(e.message) );
```

A catch() method that recovers from an error

```
const getMyPhoto = id => {
    if(id > 0) {
        return fetch(`${domain}/photos/${id}`)
                    .then( response => response.json() );
    } else {
        return Promise.reject(new Error("id must be greater than zero."));
    }
};
const getGenericPhoto = () => ( {url: "images/genericPhoto.jpg"} );
const displayPhoto = photo => console.log(photo.url);
const logError = e => console.log(e);

getMyPhoto(0)
    .catch(getGenericPhoto)
    .then(displayPhoto)
    .catch(logError);
```

A finally() method that makes sure a file is closed

```
readFile()
    .then(displayContents)
    .catch(logError)
    .finally(closeFile);
```

Description

- It's a good practice to end every promise chain with a catch() method for general errors. You can also include a catch() method earlier in a promise chain for specific errors that can be recovered from.

- It's also possible to handle errors by passing an optional second callback function to the then() method. However, it's a better practice to use the catch() method.

- The finally() method is typically used for cleanup activities.

Figure 18-10   How to handle errors

The Photo Viewer application

Figure 18-11 presents a Photo Viewer application that displays a photo for the specified ID. In addition, it displays some related data such as the album title, photo title, and username. To make this possible, the Photo Viewer application gets its data from the JSON Placeholder API described earlier in this chapter.

This API doesn't provide realistic photos and text. Instead, it provides placeholder photos that are squares of different colors, and it provides placeholder text that's mostly in Latin. Still, this API provides related photo, album, and user data that requires you to make additional Ajax requests based on the data returned by the response to an initial Ajax request. As a result, it's useful for testing these types of Ajax requests.

The HTML and CSS

The HTML for this application displays the title of the application as well as a text box that allows the user to enter an ID for the photo. In addition, it displays a View button that allows the user to view the photo data for the specified ID. Here, the text box has an id of "photo_id", and the View button has an id of "view_button".

Below the View button, this HTML includes a div element with an id of "photo". This is where the application displays the photo and its related data. It's also where the application displays any error messages.

The CSS aligns the label and input elements. To do that, it specifies that the label should be displayed as an inline block and sets the width of the label to 10em. In addition, it sets the right margin of the all input elements including the text box to 1em.

The Photo Viewer application

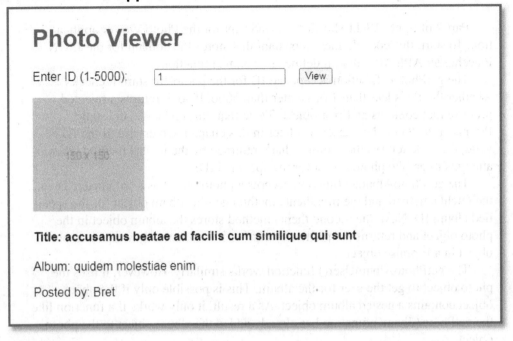

The HTML

```
<body>
    <main>
        <h1>Photo Viewer</h1>
        <div>
            <label for="photo_id">Enter ID (1-5000):</label>
            <input type="text" name="photo_id" id="photo_id" value="1">
            <input type="button" id="view_button" value="View">
        </div>
        <div id="photo"></div>
    </main>
    <script src="https://code.jquery.com/jquery-3.4.1.slim.min.js"></script>
    <script src="photo_viewer.js"></script>
</body>
```

Some of the CSS

```
label {
    display: inline-block;
    width: 10em;
}
input {
    margin-right: 1em;
}
```

Description

- The Photo Viewer application allows the user to enter an ID for the photo. Then, it displays a thumbnail image for the ID. In addition, it displays some related data such as photo title, album title, and username.

Figure 18-11   The Photo Viewer application (part 1)

The JavaScript

Part 2 of figure 18-11 shows the JavaScript for the Photo Viewer application. To start, this code defines a constant that stores the domain for the JSON Placeholder API. After that, it defines five named functions.

The getPhoto() function accepts an ID for the photo. To start, it checks whether the ID is less than 1 or greater than 5000. If so, it returns a rejected promise that contains an Error object. To do that, this code uses the static Promise.reject() method described later in this chapter. Otherwise, if the ID is valid, the code returns the promise that's returned by the fetch() method when it attempts to get the photo object for the specified ID.

The getPhotoAlbum() function accepts a photo object as a parameter. Then, the fetch() method and the first then() method get the album object for the specified album ID. Next, the second then() method stores the album object in the photo object and returns the photo object after it automatically wraps that photo object in a Promise object.

The getPhotoAlbumUser() function works similarly. However, it uses the photo object to get the user for the album. This is possible only if the photo object contains a nested album object. As a result, it only works if a function like the getPhotoAlbum() function has already added the album object to the photo object.

The displayPhotoData() function accepts a photo object and uses it to generate the HTML that's displayed. Within this function, the first statement creates the img element that uses its src attribute to display a thumbnail image. The second statement creates the h4 element that displays the title of the photo album. The third statement creates a <p> element that displays the title of the photo. The fourth statement adds plain text that displays the username. And the fifth statement adds this HTML to the div element that has an id of "photo".

The displayError() function accepts an Error object and uses it to display the error message that it contains. To do that, it creates the HTML for a span element that displays the error. Then, it adds this HTML to the div element that has an id of "photo".

The ready() event handler registers the click() event handler for the View button. This event handler begins by getting the photo ID entered by the user. Then, it uses a chain of promises to get the photo object from the JSON Placeholder API. Here, the getPhoto() function gets the photo object with the specified ID. Next, the first then() method stores the album object in the photo object, the second then() method stores the user object in the photo object, and the third then() method displays the photo and its related data. However, if an error occurs, the catch() method displays an error.

The JavaScript

```javascript
"use strict";

const domain = "https://jsonplaceholder.typicode.com";

const getPhoto = id => {
    if (id < 1 || id > 5000) {
        return Promise.reject(
            new Error ("Photo ID must be between 1 and 5000."));
    } else {
        return fetch(`${domain}/photos/${id}`)
            .then( response => response.json() );  // resolves to photo obj
    }
};

const getPhotoAlbum = photo => {
    return fetch(`${domain}/albums/${photo.albumId}`)
        .then( response => response.json() )   // resolves to album obj
        .then( album => {
            photo.album = album;               // add album property
            return photo;                      // resolves to photo obj
        });
};

const getPhotoAlbumUser = photo => {
    return fetch(`${domain}/users/${photo.album.userId}`)
        .then( response => response.json() )   // resolves to user obj
        .then( user => {
            photo.album.user = user;           // add album.user property
            return photo;                      // resolves to photo obj
        });
};

const displayPhotoData = photo => {
    let html = `<img src="${photo.thumbnailUrl}" alt="${photo.title}">`;
    html    += `<h4>Title: ${photo.title}</h4>`;
    html    += `<p>Album: ${photo.album.title}</p>`;
    html    += `Posted by: ${photo.album.user.username}`;
    $("#photo").html(html);
};

const displayError = e => {
    let html = `<span>${e}</span>`;
    $("#photo").html(html);
};

$(document).ready( () => {
    $("#view_button").click( () => {
        const photo_id = $("#photo_id").val();
        getPhoto(photo_id)
            .then(getPhotoAlbum)
            .then(getPhotoAlbumUser)
            .then(displayPhotoData)
            .catch(displayError);
    });
});
```

Figure 18-11 The Photo Viewer application (part 2)

More skills for working with promises

So far, this chapter has shown how to work with the Promise objects that the fetch(), then(), and catch() methods return. However, you can use promises outside of these methods too.

How to create and use your own Promise objects

If necessary, you can create your own Promise objects. This is sometimes useful for converting code that uses callbacks so it can use promises instead. To do that, you use a Promise constructor as shown by the syntax at the top of figure 18-12. This constructor accepts a single parameter that's a callback function. In turn, this callback function accepts two parameters, which are also callback functions. Typically, these two callback functions are named resolve and reject.

The resolve() callback is the callback that's registered by the then() method of a promise. Similarly, the reject() callback is the one that's registered by the catch() method.

The first example below the table shows how this works. Here, the myFetch() function wraps the XMLHttpRequest object in a promise. This function is similar to the fetch() method, but it supports older browsers.

The myFetch() function returns a Promise object by calling the Promise constructor and passing it a callback function with two parameters named resolve and reject. In the body of the Promise constructor, the code creates a new XMLHttpRequest object, configures it, opens the connection, and starts the request. As a result, when this function returns this Promise object, the request made with the XMLHttpRequest object has been made and is waiting for a response. In other words, the promise is pending.

In the callback function for the onreadystatechange event, the code uses the readyState property to check whether the request is done. If so, the code checks the status property. If the status is 200 (OK), the code calls the resolve() callback that was registered by the then() method and passes it the data returned by the request. Otherwise, the code calls the reject() callback that was registered by the catch() method and passes it a new Error object.

The code that calls the myFetch() function passes it a URL for an Ajax request. Next, it calls the then() method to register the callback to execute when the request completes successfully. In other words, it registers the callback to use for the resolve() function. After that, it calls the catch() method to register the callback to execute when the request fails. In other words, it registers the callback to use for the reject() function.

The second example shows a function named wait() that wraps the setTimeout() function. Here, if the milliseconds value is valid, the code passes the milliseconds value and the resolve() callback to the setTimeout() function. This executes the resolve() callback after the specified number of milliseconds. Otherwise, if the milliseconds value isn't valid, this code calls the reject() method and passes it a RangeError object. The code that calls the wait() function retries a function that fails intermittently. This can be useful if you need to recover from intermittent errors caused by network traffic.

The syntax of the Promise constructor

```
const myPromise = new Promise(callback);
```

The two parameters of the callback passed to the Promise constructor

Parameter	Description
resolve	The callback function that is passed to the then() method to execute when the promise is resolved.
reject	The callback function that is passed to the catch() method to execute when the promise is rejected.

A function that wraps the XMLHttpRequest object in a promise

```
const myFetch = url => {
  return new Promise( (resolve, reject) => {
    const xhr = new XMLHttpRequest();
    xhr.responseType = "json";
    xhr.onreadystatechange = () => {
        if (xhr.readyState == 4) {
            if (xhr.status == 200) {
                resolve(xhr.response)
            } else {
                reject(new Error(`Error code: ${xhr.status}`));
            }
        }
    };
    xhr.open("GET", url);
    xhr.send();
  });
};
```

Code that uses the function

```
myFetch(`${domain}/todos/`)
    .then( todos => console.log(todos) )
    .catch( e => console.log(e) );
```

A function that wraps the setTimeout() function in a Promise

```
const wait = milliseconds => {
    return new Promise( (resolve, reject) => {
        if (milliseconds > 0) {
            setTimeout(resolve, milliseconds);
        } else {
            reject( new RangeError("Milliseconds must be positive.") );
        }
    });
}
```

Code that uses the function

```
actionThatFailsIntermittently()
    .catch( e => wait(200).then(actionThatFailsIntermittently) ) // retry
    .then(doSomethingWithDataReturnedByAction)
    .catch(logError);
```

Description

- You can create your own Promise objects with the Promise constructor.

Figure 18-12   How to create and use your own Promise objects

Static methods of the Promise type

Figure 18-13 presents five of the most useful static methods available from the Promise type. The Promise.all() and Promise.allSettled() methods are similar in that they both accept an array of promises, execute these promises asynchronously, and return a promise that resolves to an array of values.

However, there are two important differences between these two methods. First, if any promise in the array that's passed to Promise.all() is rejected, Promise.all() immediately resolves to an array that contains only the return value of the rejected promise. In contrast, Promise.allSettled() resolves to an array that contains the return values for all of the promises, whether those promises resolve or reject.

Second, these two methods resolve to arrays that contain different types of data. The array returned by Promise.all() contains the values that the promises resolve to. In contrast, the array returned by Promise.allSettled() contains objects with two properties. The first property is named status and contains a string of "fulfilled" or "rejected". The second property depends on the status of the promise. If it was fulfilled, the second property contains the value the promise resolved to. But if the promise was rejected, the second property contains the reason the promise was rejected.

Like the first two methods, the Promise.race() method accepts an array of promises and executes them asynchronously. Unlike those methods, though, Promise.race() resolves to the return value of the first promise that's resolved or rejected. In other words, it returns the promise that wins the race.

The first three static methods in the table return Promise objects that are pending. Eventually, these Promise objects resolve or reject. In contrast, the Promise.resolve() and Promise.reject() methods each return a Promise object that is already resolved or rejected.

The examples in this figure show how some of these static methods work. To start, the first and second examples define an array of promise objects that are used by the next two examples. Here, the second example uses the Promise.reject() method to add a rejected Promise object to the array of promises defined in the first example. As a result, the array named fetchUsers contains three pending promises and one rejected promise. The three pending promises may also eventually reject, but the fourth promise has already been rejected. This rejected promise provides a way to test the Promise.all() and Promise.allSettled() methods.

The third example uses the Promise.all() method to resolve the promises stored in the array of promises. However, since the fourth promise is rejected, this method only returns the value for the rejected promise.

The fourth example uses the Promise.allSettled() method to resolve the same promises. This time, the method continues executing until all promises are fulfilled or rejected. This shows that the first three objects in the array that's returned have a status of "fulfilled" and a value property that contains the JSON returned by the request. However, the fourth object in the array has a status of "rejected" and a reason property that contains the Error object.

Five static methods of the Promise type

Method	Description
all(*promises*)	Accepts an array of Promise objects and executes the asynchronous requests for each promise. If all promises are fulfilled, returns a Promise object that resolves to an array of the values that each promise resolves to. If any promise is rejected, this method returns the rejected promise and no others.
allSettled(*promises*)	Accepts an array of Promise objects and executes the asynchronous requests for each promise. Returns a Promise object that resolves to an array of objects for all promises. Within this array, each object has a status property that indicates whether it was fulfilled or rejected.
race(*promises*)	Accepts an array of Promise objects and executes the asynchronous requests for each promise. Returns a Promise object that resolves to the return value of the first promise that's resolved or rejected.
resolve(*value*)	Returns a Promise object that's resolved with the specified value.
reject(*value*)	Returns a Promise object that's rejected with the specified value.

An array of Promise objects

```
const fetchUsers = [
    fetch(`${domain}/users/1`).then(r => r.json()),
    fetch(`${domain}/users/2`).then(r => r.json()),
    fetch(`${domain}/users/3`).then(r => r.json())
];
```

Add a rejected promise to the array of Promise objects

```
fetchUsers.push( Promise.reject(new Error("Dang!")) );
```

Execute an array of promises

```
Promise.all(fetchUsers)
    .then( users => console.log(users) )
    .catch( e => console.log(e) );
```

Only the return value of the rejected promise is displayed

```
Error: Dang!
```

Another way to execute an array of promises

```
Promise.allSettled(fetchUsers)
    .then( users => console.log(users) )
    .catch( e => console.log(e) );
```

The return values of all the promises are displayed

```
▼ (4) [{…}, {…}, {…}, {…}] 
  ▶ 0: {status: "fulfilled", value: {…}}
  ▶ 1: {status: "fulfilled", value: {…}}
  ▶ 2: {status: "fulfilled", value: {…}}
  ▶ 3: {status: "rejected", reason: Error: Dang!
```

Figure 18-13   Useful static methods of the Promise type

How to use the *async* and *await* keywords

So far, this chapter has shown how promises can make asynchronous code more readable. Still, most developers are used to synchronous code, and code that works directly with promises just *looks* different, which can make it harder for some developers to understand. Fortunately, the *async* and *await* keywords make asynchronous code look more like synchronous code. In turn, this makes working with promises even easier.

When you define a function, you can use the *async* keyword to create an *asynchronous function* that wraps the return value of that function in a Promise object. For instance, the first example in figure 18-14 presents a function named getPI() that returns the value of the Math.PI property. This looks much like a normal arrow function, except that it's prefixed with the *async* keyword. As a result, the value returned by Math.PI is automatically wrapped in a promise. That's why the code that calls this function uses the then() method of the promise to get the value that the promise resolves to.

The *await* keyword tells JavaScript to wait until a promise is settled and then return its result. It can only be used in asynchronous functions. For instance, the second example defines an asynchronous function named loadPhoto() that uses the fetch() method to get a photo object. Then, it uses that photo object to get the album object that's related to the photo. Here, the *await* keyword makes this code look like "normal" synchronous code because it doesn't use callback functions. Also, since the function is defined with the *async* keyword, it wraps the photo object that's returned in a promise. That's why the code that calls the loadPhoto() function uses the then() method to access the photo object.

The third example shows how to pass an asynchronous event handler to the jQuery ready() method. To do that, this code includes the *async* keyword before the function that's passed to the ready() method. Then, within that function, the code uses the *await* keyword to get the values that the promises returned by the fetch() and json() methods resolve to. Because the function doesn't need to return a result, it doesn't create a single return object that contains all the data like the second example does. Instead, the third example just retrieves the data asynchronously and uses it to update the DOM.

The *async* keyword can also be used with IIFEs as shown by the fourth example. Then, you can use the *await* keyword with promises within the IIFE.

The examples in this figure also show how to handle errors when you use the *async* and *await* keywords. You can use the catch() method with the promise that an asynchronous function returns. However, within an asynchronous function, you can use a normal try-catch statement.

A simple asynchronous function

```
const getPI = async () => Math.PI;
```

Code that calls the function and uses the promise it returns

```
getPI().then( pi => console.log(pi) );    // displays 3.141592653589793
```

An asynchronous function that uses await instead of a chain of promises

```
const loadPhoto = async photoId => {
    const photoResponse = await fetch(`${domain}/photos/${photoId}`);
    const photo = await photoResponse.json();

    const albumResponse = await fetch(`${domain}/albums/${photo.albumId}`)
    const album = await albumResponse.json();
    photo.album = album;

    return photo;  // automatically wrapped in a Promise object
}
```

Code that calls the function and uses the promise it returns

```
loadPhoto(1)
    .then( photo => {
        let html = `<img src="${photo.url}" alt="${photo.title}">`;
        html += `<h4>In album ${photo.album.title}</h4>`;
        $("#photo").html(html);
    })
    .catch( e => console.log(e) ); // use catch() method for error handling
```

A jQuery ready() function with an asynchronous event handler

```
$(document).ready( async () => {
    try {
        const postResponse = await fetch(`${domain}/posts/1`);
        const post = await postResponse.json();
        const userResponse = await fetch(`${domain}/users/${post.userId}`)
        const user = await userResponse.json();

        let html = `<h2>${post.title}</h2>`;
        html += `<p>${post.body}</p>`;
        html += `<span>Posted by ${user.username}</span>`;
        $("#post").html(html);
    }
    catch(e) { console.log(e); }    // use try/catch for error handling
});
```

An asynchronous IIFE

```
(async () => {
    // asynchronous code goes here
})();
```

Description

- The *async* keyword declares an *asynchronous function* that wraps its return value in a Promise object.
- The *await* keyword tells JavaScript to wait until a promise is settled and then return its result. It can only be used in asynchronous functions.

Figure 18-14   How to use the *async* and *await* keywords

How to work with for-await-of loops

If you want to make multiple asynchronous requests, and the sequence of these requests doesn't matter, you can use the Promise.all() or Promise.allSettled() methods described earlier in this chapter. Sometimes, though, you need to make multiple asynchronous requests, and you need to control the sequence of these requests. To do that, you can use a for-of or a *for-await-of loop* as shown in figure 18-15.

The main difference between the two loops is that the for-await-of loop includes the *await* keyword in the for statement itself, rather than in the body of the loop. This makes the code more concise.

Both of these examples use the *await* keyword. As a result, they must be coded within asynchronous functions. In this figure, both examples are coded within asynchronous IIFEs.

The for-await-of loop is designed to work with asynchronous iterators. These are often defined with asynchronous generators and the well-known symbol Symbol.asyncIterator. Although asynchronous iterators are beyond the scope of this book, you can find lots of information about them online.

An array of Promise objects

```
const promises = [
    fetch(`${domain}/posts/1`).then(r => r.json()),
    fetch(`${domain}/posts/2`).then(r => r.json()),
    fetch(`${domain}/posts/3`).then(r => r.json())
];
```

A for-of loop that processes the promises in sequence

```
(async () => {
    for (const promise of promises) {
        const json = await promise;          // use await in body of loop
        console.log(json);
    }
})();
```

A for-await-of loop that performs the same task

```
(async () => {
    for await (const json of promises) {  // use await in loop statement
        console.log(json);
    }
})();
```

Description

- If you need to execute multiple requests, and you need to make the requests sequentially, you can use a *for-await-of loop*. This works much like a for-of loop, but it includes the *await* keyword in the loop statement.

- The for-await-of loop is designed to work with asynchronous iterators.

Figure 18-15   How to work with for-await-of loops

The updated JavaScript for the Photo Viewer application

Figure 18-16 presents the JavaScript for the Photo Viewer application after it has been updated to use the *async* and *await* keywords instead of a chain of promises. This code begins by defining a constant named domain that holds the base URL for the JSON Placeholder API. Then, it defines three helper functions.

The getPhoto() function is defined with the *async* keyword. As a result, it is an asynchronous function that can use the *await* keyword to wait for a promise to be settled. This function accepts an ID for the photo. It begins by checking whether this ID is valid. If not, it uses the static Promise.reject() method to return a rejected promise that contains an Error object with an appropriate message.

However, if the ID is valid, this code uses the *await* keyword with the fetch() method to wait for the response object that the promise resolves to. When the response resolves, this code uses the json() method to get the photo object from the JSON in the response.

After getting the photo object, this code uses the *await* keyword with the fetch() and json() methods to get the album object that's related to the photo. Then, it stores the album object as a property of the photo object.

After getting the album object, this code uses a similar technique to get the user object that's related to the album. Then, it stores the user object as a nested property of the photo object. Finally, it returns the photo object.

Because the getPhoto() function is an asynchronous function, returning the photo object automatically wraps that object in a resolved promise. If you were working strictly with promises, you'd need to pass the photo object to the Promise.resolve() method to achieve the same effect.

Note that the getPhoto() function uses the Promise.reject() method to wrap the Error object in a rejected promise. This is necessary for the try/catch statement in the click() event handler to be able to catch this error.

The displayPhotoData() function isn't asynchronous. Rather, it accepts the photo object and uses it to update the HTML in the DOM exactly as it did earlier in this chapter. Similarly, the displayError() function isn't asynchronous and works exactly as it did earlier in this chapter.

The ready() event handler uses the *async* keyword to register an asynchronous click() event handler for the View button. This event handler begins by getting the photo ID entered by the user. Then, it defines a try-catch statement. Within the try block, the first statement uses the *await* keyword to wait for the photo object the asynchronous getPhoto() function eventually resolves to. This gets the photo object with the specified ID. Then, the second statement passes the photo object to the displayPhotoData() method. This displays the photo and its related data in the browser. However, if an error occurs, the catch block uses the displayError() function to display the error in the browser.

If you compare the code in this figure with the code in part 2 of figure 18-11, you should notice that it's shorter and easier to read. Because of that, it's also easier to debug and maintain. In addition, this code looks more like the synchronous code that most programmers already understand.

The updated JavaScript for the Photo Viewer application

```javascript
"use strict";

const domain = "https://jsonplaceholder.typicode.com";

const getPhoto = async id => {
    if (id < 1 || id > 5000) {
        return Promise.reject(
            new Error ("Photo ID must be between 1 and 5000."));
    } else {
        const r1 = await fetch(`${domain}/photos/${id}`);
        const photo = await r1.json();

        const r2 = await fetch(`${domain}/albums/${photo.albumId}`)
        const album = await r2.json();
        photo.album = album;

        const r3 = await fetch(`${domain}/users/${photo.album.userId}`)
        const user = await r3.json();
        photo.album.user = user;

        return photo;   // automatically wrapped in a promise
    }
};

const displayPhotoData = photo => {
    let html = `<img src="${photo.thumbnailUrl}" alt="${photo.title}">`;
    html    += `<h4>Title: ${photo.title}</h4>`;
    html    += `<p>Album: ${photo.album.title}</p>`;
    html    += `Posted by: ${photo.album.user.username}`;
    $("#photo").html(html);
};

const displayError = e => {
    let html = `<span>${e}</span>`;
    $("#photo").html(html);
};

$(document).ready( () => {
    $("#view_button").click( async () => {
        const photo_id = $("#photo_id").val();
        try {
            const photo = await getPhoto(photo_id);
            displayPhotoData(photo);
        }
        catch(e) {
            displayError(e);
        }
    });
});
```

Figure 18-16   The updated JavaScript for the Photo Viewer application

How to make cross-origin requests

So far, the examples in this chapter work because they make requests to an API that allows *cross-origin requests*. For security reasons, though, many APIs don't allow cross-origin requests. As a result, you'll get an error if you try to make one. To handle this issue, you can start by learning more about it.

An introduction to Cross Origin Resource Sharing

For security, browsers enforce a *same origin policy* for client-side code. This means JavaScript code from one *origin* (protocol, domain, and port) can't request a resource from another origin. For instance, JavaScript code at http://mysite.com can't request a resource from an API at https://yourapi.com. Fortunately, browsers have a mechanism that allows exceptions to the same origin policy.

Browsers use *Cross Origin Resource Sharing (CORS)* to check whether JavaScript is allowed to make cross-origin requests. To do that, CORS requires the server that's hosting the API to include an Access-Control-Allow-Origin header in the HTTP response that it returns. Figure 18-17 shows two examples of this header. The first authorizes a cross-origin request from a specific website, and the second uses the * character to authorize requests from any website.

How to handle CORS issues with APIs

If you make an Ajax request to an API that doesn't allow cross-origin requests, your request will fail with an error message like the one shown in this figure. Unfortunately, if an API doesn't allow cross-origin requests, there's no way to fix this with client-side code. In that case, you can only make the request with server-side code.

In the past, some developers used iframes or JSON with padding (JSON-P) to trick the server into thinking that another server was making the request. However, these techniques aren't recommended for modern development.

These days, it's generally considered a best practice to solve this issue by using a *server-side proxy*. Such a proxy uses code that runs on the server to request data from the API and then displays it in a web page that has the same origin as your client-side application. Then, your application can use an Ajax request to get the data from that web page.

Creating your own server-side proxy is generally considered the best way to solve this issue. For example, you could use Node.js to run JavaScript on the server as described in the next chapter, and you can use the cors-anywhere module to create your own server-side proxy. However, creating such a proxy is beyond the scope of this book.

Fortunately, there are third-party proxies that function similarly. For example, this figure shows how to use the CORS Anywhere proxy. In general, using a third-party proxy isn't secure enough for a production application. However, it's useful for quickly developing a prototype or testing an API.

A CORS header that allows a specific cross-origin request

```
Access-Control-Allow-Origin: https://example.com
```

A CORS header that allows any cross-origin request

```
Access-Control-Allow-Origin: *
```

A CORS error in the console

```
Access to fetch at 'https://www.flickr.com/services/feeds/photos_public.gne' from origin
'null' has been blocked by CORS policy: No 'Access-Control-Allow-Origin' header is present on the
requested resource. If an opaque response serves your needs, set the request's mode to 'no-cors' to
fetch the resource with CORS disabled.
```

Ways to make a cross-origin request to an API that doesn't allow them

- Use iframes (not recommended).
- Use JSON-P (not recommended).
- Use a third-party proxy (only recommended for prototyping and testing).
- Create your own server-side proxy.

The URL for a third-party proxy named CORS Anywhere

```
https://cors-anywhere.herokuapp.com/
```

Code that uses the CORS Anywhere proxy to make a cross-origin request

```
const proxy = "https://cors-anywhere.herokuapp.com/";
const api = "https://www.flickr.com/services/feeds/photos_public.gne";
const url = proxy + api;  // prefix api URL with CORS Anywhere URL

const response = await fetch(url);
...
```

Description

- For security, browsers enforce a *same origin policy*. This means JavaScript code from one *origin* (protocol, domain, and port) can't request a resource from another origin unless that server returns a response that contains the appropriate *Cross Origin Resource Sharing (CORS)* headers.
- If the response from an API doesn't contain the correct CORS headers, you can't use an Ajax request to access that API.
- To make a cross-origin request, you can use a *server-side proxy*. This is server-side code in your application that requests the data from the API and makes it available as a web page. Then, you can use an Ajax request to get the data from the proxy.
- For testing and development, you can use a third-party proxy like CORS Anywhere. However, this usually isn't secure enough for a production application.

Figure 18-17   How to make cross-origin requests

Perspective

Now that you've completed this chapter, you should be able to use Ajax to get data from a web service, parse that data, and update a web page with that data without reloading the entire page. This is a powerful skill that's commonly used in modern websites. In addition, you should have a solid set of skills for working with asynchronous JavaScript. Because many scripts that run on a server should run asynchronously, these skills are often useful when writing JavaScript that runs on a server as described in the next chapter.

Terms

Ajax (Asynchronous JavaScript and XML)	rejected
	settled
XMLHttpRequest (XHR) object	resolved
Fetch API	async keyword
web service	await keyword
API (Application Programming Interface)	asynchronous function
	for-await-of loop
XML (Extensible Markup Language)	cross-origin request
JSON (JavaScript Object Notation)	same origin policy
object member	origin
callback function	Cross Origin Resource Sharing
promise	(CORS)
pending	server-side proxy
fulfilled	

Summary

- Unlike normal HTTP requests, *Ajax (Asynchronous JavaScript and XML)* requests update a page with data from a web server without needing to reload the entire page. This is called a "partial page refresh."

- When you use Ajax, you use JavaScript to make the request, process the returned data, and update the DOM so the data is displayed on the web page.

- To send an Ajax request, JavaScript can use a browser object known as the *XMLHttpRequest (XHR) object*, or it can use the *Fetch API*.

- Ajax requests are often made to *web services* that provide *Application Programming Interfaces (APIs)* that developers can use to get data from a website.

- The two most common data formats for working with Ajax are *XML* (*Extensible Markup Language*) and *JSON* (*JavaScript Object Notation*).

- A *member* of an object is one of its methods, properties, or events.

- Asynchronous code can't return values or throw exceptions like synchronous code can. Instead, you must code *callback functions* that execute when the asynchronous code eventually returns a value or throws an exception.

- The Fetch API provides methods and objects for making Ajax requests. When its fetch() method gets data, it returns a Promise object, or *promise*.

- A Promise object is in one of three states: *pending, fulfilled,* or *rejected.* A promise that is fulfilled or rejected is *settled.* A promise can be *resolved* without being fulfilled by returning another Promise object.

- The *async* keyword declares an *asynchronous function* that wraps its return value in a Promise object.

- The *await* keyword tells JavaScript to wait until a promise is settled and then return its result. It can only be used in asynchronous functions.

- A *cross-origin request* occurs when JavaScript code from one *origin* (protocol, domain, and port) requests a resource from another origin. For security, browsers enforce a *same origin policy.*

- Servers provide *Cross Origin Resource Sharing (CORS)* headers that allow JavaScript to make cross-origin requests.

- To make a cross-origin request from a server that doesn't have CORS headers, you can use a *server-side proxy* to request data from an API and make it available as a web page that has the same origin as your application. Then, you can request the data from that web page.

Exercise 18-1   Review and update the APOD application

In this exercise, you'll review and update the Astronomy Picture of the Day (APOD) application that uses NASA's APOD API.

Run the application

1. Use your text editor or IDE to open the application in this folder:
    `javascript_jquery\exercises\ch18\astronomy_pod`

2. Run the application. Note that the date text box contains today's date.

3. Click the View button and review the data that's displayed.

4. Experiment with other dates, including future dates, dates before June 16, 1995, dates not in the YYYY-MM-DD format the API requires, and invalid dates.

Review the code

5. Open the index.html file and review the HTML for the application. Note that the second div element has an id of "display". This div element is where the application displays the HTML that contains the data from the API.

6. Open the apod.js file and review the JavaScript for the application.

7. Review the URL for the API and note that it includes an API key. Note that the api_key parameter has a value of DEMO_KEY.

8. Visit the website for the NASA APIs (https://api.nasa.gov) to learn more about the limits of using the DEMO_KEY. If you want, you can get your own API key and replace the DEMO_KEY value with your own key. This removes most of the limits of using the DEMO_KEY.

9. On the website for the NASA APIs, review the documentation for the APOD API and explore any other APIs that you're interested in.

10. In the apod.js file, review the code that makes the asynchronous request to the API. Note that it uses the fetch() method and a chain of promise methods, including a catch() method at the end of the chain.

Update the application to use the *async* and *await* keywords

11. Add the *async* keyword to the click() event handler for the View button.

12. Find the chain of promises and code a try/catch statement so that the try block contains the chain of promises.

13. In the try block, code the *await* keyword before the fetch() method to get the initial response from the API. In addition, code the *await* keyword before the json() method of the response to get the object created from the JSON. To do that, you can refer to figure 18-16 for guidance.

14. Write the code that displays the data stored in the object created from the JSON. To do that, you can copy it from the second then() method.

15. Move the error handling code from the catch() method to the catch block.

16. Delete any code that remains of the original promise chain.

17. Run the application and test it to make sure it still works correctly.

19

How to work with Node.js

So far, this book has shown how to use a web browser to run JavaScript. That's because JavaScript was originally developed to provide client-side scripting for browsers in a web application. For server-side scripting, developers needed to use another language such as Java, C#, or PHP. Today, however, you can use JavaScript for server-side scripting, and the most common way to do that is to use Node.js.

An introduction to Node.js

Node.js is an open-source, cross-platform, runtime environment that executes JavaScript code outside a web browser. This provides a way to use JavaScript for server-side scripting.

When to use Node.js

Figure 19-1 begins by listing a few scenarios in which you might want to use Node.js. First, Node.js provides a way to interactively test JavaScript expressions and statements. So, if you want to experiment with JavaScript without running it in a browser, you might want to use Node.js. For example, the next figure shows how to use Node.js to test some JavaScript statements.

Second, if you want to use JavaScript to write applications that run outside of a web browser such as console applications and command-line tools, you can use Node.js to do that. For example, this chapter shows how to create a simple console application that works like the Future Value application that was presented earlier in this book.

Third, if you want to use JavaScript to write server-side scripts, Node.js provides several built-in libraries that contain APIs for working with the local file system and networking. As a result, you can use Node.js to script the local file system or to write networking applications such as web servers. Although this chapter only scratches the surface of how to write this type of server-side code, it shows how to install and use a web server that's written in JavaScript that you can use to test your applications.

How to install Node.js

If you want to use Node.js, the first step is to install it on your computer. To do that, you can use the first procedure in this figure. Since this is similar to installing most applications, you shouldn't have much trouble with it.

After you install Node.js, you can make sure it's installed correctly by starting a command line and entering the command shown in the second procedure. On Windows, you can do that by starting the Command Prompt application. Then, you should get a prompt like this:

```
C:\Users\YourUsername>
```

At this prompt, you can enter the "node –v" command.

Or, if you're a macOS user, you can start the Terminal application. Then, you should get a prompt like this:

```
Your-Computer-Name:CurrentDirectory YourUsername$
```

At this prompt, you can enter the "node –v" command. Either way, the node command should respond by displaying the version of Node.js that you just installed.

The Node.js website

www.nodejs.org

Use Node.js when you want to...

- Interactively test JavaScript expressions and statements.
- Use JavaScript to write applications that run outside of a web browser such as console applications and command-line tools.
- Use JavaScript to write server-side scripts.

How to install Node.js

1. Go to the download page for Node.js. One way to find this page is to search the Internet for "node.js download".
2. Click the button for the most current LTS (Long Term Stable) release and respond to the resulting dialog boxes.
3. If you get any warning dialog boxes, choose to continue with the installation. This should download the installer file to your computer.
4. Double-click on the installer file to start the installation.
5. Respond to the resulting dialog boxes by accepting the default options.

How to make sure Node.js is installed correctly

1. Start a Command Prompt (Windows) or Terminal (macOS) window.
2. Enter the following command:

```
C:\Users\mike>node -v
v12.18.2
```

   If this displays the version number of Node.js that's installed on your system, Node.js is set up correctly.

Description

- *Node.js* is an open-source, cross-platform, runtime environment that executes JavaScript code outside a web browser.
- The examples in this chapter have been done on a Windows system. If you're using a macOS or Linux system, the prompt will look a little different. On a macOS system, for example, the prompt is a $ sign instead of the > symbol.

Figure 19-1   An introduction to Node.js

How to use the node command

After you install Node.js, you can start a command line for your operating system. Then, you can use the node command that's provided by Node.js to interactively test code or to run a script that you've stored in a file. Remember that all of the examples in this chapter use a Windows prompt, but otherwise these examples work the same on a macOS or Linux system.

How to interactively test code

Node.js provides a *REPL* (*Read Eval Print Loop*) that interactively evaluates JavaScript code that the user enters at the command line. To start the REPL, you enter the node command at the command prompt without any parameters as shown by the first example in figure 19-2. Then, the command line should show an empty prompt. At this prompt, you can interactively test JavaScript code by typing it and pressing Enter.

The second example shows how to test JavaScript expressions. To do that, you just enter the expression and press Enter. Then, the REPL evaluates the expression, displays the result below the prompt, and displays another command prompt so you can continue testing code. This example shows how you can use parentheses to control the order of precedence in arithmetic operations.

As you enter code at the command prompt, you may want to display code that you've already entered. To do that, you can press the Up and Down arrow keys to scroll through the command prompt history. If necessary, you can edit the code that's displayed. Then, you can press Enter to execute the code again. For example, after entering the first expression in the second example, you could press the Up arrow to display it again, edit the code to add the parentheses, and press Enter to evaluate the new expression.

The third example shows how to test one-line JavaScript statements. To do that, you just enter the statement. In that case, you don't need to enter the semicolon that ends the statement. Then, you can press Enter to evaluate the statement. In this example, the first statement stores a value of 200 in the constant named subtotal. But since this doesn't return a value, the console displays "undefined". However, you can enter the name of the constant at the prompt to display it or use it in another statement.

As you enter code at the command prompt, it may suggest code completion possibilities. For example, when you enter the start of a name, it may suggest the rest of the name. To accept the suggestion, you can press the Tab key.

The fourth example shows how to enter a multi-line statement. To do that, you end the first line with an opening brace ({). Then, the Node.js command prompt lets you enter the rest of the multi-line statement. It doesn't evaluate the statement until you enter the closing brace and press Enter.

The fifth example shows how to exit the Node.js command prompt and return to your operating system's command line. To do that, you enter the .exit command.

How to start the Node.js command prompt

```
C:\Users\Joel>node
Welcome to Node.js v12.18.2.
Type ".help" for more information.
>
```

How to evaluate JavaScript expressions

```
> 3 + 4 * 5
23
> (3 + 4) * 5
35
```

How to evaluate JavaScript statements

```
> const subtotal = 200
undefined
> subtotal
200
> const taxPercent = .05
undefined
> const taxAmount = subtotal * taxPercent
undefined
> taxAmount
10
```

How to evaluate multi-line statements

```
> for (let i = 1; i < 4; i++) {
... console.log(i);
... }
1
2
3
undefined
```

How to exit the Node.js command prompt

```
> .exit
C:\Users\Joel>
```

Description

- Node.js provides a *REPL (Read Eval Print Loop)* that interactively evaluates the JavaScript code that the user enters at the command line.

- To evaluate JavaScript code, type it at the Node.js command prompt and press Enter.

- To display code that you've already entered, use the Up and Down arrow keys to scroll through the command prompt history. If necessary, you can edit the code that's displayed. Then, you can press Enter to execute the code again.

- As you type, the Node.js command prompt may suggest code completion. To accept the code completion, press the Tab key.

- The Node.js command prompt lets you enter a multi-line statement if you end the first line with an opening brace ({).

Figure 19-2   How to interactively test code

How to run a script

Figure 19-3 shows how you can use the node command to run a script. Here, the first example shows a script that has been saved in a file named index.js that's in the book_apps/ch19/future_value directory. This file contains JavaScript that calculates a future value. When you use Node.js to run this script, the four console.log() methods display four lines of data.

The second example shows how to use Node.js to run the script in the first example. To start, this example uses the cd command to change the directory to the book_apps/ch19 directory. Then, it uses the node command to run the index.js file that's in the future_value directory. When it does, Node.js displays the four lines of data on the console.

The third example shows that you don't have to supply the entire filename of the JavaScript file when you use the node command. To start, if your file ends with an extension of .js, you don't have to supply the extension. Similarly, if your file has a name of index.js, you don't have to supply the filename at all. Instead, you can code the name of the directory that contains the file. This works because Node.js uses the index.js file for a directory by default.

The script in the future_value/index.js file

```
"use strict";

// set investment amount, interest rate, and years
const investment = 10000;
const rate = 7.5;
const years = 10;

// calulate future value
let futureValue = investment;
for (let i = 1; i <= years; i++) {
    futureValue += futureValue * rate / 100;
}

// display results
console.log(`Investment amount: ${investment}`);
console.log(`Interest rate: ${rate}`);
console.log(`Years: ${years}`);
console.log(`Future Value: ${futureValue.toFixed(2)}`);
```

How to use the node command to execute the future_value/index.js file

```
>cd /murach/javascript_jquery/book_apps/ch19

>node future_value/index.js
Investment amount: 10000
Interest rate: 7.5
Years: 10
Future Value: 20610.32
```

Two more ways to execute this script

```
>node future_value/index
>node future_value
```

Description

- The console object is available to Node.js. You can use it within a script to display data on the Node.js command prompt.

- To run a script, use the cd command to change to the directory that contains the script. Then, enter the name of the script.

- If your script is in a file that has an extension of .js, you don't need to enter .js to run the file. That's because Node.js automatically adds the .js extension.

- If your script is in a file named index.js, you can enter the name of the directory that contains it instead of entering the filename. That's because Node.js uses the index.js file by default.

Figure 19-3   How to run a script

How to pass arguments to a script

In the previous figure, the script stores the investment amount, interest rate, and number of years in three constants. Typically, though, you would pass these arguments to a script. To do that, you can use the *process object* as described in figure 19-4.

The first example shows the script from the previous figure after it has been updated to accept three arguments. Here, the first three statements use the argv property of the process object to access these arguments. To understand this code, you need to know that the first two arguments of the argv property are for the path to the node command and the path to the script. As a result, the first argument that the user enters on the command line is actually the third argument, which has an index of 2. In turn, the second command line argument has an index of 3, and the third has an index of 4.

After getting the command line arguments, this code uses the parseFloat() and parseInt() functions to parse these arguments into numbers. This is necessary because the argv property stores all of its arguments as strings. Then, this code stores these arguments in the constants named investment, rate, and years.

After storing the command line arguments in constants, this code uses an if statement with the isNaN() function to check whether any of these three arguments is not a valid number. If so, the code displays an error message on the console, and calls the exit() method of the process object to exit the script. Here, the code passes a value of 1 to the script to indicate that the script exited abnormally. In contrast, if you want to exit a script and indicate that the script exited normally, you can pass a value of 0.

After validating the user entries, the code calculates the future value and displays it on the Node.js command line. This works just as it did in the previous example.

The second example shows how to use the node command to pass arguments to the script in the first example. To start, you use the node command to call the index.js script that's in the future_value folder. Then, you enter the three command line arguments, separating each argument with a space. In this example, the code passes arguments of 10000, 6.5, and 10.

The third example shows the array of arguments that are passed to the script. As you saw earlier, the first argument is the path to the node command, and the second argument is the path to the script. This is followed by the three arguments that are passed by the calling statement.

A future_value/index.js file that accepts arguments

```
"use strict";

// set investment amount, interest rate, and years
const investment = parseFloat(process.argv[2]);
const rate = parseFloat(process.argv[3]);
const years = parseInt(process.argv[4]);

// validate command line arguments
if (isNaN(investment) || isNaN(rate) || isNaN(years)) {
    console.log("ERROR: Please pass valid numbers for all arguments.");
    process.exit(1);              // exit process with an error code of 1
}

// calculate future value
let futureValue = investment;
for (let i = 1; i <= years; i++) {
    futureValue += futureValue * rate / 100;
}

// display results
console.log(`Investment amount: ${investment}`);
console.log(`Interest rate: ${rate}`);
console.log(`Years: ${years}`);
console.log(`Future Value: ${futureValue.toFixed(2)}`);

process.exit(0);                  // exit process normally
```

How to use the node command to execute a script

```
>node future_value 10000 6.5 10
Investment amount: 10000
Interest rate: 6.5
Years: 10
Future Value: 18771.37
```

The array of arguments that's passed to the script

```
[ 'C:\\Program Files\\nodejs\\node.exe',
  'C:\\murach\\javascript_jquery\\book_apps\\ch19\\future_value',
  '10000', '6.5', '10'
]
```

Description

- Node.js provides a *process object* that allows you to work with the process that runs the script.

- To access the arguments that are passed to a script, you can use the argv property of the process object. This property contains an array of all arguments that were passed from the command line to the script. Here, the first two arguments specify the path to the node command and the path to the script.

- To exit a script, use the exit() method of the process object. You can pass a value of 0 to the exit() method to indicate that the script exited normally, or you can pass other integer values to indicate that the script exited abnormally.

Figure 19-4   How to pass arguments to a script

How to work with Node.js modules

To make it possible for developers to share server-side scripts, Node.js includes a module system. By default, it uses the *CommonJS module system*. This module system is slightly older than the ES module system described in chapter 17, but it's still commonly used by many JavaScript frameworks, including Node.js.

The CommonJS module system has some similarities to the ES module system. However, the CommonJS module system uses the require() function to import modules, and it uses the exports property to export modules. In contrast, the ES module system uses import and export statements to import and export modules. In the context of Node.js, a *module* is any object or function that can be loaded by the require() function that's built into Node.js.

An introduction to modules

Figure 19-5 starts by summarizing two of the built-in modules that are provided by Node.js. These modules provide basic functionality that makes it easier for JavaScript programmers to work with the file system and HTTP networking, such as creating a web server. However, Node.js also provides many other built-in modules that provide for other types of networking, cryptography, data streams, and other core functions.

After the summary of the two built-in modules, this figure presents the require() function that you can use to import modules. To import a built-in module, you just need to pass a string that specifies the name of the module. In this figure, the second example shows how to import the built-in fs module. However, if you create your own module, you may need to specify a path to that module as described in figure 19-8.

To give you an idea of how you can use a built-in module, the three examples show how to use the fs module to read a file named email_list.txt. To start, the first example shows the contents of this file.

The second example shows a script named read.js that uses the fs module. To start, this script imports the fs module into a constant named fs. Then, it calls the readFile() function from the fs module. For now, all you need to know about this code is that it reads the contents of the email_list.txt file that's in the current working directory and displays the contents on the command line.

The third example shows how to call the script that's stored in the read.js file. To do that, this example uses the cd command to change the current directory to the directory that contains the read.js file and the email_list.txt file. Then, it uses the node command to call the read.js script. Here, it isn't necessary to include the .js extension because the node command automatically adds that extension.

Two built-in modules available from Node.js

Module	Description
fs	Functions for working with the local file system, including functions for reading and writing files.
http	Functions for creating HTTP servers that can make HTTP requests and return HTTP responses.

A built-in function for Node.js

Function	Description
require(*module*)	Imports the specified module. If the module isn't a built-in Node.js module or a module that has been installed globally, you can specify a path to the directory or file as shown in figure 19-8.

The contents of a file named email_list.txt

```
mary@murach.com (Mary Delamater)
joel@murach.com (Joel Murach)
anne@murach.com (Anne Boehm)
```

A script named read.js that uses the fs module to read the email_list.txt file

```javascript
"use strict";

const fs = require("fs");
fs.readFile("email_list.txt", "utf8", (error, text) => {
    if (error) throw error;
    console.log(text);
});
```

The commands for executing this script

```
>cd /murach/javascript_jquery/book_apps/ch19/email_list

>node read
mary@murach.com (Mary Delamater)
joel@murach.com (Joel Murach)
anne@murach.com (Anne Boehm)
```

Description

- By default, Node.js uses the *CommonJS module system*. This system uses a function named require() to import modules, and it uses a property named exports to export modules as described in figure 19-8.

- In the context of Node.js, a *module* is any object that can be loaded by the built-in require() function.

Figure 19-5   An introduction to Node.js modules

How to use the built-in file system module

Now that you have a general idea of how to use a built-in module, you're ready to learn more details about using the file system module. That's why figure 19-6 shows how to use the readFile() and writeFile() functions that are available from this module. This should illustrate some of the concepts for working with the fs module. If you understand these functions, you should be able to apply them to the dozens of other functions that are available from this module.

To start, the readFile() and writeFile() functions accept callback functions. That's because Node.js is designed for asynchronous programming. As a result, it's ideal for any server-side tasks that need to be asynchronous, and many server-side tasks do.

The first example shows how you can use the readFile() and writeFile() functions if you need to make sure that the code reads a file before it writes the file. To do that, it nests one callback within another. Here, the call to the readFile() method passes a callback function that has two parameters: error and list. The error parameter stores the error message if an error occurs while attempting to execute this function, and the list parameter stores the contents of the email_list.txt file if it's read successfully. If no error occurs, this code adds the specified email address to the list and calls the writeFile() function.

The writeFile() function accepts a callback that has a single parameter: error. If an error occurs, this code throws the error. Otherwise, it displays a message on the console that indicates that the specified email address has been added to the list.

In the real world, you wouldn't use code like this to add data to a file because there are easier and more efficient ways to do that. For example, you can use file system flags to open a file for appending data to it. Still, this code should give you an idea of how to use the fs module to work asynchronously with files.

Although the fs module is designed for asynchronous programming, it provides synchronous versions of its functions. These versions have a suffix of Sync, and the second example shows how you can use them. Since this code doesn't use callback functions, it's simpler than the asynchronous versions of the functions that are presented in the first example. However, this code also blocks any other calls, which can cause frustrating delays in your application.

When you import a module, you can use destructuring to import the functions you want to use and store them in constants. Then, you don't need to specify the name of the module to call these functions. For instance, the last example imports the readFile() and writeFile() functions and stores them in constants. As a result, you can call these functions without needing to specify the name of the module.

Two functions available from the fs module

Function	Description
readFile(*fname,encoding,callback*)	Reads the contents of the specified file, using the specified encoding, and executes the specified callback function when it's done.
writeFile(*fname,contents,callback*)	Writes the specified contents to the specified file and executes the specified callback function when it's done.

A script that reads a file, adds data to it, and writes it again

```
"use strict";

const fs = require("fs");

const fname = "email_list.txt";
const email = "mike@murach.com (Mike Murach)";

fs.readFile(fname, "utf8", (error, list) => {
    if (error) throw error;
    else {
        list += "\n" + email;
        fs.writeFile(fname, list, error => {       // nested callback
            if (error) throw error;
            console.log(email + " written to file.");
        });
    }
});
```

How to use the synchronous versions of these functions

```
let list = fs.readFileSync(fname, "utf8");
list += "\n" + email;
fs.writeFileSync(fname, list);
console.log(email + " written to file.");
```

How to use destructuring to get functions from a module

```
const {readFile, writeFile} = require("fs");
...
readFile(fname, "utf8", (error, text) => { ... });
```

Description

- Node.js is designed for asynchronous programming. As a result, it's ideal for any server-side tasks that need to be asynchronous.

- The fs module provides asynchronous and synchronous versions of its functions. The synchronous versions have a suffix of Sync.

Figure 19-6   How to use the built-in file system module

How to use the built-in file system module with promises

In the previous chapter, you learned that using promises can simplify the code that handles asynchronous calls, especially if you find yourself nesting callback functions. Fortunately, the file system module includes an API named fs.promises that provides an alternative set of asynchronous functions in which each function returns a promise instead of requiring that you code a callback function. As a result, you can use this API to simplify code that makes asynchronous calls to the file system module.

The table in figure 19-7 shows that the fs.promises API provides functions with the same names as the regular fs API. However, a function that's available from the fs.promises API doesn't accept a callback parameter, and it returns a promise. As a result, you can chain the calls to these functions.

The first example in this figure shows two ways to access the fs.promises API. With the first technique, you use the require() function to access the fs module, and you use that module's promises property to access the fs.promises API. With the second technique, you pass a string to the require() function that locates the fs.promises API.

The second example shows how to use this API to perform the same task that's presented in the previous figure. This code begins in the same way, except that it imports the fs.promises API, not the regular fs API. Then, the call to the readFile() function only passes the filename and encoding, not a callback function. Instead, this function uses the then() method of the Promise object to register the callback that specifies the code that's executed when the promise is resolved.

The code in the first callback adds an email address to the list returned by the readFile() function. Then, it calls the writeFile() function. Next, this code uses the second then() method to register the callback that's executed when the promise returned by the writeFile() function is resolved. This callback displays a message on the console that indicates that the email was written to the file. Or, if either promise is rejected, the catch() method registers a callback that displays an error on the console.

If you compare the code in this figure with the code in the previous figure, you'll see that the code in this figure is a few lines shorter. More importantly, it's easier to read and understand.

Two functions available from the fs.promises API

Function	Description
readFile(*fname*, *encoding*)	Reads the contents of the specified file, using the specified encoding, and returns a promise that resolves to the contents of the file after it has been read.
writeFile(*fname*, *contents*)	Writes the specified contents to the specified file and returns a promise that resolves when the contents have been successfully written to the file.

Two ways to access the fs.promises API

```
const fs = require("fs").promises;
const fs = require("fs/promises");
```

A script that uses the fs.promises API to read and write a file

```
"use strict";

const fs = require("fs").promises;

const fname = "email_list.txt";
const email = "mike@murach.com (Mike Murach)";

fs.readFile(fname, "utf8")
    .then( list => {
        list += "\n" + email;
        fs.writeFile(fname, list)
    })
    .then ( console.log(email + " written to file.") )
    .catch( error => console.log(error) );
```

Description

- The fs.promises API provides an alternative set of asynchronous functions where each function returns a promise.

Figure 19-7   How to use the built-in file system module with promises

How to create and use your own module

The previous two figures showed how to work with the built-in fs module. Now, figure 19-8 shows how to create and use your own module.

To create your own module, you use the techniques described in chapter 17. Then, to use the module with Node.js, you must use the CommonJS module system to export an object or function that's in your module. To do that, you add the object or function to the exports property, as illustrated by the first example in this figure.

The second example shows the filename that stores the code in the first example. This shows that the module is a regular JavaScript file. By convention, this filename uses dashes instead of underscores in its name.

The third example shows how to use the module. To start, this example imports the function from the CommonJS module system. To do that, it uses the require() function. However, when you create your own module, the require() function typically needs to include a path to the module. To do that, you can use the characters described in this figure to specify a directory. In this example, the code uses the ./ character to indicate that the module is in the same directory as the script that called it.

When the third example imports the module, it uses destructuring to store the calcFutureValue() function in a constant. As a result, it can call this function without needing to prefix it with the name of the module. Alternately, you could import the module into a constant like this:

```
const murach = require("./murach-calc-future-value");
```

Then, you could call the function like this:

```
const futureValue = murach.calcFutureValue(investment, rate, years);
```

A property that stores the functions that are exported by a module

Property	Description
exports	An object that contains the functions that the module exports.

A module that exports a single function

```
"use strict";

// export the calcFutureValue function as a CommonJS module
exports.calcFutureValue = (investment, rate, years) => {
    let futureValue = investment;
    for (let i = 1; i <= years; i++) {
        futureValue += futureValue * rate / 100;
    }
    return futureValue;
}
```

The name of the file that contains the module

```
murach-calc-future-value.js
```

Characters for specifying a path to a module

Name	Description
/	The root directory for the file system.
./	The same directory as the current file.
../	One directory up from the current file.

A file that uses the module

```
"use strict";

// import calcFutureValue() from the murach-calc-future-value.js module
const {calcFutureValue} = require("./murach-calc-future-value");

// convert command line arguments from strings to numbers
const investment = parseFloat(process.argv[2]);
const rate = parseFloat(process.argv[3]);
const years = parseInt(process.argv[4]);

// use calcFutureValue() to calculate the future value
const futureValue = calcFutureValue(investment, rate, years);
...
```

Description

- To export an object or function to the CommonJS module system, you add it to the exports property.
- To import an object or function from the CommonJS module system, you can use the require() function as described earlier in this chapter. However, when you create your own modules, the require() function typically needs to include a path to the module.

Figure 19-8   How to create and use your own module

How to use NPM to install modules

NPM (Node Package Manager) is a package manager for the JavaScript programming language. It's the default package manager for Node.js, and it's included when you install Node.js on your system.

A *package* is a module that's described by a package.json file, which is a file that provides all the data that NPM needs to share the package with other programmers. As a result, all packages are modules, but not all modules are packages. For example, the murach-calc-future-value module doesn't have a package.json file. As a result, it's a module, but not a package.

An introduction to NPM

Figure 19-9 provides an introduction to NPM. In broad terms, you can think of NPM as having two main components.

The first component is the *NPM registry*. This registry is an online database of packages that you can search via the NPM website. To do that, you can visit the URL shown at the top of this figure. Then, you can search for modules that provide many different types of server-side functionality. For example, the http-server module provides a simple web server that you can use to test web applications on a local server.

The NPM registry provides access to thousands of packages. Many of these packages provide high-quality code that extends the functionality that's available from the built-in packages of Node.js. As a result, it typically makes sense to use these packages instead of writing your own code for these tasks. However, the vetting process for the NPM registry relies on user reports to take down packages if they violate policies by being low quality, insecure, or malicious. As a result, you need to be careful when downloading and using these packages.

The second component of NPM is the npm command. You can use this to install packages from the NPM registry. For instance, the first example in this figure shows how to use the npm install command to install the http-server module.

When you use the npm command, you often need to specify options. To do that, you can use a longer but more descriptive double-dash option or a shorter but less descriptive single-dash option. For instance, the first npm install command in this figure uses the double-dash option to specify the global option that installs the package globally. The second npm install command uses the single-dash option to specify the same option.

When you use macOS (or Linux), you typically need to prefix the npm install command with the sudo (*superuser do*) command as shown by the third npm install command. Otherwise, you'll get an error that says, "permission denied."

When you use NPM to install modules globally, it installs the modules into the node_modules directory. By default, the require() function looks for modules in this directory. As a result, when you call the require() function for a module that has been installed globally, you only need to specify the name of the package, not its path. This works much like the built-in functions for Node.js.

The NPM website

www.npmjs.com

A module that's available from NPM

Name	Description
http-server	A module that you can use to test web applications on a local web server.

The npm install command for the http-server module (Windows)

With the double-dash global option

```
> npm install --global http-server
```

With the single-dash global option

```
> npm install -g http-server
```

How to use the sudo command to solve a permissions problem (macOS)

```
$sudo npm install -g http-server
```

Description

- *NPM (Node Package Manager)* is a package manager for the JavaScript programming language.

- NPM is the default package manager for Node.js, and it's included when you install Node.js on your system.

- A *package* is a module that is described by a package.json file. As a result, all packages are modules, but not all modules are packages.

- The *NPM registry* is an online database of packages that you can browse and search via the NPM website.

- You can use the npm install command to install packages from the NPM registry. With macOS, you typically need to prefix this command with the sudo (*superuser do*) command. Otherwise, you'll get an error that says, "permission denied."

- When you use the npm command, you often need to supply options. To supply an option, you often have the choice between a longer but more descriptive double-dash option or a shorter but less descriptive single-dash option.

- When you use the global option, NPM installs modules in the node_modules directory. By default, the require() function looks for modules in that directory. So, when you call the require() function, you only need to specify the name of the package, not its path.

Figure 19-9   An introduction to NPM

How to install and use the http-server module

Figure 19-10 shows how to install and use the http-server module. You can use this module to test web applications on a local web server.

For example, chapter 14 of this book presents a Task List application that uses cookies. However, this application doesn't work correctly if you run it from the file system. As a result, you need to run it from a web server. One way to do that is to use the http-server module as shown in this figure.

To start, you can use the npm install command to install the http-server module globally on your system, as shown in the first example in this figure. When you run this command, it should display messages that show that the http-server module was installed successfully. These messages should also include the path to the node_modules directory on your system.

The npm install command in this first example is for a Windows system. But to get it to run on macOS (or Linux), you typically need to prefix the npm install command with the sudo command as shown in the previous figure.

After you install the http-server module, you can use the cd command to change the directory to the directory that contains the web application you want to run, as shown by the second example. Here, the example changes the directory to the Task List application that uses cookies.

After changing the directory, you can start the http-server by entering the http-server command, as in the third example. Then, your firewall software may display a message that asks whether you want to allow Node.js to communicate on private networks. If so, you must allow this for the http-server to work.

When the http-server module starts, it should display messages that indicate that the web server is starting and where it's available. These messages show that the web server is available from port 8080 of the IP address of 127.0.0.1. In addition, they show that you can stop the web server by pressing Ctrl+C.

Since the localhost keyword is a synonym for 127.0.0.1, you can run the web application in the current directory by starting a web browser and entering "localhost:8080" for the URL. This is illustrated by the fourth example. Here, because the current directory has already been set to the ch14/task_list_cookies, the browser displays the Task List application that's in that directory.

The command for installing the http-server module

```
>npm install -g http-server
C:\Users\Joel\AppData\Roaming\npm\hs ->
C:\Users\Joel\AppData\Roaming\npm\node_modules\http-server\bin\http-server
C:\Users\Joel\AppData\Roaming\npm\http-server ->
C:\Users\Joel\AppData\Roaming\npm\node_modules\http-server\bin\http-server
+ http-server@0.12.3
added 23 packages from 35 contributors in 7.162s
```

The command for changing the directory to the web application

```
>cd /murach/javascript_jquery/book_apps/ch14/task_list_cookies
```

The command for starting the server for the web application

```
>http-server
Starting up http-server, serving ./
Available on:
  http://192.168.86.58:8080
  http://127.0.0.1:8080
Hit CTRL-C to stop the server
```

A URL you can use to display the web application

```
http://localhost:8080
```

The website displayed in the browser

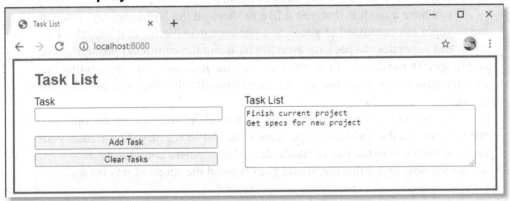

The message that's displayed when you press Ctrl-C

```
http-server stopped.
```

Description

- If your firewall software displays a message that asks whether you want to allow
  Node.js to communicate on private networks, you must allow it for the http-server
  to work.

Figure 19-10   How to install and use the http-server module

How package.json files work

Figure 19-11 presents some excerpts from the package.json file for the http-server module that show how package.json files work. These excerpts show that the package.json file identifies important aspects of a package that are necessary to share it. For example, this file identifies the name, description, and version of the package.

When developers specify version numbers for packages, they should use *semantic versioning*. This versioning system uses three numbers to indicate version compatibility. The first number indicates that breaking changes have been made so the module is incompatible with previous versions. The middle and last numbers indicate that the module remains compatible with previous versions.

The package.json file shown in this figure also identifies the repository for the package, which is where the package can be downloaded from the web. It specifies that the package requires a Node.js engine of 6 or greater. And it specifies *dependencies*, which are other packages that the package depends on.

The dependencies for a package use the caret character (^) in front of a version number to indicate that the library can use a higher version if that version is compatible with the specified version. For example, ^1.0.3 indicates that Node.js could use a newer version that's still compatible such as 1.4.2 but not a version that's incompatible such as 2.0.0.

If you have a module that you'd like to share on the NPM registry, you can use the npm init command to generate a package.json file for that module. This command generates the package.json file by using the command prompt to ask you to specify the data that's needed to share the package. After generating the package.json file, you can use a text editor to modify this file to make subsequent changes.

After you create a package.json file for a module, you can use the npm publish command to publish the package to the NPM registry. This makes your package available to the rest of the Node.js development community. However, describing how to use this command goes beyond the scope of this book.

Excerpts from the http-server module's package.json file

```
{
  "contributors": [
    {
      "name": "Charlie Robbins",
      "email": "charlie.robbins@gmail.com"
    },
    ...
    {
      "name": "Jade Michael Thornton",
      "email": "jade@jmthornton.net"
    }
  ],
  "dependencies": {
    "basic-auth": "^1.0.3",
    "colors": "^1.4.0",
    "corser": "^2.0.1",
    "ecstatic": "^3.3.2",
    "http-proxy": "^1.18.0",
    "minimist": "^1.2.5",
    "opener": "^1.5.1",
    "portfinder": "^1.0.25",
    "secure-compare": "3.0.1",
    "union": "~0.5.0"
  },
  "description": "A simple zero-configuration command-line http server",
  "engines": {
    "node": ">=6"
  },
  "homepage": "https://github.com/http-party/http-server#readme",
  "license": "MIT",
  "main": "./lib/http-server",
  "name": "http-server",
  "repository": {
    "type": "git",
    "url": "git://github.com/http-party/http-server.git"
  },
  "version": "0.12.3"
}
```

Description

- NPM packages should use *semantic versioning*. Semantic versioning uses three numbers to indicate version compatibility. The first number indicates that breaking changes have been made that make the module incompatible with previous versions.

- The caret character (^) in front of a version number indicates that the library can use a higher version if that version is compatible with the specified version.

- If you have a module that you'd like to share on the NPM registry, you can use the npm init command to generate a package.json file for that module. Then, if necessary, you can use a text editor to modify this file.

- After you create a package.json file for a module, you can use the npm publish command to publish the package to the NPM registry.

Figure 19-11 How package.json files work

Perspective

This chapter shows how Node.js makes it possible to use JavaScript for server-side scripting. Because JavaScript is well-suited to asynchronous programming, using JavaScript on the server often makes sense. In addition, this chapter shows how you can use NPM to extend the server-side functionality that's built into Node.js.

However, Node.js and NPM are huge subjects, and there's much more to learn about both of them. For example, the built-in fs module provides dozens of functions for working with the file system. So, if you need to use the fs module, you should consult its online documentation to learn more about it.

Keep in mind, though, that the fs module is only one of many built-in modules for Node.js. In addition, NPM provides access to thousands of other modules. These modules make developing server-side JavaScript code a lot easier than it would be if you had to develop these modules on your own.

Terms

Node.js	NPM (Node Package Manager)
REPL (Read Eval Print Loop)	package
CommonJS module system	NPM registry
module	semantic versioning

Summary

- *Node.js* is an open-source, cross-platform, runtime environment that lets you run JavaScript code outside a web browser. It also provides a way to use JavaScript for server-side scripting.

- Node.js provides a *REPL (Read Eval Print Loop)* that interactively evaluates JavaScript code that the user enters at the command line.

- By default, Node.js uses the *CommonJS module system*. This system uses the require() function to import modules and a property named exports to export them.

- In the context of Node.js, a *module* is any object or function that can be loaded by the built-in require() function.

- *NPM (Node Package Manager)* is a package manager for the JavaScript programming language and the default package manager for Node.js.

- A *package* is a module that's described by a package.json file. As a result, all packages are modules, but not all modules are packages.

- The *NPM registry* is an online database of packages that you can access via the NPM website. Then, you can use the npm command to install these packages.

- *Semantic versioning* uses three numbers to indicate the version compatibility of NPM packages.

Exercise 19-1   Experiment with Node.js

This exercise guides you through the process of installing Node.js on your system, testing your installation, and using Node.js to evaluate JavaScript expressions and run JavaScript scripts.

Install Node.js and test the installation

1. Install Node.js on your system as described in figure 19-1.

2. Start a Command Prompt (Windows) or Terminal (macOS) window.

3. Test the installation by entering the following command:
   ```
   node -v
   ```
   This should display the version of Node.js that you installed.

Use Node.js to evaluate JavaScript code

4. Enter the node command without any options to start a Node.js command prompt.

5. At the Node.js command prompt, enter a statement that declares a constant named numbers that's an array literal. Then, enter a statement that uses the push() method to add a number to the array. When you do, the console should display the length of the array like this:
   ```
   > numbers.push(4)
   1
   ```

6. Press the Up arrow to redisplay the previous statement and edit it so the push() method adds a new value to the array. Then, press Enter to execute this statement.

7. Repeat step 6 for another value.

8. Enter the numbers constant at the prompt. This should display the array of values:
   ```
   > numbers
   [ 4, 77, 3.14 ]
   ```

9. Use a for-of loop to iterate the array and write each array value to the console using the console.log() method. As you do that, use the Tab key to accept any helpful code completion suggestions.

10. Enter the .exit command to exit the Node.js command prompt.

Use Node.js to run JavaScript code in script files

11. Use the following command to change the directory to exercises/ch19:
    ```
    cd /murach/javascript_jquery/exercises/ch19
    ```

12. Run the index.js file for the test_scores application by entering the following command:
    ```
    node test_scores/index.js
    ```
    This should display three test scores and the average of those scores.

13. Use your text editor or IDE to open the index.js file. Then, update the code to accept arguments using the process object.

14. Enter the following command to pass three test scores to the index.js file.

    `node test_scores/index.js 97 88 92`

    This should display the three specified test scores and the average of those scores.

Use the fs module to read a text file

15. Use the following command to change the directory to ch19/fs_module:

    `cd /murach/javascript_jquery/exercises/ch19/fs_module`

16. Use your text editor or IDE to open the names.txt and read.js files in this directory. Review the contents of these files. Note that the read.js file already uses the require() function to import the fs.promises API.

17. In the read.js file, add code that uses the readFile() method of the fs.promises API to display each name in the names.txt file.

18. Use the node command to execute the read.js file. This should display the names in the text file on the console.

Use NPM to install the http-server module and run an application

19. Use the npm install command to install the http-server module as shown in figure 19-9.

20. Use the following command to change the directory to book_apps:

    `cd /murach/javascript_jquery/book_apps`

21. Use the http-server command to start the web server. If your firewall displays a message asking whether you want to allow Node.js to communicate on private networks, click Allow. If successful, this should display a message that indicates that the server is running.

22. Open a web browser and enter the following URL in the address bar:

    `localhost:8080`

    This should display a list of links for each chapter in this book.

23. Click the ch14 link followed by the task_list_cookies link. This should run the Task List application that uses cookies, and this application should work correctly because it's being run from a web server, not the file system.

24. Click the browser's back button until you return to the list of links for each chapter.

25. Click the ch17 link followed by the slide_show_module2_es link. This should run the Slide Show application that uses ES modules, and this application should work correctly because it's being run from a web server.

26. Switch to the command prompt and press Ctrl-C to stop the server. This should display a message that indicates that the server was stopped.

Appendix A

How to set up Windows for this book

This appendix shows how to install the source code for this book. It also shows how to install the software that we recommend for editing and testing the web pages and applications for this book. That includes the Chrome browser and the Visual Studio Code (VS Code) text editor.

As you read these descriptions, please remember that most websites are continually upgraded. As a result, some of the procedures in this appendix may have changed since this book was published. Nevertheless, these procedures should still be good guides to installing the software. And if there are significant changes to these setup instructions, we will post updates on our website (www.murach.com).

How to install the source code for this book

Figure A-1 shows how to install the source code for this book. This includes the source code for the web applications presented in this book. In addition, it includes the starting files for the exercises that are at the end of each chapter and the solutions for those exercises.

When you finish installing the source code, the book applications, exercise starts, and exercise solutions should be in the folders shown in this figure. Then, you can review the applications that are presented in this book, and you'll be ready to do the exercises in this book.

The Murach website

www.murach.com

The folder that contains the source code for this book

`C:\murach\javascript_jquery`

The subfolders

Folder	Description
book_apps	The web applications that are presented throughout this book.
exercises	The starting points for the exercises at the end of each chapter.
solutions	The solutions to the exercises.

How to download and install the source code for this book

1. Go to www.murach.com.
2. Find the page for *Murach's JavaScript and jQuery (4th Edition)*.
3. Scroll down to the "FREE downloads" tab and click on it.
4. Click the DOWNLOAD NOW button for the exe file for Windows. This should download a setup file named jqu4_allfiles.exe.
5. Run the exe file by double-clicking on it and responding to the dialogs that follow. This should install all the files for this book in the folder above.

If you prefer to use a zip file instead of the exe file...

1. Go to www.murach.com.
2. Find the page for *Murach's JavaScript and jQuery (4th Edition)*.
3. Scroll down to the "FREE downloads" tab and click on it.
4. Click the DOWNLOAD NOW button for the zip file. This should download a zip file named jqu4_allfiles.zip.
5. Double-click the zip file to extract the files for this book into a folder named javascript_jquery.
6. If necessary, create the C:\murach folder.
7. Copy the javascript_jquery folder into the C:\murach folder.

Description

- We recommend that you store the files for this book in folders that start with C:\murach\javascript_jquery. That way, they will match the book exactly.
- We recommend that you use the exe file to install the files for this book because that's the easiest way to install these files. However, some systems might not let you download exe files due to security considerations. In that case, you can use the zip file.

Figure A-1   How to install the source code for this book

How to install Chrome

When you develop JavaScript applications, you need to test them on the browsers that your users are likely to use. For a commercial application, that usually includes Chrome, Firefox, Edge, Safari, and Opera. Then, if an application doesn't work on one of those browsers, you need to debug it.

As you do the exercises and work with the applications in this book, though, you can test your applications on just Chrome. Then, if you need to debug an application, you can use Chrome's developer tools as described in chapter 5.

The first procedure in figure A-2 shows how to download and install Chrome. In addition, we recommend that you set Chrome as the default browser for Windows. To do that, you can use the second procedure shown in this figure.

Once you've got Chrome installed and your default browser set correctly, you can use the third procedure to make sure that your system is set up correctly. To do that, you can double-click on an HTML file to test the default browser, and you can right-click on an HTML file to test the other browsers on your system.

If you want to test your web applications in browsers that aren't already on your system, you should be able to use a similar procedure to install Firefox, Opera, or Safari.

The web address for Chrome

https://www.google.com/chrome/

How to install Chrome

1. Go to the download page for Chrome. One easy way to find this page is to search the Internet for "chrome download".
2. Click the Download Chrome button and respond to the resulting dialog boxes.
3. When you're asked what you want to do with the installer file, click the Save File button. This should download an exe file to your computer.
4. When the exe file finishes downloading, double-click on it to start the installation.
5. If you get a dialog that indicates that this app isn't a verified app from the Microsoft Store, click the Install Anyway button.
6. If you're asked if you want to allow the program to make changes to your computer, click the Yes button.

How to change the default browser

1. Start the Settings application.
2. Search for "default web browser".
3. On the Default Apps page, select a new web browser.

How to make sure your browsers are set up correctly

1. Start File Explorer and navigate to this folder:
   C:\murach\java_script\book_apps\ch01\email_list
2. Double-click the index.html file. This should display the index.html file in the default browser.
3. Right-click the index.html file and select the Open With item. This should display a menu of applications that includes all browsers that are installed on your system. From this list, select the browser you want to test. This should display the Email List web page defined by the index.html file.

Description

- Because Chrome is a popular browser that has excellent tools for testing and debugging JavaScript code, we recommend testing all of the exercises for this book in this browser.
- Because Firefox, Safari, Opera, and Edge are also popular browsers, you may want to install them too.
- You can use a procedure similar to the one above for installing Chrome to install Firefox, Safari, Opera, or Edge.
- Most Windows systems already have Edge installed.

Figure A-2   How to install Chrome

How to install Visual Studio Code

If you're already comfortable with a text editor that works for editing HTML, CSS, and JavaScript files, you can continue using it. Otherwise, we recommend using Visual Studio Code. It is a free editor that offers many features and runs on Windows, macOS, and Linux. In addition, chapter 1 shows how to get you started with it.

The first procedure in figure A-3 shows how to install Visual Studio Code (VS Code). To do that, you download the installation file from the VS Code website. Then, you run the installation file that's downloaded.

The second procedure shows how to make sure Visual Studio Code is installed correctly. To do that, you can use VS Code to open the book_apps folder described in figure A-1. Then, you can use the Explorer window on the left side of the main Visual Studio Code window to expand and collapse the folders that contain the HTML, CSS, and JavaScript files for this book. To learn how to use VS Code to work with these files, you can start by reading chapter 1.

The web address for Visual Studio Code

https://code.visualstudio.com/

How to install Visual Studio Code

1. Go to the download page for Visual Studio Code (VS Code). One easy way to find this page is to search the Internet for "vs code download".
2. Click the button for downloading the Windows version and respond to any dialog boxes.
3. When you're asked what you want to do with the installer file, click the Save File button. This should download an exe file to your computer.
4. When the exe file finishes downloading, click or double-click on it to start the installation.
5. If you get a dialog that indicates that this app isn't a verified app from the Microsoft Store, click the Install Anyway button.
6. If you're asked if you want to allow the program to make changes to your computer, click the Yes button.

How to make sure Visual Studio Code is installed correctly

1. Start VS Code.
2. Select File→Open Folder from the menu system.
3. Use the resulting dialog to select this folder:
    C:\murach\javascript_jquery\book_apps
4. This should open the folder that contains all applications for this book in the Explorer window that's displayed on the left side of the main VS Code window.
5. Expand or collapse the folders in the Explorer window to view the files for the applications presented in this book. If you can view these files, VS Code is installed correctly.

Description

* Visual Studio Code, also known as VS Code, runs on the Windows, macOS, and Linux operating systems.
* Chapter 1 of this book presents a tutorial that will get you off to a fast start with Visual Studio Code.

Figure A-3   How to install Visual Studio Code

Appendix B

How to set up macOS for this book

This appendix shows how to install the source code for this book. It also shows how to install the software that we recommend for editing and testing the web pages and applications for this book. That includes the Chrome browser and the Visual Studio Code (VS Code) text editor.

As you read these descriptions, please remember that most websites are continually upgraded. As a result, some of the procedures in this appendix may have changed since this book was published. Nevertheless, these procedures should still be good guides to installing the software. And if there are significant changes to these setup instructions, we will post updates on our website (www.murach.com).

How to install the source code for this book

Figure B-1 shows how to install the source code for this book. This includes the source code for the web applications presented in this book. In addition, it includes the starting files for the exercises that are at the end of each chapter and the solutions for those exercises.

When you finish installing the source code, the book applications, exercise starts, and exercise solutions should be in the folders shown in this figure. Then, you can review the applications that are presented in this book, and you'll be ready to do the exercises in this book.

The Murach website

www.murach.com

The folder that contains the files for this book

/murach/javascript_jquery

The subfolders

Folder	Description
book_apps	The web applications that are presented throughout this book.
exercises	The starting points for the exercises at the end of each chapter.
solutions	The solutions to the exercises.

How to download and install the files for this book

1. Go to www.murach.com.
2. Find the page for *Murach's JavaScript and jQuery (4th Edition)*.
3. Scroll down to the "FREE downloads" tab and click on it.
4. Click the DOWNLOAD NOW button for the zip file. This should download a zip file named jqu4_allfiles.zip.
5. Double-click the zip file to extract the files for this book into a folder named javascript_jquery.
6. If necessary, use Finder to create the murach folder directly on your hard disk. To make that easy to do, you can modify the preferences for Finder so it includes your hard disk in its sidebar.
7. Copy the javascript_jquery folder into the /murach folder.

A note about right-clicking

- This book sometimes instructs you to right-click, because that's common in Windows. On macOS, right-clicking is not enabled by default. However, you can enable right-clicking by editing the system preferences for your mouse. Alternately, you can hold down the Ctrl key and click instead of right-clicking.

Description

- We recommend that you store the files for this book in folders that start with /murach/javascript_jquery. That way, your file paths will correspond with the folders displayed throughout this book.

Figure B-1   How to install the source code for this book

How to install Chrome

When you develop JavaScript applications, you need to test them on the browsers that your users are likely to use. For a commercial application, that usually includes Chrome, Firefox, Edge, Safari, and Opera. Then, if an application doesn't work on one of those browsers, you need to debug it.

As you do the exercises and work with the applications in this book, though, you can test your applications on just Chrome. Then, if you need to debug an application, you can use Chrome's developer tools as described in chapter 5.

The first procedure in figure B-2 shows how to download and install Chrome. In addition, we recommend that you set Chrome as the default browser for Windows. To do that, you can use the second procedure shown in this figure.

Once you've got Chrome installed and your default browser set correctly, you can use the third procedure to make sure that your system is set up correctly. To do that, you can double-click on an HTML file to test the default browser, and you can Ctrl-click on an HTML file to test the other browsers on your system.

If you want to test your web applications in browsers that aren't already on your system, you should be able to use a similar procedure to install Firefox, Opera, or Edge.

The web address for Chrome

https://www.google.com/chrome/

How to install Chrome

1. Go to the download page for Chrome. One easy way to find this page is to search the Internet for "chrome download".

2. Click the Download Chrome button and respond to the resulting dialog boxes. This should download an install file to your computer.

3. When the install file finishes downloading, double-click on it and respond to the resulting dialog boxes.

4. If you get a dialog that indicates that Google Chrome was downloaded from the Internet and asks if you want to install it, click the Open button and respond the resulting dialog boxes.

5. In the sidebar, double click on the Google Chrome disk image and respond to the resulting dialog boxes. This should move Google Chrome to the Applications folder.

6. In the sidebar, click the eject icon that's to the right of the Google Chrome disk image.

How to make Chrome the default browser

1. Start Chrome.

2. Select Preferences from the Chrome menu.

3. If necessary, scroll to the bottom of the preferences.

4. Click the "Make default" button.

How to make sure your browsers are set up correctly

1. Start Finder and navigate to this folder:
   /murach/java_script/book_apps/ch01/email_list

2. Double-click on the index.html file. This should display the index.html file in the default browser.

3. Ctrl-click the index.html file and click the Open With item. This should display a menu of applications that includes all browsers that are installed on your system. From this list, select the browser you want to test. This should display the Email List web page defined by the index.html file.

Description

- Because Chrome is a popular browser that has excellent tools for testing and debugging JavaScript code, we recommend testing all of the exercises for this book in this browser.

- Because Firefox, Safari, Opera, and Edge are also popular browsers, you may want to install them too.

- You can use a procedure similar to the one above for installing Chrome to install Firefox, Safari, Opera, or Edge.

- Safari is already installed on most macOS computers.

Figure B-2   How to install Chrome

How to install Visual Studio Code

If you're already comfortable with a text editor that works for editing HTML, CSS, and JavaScript files, you can continue using it. Otherwise, we recommend using Visual Studio Code. It is a free editor that offers many features and runs on Windows, macOS, and Linux. In addition, chapter 1 shows how to get you started with it.

The first procedure in figure B-3 shows how to install Visual Studio Code (VS Code). To do that, you download the installation file from the VS Code website. Then, you run the installation file that's downloaded.

The second procedure shows how to make sure Visual Studio Code is installed correctly. To do that, you can use VS Code to open the book_apps folder described in figure B-1. Then, you can use the Explorer window on the left side of the main Visual Studio Code window to expand and collapse the folders that contain the HTML, CSS, and JavaScript files for this book. To learn how to use VS Code to work with these files, you can start by reading chapter 1.

The website address for Visual Studio Code

https://code.visualstudio.com/

How to install Visual Studio Code

1. Go to the download page for Visual Studio Code (VS Code). One easy way to find this page is to search the Internet for "vs code download".
2. Click the button for downloading the macOS version and respond to any dialogs. This should download the application file for Visual Studio Code.
3. Move the application file for Visual Studio Code from the Downloads folder to the Applications folder.

How to make sure Visual Studio Code is installed correctly

1. Start VS Code.
2. Select File→Open from the menu system.
3. Use the resulting dialog to select this folder:
   /murach/java_script/book_apps
4. This should open the folder that contains all applications for this book in the Explorer window that's displayed on the left side of the main VS Code window.
5. Expand or collapse the folders in the Explorer window to view the files for the applications presented in this book. If you can view these files, VS Code is installed correctly.

Description

- Visual Studio Code, also known as VS Code, runs on the Windows, macOS, and Linux operating systems.
- Chapter 1 of this book presents a tutorial that will get you off to a fast start with Visual Studio Code.

Figure B-3   How to install Visual Studio Code

Index

The software you need for this book

- **Any text editor.** We recommend Visual Studio Code (VS Code) for both the Windows and macOS operating systems because it's free and provides many excellent features.
- **At least one web browser.** We recommend using the Chrome browser because it provides excellent developer tools.

  To find detailed instructions for installing this software, please see appendix A (Windows) or B (macOS).

What's included in the download for this book

- The applications presented in this book.
- The starting files for the exercises presented at the end of each chapter.
- The solutions to those exercises.

How to download the files for this book

1. Go to murach.com.
2. Navigate to the page for *Murach's JavaScript and jQuery (4th Edition)*.
3. Scroll down until you see the "FREE downloads" tab and click it.
4. Click the DOWNLOAD NOW button to download the zip file that contains the book applications and exercises for this book.
5. If necessary, create the murach folder directly on your hard drive.
6. Unzip all files into the murach folder. This creates these three subfolders: book_apps, exercises, and solutions.

   For more detailed instructions, please see appendix A (Windows) or B (macOS).

www.murach.com